WASHINGTON

A BEST PLACES® GUIDE
TO THE OUTDOORS

RON C. JUDD

SASQUATCH
BOOKS
SEATTLE

Acknowledgments

The author thanks his parents, Ron and Gloria Judd, for pushing him outside in the first place, and Seabury Blair Jr. for helping to keep him there. Thanks also to Sasquatch editors Stephanie Irving and Kate Rogers for support; and a special thank you to Liz, for inspiration.

First Edition

Library of Congress Cataloging in Publication Data
Judd, Ron C.
     Inside out, Washington : a best places guide to the outdoors / by
Ron C. Judd.
        p.   cm.
     Includes index.
     ISBN 1-57061-098-3
     1. Washington (State)—Guidebooks. 2. Outdoor recreation—
Washington (State)—Guidebooks.   I. Title.
F889.3.J83 1997
917.5304'41—dc21   96—38105
                                                             CIP

Cover Photo: Joel Rogers/Tony Stone Images
Cover Design: Karen Schober
Interior Design: Lynne Faulk, Vashon Island WA
Maps: Rohani Design, Edmonds WA
Copy editor: Don Roberts
Proofreader: Sigrid Asmus
Composition: Patrick Barber/Apraxia Design Laboratories, with Jerret Scot Cortese

Important Note: Please use common sense. No guidebook can act as a substitute for experience, careful planning, and appropriate training. There is inherent danger in all the outdoor activities described in this book, and readers must assume responsibility for their own actions and safety. Changing or unfavorable conditions in weather, roads, trails, waterways, etc. cannot be anticipated by the author or publisher, but should be considered by any outdoor participants. The author and the publisher will not be responsible for the safety of users of this guide.

The information in this edition is based on facts available at press time and is subject to change. The author and publisher welcome information conveyed by users of this book, as long as they have no financial connection with the area, guide, outfitter, organization, or establishment concerned. A report form is provided at the end of the book.

Sasquatch Books
615 Second Avenue, Suite 260
Seattle, Washington 98104
(206)467-4300
http://www.SasquatchBooks.com

Contents

Introduction
and How to Use this Book

You might want to rope up for this.

Not that anything in these introductory pages is inherently dangerous—it's the stuff that follows that's cause for concern. The Washington outdoor world is a vortex: If you linger long on the edges, you'll invariably get sucked in. Given the addictive nature of jaw-dropping alpine views, miraculous ocean sunsets and picture-perfect campsites, nobody ever really pulls himself all the way back out. You get lured by the lush greenery of the Olympic Peninsula; seduced by the stone faces, snowy heads and flower-specked shoulders of the Cascade Mountains; or awed by the sprawling geographic wonders of the Columbia River drainage and Okanogan Highlands. The diversity of the state—really three distinct topographic regions in a single political package—surprises most newcomers and leaves even longtime residents befuddled about where to go, when, and how.

That's where *Inside Out: Washington* comes in. It's designed to be a road map, a trail-tested guide from an experienced, outdoorsy friend. Think of it as the portable, collective knowledge of an Evergreen State native who's spent a lifetime exploring the state's special nooks and outrageous crannies.

Unlike most single-sport guidebooks out there, this one was designed to offer something for *everyone*. A love of, and respect for, Washington's outdoor world is the only prerequisite. The information here is detailed enough to please specialists, but diverse enough to appeal to dabblers. It's an outdoors guide for real outdoors people: people whose choice of activities changes from season to season and decade to decade; people who love to hike and cycle, but also think they'd love to kayak; people who are equally comfortable on a sailboat and in a saddle; people young enough at heart to endure three days of remote backcountry skiing, but old enough to appreciate capping it off with a hot bath and a hot fire at a comfortable inn; and most of all, people who want to do all those things without lugging along a bookmobile full of various outdoor and travel guides.

Inside Out: Washington is a guide to every inch of Washington state written by a discriminating—and fickle—outdoor traveler. The structure is simple: The state is broken into nine separate geographic regions, which are then sub-divided into a total of 52 specific destinations (or chapters). Each chapter begins with an **introductory essay** about the area, its people, and its unique place in the world of Washington outdoor recreation. Next, in **Getting There** and **Adjoining Areas,** you'll learn the best way to get to your destination, how long it will take, and the other areas nearest it in this book. Then comes the meat and potatoes: The **Inside Out** section in every chapter offers detailed descriptions of the very best outdoor activities, ranked in order of prominence and appeal in that area. These activities vary across the state, but some are universal. Every Inside Out section, for example, describes campgrounds, hiking trails, picnic areas, fishing venues, cycling routes and some form of aquatic recreation, be it boating, kayaking, rafting or canoeing. Many sections have tips on where to view wildlife and where and when to take scenic photos. Chapters covering mountainous regions add cross-country and downhill skiing to the Inside Out activities. And dozens of specialized sports creep into the mix, from competitive kite-flying to clam-digging to long-distance horsepacking.

That's only the first half, however. Each chapter goes on to detail other worthwhile attractions in the area, from art galleries and noted shops to museums and odd natural features. These **Outside In** sections also provide Best Places® reviews—both star-rated and budget—of local restaurants and lodgings. Every chapter then concludes with **More Information,** a list of helpful phone numbers relevant to that area. It's the best of both worlds, inside and out: the wilderness experience and advice of a Washington native and veteran outdoors writer/photographer for *The Seattle Times,* coupled with the indoor expertise of the editors of the acclaimed Best Places® series.

Research for this book has dominated more than one lifetime, and would have been an onerous chore if it wasn't so much fun. Take it from me: Washington is a big, diverse place—one filled with natural treasures that even decades of exploring can't fully uncover. Compiling this evaluation of Washington's outdoor world has been exhausting and exhilarating all at once: exhausting because there's just so much of it, and exhilarating because it's introduced me to a new world of truly special wilderness places, and reacquainted me with others.

More than anything else, I hope reading this guide will do for you what creating it has done for me: reaffirmed a faith that Washington's outdoor world not only is where I want to be, but where I belong. Ropes or no ropes, I'm in too deep to turn back.

See you out there.

—Ron C. Judd

Washington Outdoors Primer

Most advice in this guide on what to do and where to do it is fairly self-explanatory. But it's important to keep some general tenets in mind before setting out into Washington's wild lands. Following is a general activity-by-activity overview, sprinkled with do's and don'ts and think-twice's. Reading it before hooking up the trailer, packing away the kids, and heading for Chewelah could save you a lot of wasted time and energy.

Camping

Washington campers are blessed and cursed all at once. They're fortunate to have a healthier-than-average number of campgrounds from which to choose. Problem is, their next door neighbors are likely to be fighting them for that last open site. Available summertime campsites are at a premium in the Evergreen State, particularly in many popular Washington State Parks. Translation: He who sets out on a Saturday in August for a weekend at Deception Pass State Park is liable to end up spending the night in the parking lot of the Oak Harbor Safeway. With Washington's population bursting at its Puget Sound seams—and camping venues not even close to keeping pace—only two things can leave you reasonably certain of finding a spot. One is camping off-season, a particularly attractive alternative for many RV owners, who laugh in the face of the cold and tune their satellite dishes from the Kalaloch parking lot. The other is a reservation.

Campsite reservations

Reservations are a four-letter word in Olympia, where Washington State Parks officials have struggled for years to develop a fair, efficient, cost-effective way to ensure that campers who drive from Seabeck to Spokane aren't left out in the cold, staring at a CAMPGROUND FULL sign. For many years, a select dozen of Washington's 82 state parks campgrounds operated on a mail-in reservation system. In 1996, the state took a giant step forward by joining forces with **Reservations Northwest,** a toll-free, computer-operated reservation center that books campground reservations for Washington and Oregon state parks. By calling (800) 452-5687, campers can reserve a space as far as 11 months in advance at any of 50 Washington State Parks (they're designated in this guide). That number has been increasing yearly, and more reservation parks are expected to be added to the Reservations Northwest system in coming years.

After some initial glitches (inadequate staffing and phone lines to handle the crush), Reservations Northwest has proven to be an effective tool for state campers. Campsites can be reserved and paid for by credit card (a reservation fee is added; at this writing it is $6), and if the campground you seek is full for the requested dates, you'll know so immediately. Telephone operators also can steer you toward alternative campsites.

Remember three things:

The **11-month advance** window is crucial. If you're looking to get a site in, say, Fort Flagler on the Fourth of July, you'd better be punching up "redial" on the preceding fourth of August.

The reservation system is in effect only from **April 1 through September 30.** All reservation campgrounds revert to first-come, first-served in the off-season.

Don't overlook the fact that many Washington State Parks are *not* on the reservation system. Sites there can still be nabbed the old-fashioned way: Show up early. Call the **State Parks information** line, (800) 233-0321, for information on campgrounds that are not part of the Reservations Northwest planning system.

An alternative is a national booking agency that handles reservations for many **U.S. Forest Service Campgrounds.** A large number of Washington's 500 Forest Service campgrounds (they're designated throughout this book) can be reserved in advance by calling (800) 280-CAMP. Since most of these campgrounds are smaller than state parks, they tend to book up faster. But keep in mind that most Forest Service campgrounds retain a number of non-reservable sites in each campground for first-come, first-served campers. At this writing, no National Parks campgrounds in Washington were accepting campground reservations.

Prices

Because campground prices change yearly, individual campsite prices are not listed with campground descriptions in this guide. Generally, however, the following rules apply.

In **Washington State Parks,** primitive campsites (no tables or fire pits) cost $5 per night; standard sites (tables and fire pits but no hook-ups) are $10 per night; and utility sites (tables, fire pits, sewer and water hook-ups) are $15 per night. A summer surcharge is added at some popular parks.

Most **national park, state Department of Natural Resources,** and **county park** campgrounds charge $6 to $12 per night for standard sites. Add about $5 more per night for hook-up sites. **Forest Service** campsites also charge between $6 and $10 per night, but many, especially those without piped water, are free.

Observant campers, particularly those in RVs, will notice that—with a few exceptions—private campgrounds are not listed in this guide. The reasoning is simple: There are far too many of them to make listings practical, and these campgrounds often change ownership, so it's difficult to vouch for their quality or level of service.

Hiking/Backpacking

Every hike listed in this guide includes both the distance, listed as **round-trip mileage,** and a difficulty rating, which ranges from easy to difficult. **Easy trails** are mostly level, sometimes paved grades that should be accessible to all family members. **Difficult trails** typically have a vertical climb ranging from 500 to 1,000 feet per mile. **Moderate trails** fall somewhere in between. Any hikes listed as **extremely difficult** typically involve extraordinary obstacles, such as snow fields or hazardous rock or stream crossings. The range included should please everyone, from the most gung-ho to the most aerobically-challenged. If you're new to hiking, there's plenty of easy stuff here to gradually build up your stamina and escort you to more difficult hikes. If you're a seasoned veteran, you'll find an equal number of off-the-beaten track routes and long-distance backpack routes. Most of you average hikers in the middle will enjoy dabbling in both.

Time estimates aren't included with the hikes, largely because round-trip times vary dramatically depending on the hiker. A good way to estimate your travel time in advance is to apply the "average-hiker" rule: An average hiker covers 2 to 2.5 miles per hour on moderate terrain. Add time if you think you're slower than average, subtract if you know you're faster.

Gear

It's not necessary to spend hundreds of dollars to become a properly equipped hiker. But there are some essentials. **Boots** are critical, particularly if you're venturing anywhere off the easiest, level trails. Consult with your local outdoor-shop experts on how much boot you'll need, but do invest in a sturdy pair of waterproof boots. We're constantly amazed at the numbers of people we see in high places clad only in tennis shoes. It's like begging for a broken bone or a sprained ankle. And with the wealth of reliable but relatively inexpensive boots on the market today, there's no excuse for not having decent footwear. Your feet will thank you for decades. **Clothing** is largely a personal choice, with necessary items fitting into the "10 essentials" category.

The **10 Essentials** list was developed long ago by The Mountaineers, a Seattle-based mountaineering group, and other frequent mountain visitors, but it still stands as the definitive list of must-have survival gear for hikers. No matter where you go—and, if you're hiking in mountainous terrain, no matter when—it's important to carry this stuff. (It needn't weigh you down or break the bank. Most of the gear is small enough to fit in a compact stuff sack, and much of it can be picked up for low cost at variety stores or used-gear shops.) These items, essentially the minimal equipment you need to survive a night in the woods or to find your way out if you lose the trail, have saved many a life in the Washington backcountry. While they're not necessary for some of the trails designated as "easy" in this guide, they should be carried—always—on longer hikes rated "moderate" or above. Most experienced canoeists, kayakers, backcountry skiers and other recreationalists carry similar supply caches. The list:

- **Map.** Get a good topographic map, and learn how to use it. For hiking, the 7.5- or 15-minute series USGS topographic maps are good, but hiker-designed specialty maps, such as those from Green Trails, Inc., are easier to follow.
- **Compass.** Use one preferably with a navigational sight.
- **Flashlight** or **headlamp.** Always carry spare batteries and bulb. Headlamps are more versatile, because they allow hands-free walking or climbing, and many headlamps come with an extra bulb already inside the casing.
- **Extra food.** Energy bars or other compact, high-energy snacks are good.
- **Extra clothing.** A warm fleece or wool pullover, rain- and windshell and pants, fleece or wool gloves, and a warm hat are all Northwest essentials, any time of the year.
- **Sunglasses.** Not just for looks, but to avoid snowblindness in high altitudes.
- **First-aid kit.** Commercially pre-packaged kits from manufacturers such as Outdoor Research are excellent, but be sure to check medicine expiration dates annually and add any specific drugs you might need, for instance bee-sting medication if you're allergic.
- **Pocket knife.** Your basic Swiss Army knife is an indispensable tool.
- **Matches.** Put them in a waterproof cylinder, and/or carry a cigarette lighter. They weigh practically nothing and light even when wet.
- **Fire starter.** Commercially packaged fire pellets are good. A candle can be even better.

I usually suggest carrying a couple additional items. One obvious one is a **water bottle,** filled before you leave to avoid risking giardiasis from drinking stream water. **Sunscreen** and **bug repellent** are also "must-haves" in our packs.

Other items that come in handy include a reflective **space blanket,** which can make long nights in exposed places far more comfortable. Get a sturdy one, and in a pinch it can be rigged with **parachute cord** (another essential!) into a decent weather shelter. A collapsible **walking stick** can be indispensable: It takes the load off on steep downhill stretches, makes impossible stream crossings possible, and even can be used to self-arrest on unplanned snow field slides. (Note, however, that it's no substitute for an **ice ax,** which is a necessary item for trips involving snow field crossings.) The walking stick also makes a grand center post for that emergency space-blanket tent condo. But if you pack only one additional "essential," make it a **candle.** Ounce for ounce, it's one of the best survival tools you can carry.

Call first

A final word to the hiking wise: Do yourself a favor and call the nearest ranger district or national park office before leaving for your hike. Washed-out roads, wildfires, rogue animals, and other acts of nature often make trails inaccessible. Increasingly, too, limited-number permit systems are creeping into the Washington hiking equation, especially in areas such as the Alpine Lakes Wilderness. The only way to be sure you'll get where you want to go is to call first. Ranger district phone numbers are listed along with all the hikes in this guide. Use them.

Another good general information source is the **Outdoor Recreation Information Center** in Seattle, (206) 220-7450, which dispenses information about all Washington national forests and national parks.

Biking

Biking in this guide is divided fairly equally between road **Cycling** routes and **Mountain Biking,** largely based on the physical character of each particular region. In most cases, only a few possible cycle routes are suggested. Most of these have multiple variations and can be made either shorter or longer by adding or subtracting some road-legs. A good map guide showing small, rural roads, such as the *Washington State Atlas & Gazeteer* (or a regional U.S. Forest Service map, if you're on a mountain bike), can be an indispensable tool for cyclists.

Specific mountain-bike roads and trails are also suggested for many destinations. But they rarely represent the net total of routes available to the creative mountain biker. Because **restrictions** vary dramatically according to jurisdiction, it's important to call the information numbers listed in each chapter to inquire about paths. Many new trails and roads are opening—and closing—to mountain bikers every year as land managers seek a balance between foot and wheeled use of wild areas. It's important to note that mountain bikes remain illegal on the vast majority of hiking trails in Washington state. Bicycles are forbidden on nearly all national park trails, in all federal wilderness areas, and on many non-wilderness Forest Service trails. Heed these restrictions: Failure to do so will only fan the fire of the handful of hikers who'd like to see mountain bikers banned from *all* trails. On the other hand, fat-tire cyclists will find a wealth of opportunities on designated dual-use trails, as well as on roads managed by the Forest Service, the state Department of Natural Resources, and the federal Bureau of Land Management. East-slope Cascade areas—such as the Wenatchee National Forest, where many trails are open to motorcycles—offer the greatest percentage of trails open to mountain bikes.

In many sections of this guide, cycle rental and repair shops are listed for visitors who didn't bring a bike, but are itching to see the countryside from the saddle. Cycling can be an amazingly productive way to tour many of the regions in this guide. You'll see much more from a bicycle than the car, and wildlife sightings increase immeasurably for cyclists. Whichever cycling speed and style you choose, **wear a helmet.**

Kayaking/Canoeing

Paddle venues in this book are listed for nearly every locale, with an eye toward difficulty and scenery. You're the best judge of your own paddling experience and ability, so it's up to you to decide if a particular waterway is within your means. **Canoe routes** listed here are almost exclusively in lakes or other flat water; all, of course, should be equally enjoyable to the sea kayaker. **Sea kayaking** routes and destinations are described in general terms only, based on the experiences of local kayakers and frequent visitors. They're not the only information you'll need before setting out on a trek, particularly in an open saltwater area. Wise kayakers will consult maps, tide charts, and other resources before putting paddle to untested waters. Another option is to make an initial visit to a new area with an experienced guide, many of whom are listed in this book.

Beginning kayakers, of course, should seek expert advice and take a lesson or two before setting out on their own. Western Washington is blessed with a large number of kayak guide services and schools, many of which, again, are listed in this book. (See particularly the Greater Seattle chapter for information on beginning kayaking courses and rentals.) Unlike many water sports, however, sea kayaking is one that should not scare away the interested newcomer. With the proper training, it's a safe, relaxing sport—one any beginner can pick up in a day.

Once you're ready to head out on your own, it's hard to imagine a sea-kayak playground as rich as the one in our backyard. Puget Sound is packed with quiet coves, protected bays, and scenic islands—all the ingredients for a memorable waterborne single- or multi-day trip. Prime day-trip waters are identified in the Kayaking sections of this guide. Stronger paddlers can link one or more (or all) of the Puget Sound sections by embarking on the **Cascadia Marine Trail,** a unique kayaking and camping circuit stretching 150 miles from Olympia to the San Juan Islands, the second-longest marine trail in the country. Cascadia began with 20 official stopover points, most of them at existing state parks or undeveloped state Department of Natural Resources beaches. The list since has grown to more than 50 campsites, and trail backers, led by the Washington Water Trails Association, hope to boost the number to 200 by the year 2000. That would leave paddlers with a campsite every 5 to 8 miles, running the gamut from swampy mudflats to cozy B&Bs. Most of the current Cascadia stopover points are noted in either the Beaches or Kayaking sections of this guide. For Cascadia maps, annual permits ($20 per person), and volunteer information, contact Washington State Parks, (800) 233-0321, or the Washington Water Trails Association, (206) 545-9161.

Fast-action **whitewater kayakers** already know their favorite spots, but we've included a full range of them in this guide, all across the state. Many "runnable" sections of Washington rivers are described in this guide, with general whitewater ratings (Class I to Class V) for notable river obstacles. In many cases, these descriptions are also applicable to whitewater rafting (see below). Whitewater kayakers should never attempt new waters, particularly those rated Class III or higher, without expert help.

Rafting

Rafting is a very popular sport in Washington, drawing some 40,000 customers a year to commercial rafting guide services. This guide contains descriptions of dozens of whitewater venues visited each year by rafters, including advice on when the rivers are best run. It does *not* contain specific guide service recommendations, for a variety of reasons. The primary reason is that commercial whitewater rafting is not regulated by the state of Washington. Any raft guide with proof of insurance and a raft can become a licensed guide, so vouching for the quality of any given raft service can be risky business. However, Washington's rafting industry in general has an excellent safety record, and the vast majority of raft outfitters are staffed by well-trained professionals. Still, it's important for the customer to ask specific questions before booking a trip: How long has the guide been in business? Do all guides escorting the float have a similar level of experience? Does the company keep log books to prove it? Are all rafters issued protective helmets and wetsuits? Use your judgment. Many rafting outfitters belong to an industry group, Professional River Outfitters of Washington, which requires voluntary safety and training standards. That's a suggestion, but not a guarantee, of quality. The best advice is to seek referrals from the Forest Service Ranger District or other managing agency under whose jurisdiction the river falls. In many cases, Forest Service officials work directly with outfitters in setting individual standards and safety requirements for specific rivers. We've included phone numbers specifically for that purpose in most sections of this guide.

Fishing

Perhaps nowhere is Washington's outdoor-recreation diversity better illustrated than in its fisheries, which are literally all over the map. You can catch anything from a 250-pound white sturgeon to a thumb-sized bullhead in Washington waters, although figuring out which waterways are open, when, and to whom, can be downright befuddling. In these pages we've offered hundreds of suggestions for local fishing venues, including what you'll catch there, how to pursue it, and generally when. Note the "generally." State fishing regulations change—and seemingly become more Byzantine—every year. Many special regulations are placed on fisheries, particularly in the Pacific Ocean and Puget Sound, where fish managers are struggling to save near-extinct salmon and steelhead stocks while protecting traditional sport fisheries.

Given all that upheaval, what we offer in this guide is primarily the "where" and "how" of Washington fishing. To get the only reliable word on "when," it's *crucial* that state anglers pick up a copy of the state Department of Fish and Wildlife's annual **"Sport Fishing Rules" pamphlet,** which lays out seasons for all species and all waterways in the state. The guide, available free in local outdoor shops each spring, has full details on seasons, catch limits, species identification, special fisheries, and—of utmost importance—licensing. Get the pamphlet and use it. There's no substitute. Of course, if you're like many people and can't make heads or tails of the constantly expanding thing, you can always call a local expert and ask. Wherever possible, we've listed such contact numbers in the Fishing section for each area.

Wildlife

One feature of this guidebook we think will appeal to almost everyone is the Wildlife listings, which give tips on what sorts of creatures roam each area of the state and how best to find and view them. In spite of its rapid suburbanization, Washington is home to an astonishing array of creatures, from the banana slug to the moose. Most listings include the best seasons for viewing. What they don't include is this common-sense admonition: For your sake and theirs, **don't approach wild animals** you might encounter in a wildlife-watching zone or elsewhere. Large mammals—such as elk, moose and, of course, bear—can be dangerous. And you can be dangerous to them. Animals that become habituated to humans, whether through feeding or just frequent contact, often develop into "problem wildlife" cases in Washington state. Admire them, but respect them. Keep your distance.

Boating/Sailing

We didn't become one of the most boat-happy states in the nation by sitting around on dry land and watching the dust blow by. When it comes to boating, we are where we live, and for most of us that's somewhere near a major waterway. Included in nearly every section of this guide are descriptions and locations of boat launches, marine-supply outlets, marinas, beachside moorage floats, and other boating facilities. These are most heavily concentrated in the Puget Sound section. Water lovers who don't have their own craft (yet) are far from out of luck. On many state waterways described in this guide, small boats (or big, huge boats, if you're looking to cruise the San Juans) are available for charter, either on your own or with a complimentary skipper. This information occasionally is combined with descriptions of fishing or kayaking venues.

Climbing

Individual approaches to rock pitches in the Cascades are best left to experts, but general descriptions of the state's most popular rock-climbing venues are included in this guide, particularly in the Leavenworth and the Icicle Valley and Snoqualmie Pass Corridor chapters. You'll also find general mountaineering information in many of the Cascade Mountain sections, as well as specific details for those interested in summit attempts on major peaks, such as Mounts Rainier, St. Helens, Baker, Adams, and Olympus. Consult those sections of this guide for more information.

Skiing/Snowplay

I've often said that the best way to survive a wet, dark Washington winter is to get out in it and participate in the weather. Toward that end, this guidebook contains descriptions of every organized downhill and cross-country skiing venue in the state, and a fair number of unorganized

ones. All seven of the state's major commercial downhill ski areas—
Mount Baker, Crystal Mountain, The Pass (Snoqualmie), Stevens Pass,
White Pass, 49 Degrees North, and Ski Bluewood—are profiled, as are all
of the state's 50-plus Sno-Parks for cross-country skiers, snowshoers, and
snowmobilers.

Seasons

Washington's downhill ski season typically begins in late November or
early December and continues through the first week of April. Cross-
country and backcountry telemark skiers begin earlier (often October, at
high elevations) and stay longer (through May, in the high country). And
intrepid skiers and snowshoers can get a taste of their addiction literally
all year long on Mount Rainier and other high Cascade peaks.

Downhill

The greater Seattle area is home to the second highest number of skiers-
per-capita in the nation (behind only Denver). The smarter ones get their
start by taking lessons, which can save years of wasted effort and painful
bruises. Washington is blessed with dozens of quality ski schools; every
major ski area has at least one. Call the mountain information numbers
listed in each section for ski-school referrals. The four singly-owned ski
areas at The Pass on Snoqualmie Summit are home to the bulk of the
state's ski schools, largely because the mountain is only 45 minutes east of
Seattle on Interstate 90. Intermediate skiers can find more than enough
challenging terrain in Washington, particularly at the big, wide-open ski
areas such as White Pass, Crystal Mountain, Stevens Pass, and Mount
Baker. And even the gustiest experts can test their mettle on black-
diamond pitches at Baker, Alpental (The Pass), and the backcountry areas
of Crystal Mountain.

Cross-Country

If downhill skiing disagrees with your knees or sensibilities, don't overlook cross-country skiing, which is a great way to exercise and shake the
winter blahs during the cold months. Nordic skiing is easy to learn
(beginners can pick up skiing on groomed, flat tracks in about an hour),
relatively inexpensive, and very easy to access. **Washington Sno-Parks,**
plowed parking lots and (sometimes) groomed trails maintained by
Washington State Parks, are one of the best recreation values in the
Northwest. A season's pass to all 50 costs only $20 per vehicle—about half
the cost of a single day's lift ticket at many major downhill resorts. Cross-
country skiing is the best—and often the only—way to visit alpine backcountry areas in the winter time, when many take on a peaceful, silent,
almost heavenly presence. Beginners can rent gear at any Seattle-area ski

shop, pick out a groomed trail with an "easy" rating, and have at it. It's safe, fun, and an uncommonly fresh breath of air in our long, often insufferably wet winter months. State Sno-Park information is found throughout the guide, but concentrated most heavily in the Snoqualmie Pass Corridor, Stevens Pass Corridor, Leavenworth and the Icicle Valley, Okanogan Highlands and Sherman Pass, Mount Rainier National Park, and Mount St. Helens chapters.

More advanced levels of cross-country skiing can be dangerous, however, particularly for expert Nordic skiers who venture out-of-bounds into the unpatrolled Cascade or Olympic mountain areas. **Avalanche danger** is a constant companion in Washington's winter backcountry. Skiers should check avalanche conditions by calling a local ranger district or the Northwest Avalanche Hotline, (206) 526-6677.

Snowshoeing/Inner tubing

Snowshoeing is making a strong comeback in Washington. While tromping across ski trails in snowshoes is a certified no-no, most of the Sno-Parks listed herein are good starting points for backcountry jaunts near ski trails. And lest we forget, entire generations of Washingtonians have received their first taste of winter seat-first, riding an inner-tube at obscene speeds down an icy hill. We've tried to identify the state's maintained, safe-and-sane tubing courses throughout the guide. See particularly the Mount Rainier National Park, Snoqualmie Pass Corridor, and Port Angeles and Hurricane Ridge chapters.

Mountain passes

A final word to winter-sport revelers: Traveling to most of these venues can be risky business when snowstorms blanket mountain passes, as they do more often than not in the winter. Roads can be very hazardous, as can other drivers, many of whom, no matter how long they live in Washington, never seem to really catch on to the art of snow driving. Always carry tire chains, chain tighteners, warm boots, gloves and a hat, and other snow gear when you're headed over a mountain pass. A collapsible snow shovel is a good idea, too. It can make installing chains much easier when the snow is really dumping and there's no such thing as bare ground, anywhere. Mountain-pass road information can be obtained by calling toll-free **(888) SNO-INFO.** Go slow, and for heaven's sake, ease off the brakes.

Windsurfing/Surfing

These two sports are picking up speed fast in Washington, and we've sought to identify reliable venues for both. Washington's coast, believe it or not, is increasingly dotted by wet-suited surfboard riders who congregate in the greatest numbers at Westport on the Southwest ocean coast. See the Grays Harbor: Westport and Ocean Shores chapter for details.

Windsurfing is popular statewide (any place equipped with long stretches of reasonably flat water and semi-reliable winds will do). But the Columbia River Gorge continues to lead the Northwest—indeed the world—in boardsailers per capita. The Gorge windsurfing culture is centered in Hood River, Oregon—a short ride as the board sails from Washington's south coast. Many of the hottest windsurfing sites, though, are actually on the Washington side. See the Bridge of the Gods, White Salmon and Bingen, and Goldendale and Maryhill chapters for full details.

Disclaimer

These pages are filled with the best, most reliable, most up-to-date information on Washington outdoor-recreation sites available at press time. But we can't be everywhere at all times (or even part of the time, for that matter). Washington's road, river, trail, campground, and water conditions can change in the blink of an eye or the spark of a lightning storm. That means any trail, paddle route, road, or other site described as safe and passable in this guide could turn miserable and deadly under the wrong set of circumstances. Risk is inherent in each and every activity described herein. Much of it can be minimized by knowledge and preparation. But risk can never be eliminated, and you assume it every time you head outdoors.

That's by no means an admonition to stay in. To the contrary. Go out, but go prepared. We've done our best to arm you with basic information in this guide, but it should be a starting point, not an end. Excellent books, classes, and seminars on wilderness safety, first aid, mountaineering, water safety, boating rules, and other outdoor-oriented topics are widely available (and sometimes free) in most residential areas of Washington State. Take advantage of them.

Finally, a plea for kindness to the lands that are the focus of all this activity. Washington is richly blessed, one of the most scenic places in the world. Its outdoor-recreation sites also are among the most heavily used and abused in the United States, thanks to a burgeoning population growth and a flood of interest in outdoor lifestyles. We can't, in good conscience, send you out the door without asking you to remember to be a good steward. Don't trash campgrounds or backcountry camps. Keep streams clean. Pack out all your litter and a little of someone else's. Play by the rules—and don't hesitate to impose them on someone else. A lot of people love the land you're hiking through, skiing over, paddling across, and sailing into. Treat it well, and it'll do the same for you.

About Best Places® Guidebooks

The restaurant and lodging reviews in this book are condensed from *Best Places* guidebooks. The *Best Places* series is unique in the sense that each guide is written by and for locals, and is therefore coveted by travelers. The best places in the region are the ones that denizens favor: establishments of good value, often independently owned, touched with local history, run by lively individuals, and graced with natural beauty. *Best Places* reviews are completely independent: no advertisers, no sponsors, no favors.

All evaluations are based on numerous reports from local and traveling inspectors. *Best Places* writers do not identify themselves when they review an establishment, and they accept no free meals, accommodations, or any other services. Every place featured in this book is recommended.

Stars

Restaurants and lodgings are rated on a scale of zero to four stars, based on uniqueness, loyalty of local clientele, performance measured against goals, excellence of cooking, value, and professionalism of service. Reviews are listed alphabetically.

☆☆☆☆	The very best in the region
☆☆☆	Distinguished; many outstanding features
☆☆	Excellent; some wonderful qualities
☆	A good place
no stars	Worth knowing about, if nearby

Price Range

Prices are subject to change. Contact the establishment directly to verify.

$$$	Expensive (more than $80 for dinner for two; more than $90 for lodgings for two)
$$	Moderate (between expensive and inexpensive)
$	Inexpensive (less than $30 for dinner for two; less than $60 for lodgings for two)

Directions

Basic directions are provided with each review; contact each business to confirm hours and location.

Cheaper Eats/Sleeps

The listings under Cheaper Eats and Cheaper Sleeps are for the budget-conscious traveler. While they are not star-rated, each establishment is recommended and is generally in the inexpensive price range (see above). These listings do not provide directions; call ahead to confirm location.

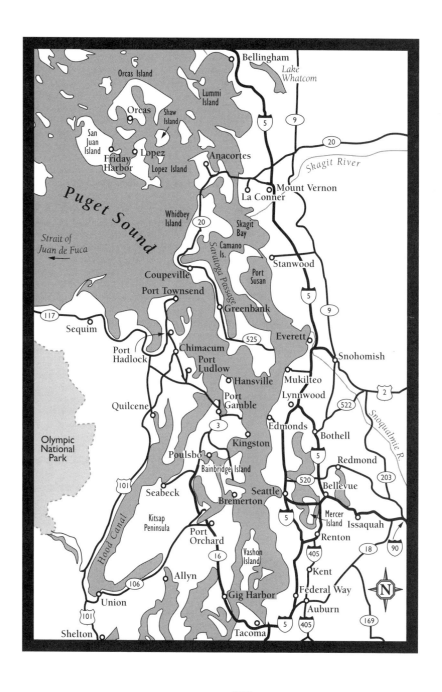

Puget Sound

Bellingham and Lummi Island

From Blaine south to Clayton Beach on Chuckanut Drive, west to Lummi Island, and east to Lake Whatcom, including Larrabee and Birch Bay State Parks, Semiahmoo Bay, Bellingham Bay, Lake Whatcom, the lower Nooksack River, the Interurban Trail, and Clayton Beach.

The moose had good taste. Not too long ago, a full-grown Bullwinkle wandered down from the Canadian north, following Interstate 5 to Bellingham, where it took up residence in the woods of Sehome Hill, in the heart of town. It's easy to see why the beast was confused. Around Bellingham, everything is a lot more like it used to be. Or *ought* to be, if a passion for outdoor frolicking in clean, uncrowded air, water, and forests happens to be chugging through your veins. From Interstate 5, the Bellingham area may look (and occasionally even smell) like another Everett. But not far off the freeway, the city resting on the banks of the Nooksack River in the shadow of Mount Baker is an undiscovered outdoor treasure trove. This region is well stocked with every conceivable ingredient for outdoor nirvana soup: abundant fresh and salt water, world-class alpine peaks, sprawling forest lands.

So how are Bellingham's parks, trails, shorelines, and rivers better than others around Puget Sound? For starters, you can still get to them. And once there, your chances for sunset solitude are much higher there than in most Puget Sound areas farther south. Bellingham, a progressive city of 57,000 heavy industrial (pulp mill, oil refinery) workers, university students and teachers, artists, farmers, retired draft dodgers, and high-tech workers, still hasn't spilled too far over its own edges. And locals have an unusual, refreshing attitude about what's inside them. This is a community very much in touch with its natural beauty. Support for parks, natural areas, and outdoor recreation is a core value.

It's no wonder. The region's sheer physical beauty is perhaps unmatched among the Northwest's smaller cities: secluded saltwater coves and islands on one side, glacier-draped mountains on the other, forest all around. A healthy slate of public facilities take full advantage of that. Waterfront parks developed and maintained here by Bellingham, Whatcom County, and Washington State Parks are among the best in the Northwest, providing unrivaled boating, kayaking, hiking, picnicking, and wildlife-watching access.

The moose, which ultimately met an untimely death in an encounter with a car, wasn't the only soul to take a quick sniff around Bellingham and decide to set up camp. Many people venture to Bellingham for a day of kayaking Lummi Island or hiking at Larrabee State Park, and just flat out disappear. They leave behind Metro bus passes, cellular phones, therapist's appointments, and a familiar, six-word epitaph: "Went to Bellingham. Never came back."

Getting There

Bellingham is an easy 90-minute freeway commute from the Seattle area. Take Interstate 5 north to exit 250 (Fairhaven area/Chuckanut Drive) or exit 253 (downtown/Lake Whatcom). To reach Lummi Island, continue north on I-5 to exit 260, following Slater Road west. Turn left (southwest) on Haxton Way, and follow it to the Lummi Island ferry, (360) 758-2190. Sailings are hourly, and the crossing of Hales Pass takes about 6 minutes.

Adjoining Areas

EAST: **Mount Baker Highway**

WEST: **San Juan Islands and Anacortes**

SOUTH: **Skagit Valley**

inside out

Beaches

Fresh- and saltwater shorelines make the Bellingham area shine, literally and figuratively. A slew of city, county, and state parks offer excellent access to waterfront areas that provide grand picnicking, strolling, swimming, windsurfing, class-skipping, and dog- or Frisbee-chasing all year long. Some favorites:

Larrabee State Park, 7 miles south of town on Chuckanut Drive, is the oldest and among the most diverse in Washington's well-stocked parks arsenal. From the park's main day-use area, a trail (short, easy enough for kids) leads to 3,600 feet of mostly flat, sandy saltwater beaches on Samish Bay. A half mile farther south on Chuckanut Drive, a newish Department of Natural Resources parking area provides access to another gentle (kid-friendly, mountain-bike accessible) trail, which leads about a half mile downhill to equally nice (and usually less crowded) **Clayton Beach.**

Nearby, just outside city limits, scenic, steep-walled **Teddy Bear Cove** is reached by lurching down a quite steep trail from Chuckanut Drive. The secluded cove has 300 yards of pleasant saltwater beach, more often than not sprawled upon by sun worshippers. At this beach, clothing is optional, gaping frowned upon.

Farther north, **Birch Bay State Park,** near the Canadian border on Helwig Road (about a 30-minute drive from Bellingham), offers good waterfront access to the saltwater beaches of the Strait of Georgia. Clamming and general beachcombing are popular here. Cinch down your hood: the beach area is gusty enough to be a hot kite-flying venue. Amid the many resort trappings at Semiahmoo is **Semiahmoo Public Park,** with a mile and a half of gorgeous, flat beach and an interpretive center detailing the once-thriving salmon canning business here that helped scoop up and ship out the bulk of the state's slippery silver resource.

In town, **Boulevard Park,** at State Street and Bayview Drive, is a delightful 14-acre spread on Bellingham Bay in the heart of the city. It's close enough to the unsightly Georgia Pacific operation to smell the plant's warm-tuna breath, but even that tends to fade into obscurity in this peaceful spot. The park has a half mile of beachfront trail (paved, in-line-skate friendly) and has become a local wind-surfer hangout. Likewise at small-but-memorable **Marine Park,** tucked behind an industrial area at the foot of Harris Street near the Alaska Ferry terminal in the Fairhaven district. Wind surfers will find the beach riprap a bit harsh on the neoprene, but it's a grand place to sit on a bench under the picnic shelter and down a quad-jammer from Tony's Coffee, just up the street.

East of town, 1,000-acre **Lake Padden Park** on Samish Way is a noted swimming, sunbathing, and windsurfing venue (also Fishing, see below), with a nice trail all the way around the lake. Also on the eastside, **Bloedel Donovan Park** (follow Lake Whatcom Boulevard east from Exit 253) has a nice Lake Whatcom swimming area that's supervised from June through September.

South of the city, **Samish Park** on Lake Samish Drive (take I-5 exit

246) has a beautiful terraced picnic area and 1,500 feet of beach for swimming. Rowboats and canoes are rented in the summer.

On steep-banked Lummi Island, many of the best beaches are accessible only by boat or kayak. Most are Department of Natural Resources sites on the island's east side. One beach accessible by trail (staircase, actually) is **DNR Beach 224,** which extends north about 100 yards from the ferry landing. Park at the landing and walk north along the road to a viewing platform, where stairs lead down.

Camping

The primary camping venue here is the aforementioned **Larrabee State Park,** which has 87 campsites, 26 with full hookups. Sites are situated in the trees, and don't have water views. They're nice in the summer, but fairly dreary in bad weather. Larrabee is open all year. Campsites can be reserved up to 11 months in advance by calling Reservations Northwest, (800) 452-5687. *7 miles south of Bellingham on Chuckanut Drive; (360) 676-2093 or (800) 233-0321.*

Equally popular, although a 30-minute drive north, is **Birch Bay State Park** (see Beaches, above), which has 167 campsites, 20 with hookups, and a trailer dump facility. This is an extremely popular park in the summer, drawing large crowds of campers from both sides of the border. Reservations are recommended. Birch Bay is open all year. Sites can be reserved up to 11 months in advance by calling Reservations Northwest, (800) 452-5687. *Follow signs west from I-5 exit 270; (360) 371-2800 or (800) 233-0321.*

Boating/Sailing

The choices are rich in Bellingham, which has been a port longer than it's been a city. The main attraction is the downtown **Squalicum Marina** (central waterfront; (360) 676-2542), a lovely, recently revamped area with public moorage (free for the first 24 hours) and a full range of marine services. The complex has a four-lane boat launch, a mall with public rest rooms, showers, shopping and restaurants, plus a nice public park.

From here, landlubbers can take to sea on numerous daylong wildlife sightseeing tours of the nearby San Juan Islands. Several charter services are open here year round. The **San Juan Islands Passenger Ferry,** (360) 671-1137, offers similar daily services from the Bellingham Cruise Center in old Fairhaven. And, of course, you can steam your way all the way up to Alaska from the same dock, via the **Alaska Marine Highway System:** (800) 642-0066.

Boat owners who'd rather do it on their own can put in at Squalicum's grand boat launch, which has ample parking. But other public boat ramps are found at **Harris Avenue,** near the Bellingham Cruise Center in Old Fairhaven, at **Larrabee State Park** (see Beaches, above) and at **Legoe Bay,** on the northwest side of Lummi Island. Avoid the latter one in bad weather; it's rather exposed. In addition, a launch hoist is available at **Gooseberry Point,** near the Lummi Island ferry landing.

Shorelines, secluded coves, and islands around Bellingham Bay are ripe for boat exploration. Favorites include **Inati Bay** on the southeast side of Lummi Island (two mooring buoys, picnic facilities) and nearby **DNR Beaches 223, 223A,** and **223B,** all of which have sandy landings. Most other DNR beaches on Lummi Island are rocky, some of them very hazardous for all but kayakers.

Many sailors use Squalicum Marina as a launching point for ventures into the heavily touristed San Juan Islands, but other small, lesser known islands in that chain are just offshore from Bellingham and make nice day trips by boat. **Eliza, Vendovi,** and **Sinclair Islands** ring the southern end of Lummi. The largest and westernmost, Sinclair, has a public dock and beach access on the south end. Tiny Vendovi has public tidelands access all the way around, below the high-tide line. Uplands are private, but some nice coves await boaters in small craft. Eliza, the closest to town, isn't well suited for beach landings and is mostly private land.

Canoeing/Kayaking

Most of the waterfront parks listed above under Beaches make fine small-craft launching points in both fresh and salt water, but there are some standouts. **Larrabee State Park**'s boat launch area in Wildcat Cove is a very secluded, all-weather launch site for kayaks, canoes, and small craft. The smooth, vertical rock walls stretching into the waters of Chuckanut and Samish Bays make for great half-day kayak trips. Lummi Island's many secluded DNR beaches also make fine kayak destinations. One of them, **Lummi Island Recreation Site,** near Reil Harbor on the southeast side of the island, is a designated beachside campsite for the state's **Cascadia Marine Trail** (a state-managed water trail including campsites from Olympia to Vancouver, BC; (206) 545-9161). Note: No running water.

Guided sea kayak tours in the area are offered by Moondance Sea Kayaking Adventures; (360) 738-7664. For canoe and kayak rentals, see Bellingham Boat Rental at Bloedel Donovan Park, (360) 676-1363, or The Great Adventure on Chestnut Street; (360) 671-4615. For windsurfing, water skis, and the like, contact Washington Wind Sports; (360) 676-1146.

Inland, **Lake Padden** and **Lake Whatcom** are good year-round pad-

dle venues, and the usually calm waters of **Lake Samish** south of town
are plied very, very early every day by Western Washington University's
crew teams.

Hiking

Some of the best trails in the area can be sampled right from the city. Park
on Fairhaven Parkway near 24th Street and follow the **Interurban Trail**
(easy, 5.6 miles one way), a fine rails-to-trails conversion, south to
Larrabee State Park. The route, former path of the old interurban electric
trolley from Bellingham to Mount Vernon, parallels Chuckanut Drive. It's
mostly flat (good for kids) and open to mountain bikes and horses. A popular option: mountain bike down the Interurban Trail to Larrabee, then
lock up the bikes and climb on the popular trail from Chuckanut Drive to
Fragrance Lake (moderate, 4 miles round trip) in the highlands above
the park's shoreline area.

The steep climb up Chuckanut Mountain to **Pine and Cedar Lakes**
(difficult, 5.6 miles round trip), an undeveloped Whatcom County Park,
yields excellent Mount Baker and San Juan Island views. The trailhead is
on the Old Samish Highway between Chuckanut Drive and I-5 exit 246.
Lake Padden Park has a delightful 2.6-mile (mostly flat) loop trail all the
way around the lake, as well as 5 miles of segregated bridle trails. Some of
the nicer trails in the region are hidden inside **Whatcom Falls Park,** a
beautiful, forested refuge with 5.5 miles of trails of varying difficulty.

Another little-known favorite, the **Sehome Hill Arboretum** (moderate, various lengths possible) is used primarily by students at abutting
Western Washington University, thanks (or no thanks) to the lack of a
single developed trailhead with good parking, except for one at the very
top of the hill. More than 5 miles of unmarked trails and abandoned roads
(mostly up and down moderate hills) skirt the mountain. At the mountaintop is one of our favorite spots in Bellingham—a tall observation platform with awe-inspiring views of Bellingham Bay, Mount Baker, and the
far northern Cascades. Sehome Hill is where the moose came to live.
You'll see why.

On Lummi Island, a popular hike leads from a Seacrest Drive trailhead to the top of **Lummi Peak** (moderate, 7 miles round trip), which has
grand views of the San Juans and the North Sound. Warning: The trail is
hard to follow at the top. Careful along the cliffs.

If you're up for a longer day trip, the Mount Baker Highway between
Bellingham and the mountain is your pathway to some of the finest day-
hiking in the Northwest. (See the Mount Baker Highway chapter.) For
hiking maps and supplies, visit Base Camp, Inc., (360) 733-5461.

Biking

The road is narrow and shoulders nonexistent, but cyclists still are drawn to the 11-mile cliff-side stretch of **Chuckanut Drive** south from Fairhaven to the northern fringe of the Skagit Valley. The views over northern Puget Sound to the San Juan Islands, provided you ever take your eyes off traffic, are stupendous. The trip often is made as a 40-mile round trip by continuing south all the way to **Bay View State Park** on Padilla Bay. Road riders also love the 7-mile triangular loop around the north end of **Lummi Island,** made by crossing on the Lummi ferry and following Nugent Road, West Shore Drive, and Legoe Bay Road. It's moderately hilly. (Stronger riders can turn this into a 30-mile round trip by starting and finishing in Ferndale.) Bicycle rentals are available at the store next to The Islander, a few yards from the ferry landing.

Mountain bikers will love riding the **Interurban Trail** (see Hiking, above), as well as a number of closed roads in the highland area of Larrabee State Park. The **Pine and Cedar Lakes Trail** is another option for mountain bikers with monster thighs.

For supplies and rentals, see Fairhaven Bike & Mountain Sports (1103 11th Street; (360) 733-4433).

Skiing

Mount Baker Ski Area, a nationally known deep-powder heaven for skiers and snowboarders, is 56 miles east on Hwy 542. For details, call (360) 734-6771, or see the Mount Baker Highway chapter.

Fishing

The mix is excellent here. Bellingham is a good homeport for summer and fall **coho, chinook, sockeye, chum,** and, during odd-numbered years only, **pink salmon** fishing in northern Puget Sound and the San Juan Islands, as well as **blackmouth** (immature chinook) fishing all winter long. Salmon charters are available from Blaine (Jim's Salmon Charters; (360) 332-6724), Bellingham Cruise Terminal (Bellingham Salmon Charters; (360) 650-9584), and Semiahmoo (Boom Town Enterprises; (360) 319-9515).

Trout anglers are in luck around here. State-stocked local lakes, such as Padden, Silver, Toad, and Cain, typically are among the strongest trout producers in Western Washington, especially in the early season of April and May. Of these, Padden has by far the best bank access, and it's stocked with some 18,000 legal-size trout every spring. State fishing access sites also are found on the east side of Samish Lake and the south end of Lake Whatcom.

Largemouth bass fans will be pleased with Lake Terrell west of Ferndale (see Wildlife, below). **Kokanee** anglers usually troll the broader, deeper waters of Lake Whatcom or Baker Lake. Local **steelheaders** catch winter-run fish on the main stem of the Nooksack in the Lynden/Everson area, but catch rates are down substantially in recent years. The river does have decent fall **coho** and winter **chum** salmon runs, however (see also the Mount Baker Highway chapter). For licenses and supplies, see H&H Outdoor Sports; (360) 733-2050. Call the Washington Department of Fish and Wildlife, (206) 775-1311, for more information.

Wildlife

Not many Puget Sound cities offer as many chances to rub binocular lenses with wild animals as the Bellingham area. **Whale** watchers and **seabird** lovers can book boat trips from Bellingham to north Sound islands (see Boating/Sailing, above). Shoreside marine wildlife lovers are hardly left out up here, however. **Semiahmoo Park,** near Blaine, provides access to the 1.5-mile-long Semiahmoo Spit, where **shorebirds** often congregate. To the west, **Lighthouse Marine Park** at Point Roberts has a viewing tower that makes a great **orca-** and **bird-watching** post, as well as a long beachfront boardwalk. The park, reached by driving north through British Columbia, makes an interesting full-day excursion from Bellingham. Winter trips are best for spotting **migratory birds** such as **loons** and numerous **duck** species. Other good **marine mammal** haunts are the rocks and small islands off the west side of Lummi Island. Most are protected portions of the **San Juan Island National Wildlife Refuge.**

Downtown, the **Maritime Heritage Center,** 1600 C Street; (360) 676-6806, provides great viewing of spawning **salmon** in the fall and winter—a good chance to enlighten and educate the kids, who'll learn something important without feeling a thing.

The **Terrell Marsh Nature Trail** at Birch Bay State Park (see Camping, above) is a good bird-watching trail. It's short and easy enough for children. Keep them quiet long enough, and you might spot beautiful **harlequin ducks,** which look like they were painted by the same guy who did the *Partridge Family* bus. To the north, the 11,000-acre **Lake Terrell Habitat Management Area** near Ferndale (I-5 exit 260) is a major stopover point for **migratory ducks.** Note: Hunting occurs here in season.

Just south of Ferndale near the mainstem Nooksack River, **Tennant Lake Interpretive Center,** operated by Whatcom County Parks, has an observation tower and boardwalk offering frequent sightings of **ducks, bald eagles,** and **hawks,** particularly in the winter.

A sometimes overlooked local wildlife hot spot is the **North Fork**

Nooksack River, where winter visitors see hundreds of wintering **bald eagles** and **elk,** with a tiny fraction of the crowds attracted to the better-known Skagit River eagle habitat to the south. (See the Mount Baker Highway chapter.)

Photography

The observation tower atop **Sehome Hill** (see Hiking, above) is a grand sunset spot. But this area's grand-champion tripod spot is farther south: summer sunsets from the pullouts along **Chuckanut Drive** are among the most spectacular you'll ever see.

Adventure Calendar

The annual **Ski-to-Sea Race** (an 85-mile team dash from Mount Baker to Fairhaven via skis, canoe, bicycle, foot, and boat), takes place Memorial Day Weekend; (360) 734-1330. There's a big street party afterward in Fairhaven. This is one of the Northwest's most notable multi-leg relay events.

The **Mount Baker Legendary Banked Slalom,** one of North America's premier snowboard competitions, is Super Bowl Sunday, followed by the Mount Baker Legendary Parking Lot Weenie Roast; (360) 734-6771.

Attractions

"Up on the hill," as the locals will say, the campus of **Western Washington University** (stop for parking info and a map at the drive-through visitors center on South College Drive) makes for a grand stroll year-round. Western's outdoor sculpture collection, (360) 650-3963, is considered among the finest in the nation. A unique audio tour lets you hear just what that artist was thinking during the shaping of the creation before you. The campus is at its scenic best in the spring, with trees abloom throughout.

The downtown **Whatcom Museum of History and Art** (121 Prospect Street; (360) 676-6981), located in the wonderfully refurbished 1892 red-brick city hall building, is Washington's second largest, and perhaps its finest. Nearby, the **Mount Baker Theatre** (106 N Commercial; (360) 734-6080) is a wonderfully refurbished movie, concert, and play house, complete with Wurlitzer.

The funky old village of **Fairhaven** on the south end of town, the legacy of an overly optimistic railroad venture in the 1890s, has a wide range of attention-holding shops and restaurants, and now the spiffy new **Bellingham Cruise Terminal,** the southern terminus of the **Alaska Marine Highway System;** (800) 642-0066.

Bellingham, formed by the union of four independently developing towns (hence the mishmash of streets), is dotted by a delightfully large number of lovingly preserved turn-of-the-century **mansions.** Drive or cycle along Utter Street between Madison and Monroe, West Holly Street from Broadway to C Street, N Garden Street from Myrtle to Champion, and Knox Avenue from 12th to 17th. Gardeners shouldn't miss the fantastic **rose collection** in Fairhaven Park or the **Gardens of Art** near Lake Whatcom; (360) 671-1069.

Restaurants

The Bagelry ☆☆☆   In 1993, The Bagelry doubled in size and diminished the lines. Thankfully, the New York–style bagels remained the same. *Railroad near Champion; (360) 676-5288; 1319 Railroad Ave, Bellingham; $.*

Cafe Toulouse ☆   The best place in town for Sunday brunch. *Downtown near Cornwall, next to the Federal Building; (360) 733-8996; 114 W Magnolia St, Bellingham; $.*

Colophon Cafe   Located in the best bookstore in town. The African peanut soup is justly famous. *11th near Harris (in Village Books) in Fairhaven; (360) 647-0092; 1208 11th St, Bellingham; $.*

il fiasco ☆☆   Under new owners, il fiasco offers excellent Northern Italian cuisine. *Across from the Parkade; (360) 676-9136; 1309 Commercial St, Bellingham; $$.*

The Oyster Bar ☆☆   A Samish Bay restaurant with a spectacular view, it has become an institution on Chuckanut Drive. Award-winning wine list. No young children. *Fairhaven exit off I-5; (360) 766-6185; 240 Chuckanut Dr, Bow; $$$.*

Oyster Creek Inn ☆   Adjacent to the Samish Bay Shellfish Farm, the Inn has a long history of dedication to seafood. The wild blackberry pie is a must. *About ½-hour drive south of Bellingham on Chuckanut Dr; (360) 766-6179; 190 Chuckanut Dr, Bow; $$.*

Pacific Cafe ☆☆   Tucked into the historic Mount Baker Theatre building, it has been a local gastronomic leader since 1985. *Off Champion on Commercial; (360) 647-0800; 100 N Commercial, Bellingham; $$.*

Pepper Sisters ☆☆   Cheerful, knowledgeable service, a great location, and a wide-awake kitchen have turned this place into an institution. *On State St south of Holly; (360) 671-3414; 1055 N State St, Bellingham; $.*

The Rhododendron Cafe ☆   The perfect starting spot or stopping point for a scenic trek on Chuckanut Drive. Homemade soups, excellent chowder, and sautéed Samish Bay oysters. *At the Bow-Edison Junction; (360) 766-6667; 553 Chuckanut Dr, Bow; $$.*

Taste of India   Tandoori meats and breads and other Punjabi creations are the specialties. *Across from Bellis Fair Mall; (360) 647-1589; 3930 Meridian Village, Bellingham; $.*

Thai House ☆   A most comfortable spot, especially for one in a strip mall. *Across from Bellis Fair Mall; (360) 734-5111; 3930 Meridian Village, Bellingham; $.*

Cheaper Eats

Bellingham's best latte is steamed up in Old Fairhaven at **Tony's Coffee & Tea** (1101 Harris; (360) 733-6319), which attracted whole-bean coffee-house aficionados long before the birth of Starbucks. A top local brewhouse, **The Archer Ale House** (1212 10th; (360) 647-7002) is nearby.

Lodgings

Best Western Heritage Inn ☆☆   One of the most professionally run hotels in the area, with elegantly furnished rooms and many thoughtful touches. Ask for a room away from the freeway. *Take I-5 exit 256; (360) 647-1912 or (800) 528-1234; 151 E McLeod, Bellingham; $$.*

DeCann House ☆   An unpretentious Victorian B&B overlooking Squalicum Harbor Marina. *West on Holly, which turns into Eldridge; (360) 734-9172; 2610 Eldridge Ave, Bellingham; $$.*

Holiday Inn Express of Bellingham   This spot on the Guide Meridian strip is a find, especially for time-pressed business travelers. Great value for your dollar. *Take I-5 exit 256A and head north on Guide Meridian; (360) 671-4800 or (800) HOLIDAY; 4160 Guide Meridian, Bellingham; $.*

Inn at Semiahmoo ☆☆   The sprawling Inn, on Semiahmoo Spit near Blaine, is situated at a stunning site with lots of amenities, including a house cruise vessel, athletic club, three restaurants, a convention center, and an Arnold Palmer–designed golf course. But lots of little things (thin walls, few view rooms, and frustrating waits for room service) make this seem more like a glorified motel than a luxury resort. *Take I-5 exit 270, travel west; (360) 371-2000; 9565 Semiahmoo Pkwy, Blaine; $$$.*

Jacob's Landing Rentals ☆☆   Jacob's Landing is Birch Bay's best local condo development. *Take I-5 exit 270, travel 5 miles west, watch for signs; (360) 371-7633); 7825 Birch Bay Dr, Birch Bay; $$.*

North Garden Inn ☆ A Victorian house on the National Register of Historic Places, with two dozen rooms and seven baths. Only 10 are rented as guest rooms, some with lovely views over Bellingham Bay and the islands. *Maple and N Garden; (360) 671-7828 or (800) 922-6414; 1014 N Garden St, Bellingham; $$.*

Schnauzer Crossing ☆☆☆ A sophisticated and unique B&B in a lovely contemporary home overlooking Lake Whatcom. *On Lakeway Dr off I-5 exit 253; (360) 734-2808 or (800) 562-2808; 4421 Lakeway Dr, Bellingham; $$$.*

The Willows ☆☆☆ Perched on a knoll 100 feet above the Lummi Island beach, The Willows offers sweeping views and an elaborate atmosphere. It's also one of the few—and definitely the best—places on Lummi for an evening meal, but you'll need reservations months in advance. *From the ferry, head north on Nugent for 3½ miles; (360) 758-2620; 2579 W Shore Dr, Lummi Island; $$$.*

Cheaper Sleeps

Wilkins Farm B&B In the cool shadow of Sumas Mountain is the ultimate family bed and breakfast. The atmosphere is low-key and friendly, and so is the price. *(360) 966-7616; 4165 S Pass Rd, Everson.*

More Information

Bellingham Parks and Recreation: *(360) 676-6985.*
Bellingham/Whatcom County Visitors and Convention Bureau: *(360) 671-3990 or (800) 487-2032.*
Whatcom Parks and Recreation: *(360) 733-2900.*
Lummi Island Ferry: *(360) 758-2190.*
Base Camp Inc. (leading local outdoors store): *(360) 733-5461.*
Fairhaven Bike & Mountain Sports (bike, ski, in-line skate sales/rentals): *(360) 733-4433.*
H&H Outdoor Sports (fishing/camping supplies): *(360) 733-2050.*

San Juan
Islands
and Anacortes

From Anacortes west to Haro Strait, north to Patos Island, and east to Rosario Strait, including Moran State Park, Mount Constitution, Lime Kiln Point State Park, the San Juan Islands National Wildlife Refuge, and the northern stretch of the Cascadia Marine Trail.

Welcome to paradise. Please don't block the ferry lane. To many Evergreen State natives, the San Juan Islands are the perfect bite-size example of everything that's always been right—but keeps going wrong—with Washington's premier outdoor treasures. As a just-far-enough-away retreat from the Seattle metro mess, the placid shorelines, quiet coves, and cool forests of the San Juans are the penultimate outdoor retreat. But as an increasingly desirable national tourist destination—and a year-round residence for the rich, super-rich, and pseudo-rich—they also have all the trappings of paradise lost.

For those of us who love the islands the way they always used to be, summertime San Juan visits have been abandoned, mostly for mental-health and sagging-spirit reasons. Summertime in the San Juans is frenetic, with thousands of condo-dwellers, kayakers, camping cyclists, and yacht skippers clogging local parks, roadways, ferry lines, and latte stands. Just getting to the idyllic archipelago can be a trying experience in June, July, or August, when Washington State ferries built to handle early 1970s loads creak, groan, and shudder under the crushing weight of tourism. And once you're in the islands, even a little noise seems like a lot, because, well, it just shouldn't be this way.

Not everyone agrees with this assessment, proving once again that many people are just plain wrong. Some summertime San Juan adventurers say the islands' soothing qualities and great weather (the islands, in the Olympic rain shadow, are drier and sunnier than Seattle, but contain one-third more fat per serving) more than make up for the trouble of getting there and back. That's a valid assessment. But we can't help believe the truly savvy Washington outdoor lover tends to avoid the islands during the peak California migration season.

Smarter island hoppers don't start jumping until mid-September. Then, after all those Midwestern kids are back in school and East Coasters are back in therapy, the islands reopen to the rest of us. And what a grand reunion it is. The islands in the off season are the islands of old. The air is crisp enough to fold into origami sailboats. The deafening roar of silence keeps you awake all night in the tent at Moran State Park. The porpoises look up at the bow of the boat and sigh in relief that it's only you. All is right with the world of water, and there's no better place to recharge the spiritual batteries than the islands called San Juan.

Perhaps we overestimate the seasonal difference. The islands—743 when the tide goes out, 428 when it comes back in—are, after all, a world-class marine getaway even in the summer, particularly to those who explore their myriad coastlines by boat or sea kayak. Few Washington summer experiences can top a week at Moran State Park or a day on the water capped by a surprise brush—and by that, we mean actual fin-to-stern contact—with an orca whale.

But you old-timers know what we mean. We love the San Juan Islands not so much for what they are as for what they were. For many of us, they're the plush winter reward for spartan summer toils. The San Juans are the cheesecake dessert on our outdoors menu. Palatable in any form. But best served cold.

Getting There

Two primary options: Go off-season, or wait in line.

The most obvious and cost-effective way of getting to the San Juans is via Washington State ferries, which run year-round from Anacortes, about 90 minutes north of Seattle; for schedule and fare information, call (800) 843-3779. Expect the ferries to be packed to the gills—and beyond—in the summer. Getting a ferry out of Anacortes can be a long, dull 3-hours-and-up wait. Bring a good book—or park the car and board with a bike. Money-saving tip: Cars only pay westbound. If you plan to visit more than one island, arrange to go to the farthest first (San Juan) and work your way east.

There are a few ways to cheat if you don't need your car (and if you work at it hard enough, you probably won't). The Victoria Clipper makes a once-a-

day trip from downtown Seattle to Friday Harbor (with a quick stop in Port Townsend) from mid-May through mid-September. The summer-only ferry departs Pier 69 at 7:30am and arrives in Friday Harbor just before noon; for Clipper information, call (206) 448-5000 or (800) 888-2535. Another summertime option is via Bellingham; the Island Shuttle Express provides passenger-only ferry service to the San Juan Islands, May through September. Call for reservations: (360) 671-1137.

For the total-express experience, fly. Kenmore Air schedules four flights a day during peak season. Round-trip flights start at about $99 per person; for more information, call (206)486-8400 or (206) 486-1257.

Adjoining Areas

SOUTH: **Whidbey and Camano Islands**

EAST: **Bellingham and Lummi Island; Skagit Valley**

Parks/Camping

The islands have one of the highest mind-boggling-picnic-spot-per-square-mile ratios in the Northwest. Camping facilities, conversely, are somewhat limited in relation to the crush of summer visitors. But what's there is first-rate. We'll take it island by island.

Orcas Island

The largest of the San Juan Islands is home to the chain's most diverse outdoor-recreation site, **Moran State Park.** The sprawling 4,800-acre park is one of the jewels of the state park system, with a rich mix of old-growth forests, freshwater lakes, pleasant campsites, and a 2,400-foot mountaintop where the view is as gorgeous as any in the Northwest. The park, named for shipbuilder and former resident Robert Moran (who donated the park land and whose mansion now is the focus of nearby Rosario Resort), often surprises first-time visitors who expect a marine environment. Even though it's the largest park in the San Juan Islands, most of the park is wooded, mountainous terrain. Waterborne activities at Moran are on fresh water, not salt. Four small, picturesque lakes are found in the park, two of them ringed by scenic campsites.

Campers pack the park's 166 campsites (no hookups) all summer. In fact, you're likely to be out of luck unless you reserve a site well in advance through the State Parks reservation system. Those who land a site are rarely disappointed. This is a big, diverse park, with two main camping areas, pleasant picnic grounds, two boat launches, bathhouses, swimming beaches, and moorage docks with rental boats. Also on site is a large Extended Learning Center, which offers cabins for rent to large groups. Activities include fishing, kayaking, canoeing, or boating in Mountain or Cascade Lake and hiking on the park's 30-mile trail system (see also the Fishing, Boating, and Hiking sections, below).

One of those trails leads from the park's lowland camping areas to Moran's highlight—2,400-foot Mount Constitution, the highest spot in the San Juans. At the summit (which also can be driven to during daylight hours), the view in all directions is spectacular. Climb up the stairway in the 12th-century replica stone observation tower, and you can see as far south as Mount Rainier and the Olympics, west to Vancouver Island, north to Vancouver, BC, and east into the North Cascades. It's an airplane-style view—not to be missed. (Note: Cyclists or walk-on ferry passengers can arrange transportation to Mount Constitution through Adventure Limo & Taxi service, (360) 376-4994.)

Moran State Park is open all year. Campsites can be reserved up to 11 months in advance by calling Reservations Northwest; (800) 452-5687. *Follow signs 13 miles northeast from the Orcas Island ferry landing; (360) 376-2326 or (800) 233-0321.*

Also on Orcas are **Doe Bay Village Resort,** (360) 376-2291, which offers 50 campsites (8 have hookups); the primitive **Obstruction Pass State Park** near the mouth of East Sound at Olga, which has 9 campsites accessible via the beach or a half-mile trail; and **West Beach Resort** at Eastsound, (360) 376-2240, a private facility with 72 campsites (36 with hookups).

Lopez Island

The favorite island of cyclists has plenty of parks providing great day-trip or overnight stopovers. Two popular westside day-use parks, **Otis Perkins** and **Upright Channel,** are great for exploring, with good beach access. **Agate Beach County Park,** on Outer Bay at the southwest tip of the island near Mackaye Harbor, has a pleasant rocky beach for the tired cyclist, with views of the lighthouse at Iceberg Point. A great place for a sunset. Nearby **Hughes Bay County Park** is another pleasant beach, accessible by stairs from a wooded upland. Seals and bald eagles can often be seen from the rocky promontory of **Shark Reef Recreation Area,** a long stone's throw away from the southernmost tip of San Juan Island. A rare stand of old-growth timber remains in this park.

Two good campgrounds are found a short distance from the Lopez ferry terminal. **Odlin County Park** is an 80-acre spread with 30 campsites (no hookups), a boat launch, and low-bank waterfront access. Sites here can be reserved (two-night minimum) by calling (360) 468-2496. On the northeast side of the island is **Spencer Spit State Park,** a 130-acre park with 40 waterfront sites (no hookups) and a group camp that can be reserved. The waterfront campsites can be reserved up to 11 months in advance by calling (800) 452-5687. The park, one of the most pleasant in the islands, is a designated Cascadia Marine Trail campsite (see Sea Kayaking, below), and its 16 moorage buoys make it a popular boat-in campground for mariners of all sorts. No matter how many visitors arrive to explore the sandy beach, however, there's still twice as many rabbits here as people. *Spencer Spit is 5 miles from the ferry terminal on Baker View Road; (360) 468-2251 or (800) 233-0321.*

San Juan Island

Popular day-use parks on the San Juans' most populous island include **American** and **English Camps** (see Attractions, below), **San Juan County Park** on Westside Road (see below), and **Lime Kiln Point State Park** (see Wildlife, below).

The best campground is **Lakedale,** which has 117 campsites (19 with hookups) and three small lakes for fishing and swimming, on Roche Harbor Road 4.5 miles from the ferry terminal. As the primary public campground on the island, it's often overcrowded, but sites can be reserved in advance by calling (800) 617-CAMP. Rental cycles, boats, and camping gear are available here. The park is open March 15 to October 15. **San Juan County Park,** 10 miles from the ferry terminal on Westside Road, near Smallpox Bay, has 20 campsites, a boat ramp and beach access. Campsites here are overcrowded, but can be reserved by calling (360) 378-2992. The offshore area of this park is a favorite of island scuba divers.

Other private campgrounds include the Pedal Inn, 5 miles from the ferry terminal on False Bay Drive, where 25 bike/hiker sites can be reserved by calling (360) 378-3049; and Snug Harbor Marina Resort, on Mitchell Bay Road 8.5 miles from the terminal, which has 16 campsites (4 with hookups), a boat launch, and other services. Sites can be reserved by calling (360) 378-4762. In Friday Harbor proper is Town and Country Trailer Park, which has 40 sites (some with hookups), showers and laundry facilities; (360) 378-4717.

Shaw Island

The sole choice for campers on the quiet island of Shaw is **South Beach County Park,** which has 12 campsites, a boat launch, beach access, and nice views along Indian Cove. Campsites cannot be reserved here. The park also is a grand picnic spot. Its sandy beach is one of the loveliest in all the islands. Canoeists and kayakers can paddle a short distance across the channel to Canoe Island, home of a summer camp for teens. The park is a popular boat-in destination for powerboaters and paddlers based in Friday Harbor, which is less than 4 nautical miles away.

Fidalgo Island

One of the San Juans' best beachfront parks isn't even technically in the San Juans. **Washington Park** in Anacortes is an island park, nonetheless. The 220-acre park on Fidalgo Head, just beyond the Anacortes Ferry Terminal, is one of the loveliest waterfront getaways in the Northwest. The day-use park has a pleasant beach, picnic area, and boat launch, but the highlight is a 3.5-mile loop road that skirts the shoreline all the way around the park. The narrow road can be driven one way, or better yet walked or cycled, to grand waterfront picnic spots with views of Guemes Channel, the San Juans, and all the pleasure craft headed toward them. It's a wonderful place to spend a few hours if you're stuck in a day-long ferry line. The park is about a 20-minute walk or 5-minute bike ride from the ferry terminal.

Cycling

All four of the San Juan Islands served by ferry—Lopez, Shaw, Orcas, and San Juan—are great places to explore by bicycle. Many visitors, particularly those returning after an initial visit, *prefer* to come by bicycle, for several reasons. One is that each of the islands is small enough to cross by bicycle in a couple of hours, although some are quite hilly. A larger advantage to a cycle visit, however, is ease of access. Cyclists get first shake in the ferry line at Anacortes. In midsummer, commuting to the islands by bicycle could shave half a day off the ferry-line wait.

Don't expect to be the only one savvy enough to figure this out. The San Juans are one of the few destinations in the country where cyclists occasionally overwhelm available facilities. As many as 150,000 cyclists are believed to invade the islands every year. In midsummer you're likely to find a line even for cycles at the ferry, and popular cycling roads on Lopez and San Juan Islands have actual bike-jams (or "gaper jams," if you're a local). That makes it even more important than usual to observe smart riding etiquette. Stay single file in groups of five or less, and get clear of the road whenever you stop.

Lopez is by far the most popular cycling venue, largely because it's almost exclusively flat. A 30-mile loop, easy enough for most riders to make in a day, circles the island, with good saltwater views and park stopovers all along the route. Or devise your own route by following a map and meandering along the island's 70 miles of county roads. You can bring your own bike on the ferry for a small fee, or rent one from several sources on the island. Vendors such as Cycle San Juans, (360) 468-3251, or the Bicycle Shop, (360) 468-3497, will deliver rented bikes to the ferry or wherever you're staying. Lopez Bicycle Works, (360) 468-2847, also offers rentals and cycling supplies. From the ferry terminal, overnighters can pedal an easy mile to Odlin County Park, or 4.5 miles to Spencer Spit State Park. See Parks/Camping, above, for details and a list of other stopover points along the Lopez cycling route.

Almost as popular among cyclists is **San Juan Island,** which is laced with 95 miles of mostly flat roads, many with good views. The scenic West Side Road is a water-view standout. Lakedale Campground (see Parks/Camping, above) is a popular cycle-in overnight spot 4.5 miles from the ferry terminal. Day trippers should consider the 10-mile ride to San Juan County Park, which has great local marine views, or nearby Lime Kiln Park, specifically designed for shore-based whale watching. Cycle rentals are available two blocks from the ferry terminal at Island Bicycles, (360) 378-4941.

Strong riders will get a good workout on hilly **Orcas Island,** where some local hills are torturous (i.e., "The Wall," a 16.5-degree grade on Enchanted Forest Road west of Eastsound, or the lung-busting 2,000-vertical-foot jaunt up 2,400-foot Mount Constitution). But it's not all that way. Many riders come specifically to wheel their way to Moran State Park (see Parks/Camping, above), 14 miles from the ferry terminal. Rentals are conveniently located near the ferry terminal at Dolphin Bay Bicycles, (360) 376-4157, and from Wildlife Cycles, (360) 376-4708, in Eastsound. Hint: Wait until the ferry traffic clears before you head out!

While it lacks amenities such as cycle rental shops, **Shaw Island,** the least cluttered in the chain, is another grand two-wheel destination because of expansive views, truly rural landscapes, and roads virtually devoid of auto traffic.

An excellent pocket-size cycle map of the islands, the "Bicyclists Touring Companion," is published by Cycle San Juans. The map, which lists point-to-point mileages and other helpful information, is available at outdoor stores and cycle shops, or from Cycle San Juans, Route 1, Box 1744, Lopez Island, WA 98261; (360) 468-3251.

Sea Kayaking

First-time visitors to the San Juans often go home disappointed that they've just spent a week in a chain of islands with very little access to a beach. The sad fact is that most waterfront property in the islands is privately owned (probably by your boss), and except for a handful of state and county parks, it's mostly off-limits.

Not so for paddlers, however. A healthy string of public beaches and take-outs rings the San Juans, including the many islands in the archipelago that are accessible *only* by water. The islands—which form a long string of protected waterways rife with hidden coves, quiet waters, and abundant wildlife—are as close to a sea-kayaking paradise as you'll find in the Northwest. Some paddlers spend entire waterborne lifetimes exploring the chain, and we won't begin to attempt to list all the possible destinations here. If you're serious about exploring the San Juans in depth from a sea kayak, we strongly suggest picking up a San Juan–specific marine guidebook. *The San Juan Islands Afoot & Afloat,* by Marge and Ted Mueller (The Mountaineers) is a good start. It lists nearly all the publicly accessible beach sites on the major islands, with an eye toward the mariner.

If you'd rather get it straight from the locals, your best bet is to consult with one of the many kayak experts in the islands. The islands have several top-notch kayak outfitters (see below), offering rental boats and gear, maps, and even guided tours. Paddlers with even a minimal degree of sea-kayaking experience can rent a boat for about $30 a day and set off on their own, get a guided tour for $40 to $50, or splurge for a full-blown $300-to-$400 weekend trip where the guide leads the way, points out the wildlife, pitches the tents, and cooks the meals. Any one of these can be—and usually is—an unforgettable experience, one you're not likely to find anywhere else in the Lower 48 states.

Experienced paddlers setting out on their own multiday trip should keep in mind the growing number of **Cascadia Marine Trail**—a state-managed water trail from Olympia to British Columbia—campsites recently established in the islands. At this writing, 14 Cascadia-designated sites dotted the island chain, all available for waterborne travelers. More will likely be added in coming years. Some are state parks sites listed under Parks/Camping, above. Others are state Department of Natural Resources sites accessible only by water (see Boating/Sailing, below, for a list). For Cascadia Marine Trail permit information, maps, and a brochure, contact Washington State Parks, (800) 233-0321, or Washington Water Trails Association, (206) 545-9161.

Many a Washington paddler has received an introduction to sea kayaking in East Sound, the large bay dividing the halves of saddlebag-shaped **Orcas Island.** Rentals are available there at Crescent Beach Kayaks; (360) 376-2464. Lessons and guided East Sound tours are available from Island Kayak Guides at Doe Bay, (360) 376-4755, or Shearwater Adventures in East Sound, (360) 376-4699. The latter also offers orca whale–watching expeditions in conjunction with the Whale Museum at Friday Harbor, (360) 378-4710. An outfitter on **Lopez Island,** Lopez Kayaks, (360) 468-2847, is open summer's only (May to September).

On **San Juan Island,** kayaks can be rented from any of a number of

Friday Harbor vendors, including Emerald Seas Diving Center, (360) 378-2772. Two leading outfitters offering single- and multiday wildlife-watching adventures are Sea Quest Expeditions, (360) 378-5767, and San Juan Kayak Expeditions, (360) 378-4436, both in Friday Harbor. Both lead fun, educational tours through fantastic surroundings. Whale and other wildlife sightings are common, and there's no more thrilling way to see an orca than from water level. Beginners shouldn't shy away from an overnight tour; most trips are led by patient, skilled guides quite accustomed to leading paddlers with virtually no experience.

Newcomers, in fact, can test the waters before they ever get to them. On the way to Anacortes, stop by Eddyline Kayaks (1344 Ashten Road, Burlington; (360) 757-2300); it is located off SR 20 at the Port of Skagit County (west of I-5). Test-paddle a kayak in their man-made pond, then rent one for a weekend in the San Juans. Reservations are necessary.

Note: Kayaks can be carried on Washington State ferries for a small charge in addition to the walk-on fee.

Wildlife

The San Juan Islands are an indescribably rich wildlife habitat, boasting healthy populations of marine and land creatures, some found in greater numbers here than anywhere else in the contiguous United States. But one species, the **orca** or "killer" whale, draws the bulk of attention from visitors. The San Juans are the permanent home to three sizable pods of orcas (80 to 90 in all), which are commonly spotted from boats, kayaks, the state ferries, and even occasionally from island streets. A literal armada of whale-watching tourist boats descends on the islands every summer, hauling binocular-armed tourists out for a brush with the friendly, fascinating mammals.

Whale watching has grown into a science here. An organized network of whale spotters throughout the island chain keeps close tab on the pods. The orcas rarely venture anywhere near the major islands without being spotted, then followed by the radio-equipped armada. So far, whales and tour boats have coexisted fairly well, although government studies are under way to determine if the whales are bothered by all the commotion. However you choose to pursue the whales, start your quest with a stop at Friday Harbor's **Whale Museum,** (360) 378-4710. It's free, and open daily.

The best time to see orcas is in the summer, when pods follow migrating salmon in close to shore. But sightings occur throughout the year. It's not hard to find a **commercial whale-watching** ride in the summer. Dozens of vendors offer whale-watching trips, and airplane whale tours also are available. Most are based in Friday Harbor, but some tours depart from Bellingham, Anacortes, or even downtown Seattle (via the *Victoria Clipper;* see Getting There, above). Daylong whale tours cost between $40 and $60, and most vendors belong to an industry group, the Whale Watching Operators Association Northwest, which heeds whale-engagement rules. A leading service is *Western Prince,* (360) 378-5315 or (800) 757-ORCA(6722). The Seattle Aquarium, (206) 386-4353, also has summer whale tours, some of which include transportation to the departure point in Anacortes. For a full list of operators, call the San Juan Islands Visitor Information Center, (360) 468-3663.

Kayak tour guides also offer whale-watching trips, with opportunities for a truly memorable encounter for those fortunate enough to come (literally) eye-to-eye with the orcas. See Sea Kayaking, above, for outfitter information.

And the whales occasionally are spotted from land. San Juan Island's **Lime Kiln Point State Park** on whale-rich Haro Strait (see Parks/Camping, above) was designed specifically for land-based whale watching. From a vantage point near the picturesque Lime Kiln Lighthouse, you can gaze across the Strait with binoculars and sometime spot pods of whales as close as ¾ mile from shore. Knowledgeable volunteer spotters from the Whale Museum are on hand daily in the summer, weekends in the fall.

Other fascinating wildlife species slither, fly, and plod across the islands, largely overlooked in the orca frenzy. **California sea lions, harbor seals, river otters, minke whales,** and **Dall's porpoises** are commonly seen in local waterways.

The islands also are a particularly important bird habitat; 84 islands in the archipelago, in fact, are designated as the San Juan Islands National Wildlife Refuge. All these islands except Matia and Turn are off-limits to the public, but they can be viewed easily from boats, including the Washington State ferries. A walk-on ferry ride through the San Juans, in fact, is about as productive (and inexpensive) a wildlife tour as you're likely to find anywhere in the Northwest. Bring the binoculars and bird guide, and you're not likely to be disappointed. Common species are **bald eagles** (which nest here in greater numbers than anywhere else in the Lower 48), **golden eagles, great blue herons, belted kingfishers,** various **owls** and **hawks, turkey vultures,** and marine birds such as **tufted puffins, cormorants, scoters, rhinoceros auklets,** and **glaucous-winged gulls.**

Bring your bicycle along (see Cycling, above), and you can combine your boat tour with a land-based wildlife venture on San Juan Island, which is particularly productive for bird- and whale-watching. Lime Kiln Point State Park (see above) is a grand whale-watching post, and Cattle Point, at the extreme south end of the island, is home to nesting **bald eagles** all year round.

Most of the common land mammals found throughout Western Washington also are present in the islands. Don't be surprised if a **black-tailed deer** pads through your campsite at Moran State Park—or if a **raccoon** burgles your cooler at Spencer Spit.

For an active, exciting education about the San Juan Island ecosystem, immerse yourself in a week of marine science activities at the Island Institute (PO Box 661, Vashon Island, WA 98070; (206) 463-ORCA), a camp for kids or adults based on the privately owned Spieden Island.

Boating/Sailing

Choose your pleasure. During the dry, sunny summer months, the San Juans are the indisputable boating capital of the Northwest—a place where 8-foot Livingstons are happily at home among 60-foot yachts. A full range of boat rentals, facilities, and services are available, both in the islands themselves and nearby Anacortes, which serves as a staging area for many island excursions. All the major islands have moorage facilities and basic services, but the primary boating havens here are found at Anacortes and Friday Harbor.

Marina facilities

In Anacortes, **Cap Sante Boat Haven,** (360) 293-0694, a very nice facility managed by the Port of Anacortes, has extensive moorage, fuels, rest rooms, showers, laundry facilities, and nearby marine-supply stores. It's a primary starting point for many San Juan guided excursions, and boats and yachts often are turned over to renters here. Cap Sante is just east of downtown Anacortes.

In the islands, the **Port of Friday Harbor,** (360) 378-2688, is the largest moorage and full-service marina facility, with ample guest moorage and full boater services. **Roche Harbor Resort,** (360) 378-2155, is another popular boater destination. On Lopez, **Islands Marine Center,** (360) 468-3377, is a full-service marina near Lopez Village. On Orcas, **Deer Harbor Resort & Marina,** (360) 376-4420, is a popular spot with guest moorage (call ahead) and other services. Other popular Orcas boater stop-ins are **West Sound Marina,** (360) 376-2314; **Rosario Resort,** (800) 562-8820; and **West Beach Resort,** (360) 376-2240. On Blakely Island, it's **Blakely Island Marina,** (360) 375-6121.

Rentals and tours

If you're looking for a small-to-medium powerboat for fishing or island exploration, most of the marinas listed above can put you in the driver's seat. San Juan Boat Rentals in Friday Harbor, (360) 378-3499, also offers a wide range of boats.

If a skippered cruise, either on a power- or sailboat, is more to your liking, there's no shortage of opportunities here. More than a dozen skippered charter services operate in the San Juans, with home bases at Friday Harbor, Deer Harbor, Eastsound, and Anacortes. Bare-boat rentals also are available from a number of yacht brokers. A small, basic sailboat costs about $100 a day, while fully skippered cruises can run several thousand dollars per person per week. Rentals are available all year, but they're substantially cheaper outside the peak tourist season. Two leading charter services with both bare-boat and skippered tours are Charters Northwest, (360) 378-7196, and Trophy Charters, (360) 378-2110. On Orcas, try Deer Harbor Charters, (800) 544-5758. The San Juan Islands Visitors Information Center, (360) 468-3663, can help you match your desires with a suitable skipper. (Note: Guided San Juan boat tours also are available from Bellingham. See the Bellingham and Lummi Island chapter.)

Boat camping

Private boaters will find an almost overwhelming array of quality public moorages with access to primitive beachfront or upland campsites, managed by **Washington State Parks** or the **Department of Natural Resources.** (Many of these also serve as Cascadia Marine Trail campsites; see Sea Kayaking, above.) Most have moorage floats or docks. Fees are charged at some during the summer, and fresh water usually is limited. Avid boaters say these parks offer some of the best boat camping (or boat-in camping) in the country.

In addition to the waterfront parks noted under Parks/Camping, above, these popular boat-in spots include state marine parks at James Island, Blind Island, Turn Island, Posey Island, Jones Island, Obstruction Pass, Doe Island, Clark Island, Matia Island, Sucia Island, Patos Island, and Stuart Island. Of these, the Northern Boundary islands—Sucia, Patos, Matia, Clark, and Barnes—are the most scenic, best developed, and most heavily used. Sucia Island, with 55 campsites and moorage for some 700 boats, is a splendid spot, but can look more like a small city than a wild refuge on summer weekends. Patos and Stuart islands also receive fairly heavy use. For information, call Washington State Parks, (800) 233-0321. A good guidebook to the marine parks is *The San Juan Islands: Afoot & Afloat,* by Marge and Ted Mueller (The Mountaineers).

Fishing

Freshwater and saltwater anglers can get their licks in on the islands. Or around the islands, if salmon is the prey of choice. The rocky shoals and kelp beds around the San Juans have been among the most productive king salmon fishing grounds in the state during the 1990s. Catch rates have remained consistent here and, more important, the islands have been spared most of the summer-long closures plaguing the nearby Strait of Juan de Fuca and North Puget Sound. Trophy kings upward of 40 pounds (most bound for the Fraser River system) are not uncommon here, although finding where, when, and how to pursue them can be tricky. First-timers should strongly consider a guided charter trip, available through Trophy Charters in Friday Harbor, (360) 378-2110; Fish Tales Charters in Anacortes, (360) 293-5766; or King Salmon Charters on Shaw Island, (360) 468-2314.

Waters around the islands are open all year for salmon fishing. Prime time for kings is July and August, and hot spots include **Cattle Point** and **Eagle Point** on the south end of San Juan Island. But the islands also boast productive summer coho, winter blackmouth (resident coho) and, during late summer weeks in odd-numbered years, pink salmon fisheries. Lingcod and halibut fishing also can be fair, particularly in the spring.

Trout and bass anglers keep themselves busy with above-average fishing in **Mountain** and **Cascade Lakes** in Moran State Park (see Parks/Camping, above), **Egg Lake** and **Sportsman's Lake** on San Juan Island, and **Hummel Lake** on Lopez. Hummel, Egg, Sportsman's, and Mountain Lakes are open all year. Fishing also is available all year on the three small private lakes at Lakedale Campground on San Juan Island, where no license is required (see Parks/Camping, above).

Hiking

Moran State Park on Orcas Island is the best—and really *only*—hiking venue in the San Juans, where most of the land is privately owned and inaccessible to long-distance strollers. Moran makes up for the lack of quantity in the island chain, however. The park has more than 30 miles of trails, most of which skirt the sides of 2,400-foot Mount Constitution. Many of these are steep, forested routes. But the access road to the top of Mount Constitution allows a cheater's option: hitch a ride to the top and walk back down, passing some fabulous scenery on the way to a pickup—or your campsite—in the lower portion of the park. A popular route is the **Mount Constitution/Twin Lakes Trail** (difficult; 1.5 miles one way), which drops more than 1,000 feet in a mile down from the lookout tower to Twin Lakes, where a side trail can be caught back to Mountain Lake and the main Moran camping area. Again, this is a good one to walk downhill. Uphill striders will struggle, but it's a grand workout.

Not all trails in the park are this extreme. The most popular route, no doubt, is the **Cascade Falls Trail** (easy; 1 mile round trip), which can be hiked either from a signed roadside pullout along the Mount Constitution

Road or as part of a 3-mile (one way) hike between the Mountain Lake and Cascade Lake camping areas.

Other popular routes in the park include the **Mountain Lake Loop** (easy; 3.5 miles round trip), **Little Summit Trail** (moderate; 4.5 miles round trip), and **North Side Trail** (moderate; 9.5 miles round trip). For more hiking information, contact the state park at (360) 376-2326.

A very pleasant hike that offers a sense of what the San Juans would be like if they were public land completely open to recreation is the **Washington Park Loop** (easy; 3.5 miles round trip), a combination one-way road/walking path at Washington Park in Anacortes (see Parks/Camping, above). The 3.5-mile loop is open to auto traffic, but cars are relatively rare, and in some places the single-track trail leaves the road and skirts the highly scenic cliffs and rocky beaches of Fidalgo Head. Throw a loaf of bread and a bottle of wine in a daypack and give it a try. It's a walk that rarely disappoints.

Scuba Diving

Many Washington divers swear the deep coves, bays, and straits between the San Juan Islands offer the best cold-water diving on the planet. A major center for gear, rentals, and instruction is Emerald Seas Diving Center, 180 First Street, Friday Harbor, (360) 378-2772.

Attractions

Lopez Island

Lopez Island, flat and shaped like a jigsaw-puzzle piece, is a sleepy, rural place, famous for its friendly locals (drivers always wave) and its cozy coves and full pastures. It has the easiest bicycling in the islands: a 30-mile circuit suitable for the whole family to ride in a day (see Cycling, above). **Lopez Village** is basic, but has a few spots worth knowing about, such as **Holly B's Bakery** in the Lopez Plaza, (360) 468-2133, with celebrated fresh bread and pastries and coffee to wash them down (open June through September), and **Gail's** (Village Center #1; (360) 468-2150), for excellent soups and sandwiches.

Orcas Island

Named not for the whales (the large cetaceans tend to congregate on the west side of San Juan Island and are rarely spotted here), but for a Spanish explorer, Orcas has a reputation as the most beautiful of the four big San Juan Islands. The sprawling mansion left by shipbuilding tycoon Robert Moran (see Moran State Park, a must-see, under Parks/Camping, above) now is the centerpiece of **Rosario Resort,** just west of the park. Unfortunately, the resort doesn't live up to its extravagant billing and prices. But the mansion, decked out in memorabilia and mahogany trim and featuring an enormous pipe organ (still in use; check for concert dates), is certainly worth a sightseeing stop; (360) 376-2222. Every small, hip town has to lay claim to a small, hip bakery, and Eastsound has **Roses Bakery Cafe,** (360) 376-4220. Roses features simple breakfasts and lunches, but locals prefer the outdoor patio for fresh blueberry scones, muffins, savory potpies, and lattes served in enormous bowls. Orcas Island is the perfect place to relax with a good book in hand and **Darvill's Book Store,** (360) 376-2135, in Eastsound, houses an impressive stock of reading material for any and all interests. Pacific Northwest authors are well represented here.

San Juan Island

San Juan Island is the most populated in the archipelago; therefore it supports the biggest town, Friday Harbor, though typically nightlife is scarce even here, especially in the off season. Attractions include the mid-19th-century sites of the **American** and **English Camps,** established when ownership of the island was under dispute, and now part of the dual-site San Juan Islands National Historical Park. The U.S.–British border dispute here led to the infamous Pig War of 1859–1860, so called because the sole casualty was a pig. The Americans and British shared joint occupation until 1872, when the dispute was settled in favor of the United States. The English camp, toward the island's north end, is wooded and secluded, while the American camp is open, windy prairie and beach, inhabited now only by thousands of rabbits. Either camp makes a fine picnic spot. The **San Juan Historical Museum** is located in an old home in Friday Harbor filled with memorabilia from the island's early days. The 90-plus-year-old founder, a third-generation islander, is there two days a week. Admission is free; (360) 378-3949. Another bit of history is hidden away at the **Roche Harbor Resort** (see Lodgings, below). Here you'll find a mausoleum, a bizarre monument that may tell more about timber tycoon John McMillin than all the rest of Roche Harbor. The ashes of family members are contained in a set of stone chairs that surround a concrete dining room table. They're ringed by a set of 30-foot-high columns, symbolic of McMillan's adherence to Masonic beliefs. Whale lovers would be remiss to pass up a tour of the Whale Museum (see Wildlife, above). And oyster fans will be happy to visit **Westcott Bay Sea Farms** off West Valley Road just north of British Camp, (360) 378-2489, where you can help yourself to oysters at bargain prices. One of the island's largest festivals is Friday Harbor's **Dixieland Jazz Festival,** which spans three days every mid- to late July; for information, call (360) 378-5509.

Anacortes

Anacortes, the gateway to the San Juans, is itself on an island—Fidalgo. Though most travelers rush through here on their way to the ferry, this town adorned with colorful, life-size cutouts of early pioneers is quietly becoming a place where it's worth it to slow down in your journey. For picnic or ferry food, try **Geppetto's** (3320 Commercial Avenue; (360) 293-5033) for Italian take-out. Those with a little more time head to **Gere-A-Deli** (502 Commercial Avenue, (360) 293-7383), a friendly hangout with good homemade food in an airy former Bank of Commerce building, or the new **Anacortes Brewhouse** (320 Commercial Avenue; (360) 293-2444) with their own brews and wood-oven pizzas. And don't forget the **Calico Cupboard,** offshoot of the well-known cafe and bakery in La Conner (901 Commercial Street; (360) 293-7315). If you need reading material for the ferry line, stop by **Watermark Book Company** (612 Commercial Avenue; (360) 293-4277), loaded with interesting reads. Seafaring folks should poke around **Marine Supply and Hardware** (202 Commercial Avenue; (360) 293-3014). Established in 1913, Marine Supply is packed to the rafters with basic and hard-to-find specialty marine items. And for the history of Fidalgo Island, visit the **Anacortes Museum** (1305 Eighth Street; (360) 293-1915).

Restaurants

Bay Cafe ☆☆☆   Entertaining a full house of both tourists and locals most nights, this storefront restaurant specializes in ethnic dishes and reasonable prices. *Across from the old post office in Lopez; (360) 468-3700; Lopez Town, Lopez Island; $$.*

Bilbo's Festivo ☆   Orcas Islanders speak of this cozy little place with reverence. The fare includes a combination of Mexican and New Mexican influences, with mesquite-grilled specials. *In central Eastsound; (360) 376-4728; Northbeach Rd and A St, Eastsound, Orcas Island; $.*

Cafe Olga ☆   You're likely to experience a wait at Cafe Olga, a popular lunch and late-afternoon stop for locals and visitors alike. Luckily, this country kitchen is part of the Orcas Island Artworks, a cooperative crafts gallery where you can browse while you work up an appetite. *East of Moran State Park at Olga Junction; (360) 376-5098; Olga, Orcas Island; $.*

Christina's ☆☆☆   Christina's continues to enjoy its long-standing reputation as the premier restaurant in the San Juan Islands, featuring an ever-changing, innovative, neo-Northwest menu that incorporates the freshest seasonal ingredients. *Eastsound at North Beach Rd and Horseshoe Hwy; (360) 376-4904; Eastsound, Orcas Island; $$$.*

Courtyard Bistro (Majestic Hotel) ☆☆   This elegant bistro has succeeded in combining the harvest of the Pacific Northwest with classic French cuisine and a Pacific Rim flair. There's also a Sunday champagne brunch, and live jazz Friday and Saturday nights in the pub. *Between 4th and 5th on Commercial; (360) 299-2923; 419 Commercial Ave, Anacortes; $$.*

Deer Harbor Lodge and Inn ☆☆   This expansive, rustic dining room with a large view deck is a cozy, soothing place, despite its size, and home to some very good seafood, with generous portions and homemade touches. *From ferry landing, follow signs to Deer Harbor; (360) 376-4110; Deer Harbor Rd, Deer Harbor, Orcas Island; $$.*

Duck Soup Inn ☆☆   Local seafoods and seasonal ingredients are featured on the successful menu limited to house specialties. Housebaked bread, a small bowl of perfectly seasoned soup, and a large green salad accompany the ample portions. Closed in winter. *4¹/₂ miles north of Friday Harbor; (360) 378-4878; 3090 Roche Harbor Rd, Friday Harbor, San Juan Island; $$.*

Katrina's   Except for the signature spinach-cheese pie and green salad with toasted hazelnuts and garlicky blue cheese dressing, you never know what you might find here. Odds are, whatever is served will be a simple sensation. With three stools inside and a few tippy tables in the ramshackle yard, the food's the real centerpiece here. *2 blocks up from the ferry terminal, across from the fire station; (360) 378-7290; 135 2nd St, Friday Harbor, San Juan Island; $.*

La Famiglia ☆   Here's a mainstream Italian lunch and dinner spot that emphasizes fresh pasta, calzone, and other hearty family fare befitting the name. *Prune Alley and North Beach Rd; (360) 376-2335; Prune Alley, Eastsound, Orcas Island; $.*

La Petite ☆☆   This restaurant at the Islands Inn motel features French-inspired food with a touch of Dutch. With only six entrees to choose from, quality is high. A fixed-price Dutch breakfast is intended primarily for (but not restricted to) motel guests. *34th and Commercial; (360) 293-4644; 3401 Commercial Ave, Anacortes; $$.*

Ship Bay Oyster House ☆☆   Ship Bay has developed a reputation as a great spot for fresh fish and local oysters. Lovers of the briny slimers will be in oyster heaven: baked, stewed, pan-fried, or au naturel. The clam chowder—a New Englandy version included with every entree—might be the best in the West. *Just east of Eastsound on Horseshoe Hwy; (360) 376-5886; Horseshoe Hwy E, Eastsound, Orcas Island; $$.*

Springtree Cafe ☆☆   The consistently excellent menu emphasizes seafood, organics, and local produce; the best food here is that which is the most adventurous. Vegetarians are well cared for since chef/owner James Boyle eschews meat. *Under the elm on Spring downtown; (360) 378-4848; 310 Spring St, Friday Harbor, San Juan Island; $$.*

Lodgings

Beach Haven Resort ☆   Regardless of the time of year, this funky family retreat with its long pebble beach, canoes, and rowboats reminds us of summer camp. No TV. No telephones. No fussy amenities. Expect a seven-day minimum summer stay. Accommodations range from rustic to modern apartments and a four-bedroom house. *8¹/2 miles NW of the ferry at President Channel; (360) 376-2288; Rte 1, Orcas Island; $$.*

Blue Fjord Cabins ☆   Lopez is the most secluded and tranquil of the three ferry-accessible islands, and the two log cabins at Blue Fjord are the most secluded and tranquil getaway on Lopez. Clean and airy chalets with full kitchens. *Elliott Rd at Jasper Cove; (360) 468-2749; Lopez Island; $$.*

Channel House ☆☆   Just a mile and a half from the Anacortes ferry dock, Channel House is a 1902 Victorian home designed by an Italian count. Choose from four antique-filled rooms with grand views or two suite-style units. *At Oakes and Dakota; (360) 293-9382 or (800) 238-4353; 2902 Oakes Ave, Anacortes; $$.*

Duffy House ☆☆   This 1920s Tudor-style farmhouse looking out upon Griffin Bay and the Olympics beyond offers five comfy guest rooms with private baths on a splendid, isolated site. Even neophyte bird-watchers won't be able to miss the bald eagles here; they nest in the backyard. *Take Argyle Rd south from town to Pear Point Rd; (360) 378-5604 or (800) 972-2089; 760 Pear Point Rd, Friday Harbor, San Juan Island; $$.*

Edenwild Inn ☆   There are eight rooms in this Victorian-style bed and breakfast, located in Lopez Village, a very easy stroll from the only restaurants on the island. Each comfortable room has its own bath, a few have fireplaces. It's the only B&B on the island to accept children, and the inn serves dinner Wednesday through Saturday. *In Lopez Village; (360) 468-3238; Eads Lane and Lopez Village Rd, Lopez Island; $$$.*

Friday Harbor House ☆☆☆   This stylish urban hotel set down in the islands is a bastion of soothing serenity. Each of the 20 rooms is decorated in muted tones, with gas fireplaces, tiny balconies, and Jacuzzis positioned to absorb the warmth from both the fireplace and the harbor view. *Turn right on 1st and right again on West St; (360) 378-8455; 130 West St, Friday Harbor, San Juan Island; $$$.*

Friday's ☆   The best of the rooms is unquestionably the third-floor nest with its own deck (and water view), kitchen, double shower, and Jacuzzi tub—though all have thoughtful touches. Note: The inn is right in the middle of town and not always the most quiet retreat. Downstairs is a bistro with good pizzas and huge salads. *2 blocks up from the ferry on 1st St; (360) 378-5848 or (800) 352-2632; 35 1st St, Friday Harbor, San Juan Island; $$.*

Hillside House ☆   This 4,000-square-foot modern house on the out-skirts of Friday Harbor distinguishes itself from other contemporary B&Bs by, among other things, its full-flight aviary. Sleep in a room adja-cent to it and you might find yourself waking up and staring into the face of Bob, an enormous Reeves pheasant! *On Carter Ave, west of the ferry landing; (360) 378-4730 or (800) 232-4730; 365 Carter Ave, Friday Harbor, San Juan Island; $$.*

Inn at Swifts Bay ☆☆☆   The most appealing accommodation on Lopez. Choose from two large and comfortable bedrooms or three luxurious suites. There's also a secluded outdoor hot tub that can be scheduled for private sittings (towels, robes, and slippers provided). Expect to be pampered. You *won't* get breakfast at the new Hunter Bay House—a cabin on a bluff over-looking the water—unless you cook it yourself, but you will get a beautiful temporary home for the two of you. *Head 1 mile south of ferry to Port Stanley Rd, left 1 mile; (360) 468-3636; #3402 Rte 2, Lopez Island; $$$.*

Kangaroo House ☆☆   The location of this bed and breakfast, next to the Orcas airport, isn't scenic, but the 2-acre grounds are, and it's conve-nient to Eastsound and North Beach. The beautiful, enormous 1907 Craftsman-style bungalow has four guest rooms upstairs and a downstairs suite. Children welcome. *North Beach Rd just north of Eastsound; (360) 376-2175; Eastsound, Orcas Island; $$.*

Lonesome Cove Resort ☆   Six immaculate little cabins set among trees at the water's edge, manicured lawns, and domesticated deer that wander the 75-acre woods make this place a lighthearted favorite. The sunsets are spectacular, and there's a fine view. No pets—too many baby ducks around. *Take Roche Harbor Rd 9 miles north to Lonesome Cove Rd (call for directions); (360) 378-4477; 5810 Lonesome Cove Rd, Friday Harbor, San Juan Island; $$.*

MacKaye Harbor Inn ☆   Location, location, location. Bicyclists call it paradise after their sweaty trek from the ferry to this little harbor. The tall powder-blue house sits above a sandy, shell-strewn beach, perfect for sunset strolls. Rent kayaks or mountain bikes. *12 miles south of the ferry landing on MacKaye Harbor Rd; (360) 468-2253; Lopez Island; $$.*

The Majestic Hotel ☆☆   Truly majestic, this 1889 hotel has been through a number of incarnations, but this is surely the grandest. Every one of the 23 rooms is unique, and up top is a cupola with a 360-degree view of Anacortes, Mount Baker, the Olympics, and the San Juans. There's no better perch for a glass of wine at sunset. *Between 4th and 5th on Commercial; (360) 293-3355; 419 Commercial Ave, Anacortes; $$$.*

Mariella Inn and Cottages ☆☆   This 11-room inn, built in 1902, is set on a 9-acre point, an easy stroll from Friday Harbor. The rooms are simple and elegant, though better value is found in the seven cabins set unobtrusively in the madronas on the waterfront (great for families). Rent sea kayaks, mountain bikes, and daysailers, or charter a 65-foot classic motor yacht (1927). *Left on 1st St, follow signs until turns into Turnpoint Rd; (360) 378-6868; 630 Turnpoint Rd, Friday Harbor, San Juan Island; $$$.*

North Beach Inn ☆   If you like funky, private settings with history and personality, this is the spot. Converted into a resort in the early '30s, the inn has 11 worn cabins laid out on a prime stretch of beach (bonfires allowed). Each comes with a kitchen, grill, Adirondack chairs, and a tremendous view. Bring Fido if you like. *1½ miles west of the airport at Mt Baker Rd (call ahead for directions); (360) 376-2660; Orcas Island; $$.*

Olympic Lights ☆☆   This tall Victorian farmhouse sits lonely as a lighthouse in a sea of open meadow. The renovated interior is more modern and elegant, with five rooms; note you must remove your shoes to tread the off-white pile carpet. Panoramic views of the Olympic Mountains and Strait of Juan de Fuca. *Take Argyle Ave out of Friday Harbor to Cattle Point Rd; (360) 378-3186; 4531-A Cattle Point Rd, Friday Harbor, San Juan Island; $$.*

Orcas Hotel ☆   The 12-room hostelry just above the ferry terminal is a gem, with period pieces (it was first built in 1904), lovely gardens, and a deck overlooking the water. The pub is a favorite local watering hole, and the bakery a good place to get bread for an afternoon picnic. *Orcas ferry landing; (360) 376-4300; Orcas Island; $$$.*

Roche Harbor Resort   Some renovation has been done since Teddy Roosevelt visited, but not tons. Still, the 107-year-old resort has a terrific view, a few renovated cottages, and condos. Between strolling the gardens, swimming, tennis, and visiting the mausoleum (really), there's plenty to do. *In Roche Harbor; (360) 378-2155 or (800) 451-8190; Roche Harbor, San Juan Island; $$$.*

Spring Bay Inn ☆☆   Set on 57 heavily wooded acres rife with wildlife and hiking trails, this waterfront inn adjacent to Obstruction Pass State Park is an outdoor enthusiast's dream. Rooms all have bay views and each morning guests are led on a two-hour sea kayak tour (beginners welcome, kayaks and equipment provided), followed by a big, healthy brunch. *Follow Obstruction Pass Rd to Obstruction Pass Park Trailhead, take right fork onto dirt road to Spring Bay gate; (360) 376-5531; Obstruction Pass Park Rd, Olga, Orcas Island; $$$.*

Trumpeter Inn ☆   Located in splendid isolation in the middle of farmlands about two miles outside of Friday Harbor. The pastoral setting is soothing, as are the simply decorated guest rooms with private baths. You may even glimpse trumpeter swans if you visit in winter. Owners will pick up guests from the ferry. *Follow Spring St from Friday Harbor, which runs into San Juan Valley Rd; (360) 378-3884 or (800) 826-7926; 420 Trumpeter Way, Friday Harbor, San Juan Island; $$.*

Turtleback Farm Inn ☆☆   Located inland amid tall trees, rolling pastures, and private ponds, Turtleback offers seven spotless rooms dressed in simple sophistication. Enjoy a pleasant, filling breakfast served outdoors in warm weather. *10 minutes from the ferry on Crow Valley Rd; (360) 376-4914; Eastsound, Orcas Island; $$$.*

Westwinds Bed & Breakfast ☆☆   Easily the most magnificent view on all of the San Juan Islands. This private glass-and-wood paradise is a two-bedroom facility (guests have the 1,200-square-foot house to themselves) set on 6 acres of mountainside abundant with deer and quail. Particularly popular with honeymoon couples (privacy is never an issue). *2 miles from Lime Kiln Whale Watch Park; (360) 378-5283; 4909 H Hannah Highlands Rd, Friday Harbor, San Juan Island; $$$.*

Wharfside Bed & Breakfast ☆   It's this region's first realization of the European tradition of floating inns. Two guest rooms on the 60-foot sailboat *Jacquelyn* are both very nicely finished with full amenities and that compact precision that only living on a boat can inspire. *On the K dock in Friday Harbor, San Juan Island; (360) 378-5661; Friday Harbor; $$.*

Cheaper Sleeps

The Island Farmhouse   This 12-acre working farm is the only resting spot that's much of a deal on Lopez. The owners have added a large room off the back of their home with deck and private entry. *(360) 468-2864; Hammel Lake Rd, Lopez Island.*

West Beach Resort   There are pine-and-burl cabins just feet from a gravel beach, and a small marina with boat rental. Two-person cabins are available, but the two- and three-bedroom ones are nicer and a better deal. *(360) 376-2240; Rte 1 in Eastsound (call for directions), Orcas Island.*

More Information

San Juan Islands Visitors Information Center: *P.O. Box 65, Lopez, WA 98261; (360) 468-3663.*

Washington State Ferries Information: *(800) 843-3779.*

Anacortes Terminal: *(360) 293-8166.*

Friday Harbor Terminal: *(360) 378-4777.*

Lopez Island Chamber of Commerce: *(360) 468-3663.*

Lopez Terminal: *(360) 468-2252.*

Orcas Island Chamber of Commerce: *(360) 376-2273.*

Orcas Terminal: *(360) 376-2134.*

San Juan Island Chamber of Commerce: *(360) 378-5240.*

Shaw Island Terminal: *(360) 468-2142.*

Whale-spotting Hotline: *(800) 562-8832.*

U.S. Coast Guard Emergencies: *(206) 286-5400.*

U.S. Customs, Friday Harbor: *(360) 378-2080.*

Skagit Valley

From Samish Island south and west to La Conner and east to Big Lake, including Bay View State Park, the Skagit River Delta, and the Padilla Bay National Estuarine Research Reserve.

For an area that's mostly flat, Skagit Valley offers plenty of depth when it comes to outdoor action.

Physically, it's unique. The valley, a sprawling, farm-studded floodplain, looks a lot like many other lowland valleys around Puget Sound: a large river (the Skagit) running through it floods several times a year, sending dairy cows and stubborn lowland homeowners scurrying. But there, the comparisons end.

What makes Skagit Valley special is its location. The combination of flat, sandy farmlands and wide, quiet saltwater bays is a delightful mix made more fascinating by looming mountains to the northeast (Mount Baker and the North Cascades) and west (Orcas Island's Mount Constitution). Climb on a bicycle and head west through the valley on a lonesome country road, and the flat pasturelands abruptly end, spilling out into the open salt water, giving the area a farmlands-to-the-sea feeling reminiscent of Holland. Stroll along one of the valley's many placid saltwater beaches, and you can watch migratory snow geese riding a saltwater breeze to a splash landing in a field already occupied by cows.

Seaweed mingling with silage can be downright confusing, but it all comes together in rather splendorous fashion during the spring bloom season. Then, the valley floor looks like it's been carpet-bombed by paint balls as daffodils, tulips, and irises jump to colorful attention in sprawling bulb-farm fields. The bloom season, mid-March to early May, is prime time in the valley, drawing thousands of motorists and, increasingly, cyclists to otherwise-deserted roads. A spring ride through the bulb fields can't be underrated. It's a uniquely Northwest experience, one of those dozen or so every Washingtonian must undertake to earn his or her veteran's stripes.

But don't make the mistake of overlooking the valley during the rest of the year, especially during the winter, our favorite time to visit. Whatever you do here, the pace is slow, deliberate, relaxed. The Skagit Valley will unwind you—even if you didn't know you were wound.

Getting There

The Skagit Valley is approximately 60 miles north of Seattle on Interstate 5. Most attractions discussed below are accessible by taking I-5 exit 226 (Mount Vernon) or exit 231 (Sedro Woolley/Hwy 20).

Adjoining Areas

NORTH: **Bellingham and Lummi Island**

SOUTHWEST: **Whidbey and Camano Islands**

EAST: **North Cascades Scenic Highway**

WEST: **San Juan Islands and Anacortes**

inside out

Camping

Bay View State Park on Padilla Bay is the primary public camping venue. The park, 2 miles north of Hwy 20 on Bay View–Edison Road, has 99 campsites (9 with hookups; maximum RV length, 32 feet). It's a pleasant, sunny park, with plenty of flat grasslands for baseball and/or Frisbee use. But the real attraction is the 1,200 feet of saltwater shoreline on Padilla Bay, much of which is protected as a National Wildlife Refuge (see Wildlife, below). The beach area, separated by the highway from the campground, is a great day-use area—the best beach spot in the valley. Picnickers or cyclists can use the beach parking lot as a base for a day's exploring. Bay View is open all year. Campsites can be reserved up to 11 months in advance by calling Reservations Northwest; (800) 452-5687. *1093 Bay View–Edison Road; (360) 757-0227 or (800) 233-0321.*

River Bend Park, a private campground along the Skagit River in Mount Vernon, is an alternative, but it's primarily an I-5 motorhome stopover, with 25 tent sites and 95 RV pull-throughs with hookups. *305 Stewart, Mt Vernon; (360) 428-4044.*

Another private campground, **Burlington KOA,** has 45 tent and 45 RV sites, many with hookups, along with the standard KOA amenities. *646 North Green Road, Burlington; (360) 724-5511.*

Some valley recreators prefer to camp at **Larrabee State Park,** a 20-minute drive north on Chuckanut Drive (see the Bellingham and Lummi Island chapter).

Cycling

Here's where the valley really shines. The Skagit flats have become one of the Northwest's premier cycling destinations, thanks to hundreds of miles of flat country roads that roll through thousands of acres of unbelievably colorful bulb fields during the spring tulip/daffodil bloomathon.

The options are so numerous that describing particular routes is almost superfluous. A good strategy is to pick a safe, reliable parking spot, consult the free daffodil-fields map available from one of the local Chamber of Commerces (see below), and design a loop with a length to your liking. Most of the largest bulb fields lie south of Hwy 536, between Mount Vernon and La Conner. One popular daylong loop, however, will take you through the full range of the best of the valley: beaches, bird-watching estuaries, tulip fields, Mount Baker viewpoints, the Skagit River, and downtown Mount Vernon. It's mostly flat, and traffic is generally very light except during the peak bloom season of mid-March to mid-May. We highly recommend it as a full valley tour; it's one of the more scenic rural routes around Puget Sound.

The full tour: Park at Bay View State Park (see Camping, above), and travel north on Bay View–Edison Road, turning east through the small towns of Edison and Bow, then south along Worline and Ershig/Avon–Allen Roads to Mount Vernon. From the city, follow Riverbend Road south along the Skagit to Penn Road, then cut back east across the valley on Calhoun Road, returning north to Bay View via Best or La Conner–Whitley Roads, then Bay View–Edison Road. It's a 40- to 50-mile loop, depending on your particular route.

Shorter rides: For a shorter, 2-hour loop circling the peaceful, less-traveled north end of the valley, follow the route above, but turn west off Avon–Allen Road onto Wilson Road and return to Bay View, rather than proceeding south across Hwy 20 and into Mount Vernon. Similarly, cyclists who want to proceed straight to the bloomfields can make a nice half-day trip from Bay View by riding the general full-circle route back-ward and eliminating the northern portion.

Wildlife

The lower Skagit Valley is one of Washington's best—and least utilized—wild bird-watching venues, particularly during the winter. While wintering bald eagles are feasting on spawning salmon and attracting (too) much attention on the middle Skagit River (see the North Cascades Scenic Highway chapter), far greater numbers of migratory birds, many of them quite rare, are quietly biding their time lower down the valley.

One of the best ways to see the valley's rich winged wildlife is from the saddle of a bicycle, which will put you up close to birds without scaring them away. Cyclists find a full range of migratory fowl in local fields during the cold season: **ducks** of all stripes, **mergansers, cormorants, great blue herons,** and even **snow geese** stop over or stay in swampy fields throughout the winter. The **north-end valley loop** described in Cycling, above, is one of the most wildlife-rich road routes we've ever found. In the winter, birds along the way will outnumber cars 10 to 1.

Most day visitors, however, are content to get their two binocular-lenses worth at the **Padilla Bay National Estuarine Research Reserve,** which has a full interpretive center, viewing blinds, boardwalks, and a nicely maintained 2.25-mile handicapped-accessible trail along a dike at the south end of the bay. Start the tour at the Breazeale–Padilla Bay Interpretive Center, just north of Bay View State Park. From a viewing blind here, winter visitors are likely to see **canvasbacks, harlequin ducks,** and **black brant**. Other common visitors are numerous small **shorebirds, great blue herons, dunlins, black-bellied plovers, bald eagles,** and an occasional **peregrine falcon. Harbor seals** also are sometimes spotted in the bay. The center is open 10am to 5pm, Wednesday through Sunday. On Bay View–Edison Road, about 3 miles north of Hwy 20; (360) 428-1558.

If time still allows, drive north to Samish Island Road and follow it west onto the long peninsula known as **Samish Island**. The "island," part of a former delta of the Skagit River, has a small but nice picnic spot and public beach on its north shore. Views to the north of Samish Bay, Mount Baker, and Chuckanut Mountain are excellent, and the sprawling Samish Bay mudflats are a prime landing zone for **migratory birds.** Bird-watchers often find a day spent here every bit as rewarding as one at the Padilla Bay area to the south. **Black brant, canvasbacks, widgeons,** and the occasional **peregrine falcon** and **snowy owl** are seen here. Follow Samish Island Road west to Wharf Road, turn north and proceed to Samish Picnic Site. The beach is accessible by stairs.

Another good birding venue, also lesser-known, is the **Skagit Wildlife Area,** at the river's mouth in Puget Sound. This is *the* place to see

snow geese, which migrate here each winter from Wrangell Island in the Arctic region. As many as 27,000 are believed to winter on this 12,000-acre river delta, a triangle of private farms and grasslands maintained as wildlife habitat. Several hundred **tundra swans** also have made a winter home here. Viewing is good all winter, provided local roads aren't flooded. Stop at the Wildlife Area headquarters near Conway for viewing advice. (Note: The area is open for hunting during duck and goose seasons.) From the Conway exit on I-5, drive west and follow the binocular signs; (206) 775-1311.

Hiking

Generally, hiking trails are few in the valley flatlands. One good one, however, is the waterfront trail at **Padilla Bay's** wildlife viewing area (see above).

Weekenders should consider stretching their wings (or wheels) a bit and partaking in excellent day hikes around Bellingham (see the Bellingham and Lummi Island chapter) or one of several wonderful and little-known trails around nearby Anacortes (see the Whidbey and Camano Islands chapter).

Picnics

The beach area at **Bay View State Park** (see above) has nice picnic facilities (windy on occasion). Another good picnicking/beachcombing site is the lightly used **Samish Island** beach area (see Wildlife, above).

In Mount Vernon, tables can be found at **Lion's Park** on the Skagit River and **Hillcrest Park** at 13th and Blackburn. Southeast of the city on Blackburn Road, **Little Mountain Park** is a good picnic spot with a sweeping view of the valley, the San Juan Islands, and the northern Olympics. Squint hard enough, and you might spot migratory trumpeter swans in January and February. Bring the camera.

Canoeing/Kayaking

Padilla Bay is fully explorable by canoe or kayak. In fact, except for a single deep channel through the center, most of its shallow, muddy waters are open only to flat-hulled craft. Good launching spots can be found at Bay View State Park and the Skagit County launch ramp below the Swinomish Channel Bridge along Hwy 20. **Samish Bay,** just to the north of the peninsula forming Samish Island, is another good paddling venue at high tide. But consider that it's less sheltered than Padilla Bay itself and more prone to strong northerly or westerly winds.

Fishing

The **Lower Skagit River,** low and milky green in the summer and often brown and powerful in the winter, is a major **steelhead** and **salmon** freeway. Well, not as major as it used to be. The Skagit used to hold the most prolific stocks of winter steelhead and summer chinook in the Puget Sound area. Not so anymore. Steelhead numbers are down, and the **chinook** stocks are so troubled you can't fish for them here anymore. (Two major reasons: wasteful fishing and incredibly destructive clearcutting on the upper river, not necessarily in that order.) But decent steelheading and good bank and boat fishing for **chum** and **pink** salmon are available in season. The chums roll in around October; look for pinks in late August and September of odd-numbered years only.

Plenty of public launch spots are found on the lower Skagit, including Hamilton, Sedro Woolley, Burlington, and Edgewater and Riverbend RV Parks in Mount Vernon.

Fishing for warm-water species such as largemouth bass, crappie, and perch can be good in **Big Lake,** just east of Mount Vernon. And several local Cascade foothills lakes—**Cavanaugh, Sixteen,** and **McMurray**—usually are excellent rainbow trout producers in the spring. Note: You'll need a boat. Bank-fishing access is poor at all three. Not far away, Heart Lake and Lake Erie outside Anacortes are perennial rainbow trout producers, especially early in the spring.

Sailing/Boating

Saltwater pleasure boaters often tie up in **La Conner,** on the riverlike Swinomish Channel (Caution: tricky tides). Two Port of Skagit County marinas are found just north of town, with guest moorage and full services. The private **La Conner Marina,** (360) 466-3118, not far away, offers full services year-round, and nearby La Conner Yacht Sales ((360) 466-3300) will rent you a boat.

Three small islands in Padilla Bay, **Huckleberry, Saddlebag,** and **Dot,** are undeveloped state parks sites popular with boaters and kayakers. Saddlebag is a designated campsite on the state's **Cascadia Marine Trail,** a state-managed water trail with campsites from Olympia to British Columbia; (206) 545-9161. (See the Washington Outdoors Primer for details.)

A public boat ramp is located at **Bay View,** but it's a single-lane job usable at high tide only. A newer, more reliable launch is the Skagit County ramp beneath the **Swinomish Channel Bridge,** just off Hwy 20. This is also a decent picnic spot.

Attractions

La Conner—so quaint and touristy you might feel the need to be hosed off—is a must stop for valley first-timers. The buildings are old and quaint, the merchandise new and quaint, and everything, right down to the waffle cones, smells like gift-shop potpourri. The artsy town is perched on Swinomish Channel at the valley's west edge. Can't miss it.

Old downtown Mount Vernon, the part west of the Skagit River, is an unexpected treat, particularly for those who mistakenly enter the Burlington–Mount Vernon area via its northern outlet-mall-marred extremes.

Another Mount Vernon curiosity, the **Chuck Wagon Drive Inn,** is worth one stop. At least. It has 50 different burgers, not to mention the world's largest collection of ceramic whiskey-bottle cowboys. Boy howdy.

In spring and summer, it's one festival after another in the valley. It all begins with the **Tulip Festival,** a valleywide celebration usually conducted in early April. Call the Chamber of Commerce, (360) 428-8547, for a full schedule.

For an interesting history lesson, drive to the north end of the valley, following directions to Samish Island (see Wildlife, above), and find the old village of Hamilton. In 1898, a utopian commune, **Equality Colony,** was formed here. The colony was inhabited and farmed for nearly 10 years, but not much remains today except a cemetery and a stream bearing the name Colony Creek.

Restaurants

Calico Cupboard ☆ Awfully cute—Laura Ashley meets Laura Ingalls Wilder—but the bakery is reason enough to go. *South end of the line on 1st; (360) 466-4451; 720 S 1st, La Conner; $.*

La Conner Seafood and Prime Rib House ☆ Every weekend those who put their name on the waiting list are rewarded with excellent seafood. Ample outdoor seating. *On the waterfront; (360) 466-4014; 614 S 1st St, La Conner; $$.*

The Longfellow Cafe Old Town Bistro ☆☆ Local people fill it because they have come to expect good food. Now downtown, the owners are turning their new digs into a showcase of Skagit Valley produce and their own solid culinary talents. *In downtown Mt Vernon; (360) 336-3684; 416 Myrtle St, Mt Vernon; $$$.*

Pacioni's Pizzeria ☆ Real hand-thrown pizza pies. Try the tri-color with pesto, ricotta, and roma tomatoes. *Everything* is made to order. *In old downtown Mt Vernon; (360) 336-3314; 606 S 1st St, Mt Vernon; $.*

Palmer's Restaurant and Pub ☆☆   La Conner's favorite restaurant, Palmer's is perched on a knoll behind town at the far end of La Conner Country Inn. *2nd and Washington; (360) 466-4261; 205 E Washington, La Conner; $$.*

Wildflowers ☆☆☆   A restaurant truly worthy of considerable attention. And attention *is* the secret—attention to the smallest detail in the kitchen, on the plate, in the surrounding ambience. *From I-5, take the 227 exit and head east; (360) 424-9724; 2001 E College Way, Mt Vernon; $$$.*

Cheaper Eats

The Deli Next Door   In the Skagit Valley Food Co-op, the Deli offers a healthy, super-tasty afternoon nosh. *(360) 336-3886; 202 S 1st St, Mount Vernon.*

Lodgings

Benson Farmstead Bed & Breakfast   Once part of a working dairy farm, the large 17-room house is packed with antiques and Scandinavian memorabilia. Kids will like this place, especially the playroom and the three cats. Open weekends only October to March, except by special arrangement. *Northwest of Burlington; exit 231 off I-5; (360) 757-0578; 1009 Avon-Allen Rd, Bow; $$.*

The Heron in La Conner ☆☆   One of the prettiest hostelries in town, with 12 rooms done in jewel-box fashion. Splurge on room 31 or 32. *On the edge of town on Maple St; (360) 466-4626; 117 Maple Ave, La Conner; $$.*

Hotel Planter   The most famous (and infamous) characters of La Conner's colorful past once inhabited this end of town. Today, owner Don Hoskins creates a style that is a tasteful blend of past and present. *End of the line on the south end of 1st St; (360) 466-4710; 715 S 1st St, La Conner; $$.*

La Conner Channel Lodge ☆☆   At the edge of the Swinomish Channel, this is a fit urban version of its slightly dowdy cousin, The Country Inn, a few blocks inland. Prime waterfront location. *On the waterfront, north end of town; (360) 466-1500; 205 N 1st St, La Conner; $$$.*

Rainbow Inn ☆☆   Set amid the acres of valley flatlands, this elegant turn-of-the-century farmhouse offers sweeping views of lush pastures, Mount Baker, and the Olympics from eight pretty guest rooms. *1/2 mile east of La Conner; (360) 466-4578; 1075 Chilberg Rd, Mt Vernon; $$.*

White Swan Guest House ☆☆   Peter Goldfarb's house is splashed with warm yellow, salmon, evergreen, and peach, and seems to soak up the sunlight—even in the rain. Good launching point for cycle trips around Fir Island. *6 miles southeast of La Conner; (360) 445-6805; 1388 Moore Rd, Mt. Vernon; $$.*

The Wild Iris ☆   Geared toward romance, with spacious suites each featuring a gas fireplace, oversize Jacuzzi, and panoramic west-facing view. *On the edge of town on Maple Ave; (360) 466-1400; 121 Maple Ave, La Conner; $$$.*

Cheaper Sleeps

The Tulip Valley Inn   There are times in life when a good motel room at a reasonable rate is all you are going to find and maybe all you really want. Comfortable beds in a no-frills 40-room motel. *(360) 428-5969; 2200 Freeway Dr, Mt Vernon.*

More Information

Mount Vernon Chamber of Commerce: *(360) 855-0974.*
La Conner Chamber of Commerce: *(360) 466-4778.*

Whidbey and Camano Islands

Clinton north to Rosario Bay at Deception Pass, including Camano, South Whidbey, Fort Ebey, Fort Casey and Deception Pass State Parks.

Whidbey and Camano Islands are like the San Juan Islands but without the ferry hassle. Reaching them requires only a fraction of the commitment imposed by a trip to the more famous San Juans. Both are but a 45-minute commute from the Seattle area. Both are separated from the mainland only by bridged channels. And each offers the great views, beautiful countryside, and stunning parks found in its neighboring islands farther north.

It's amazing how often Whidbey becomes a weekend destination for those of us who haven't planned far enough in advance to arrange transportation, lodging, and other essentials for trips to the mountains, the Olympic Peninsula, or the San Juans. Whidbey and Camano are a hassle-free alternative: San Juan Lite.

They're also relatively blue-collar outdoor venues. Both Whidbey and Camano have far fewer quaint B&Bs, restaurants, guide services, and other cheesy touristy amenities per square mile than their northern neighbors, the San Juans. But that's a large part of their charm to longtime Seattleites, who appreciate the islands as places where change, thankfully, hasn't kept pace with the rest of Puget Sound. Camano's beaches look the same today as they did when we were children. Whidbey's magnificent public places, particularly the classic Fort Casey and Deception Pass State Parks, just seem to improve with age. Indeed, the rolling farmlands around Ebey's Landing National Historical Monument look much the same as they did 150 years ago, when some of Puget Sound's first white settlements were founded there.

Early homesteaders in Coupeville, one of Washington's first towns, no doubt were drawn by the island's unique topography: high, sandy cliffs on the wind-buffeted west side, several miles of rolling, farmable plateau in the middle, and gentle beaches and curving coves on the protected eastern (leeward) side. They found firm, fertile ground underfoot. Mountains all around. And a watercolor saltwater view in every direction. What more could a settler ask?

Not much. And today, neither do we. The island's unique beauty continues to draw Puget Sound cyclists, sightseers, campers, beach walkers, kayakers, boaters, and wildlife watchers, many of whom consider Whidbey their own island playground. Poking around here for even a short time prompts admiration for Whidbey's hearty early settlers. And it makes one wonder: Did Whidbey sport the first rooflines in Puget Sound because it was a convenient site, or simply because it was the best?

Getting There

The south Whidbey Island port of Clinton is a mere 20-minute ferry ride from Mukilteo, a which is 30-minute drive north of downtown Seattle. From Clinton, Hwy 525—the main Whidbey corridor—runs north, merging with Hwy 20 at mid-island. Northern Whidbey destinations such as Oak Harbor and Deception Pass often are reached by skipping the ferry and driving Interstate 5 to Mount Vernon—60 miles north of Seattle—then following Hwy 20 west across Fidalgo Island to Whidbey. For the best of both worlds, make it a loop, commuting by ferry one way, I-5 the other.

Camano Island is a 45-minute drive north of Seattle. Travel I-5 to about 18 miles north of Everett, take exit 212 (Camano Island/Stanwood), and follow Hwy 532 about 10 miles west to the island.

Adjoining Areas

NORTH: **San Juan Islands and Anacortes**

SOUTH: **Greater Seattle**

EAST: **Skagit Valley**

WEST: **Port Townsend**

Parks/Camping

On Whidbey—45 miles long, but never more than 5 across—you're never more than about a 5-minute drive—or 500 strong pedals—away from a saltwater shoreline. Some of Washington's most pleasant, scenic saltwater beaches are found here. And public access is uncommonly good, thanks to a string of four state parks, beginning with South Whidbey at the island's far south end and culminating in drop-dead–gorgeous fashion with Deception Pass, at the north end. Three of the four Whidbey parks have campgrounds; all have magnificent saltwater access, with views of the Cascades and the entire north Puget Sound marine environment. Just to the south, Camano Island State Park, the recreational focal point of that oft-overlooked island, is a longtime favorite of many Puget Sound area residents.

All the parks are excellent, close-to-home getaways, whether for the day or overnight. But a cautionary note on camping: Unfortunately, being very popular and very close to Seattle usually adds up to very crowded, so landing a space on Whidbey can be a challenge in the summer. Thankfully, three of Whidbey's state parks—Deception Pass, Fort Ebey, and South Whidbey—are scheduled to join Washington's telephone campsite reservation system in the spring of 1997.

Make the call. Even if you don't, it's still well worth the effort to head this way off-season or midweek, or to play weekend campground roulette by staying in one of the island's less popular venues and scouting for an open site at your favorite.

Here's the list of goods for each park, from south to north:

Camano Island State Park

Multiple generations of Puget Sound area folks got their first exposure to outdoor life at Camano, a sprawling park with 6,700 feet of waterfront on sparkling Saratoga Passage. The park's unusually good weather (it's at the far end of the same Olympic Mountain "rain shadow" that keeps the Dungeness Valley dry), exceptional beaches, and plentiful wildlife make it a grand family spot. And spectacular sunsets over the Olympics have spurred many a late-night snuggle on Camano's flat, gravelly beach.

The beach is the highlight. Camano begs for large-scale, family-reunion blowout-style picnics, and it gets them. All told, the park has 113 designated **picnic** sites, plus a full-blown kitchen shelter. They're divided in two, with many on the beach and others on a bluff at the park's north end. Wherever you pop open the picnic basket, be warned: Scavenging crows have been known to fly right down and scarf sandwiches out of unsuspecting children's hands here. They like the view too.

Camano's unusually wide, flat beach has a grassy area that's great for **kite flying** and Frisbee tossing. Those more inclined to be sand spuds will find grand sunbathing spots on the upper beach, which has a soft, sandy surface and plenty of driftwood upon which to rest one's head and watch sailboats drift past.

A three-lane boat launch makes the beach area a high-traffic **boating** venue, particularly during summer salmon-fishing season. (Parking your Yugo in one of the boat-trailer spots is not couth, and could lead to accidental fish-sliming of your windshield.)

Surf fishing for bottomfish (perch, flounder) can be productive here, and if you're lucky, some steamer clams can be had at very low tide.

About 3 miles of **hiking trails** run through the park's upper, woodsy area, connecting the three main campground loops, the beach area, and the picnic area. **Campers** have their choice of 87 sites (no hookups; maximum RV length, 45 feet). The sites are wooded, and for the most part nicely separated by trees. Show up early; you can't reserve sites here. The park also has a group camp for 200 people; call the park for information.

Camano Island State Park is open all year. *Take I-5 north to Exit 212, 18 miles north of Everett. Turn west and follow signs on Hwy 532 west to the park, about 13 miles; (360) 387-3031 or (800) 233-0321.*

South Whidbey State Park

This secluded site on Whidbey's west shore is one of our favorite get-out-of-town-for-an-afternoon escapes, particularly on cold, clear winter weekend days. South Whidbey has 4,500 feet of narrow, gravelly beach on Admiralty Inlet—reached via a short, steep trail from the upland day-use area. Not much room to frolic down here at high tide, but plenty of space to take a seat on a log, watch the sun go down, and reflect on how lucky you are to be here.

The park's real attraction is upland: a stand of **old-growth forest,** mostly Douglas fir, that's unique in this area. The trees, which include some grand western red cedars, are best seen by following the **Wilbert Trail** (easy; 1.5-mile loop) on the east side of Smuggler's Cove Road, opposite the developed park area. Two other trails, each about a half mile, lead from the day-use area to the beach, and a mile-long **Forest Discovery Trail** is a pleasant, mostly flat nature path.

The wooded **camping area,** on a heavily forested bluff, offers no views, but good privacy. Choose from 54 standard and 6 "primitive" sites (no hookups; 45-foot maximum RV length). A dump station is available. Day users will find the wooded **picnic area** a relaxing, though shady, retreat with a shelter to flee to in bad weather.

South Whidbey is open daily in summer and on weekends and holidays only from November 15 to February 14. Campsites can be reserved up to 11 months in advance through Reservations Northwest; (800) 452-5687. Follow Hwy 525 9 miles north from Clinton, turn west on Bush

Point Road and follow signs to the park, on Smugglers Cove Road; (360) 321-4559 or (800) 233-0321.

Fort Casey State Park

Old Fort Casey, perched on a prominent point on Whidbey's west shore across Admiralty Inlet from Port Townsend, truly is one of the most picturesque spots in the Northwest. Choose your highlight: 137 sunny acres, much of which are wide-open, grassy uplands with stunning views of the North Sound and Mount Baker. More than 4,000 feet of saltwater shoreline, for uninterrupted beach strolling, surf fishing, or lounging. **Gun emplacements** with restored cannons—always a hit with the kids. And a beachfront campground that's highly sought all year round, particularly by RV owners.

The park's focal point is the day-use area, high on a bluff near the old gun mounts. Sprawling grass fields make a wonderful softball/Frisbee/kite-flying playground. Trails lead along the bluff to several grassy (unfenced, be careful with kids) overlooks that are as grand a place to watch a summer sunset as we've found in the Northwest. Interpretive signs describe the fort's history as a World War I–era gun emplacement and World War II–era training facility. A large picnic area is nearby.

At the north end of the day-use area is the stately **Admiralty Head Lighthouse,** built in the 1860s and moved when the area became a military base. The lovingly restored building now contains an interpretive center filled with park history. It's one of the most photographed buildings in the state (aside from Bill Gates's house).

Unfortunately, Fort Casey, one of the state's more popular parks, also has one of its smaller camping areas. The park has only 35 **campsites** (no hookups; maximum RV length, 40 feet). All are almost literally on the water, on a sand spit below the bluff-top gun emplacements. The setting is idyllic: Puget Sound just outside your tent flap or doorstep, with two of the state's most lovingly restored Washington State ferries plying the water from Port Townsend to a landing right next to the campground. Needless to say, it's a popular spot—particularly among RVers, who are less troubled by the persistent winds on the mostly exposed beach.

The park also has a **boat launch,** a couple miles of **hiking trails,** and an **underwater park** for scuba divers. The beach is a popular spot for **surf fishing** for bottomfish, salmon, and steelhead (see Fishing, below).

Immediately south of the park, on the far side of the Keystone ferry terminal, is Keystone Spit, an undeveloped state park site. Its 6,800 feet of saltwater shoreline are great for strolling, and the equally long freshwater beach on Lake Crockett is a good bird-watching venue.

Fort Casey is open all year. Campsites cannot be reserved. *Turn west off Hwy 20 on Engle Road at Coupeville, follow signs 3 miles southwest to the park, near Keystone ferry terminal; (800) 233-0321.*

Fort Ebey State Park

Fort Ebey, another abandoned military base, is smaller, more secluded, and less popular than nearby Deception Pass State Park. But it offers a similar saltwater-beach experience, and its camping area is actually nicer.

The main day-use area, perched on a high bluff above Point Partridge, is the northern starting point for a **clifftop trail** offering great views of Admiralty Inlet, plus a chance to explore gun bunkers abandoned after World War II. Unlike nearby Forts Casey, Worden, and Flagler—all built early in the 20th century—Fort Ebey was a "second-generation" Puget Sound fortress, part of a triad of 16-inch cannon emplacements built during World War II. Ebey's sister installations were built at Cape Flattery and at Striped Peak west of Port Angeles. The remains of Ebey's never-used gun battery are at the park's south end, near the campground. Also from the north (day-use) parking lot, a trail leads down to the beach (almost 3 miles of it is public property here) and the **Point Partridge Lighthouse.**

The nicely laid-out, lightly treed **camping area** has two loops with 50 standard sites (no hookups; maximum RV length, 70 feet). It's a particularly nice place to visit in the spring, when wild rhododendrons are out in pale pink splendor.

Cyclists, take note: Fort Ebey has three very nice primitive campsites at the end of a short trail to Lake Pondilla, a swampy wetland at the park's north end.

Fort Ebey is open all year. Campsites can be reserved up to 11 months in advance through Reservations Northwest, (800) 452-5687. *Follow signs from Libby Road, which turns west off Hwy 20 just under 6 miles south of Oak Harbor; information: (360) 678-4636 or (800) 233-0321.*

Joseph Whidbey State Park

This is a day-use spot, with no campground. But the park named in honor of Capt. George Vancouver's fellow 1792 north Sound explorer is one of the best **picnic** places on Whidbey. The park has 3,100 feet of saltwater shoreline, with good views across the Strait of Juan de Fuca, and 20 picnic sites upland. (Note: No water, not much shade on hot days.)

Joseph Whidbey State Park is open daily in summer, and closed September 30 to March 30. *At Swantown Road and West Beach Road, three miles west of Oak Harbor; information: (800) 233-0321.*

Deception Pass State Park

Washington's most popular state park is a showcase for all that is magnetic about the Northwest: clean, sprawling saltwater beaches, jutting cliffs, deep forest, freshwater lakes, and great views. Plus, they threw in a magnificent bridge that might be the most artful assemblage of steel in the country. All told, it's a magnificent package—one that every Washington nature lover must unwrap at least once in his/her career outside.

This is a park that can't be fully explored in a single day. Deception has an impressive 3,600 acres of wooded uplands, a remarkable 77,000 feet of saltwater shoreline, two campgrounds, multiple day-use areas, and four freshwater lakes. If you only have time for the highlights, park in one of the Hwy 20 pullouts and walk out on **Deception Pass Bridge.** After you catch your breath, get back in the car and follow the winding road from the park's main entrance (south of the bridge) downhill to the beach day-use area. From here, trails lead along North Beach to viewpoints of the impressive bridge—actually two steel spans linking Whidbey and Fidalgo Islands—over the turbulent, swift current coursing through Deception Pass. The southern end of the main day-use area fronts on both Rosario Strait and Cranberry Lake, offering fine salt- and freshwater swimming in the summer. A separate picnic area on the opposite shore of **Cranberry Lake** has a splendid picnic area, a boat launch, and a dock where trout fishing is often good.

More of the park is found on the opposite (north) side of the bridge. **Pass Lake,** a productive fly-fishing lake, is right off Hwy 20. Nearby, a road leads steeply downhill to **Bowman Bay,** where a saltwater fishing pier, small (16-site) campground, and boat launch are found.

Compared with the park's overall grandeur, the main **campground** is nothing special. Its location, however, is. Most of the 246 campsites (no hookups; maximum RV length, 30 feet) are within a short walk of the park's memorable North Beach day-use area. If you have a choice (which you probably won't), go low and get one of the more open-air sites closest to the water, thus farthest away from busy Hwy 20.

If you're a light sleeper, you might consider packing earplugs. **Whidbey Island Naval Air Station** is still close by, even though the "Please pardon our noise: It's the sound of freedom" sign isn't. And the local vocals—an early morning crow population—are quite healthy.

Deception Pass also has a 60-person **group camp** near North Beach and a separate, fully equipped group camp/Environmental Learning Center (for parties of 25 or more) on **Cornet Bay,** east of Hwy 20. A fully developed boat launch/moorage also is located here. All of this is tied together by some 30 miles of trails (see Hiking, below).

Deception Pass State Park is open all year. Campsites can be reserved up to 11 months in advance through Reservations Northwest; (800) 452-5687. At Deception Pass Bridge, 9 miles northeast of Oak Harbor on Hwy 20. Information: (360) 675-2417 or (800) 233-0321.

Beaches

Just north of Fort Casey, **Ebey's Landing State Park,** named after the first white settler on Whidbey Island, has a mile-long trail to the grave site of the park's namesake, as well as a path along the top of Perego's Bluff. Worth the walk on a nice day. **Double Bluff Beach,** southwest of Langley, is a sandy waterfront spot, good for walking or kite flying.

Hiking

All the **Washington State Parks** listed above have hiking trails worthy of the average day hiker. Most are either beach walks or up-and-down hikes along Whidbey's steep, sandy bluffs, with good views of Puget Sound, the Olympic Mountains, and Mount Baker. Lovers of pure, flat beach walking might try the 5 miles of wild but public sand between Fort Casey and Fort Ebey State Parks. Fort Ebey's excellent bluff-top trails and the old-growth forest loop at South Whidbey State Park also are Whidbey highlights (see above for both). And especially worth noting is the 27-mile trail network at **Deception Pass State Park.**

At Deception, hikes range from short nature trails to long, steep, alarming clifftop scrambles. From the main (**West Point**) parking lot on the south side of Deception Pass Bridge, spring-fed **Cranberry Lake** (easy) has a short trail along its sandy west side, with a viewpoint over a marshy area that makes for good bird-watching. On the other side of the lake, kids will like the short (half-mile) **nature trail** that loops through the woods near the Ranger Station. Nearby, at the north end of the day-use area at West Point, a slew of trails head east toward the bridge. You can walk nearly all the way to the bridge on **North Beach** during low tide, but stick to the upper, forested trail during high tides. Keep heading east, and you ll catch a path running right under the bridge and on to awesome views from 500-foot-high **Goose Rock** (moderate; round trip from West Point is about 3 miles, depending on your route).

A loop of the same **Goose Rock** area can be made from the park's **Environmental Learning Center** on **Cornet Bay**, as can a pleasant nature walk, the **Discovery Trail** (easy, 1 mile round trip). Another nice walk on Deception's east side is the long beach stroll and upland loop trail in the **Hoypus Hill Natural Forest** (easy; 3.5 miles round trip) at the end of Cornet Bay Road. The state preserve contains a rare stand of virgin old-growth timber.

On the north side of Deception Bridge, **Bowman Bay** is the departure point for the park's more challenging—and most alluring—hiking destinations (difficult; various lengths possible). One trail leads south, up a steep rock face and around the top of Reservation Head to **Lighthouse**

Point and down to **Lottie Bay.** Another trail leads from the Bowman Bay parking area west to picturesque **Sharp Cove** and **Rosario Head.** Both are good half-day hikes, with some tricky spots on the rocks.

Whidbey Island weekenders, particularly those at Deception Pass, also shouldn't overlook the excellent trails in the **Anacortes** area, such as the scramble to the top of **Mount Erie** (see the San Juan Islands and Anacortes chapter).

Cycling

Whidbey is a patchwork of glacier-smoothed rolling hills, many of which will challenge beginning cyclists, but none big enough to suck the life from more experienced ones. The island's main drag, Hwy 525, isn't the best cycling venue. It's narrow in places, with so-so shoulder space. And traffic tends to move fast over the long straightaways. But a number of Whidbey side roads make fantastic day trips, many through scenic, rolling farmland with a saltwater beach picnic for a reward at the destination.

A good day trip to **South Whidbey State Park** begins at Mukilteo, where you can park in the Mukilteo State Park lot and cycle onto the ferry, disembarking at Clinton and climbing the long hill up Hwy 525. Proceed 9 miles, turn west on Bush Point Road for 3 miles, then follow signs 1.5 miles on Smugglers Cove Road to the park. It's a round trip of about 27 miles.

At mid-island, **Fort Casey** presents a range of opportunities. Cycling onto the Keystone ferry to tour Port Townsend makes a fun day trip for Fort Casey campers. In Port Townsend, cycle up the hill to Fort Worden, where you can have lunch on the bluff and stare back across Admiralty Inlet at Mount Baker, not to mention your own campsite below. Also from Fort Casey, a ride north to Ebey's Landing or south to South Whidbey State Park via Keystone Road and Hwy 525 makes a fine day outing. And many visitors get a good taste of Whidbey cycling by parking in Coupeville and following Engle Road—which does have a cycle lane—about 3.5 miles to Fort Casey. Cycles can be rented in Coupeville. (See Attractions, below.)

Another good day-trip starting point is **Joseph Whidbey State Park.** Rural roads in this gently rolling farmland-turned-residential-area are easy on the knees, easier on the eyes.

On the island's north end, cycling from **Deception Pass State Park** is more limited, but many riders enjoy the 7.5-mile backroad journey (on Rosario and Heart Lake or Havekost Roads) to Heart Lake and **Anacortes.** True adrenaline junkies can veer off this course and try the steep climb up Mount Erie.

Longer rides: A fairly hilly, but popular, route that takes in long stretches of both sides of **central Whidbey,** begins at Fort Casey and proceeds east on Wanamaker Road to the island's east shore. From here, you can follow an obvious series of shoreside roads north to Coupeville, around Penn Cove, and all the way to Oak Harbor (about 24 miles). The route home is west on Fort Nugent or Swantown Roads, south on West Beach Road past Fort Ebey, and south to Fort Casey via Hwy 20 and Engle Road. Round-trip mileage is 40 to 45 miles, depending on your specific route.

On **south Whidbey,** a number of good routes can be devised to bypass busy Hwy 525. The most popular method: Leave your car at Mukilteo, ride the ferry to Clinton, turn west on Deer Lake Road, south on Humphrey Road, or north on Galbreath/Wilkenson Roads. Then just follow the island's east or west shores. It's a good idea to have one, but you really don't even need a map. You can navigate by shoreline. Whichever bank you choose, all south-end roads tend to lead to Freeland, at one of the island's many tiny-waist narrow spots. Lunch up at **Freeland County Park,** rest, ride back. Round-trip mileage, depending on your route, will be from 25 to 40 miles.

Bike rentals are centrally located at **All Island Bicycles** (302 N Maine Street, Coupeville; (360) 678-3351).

Canoeing/Kayaking

Deception Pass State Park offers Whidbey's best paddling venue. Canoeists will love sprawling, shallow (maximum depth, 20 feet) **Cranberry Lake,** which has a forest ecosystem on the east side, a marine environment on the west. Sea kayakers will find calm, beautiful water in **Bowman** and **Cornet Bays,** both of which have boat launches and flat beaches with easy launch access and good parking. Both areas offer beautiful scenery and rate as excellent beginner-to-intermediate areas. Deception Pass is a designated stopover on the **Cascadia Marine Trail** (a state-managed water trail including campsites from Olympia to Vancouver, BC, (206) 545-9161).

Conversely, only very experienced paddlers should venture into treacherous, 500-foot-wide **Deception Pass** or the equally nasty 50-foot-wide **Canoe Pass,** the two channels that flow on either side of Pass Island beneath the Deception Pass Bridge. Currents are wicked here, sometimes approaching 10 knots. Even powerboaters wait for slack tide to run this channel.

Many experienced kayakers also use Bowman Bay as a base to cross short open-water stretches to the park's string of offshore islands: **Deception Island**—half a mile west of Deception Pass—is rocky, with a tricky eastside beach landing possible. **Northwest Island,** half a mile northwest of Rosario Beach, is an acre of rock and grass, with not much to see. Three-acre **Strawberry Island,** on the east side of Deception Pass, has decent landing spots on the south and east sides (easiest with higher tides), and offers a jaw-dropping view into Deception Pass. Stronger paddlers can use Cornet Bay as a base for exploring farther east, to **Skagit** or **Hope Islands** in the mouth of **Skagit Bay.** The latter, a forested rock of 166 acres, has established campsites on its north side, and a sketchy trail network.

Boating/Sailing

Whidbey's sheltered coves, deep harbors, and plentiful launch ramps make it a boater's paradise. While boating facilities are found all around the island, most marine activity takes place on the island's east side, which is protected from the raucous weather buffeting the higher-cliffed west banks.

Oak Harbor, several notches below most other Whidbey towns on the schmaltz scale, shines brightly when it comes to boating. The **Oak Harbor Marina,** (360) 240-0603, is a full-scale, full-service operation, with amenities as good as any in the north Sound. The Marina has a four-lane launch ramp, transient moorage, and a range of other services. This is the site of the famed **Whidbey Island Race Week,** the Northwest's largest summer yacht race, which draws dozens of top racing yachts in mid-July.

Also on North Whidbey, Deception Pass Marina, (360) 679-4783—east of Deception Pass State Park—offers moorage and good boater services near the popular park. It's a good place to wait for slack tide to run through the pass. On the other side of Deception Pass, **Bowman Bay** has mooring floats for waiting out the tide on the Rosario Strait end. Use caution in the bay's rock-studded mouth. Bowman Bay also has a boat ramp.

On the south end, Coupeville has its own boater services, fuel, and (shallow) moorage maintained by the **Port of Coupeville;** (360) 678-5020. Nearby **Captain Coupe Park** has some moorage of its own, plus a boat launch. **Langley Marina,** (360) 221-1771, offers moorage, full supplies, launch ramps, showers and the like. On the opposite side of the island, **Bush Point Marina,** (360) 321-1824—a popular starting point for salmon-fishing ventures to Midchannel Bank—offers the only substantial westside boater services, with fuel, supplies, and rentals, but no moorage.

If you're not getting your boat in the water from Whidbey, you're not trying hard enough. Public launch ramps can be found at Keystone, Coupeville, Oak Harbor, Fort Casey, Point Partridge, Strawberry Point, Possession Beach County Park, Dave Mackie County Park, Penn Cove's

Monroe Landing County Park, Langley, Freeland, Mutiny Bay, Bush Point, Deception Pass State Park's Bowman Bay, Cornet Bay, and Cranberry Lake—and probably a few other places we haven't found yet.

Scuba Diving/Snorkeling

Whidbey's many rocky shores offer a plethora of good exploring spots for divers. But two established sites are Puget Sound standouts.

Rosario Bay at Deception Pass (northwest of the bridge off Rosario Road) has a locally famous underwater park with a rich, varied display of Puget Sound sealife. It's particularly noted for its brightly colored sea urchins, anemones, and sea pens. Very experienced divers sometimes boat out to the rocky shoals around Northwest Island for more of the same.

Underwater treasures are equally rich in **Keystone Bay,** a protected cove where old pilings and jetty riprap attract large numbers of sea creatures, bottomfish, and the occasional octopus. This is also a popular snorkeling spot in the summer. Just watch out for the ferries.

Fishing

One of North Puget Sound's perennial **salmon-fishing** hot spots, **Midchannel Bank,** lies off the north end of Marrowstone Island near Port Townsend, and is an easy boat trip across Admiralty Inlet from Whidbey's west shore. The big underwater shelf is at its best for chinook and coho during midsummer. Unfortunately, in recent years it's been closed to fishing from July to October to allow passage of wild chinook and coho to Puget Sound spawning streams. When the fishing here is on, it's hot. Same story a short run down at **Possession Bar,** a Puget Sound hot spot off the island's south end. Most boaters launch at Bush Point or Fort Casey State Park.

The deep, tricky waters around **Deception Pass** are a known lurking spot for big chinook salmon, which are present from midsummer to fall. Many a 50-pounder has been hauled into a boat below the south side of the bridge.

The island's western shores also are home to a rather unique shore fishery for passing steelhead. Surf anglers at **Bush Point, Lagoon Point, Fort Casey,** and other western beach locations do surprisingly well at snatching winter steelhead bound for lower-Sound streams from December through February. Most use a long leader with a Spin-N-Glo bobber on top of a "Hoochy squid" salmon lure. Tip: The fish run *very* close in to shore. Make frequent, short casts.

In the winter, most Whidbey salmon-fishing action shifts to the east side of the island, with boats funneling out of **Oak Harbor** to fish for blackmouth (immature chinook) salmon in the protected leeward waters.

All year long, fishing from **piers** at Deception Pass, Langley, and Coupeville can be a relaxing, though not entirely productive, pursuit.

Trout fishing can be very good on several Whidbey lakes. Near Deception Pass, **Cranberry** and **Pass** Lakes are noted trout producers (Pass is fly-fishing only). On the south end of the island, try **Goss Lake** or **Lone Lake,** both near Freeland.

For Island fishing tips, seasons, and reports, call Bush Point Resort, (360) 321-1824, or Ted's Sport Center in Lynnwood, (425) 743-9505.

Photography

The beautifully restored **Admiralty Head Lighthouse** at Fort Casey State Park is one of the most often photographed historical sites in Washington. Sunset pictures from the **Deception Pass Bridge** and environs have graced more nature calendars than we can count.

outside in

Attractions

In **Clinton,** the golfer in the crowd can try his or her luck at Island Greens (3890 E French Road; (360) 321-6042), a par-3, nine-hole "alternative" golf course. **Cultus Bay Nursery** (4000 E Bailey Road, (360) 579-2329), open four days a week April through September, has a wide array of perennials, herbs, vines, and shrubs.

In **Langley,** a slew of shops and galleries are found on First Street. One-stop shoppers looking to get to the beach might try the **Star Store,** (360) 221-5222, a mercantile outpost with a grocery, deli, clothing, gifts, and kitchen gadgets. Fans of art and collectibles hop between galleries on main street, most notably the **Artist's Cooperative of Whidbey Island,** (360) 221-7675, where 30 island artists and craftspeople sell their wares. Also worth a stop is **Blackfish Studio,** (360) 221-1274, a mile south of town, where Kathleen Miller's hand-painted silk and wool clothing and enamel jewelry, and husband Donald Miller's art photography, are on display.

For sustenance, head to **The Dog House,** (360) 221-9996, for a pitcher of microbrew (20 on tap, 100 beers total) after a movie or an evening of live theater at **The Clyde,** (360) 221-5525. The pesto pizza-by-the-slice at **Langley Village Bakery,** (360) 221-3525, is a local favorite. And the **Whidbey Island Winery** (5237 S Langley Road, (360) 221-2040, open weekends year-round) has a fine tasting room. Try their rhubarb wine.

Farther north near **Greenbank,** make a stop at **Whidbey's Green-**

bank Farm, (360) 678-7700, where a self-guided tour culminates in samples of Loganberry Liqueur or Whidbey's Port. This is also a good picnic spot.

Coupeville, the second-oldest incorporated town in the state, has interesting historical sites. The Alexander Blockhouse on Front Street, part of an 1855 fort, is open for tours. The Island County Historical Museum, (360) 678-3310, also is worth a stop. While you're in town, a must-see gallery is the Jan McGregor Studio, (360) 678-5015, open on weekends throughout the year and every day in summer. For lunches, try Toby's 1890 Tavern, (360) 678-4222, or the Knead & Feed, (360) 678-5431. Early morning lattes are hot and fresh at Great Times Espresso. For cyclists, All Island Bicycles (302 N Main, (360) 678-3351) sells, rents, and repairs bikes.

Oak Harbor is the big city on Whidbey. Airplane buffs will enjoy a drive down to Whidbey Island Naval Air Station. Batteries burned out exploring Deception Pass can be recharged at Lucy's Mi Casita (1380 W Pioneer Way; (360) 675-4800), whose upstairs lounge has a notable 27-ounce "Turbo Godzilla" margarita. Up the road near Deception Pass, Strom's Shrimp/Fountain and Grill sells fresh seafood and shrimp for your cookout. They also grill up a mean oysterburger to go; (360) 293-2531.

Restaurants

Cafe Langley ☆☆   Sparkling consistency has established this downtown storefront cafe as the best bet in town. Make a reservation (especially on weekends) and prepare for a fine Mediterranean/Greek dining experience. *At the south end of town; (360) 221-3090; 113 1st St, Langley; $$.*

Kasteel Franssen (Auld Holland Inn) ☆   Half a mile north of Oak Harbor, this motel with the trademark windmill is just fine, if a shade close to the highway. The restaurant is quite delightful, with a regal, European feel and a solid reputation among locals. *8 miles south of Deception Pass on Hwy 20; (360) 675-2288; 3375 Hwy 20, Oak Harbor; $$$.*

Lucy's Mi Casita   It doesn't look like much, but locals keep coming back for the homemade Mexican food and lively atmosphere. *On the main drag; (360) 675-4800; 31359 Hwy 20, Oak Harbor; $.*

Star Bistro ☆   A steady staple of the Langley bistro scene, the Star (above the Star Store, a steady staple of the Langley shop scene) is a fun and color-splashed place that hops on weekends and after local events. *Above the Star Store on 1st St; (360) 221-2627; 201½ 1st St, Langley; $$.*

Lodgings

Boatyard Inn ☆☆   The industrial look of the green siding and corrugated metal roofs of this recently opened inn mesh well with Langley's still colorful working waterfront. The place is so close to the water that the tide rises up against the first floor. *From Clinton ferry, take Hwy 525 to 1st light, turn right onto Langley Rd and follow into Langley. Right at 3-way stop to Cascade, then right onto Wharf St; (360) 221-5120; 200 Wharf St, Langley; $$$.*

Captain Whidbey Inn ☆   Nothing much changes about this old Penn Cove inn, built in 1907 of sturdy madrona logs. The best bets are the 13 lagoon rooms, with private baths and verandas overlooking two calm inlets of water. *Off Madrona Way on W Captain Whidbey Inn Rd; (360) 678-4097; 2072 W Captain Whidbey Inn Rd, Coupeville; $$.*

Cliff House ☆☆   This striking home on a cliff above Admiralty Inlet is full of light from lofty windows, centering on a 30-foot-high atrium filled with native plants (open to the weather), and a sunken fireplace. *Bush Point Rd to Windmill Rd; (360) 331-1566; 5440 Windmill Rd, Freeland; $$$.*

Eagle's Nest Inn Bed and Breakfast   This four-story octagonal getaway is tucked into the forest on a knoll looking out on scenic Saratoga Passage, Camano Island, and Mount Baker. *Call ahead for directions; (360) 221-5331; 3236 E Saratoga Rd, Langley; $$$.*

Edgecliff ☆☆☆   Money can't buy you love, but in the case of these two retreat homes perched on a bluff overlooking Saratoga Passage, it can buy you a film-set version of a romantic getaway, set not far from the cliff's near-vertical staircase leading to the sandy beach below. *Call ahead for directions; (360) 221-8857 or (800) 243-5536; Langley; $$$.*

Fort Casey Inn ☆   Built in 1909 as officers' quarters for nearby Fort Casey, this neat row of nine houses now offers tidy, no-frills accommodations with a historical bent. Houses are divided into two-bedroom duplexes, each kitchen stocked with breakfast makings. Kids welcome. *2 miles west of Coupeville; (360) 678-8792; 1124 S Engle Rd, Coupeville; $$.*

Galittoire ☆☆   Galittoire is a sleek, contemporary B&B that's almost sensual in its attention to detail. Two-night minimum on weekends. *Off Hwy 525 on Coles Rd; (360) 221-0548; 5444 S Coles Rd, Langley; $$$.*

Garden Path Inn ☆☆   For an island getaway that feels more like an uptown city condo, book a weekend at one of the two upstairs suites above proprietress Linda Lundgren's interior design shop. *Downtown Langley; (360) 221-5121; 111 1st St, Langley; $$–$$$.*

Guest House Bed & Breakfast Cottages ☆☆☆   Seven varied dwellings are set on a pastoral clearing fringed with woodland. Everybody's favorite is the Lodge, a $285-a-night custom-built log home for two. Breakfast makings are left in the fully equipped kitchens. *1 mile south of Greenbank off Hwy 525; (360) 678-3115; 3366 S Hwy 525, Greenbank; $$$.*

Inn at Langley ☆☆☆   It's difficult to conceive of a more idyllic getaway, or one more evocative of the Pacific Northwest, than Paul and Pam Schell's first private venture, built elegantly into the bluff over the Saratoga Passage. Chef Steve Nogal continues to make waves in his country kitchen. *At the edge of town; (360) 221-3033; 400 1st St, Langley; $$$.*

Inn at Penn Cove ☆   This gracious inn consists of two historic pink homes, the Kineth House (built in 1887, and completely restored to its former grandeur) and the Coupe-Gillespie House (circa 1891, a decidedly more casual affair). *Take Hwy 20 S from Deception Pass; (360) 678-8000 or (800) 688-COVE; 702 N Main St, Coupeville; $$.*

Log Castle ☆☆   This is the house that Jack built—literally. And whenever there's time, U.S. Congressman Jack Metcalf builds on it some more, to his wife Norma's newest designs. Originally a Christian retreat center; however, the religious ambiance now isn't fanatical. *1½ miles west of Langley on Saratoga; (360) 321-5483; 3273 E Saratoga Rd, Langley; $$.*

Lone Lake Cottage and Breakfast ☆   An estimable resort with eccentric charm. One lodging option is aboard the *Whidbey Queen*, a sternwheeler permanently moored on the lake. Each room has a kitchen stocked with breakfast makings. Guests can use the private beach, canoes, rowboat, and bikes. *6 miles from the Clinton ferry, off Hwy 525; (360) 321-5325; 5206 S Bayview, Langley; $$$.*

The Old Morris Farm ☆   Owners Mario Chodorowski and Marilyn Randock have successfully transformed their 1909 farmhouse into an elegant countryside B&B. *Take Hwy 20, 3 miles from Coupeville overpass; (360) 678-6586; 105 W Morris Rd, Coupeville; $$.*

Saratoga Inn ☆☆   It's a two-minute walk from downtown to the Saratoga Inn (formerly the Harrison House Inn) with architectural touches reminiscent of New England. But the inn, opened by longtime hoteliers (and Brits) John and Kathleen Harrison, sets the Anglophile's standard of comfort plus privacy. *Corner of 2nd and Cascade Ave; (360) 221-5801; 201 Cascade Ave, Langley; $$$.*

Villa Isola ☆☆   Tucked into a pine-studded pastoral landscape, this version of an Italian country villa goes a long way in re-creating the slow, sweet life of the old country. Borrow the inn's mountain bikes or engage in a game of bocce (Italian lawn bowling) on the regulation-size court. *About 2 miles southeast of Langley on S Coles Rd; (360) 221-5052; 5489 S Coles Rd, Langley; $$$.*

Cheaper Sleeps

Coupeville Inn   An attractive blue-and-gray inn that's a 24-unit motel. What makes it an inn? The eccentric innkeeper, Alan Dutcher. Fourteen rooms slide in at just under $50 in the winter, and just over $50 as the season warms up. *(360) 678-6668 or (800) 247-6162; 200 NW Coveland St, Coupeville.*

Drake's Landing   The little blue house at the working end of Langley's waterfront is a modern-day version of the respectable boardinghouse. Four rooms are small, but each has its own private bath. This might not be the Inn at Langley, but it's a good night's sleep in the same quaint town. *(360) 221-3999; 203 Wharf St, Langley.*

Mutiny Bay Resort   One of the last old-time fishing resorts on Whidbey Island—hanging by a thread, with the salmon. The beach chalets are nice but pricey. Instead, request one of the old fisherman's cabins. They have kitchens, but showers in a separate bathhouse. *(360) 331-4500; 5856 S Mutiny Bay Rd, Freeland.*

More Information

Central Whidbey Chamber of Commerce, Coupeville: *(360) 678-5434.*
Greater Oak Harbor Chamber of Commerce: *(360) 675-3535.*
Langley Chamber of Commerce: *(360) 221-6765.*
Whidbey Island Naval Air Station: *(360) 257-2286.*

Greater
Seattle

From Saltwater State Park north to Edmonds, east to Redmond and west to West Point.

Welcome to Seattle, the city whose inside most assuredly is out. Out as in "green." Out as in "wild." Out as in "unconfined." When it comes to urban areas with faraway places packed right inside city limits, Seattle may have no equal.

It's true: We can look out the office window and see rowing crews swishing across Lake Union, anglers pulling salmon over the rail at Seacrest Boathouse, cyclists on the Burke-Gilman, or pic-nickers at Myrtle Edwards, and sigh a smug sigh. *It's all here.*

If you look hard enough, most of it surely is. Seattle is blessed with a wealth of rich outdoor experiences, thanks largely to the very thing that can otherwise make it a painful place to live and conduct business: water, water, and more water. We're surrounded by it here, whether it's salt water in Elliott Bay, fresh water in Lake Washington, or that salty-fresh hybrid mix floating all those big boats out in Lake Union. We curse it, but we love it. The water gives us scenic vistas in a city park system that surely ranks among the best on the continent, a county park system that's not far behind, and a dozen suburban city park systems that would beg to differ. Water keeps the Emerald City green, its inhabitants lean. When we're not exercising around water on miles of cycle and hiking trails, we're often lying beside it on grassy beaches—or relaxing upon it, on the deck of one of the nation's most imposing privately held pleasure-craft armadas.

The Seattle area—for all its hundreds of square miles of

(expanding) concrete and longer-than-January traffic jams—still manages to wring a smile from even the biggest urban pessimist among us. Why? Because it *really is all here.* Without driving more than 20 minutes from home, Seattle recreators can swim, boat, bike, hike, camp, kayak, climb, fly, fish, run, dive, ride, row, pedal, or raft. Ours is the choice, the opportunity, the challenge.

Of course, it could be argued that not many Seattle-area residents spend all their waking hours—or even a small slice of them—actually *doing* those things. Mostly, a critic would say, Seattleites watch a few other people do them, then plot to get out of town to do them better, somewhere else, some other time.

Little matter. For Seattle's hundreds of thousands of mental REI cardholders—scurrying around between business meetings in hiking boots, Gore-Tex, and Capilene, too busy to recreate—getting out and doing it isn't always the most important thing. Somehow, just knowing we *could* is enough.

Getting There

IMPORTANT NOTICE: In 1997, area codes in the Greater Seattle area are scheduled to change, affecting counties that currently share the (206) code. Please be advised that codes listed throughout this chapter may have been changed.

Locate Seattle by looking for the center of the big, constant traffic snarl at the junction of Interstate 5, Interstate 90, and Highway 520. Sea-Tac Airport, the way most people get here, is 30 minutes south of the city. Metro buses 174 and 194 make the trip from downtown. Shuttle Express is a reliable airport-to-front-door service, reservations required; (206) 622-1424 or (800) 942-0711.

The Metro bus is free in downtown's commercial core; otherwise the fare is 85 cents within the city ($1.10 during peak hours) and $1.10 if you cross the city line ($1.60 peak); (206) 553-3000.

Another common commute is on Washington State ferries, which cross Puget Sound to various destinations frequently. Riding the ferries also happens to be one of the most enjoyable ways to view the city's skyline; (206) 464-6400 or (800) 843-3779.

Most of the recreation areas described in this chapter are either inside the city limits, to the north in north King or south Snohomish Counties via I-5, to the south via I-5, or on the Eastside via the Highway 520 or I-90 floating bridges over Lake Washington.

Adjoining Areas

NORTH: **Mountain Loop Highway and Glacier Peak Wilderness; Whidbey and Camano Islands**

SOUTH: **Tacoma and Gig Harbor**

EAST: **Alpine Lakes Wilderness: Overview; Snoqualmie Pass (Mountains–to–Sound Corridor)**

WEST: **Kitsap Peninsula; Bainbridge and Vashon Islands**

Parks/Beaches

In 1884, Seattle pioneers David and Louise Denny donated to the city a 5-acre plot of land at what is now the corner of Denny Way and Dexter Avenue N, and Seattle had its first park. Since then the park system has grown to more than 5,000 acres, many of them designed by visionary park planners John Charles Olmsted and Frederick Olmsted Jr. (sons of New York's Central Park mastermind, Frederick Law Olmsted). Seattle's parks range from the classical (Capitol Hill's Volunteer Park, Washington Park Arboretum) to the recreational (Green Lake, Alki Beach) to the wild (Discovery Park, Seward Park) to the ingenious (Gas Works Park, Freeway Park). At last count there were 397 parks and playgrounds in the city of Seattle alone.

Surrounding suburban cities are no slouches in the parks department, either. Many of the area's most popular regional parks are run either by local cities or King County, and lie outside Seattle city limits—a short and (used to be) quick drive from downtown.

A compilation of the best parks in the region follows, in the only fair way possible—alphabetical order. To find out more about any of them, call the appropriate Parks and Recreation Department: Washington State Parks, (800) 233-0321 for general information or (800) 452-5687 for camping reservations; King County, (206) 296-4232; Seattle, (206) 684-4075; Bellevue, (206) 455-6881; Issaquah, (206) 392-7131; Kirkland, (206) 828-1217; Mercer Island, (206) 236-3545; and Redmond, (206) 882-6401.

Alki Beach: This 2.5-mile strip of beach point marks the spot where the original white Seattle settlers first established homesteads. (The Native American word *alki* meant "by and by," their wry comment on the pioneers' eager hopes of turning their settlement into the New York of the West.) Now the beach has many faces, depending on the season: cool and peaceful in the fall, stormy in winter, and jammed with cyclists and roller skaters in the summer. It also draws throngs of teenagers, who hang out along the Alki Avenue strip, which is lined with beachy eateries on one side, sandy beach on the other. Duwamish Head, at the north end of the strand, offers spectacular views, as does the Coast Guard–maintained Alki Point and Light Station (3201 Alki Avenue SW, (206) 932-5800) at the tip of the point. The scenic extension of Alki Beach continues southward along Beach Drive past windswept Me-Kwa-Mooks Park and on to Lincoln Park (see below). Along Alki Avenue SW in West Seattle.

Bellevue Downtown Central Park: You can almost feel the magnetic pull of a billion credit-card strips at Bellevue Square from this 20-acre downtown park, which reflects Bellevue's desire for an oasis in a busy urban area. Tired mall shoppers cross the street to sit by the fountain, enjoy the large formal garden, or stroll by the 240-foot-wide waterfall, which empties into a 1,200-foot reflecting canal. Teak benches placed throughout recall the park benches of London. 1201 NE Fourth Street, Bellevue.

Blake Island State Park: Once an ancestral camping ground of the Suquamish tribe, this tiny island in Puget Sound is now a densely wooded wilderness state park. There are 54 campsites, plus boat moorage. Bring your own boat. There is no ferry service to the island, except for commercial runs to the privately operated Tillicum Village, a staged-for-tourists glimpse of North Coast Indian heritage. But many private boaters overnight on the island, and kayakers paddle from South Kitsap County (see the Kitsap Peninsula chapter) or north Vashon Island (see the Bainbridge and Vashon Islands chapter) launching points to Blake Island's designated Cascadia Marine Trail campsites (the Cascadia Marine Trail is a state-managed water trail including campsites from Olympia to Vancouver, BC; (206) 545-9161). Plenty of on-island recreation awaits: 15 miles of hiking trails access about 5 miles of beaches. Information: (206) 443-1244 (Tillicum Village).

Bothell Landing: This quaint little community park across the Sammamish River from the Sammamish River Trail offers rolling green lawns for family picnics and Frisbee throwing, an amphitheater (with Friday-evening concerts in the summer), a historical museum housed in a turn-of-the-century frame building, and an adult day center. Canoes and small boats can tie up at the public pier, where ducks await bread crumbs. There is limited parking at the site itself; a parking lot at 17995 102nd Avenue NE, Bothell, on the south side of the river, has additional spaces. 9919 NE 180th Street, Bothell; (206) 486-8152.

Bridle Trails State Park: As its name suggests, this 480-acre park is a densely wooded equestrian paradise laced with horse trails (one links up with Marymoor Park) and even sports an exercise ring. Though you may feel like an alien if you come to do anything but ride (even the private homes in the area all seem to have stables), the park also has picnic sites. Watch where you step. 116th Avenue NE and NE 53rd Street, Kirkland; (206) 827-2900.

Burke-Gilman Trail: See Gas Works and Marymoor Parks, this section, and Cycling, below.

Camp Long: Run by the Seattle Parks and Recreation Department, Camp Long serves as a meeting/conference facility (a lodge holds 75 people in its upper room and 35 in the basement), an in-city outdoor experience for family or group use (10 rustic bunk-bed–equipped cabins sleep up to 12 people at $24 a cabin), and simply as a 68-acre nature preserve. The park also offers interpretive programs, perfect for school or Scout groups, and family-oriented nature programs on weekends. Climbers seeking practice can hang from a climbing rock or a simulated glacier face. 5200 35th Avenue SW; (206) 684-7434.

Carkeek Park: Here's one of the city's most under-appreciated treats: 198 acres of wilderness in the far northwest corner of the city. Forest paths wind from the parking lots and two reservable picnic areas (call (206) 684-4081) to the footbridge spanning the railroad tracks, and then down a staircase to the broad beach. (Use caution around the tracks; trains speed frequently through the park, and the acoustics can be misleading.) Grassy meadows (great for kite flying), picnic shelters, and pretty, meandering Piper's Creek are other good reasons to relax here. Visit in October to witness one of the Northwest's classic cycles of life: chum salmon return from the Pacific ocean via Puget Sound to spawn in Piper's Creek. Trails will take you close enough to get splashed. Keep dogs and kids out of the creek, please! NW Carkeek Road and 9th Avenue NW, in North Seattle's Broadview neighborhood.

Chism Beach Park: One of Bellevue's largest and oldest waterfront parks, Chism sits along the handsome residential stretch south of Meydenbauer Bay. There are docks and diving boards for swimmers, picnic areas, a playground, and a large parking area above the beach. 1175 96th Avenue SE, Bellevue.

Coulon Park: This arboreal park on the shore of Lake Washington is the prize of Renton's park system. It has won national awards for the arresting architecture of its pavilion and restaurant concession (an Ivar's Fish Bar), but is best loved for the beach. Log booms around the swimming area serve as protective barriers for wind surfers. 1201 Lake Washington Boulevard N, Renton; (206) 235-2560.

Discovery Park: Formerly the site of Seattle's Fort Lawton army base, this densely foliated Magnolia wilderness has been allowed to revert to its premetropolitan natural order. It is full of variety and even a little mystery—in 1982 a cougar was discovered in the park, and no one knew how it got there or how long it roamed free in the 534 acres. Self-guided interpretive nature loops and short trails wind through thick forests, along dramatic seacliffs (where powerful updrafts make for excellent kite flying), and across meadows of waving grasses. The old barracks, houses, and training field are the few remaining vestiges of the Army's presence. Discover the park's flora and fauna yourself or take advantage of the scheduled walks and nature workshops conducted by park naturalists. Free guided walks are offered at 2pm every Saturday, and bird tours on Saturday mornings in spring and fall. Groups can also schedule their own guided walks. **Daybreak Star Arts Center** ((206) 285-4425) sponsors Native American activities and gallery exhibits of contemporary Indian art in the **Sacred Circle Gallery.** The kids will be pleased with two marvelously equipped kids' playgrounds, along with picnic areas, playfields, tennis and basketball courts, and a rigorous fitness trail. The network of trails is a favorite among jogging enthusiasts. 3801 W Government Way; (206) 386-4236.

Fay-Bainbridge State Park: About a 15-minute drive from the Winslow ferry dock on Bainbridge Island, Fay-Bainbridge is a smallish (17-acre) park known for its camping areas and view of Mount Rainier and Seattle. The log-strewn beach has pits for fires; other features include a boat launch, horseshoe pits, and two kitchen shelters. It's a popular stop for cyclists on their way around the hilly isle. (See also Bainbridge and Vashon Islands chapter.) 15446 Sunrise Drive NE, Bainbridge Island; (206) 842-3931.

Freeway Park: One of Seattle's most original outdoor spaces, this extraordinary park forms a lid over thundering I-5—a feat of urban park innovation when it was constructed in 1976. Here, amid grassy plateaus and rushing waterfall canyons, the roar of traffic seems to disappear, and brown baggers find rejuvenating solace. Sixth Avenue and Seneca Street, downtown Seattle.

Gas Works Park: What do you do when the piece of property with the grandest skyline and lakeside view in the city is dominated by a greasy old gas-processing plant? In Seattle, you turn it into a park. Gas Works is urban reclamation at its finest. It's one of the city's most delightful parks, and the attractions are diverse. A high, grassy mound topped by a unique sundial/viewpoint offers a killer view of downtown Seattle and Lake Union, and makes a great launch pad for kite flyers. You ll also find a large picnic shelter (call (206) 684-4081 to reserve space) and a wonderful play barn. Against a sky full of dancing kites, even the rusting hulk of the old gas works looks oddly handsome. This park has a beat all its own: most summer days, drummers and other acoustic musicians gather here for impromptu jam sessions, their music reverberating through the old concrete and steel structures. The threat of lurking soil pollutants—which closed the park in 1984—has been ruled out, provided you don't eat the dirt. (Parents with toddlers, take note.) Motorists should keep eyes peeled for cyclists. Gas Works is a primary start/stop point for **Burke-Gilman Trail** (see Cycling, below) riders. N Northlake Way and Meridian Avenue N, north Seattle.

Golden Gardens: Alki Beach's spiritual counterpart to the north, Golden Gardens teems with tanning humanity on summer weekends. A breezy, sandy beach, nearby boat ramp, beach fire pit, and the pretty waters of Shilshole Bay are the biggest lures, although fully half of the park's 95 acres lie to the east of the railroad tracks along the wooded, trail-laced hillside. Watching the sun settle behind the pink Olympic Mountains from the beach at Golden Gardens reminds us why we live here. North end of Seaview Avenue NW, adjacent to Shilshole Marina.

Green Lake: When the sun shines and the jogging, tanning, and roller-skating crowd musters en masse, the greenbelt around Green Lake looks like a slice of Southern California that's been beamed to the button-down Northwest. Nature lovers will better appreciate Green Lake during winter months. But even on dreary days, the 2.8-mile paved circuit around the lake can be jammed with the Nike-and-Walkman set. For less competition, runners should try the outer, 3.2-mile unpaved path (it's also easier on the knees). What is now the center of Seattle's exercise culture is the remnant of a large glacial lake that was well on its way to becoming a meadow when the pioneers arrived (hence the name). The city scrapped plans to turn it into a golf course or storm drain for I-5 and decided to bolster its declining waters with surplus from city reservoirs. This makes for balmy dunking (though on warm days the water can be rather ripe), superlative sailing and windsurfing, and great people-watching. The lake also is open year-round for surprisingly productive fishing for stocked rainbow trout. Although the tennis courts, soccer field, indoor pool and recreation center, outdoor basketball court, baseball diamond, pitch-and-putt golf course, boat rental, thriving commercial district, and considerable car traffic around the lake make it feel like an urban beach resort, you can usually find one or two lonely grassy patches for a picnic. Take the kids to the well-equipped kids' playground on the northeast side. Limited parking can be found in three lots: the northeast lot (Latona Avenue N and E Green Lake Way N, the most crowded), northwest lot (7312 W Green Lake Way N), and the south lots (5900 W Green Lake Way N). Be forewarned: Green Lake's lots are notorious car-prowl territory. E Green Lake Drive N and W Green Lake Drive N, in North Seattle.

Hing Hay Park: Hing Hay (Chinese for "park for pleasurable gathering") is a meeting and gathering place for the International District's large Asian community. From the adjacent Bush Hotel, an enormous multicolored mural of a dragon presides over the park and the ornate grand pavilion from Taipei. A great place to get a feel for the rhythms of International District life. S King Street and Maynard Avenue S, in the International District.

Kelsey Creek Park: Kids are in their element at this excellent nature park, which comprises 80 acres northeast of the I-90/I-405 interchange. In addition to a variety of parkland habitats (marshy forests, open grassy glades, wooded hillsides), two barns and a farmyard provide an area where kids can see newborn calves, goats, lambs, and piglets in the spring. Kelsey Creek and numerous footpaths (good for jogging) wind throughout. An original 1888 pioneer log cabin adds a historical dimension. The park also has nice picnic areas and a small children's playground. 13204 SE Eighth Place, east of I-405 in Bellevue.

Kirkland Waterfront: A string of parks, from Houghton Beach to Marina Park at Moss Bay lines the shore of Kirkland's beautiful Lake Washington Boulevard. The kids feed the ducks and wade (only Houghton Beach and Waverly Beach have lifeguards); their parents sunbathe and watch the runners lope by. This is as close to Santa Cruz as the Northwest gets. Along Lake Washington Boulevard, Kirkland.

Lake Sammamish State Park: The sprawling beach is the main attraction of this state park at the south end of Lake Sammamish. Shady picnic areas, grassy playfields, barbecue grills, and volleyball courts are excellent secondary draws. Large groups must reserve day-use areas—the place can be overrun in summer. This is one of the most frequently visited parks in all the Northwest. Issaquah Creek, a major passageway for salmon bound for the Issaquah Hatchery, runs through the park's wooded area. 20606 SE 56th Street, Issaquah (follow signs from I-90); (206) 455-7010.

Lake Washington Parks: This string of grassy beachfronts acts as collective backyard for several of the neighborhoods that slope toward Lake Washington's western shore. **Bicycle Saturdays and Sundays** take place in the summer, when Lake Washington Boulevard from Colman Park to Seward Park is open to bicycles (closed to cars 10am to 6pm). **Madison Park,** the site of an amusement park and bathing beach early in the century, has shed its vaudeville image and is now a genteel neighborhood park, with a roped-in swimming area and tennis courts. If you head west on Madison and turn left onto Lake Washington Boulevard, you'll wind down to meet the beach again, this time at **Madrona Park** (Lake Washington Boulevard and Madrona Drive), a grassy strip with a swimming beach, picnic tables, a summer-only food concession, and a dance studio. Farther on is **Leschi Park** (Lakeside Avenue S and Leschi Place), a nicely manicured city park that occupies the hillside across the boulevard. The park offers great views of the Leschi Marina and the dazzling spinnakers on the sailboats, as well as a play area for kids. Another green-belt, **Colman Park** (36th Avenue S and Lakeside Avenue S), also with a play area, marks the start of the seamless strip that includes **Mount Baker Park** (Lake Park Drive S and Lake Washington Boulevard S), a gently sloping, tree-lined ravine; the hydroplane racing mecca—once a marshy slough, now a manicured park and spectator beach with boat launches—called Stan Sayres Memorial Park; and the lonely wilderness peninsula of **Seward Park** (see listing in this section). From Madison Park at E Madison Street and 43rd Avenue E to Stan Sayres Memorial Park at 3800 Lake Washington Boulevard S.

Lincoln Park: Lincoln Park, a 130-acre jewel perched on a pointed bluff in West Seattle, offers a network of walking and biking paths amid grassy forests, picnic shelters (call (206) 684-4081 to reserve), recreational activities from horseshoes to football to tennis, and expansive views of the Olympic Mountains from seawalls or rocky beaches. Tide pools can be inspected at low tide, and plenty of beach is available for roaming. Kids will love the playground equipment. Don't miss the (heated) outdoor salt-water Colman Pool (summer only), which began as a tide-fed swimming hole. Fauntleroy Avenue SW and SW Webster Street in West Seattle.

Luther Burbank Park: This park's undulating fields and endless land-and-lake recreational areas occupy a good chunk of the northern tip of Mercer Island and make it the Eastside's favorite family park. It's well equipped, with picnic areas, barbecues, a swimming area, nicely main-tained tennis courts, an outdoor amphitheater for summer concerts, a first-rate playground, several playing fields, docks for boat tie-ups (the haunt of the sun-worshipping teens in summer), and green meadows that tumble down to the shore. When the main beach is crowded, head north toward the point to find lonelier picnic spots. Parking is not a problem. 2040 84th Avenue SE, Mercer Island.

Magnuson Park: This 193-acre park fronts Lake Washington just south of Sand Point Naval Air Base, with a mile of shoreline, a boat launch, a playing field, and six tennis courts. Adjacent to the north is NOAA (National Oceanic and Atmospheric Administration, (206) 526-6046). You'll find a series of unique artworks along the beach. One sculpture, *Sound Garden,* is fitted with flutelike aluminum tubes that create eerie "music" when the wind blows. The site is open every day from 6:30am and is a hauntingly wonderful spot to sit on a bench that resembles a blue whale, listening to the wailing wind chimes and watching the sun come up over Lake Washington. Sand Point Way NE and 65th Avenue NE.

Marymoor County Park: This vast expanse of flat grasslands and playfields in Redmond is a regional treasure. Marymoor is home to the famed Marymoor Velodrome (see Cycling, below) and serves as the starting point of the Sammamish River bike (or jogging or horseback-riding) trail, which connects to the Burke-Gilman Trail in Kenmore. But plenty of open-space fun awaits non-cyclists: the Marymoor Historical Museum, (206) 885-3684, Clise Mansion, picnic facilities, a popular area for flying remote-control model airplanes, an *extremely* popular off-leash area for dogs along the Sammamish Slough, and about a zillion playing fields. 6046 W Lake Sammamish Parkway NE, just south of Hwy 520 in Redmond; (206) 296-2966.

Myrtle Edwards Park: Myrtle Edwards and adjacent **Elliott Bay Park** provide a front lawn to the downtown Seattle shoreline. This breezy and refreshing strip is a great noontime getaway for jogging (the two parks combined form a 1.25-mile trail), picnicking on sea-facing benches, or just strolling. The park is a big-time gathering spot for Fourth of July fireworks, and Michael Heizer's prominent granite-and-concrete park sculpture, *Adjacent, Against, Upon*, has truly grown on us. Parking at the Pier 70 lot just south of Myrtle Edwards is at a premium, but the Waterfront Streetcar stops nearby. Alaskan Way between W Bay Street and W Thomas Street, at the north end of the waterfront commercial strip.

Newcastle Beach Park: This Bellevue park takes full advantage of its waterfront location with a fishing dock, swimming area, and bathhouse facility (complete with outdoor showers). Walking paths—including a ³/₄-mile loop—weave throughout the 28 acres, and a wildlife habitat offers the chance to see animals and birds in their natural environment. 4400 Lake Washington Boulevard S, Bellevue.

Ravenna Park: This steep woodland ravine strung between residential districts north of the University District is a lush sylvan antidote to the city around it. At the west end is **Cowen Park** (University Way NE and NE Ravenna Boulevard), with tennis courts and play and picnic areas. Trails along burbling Ravenna Creek lead to the eastern end of the park and more picnic areas, a wading pool, and playing fields. The whole expanse is a favorite haunt of joggers, as is Ravenna Boulevard, the gracious, tree-lined thoroughfare that defines its southern flank. 20th Avenue NE and NE 58th Street.

Saltwater State Park: Folks use this 88-acre Puget Sound–front park for clamming (January to June only; call ahead for red tide report), picnicking, camping, hiking in the forested uplands, or scuba diving in the underwater reef. The views of Vashon Island and the summer sunsets are spectacular. 25205 Eighth Place S, Des Moines; (206) 764-4128.

Schmitz Park: Just east of West Seattle's Alki Beach is this 50-acre virgin nature preserve, full of raw trails through thickly wooded terrain. The largest western red cedars and hemlocks here are likely to be about 800 years old—seedlings when Richard the Lionhearted was leading his troops on the Third Crusade. It's a marvelous place for contemplation and nature study. No playgrounds, picnic areas, or other park amenities. SW Stevens Street and Admiral Way SW.

Seward Park: This spectacular wilderness occupies a 277-acre knob of land in southeast Seattle and gives the modern-day Seattleite an idea of what the area must have looked like centuries ago. At times, the park is imbued with a primal sense of permanence, especially on misty winter days when the quiet of a solitary walk through old-growth Douglas fir forest is broken only by the cries of a few birds. But at other times—hot summer Sundays, for instance—Seward turns into a frenzy of music and barbecues. You can drive the short loop road to get acquainted with the park, past the bathhouse and beach facilities; **Seward Park Art Studio** (206) 722-6342), which offers classes in the arts; some of the six picnic shelters (call (206) 684-4081 for reservations); and some of the trailheads, which lead to the fish hatchery, the outdoor amphitheater, and into the forest preserve. Cyclists and runners can make an even better loop on the scenic two-and-a-half-mile lakeside trail encircling the park. Lake Washington Boulevard S and S Juneau Street.

Victor Steinbrueck Park: Pike Place Market's greatest supporter and friend is the namesake behind this splash of green at the north end of Pike Place Market. With the Alaskan Way Viaduct right below, the park can be quite noisy during peak traffic hours. It also tends to be a favorite hangout for street people. Despite those caveats, the park's grassy slopes and tables make a fine place for a Market picnic, and the view of the blue bay and ferry traffic is refreshing. Western Avenue and Virginia Street; (206) 684-4080.

Volunteer Park: Mature trees, circling drives, grassy lawns, and lily ponds make this the most elegant of Seattle's parks—as stately as the mansions that surround it. Designed by the Olmsted brothers, and dedicated to those who fought in the Spanish-American War, Volunteer Park's 44.5 acres grace the top of Capitol Hill and offer sweeping views of the Space Needle, the Sound, and the Olympic Mountains. At the north end of the main concourse lies the elaborate **Volunteer Park Conservatory** (15th Avenue and Galer Street, (206) 684-4743), with three large greenhouse wings filled with flowering plants, cacti, and tropical flora. It's open (free of charge) to the public. At the other end of the main concourse is an old 75-foot water tower, which the hardy can climb for a splendid view of the city and the Cascades. In between is the **Seattle Asian Art Museum** (1400 E Prospect; (206) 654-3100), with one of the most extraordinary collections of Asian art in the nation. For the kids, there's a play area near the main entrance, east of the conservatory. 15th Avenue E and E Prospect Street.

Washington Park Arboretum: All year round, the Arboretum is nearly as full of people as it is of trees. Naturalists and botanists rub elbows with serious joggers and casual walkers, for this 200-acre public park doubles as a botanical research facility for the nearby University of Washington. The Arboretum stretches from Foster Island, just off the shores of Lake Washington, through the Montlake and Madison Park neighborhoods, its rambling trails screened from the houses by thick greenbelts of trees and shrubs. More than 5,000 varieties of woody plants are arranged by family; pick up maps or an illustrated guide at the visitors center if you want to find specific trees.

From spring until autumn, the Arboretum's **Japanese Garden** (1502 Lake Washington Boulevard E, (206) 684-4725) is well worth a visit. Just across the road to the north runs **Azalea Way,** a wide, grassy thoroughfare that winds through the heart of the arboretum. (No jogging is permitted on this popular walk.) Always pleasant, Azalea Way is magnificent in April and May when its blossoming shrubs are joined by scores of companion dogwoods and ornamental cherries. Side trails lead through the Arboretum's extensive camellia and rhododendron groves (the latter collection is world-famous). Follow Azalea Way to the copper-roofed **Visitors Center,** where you can find maps and Arboretum guides as well as horticulturally related books, gifts, and informational displays. On Sundays at 1pm, guided tours begin at the Center, which is open from 10am to 4pm on weekdays and noon to 4pm on weekends. North of the visitors center, a waterfront nature trail winds along the marshy shoreline to **Foster Island,** a sanctuary for birds and bird-watchers and a haven for canoeists, swimmers, fishermen, and picnickers. To explore the shoreline by boat, rent a canoe from the **University of Washington Waterfront Activities Center.** The Arboretum is open from sunrise to sunset. E Madison and Lake Washington Boulevard E; (206) 543-8800.

Waterfall Gardens: How many city downtowns can boast a park with a 22-foot crashing waterfall, even an artificial one? The waterfall in this tiny Pioneer Square park was built to honor United Parcel Service, which started in this location in 1907. It does crash (this is no place for quiet conversation), and the benches do fill up by noon on weekdays, but the park makes for a marvelous little nature fix in the middle of a busy urban day. 219 Second Avenue S, downtown Seattle; (206) 624-6096.

Waterfront Park: A park that spans three piers between the Aquarium and Pier 57 provides a break from the bustling activity of the rest of the waterfront. The park contains a tree-encircled courtyard, raised platforms with telescopes for a voyeur's view of the bay and islands, plenty of benches, and—strange for a park in this town—nary a blade of grass. Pier 57 to Pier 61 on Alaskan Way.

Woodland Park: Guy Phinney was an Englishman who wanted to turn his property into something resembling a proper English country estate. Woodland Park retains much of its previous owner's vision; no matter that six-lane Aurora Avenue plows right through the middle of it, dividing the property into two distinct areas. The east side of Aurora is the site of most of the sporting activities (lawn bowling, tennis, playing fields, minigolf, picnic areas, and Green Lake). The west side has the formal rose garden, the zoo's Education Center Auditorium, and the impressive Woodland Park Zoo (see Attractions, this chapter). 5201 Green Lake Way N in North Seattle; (206) 684-4075.

Cycling

Despite the large amount of rainfall and fairly hilly terrain, cycling—from cruising to commuting to racing—is all the rage in and around Seattle. **Cascade Bicycle Club,** the largest cycling organization in the United States, organizes group rides nearly every day, ranging from a social pace to strenuous workouts. Call their hotline, (206) 522-BIKE, for listings for the current week and information about upcoming cycling events such as the legendary **Seattle-to-Portland Classic** (the STP), a weekend odyssey in which approximately 10,000 cyclists pedal from the Kingdome to downtown Portland (usually the third or fourth weekend in June), as well as the season-opening **Chilly Hilly.** The name says it all about this 36-mile late-February trek around the rolling terrain of Bainbridge Island. And for those worried about testosterone-laden individuals spoiling the pleasant atmosphere of their ride, **Womyn on Wheels,** (206) 324-0861, a lesbian cycling club, welcomes all women on their rides.

The Seattle Department of Parks and Recreation sponsors monthly **Bicycle Saturdays/Sundays** (the third Sunday and second Saturday of each month, May through September except August, when it's the first Saturday) along Lake Washington Boulevard, which closes to auto traffic. Anyone with a bike is welcome to participate. This great family activity offers a look at the Boulevard as it ought to be: a quiet promenade, (206) 684-7092.

If **racing** is more your speed, either as spectator or competitor, the calendar is rife with opportunities. From May through August racers gather Tuesday night at the Seattle International Raceway, (206) 631-1550, in Kent, and every Thursday evening at Seward Park. Summer weekends mean racing venues in locations throughout the state. Ask at local bicycle shops or pick up a copy of *The Bicycle Paper* or *Sports Etc.* for dates and locales. Serious racers can also join any of the dozens of racing clubs in the area. Two of the biggest are the **Puget Sound Cycling**

Club, (206) 523-1822, sponsored by Gregg's Greenlake Cycle, and **Avanti Racing Team**, (206) 324-8878.

The greater Seattle cycling community also boasts a national-quality bike-racing track located just across Lake Washington in Redmond, at Marymoor Park. The **Marymoor Velodrome** is a 400-meter concrete track with sharply banked corners. It was built in 1975 for the 1976 Olympic trials and is now home to twice-weekly races from mid-May to September. On Wednesdays the racing starts at 7pm and features entry-level and developing racers. Friday's action starts at 7:30pm with elite riders traveling from as far away as Oregon and British Columbia to compete in a variety of events. Admission is free on Wednesday and $3 on Friday (free for children under 10). The relaxed outdoor atmosphere, with a view of Mount Rainier on clear days, makes the Velodrome a perfect destination for those with kids or dogs. The **Marymoor Velodrome Association**, (206) 389-5825, offers classes which enable all levels of cyclists to get out on the track, improve their handling skills, and learn a little bit about the sport ($35 adults, $10 under 18). Bikes are provided.

Following are some of the area's favored rides; the city Engineering Department also publishes a biker's map of Seattle, available at most bike stores. (See also Mountain Biking and Running, this chapter.)

Alki Strip: This 6-mile West Seattle route from the beach at Alki to Lincoln Park is along a road wide enough for both bikes and cars, and now that motorized cruising has been outlawed here, cycling is safer. Avoid the Alki beach area on sunny Sunday afternoons, when it is crowded and often littered with broken glass. Alki Beach Park to Lincoln Park.

Bainbridge Island Loop: A pleasant, hilly 30-mile getaway for Seattle cyclists, this signed bike route follows fairly low-traffic roads around the island. This is the approximate route of the Chilly Hilly, a February bike ride that officially marks the opening day of Seattle biking. Take your own bike across on the ferry for 50 cents more than the walk-on fee. Start on Ferncliff (heading north) at Winslow Ferry Terminal (avoid Hwy 305) and work your way counterclockwise around the island (follow the signs).

Blue Ridge: The view of Puget Sound and the Olympic Mountains beyond is spectacular on this ride of less than 2 miles. Try making a big loop, from Green Lake through the Greenwood district to Carkeek and Golden Gardens Parks, then back by way of the Ballard (Hiram M. Chittenden) Locks.

Burke-Gilman Trail: It looks like a trail, but in spirit it's a park that provides a lush corridor of green from Gas Works Park on Lake Union to Kenmore's Logboom Park at the northern tip of Lake Washington. The 12½-mile path is built on an old railway bed and offers a scenic route through the leafy University of Washington, along Lake Washington, and past neighborhood parks such as the family-oriented Matthews Beach. It's crowded with cyclists, joggers, walkers, and roller skaters (speed limit, 15mph, but often ignored by training cyclists). Cyclists often continue on to the Sammamish River Trail, which connects with the Burke-Gilman in Kenmore, after about a mile on quiet surface streets, and a crossing of Juanita Drive. The Sammamish Trail leads through a placid farm valley, past the new Red Hook Brewery, local wineries, and a slew of new business parks, to Marymoor Park—about 25 miles from Gas Works. You can rent wheels at The Bicycle Center (4529 Sand Point Way NE; (206) 523-8300), about a mile northwest of UW, just off the trail.

Elliott Bay Bikeway: You get a grand view on this brief ride along Puget Sound. The trail, 1½ miles long, begins at Pier 70, skirts along the waterfront, passes between the Grain Terminal and its loading dock, winds its way through a parking lot of cars right off the ship, and continues to the Elliott Bay Marina. Full of runners and Rollerbladers at noontime.

Lake Washington Boulevard: Great views are plentiful all along this serene 5-mile stretch between Madrona and Seward Parks. The road is narrow part of the way, but bicycles do have a posted right-of-way. The southern portion (from Mount Baker Beach southward) has a separate asphalt path, safer for children. On Bicycle Saturdays and Sundays this portion is closed to auto traffic. The in-shape rider can continue south, via S Juneau Street, Seward Park Avenue S, and Rainier Avenue to the Renton Municipal Airport and on around the south end of Lake Washington, then return via the protected bike lane of I-90. This makes for a pretty 35-mile ride. Take a map with you.

Mercer Island Loop: A bicycles-only tunnel leads to the I-90 bridge on the way to Mercer Island (the entrance is off Martin Luther King Jr. Way, through a park of concrete monoliths and artwork by Seattle's Dennis Evans). You'll ride over moderate rolling hills the whole length of this 14-mile loop along E Mercer Way and W Mercer Way. The roads are curving and narrow, so avoid rush hour. The most exhilarating portion of the ride is through the wooded S-curves on the eastern side of the island. This is a great route for perusing the varied residential architecture.

Sammamish River Valley Trail: This very flat, peacefully rural route follows the quietly flowing Sammamish River for 9½ miles between Bothell Landing and Marymoor Park. Stop for a picnic at the parklike Chateau Ste. Michelle Winery, just off the trail at NE 145th (bring your own lunch or buy one there). Bike rentals are available at Sammamish Valley Cycle (8451 164th Avenue NE, Redmond, (206) 881-8442). The path connects with the Burke-Gilman Trail (see above) in Kenmore.

Seward Park: Take this paved and traffic-free 2½-mile road (S

Juneau Street and Lake Washington Boulevard S) around wooded Seward Park, which juts out into Lake Washington. The ride is extremely peaceful, and offers a look at what may be the only old-growth forest left on the shores of the lake. Eagles sometimes soar overhead, as a few still nest in the park.

Mountain Biking

The fat-tire revolution is well-ensconced in Seattle, but true mountain-biking terrain is fairly tough to find in Seattle or even its suburbs. You don't have to drive far, however. Good mountain bike routes (usually either on Forest Service roads or trails) are found all around Puget Sound's rural areas. In particular, consult the chapters on the Snoqualmie Pass Corridor, Stevens Pass Corridor and Lake Wenatchee, Mountain Loop Highway, and all chapters in the Central Cascades section of this guide.

Keep in mind that mountain bikes are forbidden on national park trails, and allowed only on certain trails maintained by the state Department of Natural Resources, state parks system, and U.S. Forest Service. Call the closest park or ranger district for advice on trails open to bikes.

Other sources of information include **TRIS** (Trail Users Information System), a computer program (allegedly updated weekly in prime outdoor sports months, less often in the winter) providing the latest trail information for mountain bikers, hikers, backpackers, and horseback riders. TRIS computers can be found at all REI stores, as well as at the **Outdoor Recreation Information Center** (Henry M. Jackson Federal Building, 915 Second Avenue, Suite 442, (206) 220-7450). Perhaps even more reliable are Internet Web sites maintained by groups such as the **Backcountry Bicycle Trails Club** (call (206) 283-2995 for addresses). The club organizes local rides for all levels of experience and is adamant about teaching "soft-riding" techniques which protect trails from the roughing-up that can eventually cause their closure. Wedgwood Cycle, (206) 523-5572, also leads rides every Sunday.

Hiking

Most of the parks and gardens listed above have hiking trails through forested or waterfront areas, usually with good views of the Olympics or Cascades. Particularly popular among walkers and joggers are **Discovery Park** in Magnolia, **Green Lake** and **Carkeek Park** in North Seattle, **Gas Works Park** (with access to the Burke-Gilman Trail) on Lake Union, the **Washington Park Arboretum** (with miles of garden trails and a unique 1-mile floating trail along Lake Washington), **Bridle Trails Park** near

Redmond, **Marymoor Park** (with access to the Sammamish River Trail) in Redmond, and **Saint Edward State Park,** between Kirkland and Bothell.

Also wildly popular in recent years are the extensive trail systems on **Mount Si** and **Cougar** and **Tiger Mountains,** sometimes known as the Issaquah Alps. See the Snoqualmie Pass Corridor chapter for information on dozens of trails in that area. Some of the more spectacular hiking trails in the country are found in the **Alpine Lakes Wilderness** (see chapter in this guide), between Stevens and Snoqualmie passes. Many can be hiked in a day trip from Seattle. Hikers looking for easily accessible day trips that sample the region's vaunted wild lands can head to **Mount Rainier** or **Olympic National Parks** (see the chapters for each in this guide), or the **Mount St. Helens National Volcanic Monument** (see the Mount St. Helens chapter), all of which offer short hiking trails that don't require a lot of planning or equipment.

While most major hiking destinations are out of town, Seattle is a virtual storehouse of hiking information. A valuable reference service is the **Outdoor Recreation Information Center** (Henry M. Jackson Federal Building, 915 Second Avenue, Suite 442, (206) 220-7450), a joint Forest Service/National Park Service public information office. Staffers have good knowledge of most Northwest trail systems, campgrounds, and backcountry roads. More important, they can refer questions they can't answer to a local ranger district or visitors center.

For gear, supplies, and maps, stop by **REI** (Recreational Equipment Inc.), which moved its flagship Capitol Hill store into huge new quarters at 222 Yale Avenue N, (206) 223-1944, in the fall of 1996. REI, which also has outlets in Lynnwood, Bellevue, Federal Way, and Spokane, has a good selection of guidebooks, USGS topographical maps, and other necessities. If you can't find the right advice at REI, guidebooks for virtually every corner of the Northwest are available from the bookstore at **The Mountaineers Clubhouse** (300 Third Avenue W, (206) 284-6310). Other good resources include the Seattle branch of **The Sierra Club** (8511 15th Avenue NE, (206) 523-2147) and the nonprofit **Washington Trails Association** (1305 Fourth Avenue, Suite 512, (206) 625-1367) whose monthly magazine, *Signpost*, contains trail reports straight from the hikers' mouths. WTA is a leading organizer of volunteer trail maintenance work parties. Call for information.

Boating

The same thing that makes Seattle such a lousy place for driving (water, water, everywhere) makes it nirvana for boat owners. A full range of services is available, from marine stores with that hard-to-find fuse, to a full-scale boatyard to build the cabin cruiser of your dreams. A wealth of boater services, suppliers, and repair shops is located in the **Ballard/Salmon Bay** area. And the city is as friendly as can be when it comes to welcoming visiting boaters. The short list of marina facilities:

Shilshole Bay Marina (7001 Seaview Avenue NW; (206) 728-3385) is huge and always open, with full services, an unbeatable location, and a nearby public boat launch, plus spacious parking. **Elliott Bay Marina** (2601 W Marina Place; (206) 285-4817) is a newish, fabulous, and well-equipped (free cable!) site at the foot of Magnolia Bluff. **Harbor Island Marina** (1401 SW Manning Street; (206) 467-9400) provides service for southern Elliott Bay. Not far away, **Seacrest Boathouse** (1660 Harbor Drive SW; (206) 932-1050) has some guest moorage and boater services. Boaters who pass through the Hiram M. Chittenden Locks (see Attractions, this chapter), the Lake Washington Ship Canal, and/or Montlake Cut will find many private marinas and moorage spaces on **Lake Union** and **Lake Washington.**

Sailing

Seattle's surplus of water doesn't necessarily translate to excess wind (at least not in the summer). Thus many local sailors reckon that the *real* sailing season runs from around Labor Day to May 1st. But more credulous souls rely on the late afternoon summer winds. The sailing territory in these parts is vast and varied: there is, for instance, the Inside Passage from Puget Sound to Alaska—taking in the San Juans, the Gulf Islands, Desolation Sound and the myriad ravine-channels between Vancouver Island and the BC mainland, the Queen Charlotte Islands, and beyond, all the way to Ketchikan. For the intrepid, the Pacific Ocean beckons via the Strait of Juan de Fuca and Cape Flattery. For weekend salts, in addition to the sailing on south Puget Sound, some fine sailing sites await in the city. They're listed below. Some in-city boat rentals are cited here as well. For more information, contact *Northwest Yachting*, (206) 789-8116.

Green Lake: No more than a mile across in any direction, Green Lake is safe, quiet, and free of the hazards of motor cruisers, cigarette boats, floatplanes, and barge traffic. It's a perfect spot to learn to sail or to reacquaint yourself with the art. The **Seattle Sailing Association** is headquartered at the **Green Lake Small Craft Center** (5900 W Green Lake Way N, (206) 684-4074), at the southwest corner of the lake; they'll let you use their boats on Green Lake for a $20 annual membership fee and proof that you know a thing or two about sailing. The association also organizes its own classes and races.

Lake Union: On Tuesday evenings, when the Duck Dodge race (high silliness) is held, Lake Union is likely to make you pine for the peace and solitude of an I-5 interchange. At other times, what with its fluky wind; banks lined with houseboats, marinas, shipyards, restaurants; and areas that double as airport waterways, Lake Union is no Walden Pond either. The most interesting maritime experience on the lake, with beautiful, vintage rental boats, lessons, and a museum is at **The Center for Wooden Boats** (1010 Valley Street, (206) 382-2628). **Sailboat Rentals and Yacht Charters** (1301 N Northlake Way, (206) 632-3302) is open year-round and has day sailers, cruisers, and racers for rent by the hour, day, or week on both Lake Union and Lake Washington.

Lake Washington: Lake Washington is long, relatively narrow, and acts as a wind funnel, with a breeze nearly always blowing either due north or due south. This means that on a good day you can zip from the top to the bottom (or vice versa) in around 3 hours; but be warned, you may take the best part of a week to get back. You can launch craft from just about any waterfront park. Sailing lessons are available at **Mount Baker Park** through the Seattle Parks Department's **Mount Baker Rowing and Sailing Center** (3800 Lake Washington Boulevard S, (206) 386-1913). For a more extensive course, Kirkland's **Island Sailing Club** at Carillon Point, (206) 822-2470, offers 18 hours of instruction on 20-foot sailboats; at the course's end, you'll receive an American Sailing Association (ASA) certification and your own logbook.

Fishing

Salmon

"Fish from your window." The old motto for Seattle's Edgewater Inn used to be taken quite literally by many guests, who would cast from their rooms and maybe hook up with a bottomfish. It was more gimmick than sales point, of course. But the truth is, one of Seattle's most famous qualities always has been its front-door salmon fishery. The city surely is one of the few metropolitan centers in the world where anglers routinely hook up with a healthy salmon from a fishing pier literally within the shadow of a downtown skyscraper. Everyone knows Northwest salmon have been on a disturbing downward spiral for the past two decades. But in spite of that, the Elliott Bay salmon fishery off downtown Seattle still can be quite productive. They're probably not tourists, but the fact is many anglers still *do* hook up with salmon right off the waterfront. If you don't believe it, get up early and watch boat anglers off the mouth of the Duwamish or spin-casters on the fishing pier at Seacrest Boathouse in West Seattle.

The city's biggest salmon-hooking trick these days isn't technique—

it's opportunity. Struggling wild salmon runs all around Puget Sound have caused a crazy quilt of seasonal closures during peak summer months. The road map you'll need to know when and where to fish is the state's fishing regulations pamphlet, available at sporting goods stores (such as Warshal's, downtown). Another way—probably easier—is to consult an expert at a local boathouse or tackle shop. You'll also need a license to catch just about any Washington game fish, and a separate catch record for steelhead, sturgeon, salmon, and halibut. Ask.

In spite of the closures, salmon fishing in Central Puget Sound has remained fair in recent years. Like the rest of the Central Sound, when fishing is open, resident **coho** are available through the spring and summer (larger migratory coho arrive in midsummer), migratory **chinook** are caught primarily from June to August, **pink salmon** are caught in August and September of odd-numbered years, and **chum salmon** are harvested in autumn months. But it's not a summer-only venture. In recent years, winter **blackmouth** (resident chinook) fishing in the Central Sound has been productive from November to March.

Where to go? For Seattle boat owners, top Central Puget Sound fishing spots are right where they have been for decades: interior **Elliott Bay** (in season); **Jefferson Head, Allen Bank,** and **Point No Point** off Kitsap Peninsula; **Midchannel Bank** near Port Townsend; **Possession Bar** south of Whidbey Island; and other local favorites. In recent years, popular north Sound fisheries, including Jefferson Head and Point No Point, have been closed from July to October, sending many Seattle anglers south to Tacoma-area hot spots such as **Point Defiance** and the nearby **"Clay Banks"** (see Fishing in the Tacoma and Gig Harbor chapter). Two City of Seattle boat ramps—Don Armeni Ramp in West Seattle and Shilshole Ramp at Golden Gardens Park—are the most popular launching spots. You'll be asked to pay a (voluntary) $3 fee.

The key to successful Puget Sound salmon fishing is timing. Learn when runs begin and peak. Fish early (the best bite often is at dawn). Concentrate on tide changes, which also tend to bring on stronger bites. And use fresh herring.

If you don't have your own boat, you're far from out of luck. Rental kicker boats are available at Seacrest Boathouse in West Seattle (1660 Harbor Drive SW; (206) 932-1050). Several charter companies with expert Puget Sound skippers operate daily from Seattle and its suburbs. Contact: A Spot Tail Salmon Guide, Shilshole Bay, (206) 283-6680 (pager (206) 918-0707); Sport Fishing of Seattle, Pier 55, Suite 201, (206) 623-6364; Ballard Salmon Charters, 1811 N 95th Street, (206) 789-6202; or All Star Charters, 1724 W Marine View Drive, Everett, (206) 252-4188.

And even though success rates aren't as high, you can catch salmon from Puget Sound fishing piers. Some of the most popular pier-casting spots are found at **Seacrest** in West Seattle, **Shilshole Bay Marina** near Golden Gardens Park, **Pier 86** (just northwest of the Grain Terminal), the **Edmonds Waterfront Pier,** and **Redondo** and **Dash Point** in south King County. All of these piers also have become popular squid-jigging sites in the winter.

Steelhead

Steelhead, sea-run trout known for their ferocity and unusual (for a fish, at least) smarts, may have surpassed salmon as the most sought-after sports fish in Washington. A number of good steelhead streams flow into Puget Sound on all sides of Seattle. The closest are the **Green, Snohomish, Snoqualmie, Tolt,** and the justly famous **Skykomish.** Other rivers, farther north or south or on the Olympic Peninsula, are usually better. Steelhead return to local streams throughout much of the year, but the winter season, which generally begins in November and lasts through early April, is the most productive. If you're a newcomer to the game and/or just visiting, your best bet is to hook up with a guide. They come and go (usually to Alaska…), so ask for a referral at one of the tackle shops listed below.

Shellfish

Seattle's public beaches are open for clamming year-round (butter clams are the big draw), unless pollution alerts are posted. Bring your own bucket, rake or shovel, mud boots, and tide table. **Alki Beach Park** (Alki Avenue SW) is the most popular in-city spot, but the digging is good at public beaches in Edmonds, Mukilteo, Everett, and on Whidbey Island as well. Clamming does, however, require a license. (Indeed, everything harvested from or near the water now requires a license—even seaweed.) And be warned: Clamming seasons are sometimes shortened or canceled altogether because of drastic decreases in the clam population, so you should consult the Fish and Wildlife Department before setting off. There is also an ongoing danger of paralytic shellfish poisoning (PSP) caused by a microscopic organism that can turn the ocean water red, thus "red tide." The organism is a tonic for bivalves but highly toxic to humans. Cooking does not reduce the toxicity. To learn which beaches are unsafe, always call the **Red Tide Hotline,** (800) 562-5632, before going shellfishing.

Trout and bass

State fish hatcheries routinely stock catchable (10- to 12-inch) rainbow trout in dozens of suburban lakes inside and all around Seattle. Many of these lakes now are open for fishing all year; others open in late April. Most local streams open in June. For seasons and limits on a lake nearest you, contact the Fish and Wildlife Region 4 Headquarters in Mill Creek, (206) 775-1311. Or ask at a local tackle shop. Some local favorites for Seattleites include **Green Lake** in North Seattle (see Parks/Beaches, this chapter) and, of course, **Lake Washington,** a truly spectacular fishing venue that holds hundreds of species, some of which are available all year long. Most Lake Washington parks have fishable shorelines or piers.

Contacts

For general fishing advice, be it on salmon or otherwise, call Linc's Tackle (501 Rainier Avenue S; (206) 324-7600); Ballard Bait and Tackle (5517 Seaview Avenue NW; (206) 784-3016); Ted's Sport Center (156th SW and Hwy 99, Lynnwood; (206) 743-9505); Kitsap Sport Shop in Bremerton (630 N Callow Avenue; (360) 373-9589); Kingston Tackle, (360) 297-2521; Salmon Bay Tackle (5701 15th Avenue NW; (206) 789-9335); or Warshal's Sporting Goods (First and Madison; (206) 624-7300).

Leading fly-fishing shops include Kauffman's Streamborn Flies, Seattle (1918 Fourth Avenue; (206) 448-0601) and Bellevue (15015 Main; (206) 643-2246); Swallow's Nest (2308 Sixth Avenue; (206) 441-4100); Eddie Bauer (1330 Fifth Avenue; (206) 622-2766); and Creekside Angling Co. (1660 NW Gilman Boulevard, Issaquah; (206) 392-3800). A leading discount gear supplier is Outdoor Emporium (420 Pontius Avenue N; (206) 624-6550).

Canoeing/Kayaking

Seattle's wealth of saltwater shorelines, calm rivers, urban lakes, and other waterways has made it a national mecca for sea kayakers and canoeists. Outside of town, wild rivers such as the Skagit, Skykomish, Sauk, Nooksack, Stillaguamish, and others make it an equally notable river kayaking destination.

Kayaking—particularly sea kayaking, which employs stable, flat-bottomed boats—is safe and easy to learn by just about anyone. But it still can be dangerous, and isn't a sport you should take on by yourself. Beginners usually come out ahead by hooking up with a club, whose members can offer expert advice and instruction. One of the oldest kayaking clubs in the nation is the **Washington Kayak Club** (PO Box 24264, Seattle 98124, (206) 433-1983), a safety- and conservation-oriented club that organizes swimming-pool practices, weekend trips, and sea- and whitewater-kayaking lessons in the spring. Dues are $20 per year, with an initiation fee of $15; you must have your own equipment. Sea kayaks, gear, guidebooks, and outfitter referrals can be found at REI (222 Yale Avenue N; (206) 223-1944), or the Swallow's Nest (2308 Sixth Avenue; (206) 441-4100). Other gear/rental stores are listed with the following suggestions for calm waterways suitable for paddlers with little or no experience. Most of these outlets also offer instruction.

Duwamish River: From Tukwila (where the Green River becomes the Duwamish) to Boeing Field, this scenic waterway makes for a lovely paddle. Beyond Boeing, you pass industrial salvage ships, commercial shipping lanes, and industrial Harbor Island, until the river empties into Elliott Bay. Rent a canoe or kayak at Pacific Water Sports (16055 Pacific Hwy S, (206) 246-9385) near Sea-Tac Airport—the staff can direct you to one of several spots along the river where you can launch your craft. The current is strong at times, but not a serious hazard for moderately experienced paddlers.

Green Lake: Green Lake's tame waters are a good place to learn the basics. The **Green Lake Small Craft Center** (5900 W Green Lake Way N, (206) 684-4074) at the southwest corner of Green Lake offers year-round sailing, rowing, canoeing, and kayaking instruction, and special boating programs. The **Seattle Canoe Club** operates out of here, with canoes and kayaks for members. Green Lake Boat Rentals (7351 E Green Lake Drive N, (206) 527-0171), a Parks Department concession on the northeast side of the lake, also rents kayaks, rowboats, paddleboats, canoes, sailboards, and sailboats (open every day, except in bad weather).

Lake Union: Lake Union offers fine paddling, great city views, and a lot of boat traffic. If you don't mind that, you can rent sea kayaks at Northwest Outdoor Center (2100 Westlake Avenue N, (206) 281-9694) for use on Lake Union (Gas Works Park is nearby) and beyond, including Lake Washington, Shilshole Bay, and the Arboretum. (NWOC also offers classes and tours to the San Juan Islands and the Olympic Peninsula.)

Lake Washington: The massive lake has many public launch sites at dozens of waterfront parks, in addition to the **University of Washington Waterfront Activities Center** by the Montlake Cut (see below).

Montlake/Arboretum: A cruise through the marshlands of the Arboretum is the most popular, yet peaceful, in-city canoe excursion. You can rent a canoe or rowboat at low rates across the Montlake Cut at the **University of Washington Waterfront Activities Center**, (206) 543-9433, behind Husky Stadium. Here the mirrored waters are framed by a mosaic of green lily pads accented by white flowers. Closer to shore, vibrant yellow irises push through tall marsh grasses, while ducks cavort under weeping willows. Pack a picnic lunch and wander ashore to the marsh walk, a favorite bird-watching stroll that meanders from just below the Museum of History and Industry to the lawn of Foster Island. Be sure to have the boat back by 8:30pm.

Puget Sound: Seattle's proximity to the open waters and scenic island coves of Puget Sound makes for ideal sea kayaking. Bainbridge

Island's **Eagle Harbor** is a leisurely paddle in protected waters. Tiny **Blake Island,** a state park, is a short trip from Vashon Island, Alki Point, or Fort Ward Park on Bainbridge Island (see the Bainbridge and Vashon Islands chapter for details on both). Bird-watchers can head for the calm waters of the Nisqually National Wildlife Refuge (see the Olympia and the Nisqually Delta chapter). Note: For other regional sea kayaking trips, see the chapters on the San Juan Islands and Anacortes, Port Townsend, Hood Canal, Kitsap Peninsula, Sequim and the Dungeness Valley, Port Angeles and Hurricane Ridge, Tacoma and Gig Harbor, Bellingham and Lummi Island, Skagit Valley, and Whidbey and Camano Islands.

Sammamish River: The trip up the gently flowing Sammamish Slough is quiet and scenic. Ambitious canoeists can follow the river all the way to Lake Sammamish, about 15 miles to the southeast, passing golf courses, the town of Woodinville, Chateau Ste. Michelle Winery, and Marymoor Park along the way.

Kite Flying

In Seattle, you'll find almost as many good places for kite flying as there are parks (see Parks/Beaches, above). For advice on kite-flying conditions, suggestions on where to find breezy areas, and grand selections of colorful wind vessels, wind socks, and kite parts, visit Good Winds Kite Shop (3333 Wallingford Avenue N, (206) 633-4780); City Kites (1501 Western Avenue, (206) 622-5349); or Great Winds (402 Occidental Avenue S, (206) 624-6886). Thanks to its windswept location, **Gas Works Park**—and particularly the grassy hill to the west of the Works (check out the sundial at the top)—is a very popular kite-flying spot, attracting stunt fliers and novices alike. **Magnuson Park** is another popular kite-flying spot.

In-line Skating

Roller skaters—and their ubiquitous subset, the in-line skaters—compose an ever widening wedge of the urban athletic pie. In fair weather, skaters are found anywhere the people-watching is good and the pavement smooth, including the tree-shaded **Burke-Gilman Trail,** the **downtown waterfront,** and along **Lake Washington Boulevard.** Farther afield, fine skating is found on the **Interurban Trail** south out of Renton, and north on the **Sammamish River Valley Trail** to Redmond's Marymoor Park (see Cycling, above). Note: Skate-rental shops won't let you out the door if the pavement is damp.

Green Lake is the skate-and-be-seen-skating spot in town, where hotdoggers in bright spandex weave and bob through cyclists, joggers, racewalkers, and leashed dogs. The 2.8-mile path around the lake is crowded on weekends, but during the week it's a good place to try wheels for the first time. When the wading pool on the north shore of the lake isn't filled for kids or commandeered by roller-hockey enthusiasts, it makes a good spot to learn to skate backward or to refine some moves. You can rent or buy skates and elbow and knee pads at Gregg's Greenlake Cycle (7007 Woodlawn Avenue NE, (206) 523-1822).

Another urban skating site excellent for practicing is the grounds of the **National Oceanic and Atmospheric Administration** (7600 Sand Point Way NE, next to Magnuson Park). The facility can be reached via the Burke-Gilman Trail, and offers a quiet workout along a smooth 1-kilometer loop, with one low-grade hill and some exciting turns. NOAA is gracious in sharing its roads, even allowing an informal group-skate every Wednesday evening around 5pm.

Rowing/Crew

In a city graced with two major lakes, many people opt to exercise on the water instead of jogging through exhaust fumes or skating through the crowds at Green Lake. They've discovered an affinity for the sleek, lightweight rowing shells, and relish slicing across the silver-black water of early morning. The **Seattle Parks and Recreation Department**, (206) 684-4075, runs two rowing facilities: one on Green Lake out of the **Green Lake Small Crafts Center** (5900 W Green Lake Way N, (206) 684-4074) and another on Lake Washington through the **Mount Baker Rowing and Sailing Center,** at Sayers Park (3800 Lake Washington Boulevard S, (206) 386-1913). Both operate year-round, offer all levels of instruction, host yearly regattas, and send their top boats to the national championships. **Moss Bay Rowing Club,** (206) 820-1429, which operates in Kirkland, also oversees a club out of **Yale Street Landing** on Lake Union, (206) 682-2031.

The **Lake Washington Rowing Club** (PO Box 45117, Seattle 98145-0117, (206) 547-1583) is an excellent organization for self-starters. A coach is available three days a week, but the rest of the time you're on your own. Open to all levels, from beginners to elite rowers training for international competition, with a very reasonable yearly fee. Another club for all skill levels and also with very reasonable fees is the **Falcon Rowing Club,** (206) 281-2743, which launches out of the Seattle Pacific University gymnasium (Royal Brougham Pavilion) in Fremont. Numerous other women-only, men-only, or age-specific clubs thrive in the Northwest. For a full list, call Ann Day, regional coordinator, Northwest Region of U.S. Rowing, (206) 625-9003.

Running

Step out just about any door in the area and you're on a good running course. The mild climate and numerous parks make running solo appealing, yet there is also a large, well-organized running community to link up with for company or competition. Club Northwest's *Northwest Runner* is the best local source for information on organized runs, and has a complete road-race schedule. Racers, both casual and serious, can choose from a number of annual races (at least one every weekend in spring and summer). Some of the biggest are the **College Inn Stampede** in July, the **St. Patrick's Day 4-Mile,** the 6.7-mile **Seward-to-Madison Shore Run** in July, the 8-kilometer **Seafair Torchlight Run** through the city streets in August, and the **Seattle Marathon** in November. Outside of Seattle, runners can test their mettle in the 12K Sound-to-Narrows Run in Tacoma or Spokane's Bloomsday Run, which, with its 50,000 participants, is the world's largest timed road race (see the Spokane chapter). One of the finest running outfitters in town, Super Jock 'N Jill (7210 E Green Lake Drive N, (206) 522-7711), maintains a **racing hotline, (206) 524-RUNS.** Popular running venues include Washington Park Arboretum, Green Lake, Kelsey Creek Park, Kirkland Waterfront, Lincoln Park, Magnolia Bluff/Discovery Park, Medina/Evergreen Point, Ravenna Boulevard, and Warren Magnuson Park. (See Parks/Beaches or Cycling, above, for details.)

Horseback Riding

Stables and outfitters abound on the Eastside and in the Cascade foothills. For weekend or extended trips (camping, exploration, or cattle round-ups) on both sides of the Cascades, call High Country Outfitters (3020 Issaquah–Pine Lake Road, Suite 554, Issaquah, (206) 392-0111). Some other day-trip outfitters:

Aqua Barn Ranch: One of the oldest ranches in the area, Aqua Barn (you can swim there too, though, we assume, not with the horses) offers easy, guided rides in the evenings and on weekends through 100 acres of pasture and foothills. The cost is $19.50 an hour, and reservations are required. Anyone over age 8 can ride. For advanced riders, Aqua Barn also offers a 2-hour Ridge Ride for $39; children must be 10 years old. The ranch also has a large campground (see Camping, this chapter). 15227 SE Renton–Maple Valley Hwy, Renton; (206) 255-4618.

Eliel Ranch: Greg Eliel runs this riding and training facility, just past Issaquah, offering lessons, clinics, and short trail rides ($35 per hour, no children under 10). 11606 Upper Preston Rd, Preston; (206) 222-4625.

Horse Country: Horse Country offers lessons, horse leasing, picnics, and day camps, and features guided rides up into the Cascades and then down to the Pilchuck River. Kids age 5 and up are welcome, riders over 200 pounds are not. 8507 Hwy 92, Granite Falls; (360) 691-7509.

Tiger Mountain Outfitters: Specializes in 3-hour rides to a lookout on Tiger Mountain, often on horse celebrities. (No kidding—nobody from *Mr. Ed* here, but many were used on *Northern Exposure* and other TV shows.) Most of the 10-mile round trip is along logging roads, and the rest is in dense forest. No tykes under 10. 24508 SE 133rd Street, Issaquah; (206) 392-5090.

The neighborhood surrounding **Bridle Trails State Park** (also see Parks/Beaches, this chapter) on the Bellevue-Kirkland border looks like a condensed version of Virginia equestrian country, with backyards of horses and stables. The park features miles of riding and hiking trails through vast stands of Douglas fir.

Climbing

Most of the year, Seattle rock scalers train indoors. The Northwest boasts a number of venues, including the two very striking **Vertical Worlds** (formerly known as the Vertical Club). The Redmond location (15036-B NE 95th, Redmond; (206) 881-8826) offers 7,000 square feet of textured climbing surface, while the newer Seattle club (755 N Northlake Way, Suite 100; (206) 632-3031), which moved to Fremont from its original Elliott Avenue spot in 1995, sports 35-foot-high ceilings and a whopping 11,000 square feet of surface in addition to climbing-specific exercise stations. At either club, beginners—both adults and children—can take introductory climbing classes, and the club will even rent you shoes and chalk. REI's new Seattle headquarters (222 Yale Avenue N, (206) 223-1944) is home to a seven-story "rock," billed as the nation's largest free-standing indoor climbing structure. It's open for climbing whenever the store is open, except Friday nights which are reserved for classes.

Elsewhere, the man-made **University of Washington Climbing Rock** behind Husky Stadium, **Sherman Rock** at Camp Long (5200 35th Avenue SW; (206) 684-7434), and Wednesday night and Saturday morning open climbs at REI's Lynnwood store (4200 194th Street SW, Lynnwood; (206) 774-1300) are other convenient practice spots. **Marymoor Climbing Structure,** otherwise known as Big Pointy, just south of the Velodrome in Marymoor Park, is a 45-foot concrete-brick-and-mortar "house of cards" designed by the Godfather of rock climbing, Don Robinson, and features climbing angles up to and over 90 degrees. And, of course, plenty of the real thing surrounds the Puget Sound basin. See especially the Leavenworth and Icicle Valley and Snoqualmie Pass Corridor chapters for climbing suggestions.

Rafting

The Pacific Northwest is webbed with rivers, so it's no wonder that rafting has become one of the region's premier outdoor adventure sports. Rafting companies are sprouting up all over the state, particularly west of the Cascades, and are ready to give you a taste of wild water for $50 to $80 a day. Trips are tailored differently at each company, though there are two basic types: peaceful float trips, often in protected and scenic wildlife areas, and trips through whitewater rapids, which vary in their degree of difficulty. Spring and early summer are the seasons for whitewater trips. Eagle-watching trips on the Skagit River are scheduled between January and March. For information about specific river floats, consult the appropriate chapter in this guide.

Most guide services for those rivers, however, are based in the greater Seattle area. Here's a list of some of the more prominent guide services. For a full list, contact Professional River Outfitters of Washington (PROW), c/o Cascade Adventures (1202 E Pike; (206) 323-5485).

Downstream River Runners: The company leads day trips on 12 Washington and Oregon rivers, including the Green, Grande Ronde, Methow, and Klickitat. The bald eagle float trips down the scenic Skagit in winter (hot homemade soup included) make a great family expedition. 3130 Hwy 530 NE, Arlington; (800) 234-4644.

Northern Wilderness River Riders: A trip with the River Riders promises a day full of rapids. They provide everything you need—from wet suits to lunchtime guacamole—and feature trips for every member of the family at every level of experience. In the winter, an 8-mile float trip from Marblemount to Rockport offers a chance to watch squadrons of bald eagles feast on spawned-out salmon. PO Box 2887, Woodinville 98072; (206) 448-7238.

Orion Expeditions: The veteran guides at Orion Expeditions give lessons and lead rafting trips in Washington, Oregon, Costa Rica, and on the Rio Grande in Texas. 4739 Thackeray Place NE, Seattle; (206) 547-6715 or (800) 553-7466.

Skiing/Snow Play

All of the Puget Sound area's major ski resorts—**Mount Baker, Stevens Pass, Mission Ridge, Snoqualmie Pass, White Pass,** and **Crystal Mountain**—are within a 3-hour drive of Seattle. See the Skiing section in the Washington Outdoors Primer for an overview of Washington alpine and cross-country skiing. For detailed information on specific ski areas, consult the Mount Baker Highway, Stevens Pass Corridor and Lake Wenatchee, Wenatchee and Mission Ridge, Methow Valley, Snoqualmie

Pass Corridor, White Pass Corridor, and Mount Rainier National Park chapters in this guide.

Windsurfing

Definitely not for dilettantes, windsurfing takes athleticism, daring, and a lot of practice. The sport is big in this town, partly because the Northwest helped put it on the world map. The Columbia River Gorge (about 200 miles south of Seattle) is the top windsurfing area in the continental United States (second only to Maui in the United States), because of the strong winds that always blow in the direction opposite the river's current—ideal conditions for confident wind surfers. See the Columbia River Gorge section of this guide for detailed information. Closer to home, windsurfing can be decent on virtually any body of water. Popular locations:

Green Lake is the best place for beginners—the water is warm and the winds are usually gentle. Experts may find it too crowded, but novices will probably appreciate the company. You can take lessons and rent equipment at Green Lake Boat Rentals (7351 E Green Lake Drive N; (206) 527-0171) on the northeast side of the lake. But surfers tend to gather on the south-shore beaches.

Lake Union has fine winds in the summer, but you'll have to dodge sailboats, commercial boats, and seaplanes. You can rent equipment from Urban Surf (2100 N Northlake Way; (206) 545-9463) and take your board to Gas Works Park, the only public launch area—but the walk from parking lot to shore is farther than at many Lake Washington beaches.

Most windsurfers prefer expansive **Lake Washington.** Head to any waterfront park—most have plenty of parking and rigging space. **Magnuson Park** (Sand Point Way NE and 65th Avenue NE) is favored for its great winds. At **Mount Baker Park** (Lake Park Drive S and Lake Washington Boulevard S), you can take lessons at **Mount Baker Rowing and Sailing Center** (3800 Lake Washington Boulevard S; (206) 386-1913), a public concession. Choice Eastside beaches include Renton's **Coulon Beach Park** (1201 Lake Washington Boulevard N, Renton), where you can also rent boards and get instruction; **Houghton Beach Park** (NE 59th Street and Lake Washington Boulevard NE, Kirkland), with rentals nearby at **O. O. Denny Park** (NE 124th Street and Holmes Point Drive NE, Juanita).

On **Puget Sound,** which is warmer than Lake Washington in the winter, wind surfers head for **Golden Gardens Park** (north end of Seaview Avenue NW) or **Duwamish Head** at **Alki Beach Park** (Alki Avenue SW) in West Seattle. For rentals and lessons, try one of America's oldest windsurfing dealers: Alpine Hut (2215 15th Avenue W; (206) 284-3575).

Camping

Let's face it: few people come to the Emerald City to pitch a dome tent. But a handful of suburban campsites are available to RVers who roll into town.

In the south end, **Orchard Trailer Park** (4011 S 146th Street, I-5 exit 154, Burien; (206) 243-1210) has limited overnight facilities for RVs. In Kent is **Seattle South KOA** (5801 S 212th St, I-5 exit 152; (206) 872-8652), which has more than 140 sites for tents and RVs. **Aqua Barn Ranch** (15227 SE Renton–Maple Valley Hwy, Renton; (206) 255-4618) is one of the best local tent areas, with 240 sites, many of them grassy (see also Horseback Riding earlier in this chapter).

To the north, **Holiday Park Resort** (19250 Aurora Avenue N; (206) 542-2760 has 22 RV sites. To the east, **Lake Pleasant RV Park** (24025 Bothell-Everett Hwy (take I-405 north to exit 26); (206) 487-1785 or (800) 742-0386) is the biggest campground (and one of the nicest) in the greater Seattle area, with more than 200 campsites, including a dozen tent spots.

To the east, Trails Inn (I-90 exit 11 to 37th Street) is a popular RV park; **Blue Sky RV Park** (9002 302nd Street SE, Issaquah; (206) 222-7910) has 51 RV sites. Not far from Lake Sammamish is **Trailer Inns RV Park** (15531 I-90, Issaquah; (206) 747-9181), with 115 pull-through RV sites. **Issaquah Village RV Park** (650 First Avenue NE; (206) 392-9233 or (800) 258-9233) has 112 RV sites, no tents allowed. On the west side of Lake Sammamish (take I-90 exit 13) is **Vasa Park Resort** (3550 W Lake Sammamish Road; (206) 746-3260), a small park with decent tent sites.

Photography

Shutterbugs can't go wrong in Seattle. But to capture the city in its natural splendor, a select few sites stand out. See Parks/Beaches in this chapter for details.

Gas Works Park on Lake Union offers a nice view of the city with Lake Union in the foreground. It's also a rare place to shoot shoreline photos of kayakers in a very urban setting. Good sunset spot, too. The **Hiram M. Chittenden Locks** in Ballard are a great place to shoot boat closeups, with the Cascades or Olympics in the background. Chances are you'll also encounter sea lions here. **Washington Park Arboretum** is a sure winner in the spring. City streets along **Magnolia Bluff** are a grand place to shoot Puget Sound sunsets, as is **Golden Gardens Park** at Shilshole. The best straight-on shots of Seattle's waterfront skyline are made from West Seattle's **Harbor Drive** or **Seacrest Fishing Pier,** or better yet, from the deck of a **Seattle-Bremerton** or **Seattle-Winslow ferry.**

But if you go nowhere else, Seattle's **Kerry Park** on Queen Anne Hill (take W Highland Drive west from Queen Anne Avenue N) is *the* Seattle photo spot. This tiny park with a big reputation among pro shooters is where all those calendar twilight shots are made. Laid out before you are the Space Needle, Seattle Center's "new" KeyArena, the downtown sky-line, Harbor Island, the Kingdome (sorry about that), and, most spectac-ularly, Mount Rainier, which provides a pink backdrop to the whole thing at sunset. In the summer, you might have to line up an hour before dark to get a good tripod spot.

If your autofocus won't, the local pro camera store is Glazer's, 430 Eighth N; (206) 624-1100.

outside in

Attractions

Seattle is a charming metropolis grown up in the middle of an evergreen forest. It's a city famous for its enduring relationships with Boeing and Bill Gates, Pearl Jam and Pike Place Market, and coffee, always coffee, avail-able in steaming cups from mobile espresso carts that sprout on street cor-ners like mushrooms after a good rain.

This is a town where cops ride bikes, farmers and fishmongers hawk their wares at open-air markets, gardeners putter be it January or July, and early-morning kayakers paddle in the wake of log booms and container ships that ply the city's busy waterways. What follows are a few highlights of Seattle's attractions; for a detailed city guide, we refer you to our com-panion book, *Seattle Best Places.*

Music. Seattle Opera's productions range from creative conceptions (which don't always work) to performances of breathtaking brilliance; (206) 389-7699. The Seattle Symphony, under conductor Gerard Schwartz, maintains a high level of consistency; its Distinguished Artists series brings in superb recitalists; (206) 443-4747. Chamber music has become a local passion, with the International Music Festival of Seattle in June (showcasing many top Russian and European musicians, and including orchestral and vocal performances), and the Seattle Chamber Music Festival in July (at Lakeside School). The Early Music Guild, Seattle Baroque Orchestra, Northwest Chamber Orchestra, Ladies Musical Club, and the International Chamber Music and President's Piano Series at the University of Washington's Meany Hall, plus many indigenous performances, round out the winter and spring seasons. Choral music is experiencing an upsurge, with the Tudor Choir, the Esoterics, Seattle Men's Chorus, and Seattle Choral Company, among others.

Theater. Seattle's big professional theaters used to hire most of their actors from the bounteous local talent pool, and each had its specialty: you went to the Seattle Repertory Theater (The Rep) for mainstream comedy and drama, Intiman for the classics, A Contemporary Theater (ACT) for racier, modern stuff. Now the repertory is more homogenized, and the practice of hiring most actors from out of town has blurred the style boundaries further. Best advice: Scan the theater listings and shop by show.

More adventurous theatergoers have a far wider selection: among the dozens of smaller theater companies around town, good work often emerges from The Empty Space (funky, often musical, fun), the Annex (far-out fringe), New City Theater (mainstream avant-garde), the Bathhouse (intimate, emphasis on the classics), the Velvet Elvis Arts Lounge (from campy to just plain crazy), and many more.

Dance. Pacific Northwest Ballet has evolved into a company of national stature; its regular season mixes masterworks with new pieces, and the Christmas highlight is a breathtaking realization of *The Nutcracker* with sets by Maurice Sendak; (206) 292-2787. Meany's World Dance series and On the Boards present touring companies.

Visual Arts. Seattle Art Museum, designed by Robert Venturi, is an established part of the downtown skyline, with Jonathan Borofsky's towering sculpture *Hammering Man* at the main entrance. This building on University Street between First and Second Avenues houses the museum's permanent collections, while the Seattle Asian Art Museum, in the former SAM location in Volunteer Park, offers one of the most extraordinary collections of Asian art in the country. Henry Art Gallery, at UW, mounts thoughtful and challenging shows. The main art galleries are found predominantly (though not exclusively) in the Pioneer Square area; gallery openings are usually the first Thursday of every month.

Nightlife. There are clubs all over town, but Seattle's music scene is neighborhood centered. Pioneer Square offers various acts, from jazz to rock 'n' roll; Ballard brings in the blues, as well as traditional and new folk music; the alternative music scene is found in clubs primarily in the Denny Regrade and Belltown neighborhoods. Dimitriou's Jazz Alley, one of the West Coast's finest jazz clubs, provides an intimate venue and draws an internationally renowned roster of performers. There are good coffeehouses everywhere, but particularly in the University District and on Capitol Hill, which is also the unofficial playground for Seattle's sizable gay and lesbian community.

Exhibits. The Woodland Park Zoo is a world leader in naturalistic displays, particularly the uncannily open African Savannah, the exotic Asian elephant forest, and the award-winning Northern Trail Exhibit, which mimics Alaskan tundra and wildlife; (206) 684-4800. The Museum of Flight, south of the city, is notable for its sophisticated design and impressive collection. Pacific Science Center, with a planetarium and revolving displays on all sorts of subjects, graces Seattle Center, the legacy of the 1962 World's Fair; there is a decent aquarium on the waterfront; and at the Hiram M. Chittenden Locks in Ballard, where ships are lifted to Lake Washington, you can watch salmon climb fish ladders on their way to spawn.

Greater Seattle

The area thought of as **Edmonds** is just a small village in a much larger area. "Downtown Edmonds" is a throwback to another era, with a small movie theater, friendly shopkeepers, wide sidewalks, and waterfront views that encourage evening strolls through town. The ferry departs to Kingston; for information, call (206) 464-6400. Edmonds bills itself as the City of Celebrations. Most popular are the Edmonds Art Festival (in June) and **A Taste of Edmonds** (third weekend in August). Brackett's Landing, just north of the ferry terminal, has a jetty and an offshore underwater marine-life park that draws lots of scuba divers. Edmonds Historic Walk was prepared by the Centennial Committee and offers a look at old Edmonds. Stop by the Chamber of Commerce (120 N Fifth Avenue; (206) 776-6711) for a free map of the walk.

The suburbs have caught up with **Woodinville,** a formerly rural outback, paving the dirt roads and lining them with strip malls. Some of the country ambience remains, however, especially to the east where Woodinville fades into the dairy farms of Snoqualmie Valley. Woodinville's claim to fame is Chateau Ste. Michelle, the state's largest winery. The grapes come from Eastern Washington, but experimental vineyards are on site, and tours of the operation, complete with tastings, run daily every half hour between 10am and 5pm (14111 NE 145th; (206) 488-1133). Just across the street from Ste. Michelle is Columbia Winery, the state's oldest premium-wine company. Columbia offers tours on weekends between 10am and 4pm, and the tasting room is open daily from 10am to 7pm (14030 NE 145th; (206) 488-2776). Gardeners from around the region flock to Molbak's, the massive nursery and greenhouse at 13625 NE 175th; (206) 483-5000.

Redmond may be known for its corporate top gun, Microsoft, but this city at the north end of Lake Sammamish is also the hub of a lot of local (and national) cycling activity (see Cycling, this chapter). Redmond's downtown is a traditional suburban amalgamation of strip malls and shopping centers, but Anglophiles should stop for afternoon tea at the British Pantry (8125 161st Avenue NE; (206) 883-7511).

Kirkland's comfortable downtown on Lake Washington's Moss Bay is a popular summer strolling ground. Art galleries, restaurants, bookstores, and boutiques line the two-story main street. Several restaurants look out over boats docked at the marina. Grab a muffin and coffee at Triple J's (101 Central Way; (206) 822-7319), a storefront coffee shop, and walk a block to the recently renovated waterfront park, where ducks beg scraps and dodge children on the sandy beach. On Yarrow Bay at the south end of town lies Carillon Point, a glitzy hotel and shopping complex lining a round, red-brick courtyard with views of the lake and the Olympic Mountains in the distance.

A former quiet suburban hamlet, **Bellevue** is developing into a sister city of Seattle, boasting its own downtown skyline. Bellevue is the heart of the Eastside—the former suburbs of Seattle, east of Lake Washington, that now stand on their own. As many commuters now leave Seattle in the morning for work on the Eastside as make the traditional suburb-to-Seattle trek. At the core of downtown Bellevue is Bellevue Place, a hotel, restaurant, and shopping complex. Daniel's Broiler on the 21st floor of the Seafirst Office Building offers stunning views of Seattle, Puget Sound, and the Olympics. Across the street, Bellevue Square hosts Nordstrom and hundreds of other stores, but it's also one of the first malls in the country to house a museum—The Bellevue Art Museum, specializing in Northwest crafts; (206) 454-6021.

Fast-food franchises now line I-90, but the center of **Issaquah**, an old coal-mining town, still resembles small-town America, complete with a butcher shop and a working dairy. On good days, Mount Rainier appears between the hills that form the town's southern and eastern borders. Gilman Village on Gilman Boulevard is a shopping complex with a twist: the developers refurnished old farmhouses, a barn, and a feed store, then filled them with craft and clothing shops, restaurants, and a woodworking gallery. Boehm's Chocolates on the edge of town still dips its chocolates by hand and offers tours for groups (reservations are needed); (206) 392-6652. The Issaquah Farmers Market is open Saturdays throughout the summer, across from the Issaquah State Salmon Hatchery on Sunset Way, which is open to visitors daily from 8am to 7:30pm (there aren't any tours, but there are instructional displays in the lobby).

Restaurants

Adriatica ☆☆☆   Climbing its two challenging flights of stairs may be the culinary equivalent of climbing Mount Rainier: always worth the effort. The menu features herb-kissed grilled meats and other Mediterranean-inspired fare. Only a fool would skip dessert here. *Across from corner of Aloha and Dexter; (206) 285-5000; 1107 Dexter Ave N, Seattle; $$$.*

Al Boccalino ☆☆☆   Housed in a rustic brick building just off Pioneer Square. The menu features regional Italian. The wine list is solidly Italian too, as is the noise level when things get busy. A great place to do lunch, too. *At Yesler and Alaskan Way; (206) 622-7688; 1 Yesler Way, Seattle; $$$.*

Armadillo Barbecue ☆   A West Texas barbecue joint plopped down in the wilds of Woodinville. Tender, lean pork and extra-moist chicken, all thoroughly and powerfully smoked, served up with a rich hot-sauce tang, and sides of molasses-heavy beans and cakey corn bread. *Take Woodinville exit from 522E; (206) 481-1417; 13109 NE 175th St, Woodinville; $.*

Ayutthaya ☆   Carefully and authentically prepared Thai food on Capitol Hill. With the exception of the fried noodles (too sweet), everything is good and the seafood is excellent. One of the best lunch deals in town. *1 block west of Broadway at Harvard and Pike; (206) 324-8833; 727 E Pike St, Seattle; $.*

Azalea's Fountain Court ☆☆   A romantic dining spot, with live jazz on weekends and courtyard seating in summer. Any time, the dining room's country/continental ambience provides a warm backdrop for seasonal menus. *Between Main and 1st Sts on 103rd Ave NE; (206) 451-0426; 22 103rd Ave NE, Bellevue; $$$.*

Big Time Pizza ☆   Pizzas built on a rich, flavorful crust from hand-tossed dough with toppings ranging from Greece to Mexico to Thailand. Twenty-odd wines offered by the glass, calzone that oozes mozzarella, a few pan-tossed pastas, and green salads round out the menu. *Leary Way and W Lake Sammamish Pkwy; (206) 885-6425; 7281 W Lake Sammamish Pkwy NE, Redmond; $.*

Bistro Provençal ☆☆   You won't find a more reliable restaurant on the Eastside. The menu emphasis is bistro, with a terrific four-course prix-fixe meal. You can also choose from more upscale items on the à la carte menu, or try the deluxe, five-course prix-fixe "menu gastronomie." *Downtown Kirkland; (206) 827-3300; 212 Central Way, Kirkland; $$.*

Cafe Flora ☆☆   This very attractive, very '90s place has become a mecca for vegetarians and carnivores alike. Soups are always silky and luscious, salads sport interesting (often organic) ingredients, and those who don't do dairy will always find something cleverly prepared to suit their dietary needs. *28th and Madison; (206) 325-9100; 2901 E Madison, Seattle; $$.*

Cafe Juanita ☆☆☆ A small and unpretentious place, where the legion of regulars doesn't even need help deciding among the country-Italian offerings: about half the menu items have been there off and on for a decade and more. *116th off I-405, west to 97th; (206) 823-1505; 9702 120th Pl NE, Kirkland; $$.*

Cafe Lago ☆☆ At this rustic Montlake Italian cafe, the menu is small and features a quartet of pasta options that changes nightly. All the ingredients are fresh; even the pasta is handmade. One of the best antipasti plates in the city. *On 24th Ave E, 6 blocks south of Hwy 520; (206) 329-8005; 2305 24th Ave E, Seattle; $$.*

Cafe Veloce ☆ Amid decor celebrating the golden age of Italian motorcycle racing, creative Cafe Veloce delivers quality pasta and pizzas for fledgling connoisseurs on spaghetti-and-meatball budgets. *Kitty-corner from Totem Lake Cinemas on 120th Ave NE; (206) 814-2972; 12514 120th Ave NE, Kirkland; $.*

Campagne/Cafe Campagne ☆☆☆ Located in the Pike Place Market. Inspiration here comes from the south of France. Nightly specials reflect the day's catch and seasonal offerings. A late-night menu is available in the bar, while dining at a courtyard table is the next best thing to a trip to France. Cafe Campagne is a casual bistro-cum-charcuterie. Take-out, too. *Restaurant: At the Inn at the Market, between Stewart and Pine on Post Alley; (206) 728-2800; 86 Pine St, Seattle; $$$. Cafe: On Post Alley at Pine; (206) 728-2233; 1600 Post Alley, Seattle; $.*

Caveman Kitchens ☆ The late Dick Donley spent years experimenting with methods of smoking meat and fish over alder and applewood. What he finally achieved was outstanding. No inside seating, but most people take out, loading up on the smoked goods, accompaniments, and a terrific bread pudding with butterscotch whiskey sauce. A second Caveman (11700 Lake City Way NE; (206) 362-8464) is open in Seattle. *West Valley Hwy at the James intersection; (206) 854-1210; 807 West Valley Hwy, Kent; $.*

Chanterelle Specialty Foods ☆☆ Perhaps better known for breakfast, lunch, and baked goods, casual and kitchen-confident Chanterelle really shines at dinner, with nightly specials reflecting an ethnically diverse range. The best restaurant in town. *Up from ferry terminal, on Main; (206) 774-0650; 316 Main St, Edmonds; $.*

Ciao Italia ☆☆ Ciao Italia's Edmonds strip mall location aside, the pleasant atmosphere—at once candlelit and casual—works to fine effect. The menu is full of Italian meat and pasta standards done in better-than-standard fashion. *In the shopping center, south of 5th and Walnut; (206) 771-7950; 546 5th Ave S, Edmonds; $.*

Dahlia Lounge ☆☆☆   For many locals and out-of-towners, it's synonymous with the Seattle food scene: Northwest foods and a bold juxtaposition of cultures within one meal. The Dahlia's scenic appeal lies in a stylish two-level dining landscape of vermilion, gold, and brocade. *4th Ave between Stewart and Virginia; (206) 682-4142; 1904 4th Ave, Seattle; $$.*

El Puerco Lloron ☆   This place transports you back to that cafe in Tijuana, the one with the screaming hot pink walls, the bent Cerveza Superior tables, and the woman quietly making corn tortillas by the door. Dishes run a paltry $4 to $5. *On the Pike Place Market Hillclimb; (206) 624-0541; 1501 Western Ave, Seattle; $.*

Etta's Seafood ☆☆☆   A '90s-style seafood house that dares you to choose between such wonders as a simple wedge of iceberg lettuce topped with an extraordinary blue cheese dressing or a lively octopus and shiitake salad with a tangy citrus marinade. And that's just the start! Daily specials. *North end of Pike Place Market; (206) 443-6000; 2020 Western Ave, Seattle; $$$.*

Filiberto's ☆☆   Filiberto's is the most authentic and, on a good day, among the best of the local (and we mean local) Italian restaurants. The long menu emphasizes Old World Italian preparations of pasta, veal, poultry, and rabbit. With a bocce court out back! *Off Hwy 518; (206) 248-1944; 14401 Des Moines Memorial Dr, Burien; $$.*

Huong Binh ☆   This tidy Vietnamese restaurant, in one of the strip malls marking the expanding Vietnamese commercial area near the International District, holds its own. And you can do feasts here, huge brimming tables-full, for under $20. *At S Jackson and 12th; (206) 720-4907; 1207 S Jackson St, Seattle; $.*

I Love Sushi ☆☆   A pair of premier Japanese restaurants on either side of Lake Washington feature bustling, bright, high-energy sushi bars with exquisitely fresh fish. The sushi combinations are a veritable bargain (particularly at lunch) and the hot dishes are excellent. *On the Yale St Landing off Fairview; (206) 625-9604; 1001 Fairview Ave N, Seattle (and branch); $$.*

Il Bacio ☆☆   The beautifully rendered Italian specialties go a long way to helping you forget you're in a faux-Italian patio in a strip mall. You'd be foolish not to leave room for dessert, which comes from the nifty little adjacent Pasticcerie Il Bacio. *Downtown Redmond, on the main eastbound drag; (206) 869-8815; 16564 Cleveland St, Redmond; $$.*

Il Bistro ☆☆☆   A cherished refuge on a narrow cobblestone street in Pike Place Market in which to enjoy food, wine, and friends. The lower-level bar is a favorite spot to linger over an aperitif or share a convivial late-night supper. Il Bistro consistently serves one of the best racks of lamb in Seattle. *Just below Read All About It in Pike Place Market; (206) 682-3049; 93-A Pike St, Seattle; $$$.*

Italianissimo ☆☆   This Italian eatery consistently exceeds expectations in a relaxed, casual atmosphere that attracts more families than ultra-discerning foodies. *In Woodinville Town Center, corner of 140th and 175th; (206) 485-6888; 17650 140th Ave NE, Woodinville; $$.*

Kikuya ☆☆   No tatami rooms, no kimonos, just good, straightforward fare prepared well and efficiently served. The excellent sushi bar provides visual entertainment, and meals come with pickled cucumbers, miso, a small salad, and green tea. *Off Kirkland-Redmond Hwy on 161st NE; (206) 881-8771; 8105 161st Ave NE, Redmond; $$.*

Lampreia ☆☆☆☆   A sleek restaurant that exudes sophistication. Zealous use of seasonal, regional, and organic ingredients is akin to religion here. The wine list is carefully wrought and reasonably priced. Service is as polished as the silver. *Corner of 1st and Battery; (206) 443-3301; 2400 1st Ave, Seattle; $$$.*

Maltby Cafe ☆☆   A Saturday morning repast can fill you for the weekend: delicious omelets, good new potatoes, old-fashioned oatmeal, and thick slices of French toast. Equally satisfying lunches. *From Hwy 405, take the Monroe-Wenatchee exit onto Hwy 522, turn left at first light onto Maltby Rd, then left at the 3-way stop; (206) 483-3123; 8809 Maltby Rd, Maltby; $.*

Mandarin Garden ☆   Issaquah's best Chinese food is found here amid a drab decor. The chef handles equally well the delicate flavors of Mandarin and the heat and spice of Sichuan and Hunan. But be assured that if you order a starred dish, you're going to get hot and spicy. *Exit 17 off I-90 to Sunset Way; (206) 392-9476; 40 E Sunset Way, Issaquah; $.*

Maple Leaf Grill ☆☆   Don't let the pub atmosphere—blues on the sound system and convivial customers hoisting a brew, waiting for a seat, and trading gibes—fool you. You're just as likely to fork into a grilled breast of rabbit or a Thai-inspired pasta as a burger with fries. *89th and Roosevelt; (206) 523-8449; 8909 Roosevelt Way NE, Seattle; $$.*

Marco's Supperclub ☆☆   This stylish Belltown bistro has welcomed hordes of savvy diners who come for the warm, funky atmosphere and the trip-around-the-world menu. The bar is a great perch for those dining alone. In summer, enjoy a colorful, plant-filled deck out back. *Near 1st and Wall; (206) 441-7801; 2510 1st Ave, Seattle; $$.*

Mediterranean Kitchen ☆   Authentic Middle Eastern fare, with claims to having served over a million chicken wings marinated in vinegar and slathered with roasted garlic, just like the owner's grandfather first made in Lebanon. *Off Queen Anne Ave; (206) 285-6713; 4 W Roy St, Seattle (and branch); $.*

Metropolitan Grill ☆☆   This handsome haunt in the heart of Seattle's financial district does a booming business among the stockbrokers and Asian tourists. The bovine is divine here, so you'd do well to stick to the steaks. Large, appealing salads, sandwiches, and a daily fish special present good alternatives. *2nd and Marion; (206) 624-3287; 820 2nd Ave, Seattle; $$$.*

Neelam's Authentic Indian Cuisine ☆   This dimly lit East Indian restaurant offers bargain-priced dinner specials. For a 10-spot you'll get a choice of entree, cooling raita, fragrant dal, cumin-scented basmati rice, feathery-light naan, an appetizer, a beverage, *and* dessert. *On the Ave (University Way); (206) 523-5275; 4735 University Way, Seattle; $.*

Nicolino ☆   On warm days, the sunny brick courtyard is the place to be. On cold or rainy days, head for the cheerful little dining room, pleasantly cluttered with wine bottles and family pictures, maps and mandolins, for a steaming plate of soul-warming pasta. *In Gilman Village; (206) 391-8077; 317 NW Gilman Blvd, Issaquah; $$.*

Nikko (Westin Hotel) ☆☆   One of the few really attractive Japanese dining rooms in the city. The enormous sushi bar is the best place to enjoy impeccable raw fish, or you can always try a plate of grilled thises and thats from the robata bar. *In the Westin Hotel at 5th and Westlake; (206) 322-4641; 1900 5th Ave, Seattle; $$$.*

Piecora's ☆   People drive across town just to sit down to one of these oversized thin-crust pies and dream of New York. Sold by the pie, the half pie, and the slice. Pastas, sandwiches, and salads, too. Pizza served until midnight on weekends. *At 14th and Madison; (206) 322-9411; 1401 E Madison St, Seattle; $.*

The Pink Door ☆☆   This Italian trattoria's low-profile entrance (no sign, just a pink door off Post Alley) belies the busy scene within, especially in summer when everyone vies for a spot on the terrace with its view of the Sound. There's often live music at night. *Post Alley between Stewart and Virginia; (206) 443-3241; 1919 Post Alley, Seattle; $$.*

Place Pigalle ☆☆☆   Long on charm, short on space, this classic Seattle bistro with a Puget Sound view is tucked away in the Pike Place Market. Intriguing dishes combine fresh Northwest ingredients with recipes that speak of France and Italy here, of New Mexico and New

Orleans there. *Under the clock at Pike Place Market; (206) 624-1756; 81 Pike St, Seattle; $$$.*

Pogacha ☆   Pogacha is a chewy Croatian dinner roll baked in a wood-fired oven. Here, they stretch the dough to make what would look, to the uninitiated, like pizza. They're thin and flavorful, and there are usually a half dozen pasta dishes and a couple of serviceable meat dishes too. *In Bellevue Plaza near Main St; (206) 455-5670; 119 106th Ave NE, Bellevue; $.*

Pon Proem ☆   A nifty little Thai joint, with a no-nonsense star scale ("chok dee" next to five stars means "good luck"!). Most everything sampled here displays balance and a deft touch at the wok. Deep-fried dishes consistently please. *On the edge of downtown Mercer Island, next to Payless; (206) 236-8424; 3039 78th Ave SE, Mercer Island; $.*

Ponti Seafood Grill ☆☆☆   Beside the Fremont Bridge, Ponti inspires dreams of the Mediterranean, with its canalside perch, stucco walls, and red-tiled roof. But its true inspiration is defined by its food—fusion cuisine using an array of ethnic flavors, especially Asian. Sunday brunch. *Behind the Bleitz Funeral Home; (206) 284-3000; 3014 3rd Ave N, Seattle; $$$.*

Provinces Asian Restaurant & Bar ☆☆   A pan-Asian restaurant is a surprising find here, but we like the friendly service and the dish of sweet-and-spicy broccoli stems brought to the table gratis. The adjoining cocktail lounge is decidedly more boisterous. *In upper level of Old Mill Town Mall at 5th and Maple; (206) 744-0288; 201 5th Ave S, Edmonds; $$.*

Queen City Grill ☆☆☆   A restaurant where the menu is pared down to a short list of dishes done really, really well, offset by a couple of specials—a nice ethic in this era of multiethnic, pan-contintental eateries. The entrees are simply prepared, mostly on the grill. *Corner of Blanchard and 1st; (206) 443-0975; 2201 1st Ave, Seattle; $$$.*

Ray's Boathouse ☆☆☆   With its peerless, unabashedly romantic view of Shilshole Bay and the Olympics beyond, this is *the* place for waterfront dining. Take advantage of the fresh fish for which Ray's is famous, as well as the superb wine list. Also try the moderately priced upstairs cafe, especially popular at happy hour. *60th NW and Seaview; (206) 789-3770; 6049 Seaview Ave NW, Seattle; $$$.*

Ristorante Paradiso ☆☆   A surprisingly sophisticated culinary treat in unpretentious digs, with fresh, perfectly cooked meals and a great selection of wines. *Off Lake Washington St, across from Moss Bay; (206) 889-8601; 120-A Park Lane, Kirkland; $$.*

Saleh al Lago ☆☆☆   Some of the most consistently good central Italian food in Seattle. The place is more popular with moneyed mucky-mucks than with the city's youthful trend-seekers (who may find the room too bright, the menu too traditional). But what Saleh al Lago might lack in excitement, it makes up for in execution. *On the east side of Green Lake; (206) 524-4044; 6804 E Green Lake Way N, Seattle; $$$.*

Salvatore ☆☆   What with so many Italian restaurants going upscale and every other restaurant in town going Italian, this neighborhood dinner spot continues to impress by getting all the essentials right—the old-fashioned Italian way. *1 block north of Ravenna Blvd on Roosevelt; (206) 527-9301; 6100 Roosevelt Way NE, Seattle; $$.*

Satsuma ☆☆   Plain as a box on the outside, this tranquil Burien hideaway has captured the interest of the local Japanese, who come to enjoy the light-as-air tempura and the (merely) creditable sushi. *Off 148th on Ambaum; (206) 242-1747; 14301 Ambaum Blvd SW, Burien; $.*

Sea Garden of Bellevue ☆☆   Long a favorite in the International District, known for its subtle Mandarin flavors and consistently excellent seafood, the Sea Garden moved east a few years back. The extensive menu offers plenty of vegetarian options, plus exotics like jellyfish, sea cucumber, or fish maw. *Downtown Bellevue; (206) 450-8833; 200 106th NE Ave, Bellevue; $$.*

Seattle Bagel Bakery   Seattleites rarely match Manhattanites in their lust for the doughy rings, but this spot next to the Harbor Steps (take a bagel to go and eat by the fountains) comes close to inspiring the same passion. *Corner of University and Western; (206) 624-2187; 1302 Western Ave, Seattle; $.*

Seoul Olympic Restaurant ☆   Some of the best Korean food in the Seattle area is available in this nondescript office complex in Bellevue. *At the corner of NE 12th and 112th NE; (206) 455-9305; 1200 112th Ave NE, Bellevue; $$.*

Shamiana ☆☆   Eastern cooking meets Western chefs here in the happiest of ways: a Pakistani barbecue turns out flame-broiled meats and some mouth-watering (and mouth-igniting) versions of traditional Indian curries. Lunch is bargain city, with a buffet that changes daily. *In the Houghton Village at 108th and 68th; (206) 827-4902; 10724 NE 68th St, Kirkland; $.*

Shanghai Garden ☆☆☆   This restaurant in the International District attracts diners from every Chinese province with regional dishes that change seasonally. The menu is vast and filled with exotica. Try the chef's special hand-shaven noodles in what we're sure will be the best chow mein you'll ever eat. *Corner of 6th Ave S and Weller St; (206) 625-1689; 524 6th Ave S, Seattle; $.*

Siam on Broadway ☆   Among Seattle's multitude of Thai restaurants, tiny Siam wins the popularity contest, hands down. The menu doesn't stray far from the Bangkok standards, but distinctive dishes abound, including what might be the city's best tom kah gai. *Broadway E and E Roy; (206) 324-0892; 616 Broadway E, Seattle; $.*

Tosoni's ☆   The humble strip mall exterior belies the Old World delights awaiting inside. Generously portioned main courses are often spectacularly good (we've been less pleased with side dishes). *Off 148th Ave NE; (206) 644-1668; 14320 NE 20th St, Bellevue; $$.*

Toyoda Sushi ☆☆   Expect to wait in the bright crowded entrance, and be sure to opt for a seat at the sushi bar. This unlikely Lake City find serves some of the best gyoza in town. *125th and Lake City Way; (206) 367-7972; 12543 Lake City Way NE, Seattle; $$.*

Triangle Tavern ☆   This small space is noisy and smoky, but the food is inventive and well prepared. A Philadelphia-style cheese steak sided up with a caesar salad is cheap at twice the price. The decor is (naturally) tri-angular. *Fremont Pl N and N 35th; (206) 632-0880; 3507 Fremont Pl N, Seattle; $.*

Tulio (Hotel Vintage Park) ☆☆☆   Tables with red-checkered cloths are packed in tightly, the sweet scent of roasted garlic hangs in the air, and a wood-burning oven and open kitchen make this place ever lively. Grilled cuts of meat and fish round out dinner, while thin-crusted pizzas and calzones make a hearty lunch. *5th and Spring; (206) 624-5500; 1100 5th Ave, Seattle; $$.*

Two Bells Tavern ☆   Big, juicy burgers on sourdough, and hot beer-sausage—this food is so full of flavor and freshness and goes so well with the beer that you don't care about getting mustard all over your face. Food is served till 11pm every night, but the tavern stays open till 2am. *4th and Bell; (206) 441-3050; 2313 4th Ave, Seattle; $.*

Viet My ☆   At lunchtime, this bright, busy spot is standing room only for food that is always exact and delicious. You won't pay more than $6, and usually much less. *Just off 4th near Washington; (206) 382-9923; 129 Prefontaine Pl S, Seattle; $.*

Wild Ginger ☆☆☆   Just as the restaurants and markets of Bangkok, Singapore, Saigon, and Djakarta offer a wide range of multiethnic foods, so does the Wild Ginger, which brings together some of the best dishes from Southeast Asia. At the mahogany satay bar, order from a wide array of sizzling skewered selections. *1 block east of the waterfront on the corner of Western and Union; (206) 623-4450; 1400 Western Ave, Seattle; $$.*

Yarrow Bay Grill and Beach Cafe ☆☆   There are two restaurants here, one on top of another, each with a gorgeous Lake Washington view. The upstairs grill focuses on well-prepared seafood, while the lively cafe offers a United Nations menu. *In the Carillon Point Plaza, downtown Kirkland; (206) 889-9052 (Yarrow Bay Grill) or (206) 889-0303 (Beach Cafe); 1270 Carillon Point, Kirkland; $$$.*

Lodgings

Alexis Hotel ☆☆☆   When the Sultan of Brunei was in Seattle on business, this is where he stayed. And if it's good enough for the richest man in the world... It's small (54 rooms) and full of tasteful touches. Amenities include continental breakfasts, a morning newspaper of your choice, shoe shines, and a guest membership in a nearby athletic club. The Painted Table serves innovative Northwest cuisine. *1st and Madison; (206) 624-4844 or (800) 426-7033; 1007 1st Ave, Seattle; $$$.*

The Bellevue Hilton ☆☆   With every amenity in the book, the Bellevue Hilton is simply the best bet on the Eastside's Hotel Row. *Main and 112th NE; (206) 455-3330 or (800) BEL-HILT; 100 112th Ave NE, Bellevue; $$$.*

Chambered Nautilus ☆☆   This blue 1915 Georgian colonial in a woodsy hillside setting in the University District offers six airy guest rooms beautifully furnished with antiques. Four have private baths, and four open onto porches with tree-webbed views of the Cascades. Make prior arrangements for kids under 12. *East on NE 50th St to 20th Ave, and circle left-right-right around the block; (206) 522-2536; 5005 22nd Ave NE, Seattle; $$.*

The Edgewater ☆☆   Alas, you can't fish from the famous west-facing windows of this waterfront institution anymore. You can, however, still breathe salty air and hear the ferry horns toot. The place has been spiffed up quite a bit with a lodge style and rustic tone. A reputable restaurant, a decent bar, and an uninterrupted view of Elliott Bay, Puget Sound, and the Olympic Mountains. *Pier 67 at Wall St and Alaskan Way; (206) 728-7000; Pier 67, 2411 Alaskan Way, Seattle; $$$.*

Edmonds Harbor Inn ☆   Strategically located near the Edmonds ferry and train terminals, the inn is an attractive choice for a night in this charming waterside Seattle suburb. *Dayton and Edmonds Way; (206) 771-5021; 130 W Dayton St, Edmonds; $$.*

Four Seasons Olympic Hotel ☆☆☆☆   Elegance is yours at Seattle's landmark hotel, where grand borders on opulent, and personal around-the-clock service means smiling maids, quick-as-a-wink bellhops, and a team of caring concierges who ensure your every comfort. The venerable

Georgian Room offers a fine-dining experience you won't soon forget. Solarium spa and pool. *4th and University; (206) 621-1700 or (800) 821-8106; 411 University St, Seattle; $$$.*

Gaslight Inn and Howell Street Suites ☆☆   The Gaslight is one of the loveliest and most reasonably priced bed and breakfasts in town. This turn-of-the-century mansion has 15 guest rooms, sun decks, and a large heated swimming pool. The Howell Street Suites next door are outfitted with kitchens, contemporary furnishings and antiques, a coffeemaker, wineglasses, fruit, and flowers (they also offer phones, fax, offstreet parking, maid service, and laundry facilities). No pets or kids. *15th and Howell; (206) 325-3654; 1727 15th Ave, Seattle; $$.*

Hyatt Regency at Bellevue Place ☆☆   A 382-room hotel with 24 stories (the highest in Bellevue), the Hyatt Regency offers many extras, including a fine restaurant, Eques. *NE 8th St and Bellevue Way; (206) 462-1234 or (800) 233-1234; 900 Bellevue Way NE, Bellevue; $$$.*

Inn at the Market ☆☆☆   The setting—perched just above the fish, flower, and fruit stalls of Pike Place Market with a view of Elliott Bay—is unsurpassed. This small hotel features personalized service that approximates that of a country inn. *1st and Pine; (206) 443-3600; 86 Pine St, Seattle; $$$.*

Marriott Residence Inn/Lake Union ☆   Lake Union's first full-scale hotel is not exactly on the lake, but across a busy avenue. Still, most of the 234 rooms boast lake views. All rooms have fully outfitted kitchenettes and a continental breakfast is available. Guests can also charge meals to their room at any number of lakeside eateries across the street. *Fairview and Boren, at the south end of Lake Union across from the marina; (206) 624-6000; 800 Fairview Ave N, Seattle; $$$.*

Mayflower Park Hotel ☆☆   Renovations have paid off at this handsome 1927 hotel right in the heart of the downtown shopping district. A coolly elegant lobby opens onto **Oliver's** (bar and lounge) on one side and **Clipper's,** one of the prettiest breakfast places in town, on the other. Rooms are small, but still bear charming reminders of the hotel's past. *4th and Olive; (206) 623-8700; 405 Olive Way, Seattle; $$$.*

MV *Challenger* ☆☆   A luxury liner it's not, but if you've got a thing for tugboats, the boat-and-breakfast MV *Challenger*, a handsomely restored 96-foot workhorse, is for you. Everything—from the spotless galley to the eight cabins—is shipshape. *Yale St Landing; (206) 340-1201; 1001 Fairview Ave N, Seattle; $$.*

Salisbury House ☆☆   A welcoming porch wraps around this big, bright Capitol Hill home, an exquisite hostelry neighboring Volunteer

Park. Four guest rooms with full private baths. Classy, dignified, non-smoking, and devoid of children (under 12) and pets, the Salisbury is a sure bet in one of Seattle's finest neighborhoods. *E Aloha and 16th Ave E; (206) 328-8682; 750 16th Ave E, Seattle; $$.*

Seattle Marriott at Sea-Tac ☆ Another megamotel, the 451-room Marriott is somewhat concealed by trees, about a block from the airport strip, and offers the usual amenities. *Just east of Pacific Hwy S at S 176th and 32nd Ave S; (206) 241-2000 or (800) 228-9290; 3201 S 176th St, Seattle; $$$.*

Seattle Airport Hilton Hotel ☆☆ This streamlined four-winged building, camouflaged by trees and plantings, miraculously manages to create a resort atmosphere along an airport strip. *188th St exit off I-5, west 1 mile; (206) 244-4800 or (800) HILTONS; 17620 Pacific Hwy S, Seattle; $$$.*

Seattle Sheraton Hotel and Towers ☆☆ An 840-room tower with the Convention Center in its shadow. The rooms are smallish and standard, and much emphasis is placed on the meeting rooms and the restaurants. The outstanding four-star restaurant, Fullers, is an oasis of serenity adorned with fine Northwest art. The top floors feature a health club and a lounge with a knockout city panorama. You pay for parking. *6th and Pike; (206) 621-9000 or (800) 204-6100; 1400 6th Ave, Seattle; $$$.*

Shumway Mansion ☆☆ A gracious eight-room bed and breakfast with an equal emphasis on seminars and receptions. Children over 12 are welcome. No pets or smoking. *Near NE 116th on 99th Pl NE; (206) 823-2303; 11410 99th Pl NE, Kirkland; $$.*

Sorrento Hotel ☆☆☆ An Italianate masterpiece that first opened in 1909, the Sorrento is now a small hotel of civilized, muted good taste. Enjoy the comfortable, intimate fireside lobby lounge for afternoon tea or cognac while listening to one of the city's best jazz pianists. The Hunt Club showcases Northwest lamb, among other local culinary treasures. *Terry and Madison; (206) 622-6400 or (800) 426-1265; 900 Madison St, Seattle; $$$.*

WestCoast Sea-Tac Hotel ☆ This WestCoast outpost with 146 bright rooms is the only airport hotel that offers in-house guests free valet parking for seven days. *Across from the airport entrance; (206) 246-5535 or (800) 426-0670; 18220 Pacific Hwy S, Seattle; $$$.*

Westin Hotel ☆☆☆ Westin's international headquarters is in Seattle, so this flagship hotel has quite a few extras. The twin cylindrical towers afford spacious rooms with superb views, and convention facilities are quite complete. There is also a large pool and an exercise room. The location, near Westlake Center and the Monorail station, is excellent. *Between Stewart and Virginia on 5th; (206) 728-1000 or (800) 228-3000; 1900 5th Ave, Seattle; $$$.*

The Williams House ☆   In its 91-year history, this south-slope Queen Anne residence has been a gentlemen's boardinghouse and an emergency medical clinic for the 1962 Seattle World's Fair. Five guest rooms, four with views and two with private baths. Children are welcome by prior arrangement. *Galer and 4th N; (206) 285-0810 or (800) 880-0810; 1505 4th Ave N, Seattle; $$.*

Woodmark Hotel ☆☆☆   On the eastern shore of Lake Washington, the Woodmark claims to be the only lodging actually on the lake. From the outside, it resembles a modern office building, but on the inside one encounters the soft touches of a fine hotel. *Kirkland exit off SR 520, north on Lake Washington Blvd NE to Carillon Point; (206) 822-3700; 1200 Carillon Point, Kirkland; $$$.*

Wyndham Garden Hotel ☆   A bit classier than your standard airport hotel. Accommodations here include 180 guest rooms and 24 suites. *South of S 176th St; (206) 244-6666; 18118 Pacific Hwy S, Seattle; $$$.*

Cheaper Sleeps

The College Inn Guest House   Designed along the lines of a European pension, it's in the heart of the lively University District (with bathrooms reminiscent of a college dorm). *(206) 633-4441; 4000 University Way NE, Seattle.*

Seattle International Youth Hostel   Seattle's no-nonsense, nonsmoking hostel offers the comforts of hostels the world over: a cheap bed (under $20) and a communal kitchen. Off-season, the dormitories (male/female) are available to non-AYH members for an additional couple bucks. Rooms are closed afternoons. *(206) 622-5443; 84 Union St, Seattle.*

Vincent's Guest House   It's an AYH, but cheapies have lauded it for its unstructured atmosphere—less rigid than most hostels. Dorm beds are $12, with some private rooms available. *(206) 323-7849; 527 Malden Ave E, Seattle.*

More Information

Downtown visitors information center, Seattle: *(206) 461-5840.*
Seattle Parks and Recreation Department: *(206) 684-4075.*

Washington State Parks: *(800) 233-0321, general information; (800) 452-5687, camping reservations.*

Amtrak: *(800) 872-2245.*

Greyhound: *(800) 231-2222.*

Metro Transit: *(206) 553-3000.*

Washington State Ferries: *(206) 464-6400.*

Marmot Mountain Works: *827 Bellevue Way NE, Bellevue; (206) 453-1515.*

The North Face: *1023 First Avenue, Seattle; (206) 622-4111.*

Outdoor Recreation Information Center: *(206) 220-7450.*

REI: *222 Yale Avenue N; (206) 223-1944. Also Bellevue, (206) 643-3700; Federal Way, (206) 941-4994); and Lynnwood (206) 774-1300.*

Swallow's Nest: *2308 Sixth Avenue, Seattle; (206) 441-4100.*

Warshal's Sporting Goods: *First and Madison, Seattle; (206) 624-7300.*

Wilderness Sports: *14340 NW 20th, Bellevue; (206) 746-0500.*

Bainbridge and Vashon Islands

Encompassing the whole of Seattle's nearest two Puget Sound commuter islands, including Eagle Harbor, Dockton County Park, and Fay-Bainbridge and Fort Ward State Parks.

For all the hype about quaint, natural island living on upscale-chic Bainbridge and organic-chic Vashon, a day spent on either leaves you with a single burning question: What's the use of an island if you can't get to the water?

You would think that dual islands in the heart of Puget Sound would be bursting at the shorelines with good public beaches. You'd be mistaken. The truth is that much of the best beach land on either island, particularly Bainbridge, has already been bought, fenced off, and posted.

Sadly, lack of good public shoreline—or park space of any kind—is a fact of life on these two suburbanized, bedroom-community islands. But the truth is that the ferry trip to the islands—especially for visitors or those hordes of recently transplanted Right Coasters—really *is* charming enough in its own fresh-air way to make you buy into the island mystique. And what little public space is available on Bainbridge and Vashon is almost nice enough to ameliorate it for the rest of us.

Actually, we're probably too hard on the islands—especially Vashon, where some prime waterfront park lands have been acquired and hold great promise for the future. Even now, marine explorers can find a number of water-accessible public beaches on Vashon. Both islands provide hundreds of miles of attractive shorelines for sea kayakers, canoeists, and small-boat owners. And each island, thanks to its convenient "walk-on" access from Seattle, has become a noted bicycle destination.

In the grand outdoor-world scheme of things, each of these islands deserves at least one full day of exploration, several times a year. Lucky for the islands—if not the islanders—their stone's-throw location means that's all the time you'll need to invest.

Getting There

Both islands have a front and back door. Keys to the front way are held by Washington State ferries, which operates large auto ferries from Colman Dock in Seattle to Bainbridge; auto ferries from Fauntleroy in West Seattle to Vashon; and passenger-only ferries from Colman Dock to Vashon. Vashon has two alternate access routes: a short ferry crossing from the main Vashon terminal to Southworth in south Kitsap County, and a ferry from a southern terminal on Tahlequah Road to Tacoma's Point Defiance Park. From Bainbridge, the back entrance/exit is Hwy 305, which crosses Agate Passage by bridge to the Kitsap Peninsula near Poulsbo. For ferry schedules and information, call (206) 464-6400 or (800) 84-FERRY.

Adjoining Areas

NORTH: **Whidbey and Camano Islands**

SOUTH: **Tacoma and Gig Harbor**

EAST: **Greater Seattle**

WEST: **Kitsap Peninsula**

Parks/Beaches

Fay-Bainbridge State Park, the very best thing about Bainbridge Island, is a wonderful place to laze away a breezy summer afternoon. The 1,400-foot beach at this north-island park is sandy smooth, with just enough driftwood to lean on and very nice picnic facilities nearby. But the main draw is the view: you look straight across the Sound into the teeth of the beast—downtown Seattle—whose skyline buildings look a lot less imposing from here than when you're stuck in traffic between them. Fay-Bainbridge is on Sunrise Drive NE. Take the Day Road turnoff from Hwy 305 and follow signs northeast to the park. The park is open all year. (Also see Camping, below.) And since you asked: there is not, and never was, a "Fay Bainbridge." The park's hyphenated name combines that of the island and the original property owner, Temple S. Fay.

On the opposite shore, a largely undeveloped recreation area, **Fort Ward State Park,** provides more-solitary beach walking. The park has 4,300 feet of saltwater shoreline, but it's not easy to get to. The shoreline is best seen by walking or cycling Pleasant Beach Road (it's closed to auto traffic), which runs parallel to—but a ways up from—the rocky beach. This is a good shorebird-watching area; bird blinds are found at the north and south ends of the beach. It's also a popular summertime scuba-diving venue. Orchard Rocks, an offshore formation near the park's south end, is a designated marine park. Note that it's probably too far offshore for most divers to swim to from the beach; use a boat. A launch is available at the park's north end, near Battery Thornburgh. Fort Ward—reached by Pleasant Beach Drive NE or Fort Ward Hill Road (you'll need a map to find it from Winslow)—was a turn-of-the-century companion fort to Manchester on the other side of Rich Passage. (See the Kitsap Peninsula chapter.) Together, their mission was to employ cannons, mines, and submarine nets to protect Puget Sound Naval Shipyard. They succeeded; it's still there.

Vashon Island has a broader mix of somewhat hard-to-find public beach. There's a decent beach access just east of the main Vashon ferry terminal, as well as a 12-acre, undeveloped beachfront campsite, **Winghaven Park,** which is a designated Cascadia Marine Trail site (the Cascadia Marine Trail is a state-managed water trail including campsites from Olympia to Vancouver, BC, (206) 545-9161). It's three quarters of a mile from the ferry terminal, below Vashon Hwy SW.

If the thought of right-wing–oriented radio waves silently penetrating your brain is palatable, the sandy beach below the KVI radio tower (off SW 204th north of Portage) at Point Heyer is a very nice waterfront spot. **"KVI Beach"** is private property, but the station traditionally has left it open to the public. Caution: Parking is limited.

Many of the best beach sites on Vashon are clustered around Maury Island, connected by an isthmus to Vashon's east side. Perhaps the most scenic beach access on the island is the beach area at **Point Robinson Park** (SW 243rd Place and Skalberg Road, at the far eastern tip of Maury Island), where a trail loops down from the grassy, upland picnic area to a nice beach below the 1915 Point Robinson Light. The beach here is directly across Puget Sound from **Saltwater State Park** in Des Moines (see the Greater Seattle chapter), which looks close enough to paddle to by kayak. It is, if you know how to handle your craft in open water. Up the beach to the southwest is **Maury Island Marine Park,** a prime 340-acre beachfront property recently acquired—but as yet undeveloped—by King County Parks.

Quartermaster Harbor, the protected water between Maury and

Vashon Islands, is accessible through several waterfront parks. **Burton Acres,** a Vashon Island park, is a delightful site on a peninsula inside the harbor, with a boat launch, beach access, and miles of trails through a woodsy upland area. Across the harbor on the inside shoulder of Maury Island is **Dockton County Park,** a nice King County facility at the site of an old boatyard. The park has a boat launch, beach access, and modern moorage for visiting boaters. The upland area has about a mile and a half of hiking trails. Both parks are good places to launch a canoe or kayak to explore the quiet harbor waters.

Cycling

What these two islands lack in good beach access, they make up for in vigorous cycling routes. Both islands are hilly, but the backroads are very scenic. Leaving the car at home and taking the ferry to cycle the islands adds a unique touch of Northwest mystique to a Bainbridge or Vashon tour.

On Bainbridge, cyclists exiting at the Winslow ferry terminal have a wealth of choices. Our advice: Map a route that gets you, as quickly as possible, off of the main drag—Hwy 305. Bainbridge backroads are pleasant, with mostly slow-moving Explorers and Range Rovers providing occasional accompaniment. **Fay-Bainbridge State Park** (see Parks/Beaches, above) is a popular day-trip destination from Seattle. It's about 7 miles (one way) from the Ferry Terminal via Hwy 305, Day Road, and Sunrise Drive NE.

If you're up for a bigger trip, make a 30-mile loop around the island by following the general course of the Chilly Hilly, Cascade Bicycle Club's annual spring cycling-season kickoff. Start on Ferncliff (heading north) at Winslow ferry terminal (avoid Hwy 305) and work your way counterclockwise around the island (follow the signs).

Vashon is a great place to explore from a cycle seat. If you survive the first uphill stretch out of the ferry terminal, the rest of the island is all downhill. Sort of. The number of possible routes is endless here. A ride south down the island's main drag, 99th Avenue SW, then onto and around Maury Island, makes a solid day trip. Robinson Point Light or Dockton County Park—a nice, secluded spot above the salt water—are good lunch destinations. Round-trip distance is about 25 miles. Note: Bring your own bike. Rentals are not available on Vashon.

Camping

These islands are neither the land of the RV nor the home of the tenting brave. But campers do have one decent option. **Fay-Bainbridge State**

Park, on the north end of Bainbridge (see Parks/Beaches, above) has 36 sites (10 have water hookups; maximum RV length, 30 feet), just a short distance from the beach. They're fairly tightly bunched, and cramped by most standards, in this small (17-acre) park. The tent sites, mostly open to the wind, are rather exposed to the crowds. But hey, it's camping, and this park often fills up in the summer. The park also has a group camp and good picnic facilities with covered kitchen shelters, a boat ramp, and mooring buoys. Fay-Bainbridge is open all year. Campsites cannot be reserved. *On Sunrise Drive NE, at the north end of the island; follow signs from Hwy 305; (206) 842-3931 or (800) 233-0321.*

Fishing

Fishing action is relatively dead on both islands. But it's still very much alive all around them. Bainbridge and Vashon both lie at the epicenter of an interior **Puget Sound salmon** fishery that's often quite productive all year for anglers who can land a trip on a boat. Two areas in particular— the **Agate Passage** area west of Bainbridge and the **Dolphin Point** area off the northern tip of Vashon Island—have become well known to anglers in recent years. The reason: both areas have been designated special "bubble fisheries" during peak summer salmon seasons—while many other north and central Sound hot spots have been closed. Check with the state Department of Fish and Wildlife for seasons, limits, and restrictions. They change annually. Consult the fishing sections in the Greater Seattle or Kitsap Peninsula chapters for Puget Sound hot spots and charter information.

Also, Vashon offers a decent shore-fishing opportunity. The **Tramp Harbor Fishing Pier,** operated by King County Parks, juts 300 feet out into Tramp Harbor. It's off Dockton Road, between Portage and Point Heyer. Bottom-fishing fans should take note of the **artificial reef** just off Point Heyer.

Kayaking/Canoeing

Saltwater kayakers have adopted the shorelines of interior Puget Sound islands. And these two, being as close as they are to the people centers, are no strangers to the paddle dippers. In many ways, the kayak is the tool of choice for exploring the natural beauty of these two islands. Once you set foot on them, most of their watery charm is hidden from view. Not so from a kayak, where all the water is public, all the views memorable.

Popular kayak destinations include the interior waters of **Eagle Harbor** (launch just south of the ferry terminal at Winslow), where beginners can ply the calm waters inside the bay and more experienced kayakers can depart for a day trip through Rich Passage to Bremerton (see the Kitsap Peninsula chapter). **Fay-Bainbridge** is another good launch site for north-island exploration, or a base for exploring the narrow Agate Passage. Note that the launch site here is unprotected from the wind. For exploration of the southern shores of Bainbridge, put in at the **Fort Ward State Park** boat launch (see above).

On Vashon, a particularly good day trip is the quiet water inside **Quartermaster Harbor** at Maury Island. Good launch sites are available on the harbor side of Portage (the isthmus connecting Maury Island to Vashon) or at nearby **Dockton** or **Burton Acres** parks. Launch at the Portage site, and you can circumnavigate the whole of Maury "Island" and return to the same spot.

Many kayakers putting in at Vashon's **Dolphin Point** do so to make the 1.5-mile exposed crossing to **Blake Island,** the southern half of which is an undeveloped state park site with good, though primitive, campsites. For experienced paddlers, the island also is a reasonable hop from either **Fort Ward** or **Manchester** State Parks.

Four sites in this area—**Fay-Bainbridge** and **Fort Ward** State Parks on Bainbridge and **Wingehaven** (near the ferry terminal) and **Lisabeula** (southwestern shore, on Colvos Passage) Parks on Vashon—are designated campsites for the **Cascadia Marine Trail** from Olympia to Vancouver Island. Kayakers also should note several other Vashon public beaches accessible only from the water: **Department of Natural Resources (DNR) Beach 85** near Point Beals; **DNR Beach 83** on Maury Island near Portage; **DNR Beach 79,** northeast of Tahlequah; and **DNR Beaches 77 and 78,** two small beach patches on Colvos Passage on Vashon's west shore.

For kayak rentals and lessons, see the Greater Seattle chapter.

Boating/Sailing

On Bainbridge, a wide range of marine services is available on Eagle Harbor, near Winslow. **Eagle Harbor Waterfront Park** has guest moorage and great access to Winslow stores. **Harbour Marina,** (206) 842-6502, has guest moorage available if scheduled ahead. It's also the site of the Harbour Pub, a favorite local brewhouse. **Winslow Wharf Marina,** (206) 842-4202, has full boater services, plus a supply store, The Chandlery. **Eagle Harbor Marina,** (206) 842-4003, has limited moorage on the south side of the harbor.

On Vashon, **Dockton Park** in Quartermaster Harbor, (206) 463-2947, has 60 guest slips and other facilities, including a nice park area on the upland portion. Between the two islands, **Blake Island Marine State**

Park is a favorite local boater destination, with ample dock space, hiking trails, campsites, and picnic facilities.

outside in

Attractions

You could spend an entire day just visiting all the **Vashon Island**–based companies that market their goods both locally and nationally. Some of these offer tours (call ahead to make arrangements). The list includes **K2 Skis Inc.,** (206) 463-3631, one of the world's largest manufacturers of alpine skis and snowboards; **Seattle's Best Coffee** (formerly SBC), Island Hwy, (206) 463-3932; **Maury Island Farms** (99th and 204th on Island Hwy; (206) 463-9659), with berries and preserves. **Wax Orchards** (131st SW north of 232nd; (206) 463-9735) is no longer open for tours, but you can stop by and pick up fresh preserves, fruit syrups, and apple cider.

Many of these island products are available at **The Country Store and Farm** (20211 Vashon Hwy SW, south of Vashon Center; (206) 463-3655), a wonderful old-fashioned general store that also stocks potted herbs, gardening supplies, and natural-fiber apparel. Across the street is **Sound Food Restaurant** (20312 Vashon Hwy SW at SW 204th Street; (206) 463-3565), a mellow, wood-floored place with healthy soups, salads, sandwiches, and aromatic home-baked goods. Good espresso, too.

Stop by **Blue Heron Art Center** (19704 Vashon Hwy SW, (206) 463-5131), an art gallery displaying changing exhibits that is also home to **Vashon Allied Arts,** offering live arts events—from literary, to dance, to folk music, to theater—on weekends from September through June (and sometimes in the summer). The new **Heron's Nest Gallery** in the center of town now houses the Blue Heron's former crafts gallery, featuring the crafts of many local artisans.

Vashon's biggest affair is the **Strawberry Festival** in mid-July, when a parade, music, and crafts celebrate the island's prolific berry. Some farms on Vashon have **U-pick strawberries and raspberries,** in case you miss the big day, and foragers will be pleased to note that wild raspberries abound, roadside and elsewhere in late summer. Bring along a bucket.

Must-see stops on **Bainbridge Island** include **Bloedel Reserve,** (206) 842-7631, which comprises 150 acres of lush, tranquil gardens, woods, meadows, and ponds. Plants from all over the world make the grounds interesting at any time of the year. Open Wednesday through Sunday; reservations are required and limited. For a simpler trip, ride over on the ferry, sans car, and walk a short way up the road to the small, family-owned **Bainbridge Island Winery** (682 Hwy 305, (206) 842-WINE), which makes a number of good wines, including a superb strawberry (informal tours Sunday at 2pm, tastings Wednesday through Sunday, noon to 5pm). If it's early in the day, stroll a few blocks through downtown Winslow and have coffee and pastry at **Pegasus Espresso House** (131 Parfitt Way SW; (206) 842-3113) or at **Bainbridge Bakers** in Winslow Green. In the evening, saunter down to the **Harbour Pub** (231 Parfitt Way SW; (206) 842-0969), overlooking Eagle Harbor, to partake in fish 'n' chips and catch up on the local microbrews and micronews. If you're in a car, make your way to **Lynwood Center,** the island's lesser commercial enclave, featuring two excellent restaurants and Bainbridge's only movie theater.

Restaurants

Back Bay Inn ☆☆ The restaurant at the Back Bay Inn, a treat for islanders, is beginning to make Vashon a destination for dinner (luckily there are four antique-filled rooms upstairs if you want to avoid the ferry ride home). *In the community of Burton; (206) 463-5355; 24007 Vashon Hwy SW, Vashon; $$$.*

Dog Day Cafe and Juice Bar ☆ A stylish street-side cafe with great espresso (made with SBC, of course), interesting lunch fixings, and squeezed-to-order juice. *Corner of Vashon Hwy and SW Bank Rd; (206) 463-6404; 17530 Vashon Hwy SW, Vashon; $.*

Pleasant Beach Grill ☆☆ Bainbridge Island's only white-linen restaurant is tucked away in a large Tudor house on the island's southwest corner. Locals have always favored the pine-paneled bar, warmed by a fireplace, and appreciated the grill's pleasant consistency. *Follow signs toward Fort Ward State Park; near Lynwood Center; (206) 842-4347; 4738 Lynwood Center Rd NE, Bainbridge; $$.*

Ruby's on Bainbridge ☆☆ A steamy, garlicky little place—just casual enough for the locals, just sumptuous enough for weekend guests and day trippers. *Follow signs toward Fort Ward State Park; in Lynwood Center; (206) 780-9303; 4569 Lynwood Center Rd, Bainbridge; $$.*

Sawatdy Thai Cuisine ☆☆ Some of the best Thai food in Seattle can be found here on Bainbridge Island. Every fragrant dish is well executed and each customer well cared-for. Reservations are a good idea. *Take Hwy 305, turn west on High School Rd, north on Fletcher Bay Rd to Island Center; (206) 780-2429; 8770 Fletcher Bay Rd, Bainbridge; $.*

Streamliner Diner ☆   An island institution since 1981 and a short walk from the ferry dock, the Diner built its reputation on satisfying breakfasts and inventive entrees—Mom food with a creative twist. Expect a line on weekends. *Winslow Way and Bejune; (206) 842-8595; 397 Winslow Way, Bainbridge; $.*

Turtle Island Cafe ☆   Just off the main drag through downtown Vashon is Turtle Island Cafe, a small, friendly restaurant with wonderful food. A favorite of many islanders. *Near intersection of Vashon Hwy and SW Bank Road; (206) 463-2125; 9924 SW Bank Rd, Vashon; $$.*

Lodgings

Beach Cottage B&B ☆   This charming four-cottage setup is across Eagle Harbor from the town of Winslow. Each cottage has a queen-size bed, a kitchen (stocked with breakfast fixings), logs for the fireplace, and a deck with views of Eagle Harbor. Smoking is allowed (pets and children under 16 are not). *4 miles from the ferry off Eagle Harbor Dr; (206) 842-6081; 5831 Ward Ave NE, Bainbridge; $$$.*

The Bombay House ☆☆   This sprawling turn-of-the-century house with a widow's walk, set in a lavish flower garden with a rough-cedar gazebo overlooking scenic Rich Passage, is just a sweet stroll from Fort Ward State Park. Children over 6 years are welcome. *4 miles south of the ferry, just off W Blakely Ave (call for directions); (206) 842-3926 or (800) 598-3926; 8490 NE Beck Rd, Bainbridge; $$.*

Vashon Chamber of Commerce can offer bed and breakfast and lodging information on the island; call (206) 463-6217.

Cheaper Sleeps

AYH Ranch/Hostel   This 10-acre Vashon spread with a wonderfully hokey Old West theme is wonderfully cheap. Sleep in a covered wagon or a Sioux-style teepee, or bunk in hostel dorm rooms. Everyone gets access to firewood, bicycles, and do-it-yourself pancake breakfasts at no extra charge. *(206) 463-2592; 12119 SW Cove Road, Vashon.*

More Information

Bainbridge Chamber of Commerce: *(206) 842-3700.*
Vashon Island Chamber of Commerce: *(206) 463-6217.*
Washington State Ferries: *(800) 84-FERRY.*

Tacoma and Gig Harbor

From Fort Lewis north to Key Peninsula, east to Dash Point, and south to Spanaway Lake, including Commencement Bay, Point Defiance Park and Kopachuck, Penrose Point, Joemma Beach, and Dash Point State Parks.

Tacoma has never quite gotten over the image thing: polluted waterfront, toxic soils, high crime rate—and the ubiquitous aroma of industrial activity. The truth, much to the chagrin of city leaders, is that the image lingers because it is, at least in part, based in fact. In spite of their protestations to the contrary, Tacoma's aroma—both in its figurative and literal senses—persists.

But a larger truth is starting to seep out around the edges of Puget Sound's second most powerful urban base: Tacoma has turned the corner. Granted, the town still can smell like month-old tuna when the wind blows in, and some downtown streets are places where you definitely don't want to run out of gas on Saturday night. But to focus solely on that would be to ignore the amazing amount of good that's sprouted in the past decade along Commencement Bay.

The city is rebuilding itself the only way it can, and the only way it should—from the waterline up. Decaying industries have been blown up, scooped up, and hauled away, and replaced by waterfront parks, walkways, and marinas. Arts, business, and educational institutions are reclaiming downtown. Tourists are returning. Location is the lure: Tacoma occupies the ultimate site for a Puget Sound city—right on the salt water, yet close enough to Mount

Rainier for its residents to feel the cold wind rolling off the mountain's glaciers. The city's idyllic setting, in fact, probably has fanned much of the regional scorn for its squandered opportunities.

Today, finally, the city is learning to embrace its location, treating it as a drawing card instead of a pleasant sidelight. Walkers, joggers, anglers, and cyclists have proliferated along the waterfront. On the water, garbage barges are outnumbered by kayaks. Make no mistake: Tacoma still is a dyed-in-the-wool industrial center. But its new industry, which includes an aggressive waterfront container-shipping operation, is one that can live with, rather than exploit, the environment. The mix is sort of refreshing. And it's working. Tacoma has come so far in this respect that it now competes for, rather than waves through, Saturday-afternoon recreators who once took their canoes and picnic baskets across Tacoma Narrows to the sparkling beaches and parks around Gig Harbor.

Combined, Tacoma, Gig Harbor, and the rural Key Peninsula are a maritime combination tough to beat. From the seat of a boat off Point Defiance, gazing at Mount Rainier on one side, the Olympics on the other, we're almost tempted to pack a Ryder and move south. Then the wind shifts, and...We'll be honest. We *still* don't want to live here. But we sure are getting used to visiting.

Getting There

IMPORTANT NOTICE: In 1997, area codes in the Greater Seattle area are scheduled to change, affecting counties that currently share the (206) code. Please be advised that codes listed throughout this chapter may have been changed.

Tacoma, strategically located dead center in the Puget Sound basin, is 32 miles south of Seattle and 30 miles north of Olympia on Interstate 5. Any of the main downtown exits will take you to the city center and to most of the waterfront attractions described below. To reach the Gig Harbor area, take exit 132 (Gig Harbor/Bremerton) from I-5 and drive west across the Tacoma Narrows Bridge, following signs to the small town on the east side of the highway. Bus service to Tacoma from the Seattle area is available from Pierce Transit; (800) 562-8109.

Adjoining Areas

NORTH: **Greater Seattle; Kitsap Peninsula**

SOUTH: **Olympia and the Nisqually Delta**

EAST: **Snoqualmie Pass Corridor (Mountains-to-Sound Greenway); Mount Rainier National Park**

WEST: **Hood Canal**

Parks/Beaches

Point Defiance Park

This is the waterfront sun around which Tacoma's recreation world orbits. Fittingly so, since all the best natural features of Tacoma and the South Sound are found here: miles of sparkling saltwater beaches, scenic mountain views, a healthy trail system for hikers and cyclists, some rare old-growth timber, well-kept gardens, and even a zoo for the kid in all of us. Point Defiance is truly one of the most magnificent city parks in the country. It's also one of the largest—only New York's Central Park has more acreage.

This 700-acre outdoor smorgasbord is best sampled on foot. Many miles of trails interlace in the park. Not all of them are well signed, but they do wander past some impressive old trees—a rarity this close to Puget Sound. From the main parking area just inside the entrance, you can take a 5- to 7-mile stroll around the park's perimeter by using **Five Mile Road** as a navigational aid. Trails generally parallel this popular one-way drive that offers Puget Sound and Olympic Mountain views from pullouts. On Saturday mornings, you can forget the often-confusing trail network and just use the road: it's reserved for bikes and walkers until 1pm.

The **Point Defiance Zoo and Aquarium**, a well-run, progressive facility, is just inside the main entrance off Park Way. The beluga whale exhibit is particularly good. Watch it, though: Belugas spit. A nearby road leads down to the park's northeast shore, then to a boathouse and nearby **Owen Beach,** a very popular sunbather hangout just west of the Vashon ferry terminal. The upper beach is a good picnic area, and (depending on tides) you can walk more than a mile west toward Point Defiance before you run out of beach. This is the only established beach access in the park, which is mostly on a high bluff bordered on one side by Dalco Passage and on the other by Tacoma Narrows. The massive boathouse here has launching elevators and a fishing pier (see below).

In the park's interior, Fort Nisqually, a replica of an 1833 Hudson's Bay outpost, is open for exploration. Some of the buildings are genuine, moved from an actual Hudson's Bay settlement near Dupont and restored for display. The park also holds a logging/railroad museum with a working steam engine, a kids' playland, and other things that will make adults cringe if all they're looking for is a quiet picnic table. Be prepared: This park might be huge, but it gets FULL of people in the summertime. *Take the Bremerton/Hwy 16 exit from I-5, the Vashon Ferry (6th Avenue) exit from*

Hwy 16, follow 6th to Pearl Street, which leads north to the park. Information: (206) 305-1000; Zoo/Aquarium (206) 591-5335.

Others

Brown's Point Park on the north side of Commencement Bay, just off Marine View Drive, offers a great view of the city. A lighthouse (complete with caretaker and historical exhibits) marks the point, where massive container ships and other waterborne behemoths traverse the narrow passage between here and the south tip of Vashon Island.

Dash Point State Park, north of Brown's Point, has a popular saltwater swimming and scuba beach. **Dash Point City Park,** which has a major saltwater fishing pier, is nearby.

Wright Park, at Division and I Streets, has nice floral gardens, a fascinating old conservatory—and the highest downtown duck-per-acre concentration.

The Thea Foss Waterway, the Commencement Bay boating channel nearest the downtown area, has its own, parklike pedestrian walkway, stretching more than a dozen blocks along the west side of the waterway to **Northwest Point Park,** a grassy picnic spot with nice bay views. You can pick up the walkway just a couple blocks north of the Tacoma Dome and walk the entire waterway.

The best waterfront facilities around Tacoma, however, are a bit farther from downtown. A slew of scenic waterfront parks and public spaces adjoins **Ruston Way,** whose 2-mile-long waterfront sidewalk is Tacoma's version of Seattle's Alki Way. It's the city's leading walking/in-line skating/skateboarding/bike route. To get started, follow Schuster Parkway west from downtown to Ruston Way, and park in one of the streetside lots, preferably one on the east end of Ruston Way. Waterfront highlights along the route are **Commencement Park,** topped by a big sundial; **Old Town Dock,** a public fishing pier/public moorage site; **Les Davis Pier,** one of the more notable public shore-fishing venues in the state (see Fishing, below) and **Marine Park,** which has a grand picnic area, beach access, and a fitness trail, among other charms. A definite be-seen place for the Lycra crowd. In the middle of all this Mount Rainier–view bliss, a fireboat station is an interesting diversion. On foot, skates, or a mountain bike, this stretch can make a great afternoon outing.

Around Point Defiance, on the Tacoma Narrows side of town, several more notable city parks await. **War Memorial Park,** at the south foot of Tacoma Narrows Bridge (Jackson exit off Hwy 16) is the best place to get an up-close look at the bridge—and to argue with your friends about just what holds the thing up. (To start the argument, just suggest "Gravity," then stand back and listen.) A trail leading down from this park to the water is a favorite entry point for scuba divers, who've taken up the intriguing (and dangerous, due to ripping-strong currents) sport of diving along the sunken remains of the former Galloping Gertie. One of them tells us he's seen octopuses down there bigger than his car. But then, it's only a VW Bug.

Farther south is **Titlow Beach Park,** a 60-acre getaway with picnic facilities, a fitness trail, hiking trails, tennis courts, a pool, several bird-inhabited ponds, and grand views of the Narrows Bridge, just up the way. The beach area, reached by following Sixth Avenue past the first entrance, all the way to a dead end, is rocky but very explorable. This is another local scuba hot spot. Mooring buoys float offshore.

In the Steilacoom area, check out **Pioneer Park** on Commercial Street (good view/picnic spot); **Saltars Point Park** (small, but there's a nice beach down some wooden steps); or **Sunnyside Beach Park** (the best local swimming/sunbathing beach; follow Lafayette Street north from the downtown area).

On the other side of the narrows, Gig Harbor offers visitors a choice of great waterfront parks on opposite shores of Carr Inlet. One of the closest, **Kopachuck State Park** (follow signs from Hwy 16 near Gig Harbor) has 3,500 feet of prime saltwater shoreline—all flat, shallow areas good for clamming and beachcombing. Kopachuck includes an underwater scuba park, and a short kayak paddle away is **Cutts Island,** a tiny marine state park. On the opposite shore is **Penrose Point State Park** (take the Hwy 302 exit from Hwy 16; follow signs), a spectacular site with nearly 12,000 feet of shoreline on Carr Inlet and Delano Bay. On the other side of Key Peninsula, along Case Inlet, is **Joemma Beach State Park,** the former Robert F. Kennedy State Park. (See Camping, below, for more on all three.)

Boating/Sailing

Perhaps no city of its size in the state can match the Tacoma area's wealth of maritime facilities. Boaters, whether their craft is a 7-foot Livingston or a 60-foot Grand Banks cruiser, probably will find what they're looking for here. Downtown Tacoma, the Narrows, Steilacoom, Gig Harbor, and a dozen other smaller waterfront communities all have marinas with guest moorage, boat launches, and other boater services. In addition, nearly all of the waterfront parks noted above have at least moorage floats, and usually dock space, for visiting boaters.

All serve as departure points for a rich choice of day trips on South Puget Sound. Popular summer boating destinations include **Gig Harbor** and waterfront parks and islands on **Key Peninsula** and in nearby **Carr** or

Case Inlets. Penrose Point State Park is a particularly popular destination, as are bays and parks along southern Vashon Island, such as **Dockton Park** in Quartermaster Harbor (see Bainbridge and Vashon Islands chapter).

Point Defiance Boathouse Marina, at the base of Point Defiance Park, offers the full works: extensive marine services, restaurants, a tackle shop, fishing charters, boat rentals, launch facilities, and more. It's also salmon-fishing central in Tacoma; (206) 591-5325. **Old Town Dock** on Ruston Way has guest moorage, rest rooms, and access to waterfront parks. **The 15th Street Dock,** inside the Thea Foss Waterway, is very close to downtown. You'll find moorage space here, but floatplanes have first priority. Inside Hylebos Waterway is the spiffy new **Chinook Landing Marina;** (206) 627-7676. In Steilacoom, **Steilacoom Marina** has guest moorage and other services; (206) 582-2600. To the north at Day Island is **Narrows Marina Bait and Tackle,** a noted salmon-fishing tackle shop: (206) 564-4222. This is but a sampling of the major marine facilities in the area.

On the west side of the narrows in Gig Harbor, boater moorage and services are available at **Jerrisch Park City Dock,** (206) 851-8136; **Peninsula Yacht Basin,** (206) 858-2250; and **Arabella's Landing,** (206) 851-1793. Gig Harbor's waterfront has a distinct sailing flavor. You can join the action by booking a sailboat charter trip (or powerboat rental) through Rent-A-Boat Charters; (206) 858-7341.

Fishing

Boathouses at Point Defiance and Tacoma Narrows are the epicenter of a still-thriving South Sound salmon fishery. Success in these waters has been mixed in the past decade, but the past several years have seen strong catches of hatchery-produced coho and chinook from the **Nisqually** and **Puyallup** river systems. Those fish usually arrive in late summer and are available through fall. Popular fishing spots include the immediate **Point Defiance** area, the "**Clay Banks,**" just to the east; **Point Dalco,** at the south tip of Vashon Island; and inside **Commencement Bay,** where Puyallup River–bound fish often are intercepted. Farther south, the west side of **Tacoma Narrows** (north of the bridge) and **Gibson Point** at the south end of Fox Island are good blackmouth (resident chinook) areas. Most of these areas are open all year, and have proven productive for winter blackmouth fishing.

For shore anglers, options include waterfront fishing piers at **Old Town Dock** and **Les Davis Pier,** both on Ruston Way; and **Point Defiance Boathouse,** and **Dash Point City Park.** The Les Davis Pier is particularly well equipped, with rod holders, rest rooms, and other rare niceties. Try casting a Buzz Bomb or other weighted lure, with a slow retrieve. For general salmon-fishing information, including charter bookings and boat rentals, call Point Defiance Boathouse, (206) 591-5325; or Narrows Marina Bait and Tackle, (206) 564-4222.

Good freshwater fishing in the area can be found at **Spanaway Lake** in Parkland (many planted trout, some bass), **American Lake** (rainbows, some big), and **Steilacoom Lake** (bass), both south of Tacoma near Lakewood. The **Puyallup River** upstream from Sumner can be good in the fall for migratory salmon, and fair to good in the winter for steelhead.

Hiking

Point Defiance Park, of course, is the in-city favorite, with many miles of hiking trails through cool forest. The urban walkway along the **Thea Foss Waterway** makes for a scenic, 23-block stroll for downtown visitors, as does the **Ruston Way** waterfront sidewalk, which stretches about 2 miles west. For the carless, Ruston Way is connected to the downtown area by the 2.5-mile **Bayside Trail,** which stretches from Stadium Way to Commencement Park. Parts of the wooded path seem unkempt and a bit creepy, though. **Snake Lake Nature Center,** on Tyler Street, has almost 2 miles of interesting nature trails that loop around a wildlife-rich wetland area in the middle of the city; (206) 305-1000.

Other day hikes—long enough to wear out the kids, but short enough to save the parents—can be found at **Titlow Beach Park** on the Narrows or at **Penrose Point, Joemma Beach, Kopachuck,** or **Dash Point** State Parks, all on the outskirts of town (see above for details). If none of those is enough to scratch your hiking itch (and for serious hoofers, they might not be), remember that **Mount Rainier National Park** is a mere 90 minutes away via Hwy 7, and the **Nisqually National Wildlife Refuge** is about 20 minutes south on I-5.

Kayaking/Canoeing

If the shipping traffic and the sense of general toxicity don't bother you, inner **Commencement Bay** is an adventuresome paddle. Actually, the city's inner waterways make for a fascinating day trip, mixing the heavy industry of the inner harbor with the natural feel of the Point Defiance area. Good launch points include **Point Defiance Boathouse, Owen Beach** at Point Defiance Park, **Commencement Park** on Ruston Way, **Northwest Point Park** (downtown), or **Brown's Point Park,** for cross-bay journeys.

An extensive series of canoe and kayak tours and classes is offered by Tahoma Outdoor Pursuits, located at Backpackers Supply, 5206 S Tacoma

Way; (206) 474-8155. They also offer canoe and kayak rentals and supplies.

For a more natural setting, sparkling waters, clean beaches, and a killer Mount Rainier view, cross the Narrows and try the waters inside **Case** or **Carr** Inlets. Great launching sites are found at **Joemma Beach, Kopachuck,** and **Penrose Point** State Parks. From Kopachuck (a great beginner's spot), novices can paddle a short distance to **Cutts Island,** an undeveloped state park site. Likewise, paddlers setting out from Joemma Beach can undertake a longer voyage to primitive campsites at **McMicken Island Marine State Park,** just east of Hartstene Island. Kopachuck and Joemma Beach State Parks are designated **Cascadia Marine Trail** campsites (the Cascadia Marine Trail is a state-managed water trail with campsites from Olympia to British Columbia; (206) 545-9161; see Washington Outdoors Primer).

Cycling

In downtown Tacoma, take the **Ruston Way Waterfront Tour.** Follow Pacific Avenue to Schuster Parkway, heading northwest from downtown to Ruston Way, proceed along the waterfront 2 miles to Marine Park (see Parks/Beaches, above). Not a long ride, but there's enough to do along the way to make this a good half-day venture.

Another Tacoma treat comes once a week only, when **Five Mile Road,** which loops around most of **Point Defiance Park,** is closed to auto traffic on Saturday mornings. It's a great ride for the whole family. Call Tacoma Parks, (206) 305-1000, for information.

In Gig Harbor, a popular route is the 34-mile **Crescent Lake Loop,** which takes you north on Crescent Valley Road to the lake, then back along a waterfront route. The **Key Peninsula** across Carr Inlet also offers many miles of quiet, backcountry road cycle touring.

For general cycling information, including a Pierce County Parks map of cycle routes, call Tacoma Parks, (206) 305-1000.

Camping

Finding a restful campsite in Tacoma proper is like trying to find a Kingdome supporter at an NFL owners meeting. Not likely. Luckily, plenty of beautiful sites await within 30 minutes of downtown.

Kopachuck State Park, a mere 12 miles out of town, offers 41 campsites (no hookups; maximum RV length, 35 feet) in a wooded upland area (alas, no views). The park also contains great picnic facilities (Olympic views), a sprawling clamming/beachcombing beach, and an underwater park for scuba fans. The park is open all year. Sites cannot be reserved. *Follow signs from Hwy 16 near Gig Harbor; (206) 265-3606 or (800) 233-0321.*

Penrose Point State Park, tucked inside Carr Inlet's Mayo Cove on the east shore of Key Peninsula, is an idyllic place with 83 campsites (no hookups; maximum RV length, 35 feet), a group camp, picnic facilities, boat moorage, a shallow swimming beach, and miles of hiking trails. It's a local camping hot spot, whether you arrive by car, cycle, or boat. Penrose Point is open all year. Campsites can be reserved up to 11 months in advance by calling Reservations Northwest; (800) 452-5687. *From Hwy 16 near Gig Harbor, follow signs 17 miles southwest; (206) 884-2514 or (800) 233-0321.*

Joemma Beach State Park, on Key Peninsula's west shore, is the former R. F. Kennedy Multiple Use Area. In 1995, the 22-acre park was transferred from Department of Natural Resources management to the state park system, and the name was changed to honor Joe and Emma Smith, two early residents. The nicely upgraded park now has 19 campsites (no hookups) in two loops. Also on the premises are a couple of short hiking trails, 1,000 feet of gravelly beach, and a very nice moorage dock for overnighting boaters. Joemma Beach is open all year. Campsites cannot be reserved. *Follow signs southwest from Hwy 16; (206) 884-2514 or(800) 233-0321.*

North of Tacoma along East Passage, **Dash Point State Park** is a major camper's destination, with 138 sites (28 with hookups; maximum RV length, 35 feet) on two wooded loops. The park, divided by Hwy 509, also has an extensive hiking trail system, a bluff-top picnic area with good Sound views, and a shallow beach that's a popular late-summer swimming spot. Just to the west along the shore is Dash Point City Park, with a heavily used salmon fishing pier. Dash Point is open all year. Campsites can be reserved up to 11 months in advance by calling Reservations Northwest; (800) 452-5687. *Follow signs from I-5 exit 143 near Federal Way; (206) 593-2206 or (800) 233-0321.*

Skiing/Snow Play

Washington's premier alpine ski destination, **Crystal Mountain,** is less than 90 minutes (64 miles) away, on the north foothills of Mount Rainier. Crystal has the state's greatest vertical drop (3,100 feet), extensive backcountry skiing, full ski and snowboard services, and overnight lodging; (360) 663-2265. On the southwestern slopes of the mountain is a unique cooperative **cross-country ski trail system** operated by Mount Tahoma Scenic Trails Association. Paradise Visitor Center in **Mount Rainier National Park** gives access to one of the state's best unmaintained cross-country ski venues. Call (360) 569-2211 for recorded information, and see the Mount Rainier National Park chapter of this guide.

Wildlife

Minter Creek State Hatchery is one of the best places in the state to learn about the **salmon-spawning** process. About 15 minutes from downtown Gig Harbor, the recently rebuilt hatchery is open to the public daily or for group visits by special arrangement. Always popular with the kids. Call (206) 857-5077 for directions or information.

outside in

Attractions

Much of the heavy industry that once dominated Tacoma's waterfront has left, although the tideflats are still home to one of the largest (and perhaps most ambitious) ports on the West Coast. From the observation deck at the **Port of Tacoma** (E 11th Street), you can watch as dozens of giant mechanical pincers drop like spiders from cranes overhead to pluck cargo from ships shuttling in and out of Commencement Bay throughout the day.

Buildings in the **downtown warehouse district** are being converted from industrial use to residential and commercial, and some of the old warehouses are slated for a University of Washington branch campus. The stately homes and cobblestone streets in the North End are often used as sets for Hollywood's moviemakers, and students still fill the turreted chateau of Stadium High School. **Old City Hall,** with its newly coppered roof, Renaissance clock, and bell tower; the Romanesque **First Presbyterian Church**; the rococo **Pythian Lodge**; and the one-of-a-kind coppered **Union Station**—now the much praised Federal Courthouse—delight history and architecture buffs. The old Union Station rotunda is now graced by some spectacular work by glass artist and Tacoma native Dale Chihuly. It's open at no charge during business hours.

The **Ruston Way Waterfront,** a 6-mile mix of parks and restaurants, is thronged with people in any weather (see Restaurants, below). **Pantages Center** (901 Broadway Plaza; (206) 591-5894) contains the 1,100-seat **Pantages Theater,** designed in 1918 by nationally known movie theater architect B. Marcus Priteca. It's the focal point of the reviving downtown cultural life. The nearby **Rialto Theatre** has been restored for smaller performance groups. **Tacoma Actors Guild,** Tacoma's popular professional theater—at the Commerce Street level atop the park-covered transit center, (206) 272-2145—offers an ambitious and successful blend of American classics and Northwest premieres which draw an audience from throughout the Puget Sound region.

The **Tacoma Art Museum** (12th and Pacific, (206) 272-4258) is housed in a former downtown bank, with paintings by Renoir, Degas, and Pissarro. The **Washington State Historical Museum,** (206) 593-2830, has left its previous home near Stadium High School for a new facility just south of Union Station at 1911 Pacific Avenue, with many times the previous exhibit space.

Lakewold Gardens (12221 Gravelly Lake Drive SW, (206) 584-3360), on a beautiful 10-acre site overlooking Gravelly Lake in Lakewood, is just 10 minutes south of Tacoma. Recognized nationally as among the outstanding gardens in America, they are open Thursday through Monday for guided and nonguided tours (call for details).

The **Tacoma Dome,** the world's largest wooden dome, is the site of many entertainment and trade shows as well as a sports center. Call (206) 272-6817 for ticket information. Fans who like their baseball played outdoors in a first-class ballpark come in enthusiastic droves to **Cheney Stadium** to watch the **Tacoma Rainiers,** the Class AAA affiliate of the Seattle Mariners; (206) 752-7707.

On the other side of town, the **Tacoma Narrows Bridge** connects the city to the Kitsap Peninsula via Hwy 16. The 188-foot-high and 2,800-foot-long bridge is the fourth-longest suspension bridge in the United States. Almost directly below, sitting on the bottom of the Tacoma Narrows, is the old bridge—nicknamed "Galloping Gertie" because it rippled and swayed in high winds—that collapsed in 1940. The remains of the bridge were recently added to the National Registry of Historic Sites to ensure that no one disturbs the structure in its watery grave.

Take a drive just south of Tacoma to **Steilacoom,** once a native American village and later Washington Territory's first incorporated town (1854). October's **Apple Squeeze Festival** and midsummer's **Salmon Bake**—with canoe and kayak races—are popular drawing cards. **Steilacoom Tribal Museum** is located in a turn-of-the-century church looking out upon the south Sound islands and the Olympic range. Ferries run to **Anderson Island,** with restricted runs to McNeil Island (a state penitentiary); call Pierce County Public Works Department for more information; (206) 591-7250.

A short drive (and long wait, at times, over the Narrows Bridge) north is **Gig Harbor,** a small town with big views and attractions. The town was planned for boat traffic, not automobiles (with resulting traffic congestion and limited parking), yet it is still a good place for celebrations and weekend escapes.

The action is along the waterfront, where a well-developed marina (see Boating/Sailing, above) attracts thousands of summertime boaters, and the Mount Rainier view is impressive. A variety of interesting shops and galleries lines **Harborview Drive,** the single street that almost encircles the harbor. It's a most picturesque spot for browsing and window-shopping.

An arts festival in mid-July and a jazz festival in mid-August are two main events. May through October (on Saturdays) **Gig Harbor Farmers Market** features locally grown produce, flowers, plants, and Northwest arts and crafts; Pierce Transit Park and Ride, off Hwy 16, (206) 884-2665.

Performance Circle (6615 38th Avenue NW, (206) 851-7529), Gig Harbor's resident theater group, mounts eight enjoyable productions each year, with summer shows staged outside in the meadow at 9916 Peacock Hill Avenue NW. Theatergoers bring picnics and blankets, and watch the shows beneath the stars.

Restaurants

Antique Sandwich Company   Plastic bears filled with honey adorn the shared tables; a roomy couch usually has several students curled up on it studying and eating. On the way to Point Defiance Park, it's also a favorite luncheon gathering place for the diaper set and their parents. *2 blocks south of Point Defiance Park main entrance; (206) 752-4069; 5102 N Pearl St, Tacoma; $.*

Bair Drug and Hardware Store   Except for the customers, little has changed since Bair's was built in 1895. Old post office boxes mask the bakery, which turns out pies and pastries, and there's a 1906 soda fountain still serving genuine ice cream sodas. Friday nights, come to the Bair for a steak or crab cake dinner. *Lafayette and Wilkes; (206) 588-9668; 1617 Lafayette St, Steilacoom; $.*

Bimbo's ☆   A seedy name, a seedy location, but here's a family Italian restaurant that's been attracting regulars for almost 75 years. Members of the original owner's family are still cooking their native Tuscan recipes with little regard for today's trends. *15th and Pacific; (206) 383-5800; 1516 Pacific Ave, Tacoma; $.*

Cedars III ☆   Tacoma is awash with restaurants of various ethnic bents, but Mediterranean cuisine is a rarity. For those baba ghanouj and garlic-bathed chicken cravings, be thankful for Nadim Alawar and his Cedars III restaurant (his first two are in Seattle), not far from the Narrows Bridge. *Take 6th Ave exit from Hwy 16, head west; (206) 564-0255; 7104 6th Ave, Tacoma; $$.*

The Cliff House ☆☆   A commanding view of Commencement Bay and Tacoma's north end is enhanced by formal airs and delicious, inventive

European cuisine. *Follow East Side Dr to the top of the hill; (206) 927-0400; 6300 Marine View Dr NE, Tacoma; $$$.*

East & West Cafe ☆   What this restaurant lacks in location, it makes up for tenfold in great food and charm that you'll find at this haven of Asian delights on the busy thoroughfare south of the Tacoma Mall. For the price, it's hard to have a better meal in Tacoma. *Just west of I-5, take 56th St exit; (206) 475-7755; 5319 Tacoma Mall Blvd, Tacoma; $.*

Engine House #9 ☆   A friendly neighborhood, beer-lover's dream of a tavern (minus the smoke). A sister brewpub called the **Powerhouse** opened during the summer of 1995. *6th and Pine; (206) 272-3435; 611 N Pine St, Tacoma; $.*

ER Rogers ☆   A restored 100-year-old home with an exceptional Sound view. The Steilacoom special prime rib—first roasted, then sliced and quickly seared—is tops, and you can't beat the Sunday buffet brunch with its huge selection of seafood. *Corner of Commercial and Wilkes, off Steilacoom Blvd; (206) 582-0280; 1702 Commercial St, Steilacoom; $$.*

Fujiya ☆☆   Absolute consistency continues to attract a loyal clientele from near and far to this stylish downtown Japanese restaurant. The best sushi and sashimi around. *Between Broadway and Market on Court C; (206) 627-5319; 1125 Court C, Tacoma; $$.*

Harbor Lights ☆   Decor is circa 1950, with glass floats, stuffed prize fish, and a giant lobster, but Tacoma's first Ruston Way waterfront restaurant still packs them in (reserve early) to consume buckets of steamed clams and mounds of perfectly pan-fried oysters. *City Center exit off I-5 and follow Schuster Pkwy to Ruston Way; (206) 752-8600; 2761 Ruston Way, Tacoma; $$.*

Katie Downs ☆   Katie Downs's Philadelphia-style deep-dish pizza is a winner. This place is noisy, boisterous, and fun, but remember, it is a tavern (no minors). *City Center exit off I-5, follow Schuster Pkwy onto Ruston Way; (206) 756-0771; 3211 Ruston Way, Tacoma; $.*

Lessie's Southern Kitchen ☆   If you have a hankering for the authentic fare of the South, abandon all restraint and order up some pork chops smothered with gravy, sided by long-cooked collard greens, black-eyed peas, or sweet nuggets of yams. *6th and Division; (206) 627-4282; 1716 6th Ave, Tacoma; $.*

The Lobster Shop/The Lobster Shop South ☆   This sea-weathered restaurant is a welcome change from the increasing number of pricey, slick eateries blossoming along the waterfront. The larger, swankier Lobster Shop South has a distinctly different atmosphere and menu. It provides good seafood dishes, a full bar, and elegant surroundings, but not quite the same charm of the original. *Off Dash Point Rd; (206) 927-1513; 6912 Soundview Dr NE, Tacoma (and branch); $$.*

Marco's Ristorante Italiano ☆   A busy, crowded, bustling place, with a menu ranging from the traditional to more original specials. *Two blocks up Pioneer Way from the harbor in Gig Harbor; (206) 858-2899; 7707 Pioneer Way, Gig Harbor; $$.*

Marzano's ☆   The reputation of the voluptuous cooking here still has people arriving from miles away. Reservations are needed. *Adjacent to Pacific Lutheran University; (206) 537-4191; 516 S Garfield, Parkland; $$.*

Stanley and Seaforts Steak, Chop, and Fish House ☆☆   Every seat in this restaurant has a panoramic view of Tacoma, its busy harbor, and, on a clear day, the Olympic Mountains. But it's the interesting menu selections and dependability that have made it a favorite for over 15 years. *City Center exit off I-5 (follow Hwy 7, take 38th west, right on Pacific Ave, right on 34th); (206) 473-7300; 115 E 34th St, Tacoma; $$.*

Tides Tavern   "Meet you at the Tides" has become such a universal invitation that this tavern perched over the harbor is often standing room only, especially on sunny days when the deck is open. Indulge in man-sized sandwiches, gargantuan salads, or the highly touted fish and chips. *Where Harborview and Soundview Drs meet; (206) 858-3982; 2925 Harborview Dr, Gig Harbor; $.*

Cheaper Eats

The Spar   A classic Northwest tavern in gentrified Old Town. *(206) 627-8215; 2121 N 30th St, Tacoma.*

Frisko Freeze   Tacoma's answer to (Seattle's) Dick's: A true '50s burger hangout; popular as ever. *(206) 272-6843; 1201 Division, Tacoma.*

Java Jive   The former dance hall and speakeasy turned bar is still shaped like a mondo teapot. *(206) 475-9843; 2102 S Tacoma Way, Tacoma.*

Lodging

Anderson House on Oro Bay (Anderson Island) ☆☆   A short ferry ride from Steilacoom and a few miles from the dock is a large house surrounded by 200 acres of woods. Guests have exclusive use of the whole house, with its four large bedrooms, or the option to rent an updated three-bedroom cedar fishing cabin on outer Amsterdam Bay, with a sweeping view of the Olympics. *Head up the hill from ferry to Eckenstam-Johnson Rd* *past the church, bear left at Y and continue for 3 miles to head of Oro Bay; (206) 884-4088; 12024 Eckenstam-Johnson Rd, Anderson Island; $$.*

Commencement Bay Bed & Breakfast   ☆   For business clients, this B&B offers fax, modem, and other amenities. Two of the three rooms have Commencement Bay views. Breakfast is copious. An ideal spot for University of Puget Sound visitors. *From Hwy 16, take Union exit north; west on N 26th, north on Proctor, east on N 34th, south on Union; (206) 752-8175; 3312 N Union Ave, Tacoma; $$.*

No Cabbages B&B   ☆   A relaxed environment in an old, well-loved beach house (filled with knotty pine and Northwest arts and crafts). There's boating and bird-watching—great blue herons nest nearby, and a clutter of gulls, terns, grebes, ducks, and cormorants are always around. *Take City Center exit off Hwy 16, on the east side of the bay (call for directions); (206) 858-7797; 7712 Goodman Dr NW, Gig Harbor; $.*

The Pillars   ☆☆   From the windows of this landmark house, you can see Colvos Passage, Vashon Island, and Mount Rainier. All three guest rooms are beautifully decorated with large private baths and separate reading areas furnished with writing desks and telephones. *Take the first Gig Harbor exit off Hwy 16; (206) 851-6644; 6606 Soundview Dr, Gig Harbor; $$$.*

Sheraton Tacoma Hotel   ☆☆   Adjacent to the Tacoma Convention Center; most rooms have a view of Commencement Bay or Mount Rainier. Concierge rooms include a continental breakfast and early-evening hors d'oeuvres. The mezzanine cafe is pleasant for casual meals, and **Altezzo** on the top floor has excellent Italian food. *Downtown between 13th and 15th on Broadway; (206) 572-3200; 1320 Broadway Plaza, Tacoma; $$$.*

The Villa Bed & Breakfast   ☆☆   In the heart of Tacoma's historic residential North End is a gracious home that stands out from the crowd: open and airy, with high arched windows, tiled roof, and a palm tree out front. *Call for directions; (206) 572-1157; 705 N 5th St, Tacoma; $$.*

More Information

Tacoma/Pierce County Visitors and Convention Bureau: *(360) 627-2836.*

Tacoma Parks: *(206) 305-1000.*

Pierce Transit: *(800) 562-8109.*

Backpackers Supply: *(206) 472-4402.*

Point Defiance Boathouse (fishing gear and licenses): *(206) 591-5325.*

Tahoma Outdoor Pursuits (guided trips): *(206) 474-8155.*

Olympia
and the Nisqually
Delta

From Squaxin Island south to Black Lake, east to Nisqually Delta, and north to Johnson Point, including Budd Inlet, Capitol Lake, the lower Deschutes River, Tumwater Falls, Squaxin Island and Millersylvania Memorial State Parks, Percival Landing, and the Nisqually National Wildlife Refuge.

Two things would happen if large numbers of hikers, kayakers, picnickers, and cyclists began converging en masse on Olympia. Nervous legislators would panic, wondering what they did to offend these usually placid beasts of the forest and field. And large numbers of hikers, kayakers, picnickers, and cyclists would find out they've been missing a great outdoors getaway. In many ways, our state capital typifies Puget Sound–area recreation offerings: it doesn't look like much from the freeway, but once you get in up to your knees…Whoa: nice place!

This quiet, unassuming city at the southern tip of Puget Sound had big aspirations back in 1846 when it marked the northern end of the Oregon Trail. Its aspirations grew even bigger in the early 1870s, when city fathers banked on Olympia becoming the northern terminus of the approaching Northern Pacific Railroad. Nice try. The railroad went to Tacoma instead (and likely still regrets its choice…). Olympia fought tooth and nail for—and won—state government.

The city may have settled for a second choice. But in doing so, residents picked up a lifestyle that's purely first class. Olympia's 30,000 government workers, students, and other inhabitants

gained a permanent job base (indeed, a growth industry)—government—
without sacrificing the area's greatest resource, its pleasant natural setting.
(For the opposite, big-industry alternative, see Tacoma, the "winner" in
this game, just up the road.) The result: hidden treasure remains stashed
all around Olympia. And we don't mean gold coin, or even fine works of
art squirreled away from the Capitol Rotunda. Tucked away on the shores
of Budd and nearby Eld Inlets are a series of deliciously fresh waterfront
parks, quiet cycling paths, and a largely man-made freshwater body,
Capitol Lake, that's as rich in history as it is in recreational splendor.

Olympians are a deceptively hip bunch, and they have a good thing
going here. It's up to you to find out how good. Plan on spending a long
day. That should allow plenty of time to explore Capitol Lake, at least one
of the saltwater parks, and perhaps to stroll through a portion of the
nearby Nisqually National Wildlife Refuge—one of the last unspoiled
estuaries on the West Coast—on the way home.

We have but one plea: when you go, park your rig in a parking lot at
the Capitol Campus. The mere sight of all those Yak Racks in one place
could do those shut-in legislators—and, ultimately, all of us—a world of
good.

Getting There

Olympia is a 60-mile drive south of Seattle on Interstate 5. The Nisqually
River Delta is 50 miles south of Seattle on I-5. The best access is through the
Nisqually National Wildlife Refuge, exit 114.

Adjoining Areas

NORTH: **Tacoma and Gig Harbor; Hood Canal**

EAST: **Mount Rainier National Park**

WEST: **Grays Harbor: Westport and Ocean Shores**

Wildlife

For bird lovers, it doesn't get much better than the **Nisqually National**
Wildlife Refuge, a sprawling 2,818-acre river-bottom wildlife magnet at
the Nisqually River Delta. In recent years, the Nisqually has become the
proverbial line in the sand for many Puget Sound area conservationists,
who seek to prevent suburban and light industrial development here.
They have good reason: the Nisqually is the only undeveloped drainage
basin left between Mount Rainier and Puget Sound. The lower valley also

is a fertile crescent, of sorts, for the Puget Sound basin. Some of the oldest human remains ever discovered in Washington were unearthed here.

The lower Nisqually drainage has been protected since 1974 by the wildlife refuge, which has become an extremely popular outdoor getaway. More than 70,000 visitors a year lug their binoculars and Audubon field guides down here every year. Most head straight for the 5-mile Brown Farm Dike Trail, which follows the top of a berm separating the former Brown Farm from the salt water and the Nisqually. It's a favorite walkway of bird-watchers and hikers, who enjoy the flat, peaceful grade. This truly is a great place to watch birds. The loop trail puts you right in their midst: On the outer portions, flocks of small **shorebirds** hop through the mudflats of the river delta or the saltwater shoreline. On the inner side, **raptors,** small **perching birds,** and thousands of **ducks, geese,** and other **waterfowl** are attracted to the flat, marshy terrain. For the serious birdwatcher and photographer, side trails lead inside the refuge to nicely placed photo blinds.

The Nisqually Refuge, open all year but most heavily bird-populated in the winter, is a major migratory stop for **mallards, widgeon, teal, Canada geese,** and many other birds. **Redtailed hawks** and **bald eagles** are year-round residents. Also commonly seen on the grounds are **coyotes, deer, otters,** and other friendly mammals. Much of the wildlife is best viewed by canoe or kayak (see below for launch information).

This is an educational facility, as well. The **Twin Barns Education Center,** a short walk from the parking lot, is filled with interpretive displays. It's open from 10am to 3pm weekends. Separate 1-mile and ½-mile nature loops are available for those who don't want to stroll the entire 5-mile outer loop. Most of the refuge is wheelchair accessible.

One word of caution: The entire lower Nisqually was hit with record flooding during the winter of 1995–1996. Damage to trails and facilities closed the refuge for several months. Call the refuge at (360) 753-9467 to check on repair status before visiting. Also, note that local hunting closes the dike trail for short periods. Call first. The refuge is off I-5, exit 114, about 10 miles north of Olympia. You can pay a voluntary $2-per-family admission fee at the main trailhead, near the parking lot.

For a unique trip along the refuge shorelines, guided raft tours can be booked through Nisqually Reach Nature Center in Olympia; (360) 459-0387.

Parks

Here's where our capital city really shines. Some extremely nice saltwater shorelines are to be found among Olympia's myriad south Puget Sound rocky points, inlets, and bays. The best day trip is actually a four-in-one: Percival Landing waterfront park, Capitol Lake Park, Tumwater Historical Park, and Tumwater Falls Park are connected by a trail and the Capitol Lake Causeway (about 3 miles), nearly all of it along the saltwater or freshwater shoreline.

We'll consider them one at time. On the downtown waterfront itself is **Percival Landing,** a waterfront gathering spot with an observation tower to scan the Olympic Mountains, Budd Inlet, and the south Sound. It's at the foot of W State Street.

Just to the south, within easy walking distance from Percival Landing on the waterfront boardwalk, lies **Capitol Lake,** a great day-trip destination for walkers, joggers, in-line skaters, or picnickers. The lake was created nearly 50 years ago, when city leaders got fed up with the pungent Deschutes river-mouth mudflat and built a dam to seal the fresh water in, the salt water out. Today, the lake is a nice scenic area connected by waterfront paths and streets to the downtown waterfront.

The focus is on the northeast shore, at **Capitol Lake Park,** a good picnic and swimming area. From here, you can catch the Capitol Lake trail and walk south toward the Capitol, cut across the lake on a small fishing pier/tidal dam to **Marathon Park,** then return on the opposite shore, along Deschutes Parkway. The entire route is along the water, with good views of the Capitol dome. A series of docks and beach accesses make this lake a favorite of canoeists, kayakers, and sailors in training. Another option from Marathon Park is to continue south up the trail on the west shore of the lake, crossing beneath I-5 and continuing to Tumwater Historical Park and Tumwater Falls (see below).

A short distance upstream from Capitol Lake is one of the area's best grounds for exploring, **Tumwater Historical Park.** The park—on a peninsula jutting into Capitol Lake just east of the I-5 overpass—has two boat launches, historical homes open for tours (one of them built—no joke—by Bing Crosby's grandfather), and nice waterfront trails. You can walk here on the Capitol Lake causeway trail—about 3 miles (one way) from Percival Landing.

Keep walking, to another close-by scenic park, **Tumwater Falls,** a short distance up Deschutes Parkway. It's the water: a trail leads down one side of the long, cascading falls on the Deschutes, then crosses the river on a footbridge, and returns on the opposite bank, near the Deschutes Brewery. To reach both parks, take the Brewery exit from I-5 and follow signs to Deschutes Parkway.

Northeast of downtown—a nice bike ride from the downtown waterfront—is **Priest Point Park,** a city park that was Olympia's first, best waterfront recreation area. The park, built on an old mission site, straddles Boston Harbor Road. You ll find miles of upland hiking trails (some through old-growth fir and red cedar), multiple paths to the saltwater beach on Budd Inlet, an extensive floral garden, picnic facilities, and other attractions. To get there, follow Plum Street (it becomes Boston Harbor Road) north from downtown. A marked cycle route runs all the way to the park, about 2 miles from the city center.

North of Priest Point, between downtown and Boston Harbor, is another popular Thurston County getaway, **Burfoot Park.** This park, about 7 miles outside Olympia on Boston Harbor Road, has a great fine-gravel beach area (a major sunbather hangout), good picnic facilities, and a surprisingly interesting trail system that includes a short, family-friendly nature trail.

Northwest of downtown, **Geoduck Beach** at The Evergreen State College is worth exploring. Ask for directions at the parking booth just inside the main entrance. Nearby **Fry Cove County Park** has 2,000 acres of shoreline and a nice wooded upland area. This pleasant picnic spot is on Eld Inlet, at the end of Boardman Road NW.

Northeast of town along Nisqually Reach is **Tolmie State Park,** a day-use area with an extensive trail system, picnic facilities, and an offshore underwater park/fishing reef. Follow signs from I-5 exit 111.

Hiking

The **Capitol Lake causeway** walk described above is a great half-day hiking trip for visitors parked either at the waterfront, capitol campus, or near Tumwater Falls. Most of the beachfront day-use parks described above also offer short day-hiking trails.

The **Nisqually National Wildlife Refuge** (see Wildlife, above) is a favorite day-hiking spot for many Olympians. Farther south down I-5, **Millersylvania Memorial State Park** (see Camping, below) has more than 7 miles of mostly easy trails, plus an exercise track.

Also south of town, in the Black Hills area, is a sprawling series of backcountry trails in the hills of **Capitol State Forest,** which lies between the south edge of Olympia and the western leg of US 12. The forest, managed by the state Department of Natural Resources, is on the northern edge of a vast sea of heavily logged foothills, stretching from the outskirts of Olympia southwest all the way to Willapa Bay. Many miles of trails are marked here, some connecting to DNR campgrounds (see Camping, below), many leading to stunning mountaintop vistas, such as the summit of **Capitol Peak.** Alas, most of these trails are open to—and heavily used by—dirt bikes and other annoying industrial-revolution byproducts. Trails here are becoming quite popular with mountain bikers, but hikers walk them at their own risk. It should be noted that some trails, such as those emanating from **Fall Creek** and **Margaret McKenny** campgrounds (see Camping, below) are closed to ORV use.

Finally, a historical/geologic mystery for centuries, the **Mima Mounds,** make for an interesting walk in a setting you won't soon forget. (See Attractions, below.)

Camping

The best public camping venues in the Olympia area are outside the city. **Millersylvania Memorial State Park** once was the 850-acre estate of Johann Mueller, an Austrian general exiled to these parts in the late 19th century. Now it's a very pretty, diverse state park with a nice camping area, hiking trails, and swimming (and good trout fishing) in Deep Lake. The park's 187 campsites (52 with hookups; maximum RV length, 45 feet) are nicely set in a stand of stately firs. It's popular with both tenters and RVers. The completing touch is a series of historic Civilian Conservation Corps-era buildings. This is a good family park, with convenient I-5 access. Millersylvania is open all year. Campsites can be reserved up to 11 months in advance by calling Reservations Northwest; (800) 452-5687. *I-5 exit 95, east on Maytown Road, north on Tilley Road; (360) 753-1519 or (800) 233-0321.*

For boaters and paddlers, **Squaxin Island State Park,** a boat-in-only campground at the long, skinny island's south tip, is a nice retreat. Its 20 primitive campsites are well suited for small tents. Call (800) 233-0321.

The **Capitol State Forest** (see Hiking, above) has a series of small campgrounds, all managed by the Department of Natural Resources. They are **Porter Creek, Middle Waddell, Yew Tree, Mount Molly, Fall Creek,** and **Margaret McKenny.** Only the latter two are off-limits to the noisy dirt bikes and ORVs that frequent this area, and even they are too close for comfort for many campers. Also, most of these campgrounds are used by hunters in the fall. A DNR-managed campsite (small) is **Mima Falls Trailhead,** off Hwy 121 near Little Rock. All these campgrounds are free, and are accessed either from US 12 or Hwy 121, both west of I-5. *Call the DNR at (360) 902-1000 or (360) 902-1234.*

Boating/Sailing

Olympia is a boater's heaven. On the downtown waterfront along Budd Inlet, three modern marina facilities await: private **West Bay Marina,** (360) 943-2022; the Port of Olympia's **East Bay Marina,** (360) 786-1400; and **Percival Landing Park,** (360) 753-8382, home of the Olympia Yacht Club. All have guest moorage, nearby marine services, and good access to downtown shopping, restaurants, and walkways to Capitol Lake parks. A day trip from here, out the inlet and across to **Squaxin Island State Park,** is a great summer outing. (Ask about boat rentals at the marina offices.) Another nearby moorage and marine-services site is quaint **Boston Harbor Marina**; (360) 357-5670. **Zittel's Marina** near Johnson Point is a popular angler's departure point; (360) 459-1950.

Launch ramps are found at **Tumwater Historical Park, Boston Harbor,** and **Eld Inlet,** as well as **Luhr Beach,** near the mouth of the Nisqually River.

Fishing

Fittingly, **salmon** is king in Washington's capital city. South Sound areas outside the city are byways for many runs of migratory hatchery **coho** and **chinook,** as well as **blackmouth** (resident chinook). Many of the latter are raised in net pens in Capitol Lake, then trucked and released in streams around the state. Unlike many areas in the Central and North Sound, where concern over threatened wild stocks has vastly curtailed summertime fishing, salmon angling is still a year-round activity from the Port of Olympia. The reason: nearly all the fish migrating to and from south Sound streams are hatchery-produced, thus subject to fewer restrictions. Seasons and runs change annually, but in recent years, the south Sound has been one of the few Washington saltwater areas open for fishing all year. Typically, **blackmouth** are taken all year (but fishing is best in the winter); **migratory chinook and coho** peak in July and August; and some **resident coho** are available in midsummer and midwinter.

Most of the best salmon action is found to the north, off **Johnson Point**; off the east side of **Hartstene Island**; off **Devil's Head;** and at Tacoma-area hot spots such as the **"Clay Banks"** and **Point Defiance** (see the Tacoma and Gig Harbor chapter). Tacoma-area boathouses also are your best bet for lining up a charter trip to hook a summer chinook bound for the **Puyallup** or **Nisqually Rivers.** But anglers with their own boats can find decent fishing close to Olympia. The circle of open water formed by **Cooper Point, Hunter Point, Squaxin Island,** and **Boston Harbor** can be a good blackmouth producer all year long, especially in late winter. **Lyle Point,** at the south end of Anderson Island, also is a known blackmouth producer. For general salmon and boat rental information, call Zittel's Marina, (360) 459-1950.

Smelt dippers often report success all year round from beaches near Boston Harbor, off the north side of Squaxin Island, and at the inner banks of Totten Inlet. Call the Boston Harbor Marina, (360) 357-5670, to find out when the smelt are running.

Trout fishing can be productive in Black, Ward, Hicks, Long, Patterson, St. Claire, Offut, and Deep Lakes. For fishing tips and licenses, call Tumwater Sports, (360) 357-6775.

Also, the **Deschutes River** produces a few winter steelhead. Where the river enters Capitol Lake, a **fall chinook** fishery has been a well-kept secret.

Kayaking/Canoeing

Budd, Totten, Eld, and **Henderson Inlets** are excellent kayak territory. Their waters are fairly protected, and beach landings at waterfront parks are many (see Waterfront Parks, above). A good launching spot is Boston Harbor. Experienced paddlers also can begin here and make an overnight trip north across Dana Passage to **Squaxin Island State Park.** Currents in the passage can be dangerous for beginners, however.

Beginning kayakers and canoeists will love the quiet waters of **Capitol Lake.** Launch at Capitol Lake Park, Marathon Park, or Tumwater Historical Park, and miles of smooth, scenic waters are at your disposal. You can even paddle up to the frothy waters at the base of Tumwater Falls.

The saltwater estuary around the **Nisqually Delta** is another very popular canoe/kayak destination. A good launch site is **Luhr Beach,** at the mouth of McAlister Creek. Follow Old Hwy 99 and Meridian Road from I-5 exit 114. (Note: No launch facilities are found inside the Nisqually National Wildlife Refuge.)

Biking

The Capitol Campus and downtown Olympia both are good starting points for urban bike ventures. Head south up the shores of **Capitol Lake,** following Deschutes Parkway several miles to Tumwater Falls. Or scoot the other way out of town, following Plum Street to East Bay Road, which becomes Boston Harbor Road, for a great day trip with stops at **Priest Point Park, Burfoot County Park,** and finally, the quaint Sound-side village of **Boston Harbor.** Round trip is about 15 miles, and much of the road there has a marked cycle path.

Some mountain bikers don't share hikers' disdain for the ORV activity in the **Capitol State Forest** (see the Hiking and Camping sections, above.) Several routes there, particularly the 20-mile **Capitol Peak Tour** off Hwy 121, as well as numerous routes near the **Rock Candy Mountain** entrance off Hwy 8, have become popular mountain bike tours. Call the Department of Natural Resources, (360) 902-1000 or (360) 902-1234, for information about seasonal openings and closings, and other routes in this rugged area.

Adventure Calendar

Capital Lakefair: third weekend in July; (360) 943-7344.
Harbor Days (tugboat races): Labor Day weekend; (360) 357-3370.
Wooden Boat Show, Percival Landing: mid-May; (360) 357-3370.

outside in

Attractions

As home of the state capitol and three colleges, Olympia is an interesting mix of bureaucrats, lawmakers, students, and professors. You can plan an entire afternoon visit around the capitol campus alone, but much of the town closes up shop over the summer; the best time to visit is springtime, when the Legislature, the universities, and the businesses are all in full swing.

Most stages of the lawmaking process are open to the public. The **Legislative Building,** with the fourth-tallest dome in the world, is home to the Senate and House of Representatives chambers, as well as the Governor's office. Legislative sessions, always good entertainment, can be viewed from above. Just opposite the Legislative Building rises the pillared **Temple of Justice,** seat of the State Supreme Court. Stop by the **State Capitol Visitors Center** (14th Avenue and Capitol Way; (360) 586-3460) for guidance about sights. Free tours of the Capitol buildings, including the **Governor's Mansion,** can be arranged by calling (360) 586-TOUR. The grounds themselves are beautifully strollable, with their well-manicured lawns, centerpiece sunken garden, and conservatory greenhouse. The **State Capitol Museum** (211 W 21st Avenue; (360) 753-2580), a few blocks south of the Capitol's campus, houses a permanent state-history exhibit, including an outstanding collection of Native American baskets.

In the town is a surprising variety of galleries, offbeat shops, cafes, and restaurants. **Dancing Goats Espresso** (124 E Fourth Avenue; (360) 754-8187) offers fine espresso, sweet treats, and a mellow and slightly upscale atmosphere. Environmentally friendly **Radiance** (113 E Fifth Avenue; (360) 357-5250) has an entire wall of herbs, teas, and spices. Meanwhile, some of the best coffee you'll find anywhere brews a block away. **Batdorf and Bronson Coffee Roasters** (513 S Capitol Way; (360) 786-6717) has a large following of folks who don't care if there *is* a Starbucks across the street.

In downtown proper, the **Washington Center for the Performing Arts** (512 Washington Street SE; (360) 753-8586) has brought new life.

In the same block is the **Marianne Partlow Gallery,** a leading outlet for contemporary painting and sculpture. The **Capitol Theatre** (206 E Fifth Avenue; (360) 754-5378) is a showcase for locally produced plays, musicals, and Olympia Film Society–sponsored flicks.

On Seventh Avenue between Washington and Franklin Streets is the restored **Old Capitol,** whose pointed towers and high-arched windows suggest a late medieval chateau. In another part of the downtown, just off the Plum Street exit from I-5 and adjacent to City Hall, is the newly installed **Yashiro Japanese Garden,** which honors one of Olympia's sister cities.

Wholly different in character is **West Fourth Avenue** between Columbia and Water Streets, a hangout for students and ex-students, artists and would-be artists, and various counterculture members. Increasingly, **Percival Landing** (a new park, see Parks, above) is becoming a community focal point, the site of harbor festivals of all kinds.

At the northernmost end of Capitol Way, on Olympia's waterfront, is the lively **Olympia Farmers Market,** which displays produce, flowers, and crafts from all over the south Sound area; open Thursday through Sunday during the growing season (days vary monthly); (360) 352-9096.

A triad of colleges is found here: **The Evergreen State College** (TESC), west of Olympia, on Cooper Point; **St. Martin's,** a Benedictine monastery and college in adjacent Lacey; and **South Puget Sound Community College,** just across Hwy 101. TESC—one of the top-rated liberal arts schools in the country—offers a regular schedule of plays, films, and experimental theater, as well as special events such as its annual February Tribute to Asia. Its beautiful, woodsy campus includes an organic farm and 3,100 feet of beachfront property. The campus library and pool are public; (360) 866-6000, ext. 6128.

The historic heart of the whole area (Olympia, Lacey, and Tumwater) is **Tumwater Falls,** where the Deschutes River flows into Capitol Lake. Established here today is the chief local industry, the Tumwater Division of the **Pabst Brewing Company,** with free daily tours.

In Tenino, the educational **Wolf Haven** (3111 Offut Lake Road, Tenino, off the Tenino exit from I-5; (800) GIV-WOLF) is a nationally renowned sanctuary/research facility that's home to nearly 40 wolves. Staff members teach wolf appreciation and invite the public to join the wolves in a summertime "howl-in" (Friday and Saturday nights, May through September, by reservation only). They operate hourly tours year-round (closed Tuesday). Admission is $5 for adults, $2.50 for kids; prices are a bit higher for howl-ins.

In Littlerock (I-5 exit 95), the mysterious **Mima Mounds** cover a 450-acre plot of public land, with a primitive trail and a few information signs. The curious geological features, which average 8 to 10 feet high, are thought by many to have been caused by rapid glacier recession. We're still guessing big hurkin' moles.

Restaurants

Alice's Restaurant ☆   Located in a turn-of-the-century farmhouse on a lively little creek, Alice's serves hearty dinners, all including cream of peanut soup, a salad, trout, an entree, and choice of dessert. In conjunction with the restaurant, Vincent de Bellis operates the Johnson Creek Winery. Advance reservations are required. *Call for directions; (360) 264-2887; 19248 Johnson Creek Rd SE, Tenino; $$.*

Arnold's Country Inn ☆   Long known as one of Olympia's most accomplished chefs, Arnold Ball has established his latest restaurant just outside Yelm on the road to Mount Rainier. Steaks and meat dishes dominate here. *Across from Texaco; (360) 458-3977; 717 Yelm Ave, Yelm; $$.*

Ben Moore's ☆   Ben Moore's plain exterior, which looks as though it hasn't changed much since the time of the New Deal, can't hide from anyone the fact that inside there is good food to be had at very reasonable prices. You'll get a lot to eat, and none of it is likely to disappoint. *On 4th Ave, west of Columbia; (360) 357-7527; 112 4th Ave, Olympia; $.*

Bristol House ☆☆   Adolf Schmidt (of the Olympia Brewery founding family) is owner and chef at this cheerful place, located south of the Thurston County courthouse. Go at dinner if you want to take full advantage of the chef's ingenuity; lunches are relatively uninspired. Service is fast and professional. *Off Evergreen Park Dr; (360) 352-9494; 2401 Bristol Ct SW, Olympia; $$.*

Budd Bay Cafe ☆   The Budd Bay Cafe, with its long row of tables looking out across Budd Inlet, is a preferred after-hours haunt of many of today's legislators, lobbyists, and state government movers and shakers. Don't look for elaborate dishes here; the menu is designed for boaters and people to whom good talk matters more than haute cuisine. *Downtown Olympia, off State St; (360) 357-6963; 525 N Columbia Ave, Olympia; $$.*

Capitale ☆   In downtown Olympia, across Sylvester Square from the old courthouse, is a tiny, casual place serving up interesting, Italian-esque food in a pleasant atmosphere. The walls are lined with the work of local artists, and jazz music often complements the meals. *Capitol Way and Legion St; (360) 352-8007; 609 Capitol Way S, Olympia; $$.*

Falls Terrace ☆   It would be hard to find an Olympian who hasn't had at least one meal at this longtime Tumwater institution; during regular hours, get reservations. Part of the reason for its popularity is its splendid setting overlooking the Tumwater Falls of the Deschutes River. *Across the Deschutes River from the Olympia Brewery; (360) 943-7830; 106 Deschutes Way SW, Tumwater; $$.*

The Fish Bowl   If you're a beer lover looking for a great place to kick back in the Olympia area, the Fish Tale Ales brewpub is the perfect spot. The beers are also available to go; bring your own container. *Corner of Jefferson and Legion; (360) 943-3650; 515 Jefferson, Olympia; $.*

Gardner's Seafood and Pasta ☆☆   Gardner's is the hands-down favorite in Olympia, with good reason. This homey place—with its exposed wood floors and profusion of fresh flowers on all the tables— makes you feel in the home of a good friend who cooks like a dream. Reservations important. *North on Capitol Way to W Thurston; (360) 786-8466; 111 W Thurston St, Olympia; $$.*

La Petite Maison ☆☆   This tiny, converted 1890s farmhouse—now overshadowed by an office building—is a quiet, elegant refuge for Olympians seeking skillfully prepared Northwest cuisine (the menu changes daily). In spring or summer, it's pleasant to sit on the glassed-in porch. *1 block south of Harrison; (360) 943-8812; 101 Division St NW, Olympia; $$.*

Seven Gables ☆☆   This is the most striking restaurant in Olympia, occupying as it does the fine old Carpenter Gothic residence built by a city's turn-of-the-century mayor. A splendid Mount Rainier view. Daily specials include a vegetarian feature. *¾ mile north of the 4th Ave bridge; (360) 352-2349; 1205 W Bay Dr NW, Olympia; $$.*

The Spar   Above the restaurant's old-fashioned booths are photos of old-time loggers beaming over mammoth trees they've just felled. Indeed, 60-odd years ago, the Spar was known as a workingman's hangout; today it's a mixture of students, attorneys, artists, politicians, fishermen, and tourists. The milk shakes and bread pudding are locally acclaimed, although much of the menu is purely average. *1 block north of Capitol Way; (360) 357-6444; 114 E 4th Ave, Olympia; $.*

Sweet Oasis Mediterranean Restaurant ☆   This informal spot on Capitol Way offers some delicious Mediterranean foods, including home-made dessert pastries. Saturday nights, you get a bonus belly-dancing show—a very artful performance—winding casually between the tables. *Capitol Way and 5th Ave; (360) 956-0470; 507 Capitol Way S, Olympia; $.*

Urban Onion ☆   The site of many a power lunch for Olympia's rising breed of feminist politicians, the Urban Onion retains a faint flavor of the counterculture of the '60s. It has expanded into the lobby of the former Olympian Hotel, and meeting space is available. *Legion and Washington; (360) 943-9242; 116 Legion Way, Olympia; $$.*

Wagner's European Bakery and Cafe ☆   Almost as *echt deutsch* as an opera by that other well known Wagner is the formidable collection of pastries produced by Rudy Wagner's bakery: decorated cakes, apricot squares, raspberry mousse tortes, cream horns, doughnuts, and all kinds of freshly baked breads. *Capitol Way and Union; (360) 357-7268; 1013 S Capitol Way, Olympia; $$.*

Cheaper Eats

Olympia Farmers Market   You can lunch here on the weekends cheaply and reasonably well. Choose from Bavarian wurst, Oriental noodles, salmon burgers, and more. *(360) 352-9096); corner of N Capitol Way and W Thurston St, Olympia.*

Saigon Rendezvous   A Vietnamese restaurant with a good vegetarian selection. *(360) 352-1989; 117 W 5th Ave, Olympia.*

Lodgings:

Harbinger Inn ☆   Occupying a restored 1910 mansion, this bed and breakfast offers Edwardian furnishings, a fine outlook over Budd Inlet and the distant Olympic mountains, and several choice guest rooms. The inn is situated near excellent routes for bicycle riding, with complimentary bicycles available. *1 mile north of State St; (360) 754-0389; 1136 E Bay Dr, Olympia; $$.*

Cheaper Sleeps

Golden Gavel Motor Hotel   The folks are friendly, the rooms are well maintained, and the price is good for the location—three blocks north of the capitol and four blocks south of downtown. Wander over to Wagner's European Bakery, just up the street, for morning espresso and good pastries. *(360) 352-8533; 909 Capitol Way, Olympia.*

More Information

Greater Olympia Visitors and Convention Bureau: *(360) 357-3370.*
Olympia/Thurston County Chamber of Commerce: *(360) 357-3362.*
Tumwater Area Chamber of Commerce: *(360) 357-5153.*
Intercity Transit: *(360) 786-1881.*
Pierce Transit: *(800) 562-8109.*

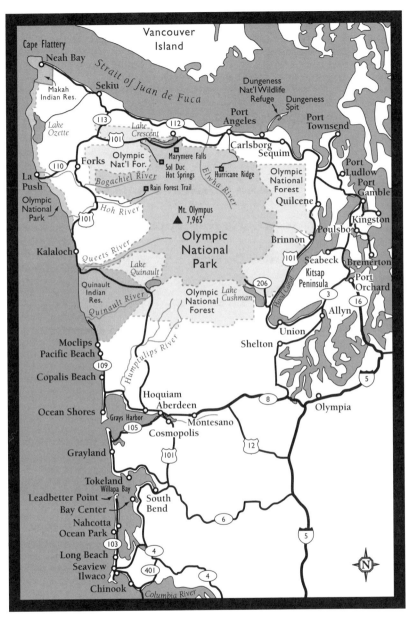

Vancouver Island

Cape Flattery
Neah Bay
Strait of Juan de Fuca
Makah Indian Res.
Sekiu
Dungeness Nat'l Wildlife Refuge
Dungeness Spit
Port Angeles
Port Townsend
Lake Ozette
113
Lake Crescent
112
Carlsborg
Sequim
101
Forks
Olympic Nat'l For.
Marymere Falls
Sol Duc Hot Springs
Elwha River
Hurricane Ridge
Olympic National Forest
Quilcene
Port Ludlow
Port Gamble
La Push
110
Bogachiel River
Rain Forest Trail
Kingston
Olympic National Park
101
Hoh River
Mt. Olympus
7,965'
Olympic National Park
Brinnon
Poulsbo
Kalaloch
Queets River
Lake Quinault
101
Seabeck
Bremerton
Port Orchard
Kitsap Peninsula
Quinault Indian Res.
Quinault River
Olympic National Forest
Lake Cushman
206
Hood Canal
3
16
Allyn
Union
Moclips
Pacific Beach
Humptulips River
Shelton
109
Copalis Beach
5
Ocean Shores
Grays Harbor
Hoquiam
Aberdeen
8
Olympia
105
Montesano
Cosmopolis
Grayland
12
101
Tokeland
Willapa Bay
Leadbetter Point
Bay Center
Nahcotta
Ocean Park
South Bend
6
103
5
Long Beach
Seaview
Ilwaco
4
401
Chinook
Columbia River
4
N

Olympic Peninsula and the Pacific Coast

Kitsap Peninsula

From Manchester north to Foulweather Bluff, west to Hood Canal, and south to Belfair, including Point No Point; Scenic Beach, Illahee, Manchester, and Kitsap Memorial State Parks; and the Foulweather Bluff Preserve.

Welcome to the great in-between. Kitsap Peninsula, a long thumb of land that's almost an island unto itself, sits smack dab between the height of civilization (Seattle) and the depths of wilderness (the Olympic Peninsula). That's perfectly fitting, because Kitsap's mix of mild and wild incorporates a bit of each.

For outdoor lovers, the peninsula, which runs from the Gig Harbor area north to Foulweather Bluff at Hansville, is a grab bag of the good and bad qualities of suburban Puget Sound. The good here is the endless shoreline: Kitsap Peninsula has 236 miles of saltwater beach. But only a small fraction of it is publicly accessible, the rest dominated by private home development or military installations, which have held sway over the landscape here for a century. That's the bad.

But whether that defeats the good, or vice versa, largely lies in the eye of the beholder. We know one thing for sure: select portions of the Kitsap Peninsula provide sweet, clean outdoor experiences you're not likely to find around any other populated areas in the country. And most of them are 60 minutes or less from downtown Seattle.

Secluded pockets of peninsula shoreline—most notably the inner bays near Poulsbo and Suquamish, and the fantastic, relatively unspoiled stretch of Hood Canal to the west—are great same-day outdoor getaways from the Seattle area. And they're often less crowded than similar places much farther away, such as the San Juan Islands or the coast of the Strait of Juan de Fuca.

Those who take the time to discover the beaches along Foulweather Bluff, or take in the view from Scenic Beach State Park, quickly learn that Kitsap County doesn't always have to be a launching point to somewhere else. When Seattle gets too hot, but the coolness of the Olympic Peninsula is simply too far, two options come to mind: stay hot and shut up, or lower your sights and aim for Kitsap County, the happy medium. Sometimes, lukewarm feels just right.

Getting There

The Kitsap Peninsula, directly across central Puget Sound from Seattle, is reached by driving 30 miles south on Interstate 5 to Tacoma and 18 miles northwest on Hwy 16 to Port Orchard and Bremerton. For the water route, take the Edmonds-Kingston, Seattle-Bainbridge, Seattle-Bremerton, or Fauntleroy-Southworth ferry. Call (206) 464-6400 or (800) 84-FERRY for rates and schedules.

Local's advice: In the summer, it's almost always faster (by about an hour) to drive by way of Tacoma, particularly if your destination is in the south or central portion of the Kitsap Peninsula. If you choose a ferry, avoid the Edmonds-Kingston run at all costs during summer months. Rule of thumb: every two hours in the Edmonds-Kingston ferry line shaves two years off your life.

Adjoining Areas

NORTH: **Whidbey and Camano Islands**

SOUTH: **Tacoma and Gig Harbor**

EAST: **Greater Seattle**

WEST: **Hood Canal; Olympic National Forest and the East Slope Olympics**

inside out

Camping

Kitsap County isn't widely considered a camping haven, but several choice spots remain favorites among people who know the place. Chief among them is **Scenic Beach State Park,** a wonderful waterfront site on Hood Canal near Seabeck. On clear summer days, this is one of the prettiest state parks in the Northwest. Wild rhododendrons burst into bloom in May, and the view across Hood Canal into the Olympics is stunning; from this angle, you're looking right up east-slope Olympic valleys (namely the Duckabush and Dosewallips), and the mountains appear many times larger than when they're viewed from Seattle.

The park also has a nice saltwater beach, some hiking trails, and a beach-bluff picnic area that's truly special. Also on the park property is Emel House, the old homestead for this former resort property. The house can be reserved for weddings and other functions. Also reservable is the park's group camp, which holds 50 campers. Call (360) 830-5079 for more information.

The camping area is simple but very nice, with 52 campsites (no hookups; maximum RV length, 40 feet) spread through two forested loops in the upland section of the park. Scenic Beach is open daily in summer, weekends and holidays only from the end of September until early March. Campsites cannot be reserved. *Follow signs from Hwy 3 near Silverdale; (360) 830-5079 or (800) 233-0321.*

Farther north, between Poulsbo and the Hood Canal Floating Bridge, is **Kitsap Memorial State Park,** another Hood Canal waterfront site. The park has 1,800 feet of rocky shoreline, although the views can't compare with those at Scenic Beach. Kitsap Memorial is a good day-use site, with acres of open, grassy fields attracting softball players, kite fliers, and dog runners. The campground has 51 campsites (no hookups; maximum RV length, 30 feet) situated in a somewhat dreary, dark, forested area. A 30-person group camp also is available. Kitsap Memorial is open all year. Campsites cannot be reserved. *On Hwy 3, west of Poulsbo, 3 miles south of Hood Canal Floating Bridge; (360) 779-3205 or (800) 233-0321.*

Another interesting park, in an odd location, is **Illahee State Park,** a waterfront site tucked below one of Bremerton's suburban neighborhoods. The park is split in two, with a boat launch and small saltwater mooring dock in the lower, waterfront portion, and a picnic area and campground in the wooded upper sector. The waterfront area is the primary draw. It's a popular shore fishing, picnicking, and sun-worshipping spot. The mooring docks are protected by a breakwater, and often draw anglers and scuba divers.

The small camping area has 25 sites (no hookups; maximum RV length, 30 feet), and a group camp can be reserved. This is another popular day-use park, with extensive picnic facilities. Illahee is open all year. Campsites cannot be reserved. *Follow Sylvan Way west from Hwy 303 in East Bremerton, look for signs; (360) 478-6460 or (800) 233-0321.*

In the south county, **Manchester State Park** is a pleasant Puget Sound waterfront park with an intriguing history. It was built in the early

1900s as a base to mine the waters of Rich Passage to protect Puget Sound Naval Shipyard in the event of war. Remnants of that operation remain, including a giant concrete shell of a torpedo warehouse that's now used as a picnic shelter. (And you thought none of that military spending ever comes home to roost!) A trail leads from the day-use area to the rocky beach and some lingering gun emplacements. You're liable to see scuba divers here in the summer months. The camping area has 50 sites (no hookups; maximum RV length, 42 feet) split into two unremarkable wooded loops. Manchester State Park is open daily in summer, weekends and holidays only from the end of September to the end of March. Campsites cannot be reserved. *From Port Orchard, follow signs from Beach Drive; from the Southworth Ferry Terminal, follow Hwy 160 and Colchester Drive to Manchester, proceed north on Beach Drive, and follow signs; (360) 871-4065 or (800) 233-0321.*

Beaches

Give one peninsula 236 miles of shoreline, and you ought to be able to find a place to walk on the beach. That's not as easy as you might think in Kitsap County, where the vast majority of saltwater shoreline surrounding the island-like Kitsap Peninsula has been snatched up by private or government landholders, chief among them Uncle Sam and his nuclear Navy. Still, a bit of minor scratching, digging, and map-reading will yield some very worthwhile beach-strolling results.

On the north end, the beach area around **Foulweather Bluff** and **Point No Point** near Hansville is a great spot. In fact, given its close proximity to the Kingston Ferry Terminal, we've never been able to figure out why it's not more heavily populated. Don't tell your neighbors. For a short outing, the beach east of the **Point No Point Lighthouse** is a nice stretch, often frequented by surf fishers casting for salmon off the point. Parents like this place, because you can park practically on the beach. Tours of the lighthouse can be arranged; call (360) 638-2261. Public beach here extends around the point and about a half mile to the south, on beachfront that's part of a mostly undeveloped 35-acre Kitsap County park.

In the other direction, 3 miles west of Hansville along Twin Spits Road, is the Nature Conservancy's **Foulweather Bluff Preserve.** Watch for the easily missed sign on a tree on the left (south) side of the road. A trail leads through the woods to a marshy area, separated from Hood Canal by a sand bar. The swampy area, a nesting area, is prime bird-watching habitat. Note: No fires, mountain bikes, clam digging, unleashed dogs, or other even mildly destructive activity is allowed in this quiet refuge. Heed the signs near the trailhead, and the Conservancy might let you come back.

For short strolls or sunny summertime picnicking, consider the public beaches at **Kitsap Memorial, Scenic Beach, Illahee,** and **Manchester State Parks,** the **waterfront park in Silverdale,** or **Salsbury Point County Park,** just north of the Hood Canal Floating Bridge near Port Gamble. The latter is a particularly nice picnic spot that sees surprisingly little use. (Watch for the "County Park" sign just north of the floating bridge.) Another very nice picnic spot on the north end is **Fay-Bainbridge State Park** on Bainbridge Island (see the Bainbridge and Vashon Islands chapter).

Cycling

Kitsap County hasn't gone out of its way to be cycle-friendly, but it's not unfriendly, either. Many of the county's rural roads make good bike-touring thoroughfares.

North end tour (moderate; 31 miles): Start at the west side of the Agate Pass Bridge on Hwy 305 near Bainbridge Island, where ample parking is available. Follow Suquamish Road several miles north to Suquamish, and another 10 miles north (the road becomes Hwy 104) to Port Gamble, a good lunch stop. Proceed about 5 miles west on Hwy 104 to Kitsap Memorial State Park, then another 6 miles south on Big Valley Road and Bond Road NE to Poulsbo. From here, it's about 6.5 miles west on Hwy 305 to your starting point.

South end tour (moderately hilly; 25 miles): A good loop begins at the **Southworth Ferry Terminal** (leave your car in Seattle and walk your bike on). Follow Hwy 160 and SE Colchester Drive north along the shoreline to Manchester State Park (about 6 miles), then continue another 7 miles on Beach Drive to Port Orchard. From here, ride south on Bethel Road SE and west on Sedgwick Road, about 12 miles, back to the Southworth Terminal.

Central peninsula (about 25 miles; very hilly): A good scenic route skirting Hood Canal can be ridden from Silverdale. From downtown, follow Anderson Hill Road and Seabeck Hwy NW 9 *very* hilly miles to Seabeck. Scenic Beach State Park (see Camping, above) is a 2-mile side trip from here. Continue 4 miles south on Seabeck-Holly Road to Camp Union. Turn left on NW Holly Road and ride 6 miles east, past Wildcat Lake County Park, to Seabeck Hwy NW. Turn left and proceed 3 miles to Newberry Hill Road, which dips another 3 miles east back to Silverdale. This is a major up/down ride, with some world-class whoop-de-doos—

not for the faint of heart or aerobically challenged. But it's particularly beautiful during the spring, when wild rhododendrons bloom all along the route.

For supplies and rentals, consult Mount Constance Mountain Shoppe in Bremerton, (360) 377-0668, or Silverdale Cyclery, (360) 692-5508.

Fishing

Salmon fishing has been a favorite pastime for Kitsap County residents for generations. Nearby Puget Sound waters continue to produce decent results, in spite of slowdowns in Washington's salmon fishery. For boat anglers, the most popular salmon-fishing spots from Kitsap County ports are the same as those fished by Seattle-area anglers: **Point No Point, Jefferson Head, Midchannel Bank, Allen Bank** off Southworth, and dozens of other Puget Sound spots. Keep in mind that interior Puget Sound fishing is seasonal: some areas close for months at a time during the peak summer season, for example. Fishing for blackmouth (immature chinook) is productive all winter long, when weather allows.

West Sound residents do enjoy one hometown salmon advantage. **Point No Point**—a deep-water hole near Hansville that's a perennial hefty chinook producer, awaits at the north end of the peninsula for boat or shore anglers. **Point No Point Resort,** (360) 638-2233, rents kicker boats, which need be driven only a short distance offshore to reach productive waters.

One unique thing about Point No Point is that salmon can be—and often are—hooked right from the beach. The rapid drop-off from the point makes it possible to reach deep water fairly easily with a casting lure, such as a Buzz Bomb. Fly casters even occasionally hook into a chinook off the beach here. Remember that you'll want insulated waders to fish here, even in the summer.

A leading local gear shop is Kingston Tackle and Marine, (360) 297-2521. Others include Kitsap Sports Shop in Bremerton, (360) 373-9589, or Silverdale, (360) 698-4808; and Viking Marine in Poulsbo, (360) 779-4656.

Trout fishing in lakes on the peninsula is better than average for the Puget Sound area. Popular fishing spots are **Wildcat Lake** and **Kitsap Lake,** both west of Bremerton, **Buck Lake** near Hansville, and **Tiger, Panther, Horseshoe,** and **Long Lakes** farther south. Most lakes are open from the last Saturday in April to October 31. For trout-fishing advice, not to mention fine flies and other supplies, consult the Northwest Angler in Poulsbo, (360) 697-7100.

A rather unique fishing opportunity was born with construction of the new (replacement) **Hood Canal Floating Bridge,** which includes a finger fishing pier on the north side of the structure. Park in the westside parking lot and follow signs to the pier, which leads far out on Hood Canal. Fishing can be decent for bottomfish here, and a rare salmon might happen by.

Another little-known, little-used bottom-fishing area is found to the south, off **Misery Point** near Seabeck, where an underwater fishing reef attracts some bottomfish. The closest launches are at Seabeck or Miami Beach, just around the corner to the southeast. Boat rentals, tackle, and licenses are available at Seabeck Marina; (360) 830-5179. (This is a popular launching spot for boaters going after Hood Canal shrimp. See the Hood Canal chapter).

Canoeing/Kayaking

The protected waters between the Kitsap Peninsula and Bainbridge and Blake Islands are favorite haunts of many Seattle-area sea kayakers. Paddlers often make use of Washington State ferries to Bainbridge Island and Bremerton, carrying their boats on one ferry, paddling between **Bremerton** and **Winslow,** then packing the boat home on the other. It's a one-way trip of about 10 water miles, and can be expanded into an overnighter by stopping at Manchester, Illahee, or Blake Island State Parks. Remember to watch your rear-view mirror: ship traffic is heavy in relatively narrow Rich Passage between Manchester and Bainbridge.

For shorter, partial-day trips, **Eagle Harbor** near Winslow and **Sinclair Inlet** between Bremerton and Port Orchard both provide interesting waters with good launch points. For a short, safe, beginner trip, **Liberty Bay** in Poulsbo is a great spot, and a local vendor, Olympic Outdoor Center (18971 Front Street; (360) 697-6095), makes it easy to dip your toes in the water. The center offers short- or long-term rentals, supplies, and expert advice. But it's more than a kayak store. Olympic Outdoor's staff also offers an impressive array of classes, and leads guided tours of nearby kayak getaways such as the Dungeness National Wildlife Refuge in Sequim (see the Sequim and the Dungeness Valley chapter).

If that's not enough territory, consider that nearly all of **Hood Canal** is a prime waterway, lightly used by boat traffic of any kind. One popular destination is **Salsbury Point County Park,** near the east foot of the Hood Canal Floating Bridge. Paddlers launching here can make a short trip north into the protected waters of **Port Gamble.**

Boating/Sailing

Nearly every town on the Kitsap Peninsula is located on the water, and a full range of marine services and moorage is available.

In the south end, the **Port of Manchester,** (360) 871-2510, has 200 feet of guest moorage, available for day use only, but minimal facilities. The highly popular **Port Orchard Marina,** (360) 876-5535, home of the Port Orchard Yacht Club, offers a full range of marine services, plus extensive guest moorage (no charge for day use). Most Port Orchard sights and services (see Attractions, below) are within walking distance.

In the central county, Bremerton-area visitors have their choice of marinas. **Bremerton Marina,** (360) 373-1035, next to the ferry terminal, is a new facility with full marine services, ample guest moorages, and walking-distance access to downtown attractions such as the battleship USS *Turner Joy*. In the Port Washington Narrows is **Port Washington Marina;** (360) 479-3037. Around the corner in Silverdale, the **Port of Silverdale Marina,** (360) 698-4918, has 60 guest slips and minimal services. Farther west, **Illahee State Park** has some moorage, and the **Port of Brownsville Marina,** (360) 692-5498, offers full services and is close to the Keyport Undersea Warfare Museum.

To the north, Poulsbo is a popular boating center. The **Port of Poulsbo Marina,** (360) 779-3505, has guest moorage and full services, and it's very conveniently located to downtown Poulsbo attractions, such as Liberty Bay Park and the Marine Science Center. The **Kingston Marina,** (360) 297-3545, near the ferry terminal is a protected spot with 39 guest slips and basic services.

Boat launches or slings are found at Miami Beach, Seabeck, and Salsbury Point County Park on Hood Canal, Point No Point, Kingston, Miller Bay, Poulsbo, Keyport, Brownsville, Illahee State Park, Port Washington Narrows, Tracyton, Silverdale, Chico, downtown Bremerton, Port Orchard, Retsil, and Manchester.

Hiking

Hiking trails aren't one of Kitsap County's stronger suits. The primary hiking venue here is 1,700-foot **Green Mountain,** a minor, antenna-farmed peak in the center of the county to which you can also drive (and, alas, ride dirt bikes). The trailhead is off NW Holly Road, west of Bremerton. It's about 2 miles to the top. If you're looking for a good day hike on Kitsap Peninsula, consider a stroll on one of the saltwater beaches described in Beaches, above. Or zip around Hood Canal and partake in one of the nearby leeward Olympics hikes. Most are within about an hour of the Kitsap Peninsula. (See the Hood Canal, and the Olympic National Forest and the East Slope Olympics chapters).

Photography

We've shot some fine sunset panoramas of the **Olympics** from the Seabeck area. Scenic Beach State Park is a good place to set up your tripod. Nice pictures across **Central Puget Sound** to downtown Seattle can be captured from the top of Green Mountain, a short hike or drive in central Kitsap County.

Attractions

The small town of Port Orchard, nicely situated along Sinclair Inlet, has become the antique capital of the Kitsap Peninsula. **The Olde Central Antique Mall** (801 Bay Street; (360) 895-1902) occupies the former Central Hotel and accommodates some 70 shops. **Sidney Gallery** (202 Sidney Street; (360) 876-3693) shows and sells fine art in a restored historic building, two blocks uphill from Bay Street. It's worth a walk up the creaky stairs to visit the small historical museum. On Saturdays, from the end of April through October, the **Port Orchard Farmers Market** (Marina Park, one block from Bay Street) is a big draw. **Horluck Transportation,** a privately owned foot ferry that runs every half hour, seven days a week, provides an economical means of travel between the main ferry terminal at Bremerton and downtown Port Orchard; (360) 876-2300.

Most of tiny Seabeck is taken up by the **Seabeck Conference Center,** the nicely preserved site of the old logging-mill community here. It can be rented by nonprofit groups; (360) 830-5010. For drama in the woods, seek out **Mountaineers' Forest Theater,** on Seabeck Hwy NW; (360) 284-6310 for information and reservations.

How closely is Bremerton linked with the **Puget Sound Naval Shipyard (PSNS)** that dominates its waterfront? The Navy was here first. The town grew up around it in the first half of the 20th century, then shrank with it during the second. Through boom or bust, the two remain inextricably linked, and Bremerton today continues to be best known for its ghostly waterfront rows of mothballed ships and submarines.

That fleet once again includes its most famous member, the 45,000-ton battleship **USS** *Missouri*—at least for now. City officials are fighting to have the ship, whose deck was the site of the 1945 Japanese surrender ending World War II, permanently moored in Bremerton, where it would be opened as a museum. City officials in Long Beach, California, and Honolulu also are lobbying for the Mighty Mo'. Meanwhile, the historic battlewagon is impressively visible—all 887 feet of her—from shore or from the *Admiral Jack,* which tours the harbor hourly, daily in summer and on weekends in winter; call Kitsap Harbor Tours, (360) 377-8924.

Securing the *Missouri* as a permanent attraction would cement Bremerton's role as a tourist center. But the town isn't banking on that alone, this time around. The ever-improving waterfront district here now includes **Overwater Park,** just north of the ferry terminal. The park's concrete promenade leads to the destroyer **USS** *Turner Joy,* which still claims fame for its role in the Gulf of Tonkin off Vietnam. The ship is open for self-guided tours, daily in summer, Thursday through Sunday in winter; (360) 792-2457. Nearby is the excellent **Bremerton Naval Museum** (130 Washington; (360) 479-7447), with great nautical displays and detailed ship models. Open daily in summer, closed Mondays in winter, 10am to 5pm.

Not all the ships at PSNS are retired. A handful of ships are home-ported here, most notably **USS** *Nimitz,* one of the Navy's mightiest aircraft carriers. Look for the *Nimitz* in carrier row when it's not out at sea.

Other notable Bremerton attractions are the **Amy Burnett Fine Art Gallery** (412 Pacific Avenue; (360) 373-3187); and **Kitsap Harbor Tours,** (360) 377-8924, which depart the Bremerton Boardwalk for 45-minute cruises to Blake Island or summer cruises to Keyport and Poulsbo.

Naval Submarine Base Bangor, home to the Navy's Pacific Trident nuclear sub fleet, occupies 7,000 acres west of Silverdale on Hood Canal. One look at the Marines by the gate will tell you it's not open for drop-in tours. But tours are available on a limited, prescheduled basis (all applicants are screened). Call the base: (360) 396-6111. Outside the base itself, one of the mammoth Tridents is occasionally seen slipping into and out of Hood Canal—passing through the center span of the Hood Canal Floating Bridge, which opens just for this purpose.

In Silverdale, cow pastures have grown into Retail Central, with the huge **Kitsap Mall** dominating things. But those who make their way to **Old Towne Silverdale** will find a nice waterfront park at the end of Washington Street (see Beaches, above). Other worthy stops include the **Waterfront Park Bakery & Cafe** (3472 Byron, across from the Old Town Pub; (360) 698-2991); **Silver Bay Herb Farm** (9151 Tracyton Boulevard; (360) 692-1340); and the **Kitsap County Historical Museum,** which is housed in cramped quarters in Old Towne Silverdale (3343 N Byron Street; (360) 692-1949) but plans to move to the former Seafirst Bank building on Fourth Street in Bremerton; open Tuesday through Saturday.

Keyport—"Torpedo Town, USA"—has been the Navy's major torpedo-testing site since 1915. Now it also is home to an extraordinary **Naval Underseas Museum** (610 Dowell Street; (360) 396-4148), housing the first Revolutionary War submarine and other interesting naval memorabilia.

Early settlers Scandinavian heritage lives on—to a nearly alarming extent—in Poulsbo, a little waterfront town on Liberty Bay. Worthwhile stops include the **Poulsbo Smokehouse** (18881C Front Street; (360) 779-1099); **The Poulsbo Country Deli** (across from the Anderson Park gazebo; (360) 779-2763); the famous **Sluy's Bakery** (18924 Front Street NE; (360) 779-2798); and an outpost of Issaquah's **Boehm's Chocolates** (18864 Front Street, (360) 697-3318).

On the waterfront itself, **Liberty Bay Park** is nicely landscaped and generously furnished with picnic tables, rest rooms, and big rocks for kids to scramble over. The **Marine Science Center** (215 Third Avenue S; (360) 779-5549; free) offers youngsters a good chance to shake fingers with a sea cucumber. Farther afield, the **Kemper Brewing Company** (2 miles north of town at 22381 Foss Road NE; (360) 697-1446) follows the classic German brewing style and makes excellent lagers, on tap at the brewery's grill, where a simple menu is served from 11am until early evening. Call ahead for brewery tour times.

Incidentally, for reasons unclear to just about everyone, Poulsbo reportedly has proclaimed itself "Geoduck Capital of the World."

In the only real town on the Port Madison Indian Reservation, the **Suquamish Museum and Tribal Center**, off Hwy 305 just west of Agate Pass Bridge, evokes a vanished way of life with a haunting video, *Come Forth Laughing: Voices of the Suquamish People*. School tours are welcome and groups may arrange for salmon feasts; (360) 598-3311. Down the road to the west on the grounds of **St. Peter's Catholic Mission Church**, is the grave of Chief Sealth, the Suquamish chief whose people once inhabited much of central Puget Sound. Twin dugout canoes rest on a log frame over the stone, which reads, "The firm friend of the whites, and for him the city of Seattle was named." Not far away is **Old Man House**, a state park at the site of a massive, spectacular longhouse that once housed Sealth and other chiefs—until it was torched by federal agents in 1870.

Built in the mid 19th century by the Pope & Talbot timber people, who traveled here by clipper ship from Maine, Port Gamble is the essence of a company town. Unfortunately, the company has left. **The Pope & Talbot mill**—long touted as North America's oldest continually operating lumber mill—has closed. But the town, a National Historic Site, remains, and the drive along its maple-shaded streets lined with immaculate, authentic Victorian-era homes continues to provide visual enchantment. The town's **historical museum** is a gem, with re-creations of a ship's cabin, a sawdusty mill room, the lushly decorated lobby of the late Hotel Puget, and an Indian longhouse. The museum is open daily, 10am to 4pm, Memorial Day through Labor Day, closed in winter; (360) 297-3341. The **Port Gamble General Store**, (360) 297-2623, just above the museum, is the place to stop for a galvanized washtub, a kerosene lantern, a sandwich, or a mile-high ice cream cone.

Hansville, the little town at the north end of the peninsula, still draws plenty of salmon anglers (see Fishing, above). But it's a wonderful family destination, as well (see Beaches, above). **The Point No Point Lighthouse** at the end of the sandy spit has been flashing since 1878 and is available for tours; (360) 638-2261. Near the lighthouse, look for the woefully small plaque in the sand commemorating the signing of the 1855 **Treaty of Point No Point**, in which Sealth and chiefs of other local tribes ceded much of central Puget Sound to white settlers.

Restaurants

Bahn Thai ☆☆   Benchai (Benny) Sunti has established a new version of the highly esteemed Seattle Bahn Thai that his wife and brother still run—and this Silverdale edition is equally as good and arguably even better, with the same personal service and a similar menu, but with a much different look. This is a place to come with a group of hungry eaters to share a wide variety of the brightly flavored dishes of Thailand. *½ block north of Bucklin Hill Rd; (360) 698-3663; 9811 Mickelberry Rd, Silverdale; $.*

Boat Shed ☆   This casual seafood restaurant overhanging the Port Washington Narrows in Bremerton is aptly named. Rough wood panels the walls inside and out, and boats of every size pass by the front windows. Whenever possible, hit the deck to eat. *East side of Manette Bridge, on the water; (360) 377-2600; 101 Shore Dr, Bremerton; $.*

Hakata ☆   For those searching for sushi with a difference, Hakata offers some intriguing selections in this immaculate restaurant in an out-of-the-way Silverdale shopping plaza. *Take the Kitsap Mall exit off Hwy 3, behind the post office in Pacific Linen Plaza; (360) 698-0929; 10876 Myhre Pl #108, Silverdale; $.*

Judith's Tearooms and Rose Cafe ☆   The small storefront of this charming Poulsbo spot disguises a large interior space that runs back through several rooms. The farther back you go, the more claustrophobic you feel, but the food more than makes up for a bad seat. A special menu section offers Scandinavian delicacies, and Judith's serves afternoon tea. *At the east end of Front St; (360) 697-3449; 18820 Front St, Poulsbo; $.*

Kingston Hotel Cafe ☆☆   This two-story, Western-front building over-looks the Sound and is truly an inviting eatery with enticing food. When the mood's right, the owner's husband plays music—occasionally joined by others. If every town had a spot like this, the world would be a better place. *A block north of the ferry terminal at Washington Blvd and 1st Ave; (360) 297-8100; 25931 Washington Blvd, Kingston; $.*

Molly Ward's Gardens ☆☆   Sam and Lynn Ward's homespun Poulsbo establishment shines best when the open French doors welcome the garden scents. Breakfast begins at a leisurely time and lunch might take up the rest of the afternoon. Everything is accompanied by a delicate garden soup and fresh-picked salad. Sam designs a five-course feast on Saturday nights. BYOB. *Just past Manor Farm Inn on Big Valley Rd; (360) 779-4471; 27462 Big Valley Rd NE, Poulsbo; $$.*

Yacht Club Broiler ☆   A simple Silverdale restaurant with some elegant touches and a water view. As might be expected by its name and location (on Dyes Inlet), seafood is a major menu item here. What is *unexpected* is the excellent quality of that seafood (as the commercial fishermen who eat here will attest). *From Hwy 3, take Newberry exit, right at Silverdale Way, right onto Byron, left on Washington, and then right onto Bayshore Dr; (360) 698-1601; 9226 Bayshore Dr, Silverdale; $$.*

Lodgings

Manor Farm Inn ☆☆☆   Manor Farm is a working farm with horses, pigs, sheep, cows, chickens, and a trout pond. The cottages are the best, and breakfast happens twice: first at your door; then (for nonguests as well) magnificently at 9am. Call ahead for a legendary special-occasion dinner. *Off Hwy 305 on Big Valley, ½ hour from Winslow ferry dock ; (360) 779-4628; 26069 Big Valley Rd NE, Poulsbo; $$$.*

Reflections Bed and Breakfast Inn ☆☆   Every cliché used to describe an excellent Northwest bed and breakfast applies to this sprawling B&B set on a hillside overlooking Sinclair Inlet, with the Olympics as background. Warm hospitality and a hearty breakfast are offered, and the largest room has a private porch and Jacuzzi tub. *East of Port Orchard off Beach Dr; (360) 871-5582; 3878 Reflections Lane E, Port Orchard; $$.*

Silverdale on the Bay ☆   This tastefully designed resort hotel serves equally well as a conference site or a getaway destination. Many rooms have balconies with views; mini-suites are the best. Extras include an indoor lap pool, a large brick sun deck, a sauna, weight room, video game room, and boat dock. *Turn east at the intersection of Silverdale Way and Bucklin Hill Rd; (360) 698-1000 or (800) 544-9799; 3073 NW Bucklin Hill Rd, Silverdale; $$.*

Willcox House   ☆☆☆   This copper-roofed, art deco, 10,000-square-foot manse on Hood Canal has oak parquet floors, walnut-paneled walls, and a mammoth copper-framed marble fireplace. Downstairs is a bar, a game room, and a clubby library, where you can look out over the canal, the gardens, and a saltwater lap pool. Comb the beach for oysters (gloves and knives available), fish from the dock, or hike the hillside trails. *Call or write for directions; (360) 830-4492 or (800) 725-9477; 2390 Tekiu Rd, Seabeck; $$$.*

More Information

For general outdoors information—including fishing columns by local guide Drew Hathorne and stories and columns by Seabury Blair Jr., one of the Northwest's leading outdoor writers, read *The Sun,* Kitsap County's daily paper: *(360) 377-3711.* For supplies and advice, contact Mount Constance Mountain Shoppe in east Bremerton: *(360) 377-0668.*

Kitsap Peninsula Visitors and Convention Bureau: *(360) 698-7411.*
Kitsap County Parks: *(360) 895-3895.*
Kitsap Maritime Attractions: *(800) 56-FERRY.*
Kitsap Transit: *(360) 373-BUSS.*
Olympic Outdoor Center, Poulsbo: *(360) 697-6095.*

Port Townsend

From Oak Bay north to Point Wilson, west to Discovery Bay, and east to Midchannel Bank in Admiralty Inlet, including Fort Flagler, Fort Worden, and Old Fort Townsend State Parks.

Port Townsend brings out the pirate in all of us. Also the Victorian-era industrial titan, the rich socialite world traveler, the visiting diplomat, and the freeloading scalawag.

No surprise there, given the historical development of the little port town perched like a hangnail on the Quimper Peninsula, a thumb of land jutting into Puget Sound toward Whidbey Island. Port Townsend is, always was, and always will be a port. Its deepwater harbor, strategically located between the foot of the Strait of Juan de Fuca and the head of Puget Sound, made it a force to be reckoned with in Washington's interior waters well before the little town of Seattle got up and running. This was a swanky place during the Tall Ships era, and most folks expected it to get swankier.

Several tons of money, most of it venture capital, came ashore here between 1851 and 1890, fueling a building boom most people expected to pay dividends when the Union Pacific Railroad made this its far-northern terminus. Victorian mansions, hotels, restaurants, and other fineries sprang up like blackberry vines. Which is exactly what they were covered with by 1900, when most of Port Townsend's people, money, and prospects fled south after the railroad dream went up in smoke.

But the infrastructure remained, much of it essentially mothballed for decades. Nearly a hundred years later, Port Townsend is entering its second boom. A walk into the little port city is a stroll into the past, with most of the old buildings painstakingly restored and maintained as lovingly as the family china by a new generation of merchants—tourist capitalists.

Port Townsend is thriving as a Seattle-area getaway. Its convenient access, counterculture feel, and amazing wealth of bed-and-breakfast, restaurant, and performing arts finery create an irresistible lure to many city dwellers. Once they get there, most of them sweep aside the fine lace curtains, peer out the window, and discover something truly powerful: a stunning natural setting, much of it also effectively mothballed for generations.

Port Townsend's extensive shorelines have been protected in something close to their natural state by a totally different force—the U.S. military. While other Puget Sound locales with abundant waterfront property, sweeping views of snow-clad mountains, and a ready supply of local timber were being swept up in a tide of single-family waterfront estates, Port Townsend's most spectacular beaches, bluffs, and forests were locked behind gates. The government held the keys. Thanks again to the area's strategic location, three major artillery batteries were built here between 1856 and 1902.

The oldest fort, Old Fort Townsend, burned in 1895 and never was effectively rebuilt. But the other two, mighty Forts Worden and Flagler, lived long lives as keepers of the gates to Puget Sound. Big artillery guns at the two forts, coupled with similar firepower at Whidbey Island's Fort Casey, combined to form a "triangle of fire," guarding the door to the inner waters' thriving population centers. (Another, more modern, layer of artillery defense—guns at Whidbey's Fort Ebey, Striped Peak west of Port Angeles, and Cape Flattery near Neah Bay—was built later to prevent Japanese invasion during World War II.)

By the early 1950s, the wars were over, big guns were obsolete, and Washington State Parks was fortunate—and far-sighted—enough to latch onto the abandoned gun sites. Today, the two big forts on either side of Port Townsend are reverting to nature—and a splendorous nature it is. In spite of the constant concrete-bunker reminders of the military past, the physical features of this priceless real estate are basically unaltered. The view across Admiralty Inlet hasn't changed much in the past century, adding a pure, natural flavor to the already clean air.

Saltwater shorelines, picturesque lighthouses, and abundant wildlife make these parks favorites among campers, anglers, cyclists, and paddlers—as all-around marine-oriented recreation venues, they might be unequaled in Western Washington. Coupled with the surviving—and thriving—finery of Port Townsend, the parks and waterways make this region an absolute classic, must-visit outdoors venue.

Getting There

Port Townsend and Marrowstone Island lie at the northeast corner of the Olympic Peninsula, 50 miles northwest of Seattle via the Seattle-Bainbridge Island or Edmonds-Kingston ferries and Hwys 104 and 19 or 20. For ferry schedules and information, call (206) 464-6400 or (800) 84-FERRY. From Port Townsend, ferries also travel to Keystone on Whidbey Island, and, in the summer, the Puget Sound Express (431 Water Street, (360) 385-5288) runs a daily ferry to Friday Harbor on San Juan Island.

Adjoining Areas

NORTH: **San Juan Islands and Anacortes**

SOUTH: **Kitsap Peninsula; Hood Canal; Olympic National Forest and the East Slope Olympics**

EAST: **Whidbey and Camano Islands**

WEST: **Sequim and the Dungeness Valley**

Beaches

Port Townsend's heritage grew from the waterline up, and its many miles of shorelines remain its chief drawing card for outdoor lovers. A sampling:

Fort Flagler State Park, at the north tip of Marrowstone Island across the bay from Port Townsend, is a favorite. The park has more than 19,000 feet of saltwater shoreline on Admiralty Inlet, Port Townsend Bay, and Kilisut Harbor, but the far northern beach is a standout day-use area. It's accessible either from the campground area or a narrow road that drops from the blufftop Environmental Learning Center to the picturesque Marrowstone Point Lighthouse. The entire stretch of fine-graveled beach in between—more than a mile—is open for strolling, and the views across the water to Port Townsend, east to Whidbey Island, and northeast to Mount Baker are sublime. Seals often are seen playing offshore here, and it's a favorite destination of sea kayakers, scuba divers, beachcombers, and salmon anglers. The large, open playfield just off the beach south of the camping area is a highly popular kite-flying venue. See also Camping, Fishing, and Cycling, below.

Closer to town, **Fort Worden State Park,** the epicenter for Port Townsend fresh-air activities, has a fine beach of its own. The historic park has 11,000 feet of shoreline, nearly all of it walkable at low tide.

Follow signs to the boat launch, or beyond to the Point Wilson light-house, to get your start. From here, with an occasional upland detour, the beach can be walked west to **North Beach County Park,** or you can head toward town on the beach to **Chetzemoka City Park.** Both are good pic-nicking spots for those who'd rather relax on the beach than stroll upon it; the latter has a nice grassy area that runs right to the waterline.

South of town off Hwy 20, **Old Fort Townsend State Park** has a pleasant, less heavily used stretch of saltwater beach marked by tall pil-ings and other reminders of this 1850s-vintage military outpost.

Camping

Fort Flagler State Park is a winner, which is no secret to Washington campers. The picturesque beachfront campground here is one of the most popular in the state. You'll probably need to get a reservation to land a site here in midsummer, particularly on or anywhere near a holiday.

The campground has 116 sites (14 with water and electricity; maxi-mum RV length, 50 feet). They're on a flat, tidal upland with very little privacy between sites. But the setting is spectacular, and the campground is a great base from which to explore this unique 800-acre park. Fort Flagler has a stunning stretch of beach, its own lighthouse, a fascinating collection of abandoned gun emplacements and other military artifacts, two boat launches, moorage floats, a fishing pier, an underwater park, a youth hostel, hiking trails, extensive group camping and group cabin facilities in old barracks, and a host of other wonders.

We've been going here for years, and probably still haven't seen it all. Because the park is so big and spread out, this is a good place to bring your bicycle. Fort Flagler is open all year. Campsites can be reserved up to 11 months in advance by calling (800) 452-5687. *At the north end of Marrowstone Island, 8 miles northeast of Hadlock on Fort Flagler Road (fol-low "Marrowstone Island" signs from Hwy 20); (360) 385-1259 or (800) 233-0321.*

Fort Worden State Park has a full slate of overnight accommoda-tions (see Lodgings, below). But its campground is nothing to sneeze at, either. While it's not as scenic as the one at Fort Flagler, the RV-equipped campground is one of the region's most extensive. The camping loops, on a bluff over the beach on the east side of the park, offer 80 sites (all with hookups; maximum RV length, 50 feet). Views across Admiralty Inlet to Whidbey Island are grand on clear days. The park's wealth of other attrac-tions—abandoned gun emplacements, lighthouse, sprawling saltwater beaches, marked hiking and cycling trails, museum exhibits, and more—make this a great place to camp with children. Fort Worden is open all year. Campsites can be reserved up to 11 months in advance by calling Reservations Northwest; (800) 452-5687. *Follow signs 1 mile north of downtown Port Townsend; 385-4730 or (800) 233-0321.*

Old Fort Townsend State Park, 3 miles south of town, just east of Hwy 20, has 43 sites (no hookups; maximum RV length, 40 feet). The campsites aren't as close to the beach as they are at the other two nearby forts, but beach access is easy, and the campground doesn't fill up quite as fast. The park also has a nice picnic area and several miles of good hiking trails through its wooded uplands. Old Fort Townsend is open all year. Campsites cannot be reserved. *Follow signs from Hwy 20; 385-3595 or (800) 233-0321.*

Kayaking

Many paddlers consider Port Townsend to be Washington's kayak central. For good reason—nearly everywhere you look on the Quimper Peninsula, an inviting beach or bay beckons. All three Port Townsend–area state parks, **Fort Flagler, Fort Worden,** and **Old Fort Townsend,** are popular day-use areas for paddlers who enjoy skimming along near the beach, with fantastic maritime and North Cascades views all along the route. Fort Flagler, in particular, is a good day-use area. Launching facilities are excellent, with two boat ramps and thousands of feet of flat, sandy beach, usually without significant surf. Also, the camping area is within easy portage distance of the beach and one of the boat ramps, making this a great vacation getaway for kayakers who like to build their camping trips around daily paddle expeditions.

The scenic, placid waters of **Kilisut Harbor** (between Marrowstone and Indian Islands) make a great day trip from Fort Flagler. Or the bay can be reached more directly by launching at **Mystery Bay State Park,** a tiny launch and moorage site halfway up Marrowstone Island on the way to Fort Flagler.

Just to the west, the waters all around **Indian Island,** an off-limits Naval facility (it holds one of the Navy's major West Coast ammunition dumps) are a favorite of many adventuresome paddlers. No beach landings are permitted, but a paddle all the way around the island is a unique trip, because it includes passages through the narrow Port Townsend Canal between Indian Island and the mainland, and through the swift-moving Marrowstone–Indian Island Causeway, which barely separates the south ends of the two islands. Good launching points for this daylong trip are **Indian Island** or **Oak Bay County Parks,** both near the island's south end. Other good launch points are the boat ramps at Mystery Bay and Fort Flagler. A total circumnavigation of the island is a trip of between 11 and

12 water miles. Warning: Tricky currents at the canal and causeway make this a trip recommended for more advanced paddlers only.

Those are just a couple examples of dozens of good day trips in this area. For strong paddlers, it's possible to launch at Fort Worden, run across Port Townsend Bay and explore the entire shorelines of **Marrowstone** and **Indian Islands** in one very long day.

For advice, supplies, no-experience-required guided tours, and rentals, see Kayak Port Townsend (435 Water Street; (360) 385-6240), Sport Townsend (1044 Water Street; (360) 379-9711), or Olympic Outdoor Center (in Poulsbo; (360) 697-6095).

Fishing

Port Townsend Boat Haven is a hot spot for Puget Sound salmon fishing action. It's a very short hop from here to known North Sound salmon hot spots, such as **Possession Bar, Midchannel Bank,** and **Bush Point.** In recent years, the most productive waters—at the entrance to Puget Sound, between Port Townsend and Whidbey Island—have been closed from July to October—peak summer months—in an effort to protect struggling wild coho stocks. But for much of the year, fishing is on up here. If fishing is open, coho are available in August, September, and early October; migratory chinook are caught primarily from mid-May through August; pink salmon are caught in August and September; and chum salmon are harvested in autumn months. In recent years, winter blackmouth (immature chinook) fishing in the North Sound has been productive from December through March.

Charter trips are available from mid-April to mid-November at Sea Sport Charters in the Port Townsend Boat Haven; (360) 385-3575. The company also will go fishing for bottomfish, or chase after whales and shorebirds, when the salmon fishing slows or closes. There's a local **salmon derby** the first weekend in August, and the annual **Discovery Bay Salmon Derby** is the third weekend in February.

Decent bottom fishing can be found at the **Fort Flagler pier,** as well as off most local beaches, particularly deep-water sites such as **Point Wilson** and **Marrowstone Point.** When the salmon season is on, expect to see plenty of hip-wadered anglers in up to their waists at both spots. These are surprisingly productive beach salmon fisheries. Tie on a weighted Buzz Bomb or Point Wilson Dart (the name is no coincidence; the heavy candlefish lure was invented in Port Townsend and named for the local landmark), heave it as far as you can, and hope for some excitement on the retrieve. Catching a salmon off the beach is a rare thrill.

For licenses, supplies, and gear, see The Fish in Hole at the Port Townsend Boat Haven; (360) 385-7031.

Boating/Sailing

Port Townsend got its start as a rather extravagant boat dock, and it's still a central passageway and moorage point for most traffic into and out of Puget Sound. The town, with a deep-water port strategically located between the Strait of Juan de Fuca and Puget Sound, is well equipped to handle the traffic. The downtown **Port Townsend Boat Haven,** operated by the Port of Port Townsend, (360) 385-2355, is about as centrally located as a marina can get. Daily, monthly, and permanent moorage is available, as are a full slate of marine services. Boat rentals and guided excursions also are readily available here; call ahead for rates and schedules. The nearby private facility, **Point Hudson Resort and Marina,** just northeast of the ferry terminal, also has full marine services; (360) 385-2828. To the south of town, moorage and supplies can be found at Port Ludlow Marina; (360) 437-0513.

Day-use boaters and sailors also are well treated in the Port Townsend area. **Launch facilities** are found at Fort Flagler and Fort Worden State Parks, downtown near the Ferry Terminal, and at Oak Bay and Mystery Bay. In addition to the two marinas above, transient moorage is available at Mystery Bay (dock space), Fort Flagler (dock and mooring buoys), Fort Worden (dock and buoys), and Old Fort Townsend (buoys).

Scuba Diving

Established marine sanctuaries are located just offshore at **Fort Flagler** and **Fort Worden State Parks.** Boaters and kayakers should take heed and watch for divers' flags.

Cycling

Even though many road cyclists pass through this area on a tour of the Olympic Peninsula, it's frankly not a great place for street riding. Once you get outside Port Townsend city limits, most highways on the Quimper Peninsula are narrow two-laners, with little to no shoulders for quick escapes. And traffic can be quite heavy. But the Port Townsend area still can be a wonderful place to explore from a bicycle seat. A couple of suggestions:

The "back route" out of Port Townsend, from Fort Worden State Park west on Hastings Avenue and south on Beckett Point Road, makes a nice half-day tour, with good views down into **Discovery Bay** and across to the Miller Peninsula. Shoulders are still narrow, but traffic is relatively light.

Park and ride at **Fort Flagler** or **Fort Worden.** Both of these sprawling state parks have many miles of either marked cycle paths or winding park roads where traffic is limited to 25mph. A day exploring one or both parks from a cycle saddle is a great way to enjoy them even if you didn't plan ahead far enough to snag a campsite. From Fort Worden, it's a short, downhill ride to downtown Port Townsend.

Another fun Port Townsend ride—a guaranteed hit with the kids—is a daylong tour involving a run across Admiralty Inlet on the **Port Townsend-Keystone Ferry.** Park downtown near the ferry terminal and walk the bikes onto one of the two nicely restored, classic old ferries, and enjoy the scenery, the Mount Baker view, and perhaps even an orca sighting on the 20-minute ride across. At Keystone, hang a left and pedal up the hill to spectacular Fort Casey State Park (see the Whidbey and Camano Islands chapter), where you can spend hours roaming the old gun bunkers, touring the scenic Admiralty Head Lighthouse, or building or flying kites on the grassy fields. If time allows, ride east toward Keystone, along Keystone Spit, with Crockett Lake on one side of the road, Admiralty Bay on the other. This is a good bird-watching area. Hop the ferry back and go to bed early.

Photography

The beaches of **Fort Flagler**—we hate to go on and on about them—make for some highly productive photo sessions, with the deep blue waters of Admiralty Inlet in the foreground, Mount Baker in the back. This is especially true of the park's east side, where the Marrowstone Point Lighthouse can be drawn into your photos. Try it at sunset for some intriguing light.

An impressive vista of the entire area is found at **Chetzemoka Park** (named after a local chief) at the northeast corner of Port Townsend. This also is a very fine picnic spot.

Attractions

Port Townsend's historical and architectural charm can be quickly taken in on a walking tour of **Water Street,** an agreeable stretch of ornate old brick-and-stone buildings mostly erected about the same time Seattle's

Pioneer Square was being rebuilt after the fire of 1889. Notable among the town's historic mansions are the **Daniel Logan House** (Taylor and Lawrence), with an iron roof crest; **Bartlett House** (end of Polk Street on the bluff), with its famous mansard roof; and the **Ann Starrett Mansion** (Adams and Clay), with a bed and breakfast in its 1890 Stick-style architecture. Old homes can be toured during the first weekend in May and the third weekend in September. Interesting buildings open for public tours are the **Jefferson County Courthouse** (Walker and Jefferson), with its clock tower and fantasy-castle appearance; **City Hall** (Water and Madison), with a fine museum, a jail, a restored Victorian hearse, and every imaginable whatnot; **Rothschild House** (Jefferson and Taylor; (360) 385-4730), with an antique rose garden and period rooms with breathtaking views; and the **Commanding Officer's House** at Fort Worden. The **Jefferson County Historical Society** (210 Madison Street; (360) 385-1003) has a fascinating museum, with old jail cells; the society's collection of Northwest Indian artifacts is extensive.

On Water Street, you'll find colorful shops. **North by Northwest** (918 Water Street; (360) 385-0955) has a wide selection of historic and contemporary Indian baskets; wood, ivory, and soapstone carvings; jewelry; and related books. Next door is **Melville and Co.** (914 Water Street; (360) 385-7127), offering an extensive selection of English mysteries, old comics, and rare books. **Williams James Bookseller** (829 Water Street; (360) 835-7313) has a vast and well-organized inventory of used books. **Earthen Works** (702 Water Street; (360) 385-0328) specializes in high-quality Washington craft items. The best ice cream cones can be had at **Elevated Ice Cream** (627 Water Street; (360) 385-1156); the best antique selection at **Port Townsend Antique Mall** (802 Washington Street; (360) 385-2590), where about 40 antique merchants have convened under one roof. The best pastry is to be had at **Bread and Roses Bakery** (230 Quincy Street; (360) 385-1044). At **Riley's General Store** (1020 Water Street) you can buy incredible chocolates. For wonderful wines, try **The Wine Cellar** (940 Water Street; (360) 385-7673). For live music and local color, check out the historic **Town Tavern** (Water and Quincy Streets), where the enormous historical back-bar, pool tables, and the owner's great taste in music draw an interesting assortment of people. **Sirens** (823 Water Street; (360) 379-0779), hidden way up three flights of stairs in the historic Bartlett Building, is a delightful place to enjoy a glass of wine, have a snack, and listen to music from the Bay View deck. Don't overlook the revitalization of uptown, especially **Aldrich's** (Lawrence and Tyler Streets; (360) 395-0500), an authentic 1890s general store come to life with an upscale twist; the **1004 Gallery** (1004 Lawrence Street; (360) 385-7302), for excellent contemporary art; **Jack and Jill** (1044 Lawrence

Street; (360) 385-3166), for tasteful children's clothing displayed in a historical setting.

Just outside town, **Fort Worden** (see Beaches, above), along with sister forts on Marrowstone and Whidbey Islands, was part of an early defense system established to protect Puget Sound. The 433-acre complex overlooking Admiralty Inlet now incorporates turn-of-the-century military structures, campgrounds, gardens, and a theater. A huge central field is perfect for games or kite flying. This setting may look familiar to those who saw the movie *An Officer and a Gentleman*, which was filmed here. At the water's edge, an enormous pier juts into the bay—it's the summer home for the **Marine Science Center,** with touch tanks and displays of sea creatures. Fort Worden is also home to **Centrum,** which sponsors a variety of concerts, workshops, and festivals.

Port Townsend is alive with festivals throughout the year. A **historic homes tour** happens the first weekend in May and again the third weekend in September. **Centrum Summer Arts Festival,** (360) 385-3102, presents one of the most successful cultural programs in the state, with dance, fiddle tunes, chamber music, a writers conference, jazz, and theater performances, and the celebrated Marrowstone Music Festival; at Fort Worden from June through September. **The Rhododendron Festival** in May, with a parade and crowning of the queen, is Port Townsend's oldest festival. The **Wooden Boat Festival** at Point Hudson Marina, (360) 385-3628, the weekend after Labor Day, is a celebration of traditional crafts and a showcase for everything from prams to kayaks to yachts to tugboats.

Restaurants

Ajax Cafe ☆   Most everyone agrees that Tennesseans are right at the top when it comes to barbecuing pork, and the tender barbecue pork ribs, here blessed with a thick barbecue sauce containing a goodly splash of Jack Daniels Tennessee whiskey, reflect this tradition. Owner/chef Rudy Valiani has given Ajax a style all its own. *In lower Hadlock on the waterfront, off Oak Bay Rd; (360) 385-3450; 271 Water St, Port Hadlock; $$.*

Belmont ☆☆   In a town where good seafood is almost "ho-hum," the Belmont is a special treasure. And in a town where sweeping water views are as common as seagulls, the Belmont stands out. Ask about staying in one of the renovated Victorian-era hotel rooms (two overlook the water). *Center of town, waterside; (360) 385-3007; 925 Water St, Port Townsend; $$.*

Blackberries ☆   A delightful little restaurant attached to the conference center dining hall in Fort Worden State Park, Blackberries features ingredients utilized by the Makah, S'Klallam, and other Native Northwest tribes. You'll find a definite emphasis on healthy food served in portions that won't leave you hungry. (Closed for the winter, but a new Blackberries has opened downtown that serves year-round.) *Fort Worden State Park Conference Center, 1 mile north of downtown; (360) 385-9950; 210 Battery Way, Port Townsend; $$.*

Fountain Cafe ☆ Locals like to bring their out-of-town guests here, especially for lunch—they can check out the art on the walls while waiting for a table. This really is good cafe food—an Asian-style ginger chicken is pleasantly piquant while a vegetarian pasta with artichokes, olives, and feta is a longtime favorite with the regulars. *At the fountain steps; (360) 385-1364; 920 Washington St, Port Townsend; $$.*

Khu Larb Thai ☆ This gracious restaurant with its muted cool greens is a welcomed balance to the tingling heat and vibrant flavors that unmistakably identify the food as Thai. One of the best of the aromatic curries is a gently steamed salmon fillet with cabbage and a slightly sweet but still spicy sauce. The helpful, attentive staff carefully explain how to order a balanced selection of dishes. *Off Water St on Adams; (360) 385-5023; 225 Adams St, Port Townsend; $$.*

The Public House ☆ The Public House is a large space with soaring ceilings, brought into human scale by clever interior design. It's both comfortable and casual (a great place for ribs or a burger with a side of sweet, crispy onion rings). Select a beer from the impressive list of drafts and watch the world go by through the big front windows. Live music at night. *On the north side of Water St; (360) 385-9708; 1038 Water St, Port Townsend; $.*

Salal Cafe ☆ Breakfasts are justly famous here, with a couple of morning newspapers circulating and locals trading stories back in the solarium. The omelets are legendary—both in quality and variety. The light, cheerful cafe serves lunch with a smattering of basic Mexican plates, but breakfast is where this place really shines. *Quincy and Water Sts; (360) 385-6532; 634 Water St, Port Townsend; $.*

Silverwater Cafe ☆ If you consider seafood one of life's great pleasures, the Silverwater Cafe shares your passion, providing simple preparations of whatever is in season—and if it is fresh frozen, the waitstaff will point that out. The Silverwater has recently moved to Taylor Street, next to the Rose Theater and beneath the historic Elks Club. *Washington and Taylor Sts, across from the fountain; (360) 385-6448; 237 Taylor St, Port Townsend; $$.*

Cheaper Eats

Chimacum Cafe   This cozy restaurant south of Port Townsend on Hwy 19 does wondrous things with basics like fish 'n' chips, steaks, oysters, and burgers—all at rock-bottom prices. *(360) 732-4631; 9253 Rhody Dr, Chimacum.*

Landfall   Overlooks the harbor and serves respectable seafood, sandwiches, salads. *(360) 385-5814; 412 Water St, Port Townsend.*

Lodgings

Ann Starrett Mansion ☆☆   The most opulent Victorian in Port Townsend, this multigabled Queen Anne hybrid was built in 1885 and sports a spiral stairway, octagonal tower, and "scandalous" ceiling fresco. All rooms are antique-furnished and have lovely decorative touches, with a florid color scheme throughout. Afternoons, the house is open for public tours, when unoccupied bedrooms are tied off for viewing. *Corner of Clay and Adams; (360) 385-3205; 744 Clay St, Port Townsend; $$.*

The Ecologic Place   This is your basic gathering of rustic cabins in a natural setting. And what a setting. Bordering on a tidal estuary, The Ecologic Place offers a view of the Olympics and Mount Rainier, conditions permitting. The cabins are simple but have everything you need to enjoy the beauty of the place—wood stoves, equipped kitchens, and bunks for the kids. Bring bikes, boats, books, bathing suits, binoculars, children, and groceries too. *Turn right at "Welcome to Marrowstone" sign; (360) 385-3077; 10 Beach Dr, Nordland; $$.*

Fort Worden ☆   Fort Worden was one of three artillery posts built at the turn of the century to guard the entrances to Puget Sound. The beautifully situated fort now is a state park, a conference center, a youth hostel, the site of the splendid Centrum Arts Festival, and an unusual place to stay. Twenty-four former officers' quarters have been made into spacious lodgings, each with a complete kitchen. Favorite lodgings are Bliss Vista and Alexander's Castle. Make reservations at least a year in advance. *1 mile north of downtown; (360) 385-4730; 200 Battery Way, Port Townsend; $$.*

Hastings House/Old Consulate Inn ☆☆   This ornately turreted red Victorian on the hill is one of the most frequently photographed of Port Townsend's "Painted Ladies." It is also one of its most comfortable (a hot tub adds a relaxing element). A mammoth seven-course breakfast is served. *On the bluff, at Washington and Walker; (360) 385-6753 or (800) 300-6753; 313 Walker St, Port Townsend; $$$.*

Heritage House   Visitors to this hillcrest Victorian bed and breakfast will find a sprightly variety of refinished antiques matching guest rooms with names like Lilac and Morning Glory. Relax in the evenings on the porch swing. Children over 12 are permitted, but pets are not. *Corner of Washington and Pierce; (360) 385-6800 or (800) 385-6867; 305 Pierce St, Port Townsend; $$.*

The James House ☆☆☆   The first bed and breakfast in the Northwest (1889) is still in great shape, though when a gale blows off the strait and hits the high bluff, you are glad to be in one of the three rooms with a fireplace or wood-burning stove. The main floor offers two comfortable parlors, each with a fireplace and reading material. *Corner of Washington and Harrison; (360) 385-1238; 1238 Washington St, Port Townsend; $$.*

Lizzie's ☆   Lizzie, the wife of a tugboat captain, put the deed of this model of Victorian excess in her own name; her name now also graces a line of bath lotions created by owners Patti and Bill Wickline. Breakfast can turn into a friendly kaffeeklatsch; a soak in the tub in the black-and-white corner bathroom—especially if the sun is slanting in—is a Victorian treat. *Near the corner of Lincoln and Pierce in the Historic District; (360) 385-4168 or (800) 700-4168; 731 Pierce St, Port Townsend; $$.*

Palace Hotel ☆   The 1889 Romanesque Palace places visitors in the midst of Port Townsend's shopping and gawking district. The rooms retain the building's ex-bordello atmosphere; Marie's (the venerable madame of the house until the mid-1930s) Room is decorated in original shades of burgundy and forest green. *On the corner of Water and Tyler; (360) 385-0773 or (800) 962-0741; 1004 Water St, Port Townsend; $$.*

Quimper Inn ☆☆   The light from all the windows plays across richly hued walls, suffusing every corner of the house with a mellow glow. Sue and Ron Ramage treat their inn and their guests with thoughtful care. Breakfasts are well executed. *Corner of Franklin and Harrison; (360) 385-1060 or (800) 557-1060; 1306 Franklin St, Port Townsend; $$.*

Ravenscroft Inn ☆☆   A nonconformist among the surrounding Victorians, Ravenscroft Inn was built in 1987, and has a long front porch, redwood-stained clapboards, and graceful end chimney. A suite on the third floor sports dormer windows that overlook the town and harbor. Guests enjoy a gourmet meal from the immense open-style kitchen. *On the bluff at Quincy and Clay; (360) 385-2784 or (800) 782-2691; 533 Quincy St, Port Townsend; $$.*

Cheaper Sleeps

Fort Flagler Hostel   You needn't be a confirmed hosteler to fall in love with this one, amid Fort Flagler's views, hiking trails, fishing, and other attractions. It's short on charm, long on utility, with one room set aside for families. Bring food and sleeping bags. It's a *real* bargain if you arrive on a bike. Open April through September. *(360) 385-1288; Fort Flagler State Park, Marrowstone Island.*

Point Hudson Resort   A derelict Coast Guard station that's evolved into a resort (including a motel, marina, and RV park), this is a heavily maritime-industry flavored spot. The plain 26-room motel has an engagingly informal mood. *(360) 385-2828 or (800) 826-3854; Point Hudson, 103 Hudson St, Port Townsend.*

Water Street Hotel   Up the steps from the mythic Town Tavern, this hotel's spare, clean rooms are the kind in which Thomases Merton, Wolfe, or Pynchon might have holed up in contemplation. *(360) 385-5467 or (800) 735-9810; 635 Water St, Port Townsend.*

More Information

Port Townsend Chamber of Commerce: *(360) 385-2722.*
Centrum: *(360) 385-0440 or (800) 733-3608.*

Sequim and the Dungeness Valley

From Sequim Bay west and north to Dungeness Spit and south to the Upper Dungeness River Trail in Olympic National Park, including John Wayne Marina, Cline Spit, Dungeness Recreation Area, Sequim Bay State Park, and the Dungeness National Wildlife Refuge.

Sequim is a work in progress. This is true of Sequim, the city—an adolescent town in the awkward stage of a transition from farm town to suburban refuge for retirees and telecommuters. It's also true of Sequim, the place—a broad, peaceful plain serving as a demilitarized zone of sorts between the warring Olympic Mountains and Strait of Juan de Fuca.

The continuing change in town and landscape leaves the strong impression that the Sequim (it's pronounced "Skwim") you enjoy today in a car, from a boat, or on the beach isn't necessarily the Sequim your great-grandchildren will know. The exploding business district is in constant flux; so is the Dungeness Valley's greatest single attraction, the Dungeness Spit. Both are sprouting from the ends—one from incoming silt, the other from migratory cash.

For recreators, this flux is a plus. No two days spent in the Dungeness Valley are ever alike. The beaches change with every winter storm, the Dungeness River with every flood, the Olympic Mountain lowlands to the south with every season.

And the weather is truly remarkable. Many people are drawn to Sequim by its vaunted sunshine: the valley is tucked directly into the armpit of the Olympic Mountains' rain shadow. Because the

Olympics go from sea level to nearly 8,000 feet in less than 30 miles, they suck out most moisture from nasty southwesterly storms that wrack the coast every winter. Sequim, directly opposite the storm path in the Olympics' northeast corner, just gets the wimpy leftovers—high, poofy clouds that left every ounce of ferocity up on the face of Mount Olympus. The result: Sequim's annual rainfall averages about 16 inches, a fraction of that for the rest of the peninsula, and about half the average of the greater Seattle area.

But it's not so much the pure sunshine that endears Sequim to outdoor lovers. It's the stark contrast between alpine and marine climates. Seated in a kayak in the quiet, relaxing waters inside the Dungeness Spit, you often can look directly up the Dungeness Valley and watch the weather wars unfold: clouds dashed apart, lightning flashing in protest, streaks of triumphant sunshine declaring victory—all the while secure in the knowledge that down here, you're untouchable.

This can all be very heady stuff. But don't worry: if you lose yourself in the grandeur, a quick stop at the Sequim Costco can send you homeward with a 2-gallon jar of mayonnaise and a renewed sense of reality.

That s the charm of Sequim, a great place to be, whether you can pronounce it or not.

Getting There

Sequim is a 60-mile drive west of Seattle on US 101. For the most direct approach, take the Edmonds-Kingston or Seattle-Bainbridge ferry to Kitsap County and follow signs to the Hood Canal Floating Bridge. Cross the bridge into Jefferson County and follow Hwy 104 to US 101, which leads along the lower west side of Discovery Bay to Sequim and the Dungeness Valley. Travel (in)sanity note: Summer weekend travelers should strongly consider skipping the ferry and driving south around Puget Sound to Kitsap Peninsula and the Hood Canal Bridge. It adds about 60 miles to the trip, but could save hours of mind-numbing waiting lines at ferry terminals. Call (206) 464-6400 or (800) 84-FERRY for ferry rates and schedules.

Adjoining Areas

WEST: **Port Angeles and Hurricane Ridge**

EAST: **Port Townsend**

SOUTH: **Olympic National Park: Overview; Hood Canal**

inside out

Beaches

The sandy flats jutting into the Strait of Juan de Fuca north of Sequim just might be the best beach-wandering territory in the Northwest. The beaches are incredibly scenic, and the local weather is far more agreeable than beaches on the Pacific Coast or even farther west on the strait. But two special, magical factors draw explorers of all ages to the Dungeness Valley. One is wildlife. You'll find a wealth of shorebirds and marine life here. The other is archaeological intrigue. Shores around Sequim have proven to be virtual gold mines of bones, teeth, tusks, and other remains of giant woolly mammoths that frequented these plains as long as 10,000 years ago. Keep your eyes peeled. You might be stubbing your Teva sandals on history.

Much of the area's marine wildlife—and more than a fair share of its awesome views—is found at the **Dungeness National Wildlife Refuge,** Sequim's primary draw. The refuge encompasses Dungeness Spit, a 5.5-mile long sand finger jutting into the Strait of Juan de Fuca. The spit, a low, flat landmass formed by silt from the Dungeness River, is hidden from sight by high bluffs separating the strait from the Dungeness valley. But it's absolutely worth seeking out.

Walking the length of the spit gives you the unique sensation of crossing a land bridge right out into the ocean. On the north (windward) side, surf laps—or pounds, depending on the season—up onto the steep, sandy beach. Ships bound for Puget Sound cruise offshore, as do **seals, sea lions,** and the occasional **orca.** On the south (leeward) side, the beach often is alive with **shorebirds.** The quiet, protected inner waters are prime habitat for more than **250 bird species,** including herons, loons, ducks, bald eagles, and cormorants. Bring binoculars. The inner waters also are frequented by windsurfers and kayakers, and the broad spit makes a great kite-launching strip.

After the first mile or so of struggle, most walkers will learn how much easier it is to walk the spit near the waterline, on firm sand. Waterproof shoes—or just cold-proof toes—are nice to have along.

Hikers with strong legs and good wind shells will want to walk the entire 5 miles (check a tide table, the spit gets pretty skinny at extreme high tides) to the picturesque New Dungeness Lighthouse, built in 1857. A lightkeeper lives in the adjacent 1905 residence, and gives tours of the light on weekends, or other times when practical.

Note where the light stands. It was built at the tip of the spit, which grows some 30 feet a year and now extends a half-mile farther east. The beach beyond here is off-limits, as is the adjoining Graveyard Spit, named to commemorate 18 Tshimshians raided and killed by warring Clallams in 1868.

The refuge is open from dawn to dusk daily. A $2-per-family donation is requested at the entrance. A good campground, Dungeness Spit Recreation Area, is adjacent to the refuge. (See Camping, below.) The refuge is open all year. From Sequim, drive 4.5 miles west on US 101 and turn right (north) on Kitchen-Dick Road. Proceed 3.5 miles and follow signs. Information: (360) 457-8451.

Several miles to the east, savvy beach walkers and picnickers enjoy little-known **Marlyn Nelson Park**, on the waterfront at the end of Port Williams Road (an extension of the Old Olympic Hwy). Facilities are basic, with picnic sites and rest rooms. The beach is the attraction. From here, it's possible to walk fairly long distances east and west along the strait. This area has yielded an astonishing number of archaeological artifacts, including beautifully preserved, football-size woolly mammoth teeth and bones that land on the beach when high clay bluffs collapse during winter storms. It's a wonderful stroll, and a good foul-weather alternative to Dungeness Spit. Take Sequim-Dungeness Way north from US 101, turn right (east) on Port Williams Road and follow it to the water.

Camping

High on a bluff where the northern Olympic Peninsula drops into the sea is **Dungeness Recreation Area,** a nicely maintained Clallam County Park adjacent to the popular Dungeness National Wildlife Refuge. Dungeness has 65 sites (no hookups), some with good back-window views of the Strait of Juan de Fuca.

Campsites are separated either by head-high shrubbery or short, thick trees, offering good privacy but ample sunlight. The campground is open from February to October. Campsites ($8 to $10) cannot be reserved. *From Sequim, drive 4.5 miles west on US 101 and turn right (north) on Kitchen-Dick Road. Proceed 3.5 miles and follow signs; (360) 683-5847.*

East of town, easy to miss off busy US 101, is **Sequim Bay State Park,** where you'll find nice picnic and marine facilities, a lot of so-so campsites, and a handful of very nice ones, near the water. Because it's the only state park in this area, it's a popular stopover for RVers and campers making the Olympic Peninsula loop. The 90-acre park has 86 campsites (26 with hookups; maximum RV length, 30 feet). The park also fronts on Sequim Bay, providing boater services, moorage, and launching. (See

Boating, below.) Sequim Bay is open all year. Sites cannot be reserved. *On US 101 4 miles southeast of Sequim; (360) 683-4235 or (800) 233-0321.*

For a more rustic, woodsy stay, trek into the hills of nearby Olympic National Forest to **Dungeness Forks Campground,** a nice spot with only nine sites at the confluence of the Dungeness and Gray Wolf Rivers. The summer-only campground is a favorite layover spot for hikers and backpackers (see Hiking/Backpacking, below). *11 miles south of Sequim via Forest Service Roads 28 and 2880; (360) 765-3368.*

Hiking/Backpacking

Beach walking gets most of the attention in Sequim, but don't overlook those mountains forming the rain shadow that keeps the valley dry. The upper Dungeness River drainage, in particular, harbors some of the Olympic Peninsula's finest long day hikes and backpack trips. They're typical Olympic ascents, beginning in deep, peaceful forests, climbing along silvery streams, and opening up into spectacular alpine meadows, tarns, and vistas. Most begin in Olympic National Forest (see Olympic National Forest Rules and Regulations in the Olympic National Forest and the East Slope Olympics chapter) and wind up in Olympic National Park (see Olympic National Park Rules and Regulations in the Olympic National Park: Overview chapter).

To some degree, trails in this area benefit from the same rain shadow effect as Sequim. Experienced Olympic hikers head to this region when weather looks iffy elsewhere on the peninsula. For full information and trailhead directions for hikes in the Dungeness and nearby Gray Wolf river drainages, contact the Olympic National Forest Quilcene Ranger District; (360) 765-3368. Also see the Olympic National Forest and the East Slope Olympics chapter, which has full information on many upper Dungeness hikes. A sampling:

The first part of the trail isn't among the more spectacular in the Olympics, but the **Deer Ridge to Deer Park Trail** (difficult; 10 miles round trip) will challenge even the most gung-ho hiker. From the trailhead near Slab Camp, off Forest Service Road 2875, this trail climbs fast, gaining about 3,000 feet in the 5 miles to the breathtaking (view-wise and fatigue-wise) panorama from Deer Park, on the shoulder of 6,007-foot Blue Mountain. The vista, taking in Vancouver Island and Mount Baker to the north and much of upper Puget Sound to the east, is one of the best in the state. For a shorter day hike, follow the trail 1.5 miles to a lesser, but still grand, view at View Rock.

Just to the south, Dungeness Forks Campground (see Camping, above) is the takeoff point for the **Lower Gray Wolf River Trail** (moderate; 20 miles round trip). For wild-river lovers the Gray Wolf is as good as it gets in Western Washington. It's one of the best-protected watersheds in the region, with its upper stretches in Olympic National Park, the lower portions in the Buckhorn Wilderness. The Gray Wolf Trail makes a great day hike, short backpack trip (good campsites are found 2, 3, 5, and 7.5 miles up the trail), or first leg of a longer trip to Graywolf or Cameron Passes in Olympic National Park.

Backpackers can hike to the Lower Gray Wolf junction and head due south, following the **Upper Gray Wolf River Trail** (difficult, various lengths) through stunning Gray Wolf Basin to Gray Wolf Pass (9.5 miles from the Lower Graywolf junction) and another 3.5 miles south to the **Dosewallips River Trail.** Strong backpackers can combine the Lower Graywolf, Cameron Creek, Dosewallips, and Upper Graywolf Trails for a fantastic six- to eight-day, 50-mile climb through some of the Olympics' most memorable wildlands.

Similar to the Lower Graywolf Trail is its nearby cousin, the **Upper Dungeness Trail** (moderate; 12.8 miles round trip). The trail attracts backpackers and day hikers alike. It's a good beginner's backpack trip, as good campsites are found at Camp Handy (3.2 miles) and farther up the trail at a major junction, Boulder Shelter (6.4 miles). Longer backpack trails fan out from here, leading south to **Constance Pass** in the Dosewallips drainage and east to **Marmot Pass** on the Big Quilcene Trail.

For an overnight or weekend backpack trip, the nearby **Royal Basin Trail** (moderate; 14 miles round trip) is a Northwest favorite. The trail, which branches off about 1 mile up the Dungeness River Trail (see above), switches back through a church-quiet forest before opening into a stunning alpine valley, with snow-covered peaks (watch for mountain goats) on three sides and a small lake at the valley head. In the early summer, the wildflower explosion makes this a magical spot.

Good medium-length day hikes in the same area include **Gold Creek** (moderate; 12.8 miles round trip and a good mountain-bike venue) and **Tubal Cain Mine** (moderate; 17.6 miles round trip), which leads to good campsites in nice meadows, beyond an abandoned mine site and all the way up to Marmot Pass, 6,100 feet.

Boating/Sailing

A lot of the retired folks living out their golden years around Sequim were into boating long before they arrived here. But even the ones who weren't are now getting started, thanks to top-notch marine facilities like the **John Wayne Marina** on Sequim Bay; (360)417-3440. The marina, built on land bought and donated for the purpose by the Duke himself, who used to cruise here in his yacht, is one of the finest in the state. Wayne would be proud: the marina has full services year-round, a delightful waterfront park overlooking the bay and Miller Peninsula, 30 guest moorage slips, and good beach access. This is a pleasant spot to spend an afternoon, whether you're a boater, sailor, or just a hapless motorist tired of breathing tour-bus fumes on US 101. The marina also is a great launching point for kayaks or small craft. On W Sequim Bay Road; follow signs from US 101.

The marina also has a popular launch ramp, one of only a few in the area. Others are found at **Sequim Bay State Park** (see Camping, above), which offers overnight moorage at a dock and several mooring buoys; and **Cline Spit County Park** (see Sea Kayaking/Windsurfing, below).

Fishing

The **John Wayne Marina** is a decent home port for **Strait of Juan de Fuca** salmon fishing, when the season is open (which is rare of late). It's also within striking distance of northern Puget Sound salmon hot spots around Port Townsend, such as Midchannel Bank. Those traditional hot spots have been closed during peak summer months in recent years. But salmon fishing activity in this region has been almost as productive in the winter when anglers pursue blackmouth (immature chinook).

A number of **Olympic National Forest streams,** including the Dungeness and Gray Wolf Rivers, can be productive trout fisheries. A state license is required in the national forest; check the state regulations pamphlet for limits and restrictions. No license is required on upper-river portions inside Olympic National Park. Check with park rangers for regulations.

Photography

The **New Dungeness Lighthouse,** described in Beaches above, is a wonderful bit of coastal architecture, the perfect anchor for a seascape photo. But you'll have to walk the Dungeness Spit to shoot it. Even with a strong lens, angles from elsewhere in the valley are all wrong. The trick is to shoot it at sunset, but somehow get off the spit before dark. Let us know when you figure it out.

Many hiking photographers make award-winning photos on east-slope **Olympic Mountain trails** in the spring (May, typically), when the deep green forests come alive with pink blobs—**wild rhododendrons** breaking into bloom. Call the Quilcene Ranger District for a current bloom update before setting out. Note: This is one activity that might be best in a warm spring rain, which adds a silvery sheen to the forest landscape.

For a unique, airplane-style view of the entire northern Peninsula, drive up Happy Valley Road and take one of the new residential streets to the top of **Bell Hill.** It's truly breathtaking, and even though there's no real public space up here, the wealthy retirees who get to see the view every day probably won't call the cops unless you do something obnoxious.

Sea Kayaking/Windsurfing

The protected waters on the leeward side of Dungeness Spit were long ago discovered by paddlers, and they've increasingly become home port for board sailors. The center of activity here is **Cline Spit,** a county park that's really little more than a flat spot, parking lot, and boat ramp below view homes on the bluff overlooking Dungeness Spit. For windsurfers, the open water is a hot setup: plenty of wind from the strait sails right over the spit, but the accompanying tidal action does not. Kayakers launching from Cline Spit will love cruising the Dungeness Spit's inner shore, rich with bird and marine life attracted to the Dungeness National Wildlife Refuge (see Beaches, above). A local guide service, Kayaks and More, (360)683-3805, offers tours and trips through the refuge and along the Port Williams and Miller Bay waterways to the east. Off Marine Drive; follow Sequim-Dungeness Way north from downtown Sequim; (360) 683-5847.

Sequim Bay, with ample access at John Wayne Marina and Sequim Bay State Park, is the region's next-best kayaking water. Just outside the bay, Marilyn Nelson Park (see Beaches, above) is a good launch site for exploration of the Port Williams area.

Cycling

The **Dungeness Scenic Loop,** a 12-mile route from one end of Sequim through the Dungeness Valley to the strait and back, was designed for cars. But it's better on a bike. The loop, an ideal regional sampler, begins on Sequim Avenue and proceeds north to Sequim-Dungeness Way. Signs direct riders out to the strait, across the Dungeness River to the Dungeness National Wildlife Refuge, then back across the valley west of town to Olympic Game Farm, and back to the starting point. Maps are available at the Sequim–Dungeness Valley Visitors Center (US 101 at Washington Street). But the route is easy to follow. Shoulders are good, traffic fairly light.

Wildlife

The star of the show most of the year is the Dungeness National Wildlife Refuge. But that's not necessarily true in the winter. In recent years, Sequim has become one of very few towns in the West (Banff, Alberta comes to mind) where **wild elk** roam the streets, take up residence in city parks, and generally help themselves to local farmers' hay. The elk, loved by some Sequimites, loathed by others, are a herd of about 50 Roosevelt elk that live in the Dungeness River drainage most of the year. In the winter, encroaching snows—and deer hunters in the Olympic National Forest to the south—chase the elk into the lowlands of Happy Valley, just south of town. And in recent years, rapid residential development there has pushed the elk even farther north, right into town. Watch for the gentle beasts from mid-October to March on either side (and, regretfully, occasionally in the middle) of US 101, on the east side of Sequim. Also see Beaches, above, for additional wildlife viewing information.

Attractions

For visitors arriving from Seattle, the touristy stuff begins even before you get to Sequim. On Sequim Bay, near Blyn, the S'Klallam Indians operate the unique **Native Art Gallery** (East Sequim Bay Road). Across the highway is the recently opened, tribal-run **Seven Cedars** (800) 4LUCKY7), a truly mammoth gambling casino with valet parking and good food.

In Sequim proper (assuming there is such a thing), **Cedarbrook Herb Farm** (360) 683-7733; open March through December 23, daily) is Washington's oldest. It has a vast range of plants, scented geraniums, fresh-cut herbs, a pleasant gift shop—and the occasional visiting elk.

On the Sequim outskirts, two small but notable wineries are found: **Lost Mountain Winery** (3174 Lost Mountain Road; (360) 683-5229) offers tastings mainly by arrangement or chance; **Neuharth Winery** (885 S Still Road; (360) 683-9652) is open daily for tastings in summer (Wednesday to Sunday in the winter).

Also worthy of note are the downtown **Museum and Arts Center** (175 W Cedar Street; (360) 683-8110), which displays locally discovered ancient artifacts, including a display based on the nearby Manis Mastodon site, where a complete skeleton was unearthed by a farmer in 1978.

And if you're headed north toward the strait on Sequim-Dungeness Way (it begins as Sequim Avenue), keep your eyes peeled for the **New Dungeness Schoolhouse,** which dates to 1892.

Restaurants

Anything Goes ☆   Word of the casual Italian, off-beat Thai, and soon-to-be French food—all at reasonable prices—is slowly spreading, with regulars finding the relaxed atmosphere and friendly service a particular treat. *In Creamery Square, east of the center of town on US 101; (360) 683-1061; 235 E Washington, Sequim; $.*

The Buckhorn Grill   It may be a motel restaurant, but the Buckhorn Grill—which shares 17 wooded acres with the Best Western Sequim Bay Lodge—brings in hungry eaters from nearby Sequim and Port Angeles. The reason is simple: enjoyable food, well presented, served quickly and politely. *Hwy 101, 2 miles east of Sequim; (360) 683-9010; 268522 US 101, Sequim; $$.*

Eclipse ☆   Cambodian-born Lay Yin starts cooking and serving at 8am and closes by 3pm—and many or all of the dishes may disappear even before noon. Diners enter through the back door of this tract home, sit at a minuscule counter or at one of the two tables, and eat whatever is available from the predominantly southeast Asian menu. *Corner of 3rd and W Alder 3 blocks north of Washington (US 101); (360) 683-2760; 139 W Alder, Sequim; $.*

Hi-way 101 Diner   A neon-lit nostalgic kind of place where the back end of a '56 T-bird serves as a jukebox playing old *Hit Parade* songs. You can sit in a booth with sweet June Allyson smiling down on you, listen to "Two to Tango," and wrap your fist around a juicy "Awful Awful Burger." *On US 101; (360) 683-3388; 392 W Washington, Sequim; $.*

Jean's Mini Mart and Deli   An old corner minimart is what you see from the road, but what you can't see is the cozy little cafe tucked in the back where Jean started baking a little here and making soup there for the odd customer. The word got around, and now her cooking is in demand full-time during the weekdays. Hikers, take note: Good muffins, cinnamon rolls, and honey buns are offered as early as 5am. *½ block off US 101; (360) 683-6727; 134 S 2nd, Sequim; $.*

Oak Table Cafe ☆   Lunch only, now, at this noisy, boisterous, and chatty cafe. *At Third and Bell 1 block south of US 101; (360) 683-2179; 292 W Bell St, Sequim; $$.*

Lodgings

Greywolf Inn ☆   In a peaceful gray frame home on the east side of Sequim, transplanted Southerners Bill and Peggy Melang built this B&B offering several tasteful guest rooms. The wooded hillside has a trail for walkers and bird-watchers. *On Keeler Rd, 1 mile east of Sequim; (360) 683-5889; 395 Keeler Rd, Sequim; $$.*

Groveland Cottage ☆   At the turn of the century this was a family home in Dungeness, just a half mile from the beach. Now the place has the comfortable salty-air feel of an old beach house where you might have spent a summer holiday with a favorite aunt, with four cheerful rooms over a country-style store that sells a bit of everything. *Follow signs from Sequim toward Three Crabs; (360) 683-3565; 4861 Sequim-Dungeness Way, Dungeness; $$.*

Juan de Fuca Cottages ☆　Any of these comfortable cabins—either overlooking Dungeness Spit or with a view of the Olympics—is a special hideout in summer or winter. (A two-bedroom suite has both views and a welcoming fireplace.) Outside is the spit, begging for beach walks and clam digging. Two-night minimum stay July and August (and weekends year-round). *7¹/₂ miles north of Sequim; (360) 683-4433; 182 Marine Dr, Sequim; $$.*

Cheaper Sleeps

Sequim Bay Lodge　An attractive 54-unit resort with a putting course and outdoor heated pool, hot tub, and fireplace suites. *(360) 683-0691 or (800) 622-0691; 268522 US 101, Sequim.*

More Information

Sequim-Dungeness Chamber of Commerce (US 101 and E Washington): *(360) 683-6197.*

Olympic National Park: Overview

Nearly one million acres of pristine wilderness in the central Olympic Peninsula.

Choose your adjective. Wild. Unique. Thrilling. Pristine. Awesome. They all fit Olympic National Park, 922,000 acres of protected alpine, rain-forest and ocean-coast heaven separating the Puget Sound basin from the Pacific Ocean.

Olympic National Park, riding bucking-bronco tectonic plates beneath the North American mainland and the Pacific Ocean, literally is an island unto itself: a wildlife-rich wonderland walled off from the rest of the world. In ancient times, the Olympics were isolated by miles-thick glaciers. In more modern times, their deep, impenetrable forests and steep mountain walls have conspired to keep human interlopers out. The mountainous region was so foreboding and daunting that it wasn't fully explored by man until the end of the 19th century. The Olympic Peninsula indeed was, as historian Robert Wood has aptly noted, "the land that slept late."

The isolation that kept people out kept plants and animals in. Several species unique on the planet live here. Even some of the park's climatic zones are considered world treasures. Most notable is the park's westside temperate rain forest, where Douglas fir, western red cedar, Sitka spruce, and hemlock, gorged by an average of *14 feet* of rain a year, grow to almost ridiculous proportions. The park contains nearly a dozen world-record trees, some believed to be 1,000 years old. The great forests—the last surviving remnants of a once-great sea of Herculean trees stretching from the Pacific Coast to the Olympic crest—are largely responsible for the park's listing as a World Heritage Park and World Biosphere Site, honors granted to places with unique physical and biological features. The park's great westside rivers— the Soleduck, Bogachiel, Hoh, Queets, and Quinault—flow through some of the wildest river valleys left on the Pacific West Coast.

Just over the crest of Olympic's westernmost peaks lies an alpine wonderland: hundreds of square miles of snow-filled valleys, soothing tarns, inspiring peaks, and ridgetop meadows. Ninety-five percent of the park is wilderness, and the backcountry, negotiated only by a nearly 600-mile trail system winding through the deep river valleys, is where the park really shines. Here, you'll find large roving herds of Roosevelt elk, a majestic herd of mountain goats (threatened, ironically, by the park itself), plentiful Olympic marmots, black-tailed deer, black bears, coyotes, and cougars.

On the northern half of the Olympic Peninsula, a 57-mile-long coastal strip of the park clings to the Pacific shoreline, separated from the bulk of park lands by heavily logged private and Forest Service timberland. The coastal strip is the longest stretch of undeveloped ocean beach in the country, and most of it truly is wild. Very few roads penetrate the forest lands to the ocean here, and access is possible only by long, often wet hikes from the south, around La Push, or from the north, near Lake Ozette or from scenic Shi Shi Beach. The full length of coastal terrain here recently was designated as the Olympic Coastal Marine Sanctuary, and four separate national wildlife refuges add another layer of protection.

Olympic National Park is a special place, a land held in sacred trust not only by the federal government, but also by the many thousands of Washington recreators who feel a deep emotional connection to its unspoiled interior. Those of us who grew up in its valleys and high meadows, and on its alpine lakes and ocean beaches guard it with an almost ferocious jealousy—a rare level of devotion, even among notoriously protective conservationists.

People who never visit the Olympics might find this fervent emotional tie to a physical place fairly odd. But the park's regular worshippers believe the connection is as natural as water running downhill. It's a soul-searching link passed down to us from our grandfathers. For the expanding Lower 48 states, Olympic National Park was the very last frontier. For many of us, it remains so today.

Getting There

Only a few access roads lead into Olympic National Park. But US 101 loops almost completely around it. Most visitors from the Seattle area journey to the park's northern entrances near Port Angeles, a 77-mile trip northwest of Seattle on US 101 (plan on about 2 hours, assuming no ferry backups). For the most direct approach, take the Edmonds-Kingston or Seattle-Bainbridge ferry to Kitsap County and follow signs to the Hood Canal Floating Bridge. Cross the bridge into Jefferson County and follow Hwy 104 to US 101, which leads through Sequim and the Dungeness Valley to Port Angeles.

Bus service is available from Seattle to Port Angeles on Olympic Van Tours in Port Angeles, (360) 452-3858, which also has daily scheduled sight-seeing tours. Arrangements can be made for drop-offs and pickups at trail-heads throughout the park. Clallam Transit, (360) 452-4511, offers shuttle service to Lake Crescent, Forks, Neah Bay, and La Push. Grays Harbor Transit, (360) 532-2770, provides service from Olympia and Aberdeen to Lake Quinault.

Adjoining Areas

Portions of Olympic National Park are described in each chapter of the Olympic Peninsula and Pacific Coast section.

inside out

Olympic National Park Rules and Regulations

Keep in mind that **trail regulations** inside Olympic are substantially more restrictive than those on most national forest trails in Washington:

Campfires are prohibited in most alpine areas above 3,500 feet and at most other popular backcountry camps at lower elevations. Check with the park visitors center for specific rules for the area you plan to visit. Better yet, avoid the problem by carrying a stove for any overnight trip in the park. Olympic's backcountry is too valuable to mar with fire rings, let alone destroy with a wildfire sparked by a careless camper. A stove is the best investment you can make in your grandchildren's backpacking future.

Pets and **mountain bikes** are forbidden on all Olympic National Park trails except the Spruce Railroad Trail and Boulder Creek (Olympic Hot Springs) Trail, where cycles are allowed. If you can't live for a day without your dog or fat tires, pick a trail in the Olympic National Forest, where both are allowed. Backcountry rangers can—and do—issue cita-tions. Dogs are allowed in campgrounds, on paved roads, and on ocean beaches, providing they're on a leash.

Hiking permits are not required for day hikes. But **backcountry permits** are required for all overnight stays on park trails. They're free and available at all ranger stations and visitors centers. At this writing, daily entry quotas were in force to prevent overcrowding in three popular areas from Memorial Day through Labor Day: Seven Lakes Basin, below High Divide in the upper Soleduck drainage; Lake Constance and Flapjack Lakes in the eastern Olympics; and the Cape Alava/Sand Point ocean beach area west of Lake Ozette. Call the Visitors Information Center, (360) 452-0330, for reservations and information.

Groups are limited to 12 in the backcountry. Larger groups should divide up, then travel and camp at least a half-mile apart. **Pack stock** are allowed on most trails, but forbidden in some sensitive areas. Call the park for a current list of trails open to horses and other pack animals, as well as wilderness guidelines for stock use.

A word about fees: Nothing is free anymore, and our national parks are no exception. In Olympic, fee-collection stations have sprung up like warts on many roads, notably Hurricane Ridge, Elwha, Sol Duc, and the Hoh River Valley. Fees increased in 1997 for the first time in many years. But you only pay once a week: the $10 entrance permit is good for seven days at all park entrances. Annual passes ($20; Olympic National Park only) and Golden Eagle Passports (at this writing, $25; all U.S. National Parks—your best value) are available at the entrance booths. Fees generally are collected at all gates from May through September, and on winter weekends at the Heart o' the Hills entrance near Port Angeles. Hint: If you show up really early in the morning, Mr. or Ms. Gatekeeper often is still home in bed, dreaming about issuing wheels-off-the-pavement citations.

Scenic Drives

Depending on your outdoor persuasion, the best or worst thing about Olympic National Park is that, with a few exceptions, you can't really drive into it. About 95 percent of the park, or about 900,000 acres, is wilderness, with no roads to speak of. The 5 percent of developed park lands are concentrated around Hurricane Ridge, Kalaloch, the Hoh and Soleduck Rivers, Lake Crescent, and Lake Quinault—all places you can drive to, and around once you get there.

Fortunately, US 101 provides a chance to drive *around* the entire park, providing easy access to its most popular road-accessible attractions. If you're a visitor with only a week to spare, or a newcomer hoping to sample the entire park on one trip, the US 101 loop is a great way to go. Most travelers like to drive only a few hours at a time, then set up camp or check in for lodging at a campground or inn before exploring the area by foot or boat. Follow that schedule, and you ll need about a week to make the entire loop.

Remember, driving the Olympic Loop isn't like making a loop trip through Yellowstone. Olympic's natural wonders won't wander up to your car and press their nose against the window. You need to go find them, usually by following a side road 20 to 30 miles into the park's interior. A hasty traveler could, in fact, drive the entire US 101 loop in one day—and see fewer of the park's attractions than someone sitting at home staring at a map.

US 101 is the connector for this trip, not the main attraction. Aside from short stretches along Lake Crescent and the Kalaloch beach strip, in fact, much of the road passes through downright ugliness. As it travels through the heart of the peninsula, sprawling forest lands on either side of 101 have been devastated by clearcutting. Logging on state, federal, and even tribal lands here has taken a heavy toll. Most of the western peninsula's great rain forest—lush, unique ecosystems with rapid tree growth unequaled on the planet—was wiped out here between 1910 and the 1970s. Logging practices have improved in recent years, but much of this land was logged early in the century, when environmental restrictions were unheard of. The resulting moonscape surface is a tragic reminder of the long-lasting consequences of industrial greed. So leave yourself enough time to venture into Olympic National Park—the peninsula's only surviving significant rain forest refuge—for a taste of what this great land once was.

That established, a typical Olympic loop driven counterclockwise from north to south would include stops at these **park highlights:** Hurricane Ridge, Lake Crescent, Sol Duc Hot Springs, Rialto Beach, Hoh Rain Forest, Kalaloch, and Lake Quinault. From here, the route exits the park and detours south on Hwy 12 and Hwy 8 before turning north up the western shore of Hood Canal on US 101, through scenic Olympic National Forest terrain (see the Hood Canal, and Olympic National Forest and the East Slope Olympics chapters). From here, you can access popular eastside national park venues such as the North Fork Skokomish, Dosewallips, and Gray Wolf river valleys.

Be prepared to poke along. US 101 is two lanes almost all the way, often winding, and frequented by slow traffic. The route used to be plugged with logging trucks. Their numbers have declined of late. But gapers have replaced cutters: it seems as though four Winnebagos have sprung up to replace each dearly departed log hauler. Traveling the peninsula frequently for many years has taught us a lesson, which we'll pass on as **locals advice:** If you live in Western Washington and plan to return to Olympic many times over the years, don't kill yourself fighting traffic on the Olympic Loop. Pick one area and get to know it personally by spending several days there, or a week. The rest of it—Congress cooperating—

will still be there next time you get a vacation. Further advice: If your Olympic destination is the Kalaloch area or anywhere south, it's probably faster to drive onto the peninsula via Olympia, Aberdeen, and Hoquiam, than via the busier northern, Port Angeles route.

Hiking/Backpacking

It may be tough to find any single area in the country with a richer mix of hiking terrain. Because 95 percent of its terrain is wilderness that can't be reached by car, foot travel long has been the preferred mode of transport in Olympic. In the early days, John Huelsdonk, the Iron Man of the Hoh, is said to have carried a cast-iron stove far up a river valley trail, commenting to passersby that the stove was no trouble, but the shifting 50-pound sack of flour inside was giving him fits. In modern days, backpackers whine and bellyache about being forced to carry an extra tent rain fly. But it's safe to say that both parties felt the same satisfaction upon getting where they were going. In Olympic, the carry-your-own-weight-and-then-some tradition lives on.

Detailed descriptions of many of Olympic's best short, medium, and long hikes can be found in the Port Angeles and Hurricane Ridge; Neah Bay, Lake Ozette, and Sekiu; Lake Crescent and the Upper Soleduck; Forks and La Push; Central Coast: Hoh, Kalaloch, and Queets; Lake Quinault and Quinault River Valley; Hood Canal; and Olympic National Forest and the East Slope Olympics chapters. But this list of don't-miss trails might serve as a good starting point.

Short 'n' easy

Even if you're zipping around the Olympic Peninsula by car, with little time to waste on the trail, it's still possible to take a roadside sip of wilderness. Consider a short hike to Hurricane Hill Summit; Humes Ranch on the Elwha River; Marymere Falls; Spruce Railroad on Lake Crescent; Cape Alava near Lake Ozette; Soleduck Falls; Rialto Beach; Hoh River's Hall of Mosses; the Queets River 3-mile nature loop; Lake Quinault's Rain Forest Loop, Graves Creek Loop or Maple Glade Rain Forest; or Kalaloch's Beach 4 or Ruby Beach. The list could go on indefinitely. But if you can hit even a fourth of those, you're guaranteed to be back to discover more on your own.

Weekend backpack routes

Popular one- to three-day destinations are too numerous to list here. Hikers should consult a guide such as *Pacific Northwest Hiking* (Foghorn Press), co-written by this author and Dan A. Nelson, or *Olympic Mountains Trail Guide* by Robert S. Wood (The Mountaineers). But some personal favorite backpack routes include Grand Valley and Grand Pass near Hurricane Ridge; Appleton Pass in the upper Elwha drainage; Deer Lake in the Soleduck area; the Sand Point/Cape Alava Loop near Lake Ozette; the North Fork Skokomish Trail; the Lower Gray Wolf Trail, the West Fork Dosewallips Trail to Honeymoon Meadows; Royal Basin; the Hoh River Trail to Glacier Meadows; and the East Fork Quinault Trail to Enchanted Valley.

Long-distance treks

Once the appetite is whetted, many Olympic veterans answer the same call as the legendary Press Expedition heard in the 1890s: "Cross the Olympics." Several routes are possible, ranging from 35 to 46 miles and requiring strong legs, a strong back, and a week of spare time. The Elwha River/Low Divide/North Fork Quinault traverse, which follows the Press Expedition route nearly exactly, is the best north-south Olympic traverse. The 45-mile crossing is only moderately difficult, and hikes about the same way in either direction. The high point is Low Divide, 3,650 feet. The most popular east-west traverse is the East Fork Quinault/Anderson Pass/Dosewallips River route (about 30 miles), which can allow stops at two of the park's most spectacular backcountry sites: O'Neil Pass and Enchanted Valley.

Other long treks considered park classics include the entire 57-mile coastal strip (careful tide planning is required); the 47-mile Skyline Loop between the Queets and Quinault drainages; the 19-mile High Divide Loop between the Soleduck and Hoh drainages; the Gray Wolf, Dosewallips, Duckabush, and North Fork Skokomish river valleys in the eastern slope Olympics; and the rugged, isolated Bailey Range Traverse, an off-trail journey in the park's northern interior for experienced trekkers only.

Camping

Olympic offers **925 campsites,** which range from usually full to usually vacant depending on season and location. The bulk are found in the park's five largest campgrounds, Heart o' the Hills on Hurricane Ridge Road (105 sites); Kalaloch on US 101 (177 sites); Mora near La Push (94 sites); Hoh (89 sites); and Sol Duc (80 sites; closes during snow). Those campgrounds usually are open all year, as are Staircase, Ozette, July Creek, North Fork, Queets, Graves Creek, and Elwha. The remaining campgrounds—Altaire, Deer Park, and Dosewallips—are open from May to November. In spite of this schedule, if you're camping in winter months, it's always a good idea to call before departing. Wicked weather can and often does close roads.

Campsite fees are $10, and are collected at all campgrounds except

Deer Park, North Fork, Ozette, and Queets. Some parks, open during the winter without services such as water, revert to a no-fee status until spring. For heartier campers, particularly those with warm RVs, the colder, off-season months can be a great time to visit Olympic in its natural state, without swarming summer crowds.

No sites can be reserved in Olympic, and in the summer, landing a space can be frustrating. That's especially true at the park's most popular destinations: Kalaloch, Hoh, and Mora. See individual chapters on those areas for some tips on getting in—or alternative campgrounds in case you can't. Worth noting are the string of Olympic National Forest campgrounds perched near the park's borders, particularly on the east and west sides. Campsites often are available there even when they're full in national park campgrounds a short distance away. See the Olympic National Forest and the East Slope Olympics chapter for details.

Olympic's campgrounds have a maximum stay of 14 days. Group campsites are available at Kalaloch (30 person maximum) and Mora (40 person maximum). Group camps can be reserved in advance by calling the park. A fee of 50 cents per camper is charged; RVs and multiple vehicles are discouraged.

Fishing

With productive **surf fishing** on the coast, excellent salmon and steelhead fishing in its western **rivers,** and good trout fishing in **Lake Crescent, Lake Quinault,** and dozens of **high alpine lakes,** Olympic's angling opportunities are uncommonly good, especially for a national park. State fishing licenses are not required inside park boundaries, but anglers do need special anadromous fish permits, such as a state steelhead or salmon punch card, to fish for those species. Special state licenses also are required to dig razor clams during open seasons at **Kalaloch.**

Most park waters adhere to general state fishing regulations (pick up a regulation pamphlet at sporting goods stores). But many park lakes and streams also have special restrictions on bait, minimum size, bag limits, and seasons. Some of those rules might differ from the same waters downstream, outside the park. And regulations change frequently. So it's always important to check regulations at local ranger stations.

Consult individual chapters on Olympic destinations for location-specific fishing information.

Canoeing/Kayaking

Surf kayaking is an increasingly popular activity at Olympic's coastal beaches, particularly those with good vehicle access, such as Kalaloch and

Rialto Beach near La Push. Canoeists and sea kayakers love the sprawling waters of Lake Ozette (where a boat-in campground is available), Lake Crescent and Lake Quinault. River kayakers can be found in most of the park's major rivers, but the lower Elwha and upper and lower Soleduck are favorites.

Remember, Olympic's rivers aren't places for amateurs. Some waterways, such as the Hoh River, have proven particularly dangerous to boaters because of fluctuating water levels and nasty log jams.

Boating/Sailing

Olympic National Park isn't a major destination for boaters. But park visitors can get out on the water in rental craft at **Lake Quinault** and **Lake Crescent.** Many visitors also launch small craft in Lake Ozette. In addition, interpretive tours of Lake Crescent are conducted on a paddlewheel replica, the M.V. *Storm King,* during summer months. See the Lake Crescent and the Upper Soleduck chapter for more information.

Beaches

Sandy shorelines on Olympic's 57-mile coastal strip are among the last remaining undeveloped saltwater beaches in the nation. You can't really go wrong with an Olympic saltwater beach, but enduring favorites remain the beaches around **Kalaloch, Rialto Beach** near La Push, **Cape Alava** and **Sand Point** near Lake Ozette, and **Shi Shi Beach** just south of Neah Bay. All the park's beaches are wilderness, and most offshore islands are protected by **Flattery Rocks** and Quillayute Needles National Wildlife Refuges. In 1994 the entire coastal area from Cape Flattery south to Copalis and west for 30 miles was designated as the **Olympic Coast National Marine Sanctuary**, protecting it from heinous threats such as offshore oil drilling. This makes the park's beach strip a favorite destination for wildlife watchers in search of shore birds, marine mammals, or migratory whales.

Biking

Olympic is not a cyclist's paradise. Far from it, in fact. While some access roads make adequate cycle routes for those determined to turn the pedals, general cycle access is poor. That's due largely to the park's physical layout. The main access route, US 101, is of course open to road cyclists. But it's far from ideal, with heavy truck and RV traffic and inadequate shoulders along many stretches.

The lack of interior roads in the park cuts down on opportunities to cycle less traveled highways. And the predominantly wilderness designation inside the park leaves almost every backcountry trail off-limits to mountain bikes. As you'll see from the chapters on park destinations, road cycling is possible in most areas of the park. But with minor exceptions such as the Spruce Railroad Trail, where mountain biking is allowed, it's simply not what most people come here to do.

Rafting

Guided raft trips are available on most westside park rivers. Call park headquarters, (360) 452-4501, for a list of outfitters.

Winter Activities

Three small ski lifts are operated by a private ski club at **Hurricane Ridge** during winter months. The vertical drop is tiny compared to other Northwest ski destinations. But Port Angeles locals enjoy the diversion. Hurricane Ridge also is a good cross-country ski destination, with several miles of snow-covered roads—and millions of acres of wide-open backcountry—open to skinny skis. **Ski rentals** are available in Port Angeles and at the Hurricane Ridge Visitors Center. Guided snowshoe tours also are conducted by park rangers on some winter weekends, and a sliding area usually is maintained for snow tubers.

Be aware that strong winds and wet weather often create icy conditions that can make cross-country skiing and snowshoeing a little bit more adventurous than most people prefer. The same weather often wreaks havoc on the park's plowing schedule for Hurricane Ridge Road. Generally, the road is plowed and open by 9am on Friday, Saturday, and Sunday. But the schedule is always tentative. Call the park before you leave. See the Port Angeles and Hurricane Ridge chapter for more information.

Wildlife

Olympic is rich with animal life, some of it found only here. By most accounts, the park's most majestic creature is the **Roosevelt Elk,** which in many respects deserves credit for creation of the park in the first place. President Theodore Roosevelt's passion for big game led in 1909 to protection of much of what now is Olympic National Park. Unlike its cousin, the smaller Rocky Mountain elk, the Roosevelt elk is a shy herd animal that's particularly wary of humans. Most park visitors never see one. That makes happening upon a herd of these gentle beasts an especially rare treat. During summer months, most of the park's herd retreats to high alpine valleys. In the winter and early spring, they're most often seen in westside river valleys. The Queets, North and East Fork Quinault, and

Hoh River Trails provide good chances to encounter an elk during off-season months. Watching a herd pass silently across your path is a memory that will stick with you for life. Your best chance to see one from a road is Lake Quinault's North Shore Road. Look for them in the flats on both sides of the road between the Quinault Ranger Station and the Quinault Bridge, which connects North and South Shore Roads.

Conversely, the park's most ubiquitous creatures, friendly **black-tailed deer,** are found throughout the park and often seen in campgrounds and other public places. They're quite bold in the alpine backcountry, where they'll sometimes wander right up to tents filled with sleeping backpackers. Another alpine creature, the **Olympic marmot,** is unique to the park and is a constant friendly companion to backcountry visitors, who watch them whistle, cavort, and play marmot-tag in alpine meadows. They're commonly seen in the Hurricane Ridge area, as well.

Black bear are common in the park, and are often spotted in the high, treeless alpine terrain. They generally keep to themselves. While basic, common-sense food handling is a good idea in the backcountry, human-bear conflicts are exceedingly rare here. Most black bears encountered on a trail will do their best to steer clear of human interlopers. But keep in mind that bears should never be approached or provoked, *especially* a mother with a cub or cubs.

Another park predator, the **cougar,** is thriving, and some menacing encounters with humans have been reported in recent years. Keep a watchful eye for cougars (and **bobcats,** also common in the park), especially when traveling in the backcountry with children. Unlike the continent's other feared predator, the grizzly bear (which you will not find in Olympic), cougars can be intimidated into leaving you alone. If you encounter one, make yourself appear as large, ornery, and formidable as possible. Chances are good you'll go home unscathed—with a great story.

Olympic's backcountry also presents occasional encounters with **coyotes, raccoons, red foxes** (rare), and a rich community of other small mammals. The native **Olympic wolf,** sadly, was hunted to extinction here in the early 20th century, before the park was protected. Olympic seems a prime candidate for wolf reintroduction, but the park hasn't publicly touched that hot issue yet.

Another warm-blooded Olympic creature, the **mountain goat,** has stirred up a storm of controversy in the past two decades. The park's current goat herd was introduced by hunters in the 1920s (debate continues as to whether goats inhabited the park previously). After national park status in 1938, goat hunting inside the park ceased, and goat numbers grew. Park scientists estimate Olympic's herd grew to more than 1,000 animals in the mid-1980s. Concern about the goat's impact on some rare alpine plants prompted a live-capture-and-removal program in the late 1980s. A 1994 census indicated fewer than 300 goats remained in the park.

In spite of that reduction, park officials continue to maintain that the remaining goats should be shot—probably from helicopters—to protect the park's plants. (Federal policy allows the park to eradicate an "introduced" species if it's doing irreparable harm to an ecosystem. Park scientists say that is true of the Olympic goat, even though they have conceded in studies that none of the park's rare alpine plants are in danger of extinction.)

At this writing, park officials are still working on a long-delayed final environmental impact statement justifying the extermination of the park's goats. That decision likely will meet with strong opposition—surveys have indicated three of four Washington residents oppose killing the gentle beasts. The Washington Department of Fish and Wildlife, which manages goats on Olympic National Forest lands surrounding the park (many goats migrate between jurisdictions) also oppose killing. And animal welfare groups have vowed to sue if a goat-kill policy is approved. But the animals' long-term future is uncertain.

One thing is for sure: hikers who want the rare thrill of seeing an Olympic goat in its well-established wild habitat should do so soon. Because of the park rangers' helicopter harassment, that's a lot more difficult than it used to be. Most of the park's remaining goats are concentrated in hard-to-reach interior alpine areas, such as the secluded Bailey Range.

Finally, the park's coastal strip, a fully protected wilderness that surely qualifies as a national treasure, is teeming with marine mammals. **Sea** and **river otters, bald eagles, harbor seals,** and **sea lions** are common sights on the coast. Special visitors seen only rarely include **elephant seals** and **gray, minke,** and **humpback whales,** which migrate near the coast in spring and fall months. **Harbor porpoises, orca whales, Dall's porpoises,** and **Pacific dolphins** also have been known to swim through the park's protected coastal waters.

outside in

Restaurants/Lodgings

Olympic is not all soggy trails and rugged, wild alpine terrain. Overnight lodgings with their own unique, lodge-style character can be found in several park areas, all operated by private concessionaires. The most popular inside the park are **Lake Crescent Lodge, Kalaloch Lodge** and oceanfront cabins, and **Sol Duc Hot Springs Resort. Lake Quinault Lodge** is located outside park boundaries, but is a favorite park destination, nonetheless.

Reservations should be made several months in advance at all park lodges, particularly Kalaloch and Lake Quinault Lodges, which are open all year. Sol Duc and Lake Crescent are open during summer months only. See the appropriate chapters in this section.

More Information

Olympic National Park Headquarters, Port Angeles: *(360) 452-4501.*
Port Angeles Visitors Center (general information): *(360) 452-0330.*
Regional Ranger Stations (all area code 360):
>   **Elwha** *452-9191.*
>   **Forks NPS/USFS Information Station** *374-6522.*
>   **Heart o' the Hills** *452-2713.*
>   **Hoh Rain Forest** *374-6925.*
>   **Kalaloch** *962-2283.*
>   **Lake Crescent** *928-3380.*
>   **Mora** *374-5460.*
>   **Ozette** *963-2725.*
>   **Queets** *962-2283.*
>   **Quinault** *288-2444.*
>   **Sol Duc** *928-3380.*
>   **Staircase** *877-5569.*

Port Angeles and Hurricane Ridge

From the Port Angeles City Pier south to Hurricane Ridge in Olympic National Park, east to Deer Park and west to the Lyre River, including the lower Elwha River Valley, Tongue Point Marine Reserve, and Salt Creek Recreation Area.

Your friends from Boston deliver the fateful news by e-mail: they're coming to Seattle, want to sample the very essence of Northwest outdoor life, and they're relying solely on you to be their recreational compass. Oh, yeah: they've only got three days.

You'd be hard-pressed to send them in a better direction than Port Angeles. The city itself doesn't look like much—a big, belching pulp mill, a lot of Big Timber—era houses that saw their best days back when Lawrence Welk was only ah-one.

The thing about Port Angeles, though, is that this city doesn't *need* to look like much. The town of 18,000 has the Strait of Juan de Fuca and Vancouver Island on its back porch, the Pacific Coast and Dungeness Valley in side bedrooms, and magnificent Olympic National Park splayed out all over the front yard.

Any one of those things would make this a great place to while away a year or 10. The combination of all four makes it a place where many of us would sincerely like to sink roots. The greatest attraction is the city's immediate proximity to Olympic National Park. The park, 922,000 acres of stunning alpine and coastal wilderness, isn't merely unique in Washington state. In many ways it's unparalleled on the planet. And Port Angeles is the closest thing to a bustling city anywhere near its borders.

Its location makes the old port city a natural jumping-off point for the wonders of the northern Olympics, the park's most spectacular terrain. City residents haven't overlooked this bit of good fortune, and in the past two decades have shifted to a tourist-driven marketing strategy. One result is that Port Angeles—once little more than a supply stop on the way to Lake Crescent, Appleton Pass, or the Elwha River Valley—has become a pleasant outdoor-oriented destination unto itself. The city's recent trail and wharf improvements, for example, have turned an ugly waterfront industrial zone into a fairly agreeable place to spend a day on the water.

When that gets old, take a drive through the city's upper residential neighborhoods. You just might spot a guidebook author doing very early retirement-property research.

Getting There

Port Angeles is a 77-mile drive west of Seattle on US 101 (plan on about 2 hours, assuming no ferry backups). For the most direct approach, take the Edmonds-Kingston or Seattle-Bainbridge ferry to Kitsap County and follow signs to the Hood Canal Floating Bridge. Cross the bridge into Jefferson County and follow Hwy 104 to US 101, which leads through Sequim and the Dungeness Valley to Port Angeles. Travel (in)sanity note: Summer weekend travelers should strongly consider skipping the ferry and heading south to cross Puget Sound at the Tacoma Narrows Bridge and driving up Kitsap Peninsula to the Hood Canal Bridge. This route adds about 60 driving miles to the trip, but could save hours of boring waits at ferry terminals.

Adjoining Areas

EAST: **Sequim and the Dungeness Valley**

WEST: **Neah Bay, Lake Ozette, and Sekiu**

SOUTH **Olympic National Park: Overview; Olympic National Forest and the East Slope Olympics; Lake Crescent and the Upper Soleduck**

inside out

Hiking/Backpacking

The interior Olympics contain what many consider to be the cream of the nation's wilderness crop for backpack treks and long day hikes. More than 95 percent of Olympic National Park's wilderness is accessible only by trail, and some of the most magnificent hikes begin within 30 minutes of downtown Port Angeles. For a full range of options, consult with park specialists at the visitors center on Hurricane Ridge Road; (360) 452-0330. Here's a quick guide to the very best of the best, divided by area. (Remember: Mountain bikes, dogs, and horses are forbidden on most Olympic National Park trails.)

Hurricane Ridge

Trails fan out literally in every direction from the Ridge, Olympic National Park's high-alpine visitors' heaven 17 miles south of Port Angeles. For a short walk offering a brief sip of the majestic Olympic high country, head out on one of the short **Nature Loop** (easy, less than 1 mile) trails from the Hurricane parking lot. They lead north through beautiful alpine meadows (aburst with wildflower colors after the snowmelt in June and July), past peaceful black-tailed deer to mile-high views of Port Angeles, the Strait of Juan de Fuca, and much of Vancouver Island. Most loops are short, relatively flat (wheelchair accessible), and take 30 minutes or less.

For a slightly more aggressive, much more exhilarating walk, head north on the **Lake Angeles–Klahhane Ridge Trail,** (moderate; 7 miles round trip), which leaves from the east end of the parking lot, climbs up along Sunrise Ridge below the stony face of 6,100-foot Mount Angeles, and at 3.5 miles connects with the trail down to Lake Angeles and Heart o' the Hills. Grand views all the way. Warning: Much of the route is wind-exposed. Bring water and a good parka. Energy-burst option: If you're liking what you see and want more, follow the path down (way down) to Lake Angeles and arrive, bleeding toes and all, at the Heart o' the Hills Trailhead. Total one-way distance: about 10 miles, and 4,000 vertical feet. Wise veterans walk it one way, downhill.

An easy, popular trail that rates as one of the best half-day hikes in the Northwest is the **Hurricane Hill Trail** (moderate; 3 miles round trip), which departs from the ends of Hurricane Ridge Road, about a quarter-mile beyond the Hurricane Picnic Area. This route, a former road, is a moderate uphill climb that starts and ends above treeline in Olympic's amazing alpine country. It's 1.5 miles to the 5,700-foot summit, the site of an old lookout. The 360-degree panorama is awesome, with views north to Victoria and south to the alpine peaks of the Olympics. This trail is at its best in early summer, when wildflowers paint the rolling slopes—and just enough snow lingers to whip up a trail margarita at your lunch stop. The first half-mile of this trail is wheelchair-accessible, with grades of 2 to 6 percent.

If you're looking for an endorphin rush, proceed directly to the notorious **Switchback Trail** (very difficult, 3 miles round trip), which begins in a pullout several miles below the Hurricane Ridge parking lot. The trail (surprise!) switches back about 17 million times on its steep, torturous, 1.5-mile, 1,600-vertical-foot ascent to Klahhane Ridge. Here, you either A) drop dead, B) sit and admire the view, C) climb Mount Angeles, or D) continue merrily on your way down the Klahhane Ridge and Lake Angeles or Heather Park Trails.

One of Olympic's premier weekend backpacking trails begins east of Hurricane Ridge, at the end of **Obstruction Point Road.** The narrow gravel road, which begins at the east end of the Ridge parking lot, leads 7.5 miles to a turnaround/trailhead. Here, hikers can embark on the **Grand Ridge Trail** (moderate; 7.5 miles one way), a high-altitude ridgetop walk to Deer Park (see Camping, below). From the same trailhead at Obstruction Point, a separate path leads over Lillian Ridge and down into majestic **Grand Valley** (moderate; various lengths possible), where a string of three lakes (Grand, Moose, and Gladys) awaits backpackers and strong day hikers. Campsites and wildlife are present at all of the lakes, and hikers will want to walk to the end of the trail at Grand Pass (8 miles from Obstruction Point) for a stupendous all-around Olympic Mountains view. Note: Obstruction Point Road is open during summer months only. The rest of the year, the road makes a fine winter cross-country ski or snowshoe trek, or a spring snow hike.

Heart o' the Hills

A trailhead across Hurricane Ridge Road from Heart o' the Hills, Olympic's primary north-end campground, offers two fine day hikes. One is the lower extension of the **Lake Angeles and Klahhane Ridge Trail** (moderate; 7 miles round trip to lake) mentioned above. The first 3.5 miles are a moderate-to-steep uphill walk through deep forest, before the path opens up to beautiful, emerald-green Lake Angeles. The aerobically challenged will want to stop here. But gung-ho hikers can continue on around the lake, up an unsettlingly steep pitch to the top of Klahhane Ridge, and on to Hurricane Ridge parking lot (10 miles) or a junction with the Heather Park Trail (6.2 miles).

The other path is the **Heather Park Trail** (difficult; 12.4 miles round trip), which climbs at a similar pace through wooded terrain to a terraced, rocky, parklike area at the base of Mount Angeles, a popular climbing venue. Views from Heather Park are breathtaking, looking mostly north over the Strait of Juan de Fuca. Continue on to a junction, at 6.2 miles, with the Lake Angeles Trail. Strong hikers, you're already ahead of us; you can hike the whole circuit as a 12.4-mile loop—up, over, and back—in a day.

Elwha River

About 8 miles west of Port Angeles, the **Elwha River Road,** which leads south up one of the Olympic Peninsula's mightiest waterways, is easy to miss. Don't. Some of the best hiking in the state is just up the way, depart-ing from two major trailheads.

The first, **Whiskey Bend,** is reached by following a gravel road 4.5 miles from the Elwha Ranger Station. This trailhead, the jump-off point for many trans-Olympic backpacking ventures, also was the jump-off point for the famed Press Expedition, which first explored the interior Olympics in 1890. It took the expedition six months (in the winter—go figure) to map a route up the Elwha to Low Divide and down the Quinault Valley. Today, some super-strong hikers follow the same 44-mile route in a single, albeit 15-hour, day.

The first 20 miles or so of the **Elwha River Trail** (moderate; various lengths) are a low-elevation walk, snow-free nearly all year. It's not replete with sweeping views, but it's a peaceful path through mostly undisturbed old-growth forest. Many backpackers will follow the Press Expedition route all the way south to the North Fork Quinault Campground, a 44-mile trip of about four days. The hike on the same trail into and back out from **Low Divide** (difficult; 28.5 miles round trip) also is a good, week-long backpack venture. Most day hikers, however, will be content to wan-der 2 miles in to **Humes Ranch** (easy; 4 miles round trip), site of Grant Humes's 1889 homestead cabin, or zip all the way into **Elkhorn,** a pleas-ant backcountry camp and seasonal ranger station 11.5 miles up the trail.

On the opposite side of this valley, the Elwha River Road climbs past Lake Mills and Glines Canyon Dam, the upper of two Elwha dams built early in the century without fish ladders, thus destroying one of the great-est salmon-spawning habitats in the West. The road eventually turns to gravel, and dead-ends about 10 miles from US 101. Here, on the other side of an automobile gate, a decaying road leads 2.4 miles to (walk-in) **Boulder Creek Campground** and **Olympic Hot Springs** (easy, 4.8 miles round trip), an always-popular park retreat. The hot springs are at the site of a former hotel and resort, a grand facility that had its own Olympic-size swimming pool. The complex closed after a fire in 1966 and ultimately was bulldozed by its owners. The park then let the hot springs, gurgling from a hillside above Boulder Creek, go natural, prohibiting any new development. (And discouraging most visitation; the hot springs don't even show up on official Olympic maps.) Today, many visitors go natural as well, flagrantly disregarding the Park's no-nudity policy in the bathwa-ter-warm hot springs. Don't worry: you won't be excluded if you wear a suit. Helpful tip: The farther up on the hillside it is, the cleaner (and smaller) the hot pool is likely to be.

For stronger hikers, however, the hot springs are just the launching point. From here, separate trails lead up the valley to **Boulder Lake** (moderately difficult; 11.6-miles round trip) and **Appleton Pass** (difficult; 15.2 miles round trip). Both are excellent day hike or weekend back-packing destinations—and can be packed to the gills on sunny summer weekends. Boulder Lake has good campsites, good fishing for brook trout, and a good side trip—a steep scramble to the summit of nearby Boulder Peak. Appleton Pass offers acres of alpine wildflowers, mind-altering views of Mount Carrie and the spectacular **Bailey Range,** and access to the **Soleduck River** trail system. Sol Duc Hot Springs Resort is 7.3 miles down and west of the pass; shuttle hikers can make a 15.5-mile one-way hike in either direction. (See the Lake Crescent and the Upper Soleduck chapter.)

Back down on the lower portion of the Elwha River Road, about 2 miles south of US 101, children or those looking for just a short stroll will enjoy the **Madison Falls Trail** (easy, 1.5 miles round trip). It's a nice pic-nic spot, and the trail to this pretty waterfall is wheelchair-accessible.

Another good day-hiking destination in the region is **Salt Creek Recreation Area** (see Camping, below), where trails lead several miles to a deep-water cove on the Strait of Juan de Fuca and to the top of **Striped Peak,** where a viewpoint offers a pilot's-eye view of the strait and Vancou-ver Island.

In Port Angeles itself, the city's new **Waterfront Trail** (easy; optional lengths) is an enjoyable, flat walk along the working waterfront and out onto Ediz Hook. Much of the trail, part of a converted railway, runs along industrial areas, but views of Mount Baker and the North Cascades are very nice, and seals and sea lions sometimes will gaze at you with moon-pie eyes from the harbor. The trail, still a work in progress, will be 10 miles long when it's finished. Park and begin at the City Pier, near the foot of Lincoln Street.

For hiking and backpacking supplies and advice, consult **Olympic Mountaineering** (221 S Peabody, Port Angeles; (360) 452-0240).

Camping

Olympic National Park

Heart o' the Hills campground (see Hiking/Backpacking, above) is the primary attraction. The park, perched at Olympic's northern gateway, is an unusually nice campground set in the tall, thin trees. It's quiet, clean, and generally packed with RVs from Nebraska all summer. But you can usu-ally stumble into a site midweek without too much trouble. The camp-ground has 105 sites (no hookups; maximum RV length, 21 feet).The evening campfire talks are usually worth your while, or at least they used to be before the federal government dispensed with such frivolities. Beware the predatory night-stalking raccoons, particularly Old Three

Legs, one of our longtime friends. Heart o' the Hills is open all year. Sites cannot be reserved. *On Hurricane Ridge Road 5 miles south of Port Angeles; (360) 452-0330.*

Farther east, **Deer Park,** open during summer months only, is a bit more primitive, a lot more remote, and…well, miserably dusty in the dry season. But hey: it's free. And the view is tough to beat. At 5,400 feet, this is one of the more lofty campgrounds in the state, and the view of the Strait of Juan de Fuca, Dungeness Valley, and most of northern Puget Sound is unique. The 18 tent sites are almost an afterthought. Deer Park, the former site of one of Washington's earliest ski lodges, is no place for RVs. Sites are too small, the 17-mile, mostly gravel road too rough (it's the kind of mountain road that makes passengers wish *they* were driving). The campground is open from mid-June to first snows in October. Campsites (free) cannot be reserved. *From US 101 about 6 miles east of Port Angeles, follow Deer Park Road 18 miles to the campground at road's end; (360) 452-0330.*

West of the city, the Elwha River entrance to Olympic (see Hiking/Backpacking, above) is the gateway to two small but very nice campgrounds on the peaceful Elwha Valley floor. The first, **Elwha,** has 41 sites (no hookups; maximum RV length, 21 feet) set in fairly thick forest. A kitchen shelter covers you in extremely bad weather, of which there is much in the winter. Elwha is open all year. Sites ($8) cannot be reserved. *On Elwha River Road 3 miles south of US 101; (360) 452-0330.*

The location of the second, **Altaire,** makes it more popular. It's right on the banks of the Elwha, with some sites fronting the clear, cold waters. Snaring a site can be challenging here. There are only 30 to be found (no hookups; maximum RV length, 21 feet). Altaire is open from June to late September. Sites ($8) cannot be reserved. *On Elwha River Road 4 miles south of US 101; (360) 452-0330.*

Clallam County

About 20 miles west of Port Angeles, **Salt Creek Recreation Area,** one of the state's best (and most-overlooked) campgrounds, sits perched on a bluff above the Strait of Juan de Fuca. Salt Creek, the crown jewel of Clallam County's park system, is the former home of **Camp Hayden,** a World War II–era 16-inch-gun emplacement. Today, the park's 80 camp-sites (no hookups; no maximum RV length for half the sites), situated either on a steep bluff above Tongue Point or in a terraced, grassy field in the center of the park, are a wonderful escape any time of the year. Nearly every site offers a gorgeous view of the Strait of Juan de Fuca, where you can watch the parade of cargo and military ships, peer across to Victoria, or scan for orca whales, otters, and sea lions in the salt water. Striped

Peak, which looms above the campground to the east, is ringed by hiking trails and old logging roads that make for fine day-long exploration (see Hiking/Backpacking, above). If your eyes are sharp, you might even stumble upon buried ruins of the park's military past. Nearby **Tongue Point** is one of Washington's best tidal-pool viewing spots (see Beaches, below). Salt Creek is open all year. Sites ($10) cannot be reserved. *Follow US 101 west to Hwy 112, proceed 10 miles west, take Camp Hayden Road 4 miles north to the campground; (360) 928-3441.*

Not far down the road on Hwy 112 is **Lyre River,** a free, semiprimitive Department of Natural Resources campground. *North of Hwy 112 .5 mile, near milepost 46; (360) 902-1000.*

Beaches

Much of the shoreline of the Strait of Juan de Fuca is inaccessible due to steep, hazardous cliffs or off-limits because of private property. But isolated access points are worth the search.

One of the best is right downtown. **Ediz Hook,** the sand finger formed over the centuries by the surging Elwha River, stretches several miles into the strait, and is accessible by trail and car. The best way to get there: park downtown near the City Pier and follow the 6-mile **Waterfront Trail,** either on foot or cycle.

While you're there, check out the pier and surrounding park, including a steel observation tower offering great views across the strait and into the Olympic foothills.

West of town, the **Tongue Point Marine Reserve** at Salt Creek Recreation Area is one of the best places in the state to explore tidal pools. The rocky point juts far into the strait, providing acres of exploration at low tide. Remember to leave everything where you found it.

Just to the west, sprawling **Crescent Beach** looks extremely tempting. It's the nicest stretch of sand in this part of the state. Regrettably, it's under private ownership, and you'll have to pay a fee at the nearby campground just to wiggle your toes in the sand. For years, we've been urging Clallam County to buy the beach and add it to Salt Creek Recreation Area. But they keep making some excuse about money.

Skiing/Snowshoeing

Hurricane Ridge is Olympic National Park's primary playground in the winter, and its only established ski venue. The 17-mile road from Port Angeles usually is plowed only Saturday through Monday by park rangers, who reserve the right not to open it at all if weather gets too rough, or if they're shorthanded—or if they don't feel like it. Be sure to call the 24-hour recorded message, (360) 452-0329, before you head out. The Park Service recently began experimenting with a shuttle bus to the summit; ask at the visitors center; (360) 452-0330.

Cross-country skiing can be very good on the Ridge. It also can be very bad. While the area gets a lot of snow, it's often wind-crusted or just plain glare ice. No fun on skinny skis, to say the least. Most XC routes begin and end in the Hurricane Ridge parking lot. A popular trail runs west along the (snow-buried) road to the Hurricane Ridge Picnic Area and beyond to the **Hurricane Hill Trail** (see Hiking/Backpacking, above). From here, backcountry telemark skiers fan out along the ridge's deep, wind-blown snow crust. Venturing very far in this direction is for the experienced only. The terrain is hazardous, particularly on the north side of the ridge, where, unbeknownst to you, the cornice you stand on might be jutting *waaay* out over sheer cliffs.

A much tamer cross-country route runs along the (closed-to-traffic) **Obstruction Point Road,** which winds 8.5 miles (13.6 kilometers) through nice alpine scenery to a ski club–maintained cabin at **Waterhole.** Experienced backcountry skiers can venture beyond, all the way to storm-blasted Obstruction Peak, for winter campouts.

Downhillers and snowboarders get their kicks at the ridge, too. A poma lift runs weekends only for skiers and tubers. The vertical isn't much, but hey, it's a lift, and if you're stuck in Port Angeles all winter, it's worth the trip. Lift tickets are $15.

Snowshoers find Hurricane Ridge snow much to their liking, whatever the conditions. Park naturalists lead guided snowshoe nature walks on Saturdays, Sundays, Mondays, and holidays through March. Call (360) 452-0330 for details. The walks last about 90 minutes, and snowshoes are provided. Those who bring their own often set off down **Obstruction Point Road**, or just ply the deep, snowy fields near the Hurricane Ridge Lodge.

For rental skis, snowshoes, supplies, and advice, stop by the Hurricane Ridge Visitors Center on weekends, or consult Olympic Mountaineering, 221 S Peabody, Port Angeles; (360) 452-0240.

Fishing

Before the big Northwest salmon crash of the 1980s, Port Angeles and nearby Strait of Juan de Fuca hot spots such as Freshwater Bay and even Ediz Hook were among the most choice **king salmon**–fishing waters in Washington. No longer, thanks to tight new restrictions to protect threatened coho runs. Unfortunately, the strait is the funnel through which all Puget Sound salmon stocks run, and it's not practical to fish for hatchery kings without hooking wild coho and other troubled stocks. Result: the strait coho and chinook fishery has been nearly shut down in recent years. But sporadic fishing for those species, and more frequent fishing for others, still goes on in the strait. Call the Department of Fish and Wildlife, or pick up a state fishing pamphlet, for current seasons and restrictions. The seasonal highlight is **Port Angeles Derby Days** in late August. It's one of the state's oldest and most prominent derbies. When fishing's open, you can still hop a charter out of Port Angeles and set out after a hefty chinook. Call Port Angeles Charters, (360) 457-7629, for rates and details.

Inland, two dams blocking salmon spawning on the mighty **Elwha River** haven't prevented trout from flourishing there. The lower river inside the park and **Lake Mills,** behind the Glines Canyon Dam, are noted trout fisheries. The Elwha is open from June 1 to October 31, artificial flies and lures only, 12-inch minimum size. Lake Mills usually is open from the last Saturday in April to October 31, artificial flies and lures only, 12-inch minimum size, two-fish limit. Licenses aren't required inside the national park, but be sure to check seasonal regulations at the Elwha Ranger Station.

West of the city toward Sekiu, the **Lyre River** is a noted trout and steelhead stream. And down US 101 to the west, **Lake Crescent** provides one of the state's most unique boat fisheries for many trout species (see the Lake Crescent and the Upper Soleduck chapter).

Boating/Sailing

Pleasure boaters can find guest moorage, fuel, and supplies year-round at the port-operated **Port Angeles Boat Haven,** (360) 457-4505, at the southwest corner of the main harbor. Just to the east, the **City Pier,** (360) 457-0411, has guest moorage and more limited facilities, summer only.

A public boat launch popular with anglers is at **Freshwater Bay County Park,** west of the city off Hwy 112. This also is a good launch point for small craft such as kayaks.

Biking

Port Angeles isn't a noted cycling venue, but the 18-mile **Hurricane Ridge Road** is a challenge many cyclists find irresistible every summer. It's incredibly long, incredibly steep, incredibly torturous. But hey: if you do it, you can pretty much take the rest of your life off.

The lower 2.4 miles of the Olympic Hot Springs Trail (see Hiking/Backpacking, above) follow an old roadway, and are open to mountain bike use. But wheels are forbidden on all other national park trails in this area, except the Spruce Railroad Trail at Lake Crescent (see the Lake Crescent and the Upper Soleduck chapter). Also, some paths in the **Olympic National Forest** to the southeast (see the Olympic National Forest and the East Slope Olympics chapter) are fat-tire friendly. Cyclists of all kinds will find the city's long, flat **Waterfront Trail** a pleasant place to ride on a hot day.

For cycle rentals, supplies, and advice, see Pedal 'n' Paddle, 120 E Front Street, (360) 457-1240.

Wildlife/Photography

Bring the wide-angle lenses. Many fantastic mountainscapes can be bagged right from the parking lot at **Hurricane Ridge** (see Hiking/Backpacking, above). Some of the park's most spectacular peaks are visible from here, including portions of 7,965-foot **Mount Olympus,** the crown jewel of the Olympic chain. Far below, the often fog-draped Elwha River Valley provides a stunning contrast to the alpine peaks.

Wildlife is plentiful at Hurricane Ridge, too. (So much so that park rangers have taken to shooting paint balls to mark "over-aggressive" **deer** that beg treats from tourists.) A weekend backpack trip to **Grand Valley** can yield delightful results, whether you're after summer wildflowers, alpine vistas, or **marmots,** deer, and **black bear.** Another good, and easier, wildflower-shooting venue is the **Hurricane Hill Trail**. Try it in June, as soon as the snow melts.

In the fall and winter, shooting on Hurricane Ridge is a tough bet, thanks to the fog, wind, and rain. Make a drive to the **Elwha River Valley,** where wildlife often is spotted beneath the valley's big broadleaf trees.

Sunset shooters note: We've seen some prize-winning shots nabbed from the rocky beach at **Salt Creek Recreation Area.**

Kayaking/Rafting

Olympic Raft and Guide Service, (360) 452-1443, runs float trips on the **Elwha, Hoh,** and **Queets Rivers.** These are primarily placid, non-intimidating tours, with an emphasis on wildlife and natural history. Definitely worth investing a day. The Elwha trip is a short run from Altaire Campground to Elwha Resort, on US 101.

That same route is popular among kayakers. The stretch of river is intermediate (Class II to III). Beware the upper stretch of river between Glines Canyon Dam and Altaire. The **Gorge Drop Rapids** just above the campground are Class IV to V, and should be attempted only by courageous experts.

Llama Trekking

Some of Olympic National Park's most fabulous trails pass through sensitive meadows closed to pack animals. But they're not closed to llamas—agile, strong packers that allow you to get deep into the wilderness without destroying your back on the way. Olympak Llamas (3175 Old Olympic Hwy; (360) 452-4475) and Kit's Llamas (Olalla, Kitsap County; (206) 857-5274) both offer guided treks into the park.

outside in

Attractions

By all means, check out the waterfront. **Port Angeles Harbor,** protected against wind and waves by Ediz Hook sand spit, is the largest natural deepwater harbor north of San Francisco. It's also a jumping-off point to **Victoria,** 17 miles across the strait on Canada's Vancouver Island via the ferry *Coho,* operated by Black Ball Transportation, (360) 457-4491, or the much quicker *Victoria Express,* a passengers-only ferry that runs two or three times daily during summer and early fall; (360) 452-8088, (800) 633-1589.

But these days, you don't have to flee to Canada to enjoy a maritime experience here, thanks to a slate of improvements on the city waterfront. At the Peninsula College–operated **Arthur D. Feiro Marine Laboratory,** (360) 452-3940, on the City Pier, 80 species from nearby waters—including octopi, wolf eels, sculpins, and sea slugs—are on display, and a touch tank keeps children occupied. Also at the main pier, at the foot of Lincoln Street, some of the U.S. Coast Guard's largest cutters are often tied up on layovers—another kid favorite. And the large steel **observation tower** offers fine views in all directions.

Downtown should-stops include **Port Book and News** (104 E First; (360) 452-6367), **Mombasa Coffee Company** (113 W First; (360) 452-3238), **Bonny's Bakery** (502 E First; (360) 457-3585), the **Clallam County Historical Museum** (319 Lincoln; (360) 417-2364), and last but certainly never least, **Swain's General Store** (602 E First; (360) 452-2357), which sells virtually everything, including that little cotter pin you need to hold the holding tank cap on the Minnie Winnie.

If you're headed west toward Salt Creek Recreation Area or farther, toward Sekiu or Lake Ozette, stop at the 100-year-old (and appropriately funky) **Joyce General Store,** (360) 928-3568, on Hwy 112. Inside the door, the phone-booth-size Joyce Post Office is the place to send a JOYCE, WA–postmarked card to all your friends named Joyce.

Restaurants

C'est Si Bon ☆☆   Yes, it *is* good—especially if you're yearning for classic pre-nouvelle French cooking with its splendid sauces. Plans are on the drawing board for an adjacent 60-room chateau-type hotel. *On Hwy 101 4 miles east of Port Angeles; (360) 452-8888; 23 Cedar Park Dr, Port Angeles; $$$.*

Chestnut Cottage ☆   *The* place to go for an exceptional breakfast in delightful country Victorian-style surroundings. *On Hwy 101, east of the center of town; (360) 452-8344; 929 E Front St, Port Angeles; $$.*

Chihuahua ☆   A notch or two above most, this small, busy eatery specializes in the foods of northern Mexico. On Sunday, ask for the menudo, a hearty soup of tender tripe in a well-flavored broth (especially recommended as a hangover cure). *1 block south of the old Clallam County Courthouse, between 4th and 5th; (360) 452-8174; 408 S Lincoln, Port Angeles; $.*

First Street Haven ☆   It's just a skinny slot of a restaurant, easily missed among the storefronts if you're not paying attention. But the cinnamon rolls, espresso, salads, hearty sandwiches, quiche, and chili draw the locals to the Haven. *1st and Laurel, next to the Toggery; (360) 457-0352; 107 E 1st St, Port Angeles; $.*

Lodgings

Domaine Madeleine ☆☆☆   Set on a bluff overlooking the Strait of Juan de Fuca among tall firs, lawns, and gardens, this modern home is an ideal spot to get away and let someone pamper you. Breakfast is indulgent. *North of Hwy 101 between Sequim and Port Angeles (call for directions); (360) 457-4174; 146 Wildflower Lane, Port Angeles; $$$.*

Olympic Lodge ☆   This Best Western hotel just seems to offer the right combination of comfort and rustic atmosphere that fits in Port Angeles— and if you don't have the time to hike the backcountry, just walk the halls to see what you are missing. Sequim photographer Ross Hamilton has a large collection of work on permanent display. *On Hwy 101, east side of Port Angeles; (360) 452-2993 or (800) 600-2993; 140 Del Guzzi Dr, Port Angeles; $$-$$$.*

Pond Motel   Several spare but exceptionally clean rooms overlook an acre-big pond where bufflehead ducks and mallards float by and two pet rainbow trout occasionally stir the serene water. There are also two bigger cabins equipped with vintage 1940s kitchenettes, and two single rooms (dark, but sort of cozy) next to the office. *½ mile west of city limits; (360) 452-8422; 1425 Hwy 101 W, Port Angeles; $.*

Tudor Inn ☆☆   One of the best-looking buildings in town, this completely restored Tudor-style bed and breakfast is located 12 blocks from the ferry terminal in a quiet residential neighborhood. Your hosts will gladly provide transportation to and from the ferry dock, and arrange for fishing charters, horseback rides, or winter ski packages. *11th and Oak; (360) 452-3138; 1108 S Oak St, Port Angeles; $$.*

More Information

Clallam Parks and Recreation: *(360) 417-2291.*

Clallam Transit System: *(800) 858-3747; (360) 452-4511.*

North Olympic Peninsula Visitors and Convention Bureau: *(800) 942-4042.*

Olympic National Park Administration: *(360) 452-4501.*

Olympic National Park Road and Weather Update: *(360) 452-0329.*

Olympic National Park Visitors Information: *(360) 452-0330.*

Port Angeles Visitors Center: *(360) 452-2363.*

Lake Crescent and the Upper Soleduck

From the northeast corner of Lake Crescent southwest to High Divide and the Bailey Range in Olympic National Park, including Fairholm Campground, Sol Duc Hot Springs Resort, Sol Duc and Marymere Falls and the Seven Lakes Basin.

Spirits lurk in every nook and cranny here. You can feel them on the eerily blue waters of Lake Crescent, smell them in the thick bark of 400-year-old fir trees standing guard over the wild lands in the upper Soleduck Valley.

The lake and the valley are the passageway to some of the Olympic Mountains' most soul-stirring spots: magnificent waterfalls plunging 100 feet through ancient trees; high mountain passes on obsidian-blade-sharp ridgelines; mountaintop vistas that challenge, combat, and ultimately defeat even the most mulish human ego.

It's no wonder the region's native people, the Quileutes and Clallams, consider much of this area sacred. Their legends live on: Lake Crescent's creation by a vengeful Storm King Mountain, who grew so angry about warring between local tribes that he hurled part of himself into the Lyre River Valley, creating Lake Crescent. The creation of Sol Duc and Olympic Hot Springs by lightning fish who battled endlessly, only to retreat in defeat by burying themselves in the earth, forever to shed steaming tears. Look high up to Storm King's face, or settle deep into the Sol Duc's waters, and it's not so hard to imagine the legends coming to life.

And new legends are created here every year by new inhabitants of the lake and valley: Nature lovers who trek here year round to pursue a rare Lake Crescent trout stand in awe at the base of a house-size tree, breathe in the soothing mist of a plunging waterfall, or watch powerful salmon and steelhead launch themselves at a wall of white water. Many a lifetime memory has been made here by explorers passing through by boot, boat, or bike.

Lake Crescent and the Upper Soleduck Valley are a highlight of Olympic National Park, thus a can't-miss stop on any outdoor lover's tour of Washington State. For us, the region today is exactly what it has been to local inhabitants for eons: a source of fear, mystery, passion, inspiration—and, inevitably, unadulterated awe.

Getting There

From Port Angeles, follow US 101 southwest 22 miles to the east shore of Lake Crescent. Proceed another 13 miles around the lake's south shore to reach the west shore (Fairholm Campground area). Other amenities, such as Lake Crescent Lodge, the Storm King Ranger Station, and the departure dock for the M.V. Storm King interpretive tour boat, are located near mid-lakeshore on US 101. To reach the Soleduck area of Olympic National Park, proceed another 3 miles west of Lake Crescent on US 101 to Soleduck River Road. Turn south and continue 13 miles to Sol Duc Hot Springs Resort, Sol Duc Campground, and the Soleduck Valley Trailhead.

Adjoining Areas

NORTHWEST: **Neah Bay, Lake Ozette, and Sekiu**

NORTHEAST: **Port Angeles and Hurricane Ridge**

SOUTHWEST: **Forks and La Push**

EAST: **Olympic National Park: Overview**

inside out

Hiking/Backpacking

Lake Crescent area

By all means, bring your boots. The northwest corner of Olympic National Park, where Lake Crescent and the upper Soleduck Valley reside, is the takeoff point for some of the most memorable day hikes and backpack treks in the Northwest. Options range from flat, easy trails—such as the Spruce Railroad grade along Lake Crescent—to the rugged, stunning alpine country of High Divide, between the Hoh and Elwha river drainages in the interior Olympics. For a full list of hikes and current trail conditions, contact the Olympic National Park Visitors Center, (360) 452-0330. Here's a list of our best bets:

An easy, popular day hike just off US 101 is the **Marymere Falls Trail** (easy; 2 miles round trip), which begins near Storm King Ranger Station on the lake's south shore (turn where signs indicate Lake Crescent Lodge). Follow the Barnes Creek Trail about a half mile to the Marymere Falls turnoff, where the trail climbs a moderate grade to the 100-foot falls, set against a brilliant green backdrop. The first half-mile of this trail is wheelchair-accessible. From the same Barnes Creek Trail, you can hang a left after about ⅓ mile, and climb up the **Mount Storm King Trail** (difficult; 6.2 miles round trip), which climbs to a fine overlook of Lake Crescent, 4,200 feet. Warning: The top portion of the trail decays into loose, crumbly rock. No place for young ones. Watch your step. Departing from the same area is the **Barnes Point Nature Trail** (easy, 1 mile round trip), a pleasant stroll through lush old-growth forest, past an old homestead to the shores of Lake Crescent.

Almost directly opposite the Storm King area on the lake's north shore, two other hiking trails depart. The first, **Pyramid Mountain Trail** (moderate; 7 miles round trip), climbs 2,400 feet to Pyramid's 3,100-foot summit, with grand views of the lake and northern Olympics. The trailhead is on North Shore Road, about 3 miles beyond Fairholm Campground (see Camping, below). It's a huffer-puffer in places. Continuing another several miles to the end of North Shore Road brings you to the western trailhead of the **Spruce Railroad Trail** (easy; 8 miles round trip). The Spruce Trail, one of the more underrated hikes in this part of the park, follows Lake Crescent's north shore on the path of a World War I–era railroad, which once hauled Sitka spruce logs to build warplanes. Now it hauls only Vibram soles and mountain bikes. This is one of the few trails in Olympic National Park where mountain biking won't get you a big fat ticket. (Many cyclists choose to circumvent the narrow, windy stretch of US 101 on the opposite shore of Lake Crescent by riding this trail.) The path is a peaceful stroll along a truly unusual lake, with plenty of oddities—abandoned railroad tunnels, bridges, and the like—along the way to keep the whole family engaged. it's also a good trail to consider in the winter, when most Olympic trails are under snow. The eastern trailhead is near Log Cabin Resort (see Camping and Lodgings, below).

Soleduck River area

From the main trailhead in the Soleduck area, separate trails lead up either side of the river into the stunning Soleduck Valley, filled to the brim with ancient fir and hemlock behemoths. For a cool, easy day hike, follow the Soleduck River Trail up the north bank to refreshing **Soleduck Falls** (easy, 1.5 miles round trip). It's a picturesque, 40-foot silvery free fall—well worth your valuable vacation time and effort, and easily photographed from the footbridge over the river. Return the way you came, or cross the river here and return on the south bank. Stronger day hikers or overnighters can cross the bridge and follow the **Canyon Creek Trail** another 3 miles up to **Deer Lake** (moderate/difficult; 7.5 miles round trip). The lake is an ideal overnight backpack spot, with plenty of choice campsites. It's also a perfect first-night stopover for those continuing on to High Divide. And as if you needed to ask: yes, there are deer. Cute to the point of being annoying.

The **High Divide Loop** (difficult; 19 miles round trip) is the granddaddy of all backpacking routes in this area, if not on the entire peninsula. From Deer Lake, the High Divide Trail climbs above the treeline into spectacular **Seven Lakes Basin,** a string of jewel-like tarns on the north side of High Divide. Campsites are excellent, but smooshed to death by overuse. Limits are now in effect for summer overnight visitors. Call (360) 452-0330 for permit information. From here, the trail climbs up the spine of the sharp ridge dividing the Hoh and Soleduck river drainages. The walk along the top is nothing short of spectacular, with acres of wildflowers at your feet, unimpeded views of the interior Olympics before your eyes. The loop tops out at the summit of **Bogachiel Peak** (7.8 miles, 5,474 feet), where the view across the Hoh to Mount Olympus will sear itself on your memory. The loop continues to **Heart Lake,** then intersects with the **Appleton Pass Trail** (see the Port Angeles and Hurricane Ridge chapter) at about 15 miles, before dropping 5 miles back down the Soleduck River to the trailhead. Note: The High Divide Loop is impassable until midsummer, usually July. Basic mountaineering skills (ice ax and rope-rescue knowledge) are necessary to negotiate the divide any time snow is present.

Also from the Soleduck area, the **Mink Lake Trail** (easy; 5 miles round trip) is a good day hike from Sol Duc Hot Springs Resort, and the **Ancient Groves Nature Trail** (easy; 1 mile loop) is a pleasant, kid-friendly walk through a stand of old-growth trees along Soleduck River Road. If getting away from people is high on your list, head 4 miles back down the Soleduck River Road to the **North Fork Soleduck Trail** (moderate; 18 miles round trip). It's a peaceful, up-and-down trail through old-growth forest to the North Fork, a noted trout-fishing stream. The river is reached at about 2.5 miles, but you can continue much farther upstream, leaving tourists and/or annoying family members far behind.

Camping

Choices are somewhat limited, so site-sleuthing is a key skill in summer months. On Lake Crescent, **Fairholm Campground** on the far western shore has 87 sites (no hookups; maximum RV length, 21 feet), all within a short stroll of Lake Crescent. The campground has a nice play area and swimming beach (brrrrr!), and good campfire programs in the summer. It's by far the best local camping area. All the Lake Crescent–area hikes described above are within a short drive or cycling distance. Fairholm, an Olympic National Park site, is open all year. Sites ($10) cannot be reserved. *On North Shore Road, just north of US 101 on the west side of Lake Crescent; (360) 452-0330.*

Sol Duc Campground near Sol Duc Hot Springs has 80 sites, all in the trees (no hookups; maximum RV length, 21 feet). This is the place to stay if you're day hiking in the Soleduck Valley. Sol Duc, a national park site, is open all year, but closes when snow is on the ground. Sites ($10) cannot be reserved. *On Soleduck River Road 13 miles south of US 101; (360) 452-0330.*

A somewhat pricey private camping option on Lake Crescent is **Log Cabin Resort,** which has 40 sites (full hookups; unlimited RV length) within a short distance of the lake's east shore. Great access to the Spruce Railroad Trail (see Hiking/Backpacking, above). Log Cabin Resort is open from April to November. Sites can be reserved. *From US 101, turn north on East Beach Road and proceed 3 miles to the end; (360) 928-3325.*

A bit farther removed is **Klahowya,** an Olympic National Forest campsite farther down US 101. The campground has 25 tent sites and 30 RV sites (no hookups; maximum length, 30 feet). Klahowya is open summer months only. Some sites can be reserved by calling (800) 280-CAMP. *Just south of US 101, about 8 miles west of Lake Crescent; (360) 374-6522.*

Fishing

Lake Crescent holds some monsters. And we don't mean a Nessie or Ogopogo sea creature. When the region's first settlers built cabins on the shores of Lake Crescent, the deep, icy waters held two trout species not found anywhere else on the planet: the **Beardslee trout** (a sort of oversize rainbow), and the **Crescentii** (a member of the cutthroat family). Sadly, both breeds now have intermingled with other hatchery-produced species. But that doesn't reduce the thrill of trolling the lake's incredible depths for big fish. They're a tricky prey, especially since fishing with bait is illegal in the lake. You'll need a boat, a trolling motor, and the right gear. Inquire about all three at Lake Crescent Lodge, (360) 928-3211, or Log Cabin Resort, (360) 928-3325. The lake is open from the last Saturday in

April to October 31, artificial flies and lures only, two-fish limit, 20-inch minimum size.

River fishing also can be fine in this area. The **Soleduck River** is open below Soleduck Falls from June 1 to October 31, and the minimum-size restriction says something about the size of the trout: bag limit is two, minimum length 14 inches. The river is closed between August 1 and October 31 within 100 yards upstream and 250 yards downstream of the Soleduck's Salmon Cascades (see Wildlife, below). Native steelhead, bull trout, and Dolly Varden must be released. Licenses are not required for fishing inside the national park.

Biking

Road cycling isn't ideal in this area, thanks—or no thanks—to winding roads and narrow shoulders. Only truly determined US 101 through-riders take the challenge of the long, winding traverse around Lake Crescent. The **Soleduck River Road,** however, makes a nice 13-mile one-way ride for cyclists camped at Fairholm or Sol Duc Campgrounds.

Mountain bikers who love Olympic National Park often wind up in the Fairholm area, because the nearby **Spruce Railroad Trail** is one of the few trails in the park accessible to mountain bikes. From the campground, the 5-mile ride on North Shore Road to the Spruce Trailhead leads to an 8-mile round-trip ride on the Spruce Trail, along Lake Crescent's north shore. The total trip up the lake and back to Fairholm is about 18 miles—a good day's outing for average riders. Pack a lunch, pick a scenic spot along the lake, and make a day of it. For rentals, see the Port Angeles and Hurricane Ridge chapter.

Boating/Canoeing/Kayaking

Small boats can be launched at **Fairholm** and **Log Cabin Resort.** Both places also rent small boats, as does **Lake Crescent Lodge.** Beaches at Fairholm and East Beach are good launching points for canoes and sea kayaks.

Experienced river runners can get a workout on the **Upper Soleduck,** a stretch of river rated as advanced, with many Class III rapids. Most floaters put in at the bridge several miles up South Fork Soleduck Road. Klahowya Campground on US 101 (see Camping, above) has another good river access. Below there, the river is often dotted by angler's drift boats. But some floaters continue downstream to the Bear Creek fishing access, or all the way to the Sol Duc Hatchery near Sappho. The Soleduck is in best running shape during the spring runoff, generally from April to June.

Wildlife

Deer, black bears, and **marmots** are common sights in the Upper Soleduck River Valley, especially at aptly named Deer Lake and along High Divide, where friendly black-tails literally will shove their snout through the crack in your tent's rain fly.

Bald eagles and other predatory birds can be seen high in the trees along Lake Crescent's shores.

One of the Olympic peninsula's most engaging wildlife spectacles is the Salmon Cascades, a long, steep rapid on the Soleduck River (well marked from Soleduck River Road). A short trail leads to a whitewater overlook, where migrating **steelhead** and **salmon** often are seen launching themselves at the falls. It's mesmerizing, and keeps people coming back year after year. It's possible to see fish jumping here throughout the summer, but fall months are the peak.

Photography

Waterfall shooters can lace up their boots and shoot both **Marymere** and **Soleduck Falls** in the same day. Bring either a tripod or fairly fast film; light is a precious commodity.

The high vista atop **Bogachiel Peak** on the High Divide Loop (see Hiking/Backpacking, above) is one of the best scenic photo stops in the Northwest. On one side, glacier-capped 7,950-foot Mount Olympus looms above a blanket of old-growth greenery in the Hoh River Valley. On the other is an eagle's-eye view straight down to the magnificent Seven Lakes Basin, with Pacific Ocean sunsets serving as a backdrop. An overnight trip to the divide with a lightweight tripod can yield spectacular results. But be warned: Bogachiel Peak's weather gods seem to have their own lens detector. Every time we get here with the right gear, the clouds roll in.

Picnics/Swimming

Fairholm Campground (see Camping, above) has a good swimming/picnicking beach on the west shore of Lake Crescent. Similarly, **East Beach** picnic area on East Beach Road is a sunny spot with an enjoyable flat beach. If you can stand the cold, this is your place. About halfway up the lake, between Barnes Point and Fairholm, is **La Poel,** a nice lakeside pullout for picnickers.

outside in

Attractions

The main show here is a new one: the **MV *Storm King*,** a paddlewheel-style interpretive tour boat that plies the silent waters of Lake Crescent. The tours operate from mid-May to early October, with an Olympic National Park naturalist aboard to describe the lake's flora, fauna, and fascinating history. (Make sure to ask about the legend of the Lady of the Lake—a woman whose body turned to soap in the cold water and still bobs up from time to time.) The boat docks at Barnes Point near Lake Crescent Lodge, but tickets and parking are found at Shadow Mountain Store, 13 miles west of Port Angeles on US 101. Reservations are a good idea. For departure times and rates, call Mosquito Fleet, (360) 452-4520.

In the Soleduck Valley, **Sol Duc Hot Springs** (for the resort and campground, the park has preserved the old spelling of the native name, which means sparkling waters) is a fully developed resort—one of only a handful in the park. The hot springs, popular even among the earliest settlers, long have been believed to have magical healing powers. We can't vouch for that, but suffice it to say the water feels mighty good after a 20-mile backpack trip to High Divide.

This is the park's "civilized" hot springs. Unlike the au naturel Olympic Hot Springs over the divide (see the Port Angeles and Hurricane Ridge chapter), the Sol Duc's 102°F to 109°F waters are channeled into three big pools, which you can dunk into for a small admission fee. The resort also has a restaurant, snack bar, and a full range of lodging options (see Lodgings, below). It's open all year, but weekends only from October to April; (360) 327-3583.

Restaurants

For recommended restaurants, see the Adjoining Areas to this chapter.

Lodgings

Lake Crescent Lodge ☆ Built more than 80 years ago, the well-maintained Lake Crescent Lodge has a grand veranda overlooking the deep, crystal-blue waters of Lake Crescent, a so-so restaurant, and a very comfortable bar. The motel rooms are the best for the money, but 1930s cabins, with their porches and fireplaces, can be fun. Open summers only. *On Hwy 101, 20 miles west of Port Angeles; (360) 928-3211; 416 Lake Crescent Rd, Port Angeles; $$.*

Log Cabin Resort   Located on the "sunny side" of Lake Crescent, this venerable resort has served visitors for over a century, although none of the present buildings are over 70 years old. No frills, but very livable. A choice of lakeside chalets (refrigerator, but no kitchens); cabins with kitchenettes; and one-room log "Kamper Kabins." Closed in January. *On E Beach Rd, 3 miles north of Hwy 101; (360) 928-3325; 3183 E Beach Rd, Port Angeles; $$.*

Sol Duc Hot Springs   Surrounded by forest, 32 small cedar-roofed sleeping cabins are clustered in the grassy meadow. The favorites are those with their porches facing the river and, in keeping with the natural serenity, there are no TVs anywhere. Hot springs and pool use are included in the cabin rental fee. Open daily in summer; weekends only, October to April. *12 miles south of Hwy 101, west of Lake Crescent; (360) 327-3583; Port Angeles; $$.*

More Information

Sol Duc Ranger Station: *(360) 374-6522.*
Sol Duc Hot Springs: *(360) 327-3583.*
Storm King Ranger Station (summer only): *(360) 928-3380.*
Lake Crescent tour boat information and reservations: *(360) 452-4520.*

Neah Bay, Lake Ozette, and Sekiu

From Sekiu west to Cape Flattery, south to Sand Point, east to Lake Crescent, including Cape Alava, Shi Shi Beach, Point of the Arches, Clallam Bay, Sekiu, Pillar Point, and the Flattery Rocks National Wildlife Refuge.

Neah Bay is as close as you can get to Homer, Alaska, without leaving Washington State. Literally. And probably figuratively, too.

It really is the end of the road. Lots of roads. And the farthest northwest point in the U.S. has all the rustic (emphasis on rust) charm you'd expect, with clean air, mind-boggling scenery, and truly spartan creature comforts. You won't find any four-star resorts out here (or many two-story buildings, for that matter). But the triangle of wild land marked by Neah Bay, Sekiu, and Ozette is a truly grand piece of geometry.

At triangle's top, Neah Bay is a small, struggling fishing village—the longtime home of the Makah Tribe, which has been whaling, fishing, and logging here for at least three millennia. With the decline of the Northwest salmon, fishing has dropped off dramatically. But Neah Bay continues to hack out a decent living on bottomfishing, sporadic salmon charters, and, increasingly, whale watching, hiking, and camping on its fantastic ocean beaches.

Sekiu—due southeast down the Strait of Juan de Fuca as the cormorant flies—also is a small, struggling fishing village, minus the historical inhabitants. For decades, the town has owed its existence to what until recently was a robust recreational salmon fishery—

particularly for hefty chinook salmon—in the strait. That changed radically in the early 1990s, when concerns for troubled Puget Sound salmon stocks led to a near fishing shutdown in the strait. Like many other small Washington coastal communities, the quaint waterfront berg of Sekiu will be forced to adapt or die if fishing fails to recover.

Lake Ozette, the southern end of the triangle, is one of the most popular destinations in Olympic National Park and is the largest natural lake in the state. But the beach strip to its west—including the park's pencil-like, 57-mile coastal strip—is the big show, drawing tens of thousands of visitors each year down a boardwalk trail to Cape Alava.

The Northwest triangle is a must-do for Washington recreators. You'll stand on the very tip of the Lower 48, staring down at the roiling Pacific. And the sunset from Shi Shi Beach makes you wonder how heaven could do it one better.

Getting There

Neah Bay, 75 slow miles west of Port Angeles, is a long haul from Seattle. Plan to spend the bulk of a day getting there, and if you're driving in the summer, pack plenty of slow-traffic patience. Follow directions to Port Angeles (see the Port Angeles and Hurricane Ridge chapter). Proceed west on US 101 to Hwy 112. Follow 112 west and northwest about 60 miles (the last 20 are winding and narrow) through Sekiu to Neah Bay. Lake Ozette is reached by turning south on Hoko-Ozette Road, 2 miles west of Sekiu. Drive 18 miles south to the lake and Olympic National Park ranger station.

Adjoining Areas

EAST: **Port Angeles and Hurricane Ridge**

SOUTHEAST: **Lake Crescent and the Upper Soleduck**

SOUTH: **Forks and La Push**

inside out

Hiking/Backpacking

Cape Flattery (moderate; 1 mile round trip), west of Neah Bay, is one of the more memorable day hikes in the Northwest. It doesn't look like much at first, just a stroll through scrubby forest, across a swamp, and toward a bluff. But the view from the end, about a half-mile down the trail, will brand itself on your memory. The path ends dramatically at a sheer cliff, with the stormy Pacific bashing itself indefatigably on rocks below and against scenic—and eerie—Tatoosh Island, a half-mile offshore. The island, a traditional whaling/fishing base and burial ground for the ancient Makahs, holds a Coast Guard lighthouse, built in 1857. Try to imagine being stuck as the lightkeeper. Not many people could. Some of the earliest keepers reportedly fled in terror of storms, ghosts, and other calamities—real or imagined—before the light was finally automated.

This high bluff is a good spot from which to scan for seals, sea lions, and gray whales, which migrate just offshore in April-May and October-November. Warnings: The trail can get quite muddy, and be sure to use extreme caution around the cliffs. It's 100 feet down in places, and at this writing, no fences were there to separate you from the plunge. Local officials promise trail work, guard railings, and other trail improvements soon. Follow Cape Loop Road 8 miles southwest from Neah Bay, following signs to, then beyond, "Cape Flattery Resort."

A few miles to the south, **Shi Shi Beach** (easy; 7 miles round trip), the Northwest's most picturesque oceanscape, is officially (wink, wink) off-limits, thanks to a land squabble between Olympic National Park, which owns the beach, and Makah residents, who own the trail through the uplands. Several years ago, both parties declared the trail closed until the path could be rerouted and a new trailhead built. But neither party actively discourages hikers from making their way to Shi Shi. Local Makah residents, in fact, encourage it. They've established a cottage industry here, allowing hikers to park in their yards for a fee. Makah tribal officials say they have no intention of citing hikers for using the trail. So while it's officially closed, Shi Shi remains very much open, and still heavily used.

The trail wanders about 3.5 miles along the headlands, then down to the spectacular beach area. To the north is Portage Head and a decaying wreck—what's left of the *General M.C. Meigs,* a World War II–era troop ship. A mile to the south is **Point of the Arches,** a picturesque series of pyramidal sea stacks marching into the Pacific like some half-submerged, stony-spined serpent. Good campsites are found here and there, and fresh stream water is available. This is one of the finest beaches in the country for seascape photography. Many coastal backpackers walk south from here to Cape Alava (see below). From Neah Bay, follow signs to the Air Force base, turning left across the Waatch River after several miles. Follow signs for Sooes Beach and the Makah Hatchery until you see signs for parking near homes on Mukkaw Bay.

The Lake Ozette area is home to another Northwest classic beach hike, the **Cape Alava/Sand Point Loop** (easy to moderate; 6.6 to 9.3 miles round trip). It's actually more of a triangle than a loop. The Cape Alava Trail cuts 3 miles west, mostly on a boardwalk (wear sneakers, not lug soles), through grasslands and forest and past an old homestead, where deer and other wildlife are plentiful. At the ocean, you can wander through what's left (not much) of an archeological dig where Makah long-houses buried in mud 500 to 1,000 years ago were excavated throughout the '70s (the artifacts are in the Makah Tribal Museum in Neah Bay). Many good (and overused; see permit information, below) campsites are found at the Cape Alava beach headland. Day hikers can return the way they came, but there's much more to see. Gray whales are often spotted during their spring and fall migrations, and sea lions, seals, otters, and other creatures are seen all year.

About a mile south of Cape Alava are **Wedding Rocks,** which contain a fascinating set of petroglyphs. Two more miles south, the Sand Point Trail emerges on the beach. This southern leg of the loop leads 3 miles northeast, back to where you started. But keep in mind that in foul, windy weather, it's usually better to hike the loop from south to north, thus keeping the wind at your back on the beach section.

More experienced coastal backpackers (those familiar with tide tables and with skills to cross steep, rocky headlands) can continue south, about 18 miles, to **Rialto Beach** (see the Forks and La Push chapter).

Important note: Cape Alava is accessible year round, but overuse in the summer has led to new permit restrictions. Between Memorial Day and Labor Day, all overnight campers must have a free backcountry permit; these are limited to 300 per day and should be reserved in advance. Call the Ozette Reservation Line, (360)452-0300. The Cape Alava/Sand Point trailhead is well marked; follow signs from Ozette Ranger Station, near the north end of the lake.

Beaches

The trail to Shi Shi Beach (see Hiking/Backpacking, above) leads to this area's most spectacular shoreline. But you don't have to hoof it to the Pacific to spend a memorable day on the salt water here. Hwy 112 between Salt Creek Recreation Area (see the Port Angeles and Hurricane Ridge Chapter) and the town of Neah Bay is narrow, winding, and frustrating. But it offers plenty of opportunities for seaside leg-stretching and exploring on the **Strait of Juan de Fuca.** Here's a sampling:

The county park at **Pillar Point** (see Camping, below) is a fantastic beach access. Its launching ramp makes it a good place for kayakers and small-craft owners, although caution should always be exercised in the strait, where vicious winds can appear seemingly out of nowhere.

Up the road a bit, the seaside village of **Clallam Bay** also offers up a public beach. At the waterfront **Clallam Bay County Park,** you can walk 9,500 feet of shoreline, past the mouth of the Clallam River and out to intriguing tide pools near the **Slip Point Lighthouse.** Like the Sequim area to the east, Clallam Bay has served up its share of natural history. A number of ancient marine fossils have been found at **DNR Beach 426,** a stretch of tidelands beyond the lighthouse.

Just around the corner, downtown **Sekiu** has beach access, as well. The "One Mile Beach" trail begins at Olson's Resort and extends along a former railroad grade. It's mostly above the beach, but separate trails lead down to several very nice sandy spots on the water. This is also a semi-popular scuba-diving venue.

Between Sekiu and Neah Bay, stop at the beach pullouts for **Snow Creek Campground** (see Camping, below) and **Beach 429,** a state Department of Natural Resources access just east of Neah Bay. Both offer good beach access and views of sea stacks just offshore, and are noted for frequent seabird and marine mammal sightings.

In Neah Bay itself, the Makah Tribe's **Hobuck Beach** is open for picnics, horseback riding, and other activities.

Fishing

Salmon is king in **Sekiu** and **Neah Bay.** Or was. Washington's coastal and Strait of Juan de Fuca salmon-fishing seasons change substantially from year to year. Call the state Department of Fish and Wildlife or pick up a state game fish pamphlet at an outdoor store to get current season and bag limit information. In recent years, much of the strait has been shut down all summer long, to protect threatened wild coho stocks. But even in off years, the area remains a popular winter blackmouth (immature chinook) salmon fishery, when weather allows. Also, Neah Bay skippers go fishing for halibut in April and May.

Once you decipher the fishing seasons, plenty of reputable charter skippers will be standing by, waiting. In Neah Bay, try Farwest Resort, (360) 645-2270 or -2240; Big Salmon Resort, (360) 645-2374; or Raven Charters, (360) 645-2121. In Sekiu, contact Van Riper's Resort, (360) 963-2334, or Olson's Resort, (360) 963-2311. If salmon season is off, most charters will go in search of halibut, cod, rockfish, or other species. Ask the skippers.

Fishing is permitted without a license in **Lake Ozette,** which contains trout, perch, kokanee, and other species. Consult the ranger station for limits and restrictions. Boat ramps are found at Swan Bay and at the north end of the lake.

In the spring, **Pillar Point Recreation Area** (see Camping, below) is a popular spot to dip smelt from the surf.

Camping

The primary public campground in the region is **Lake Ozette,** an Olympic National Park facility that's free but has only 14 sites (no hookups; maximum RV length, 21 feet). The park is open all year. Sites cannot be reserved. *On the north end of Lake Ozette; (360) 452-0330.*

Also at Lake Ozette, **Erickson's Bay** is a small, primitive campground accessible by foot or boat only. It's a great overnight spot for canoeists exploring the lake—and the shallow shoreline here is a great swimming hole in summer, when the water warms nicely. A swampy trail leads about 2.2 miles west to the ocean. *On the northwest shore of Lake Ozette; no fee, no reservations; (360) 452-0330.*

On the Strait of Juan de Fuca, **Pillar Point Recreation Area,** 40 miles west of Port Angeles, is a Clallam County facility with 20 tent sites and 18 RV sites (sewer hookups; maximum RV length, 24 feet). The sites aren't much to write home about; the camping area is essentially a gravel lot, geared toward fishermen who use the park's boat launch. It's open for camping May 15 through September 15, but accessible year round. Sites cannot be reserved. *On Pillar Point Road, just off Hwy 112, about 37 miles west of Port Angeles; (360) 963-2301.*

A similar angler-oriented campground, **Snow Creek,** is found near the end of Hwy 112. The camp, 60 miles west of Port Angeles, has 50 campsites, 16 with hookups.

A slew of **private campgrounds,** are available. Mostly gravel lots for anglers' RVs, they're not really suitable for tents, but RVers might favor amenities such as full hookups. Some have good views of the strait or the harbor at Neah Bay. The list includes Neah Bay's Tyee RV Park, (360) 645-2223; Westwind Resort, (360) 645-2751; and Farwest Resort, (360) 645-2270 or -2240. Sekiu private campgrounds include Van Riper's Resort, (360) 963-2334; Olson's Resort, (360) 963-2311; Surfside Resort, (360) 963-2723; and Coho Resort, (360) 963-2333. In the Clallam Bay area, try Sam's Trailer and RV Park, (360) 963-2402, or Silver King Resort, (360) 963-2800.

Canoeing/Kayaking

The paddle from the north end of **Lake Ozette** to **Erickson's Bay Campground** on the lake's northwest shore (see Camping, above) is a delightful canoe trip, especially for beginners. The waters of Ozette often are dead-calm in the summer, although paddlers should be prepared for a sudden blast of ferocious ocean weather. The campground is a secluded refuge with 15 sites. It's free, and open all year. A swampy trail leads from the campground to the ocean, just south of Sand Point (see Camping, above.)

On the strait, the relatively calm waters of **Clallam Bay** are a good bet for kayakers. The day-use park in downtown Clallam Bay is a good launch spot.

Wildlife

Neah Bay is a notable **seabird**-watching hot spot. More than 250 species are commonly seen at or near Cape Flattery, especially around Tatoosh Island. Mukkaw Bay, just over the Waatch River south of town, is another good birding area. A bird identification guide is available at the Makah Museum (see Attractions, below), or by contacting the Makah Planning Office, (360) 645-2201. Primary bird-watching season is the dead of winter. **Bald eagles** are most commonly seen in February and March, as they return north to British Columbia after wintering on Puget Sound rivers such as the Nooksack and the Skagit.

Also from Cape Flattery, Shi Shi Beach, and the Cape Alava/Sand Point area, **gray whales** are often seen on their Pacific migration. They're going north in April and May, returning south in October and November. The best thing about seeing them here, as opposed to farther south on the coast, is that they tend to hug the shore off Cape Flattery. You'll only need a simple pair of binoculars to get that rare close-up view.

Neah Bay's ocean beaches also are commonly inhabited by **sea lions, seals,** and **sea otters.** The entire coastal area here is protected as Flattery Rocks National Wildlife Refuge.

In the strait, watch for all of the above, plus **orca** whales.

If your heart is set on furrier mammals, the trail from Lake Ozette to Cape Alava is famous for its frequent **deer, black bear, raccoon,** and other wild animal sightings.

outside in

Attractions

Without a doubt, the tribal-run **Makah Museum,** (360) 645-2711, is the singular must-see in Neah Bay. The museum contains artifacts from the Ozette archaeological excavation, which unearthed a nearly intact Makah village buried in mud some 500 years ago. It's open 10 to 5 daily in the summer, but closed Mondays and Tuesdays in the off season.

Or, you can get a guided escort for exploring all of the Neah Bay area by contacting **Native American Adventures,** (360) 645-2554, which offers guided carpool tours of the museum, local beaches, and other sites all year round.

Canoe races and other tribal events commence during the last week of August, when the tribe celebrates **Makah Days.**

Restaurants

For recommended restaurants, see the Adjoining Areas to this chapter.

Lodgings

Van Riper's Resort   The only waterfront hotel in the area, Van Riper's is a comfortable family-operated place. Rooms facing Clallam Bay can look out on the Strait and the rugged coastline of Vancouver Island beyond. Two units are large apartments with complete kitchens. A small house up the hill is also available. The owners also operate the small store on the premises with bait and tackle, charter service, and launch ramp. *Corner of Front and Rice on the main street; (360) 963-2334; 280 Front St, Sekiu; $.*

More Information

Makah Tribal Council: *(360) 645-2201.*
Olympic National Park information: *(360) 452-0330.*
Ozette Reservation Line: *(360) 452-0300.*
U.S. Coast Guard, Neah Bay: *(360) 645-2311.*

Forks
and La Push

From the Soleduck Information Center on US 101 south to the Bogachiel River, west to La Push, and east to Bogachiel Peak in Olympic National Park, including Rialto Beach, Mora Campground, Bogachiel State Park, and the lower Soleduck, Bogachiel, and Calawah Rivers.

Most of the sparkling rivers draining the mossy west slopes of the Olympics flow together near Forks. So, too, do the dueling passions that mark the past and probable future of the Olympic Peninsula.

The Olympics in general are a study in contrasts, with small oceans of clear-cut devastation yielding views of wilderness areas as pure as any on the planet. The dichotomy is particularly glaring in Forks, a longtime timber community now struggling to cash in on its unparalleled recreation venues—without denying a rich and deeply ingrained tradition of forestry. That's a tall order, and probably wouldn't be possible almost anywhere else in the state. Fortunately, the magnificent natural features surrounding Forks and La Push (a struggling native fishing village on the coast just to the west) have proven powerful enough to accommodate both uses for generations.

For the most part, people in Forks continue to look to the woods with an eye more toward cutting than camping. Likewise, the Quileutes in La Push hope for a renaissance in their own traditional craft, salmon fishing. But economic momentum is beginning to inch the other way. Logging and fishing have largely been halted on public lands by environmental restrictions—the result, it can be argued, of a century of sloppy, wanton overharvesting. And recreation has—with only minimal urging from the local communities—begun to fill the void. That was inevitable, given the natural treasures that circle these two towns.

The string of ocean beaches on either side of La Push is the most pristine, fully accessible chunk of coastline in the Northwest, if not the nation. The surviving old-growth forests around Forks, most notably the upper Bogachiel River drainage, are priceless living memorials to the peninsula's wild past. And less than an hour away in either direction, the spectacular Hoh River Valley and Lake Crescent areas await with their own unique tourist-drawing power. Those are increasingly rare and—as the state's population continues to bulge—increasingly valuable commodities. More than any other towns on the coast, Forks and La Push are poised to take advantage of these assets. The free market of recreational opportunities might, by itself, lead both towns down a prosperous new path.

We wouldn't be surprised to drive through the old timber town of Forks in the year 2005 and see a brand-new placard popping up in local storefront windows: This business supported by Gore-Tex dollars.

Getting There

Forks is located midway on the 175-mile, north-south Olympic Peninsula coastal stretch of US 101. To reach it from the north, follow US 101 80 miles west and south of Port Angeles. From the south, Forks lies 95 miles north of Aberdeen. La Push, a small tribal fishing village at the mouth of the Quillayute River, is 14 miles southwest of Forks on Hwy 110. Clallam Transit bus service is available from Port Angeles; call (360) 452-4511 or (800) 858-3747 for details.

Adjoining Areas

NORTH: **Lake Crescent and the Upper Soleduck**

SOUTH: **Lake Quinault and the Quinault River Valley**

EAST: **Olympic National Park: Overview; Olympic National Forest and the East Slope Olympics**

Beaches

Wild ocean beaches are the primary drawing card for the Olympic Peninsula, and several of the finest are within walking distance of La Push. The center of attention is the Olympic National Park day-use area at **Rialto Beach,** just a stone's skip across the river from La Push, and a short walk or drive from Mora Campground (see Camping, below). Rialto has picnic facilities, a large parking lot, and other amenities. But the beach is the lure. It's a beauty—one of those very few picture-perfect Washington scenes you can drive right up to. A series of sea stacks lurk in the mist to the north, and the unusually steep-sloped beach makes for frothing, always picturesque surf. The beach is almost always windy, but great for strolling, with miles of unobstructed sand beckoning to the north. Rialto also is a major beach-hiking trailhead for coastal backpackers (see Hiking/Backpacking, below). Most single-day visitors walk 1.5 miles up the beach to **Hole in the Wall,** a nifty surf-carved tunnel beneath the jutting headlands. Note: Heavy flooding here in the winter of 1995–96 damaged many of Rialto's facilities. Check their status with Olympic National Park, (360) 452-0330.

Three other gorgeous ocean beaches are found just south of La Push, all reached by driving back toward Forks, turning south over the Quillayute River, and following La Push Road to the ocean. About 3 miles from the river crossing, look for the **Third Beach** trail on the south side of the road. The path leads 1.5 miles to the shore, where a nice waterfall plunges toward the beach's south end at Taylor Point, and tidal pools can be explored near Teahwhit Head, to the north. On the other side of that obstructing headland is **Second Beach,** reached via a short trail just south of La Push. **First Beach,** on the Quileute Reservation and open to the public, is near **La Push** itself. All of these are great picnic/beachcombing spots, with big, awesome rock walls, kid-luring sea caves, and tons of unidentifiable sea gunk washing up on the beach.

Camping

The best campground in the region is **Mora,** an Olympic National Park site near Rialto Beach (see Beaches, above). Mora's 95 campsites (no hookups; maximum RV length, 21 feet) are spread through several loops in a heavily wooded (dark, almost) flat not far from the Quillayute River. There's not much to see or do in the park itself, but the beach is a short walk away. A group camp for 15 to 40 campers is available and can be reserved on a first-come, first-served basis after March 1. Mora is open all year; sites ($10) cannot be reserved. *On Mora Road (Hwy 110), 12 miles west of US 101, stay right at the Y where La Push Road departs to the left;* (360) 452-0330 or (360) 374-5460.

Another good bet—especially for you multiple-days-without-showers US 101 vagabonds—is **Bogachiel State Park,** south of Forks on US 101. It's a simple place, with 40 sites (6 with hookups; maximum RV length, 35 feet) a bit too close to the highway for our taste. But Bogachiel does have hot showers, the best investment of a quarter or two you'll make all summer. The park also has a picnic area and boat launch on the lovely Bogachiel River, a noted steelhead fishery (see Fishing, below). Bogachiel State Park is open all year. Sites cannot be reserved. *On US 101 6 miles south of Forks; (360) 374-6356 or (800) 233-0321.*

The final option is rustic **Klahanie,** a small (12 sites, no hookups), primitive Olympic National Forest site east of US 101. The campground, on the Calawah River, has no drinking water or facilities. It's open summers only. Sites (free) cannot be reserved. *On Forest Service Road 29 5.4 miles east of US 101; (360) 956-2400.*

Hiking/Backpacking

Most of the prominent hikes in the area involve ocean beaches. The biggie is the **Rialto Beach to Sand Point** (moderate; 18.5 miles one way) trek north up the "Shipwreck Coast," where some scuttled seafaring remnants are still in evidence. It's a two- to three-day hike to the popular Lake Ozette area, with plenty of good streamside campsites along the way. (Note: Camping is not allowed on Rialto Beach south of Ellen Creek.) On the other side of La Push, the **Third Beach** trailhead (see Beaches, above) is the departure point for a 17-mile, three-day hike south to **Oil City,** near the mouth of the Hoh River. Long-distance beach hikers should be highly aware of tides, and be prepared to cross steep, rocky, often hazardous headlands on this stretch. Bring the rain gear, even if it *is* August.

If you're just out for the day, several good short beach hikes await. Campers at Mora often prefer to walk, roll, or run the 2-mile road from the campground to **Rialto Beach,** then walk north to **Hole in the Wall** (easy; about 3 miles round trip). The hike to **Third Beach** (easy; 3 miles round trip) is a pleasant walk from La Push Road, as is the nearby **Second Beach** (easy; 1.5 miles round trip) trail.

Forest fans aren't completely shut out by clearcuts around Forks. Just south of the town, a long finger of Olympic National Park follows the Bogachiel River toward the ocean, and the land on each side is protected. The **Bogachiel River Trail** (moderate; various lengths possible), which begins at the gated end of Undie Road, 5.5 miles east of Bogachiel State Park, is a fascinating but little-used trail up a lush old-growth valley. This is a wet and wild place. The trail has the look and feel of the famous Hoh River Trail, one valley to the south—but with a tiny fraction of the people. Great campsites are found all along the way, most overlooking the river, which will lull you to sleep at night. Strong trekkers can follow the Bogachiel Trail east all the way to **High Divide,** 31 miles (although we can't say we know anyone who's actually *done* this rather than take the shorter route up the Soleduck Valley). Weekend backpackers should consider a trek to the old **Bogachiel Shelter** site (about 6 miles, one way) or **Flapjack Camp** (8.25 miles, one way). It's a very pleasant walk, mostly flat. But the trail can be a bear (a slug?) in the spring or during winter rainy periods, when gushing streams become difficult to ford. The Bogachiel gets hit by as much as 200 inches of rain every year. Watch for Roosevelt elk—and mondo banana slugs.

Fishing

Rivers draining the rain-soaked western Olympics around Forks are among the last best steelhead and salmon waters in the Northwest. The **Soleduck, Bogachiel,** and **Calawah,** all of which merge to become the **Quillayute** just west of Forks for a short, final run to the sea near La Push, are noted highways for winter and summer **steelhead** and numerous **salmon** species. Some form of game fish season is active most of the year, but these rivers' most famous—and productive—fisheries are for spring chinook and winter steelhead.

The Soleduck River's spring chinook fishery is legendary, with many salmon up to 50 pounds returning to the Sol Duc Hatchery just north of Forks. The chinook, because they're so fresh from the ocean, are uncommonly feisty and bright. Landing one from the beach or a drift boat is a thrill not soon forgotten. Because much of the Soleduck between its mouth and the hatchery runs through private property, bank fishing is difficult. Float trips from the **Sol Duc Fish Hatchery** near Sappho downstream to a takeout off Salmon Road, just north of Forks, are popular. Guided trips are available in Forks. The spring chinook season typically runs April through May.

The winter steelhead fishery, which begins in December, peaks in January and February, and tails off by April, is more widespread, with good catch rates in all three local rivers. The trick here is timing. Because these rivers drain temperate rain forest, rain squalls can turn the waters from clear to chocolate-milk brown overnight. It's important to call for river conditions before you set out. And there's always the chance things will change by the time you drive all the way here from Seattle.

For guide referrals, tackle, licenses, season information, and river reports, see or phone Bob Gooding at Olympic Sporting Goods in downtown Forks; (360) 374-6330. For guided fishing trips, contact Three Rivers Guide Service; (360) 374-5300.

Kayaking/Surfing

First Beach in La Push has a surf often worthy of rides by surfers and/or aggressive sea kayakers. There's good parking and shore access, but you'll have to pack the gear down a substantial hill.

River runners will be challenged by the **lower Soleduck River,** which is rated intermediate (Class II to III) and is best run during the melt-off of spring and early summer. A popular route parallels a favorite fisherman's drift-boat course: from the Sol Duc Hatchery near Sappho downstream to a boat launch off Salmon Road, about 6 miles north of Forks. It's between 7 and 8 miles of river, and elk often are spotted along the banks. Note: Some major rocks lurk in this cold, fast river. Watch your bow.

The **Quillayute River,** the 6-mile stretch from the confluence of the Soleduck and Bogachiel Rivers to the coast near Rialto Beach, is another popular paddling destination. Most paddlers put in at Leyendecker Park near the confluence and take out in the salt water at Rialto.

Upstream on the **Bogachiel,** the 15-mile stretch between Bogachiel State Park and Leyendecker County Park is a more challenging daylong trip for advanced paddlers.

Photography

Rialto Beach is a photographer's favorite. The hazy beach environment, marked by looming sea stacks and pounding surf, is a sure-fire target, especially at Hole in the Wall, to the north of Rialto Beach parking lot. Big-tree shooters should not overlook the **Bogachiel River Trail** (see Hiking/Backpacking, above). We've shot some grand, tiny-hiker-amid-gargantuan-trees portraits here. In fact, the world's largest silver fir stands proudly on the river's south banks. Look for it about a quarter-mile beyond Flapjack Camp. It's that house-size thing with branches.

Wildlife

Peaceful-but-skittish **Roosevelt elk,** high on our list of favorite creatures on the planet, are common in this area, particularly in lowlands near the lower Soleduck and upper Bogachiel Rivers. Bird lovers won't be disappointed by the region's beach sites. We haven't seen them, but rare **ospreys** are said to nest often in snags just north of Rialto Beach. And hundreds of other **shorebirds** are commonly seen from here, as well as at First, Second, and Third Beaches south of La Push. The La Push area is near the geographic center of the Quillayute Needles National Wildlife Refuge and is part of the Olympic Coast National Marine Sanctuary, so all offshore rocks and islands are protected habitat. Also, we're told **gray whales** often pass very close to Hole in the Wall on their spring and fall migrations to and from Alaska. Finally, an acquaintance who knows one when she sees one reports seeing a **northern spotted owl,** of Northwest timber controversy fame, along the Bogachiel River, just up from Bogachiel State Park.

outside in

Attractions

Few things will distract you from the natural wonders here. But one stop in Forks, the **Timber Museum,** (360) 374-9633, offers a worthwhile look into the region's past. In the same vein, logging tours depart from the Forks Visitors Information Center on Tuesday and Friday summer mornings; call (800) 44-FORKS for details. Two state fish hatcheries in the region are worth viewing. The **Bogachiel Steelhead Rearing Pond** is at the end of Bogachiel Way, west of downtown Forks. The **Sol Duc Fish Hatchery,** where the big kings return every spring, is on Pavel Road, 13 miles north of Forks. If the weather turns sour—not an unusual occurrence—consider **Olympic West Arttrek,** a self-guided driving tour of native galleries and studios between the Hoh River and Neah Bay. Call (800) 44-FORKS for details.

Restaurants

Smoke House Restaurant   Stop at this big blue building north of Forks for a sampling of alder-smoked salmon: this moist, lightly smoked fish is the star ingredient on the restaurant's menu. The waitresses know most everyone, go out of their way to make strangers welcome, and dispense lots of travel advice. *North of town at the junction of Hwy 101 and La Push–Quillayute Rd; (360) 374-6258; 193161 Hwy 101, Forks; $.*

Lodgings

Eagle Point Inn ☆☆   Even if you rise before dawn to fish, a hearty breakfast will be ready when you are at this spacious, comfortable lodge built of logs. A covered outdoor kitchen down near the Soleduck River is ideal for barbecuing your own meal at night. *Between Forks and Sappho on Hwy 101; go east on Stormin' Norman Rd at milepost 202; (360) 327-3236; 384 Stormin' Norman Rd, Beaver; $$.*

Miller Tree Inn ☆   Fisherfolk will appreciate the pre-dawn breakfasts at this original homestead in Forks. Owners Ted and Prue Miller's knowledge of local river conditions, the room set aside to clean and freeze your catch, and the hot tub to relax in after a day on the river. Kids and well-mannered pets are welcome. *Next to Forks City Hall; (360) 374-6806; 654 E Division St, Forks; $.*

River Inn   A secluded private chalet on the banks of the Bogachiel River—one of the finest steelhead fishing rivers on the peninsula—now serves as a guest house. Playful otters and browsing deer are both common sights. Rent the whole house and come with friends or family. Spacious outdoor hot tub. *2.5 miles west of downtown Forks; (360) 374-6526; 2596 Bogachiel Way, Forks; $.*

More Information

Eagle Ranger Station (national park and forest and state park information): *(360) 374-6522.*

Forks Chamber of Commerce: *(800) 44-FORKS.*

Mora Ranger Station: *(360) 374-5460.*

Olympic Sporting Goods: *(360) 374-6330.*

Central Coast:
Hoh,
Kalaloch,
and Queets

From the Bogachiel River south to the Queets River, west to the Pacific, and east to Mount Olympus in Olympic National Park, including Ruby Beach, the Quillayute Needles National Wildlife Refuge, and Kalaloch and Hoh Rain Forest Campgrounds.

If they only let you out of town once a year to sample the Northwest's wilds, this is probably the place to cash in your pass.

The Hoh River, which empties into the Pacific just north of Kalaloch, is the stuff of legend. At its headwaters, 7,965-foot Mount Olympus, the Olympic Peninsula's crown jewel, provides a constant glacial water source, which empties into the Hoh proper for a swift run downstream through one of the unique ecosystems of the world—the Hoh Rain Forest. This is a special, ethereal place, where average annual rainfalls approaching 140 inches fuel a vividly green environment.

The valley is almost surreal. It's filled with massive, moss-draped spruce, maple, and red cedar trees that are among the oldest living things on the planet. The quiet, misty river bottoms are home to literally thousands of plant species, as well as herds of Roosevelt elk, one of the state's most regal creatures. The 17-mile walk up the Hoh River to the shoulders—or even the top—of Olympus is one of the nation's classic outdoor treks.

But the charms of the upper Hoh are only half the attraction here. A dozen miles downstream, the river flows into the Pacific on a broad, pristine stretch of ocean beach that's still as wild as any coastline in the United States. Just to the south, Kalaloch (newcomers will quickly learn to say CLAY-lock), the only development on this central stretch of Washington's coastline, offers just enough amenities to make a pilgrimage to the ocean comfortable. Kalaloch's campground is unforgettable, with broad ocean views and a constant breeze to mix the sweet, salty aroma of the Pacific with campfire smoke and percolated coffee. And its comfortable lodge and cabins make for the definitive Pacific Northwest wet-weekend getaway.

Just to the south, the Queets River Valley—thanks to a 1953 addition to Olympic National Park, the only rain forest valley protected from mountains to sea—is an even wilder version of the Hoh, its cousin to the north. The Queets area, accessed by a rugged gravel road stretching 14 miles east of US 101, is a backpacker's heaven, with a lightly traveled trail beginning midway up the river and winding 14.5 miles toward the mighty river's headwaters. Compared to other peninsula river valleys, the Queets is seldom visited, with anglers making up the lion's share of humans most of the year. That's too bad, given the mighty river's status: it's the most powerful single stream on the peninsula, draining much of the park's southwestern interior.

Twin magnificent rain forests sandwiching a healthy serving of pristine ocean beach: no other single area in the Northwest is packed with as much beauty, intrigue and splendor as this one. Washington, as a state and as a people, would be something much less without it.

Getting There

The Hoh River area, a 3- to 4-hour drive from Seattle via Port Angeles, is reached by traveling 13 miles south of Forks or 21 miles north of Kalaloch on US 101, then following Hoh Rain Forest Road 18 miles east to the Hoh Ranger Station, campground, and day-use area. Kalaloch, an Olympic National Park campground, resort, and day-use area, is 34 miles south of Forks and 30 miles northwest of Lake Quinault on US 101.

The Queets River basin is reached by turning east on Queets River Road, 13 miles south of Kalaloch and 20 miles north of Lake Quinault on US 101. The road is gravel, often heavily potholed, and not suited for RVs or very low-clearance vehicles.

Adjoining Areas

NORTH: **Forks and La Push**

SOUTH: **Lake Quinault and the Quinault River Valley**

EAST: **Olympic National Park: Overview**

inside out

Hiking/Backpacking

A pair of waterproof boots and a rain parka are your tickets to hiking nirvana here. Choose your pleasure: strike out from either side of Kalaloch on a sprawling ocean beach with picturesque sea stacks and more seagulls than people. Or hoist your pack and walk in awe along two long, flat valley trails through the planet's most fascinating rain forest, one leading onto the slopes of spectacular Mount Olympus. If there's a more fulfilling place to spend a summer week anywhere on earth, we haven't found it.

A series of wonderful rain forest walks begin at the Hoh Visitors Center. For kids and the aerobically challenged, the **Hall of Mosses Trail** (easy; .75-mile loop), which begins and ends near the visitors center, is a good nature-trail primer. Nearby is the **Spruce Nature Trail** (easy; 1.25-mile loop) and a separate paved, quarter-mile nature loop. The latter two trails are wheelchair-accessible.

But there's no reason just about anyone in love with the rain forest should fail to venture up the famous **Hoh River Trail** (easy; 2 to 35 miles round trip), which begins at the visitors center and runs all the way up the Hoh Valley—17.5 miles—to Glacier Meadows backcountry camp on Mount Olympus.

It's easy to see why it's so popular. The route is spectacular, winding through mile after mile of magnificent old-growth Sitka spruce, red cedar, bigleaf maple, and fir trees. Some of the trees in this valley are the largest of their kind in the world, and rank among the largest living things on earth. That's reason enough to make the trek, but the trail provides another: the first 13 miles or so are totally flat, making this an easy walk for even inexperienced hikers. Grassy flats located along the trail make fine campsites, and established camps at **Happy Four Camp** (5.75 miles) and **Olympus Guard Station** (9 miles) are popular overnight spots (they're also good lunch-stop destinations for day hikers).

At 9.2 miles, some longer-distance trekkers turn north on the **Hoh Lake Trail**, which climbs sharply to the **High Divide** area. Many backpackers who have two cars or arrange for shuttle transportation use this trail to link the Soleduck and Hoh River Valleys for weeklong backpack trips. Other long-distance hikers will want to follow the Hoh Trail for the full 17.5 miles (the last 4 being very steep) to **Glacier Meadows**, a stunning mountainside camp that serves as the base for Mount Olympus climbing expeditions. The Hoh's lower portions are hikable all year, the last 4 or 5 miles only from July to late October. Watch for stealthy herds of Roosevelt elk in the mossy forest.

Also in the Hoh Valley, the **South Fork Hoh Trail** (moderate; 7.5 miles round trip) is a more sparsely used trail that begins just beyond South Fork Hoh Campground (see Camping, below).

Beach hikes are plentiful, as well. From US 101 on either side of Kalaloch Campground, short paths lead steeply downhill to **Beaches 1, 2, 4,** and **6** (we can't figure out what happened to Beach 5, either). Each runs one-quarter to one-half mile downhill to a beach with its own appealing character. **Beach 4,** marked by sheer walls, offshore rocks, and many explorable tidal pools, is a favorite. It's also a popular surf fishing and smelt dipping area, and the upper parking lot has a wheelchair-accessible trail to a scenic beach overlook.

Kalaloch Campground itself is a good place to embark on a long beach hike. Many walkers enjoy heading north on the sand about 3 miles to Beach 6, one of the most scenic beach areas, then returning the same way. Long-distance beach backpackers often begin at **Oil City,** just north of the mouth of the Hoh River (take Oil City Road west from US 101, 15 miles south of Forks), for the rugged, spectacular 17-mile, three-day walk to **Third Beach,** near La Push (see the Forks and La Push chapter).

A dozen miles to the south, the rain forest resumes. The **Queets River Trail** (moderate; various lengths), hidden up a rough, sparsely traveled road between Kalaloch and Lake Quinault, is a spectacular walk up an old-growth river valley, with a fraction of the foot traffic on the more popular Hoh River Trail one valley to the north. You guessed it: there's a small catch. Before the journey begins, hikers have to ford the Queets River.

Some people use rafts to make this crossing during heavy flow periods in early summer. But foot crossings are practical during low-flow periods, such as late summer and early fall, when the river can be safely waded. The river flow is more key than the season. Early spring crossings can be made during spells of dry weather, for example. But be aware that during spring storms, the river can rise several feet between the time you go in and the time you go out. Call the park for information and advice. (Tip: From the main trailhead at the end of Queets Valley Road, it's usually easier to ford the Sams River, the smaller tributary flowing in from the right, and then cross the Queets farther upstream, where it's shallower.) Also be aware that two additional river fordings are required about 5 and 6 miles up the trail.

If and when you get across the river, this hike is a grand backpack trip. The trail runs 14.5 miles through lush old-growth to a dead-end at **Pelton Creek Camp,** with good campsites all along the route. Many backpackers opt to go in 5 miles to great campsites and fishing at **Spruce Bottom.** Day hikers can walk in 2.5 miles to find one of the largest Douglas firs in the world. Watch for Roosevelt elk here, particularly in the fall. The trailhead is about a mile beyond Queets Campground (see Camping, below).

Nearby, a 3-mile **loop trail** (easy) that begins and ends near the summer-only Queets Ranger Station makes a nice afternoon stroll through a rich, moss-draped rain forest. It's mostly flat, and elk sightings are possible.

Beaches

The beach right out in front of **Kalaloch Campground** is a state treasure. Incredibly broad, flat and clean, it's often fog-shrouded and windswept. But that only seems to add to the allure. Barefoot beach-walking, kite flying, Frisbee games, and just plain gaping at the sea are the favorite activities here. Razor clam digging is allowed in season. From the campground, you can stroll for miles in either direction, without ever running out of public beach—or enthusiasm. Even the least inspired walker can make it about a mile south to scenic **Kalaloch Rocks,** near the mouth of Kalaloch Creek just below Kalaloch Lodge.

The numbered beaches reached by short trails from US 101 (see Hiking/Backpacking, above) are great places to spend the day. **Beaches 4** and **6** are particularly scenic, with many sea stacks, offshore islands, and steep headlands separating them from the broader, sandy expanse to the south. We've seen sea lions, whales, and other creatures here. Both beaches are good surf fishing and, occasionally, smelt-dipping venues.

Just to the north, **Ruby Beach,** a Northwest favorite, is reached via a short trail from a highway pullout, with good views of Destruction Island just offshore.

If Kalaloch is just a short stopover on the way to somewhere else, consider pulling into the **South Beach** overflow area (summer only), about 2 miles south of Kalaloch Lodge. It's essentially a flat parking lot used to accommodate extra campers. But the lot sits just yards above a delightful, driftwood-studded beach. South Beach is a drive-in mental-health break from US 101.

Camping

Kalaloch Campground, Olympic National Park's largest, is the star. Big surprise: the campground, one of the most wonderfully situated in the Northwest, can be difficult to get into during summer months. The campground's 177 sites (no hookups; maximum RV length, 21 feet) fill up nearly every night, all summer long. It's still first-come, first-served here.

And the park takes the rules seriously, requiring that you register for your site within an hour after arrival, and strictly discouraging saving sites for friends.

The best way to snag a site is to show up at midmorning, park in the day-use lot, and patrol the loops by foot or bicycle, swooping in vulture circles waiting for someone to leave. This Kalaloch Campground Cakewalk can be extremely frustrating. But it just makes it that much sweeter when you score that spot right on the bluff, overlooking the ocean. Some campers, particularly those with anxious, must-get-out-NOW children, adopt a longer-term strategy: they grab one of the less popular, dark sites that back onto US 101, then move up to a beachfront spot later in the week. Either way, it's worth the wait. Kalaloch is open all year. Sites ($10; 14-day maximum) cannot be reserved. *On US 101, 34 miles south of Forks; (360) 452-0330 or (360) 962-2283.*

Just south of the campground is the **South Beach** overflow area, open summers only. This flat gravel lot began as a sloppy-seconds campground with no running water, tables, fire pits, or facilities of any kind. But now that a rest room has been built there, it's become the campground of choice for many, particularly RV owners who can set up just about anywhere. Reason: It's almost right on the beach, with only an 8-foot bank and a pile of driftwood separating the dinner table from the pounding Pacific surf. *On US 101, 3 miles south of Kalaloch; (360) 452-0330.*

Equally accommodating—and almost as popular—is **Hoh Rain Forest Campground,** a national park site near Hoh Visitors Center. The campground's 89 sites (no hookups; maximum RV length, 21 feet) are spread through wooded loops near the river and famous rain forest trails. Roosevelt elk are often seen in the area. One recent spring, in fact, the campground was shut down when a protective mother cow made a nursery of one of the camping loops. Hoh Rain Forest is another one of Olympic's favorite camps, and sites can be tough to land in summer months. It's open all year. Campsites ($10) cannot be reserved. *At the end of Hoh River Road, 18 miles east of US 101; (360) 452-0330.*

If Hoh Rain Forest and Kalaloch are full (or even if they aren't), don't overlook the string of very nice—and very free—state Department of Natural Resources campsites along the Hoh River. **Hoh Oxbow,** just south of the Hoh Rain Forest Road along US 101, has five sites for tents and small trailers, but no running water. A small boat launch makes it a favorite angler's hangout, especially during winter steelhead season. **Cottonwood,** just off Oil City Road (turn west 15 miles south of Forks) is similar, with six sites, primitive facilities, but no fee. On the Hoh Rain Forest Road itself are **Willoughby Creek** (3.5 miles east of US 101), which has three small campsites and limited facilities; and **Minnie**

Peterson (4.5 miles east of US 101), which has six small riverside spots. Another primitive, but private, option is **South Fork Hoh,** reached by turning east on Hoh Mainline Road (about 15.5 miles south of Forks) and proceeding 14 miles east. South Fork Hoh, part of Bert Cole State Park, has three campsites and little else, except for those mind-blowing old-growth trees that clutter the place. The South Fork Hoh Trail (see Hiking/Backpacking, above) is just up the road from here. All five camp-grounds are free and open all year. Sites cannot be reserved. *Contact the Washington Department of Natural Resources; (360) 902-1000.*

A private campground in the vicinity is **Hoh River Resort,** near the river on US 101, which has 23 sites with hookups and other facilities. The park is open all year. Sites can be reserved by calling (360) 374-5566.

On the Queets River, **Queets Campground,** an Olympic National Park site, has 20 standard (moss on the picnic tables) tent sites near the river and the Queets River Ranger Station and Trailhead. The campground and its access road aren't suitable for RVs or trailers. It's a nice spot, but primitive. No running water here. Queets is open all year. Campsites cannot be reserved. *On Queets River Road 14 miles east of US 101; (360) 452-0330 or (360) 962-2283.*

Fishing/Clam Digging

Spring and fall razor clamming seasons occasionally are available on the beach at **Kalaloch,** which gets crowded with hundred of diggers seeking the succulent bivalves. Call the state Department of Fish and Wildlife at Montesano, (360) 249-4628, for seasons and restrictions.

Beaches around Kalaloch can be very productive for surf perch fish-ing. **Beach 4,** with a steeper, rockier surface than other local areas, is a prime producer. Some surf anglers also cast deep here for Pacific skates, a raylike bottom feeder whose meaty shoulders some fishermen consider a delicacy.

The **Hoh** and **Queets Rivers** are legendary game fish haunts. Both hold winter and summer steelhead and multiple salmon species. The Hoh gets hot for steelheading in December and continues to produce through April. Then it's salmon time, with a healthy hatchery chinook run avail-able through the summer. The Queets also is a noted winter steelhead river. Most anglers head for the lower river, below the confluence of the Salmon River, where Quinault-tribe hatchery steelhead are placed. But the upper river is more scenic, and anglers searching for a big, wild steelhead can try here in March and April. Good bank access can be found all along Queets Rain Forest Road (see Camping, above). Some truly spectacular holes are found farther upstream, at Spruce Bottom on the Queets River

Trail (see Hiking/Backpacking, above). For river conditions and seasons, call Olympic Sporting Goods in Forks; (360) 374-6330.

Photography

Sunset at **Kalaloch** can be fabulous for shutterbugs. Even on foggy days, the midday sun often bursts through the clouds at Beach 4, bathing the surf and rocks in an otherworldly light.

By all means, photograph the famous **Hoh Rain Forest.** For similar pictures in an even more isolated environment, venture up the **Queets Valley,** where you can shoot magnificent moss-draped trees less than 30 feet from your car. The dark, cathedral-like canopy in both places makes for tricky light; use a tripod or bring fast film. Morning light usually is best, and bright, overcast days are better than sunny ones. A fast, 28-mm or shorter wide-angle lens is the tool of choice. And remember: The forest will be much more appreciated later if you include a human element for landscape perspective. People won't believe just how big these trees are without a known reference point.

Wildlife

The entire coastline here is rich with wildlife; **seals, sea lions, sea birds,** and migrating **gray whales** are often spotted offshore. This is the southern end of Olympic National Park's 57-mile coastal strip. All rocks, islands, and other offshore formations north of Kalaloch are protected by the Quillayute Needles National Wildlife Refuge, and the entire Olympic coastal strip recently was protected from industrial exploitation when it received National Marine Sanctuary status. The US 101 pullout just north of Kalaloch, above Destruction Island, is a good, high post from which to watch, as is a similar, wheelchair-accessible overlook at the Beach 4 Trail parking lot.

The Hoh River is a famous wildlife habitat. It's a particularly good place to find yourself amid a herd of majestic **Roosevelt elk** in the winter months, when they migrate here from the highlands. The Hoh River Trail is your best bet. Elk also are seen along the Queets River Trail.

Climbing

The route up the Blue Glacier to the summit of **Mount Olympus** is Olympic National Park's most popular climb. The route is fairly technical, but not impossible for inexperienced climbers—*providing* they have a guide who knows the mountain. From the base camp at Glacier Meadows, the summit can be bagged easily in one long day, conditions permitting. That's the catch. Weather is the biggest foe on Olympus. Because the mountain looms so high (7,965 feet) less than 40 miles from the Pacific, it's the first rain stop for approaching southwesterly storms. Major dumpage is always possible, and the route is very exposed.

Complicating matters is the relatively short climbing season. To be traversed safely, the Blue Glacier is best climbed in the spring (as early as April) or early summer. From July on, crevasses open quickly, and the route turns very hazardous. Consult with rangers at the Hoh Rain Forest Visitors Center well in advance of your climb.

The Blue Glacier route is a solid day trip. It's 8 miles and about 3,500 feet from Glacier Meadows to the summit. But consider spending a solid week on the mountain, to accommodate bad weather. Most climbers take two days to make the 17.5-mile walk in and out the Hoh River Trail. Leaving three or four days to wait for clear skies at Glacier Meadows will dramatically increase your chance of success. Note: The last pitch to the summit is a rock scramble. Helmets are advisable. For guide service information, contact Olympic Mountaineering in Port Angeles, (360) 452-0240.

Rafting

Olympic Raft and Guide Service, (360) 452-1443, runs float trips on the Elwha, Hoh, and Queets Rivers. These are primarily placid, nonintimidating tours, with an emphasis on wildlife and natural history. Well worth investing a day.

Attractions

Definitely stop and see the **Big Tree.** It's just off US 101, between Beach 4 and Beach 6. Look for the sign that says, "Big Tree." It really is big. The ancient red cedar snag originally was believed to be the largest on the peninsula, until a larger tree was located elsewhere in the park. Olympic, by the way, has nearly a dozen record trees inside its borders. Ask at the park visitors center, (360) 452-0330, for a list.

Restaurants

For restaurant recommendations, see the Adjoining Areas to this chapter.

Lodgings

Kalaloch Lodge   Kalaloch offers comfort and camaraderie in one of the most isolated beachside resorts in Washington. There are lots of accommodations: rooms in the lodge; a modern two-story lodging set amid wind-shaped trees; newer log cabins; and duplex cabins on the edge of the bluff. The older cabins should be a last choice. No phones or TVs in the rooms. The restaurant staff is friendly, but don't expect anything more than standard fare. *Hwy 101, 34 miles south of Forks, milepost 157; (360) 962-2271; 157151 Hwy 101, Forks; $$.*

More Information

Hoh Rain Forest Visitors Center, Olympic National Park: *(360) 374-6925.*

Kalaloch Information Station, Olympic National Park: *(360) 962-2283.*

Olympic National Forest Visitors Information: *(360) 374-6522.*

Olympic National Park Visitors Information: *(360) 452-0330.*

Lake Quinault
and the Quinault River Valley

From the Queets River at US 101 east to Anderson Pass in Olympic National Park, north to Low Divide, and south to Wynoochee Pass, including the Quinault and Queets River Valleys, the Colonel Bob Wilderness, the Enchanted Valley, and the Lake Quinault Lodge area.

For many Northwesterners, this rain-enriched valley is a touchstone.

The Quinault—a common name shared by an untamed river, a moss-draped valley, a glassy lake, and an indigenous people—is a survivor. The valley is in many ways an island of purity, an intact example of the startlingly beautiful rain-forest-to-glacier Olympic valleys first settled—but never tamed—by homesteaders in the late 19th century.

A sense of permanence pervades the place. Much of what was here before white settlers arrived remains. The valley's mighty rain forests, filled with Sitka spruce, western red cedar and Douglas fir that sprouted from seeds 1,000 years ago, are still intact, at least above the lake. The glacier-carved lake, a quiet, fog-draped pool marking the halfway spot on the Quinault River's 60-mile march from Mount Anderson to the Pacific, is clean and largely undeveloped. Tying it all together is the river, an unruly force which, unlike most of its peninsula neighbors, has never been harnessed, even temporarily. The Quinault is one of the Olympic's largest and most vital arteries, draining more acreage than any single river in the range except the nearby Queets. Its east and north forks, which join just above Lake Quinault, drain the entire lower portion of the Olympics, from Low Divide south.

Many of the valley's early settlers stayed. Some of them helped build Lake Quinault Lodge, a cozy south-shore getaway that feels today much as it did when the doors opened in 1926. The lodge has become a symbol of a valley recognized as a treasure by three landlords: the Quinault Tribe, which owns the lake and all the land downstream to the north and west and makes a living off their reservation land's timber and fisheries; Olympic National Forest, which controls the rugged southern valley walls; and Olympic National Park, which manages the land from the river forks upstream, through the fabled Enchanted Valley and up to the Olympic Crest at Mount Anderson.

The Quinault would be beautiful in any setting, but it seems even more precious because of its immediate surroundings. Although the upstream lands survived wonderfully intact, public and private forest lands both north and south of Lake Quinault—and tribal lands along the river to the west—were devastated by the harsh, clearcut-and-run forestry of the first half of the century. Much of the land along US 101 on either side of the Quinault looks like moonscape. But somehow, sitting beside Quinault Lodge's massive stone fireplace, walking through the old-growth forest, or straining to traverse an upper-valley trail, it's easy to forget—if not forgive—all that.

For outdoor lovers, the Quinault is a diversion powerful enough to make you forget a *lot* of things, not just clearcuts. The basin represents both ends of the activity spectrum. Some of our most relaxing days have trickled by on the eerily quiet shores of Lake Quinault. And some of our most strenuous have zipped by in the mountain valleys above. The lake offers uncommonly good camping, fishing, canoeing, and kayaking. On both sides, lowland trails wind through magnificent old-growth rain forests. The mountains hold some of Washington's best alpine destinations: Enchanted Valley, Anderson and O'Neil Passes, the Skyline Ridge, and a string of southern Olympic peaks in the Colonel Bob Wilderness.

The Quinault, unlike many other Olympic destinations, can be a year-round destination. It goes without saying, the valley gets plenty of rain—170 inches in one recent year. But even during wet season, when snows close the upper valley, the lake remains an enticement. Soggy walks along low-level rain forest trails feel, frankly, *natural* in the rain. Roosevelt elk take up winter residence on the valley floor, delighting visitors—and annoying permanent residents. Lake Quinault Lodge reverts to the quiet, relaxing (no phones or TVs) retreat that first made it popular in the 1930s.

Which is probably why some of us keep coming back here, every winter, to check in on the way things were. And the way we'd like them always to be.

Getting There

Lake Quinault is 75 miles south of Forks and 38 miles north of Hoquiam on US 101. It's a 3- to 4-hour drive from Seattle, either from the north via Port Angeles or from the south via Interstate 5 and US 101 (the southern route is probably faster for most Puget Sound residents). All Lake Quinault destinations are reached by a pair of narrow county/national park roads, North Shore and South Shore. The roads meet beyond the head of the lake, where a bridge crosses the Quinault. When both roads are open, they can be driven as a 25-mile, very scenic loop around the lake and along the upper Quinault River.

The primary route is South Shore Road, which turns east from US 101 near the lake's southwest corner. The road passes Lake Quinault Lodge and continues 19 miles up the valley to Graves Creek (East Fork Quinault) campground and ranger station in Olympic National Park. North Shore Road provides access to Olympic's Quinault Ranger Station and continues east to the North Fork campground and trailhead. Be aware that the upper half of each road is gravel, and both can be quite rough. Washouts are common in winter. It's not at all unusual for one or both roads to be closed. Call before traveling.

Adjoining Areas

NORTH: **Central Coast: Hoh, Kalaloch, and Queets**
SOUTH: **Grays Harbor: Westport and Ocean Shores**
EAST: **Olympic National Park: Overview**

inside out

Hiking/Backpacking

Whether you're in search of a short day-hike through old-growth trees or a two-week trek into some of the most spectacular alpine terrain in the Olympics, the Quinault Valley is a good place to start. Several of the best short forest walks on the entire peninsula begin within walking distance of Lake Quinault Lodge. And two of Olympic National Park's classic trans-Olympic traverses start or end at trailheads only 30 minutes away. For trail conditions and updates, contact Olympic National Park or Olympic National Forest offices listed below. Here's a quick guide to the best of the region:

South Shore Lake Quinault

Short-term visitors, campers at Falls View or Willaby Campgrounds (see Camping, below), and guests of the Lake Quinault Lodge shouldn't miss the nearby **Lake Quinault Loop** (easy; 3-mile loop), which circles along the quiet lakeshore and into a truly awesome grove of old-growth Douglas fir. This impeccably maintained trail is one of the best Forest Service paths in the state, and a great place to drain some vigor out of the kids. The setting is spectacular, particularly in Big Tree Grove where there is a stand of 500-year-old fir trees. These are some of the best examples of what's left of Washington's original old-growth forests. It's pretty tough not to be awed. If the full loop is too far, park at the **Rain Forest Nature Trail** (easy; 1-mile loop) lot on South Shore Road and walk that shorter loop through Big Tree Grove. An alternate hike, the **Willaby Creek Trail,** (easy; 3.4 miles round trip) breaks off the loop trail about a mile from the Rain Forest parking lot. More big trees. *Really* big trees.

Farther up South Shore Road, a series of popular hikes branch out from the Graves Creek Ranger Station and campground (see Camping, below). Day hikers, especially those with children, will appreciate the **Graves Creek Trail** (easy; 1-mile loop), a nature walk that begins and ends near the ranger station.

A half-mile up the road is the **East Fork Quinault Trail** (moderate; up to 26 miles round trip), which many backpackers say is as good as it gets in the Olympics, if not the country. The trail climbs gently through the river valley to a spectacular alpine basin with sheer rock walls, plunging waterfalls, and the picturesque **Enchanted Valley Chalet,** a 1930s hotel now used as a backcountry shelter for 30 or so hikers. It's often full, so bring a tent and camp in the beautiful surrounding meadows. This is one of the Olympic's most popular backcountry sites. It's usually snow-free by early summer and often remains so until late in the fall. Day hikers can go just 2.5 miles up the same trail to a truly excellent photo spot: **Pony Bridge,** which spans a deep canyon.

Backpackers should consider the worthwhile day trip from their Enchanted Valley campsite up to **Anderson Pass** (difficult; 10 miles round trip). Long-distance trekkers looking to put a full, 30-mile, one-way east-west Olympics crossing under their belts can exit down the east slope Olympics via the **West Fork Dosewallips River Trail.** Another (longer) Olympic-crossing option is a steep climb from the Enchanted Valley area up to spectacular **O'Neil Pass** and an eastern exit via the **Duckabush River Trail.**

To get away from the crowds, consider alternate destinations that branch off the same trail system. (Some of these trails lead south into the 12,000-acre Colonel Bob Wilderness.) One mile up the East Fork Quinault Trail, the **Graves Creek Trail** breaks south, leading about 8 miles to nice high country at **Wynoochee Pass, Sundown Lake,** and **Sundown Pass** near Olympic National Park's southern boundary. (Ask rangers about the fording of Success Creek, about 4 miles up the trail.) From Sundown Pass, a high, rough trail leads 2 miles east to **Six Ridge Pass** (4,650 feet; excellent views), and another 8.5 miles east to a junction with the **North Fork Skokomish River Trail.** This is a rough alpine traverse. But more than likely, solitude will be easy to come by.

Gung-ho day hikers with more stamina than common sense might consider the **Colonel Bob Mountain Trail** (difficult; 14.6 miles round trip), which departs off South Shore Road, about 6 miles from US 101. It climbs quite steeply to an old shelter at 4 miles, then even more steeply to a true Kodak-moment mountaintop view. Good campsites are available along the route for backpackers, too.

North Shore Lake Quinault Road

For a quick, easy taste of the local rain forest environment, the **Maple Glade Rain Forest Interpretive Trail** (easy, .5-mile loop) is always a good bet. The trail, which begins 8.2 miles east of US 101 at Olympic National Park's visitors center, has a smooth, easy grade. Kids will like the big trees and beaver pond. Elk sometimes frequent these flatlands.

Great backpack trips are launched from the trailhead near North Fork Quinault Campground and Ranger Station (see Camping, below.) The **North Fork Quinault Trail** (moderate; 31 miles round trip), the southern half of the popular Elwha-Quinault north-south Olympics crossing (see the Port Angeles and Hurricane Ridge chapter), follows the river 17 miles to Low Divide, 3,650 feet. Good campsites are found along the way. Many experienced backpackers use this route as the center leg of the 44-mile Skyline Loop, completed by following the **Skyline Ridge Trail** west from Low Divide and back south on the Three Lakes Trail to the North Fork Quinault Trailhead area. The Skyline route, which winds through some of the most picturesque—and rough—high country in Olympic National Park, is passable only in late summer (mid-August to September). It's for veterans only.

The southern leg of that loop, the **Irely Lake** and **Three Lakes Trail** (moderate; 2.2 to 14 miles round trip) makes a good day hike or quick backpack trip for those walking it north from the North Fork Quinault area. The trail, just west of North Fork Campground, gradually climbs 1.1 miles to Irely Lake, a good bird-watching venue (osprey have been spotted here), passing through some magnificent old growth. About a mile east of Three Lakes, you'll find the world's largest Alaska (yellow) cedar: a whopping 12 feet in diameter at the base. Have no shame: hug this baby. At 6.5 miles, the trail opens to some luscious, blueberry-filled meadows near three small lakes. Three Lakes Shelter, roughly marking the Queets-Quinault divide, is a half-mile beyond.

Camping

In the south shore Quinault area, two fine Olympic National Forest sites are popular stopovers.

Willaby is a well-kept Lake Quinault waterfront park with 16 sites (no hookups; maximum RV length, 16 feet), a boat launch, and access to the Quinault Loop Trail. A half mile to the east, **Falls View** is another nice waterfront park, with 31 sites (no hookups; maximum RV length, 16 feet) and a boat launch. Willaby and Falls View are open summer months only. Sites ($7.50 to $12) cannot be reserved. *Both parks are between 2 and 2.6 miles east of US 101, near Lake Quinault Lodge and the Quinault Ranger Station, on South Shore Road; (360) 288-2525.*

Campers who continue east to the end of South Shore Road will encounter **Graves Creek,** an Olympic National Park campground near the trailhead for the East Fork Quinault and Graves Creek Trails. The campground has 30 sites (no hookups; maximum RV length, 21 feet). They're free and open all year. *At the end of South Shore Road, 15 miles east of US 101; (360) 452-0330.*

Just to the north is **North Fork,** a quiet but nondescript Olympic National Park campground with seven tent sites set near the North Fork Quinault Trailhead. It's free but primitive, with no running water. North Fork is open all year. Sites cannot be reserved. *At the end of North Shore Road; (360) 288-2424.*

Near midlake on the north shore of Lake Quinault is one of our favorites, **July Creek,** a walk-in Olympic National Park site with 29 tent spots. It's a great campground, with sites set in between some truly massive Douglas firs near the lake and creek mouth. It tends to be much quieter here than at campgrounds on the busier south side of the lake. July Creek is open all year. Sites ($10) cannot be reserved. Fees usually aren't collected in winter months, but the water is shut off: bring your own or filter stream water. *On North Shore Road 2 miles east of US 101; (360) 288-2424.*

An hour to the south, a more remote experience awaits at **Campbell Tree Grove,** an Olympic National Forest campground on the upper Humptulips River, near the southern border of the Colonel Bob

Wilderness. It's a free campground with eight tent sites and three small RV sites. Campbell Tree Grove is open from mid-May to December. Sites cannot be reserved. *Drive 16 miles south of Lake Quinault on US 101 to Humptulips, then follow Forest Service Roads 22 and 2204 about 25 miles northeast; (360) 288-2525.*

Canoeing/Kayaking/Boating

The clear, quiet waters of Lake Quinault are ideal for daylong paddle excursions. Both canoeing and kayaking are popular activities for campers at Willaby and Falls View campgrounds on South Shore Road. Both sites have good launch areas and day-use parking. Canoes and rowboats can be rented during summer months from Lake Quinault Lodge; (360) 288-2571 or (800) 562-6672 (from Washington only). Other rentals and launch facilities are available a mile up the road at Rain Forest Resort; (360) 288-2535.

Fishing

Lake Quinault offers good fishing for (occasionally quite large) Dolly Varden, as well as kokanee and cutthroat trout. The Quinault tribe regulates the fishery. Licenses are $15. Ask at the ranger station or tribal office about restrictions, seasons, and limits.

The **Quinault River** has a strong winter steelhead run that produces some massive (25- to 30-pound) hatchery fish, as well as a respectable fall hatchery coho salmon run. Most fishable waters are below Lake Quinault, on the reservation. Anglers must be accompanied by a tribal guide to fish there. Call the Quinault Indian Nation, (360) 276-8211, for referrals. The season peaks in December and January, and anglers need a state license and steelhead punch card. Wild steelhead are harder to come by, but can be caught on the upper river (below the park boundary) in the spring. The upper-valley river inside the park can be very good trout-fishing water, no license required.

Wildlife

Lake Quinault is a birder's bonanza. On recent visits we've seen dozens of aquatic birds (**mallards, loons,** and other **waterfowl**) along the shoreline portion of the Quinault Loop Trail near Lake Quinault Lodge.

The broad floodplains along the river beyond the head of the lake are a primary winter habitat for one of Olympic's predominant **Roosevelt elk** herds. Watch for them in the bushes along North Shore Road, between the park's Quinault Ranger Station and the bridge connecting North and South Shore Roads.

Restaurants

For recommended restaurants, see the Adjoining Areas to this chapter.

Lodgings

Lake Quinault Lodge ☆   This grand old lodge was built in 1926 around sweeping lawns that descend to the lake. There are pleasant rooms in the main building, but our favorites are the lakeside rooms a short walk from the lodge. Amenities consist of a dining room, a lively bar, a sauna, an indoor heated pool, a Jacuzzi, a game room, canoes and rowboats, and well-maintained trails for hiking or running. Reserve *well* in advance. The dining room's food is uninspired. *On South Shore Rd; follow signs from Hwy 101; (360) 288-2571 or (800) 562-6672 (from Washington only); 345 S Shore Rd, Quinault; $$–$$$.*

More Information

Queets Ranger Station (summer only), Olympic National Park: *(360) 962-2283.*
Quinault Ranger Station, Olympic National Forest: *(360) 288-2525.*
Quinault Ranger Station, Olympic National Park: *(360) 288-2444.*
Quinault Indian Nation: *(360) 276-8211.*

Grays Harbor: Westport and Ocean Shores

From Moclips south to Willapa Bay and east to Aberdeen, including Westport and Ocean Shores beaches, the Grays Harbor National Wildlife Refuge, and Twin Harbors, Grayland Beach, Westhaven, Pacific Beach, and Ocean City State Parks.

If geographic areas could seek therapy, Grays Harbor would be splayed out on the couch right now.

Washington's only coastal deepwater port grew up on the bounties that put the Olympic Peninsula on the map: timber and salmon. Timber built and nurtured the inner-bay towns of Hoquiam and Aberdeen, which gladly embraced—and just as gladly shipped off—entire forests of peninsula logs. More than 30 timber mills were humming along here in 1910. On the outer harbor, the pounding surf at Westport was muted by a seawall 50 years ago, and a thriving fishing village reached west for its own squirming handful of the coast's plentiful salmon runs. Across the bay, Ocean Shores sprang up as a resort community, feeding off the fishing-fueled tourist economy.

This worked out pretty well for Grays Harbor until the logs were gone and most of the salmon had died—two unexpected, but hardly unrelated, occurrences. Since then, the region has grappled with various new identities. Hoquiam and Aberdeen—strategically located, historically significant, and just Northwest-funky enough to attract the curious—still seek one. (Being known as the birthplace of rocker Kurt Cobain wasn't too popular when he was alive. It's not even discussed now that he's dead.) Westport and Ocean Shores, meanwhile, are farther along the road to where they're going. And it's increasingly obvious that outdoor recreation is going to help get them there.

Shortly after the Northwest's salmon stocks entered a death spiral a decade ago, Westport charter boat operators scraped the fish scales off seats, installed wave-proof latte holders, and discovered that many a Seattleite would pay to go out and chase migratory whales. Desperate motel owners, realizing that "It's the beach, stupid," started marketing rooms to beachcombers, bird-watchers, kite flyers, and other nature lovers who probably like Westport *better* without all the fishing commotion. Across the harbor, Ocean Shores, a pre-fab town launched with grand aspirations of megaconvention business in the 1960s, lowered its sights and realized that it, too, could make a pretty good living off little more than the sand upon which it sits.

In the 1980s and '90s, a new generation of outdoor lovers has been turned on to Grays Harbor, the closest and most accessible ocean beach area to Seattle. The former "Fishing Capital of the United States" still fishes—for fewer salmon and a lot more bottom fish—but its outdoorsy offerings have diversified. Westport has emerged as a Northwest surfing mecca, for instance. Ocean Shores and the North Beach area have become the Seattle area's backyard beachcombing getaway. On both sides of the harbor, tourists are increasingly drawn to ocean beaches for camping, kite flying, clam digging, and sand sculpting. Even the inner harbor is taking on a Gore-Tex feel: sea kayaking is gaining in popularity, and local rivers are becoming favored fishing destinations.

It took us more than 100 years to see through the industrial commotion, but the notion of Grays Harbor as a recreator's haven is catching on. Business leaders from Aberdeen to Ocean Shores should rise from the couch and repeat their daily affirmations: "Grays Harbor is good. Our air is clean. We're folksy, friendly, and fun. We have a beach, it's only 2.5 hours from the Space Needle—and doggone it, people *like* us."

Getting There

The Grays Harbor area and its two popular oceanside destinations, Westport and Ocean Shores, are about 2.5 hours southwest of Seattle via Interstate 5 and US 12. Drive I-5 south to Olympia, turning west on US 101. Six miles west of Olympia, the highway splits, with US 101 departing north to Shelton and the Hood Canal. Stay to the left, following Hwy 8 (which becomes US 12) 42 miles west to Aberdeen. There, follow signs 18 miles south via Hwy 105 to Westport and the South Beach area, or 16 miles north via Hwys 109 and 115 to Ocean Shores and the North Beach area. Watch your signs in Aberdeen, former home of some highly confused traffic engineers.

Adjoining Areas

NORTH: **Lake Quinault and the Quinault River Valley**

SOUTH: **Long Beach Peninsula and Willapa Bay**

EAST: **Hood Canal; Olympic National Forest and the East Slope Olympics**

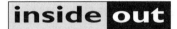

Beaches

Grays Harbor's productive tourist trade is tied to the beach. Make that *chained* to the beach. In fact, Ocean Shores wouldn't be worth supplying electricity to if it weren't for the beach. Luckily for them, some nice ones are in evidence here.

One major caveat: The state of Washington, allegedly at the urging of local citizens, allows auto traffic—that's right, auto traffic—on most public beaches in this area for much of the year. (You know you're south of Olympic National Park when you have to stop, look, and listen before stepping into the surf.) Some beach strips are autobahns all year, others "only" from September to early April. This absurd anachronism turns some otherwise lovely, natural beaches into raceways for young 4X4 punks, who rarely heed the 25-mph speed limit. If you don't like car exhaust mixed with your sea smells, write a state legislator and complain. Or do what huge numbers of state residents have been doing for decades: vote with your feet, taking your tourist dollars with you north to Olympic National Park or south to the Oregon Coast, where beaches don't have passing lanes.

North Beach (Ocean Shores to Moclips)

Twenty-two miles of beach lie between Moclips and Ocean Shores, and most of it is publicly accessible (including automobiles). The strip, known only to state-government types as the **North Beach Seashore Conservation Area,** is open for exploration, but most beach uplands are private property. Access roads to this breezy, flat beach are numerous and well marked along Hwy 109, although few public facilities have been built here. The far northern stretch near Moclips is the most scenic in this region, making it the best local beachcombing area.

Exceptions are **Pacific Beach** and **Ocean City State Parks** (see

Camping, below), both of which have good beach access, and **Griffiths-Priday State Park,** at the mouth of the Copalis River. The latter offers picnic facilities and rest rooms. From March to August, you won't be nesting in the uplands portions of the park, because the endangered snowy plover will. But the beach area is open all year. It's a fine spot for beachcombing, kite flying, surf fishing, and dumping sand on your sister's head. The river waters inside the spit are a good canoe/kayak spot, particularly for shorebird-watchers.

South Beach (Westport to Willapa Bay)

The 19-mile beach strip south of Westport comprises the **South Beach Seashore Conservation Area,** which has good public access sites along Hwy 105. The most popular beach entrances are **Westhaven State Park** and **Grayland Beach** and **Twin Harbors State Parks** (see Camping, below).

Single-day visitors should make it a point to visit **Westhaven State Park,** just a short drive or bicycle ride from downtown Westport. The day-use park is in a spectacular setting—at the southern entrance to Grays Harbor, marked by an observation platform, a foghorn tower, and the wave-splashed South Jetty. Also strings of VW buses. High winds and waves bottled in by the jetty have made this a favorite hangout of Washington surfers (see Surfing, below). But Westhaven has been in a state of flux recently. Tidal action literally is carving much of the above-beach area away, wiping out a former parking lot and other day-use facilities. State parks planners are likely to wait and see if the whole place goes bye-bye, before they pour much money into improvements.

Still, this is by far the most convenient beach access in the Westport area, and the viewing platform is a great place to taste the wind, peer into the Pacific, and watch for whales, sailing ships, or a returning charter boat. On a clear day, look behind you and scan the horizon for the rising white hulk of Mount Olympus. Early explorer John Meares, who named the 7,965-foot mountain, probably had a similar view when he first admired the peak in 1788.

Camping

Two public campgrounds await on the north side of Grays Harbor; two more on the south. None of them are much to brag about, but their locations—all within a short walk of the ocean—keep them in high demand throughout summer months. From north to south:

Pacific Beach State Park—a small (9-acre) in-town campground on Hwy 109—has 138 sites, (20 with hookups; maximum RV length, 45 feet), good beach access—and little else. Sites are crammed together, parking-lot style, with no trees or other good windbreaks. But it's a popular RV spot, particularly during razor clam seasons (see Clamming, below). Pacific Beach is open all year. Sites cannot be reserved. *On Hwy 109, 29 miles west of Hoquiam; (360) 289-3553 or (800) 233-0321.*

Ocean City State Park, just north of Ocean Shores, is much nicer, with 178 sites (29 with full hookups), spread over 131 acres of pine trees and thick shrubbery. It gets windy here, but sites are very private. This is probably the best spot in the region for tenters. Unlike other parks in the area, Ocean City has more than just the ocean competing for attention. You'll find good picnic facilities here, as well as a group camp, and a swampy area popular with bird-watchers. And, of course, the Pacific is but a short walk away. This is a summer hot spot. But you now can get a reservation here. Ocean City is open all year. Sites can be reserved up to 11 months in advance by calling (800) 452-5687. *Just north of Ocean Shores 3 miles south of the Hwy 109/115 junction; (360) 289-3553 or (800) 233-0321.*

Twin Harbors State Park is a longtime favorite of beach fans. It's a big park, with 321 sites (49 with full hookups; maximum RV length, 35 feet). The campground is split in two by Hwy 105, with half the sites on wooded lands east of the road, the other half on the windier, more exposed sand dunes on the west side. (The hookup sites, like many others installed for the benefit of visiting anglers, are crammed together, chockablock, on the east side.) The park has two trails to the ocean, as well as a nature trail that winds through the sand dune area between the campground and the beach. This is an older park, and many of its facilities are showing their age. But it's often booked during summer months. Reservations are a good idea. Twin Harbors is open all year. Sites can be reserved up to 11 months in advance by calling (800) 452-5687. *On Hwy 105, 3 miles south of Westport; (360) 268-9717 or (800) 233-0321.*

Of all the parks in this area, **Grayland Beach State Park** is probably in greatest demand. It's a newer state park, with nicer rest rooms and campsite facilities than nearby Twin Harbors. Its 63 sites (60 with full hookups; maximum RV length, 40 feet) are well situated on loops through the shrubby tidal uplands, and the large number of hookup sites makes it a favorite destination for RV owners. Campsites here also are much quieter than at Twin Harbors, which is closer to the highway. Trails lead about a half mile through sand dunes to a very pleasant—and relatively lightly used—ocean beach. A separate trail leads about a mile to and around a small, marshy lake. Wildlife alert: Grayland Beach also is a popular camp spot for otters. We ve seen them bouncing down a trail here, commuting between the lake and the ocean. Grayland Beach is open all year. Sites can be reserved up to 11 months in advance by calling (800)

452-5687. *Just south of Grayland on Hwy 105; (360) 268-9717 or (800) 233-0321.*

Fishing

Twenty years ago, fishing would have been the first Inside Out listing in this chapter. Not anymore. The gradual death spiral of Northwest wild coho and chinook stocks has reduced one of the nation's salmon capitals to a coastal community in the midst of an identity crisis (see above). But charters still run from Westport during a sharply abbreviated summer season.

That season usually isn't set until mid-April, when coastal fisheries managers dole out meager shares of dwindling salmon. In recent years, Westport's summer season has been truncated, with fishing Sundays through Thursdays only. Call to check on dates.

But if you're not picky about your prey, a **charter fishing** trip from Westport is possible just about any time of the year. Many salmon-boat skippers have switched to bottom-fishing trips for lingcod, perch, sea bass, and other species from March to October. And several companies run deep-sea tuna fishing charters from Westport's harbor during summer months. Other skippers now spend most spring months conducting whale- and shorebird-watching trips (see Wildlife, below).

Most charter companies and their rates are comparable. They include Cachalot, (360) 268-0323; Deep Sea, (800) 562-0151 or (360) 268-9300; Westport Charters, (800) 562-0157 or (360) 268-9120; Islander, (800) 322-1740 or (360) 268-9166; Washington Charters, (800) 562-0173 or (360) 268-0900; Salmon Charters, (800) 562-0157; and Travis, (360) 268-9140. (Toll-free numbers often are in operation only during the season.) A tip: Managers at Westport Charters are particularly active in the regional fish-allotment process, and usually have first word on when fishing will begin and how long it will last.

Shore fishing also can be productive in this area. **Surf fishing** for perch and other species is possible virtually anywhere on the public beach. Use a long rod, a big spinning reel, flat surf-type sinkers, and hooks baited with natural bait, such as clam necks. No license is required.

Bottom fish and even salmon are frequently caught on either side of the South Jetty, accessible through **Westhaven State Park** (see Beaches, above.) Similar fishing awaits at **North Jetty,** at Point Brown south of Ocean Shores.

An increasingly popular salmon-fishing option is a special fishery inside the **Westport Boat Basin,** where hatchery salmon can be caught from docks during September and October. A derby adds to the excitement.

Steelheaders and those who prefer drift fishing for their salmon can make the short trip inland to the **Humptulips River,** a noted fall fishing venue for chinook, coho, and chum.

Clamming

The shorelines on either side of Grays Harbor open periodically for razor clams—those sweet, meaty, highly sought coastal bivalves. State biologists usually open one or both beaches for several weeks of digging (usually on odd-numbered days only) twice a year. The fall season typically is in October; spring digging is in March, April, and/or May.

Clammers need a state license ($7). Rental shovels and clam guns (plastic or metal suction tubes for digging) usually can be rented from local shops. Popular digging spots—when they're open—include **Copalis, Moclips, Ocean City, downtown Ocean Shores,** and **Twin Harbors State Park.**

Important note: Clam seasons are largely dictated by the presence of naturally occurring marine toxins that have killed razor clams or rendered them unsuitable for consumption in the past decade. At this writing, those toxin levels are in a period of decline, and clamming seasons are occurring more regularly. But seasons and limits change frequently. To learn where and when to dig, call the state Fish and Wildlife office in Montesano; (360) 249-4628. Or contact the Westport-Grayland Chamber of Commerce at the number in More Information, below.

Wildlife

The Grays Harbor area is gaining increasing fame as a shorebird- and whale-watching destination, particularly during the spring whale-migrating season (March through May). **Whale watching** here was born largely of necessity. With dozens of fishing charter operators facing extinction because of shortened or canceled salmon seasons, whale-watching tours began sprouting like blackberry bushes around Westport. Thousands of whales migrate off Washington's coast each year, headed south to Baja in October and November, then north to the Bering Sea from March to May. Spring viewing is most productive, as whales seem to hug the coast more then, and ocean conditions are better for boat tours.

Spring whale-watching seminars are conducted by experts on March and April weekends at the Westport Maritime Museum (2201 Westhaven Drive; (360) 268-0078). Whales sometimes can be spotted from the harbor's North and South Jetties (use binoculars or a spotting scope, and look a mile or more offshore). But a whale-watching charter is your best bet. They re offered by most charter companies. (See the list under Fishing, above, or contact the Westport-Grayland Chamber of Commerce.)

The greater Grays Harbor area also is a bonanza to bird-watchers. The region has developed into a major destination for **migratory birds** in the Pacific Flyway. A half million Arctic-bound shorebirds migrate from as far south as Argentina and congregate on the beaches of the extensive North and South Beach Conservation Areas and the Grays Harbor National Wildlife Refuge at Bowerman Basin from mid-April through the first week of May. At high tide in Bowerman Basin, the birds rise in unison in thick flocks that shimmer through the air, twisting and turning, before settling back onto their feeding grounds. Trails lead through the marsh (located just beyond the Hoquiam airport). Be sure to wear boots. For more information and peak migratory days, call the Grays Harbor National Wildlife Refuge, (360) 753-9467.

Surfing

Huntington Beach, this isn't, but the coastal surfing culture has woven itself into the fabric of Westport. Watching the neoprene-clad surfers bob around has become a leading spectator sport during Westport summers. (We knew it was serious when the town's second surf shop opened a few years ago.) Surfing grabbed its first toehold more than a decade ago at **Westhaven State Park,** where the South Jetty traps incoming southwesterly waves, creating a decent surf break. Tidal conditions have made that area less desirable in recent years, and many surfers have migrated to the unnamed beach just beyond the tall riprap jetty wall in downtown Westport.

Surfing is best on incoming tides. The break is tame in the summer, but can get pretty raucous during winter months. Whenever you go, wet suits are required equipment; the water never gets above 60°F here. For rental gear, advice, wax, and enlightened philosophy, see California transplant Al Perlee at the Surf Shop in Westport, (360) 268-0992. Lessons are available if you call ahead.

Walking

Beach walking rules here, but at least one new path veers a ways off the sand. A new **Westport Nature Trail** (easy; 2 miles round trip) begins at Westhaven State Park and winds south to Ocean Avenue, near the historic Westport Lighthouse. The concrete path runs atop the beach bluff. It's about a mile one way, and is open to in-line skaters and cyclists.

Cycling

Both the Westport and Ocean Shores areas are good road cycling venues, mainly because roads are flat, traffic is slow, and many miles of backroads wind through the sand dunes near the ocean. The **Ocean Shores** vicinity has become particularly good for cycling, with more than 100 miles of sparsely traveled roads, many optimistically constructed to accommodate tourism and convention business that still hasn't arrived here. Several good bike routes are marked, fanning out from Duck Lake, Chinook Park, or North Bay Park. The best are on the town's leeward side. All sorts of cycles—including four-wheel rigs big enough for the whole family—can be rented in downtown Ocean Shores. Maps and advice are available from Olympic Outdoors; (360) 289-3736.

Kayaking/Canoeing

Hot-dog whitewater kayakers often are found out among the surfers at **Westhaven State Park.** Quieter paddlers take to the more protected waters inside **Grays Harbor.** The harbor offers a full range of fascinating quiet-water destinations, most in wildlife-rich and historically significant waterways. Rentals and guided tours ranging from 2-hour bird-watching trips to two-day bed-and-breakfast extravaganzas are available from Resonance Canoe and Kayak in Aberdeen; (360) 532-9176. **Ocean Shores** is ringed by a 23-mile chain of canals and freshwater lakes that are popular among canoeists. Rental canoes are available in town.

Kite Flying

Go fly one. You won't be alone. Kite flying has emerged as a very popular coastal sport in the past decade, and Grays Harbor beach communities are natural magnets, thanks to persistent winds. **Ocean Shores,** in particular, is dotted with several well-stocked kite shops, and hosts a kite festival in early May.

Adventure Calendar

Sea Perch Surf Fishing Derby: *Last weekend in July.*
Up Your Wind Kite Festival (Pacific Beach): *First week in September.*
Sand Sculpture Contest (Pacific Beach): *Third week in September.*
Beach Party Kite Festival (Westport): *First weekend in July.*
Westport Longboard Classic Surf Contest: *Early August.*
Ocean Shores Kite Festival: *Early May.*

outside in

Attractions

In the inner harbor area, the **Grays Harbor Historical Seaport** (east side of Aberdeen, (360) 532-8611) provides tours of a splendid replica of Captain Gray's *Lady Washington,* a 105-foot floating museum. The ship is often on tour to other ports of call, so be sure to call ahead.

In Hoquiam, tours are offered of **Hoquiam's Castle,** a 20-room mansion built for a prominent lumberman in 1897 (515 Chenault Avenue, Hoquiam; (360) 533-2005). Right next door is the equally splendid house his brother built—now the **Lytle House Bed and Breakfast** (see Lodgings, below). **Polson Park** is a fine house by Arthur Loveless, with a rose garden (1611 Riverside Avenue, Hoquiam; (360) 533-5862).

In Westport, the **Westport Maritime Museum** (2201 Westhaven Drive; (360) 268-0078), in the old Coast Guard Station, is free and worth a visit. It's open weekends April and May, daily June through September. Down the road a few miles (or down the mile-long trail from Westhaven State Park) is the 107-foot **Westport Lighthouse** (on West Ocean Avenue, off Hwy 105; (800) 233-0321). The tallest on the West Coast, it's been operating since 1895.

Restaurants

Alec's by the Sea ☆　Alec's by the Sea does a lot of things well, including grilled razor clams and steaks. A large menu, generous portions, an efficient waitstaff, and crayons for the kids add up to a high-quality, friendly family restaurant. *Point Brown Rd, left onto Chance Ala Mer Blvd NE; (360) 289-4026; 131 E Chance Ala Mer Blvd NE, Ocean Shores; $$.*

Billy's Bar and Grill ☆　Named after the infamous Billy Gohl, who terrorized the Aberdeen waterfront in 1907. Billy shanghaied sailors and robbed loggers, consigning their bodies to the murky Wishkah River through a trapdoor in a saloon only a block away from the present-day Billy's—where you get a square-deal meal and an honest drink, without much damage to your pocketbook. *Corner of Heron and G; (360) 533-7144; 322 E Heron St, Aberdeen; $.*

Bridges ☆　Sonny Bridges started out with a corner cafe 30 years ago and kept expanding his horizons—both in space and in taste. The diverse menu contains few surprises, but Sonny owns a piece of the best seafood market in town, and the clams and salmon can't be beat. *1st and G; (360) 532-6563; 112 N G St, Aberdeen; $$.*

Constantin's ☆☆   Constantin "Dino" Kontogonis is a gregarious Greek with a gift for cooking, and his place is only a stone's throw from the Westport docks, so there's fresh seafood galore. A new menu is twice as long and a lot more adventurous than its predecessor, and the wine list is ambitious. *½ block from the dock; (360) 268-0550; 320 E Dock St, Westport; $$.*

The Dunes ☆   Turn off Hwy 105 at the sign of the giant razor clam and follow the bumpy gravel road a quarter of a mile down to the dunes. You will discover a funky beachcomber's hideaway, decorated with shells, ship models, and stained glass. Most of the time you won't find fresher seafood. *Off Hwy 105; (360) 267-1441; 783 Dunes Rd, Grayland; $$.*

Galway Bay Restaurant & Pub   Guinness on tap (which everyone knows is good for you) and authentic Irish fare. Need we say more? This is surely the best way to warm up after a day of beachcombing. *In town on Ocean Shores Blvd, ½ block from Shilo; (360) 289-2300; 676 Ocean Shores Blvd NW #6, Ocean Shores; $$.*

The Levee Street ☆   Though Roy Ann Taylor spent 12 years as a cook at a logging camp, her restaurant has nothing in common with a cookhouse save generous portions of good, real food. Wonderful ambience: plum-colored carpets, soft music, and a great view of tugboats and seabirds. One of the few nonsmoking restaurants in timber country. *7th and Levee; (360) 532-1959; 709 Levee St, Hoquiam; $$.*

Parma ☆☆☆   Mario Andretti once said, "The closest thing to heaven is eating my mother's gnocchi." In Aberdeen, the closest thing to heaven is when Pierre Gabelli's mother brings you a plate of his. The dimpled potato dumplings melt in your mouth, and the French-Italian chef is always experimenting. *On Heron, 1 block west of Broadway; (360) 532-3166; 116 W Heron St, Aberdeen; $$.*

Savory Faire ☆☆   Marvelous aromas come wafting out of Candi and Randy Bactell's charming breakfast/lunch place just a block away from the handsome and historic Grays Harbor County Courthouse. The coffee is as good as you'll find anywhere in Seattle. *Take Montesano exit off Hwy 12; (360) 249-3701; 135 S Main St, Montesano; $.*

Lodgings

Rental homes   If, like many Ocean Shores weekenders, you came here to get away from it all, a good way to avoid downtown altogether is to reserve one of the private beach houses that owners occasionally rent out. Reservations need to be made weeks in advance. *(360) 289-2430 or (800) 562-8612 (in Washington only); the same numbers can also take motel reservations.*

The Best Western Lighthouse Suites Inn ☆☆   This handsome, hospitable new hotel is the best on the beach—at least until the reviews are in on the big new Shilo. Each tastefully decorated, spacious room features all the amenities. Most of the rooms have a full ocean view. *At the north city limits; (360) 289-2311 or (800) 757-SURF; 491 Damon Rd NW, Ocean Shores; $$$.*

The Chateau Westport ☆   This is considered the fanciest motel lodging in Westport, but prices for the 108 units are moderate, especially in the off-season (when beachcombing is best). It's not the quietest place, and the continental breakfast isn't exciting, but the ocean views are magnificent. *W Hancock and S Forest Sts; (360) 268-9101; 710 W Hancock, Westport; $$.*

Cooney Mansion ☆☆   For many years this 1908 Cosmopolis manse housed timber tycoon Neil Cooney, his servants, and his out-of-town guests. A clubby feel prevails: from the deck on the second floor you can sit and watch golfers on the newly expanded public course next door. *Follow C St to 5th; (360) 533-0602; 1705 5th St, Cosmopolis; $$.*

Glenacres Inn   A turn-of-the-century gem, this place has lots of lodging alternatives and a hot tub. (Note that the inn closed for the 1996–1997 winter season on a trial basis and may move to a summer-only operation.) *1 block north of the stoplight on N Montesano; (360) 268-9391; 222 N Montesano, Westport; $$.*

The Grey Gull ☆   This condominium-resort looks like a ski lodge (a rather odd style here on the beach), with jagged angles, handsome cladding, and a front door to strain the mightiest triceps. There are 36 condominium units, each outfitted with a balcony, fireplace, kitchen, TV, VCR, and attractive furnishings, *and* you are right on the beach. *In town on Ocean Shores Blvd; (360) 289-3381; 651 Ocean Shores Blvd SW, Ocean Shores; $$$.*

Lytle House Bed & Breakfast ☆   In 1897, when timber baron Robert Lytle built what was to become Hoquiam's architectural landmark, Hoquiam's Castle, his brother Joseph erected a smaller version next door. This has become Lytle House, decorated throughout with the almost requisite Victorian embellishments. *West on Emerson, right on Garfield, up hill to Chenault; (360) 533-2320 or (800)677-2320; 509 Chenault Ave, Hoquiam; $$.*

Ocean Crest Resort ☆   The Ocean Crest has always offered rooms with memorable views, and the panorama from the dining room here is magnificent, but the furnishings are old and the food (with the exception of the excellent breakfasts) has suffered from inconsistency of late. Upstairs is a cozy bar. *18 miles north of Ocean Shores on Hwy 109; (360) 276-4465; 4651 Hwy 109, Moclips; $$$.*

Sandpiper ☆☆   Here's the place to vacation with four other couples, or to bring the kids, the grandparents, and the family dog: miles of beach and a fleet of kites and volleyball players. Two four-story complexes contain large, fully equipped and spotless suites. Reservations well in advance. *On Hwy 109, 1.5 miles south of Pacific Beach; (360) 276-4580; 4159 Hwy 109, Pacific Beach; $$.*

Shilo   Our jury's still out on Shilo Inns' $10 million, 113-suite "convention resort," recently opened on the site of the landmark Ocean Shores Inn and destined to be the mother of all Ocean Shores lodgings (if we're to believe the PR hoo-ha). Each of its suites features a beachfront balcony and other niceties. There's also an indoor pool, sauna, steam room, and fitness center. *In town on Ocean Shores Blvd; (360) 289-4600 or (800) 222-2244; 707 Ocean Shores Blvd NW, Ocean Shores; $$$.*

More Information

Grays Harbor Chamber of Commerce and Visitors Center: *(800) 321-1924.*

Ocean Shores Chamber of Commerce: *(800) 76-BEACH.*

Washington Coast Chamber of Commerce (Copalis area): *(360) 289-4552 or (800) 286-4552.*

Westport-Grayland Chamber of Commerce: *(360) 268-9422 or (800) 345-6223.*

Long Beach Peninsula
and Willapa Bay

From North Cove south to Cape Disappointment and east to Chinook and Raymond; including Willapa National Wildlife Refuge and Fort Canby State Park.

We have to be careful here. A couple of years ago, we got in big trouble by referring to Long Beach, in a newspaper article, as "the cheesy souvenir capital of the Northwest." This was not at all popular with the locals, who called and wrote to extol the virtues of the Long Beach area's clean ocean beaches, friendly campgrounds, scenic lighthouses, kite-pleasing breezes, and other natural virtues. After long consideration and several more visits, we've come to a new conclusion: both of us are correct.

Long Beach, which smells like taffy throughout, is the closest thing on Washington's coast to the well-developed, Super-8-and-GO-KART!–style summer havens on the Oregon Coast. It *is* the cheesy souvenir capital of the Northwest. But it's also a quite delicious outdoor playground for those who venture off the beaten path—or boardwalk, as the case may be.

The Long Beach Peninsula, which begins at Leadbetter Point near the mouth of Willapa Bay and runs 27 straight, sandy miles south to the mouth of the Columbia River at Fort Canby, conceals a rich mix of outdoor wonders. On the inside of the long sand finger, portions of Willapa Bay are protected wildlife habitat, attracting thousands of migratory shorebirds in the spring and fall—and increasingly large hordes of chinook-salmon anglers in the summer.

The inner bay's Willapa National Wildlife Refuge—particularly Long Island, which is reached only by small watercraft—is a treasure.

On the outside is a wondrous stretch of flat, open beach—longer than any of its kind in the nation, according to the souvenir vendors. The beach leads south to one of Washington's truly memorable beach getaways, Fort Canby State Park, near the admirably untouristed town of Ilwaco. Lewis and Clark first set foot in the Pacific here, and if you walk the beach today and squint just enough to block out the lighthouse on the bluff, you can drink in nearly the same view they had that day in 1805.

Such diversions—all within a short drive of the gift shops, tourist trappings, and uncommonly fine restaurants clustered around Long Beach—provide what for many Northwesterners is the perfect recreational mix: developed and undeveloped. Raw and (slightly over-) cooked. The Long Beach Peninsula has its share of cheese. But it can be served on the side, and the rest of the course is as satisfying as it is healthy.

Getting There

The Long Beach Peninsula and Willapa Bay are approximately 150 miles southwest of Seattle via Interstate 5, Hwy 12, and US 101. Allow 3.5 hours to get there. On the peninsula itself, Hwy 103 (Pacific Hwy) runs north between Seaview and Leadbetter Point, serving as the primary access road to most sites in this section. On the inner side of the peninsula, Sandridge Road, which runs roughly parallel to Pacific Hwy, provides access to Oysterview and the west shores of Willapa Bay.

Adjoining Areas

NORTH: **Grays Harbor: Westport and Ocean Shores**

EAST: **Bridge of the Gods: Stevenson and Beacon Rock**

inside out

Camping

Nobody goes to **Fort Canby State Park** anymore; it's too crowded.

Bad joke, especially if you're stuck without a campsite. This popular park, the only major public campground in the region, is a frequent sellout during summer months. (Its popularity is further heightened during the increasingly brief ocean or "Buoy 10" salmon-fishing seasons, when anglers flock here to launch boats.) Fortunately—or unfortunately, if you're the spontaneous type—Fort Canby's campground now is on the Reservations Northwest system, meaning you can reserve sites by phone as much as 11 months in advance.

It's well worth the effort to get here. The park, sprawled out across 1,882 acres at the southwestern tip of the state, is marked on the north and south by twin-bookend lighthouses, North Head and Cape Disappointment. In between is a massive campground; a sprawling picnic area; a deliciously clean, flat ocean beach; miles of trails and a rock jetty jutting into the roiling surf of the Columbia River bar. Like most coastal campgrounds, you can't see the beach from the campsites (it's a short walk away on many sandy trails). But the proud, beautiful North Head Light is always in view, even when the fog rolls in.

The scenery is only part of the allure here. This wind-blasted land has a rich history. Lewis and Clark ended their long journey here in 1805, plunking their sore feet into the icy Pacific. The place was an important transportation and trade center from that day forward. Its significance is best understood by visiting the park's Lewis and Clark Interpretive Center, which details the explorers' journey to the Pacific, as well as the history of the two local lighthouses. (When it first blinked on in 1856, the Cape Disappointment lighthouse became the first in the state, and one of the first on the coast. North Head Lighthouse was added in 1898.)

Fort Canby, as the name implies, has a long military history. The Army was in residence here for more than a century before surplusing the land to Washington State in the late 1950s. Fort Canby, the final incarnation of the military base, stuck as the park's name. But other evidence of Fort Canby's military past remains, most notably spooky abandoned gun bunkers at McKenzie Head.

Some of us who've been visiting Fort Canby since childhood continue to make new discoveries here. It's one of Washington's recreation treasures. For more details on park hiking, boating, fishing, picnicking, beaches, and other charms, consult individual sections below. Fort Canby State Park's campground has 250 sites (60 with hookups; maximum RV length, 45 feet) that are spread in many small loops through the central part of the park, mostly between dunes. They rate only about a medium on the privacy and modernization scales. But you can't beat the setting. Trails lead to the beach, old gun bunkers, local lakes, and elsewhere. Kids love cycling on the miles of roadway. Reservations are strongly recommended. Fort Canby is open all year. Sites can be reserved up to 11 months in advance by calling (800) 452-5687. *From downtown Ilwaco, follow signs 3.5 miles south to the park, on Robert Gray Drive; (360) 642-3078 or (800) 233-0321.*

Private campgrounds in this area are more numerous than anywhere else in the state. Contact the visitors centers at the end of this chapter for referrals and information.

Hiking/Walking

A slew of good opportunities await here, ranging from long strolls through wildlife-rich marshes to quick jaunts uphill to picturesque lighthouses. On the north end of the Long Beach Peninsula, **Leadbetter Point** (easy; various distances), part of the **Willapa Bay National Wildlife Refuge** and connected to an undeveloped state park, offers about 4 miles of beach-wandering on the sand spit, with the ocean on one side, Willapa Bay on the other. This is a prime bird-viewing venue, particularly when migratory species are landing here in the spring and fall. To get there, follow Hwy 103 from Long Beach north to the end of Stackpole Road. The other, most popular, portion of the Wildlife Refuge, **Long Island** in the middle of Willapa Bay, also has a trail system, with several primitive campgrounds. Access is by small boat only. (See Canoeing/Kayaking, below.)

The central peninsula is known, of course, for its beach-strolling. **Long Beach** (easy; various distances) truly is just that: 28 miles of flat, hard, sand lie between Leadbetter Point and the mouth of the Columbia River. Long Beach is as good a place as any to start and finish, although more than a half-dozen good beach access points are marked along Hwy 103. For a short walk that won't put sand between your toes, try the city's nifty boardwalk.

To the south, **Fort Canby State Park** (easy/moderate; up to 5 miles) is a grand day-hiking destination. The prime draw here is the 43,000 feet of ocean beach. To walk the entire stretch, follow signs to the North Jetty parking area and hike the beach north about 2 miles to the rocky headland capped by the **North Head Light.** (Unmaintained way trails lead from the beach up to the lighthouse, but the light is more safely reached via one of two upland trails.) Other good day-hiking trails lead from the day-use area at Waikiki Beach, just inside the park entrance, up to the **Cape Disappointment Lighthouse** (difficult; 3.6 miles round trip) and the nearby Lewis and Clark Interpretive Center (see Camping, above).

On the far east side of the park, a pleasant nature loop, the **Coastal Forest Trail** (easy; 1.5 miles), begins and ends near the boat launch at Baker Bay, on the Columbia River. Closer to the camping area, a short trail climbs to an old gun bunker at **McKenzie Head.** Nearby, the **North Head Trail** (moderate; 3 miles one way) climbs through the east side of the park to the North Head Light. Note that both lighthouses can be reached more easily via short trails from Robert Gray Drive, the main access road to Fort Canby.

Picnics

The day-use area at **Waikiki Beach,** just inside Fort Canby State Park, is a great picnic site. Tables are spread throughout the upper beach area, which is protected from the otherwise surly weather by the tall ocean headland topped by Cape Disappointment.

The long public beach on either side of the town of **Long Beach** is accessible from many points along Hwy 103. Developed picnic sites can be found at **Pacific Pines** and **Loomis Lakes State Parks.**

Canoeing/Kayaking

The **Willapa National Wildlife Refuge** is a must-check-out scene for canoeists and kayakers. The broad tidal flat of the inner harbor is rich with bird and marine life, and paddling conditions are uncharacteristically calm for a coastal area. The one caveat is the tide: when it's low, many parts of the inner bay become chocolate pudding, without the taste appeal.

The entire bay is accessible by small watercraft, but the most popular destination is **Long Island,** reached only by boat from a parking lot/launch area near the wildlife refuge headquarters along US 101, 10 miles north of Seaview.

Long Island is unique. Scientists say the 5,000-acre refuge is the largest estuarine island on the Pacific Coast. Its most alluring attraction is an undisturbed, 274-acre grove of **ancient cedars**—believed to be the last surviving example of a coastal "terminal" forest. Because the trees have been isolated from fire damage and weren't reached by loggers who worked this island as late as the 1980s, the forest has remained much the same for thousands of years. The cedar grove is reached by a 2.5-mile trail that runs northwest from the beach landing nearest the wildlife refuge parking area. A short paddle to the landing, followed by a walk to the grove and back, makes a memorable day trip.

But the island is big enough for more lengthy explorations. More than 5 miles of trails cut through the woods, connecting four of five primitive campgrounds found here. (Most campgrounds, however, are more easily reached by boat.) Deer, Roosevelt elk, and bear often are seen on the island. It makes a perfect base camp for waterborne exploration of Willapa Bay.

Contact Refuge Headquarters (8 miles northeast of Seaview on US 101; (360) 484-3482) for more information. Kayak rentals are available from Willapa Bay Excursions, 270th and Sandridge Road, Nahcotta; (360) 665-5557.

Photography

The **North Head Lighthouse,** above Fort Canby State Park, adorns the living room wall of many a Northwest amateur photographer. It's scenic whether shot from the beach in the state park below or from the hillside above it, reached by parking at the lighthouse trailhead off Robert Gray Drive. Sunsets on partly cloudy days create nice lighting here.

Fishing/Clamming

The town of Ilwaco was a major **salmon charter** center for decades before the bottom began to fall out of Northwest salmon runs in the 1980s. Charters still head to sea—and to nearby "Buoy 10," off the Columbia's mouth—when fishing is open during the summer. In recent years, that's only been for a few weeks in July and maybe August, depending on fish allotments. Spring bottom-fishing and summer deep-sea tuna trips have picked up some of the slack. Check with local charter operators for information on seasons and limits. Popular charter operators include Sea Breeze Charters, (360) 642-2300; Coho Charters, (360) 642-3333; and Pacific Salmon Charters, (360) 642-3466 or (800) 831-2695.

When the summer salmon season is on, the **North Jetty** at Fort Canby State Park becomes a popular place. Salmon often are hooked off the jetty in late summer by anglers fishing with herring or the occasional Buzz Bomb–style lure. If the salmon season is closed, remember that the jetty also is a good place to fish for **surf perch** and other bottomfish. Spring days seem most productive for perch fishing, and anglers favor incoming tides for all jetty fishing.

While the flow of anglers to Ilwaco's ocean fishery has dwindled, it has increased almost as rapidly just up the road at **Willapa Bay.** A thriving late-summer **chinook** season inside these sheltered waters has become known as one of the "last best" chances to catch a big king salmon in Washington waters. The fish, many upward of 40 pounds, are hatchery stock, returning to their birthplace on the Naselle River. The run usually shows up around mid-August, peaks around September 1, and tails off by month's end.

The public ocean beaches around Long Beach open sporadically for razor clam digging in the spring and fall. Call the state Fish and Wildlife office in Montesano, (360) 249-4628, or the Long Beach Peninsula Chamber of Commerce, (800) 642-2400, for information on seasons.

Wildlife

The 14,000-acre Willapa National Wildlife Refuge, described above, is rich with **shorebirds, migratory birds,** and other creatures. More than 250 bird species have been cataloged here. The best day-use area in the refuge, particularly for those on foot, is Leadbetter Point, on the northern tip of the peninsula. The Wildlife Refuge property here, which adjoins an undeveloped (except for trails) state park, is a stopover site for more than 100 species of migratory birds in the spring and fall. Follow signs to the parking lot at the end of Stackpole Road, 3 miles north of Oysterville. For information, stop at the refuge visitors center, 8 miles northeast of Seaview on US 101, or call (360) 484-3482.

Cycling

The many miles of rural roads between the main drag (Hwy 103) and Willapa Bay are a favorite haunt of cyclists. Most of the roads are narrow, but traffic is light and plenty of turnouts are available. Several scenic cycling tours are marked and easy to follow. Rentals are available at Willapa Bay Excursions; (360) 484-3482.

For a good half-day trip, park in Long Beach and cycle north up Sandridge Road (it runs parallel to Hwy 103, about a half-mile east) all the way to Oysterville, then another 2 miles north to Stackpole Road and **Leadbetter Point State Park,** part of the Willapa National Wildlife Refuge. Follow one of the trails down to the beach for lunch, then ride back. It's a round trip of about 25 miles, taking you along some of the peninsula's most scenic, placid roadways near the shores of Willapa Bay.

Longer trips are possible on the east side of Willapa Bay. One highly popular route is the **Naselle-Seaview Loop,** a 42-mile circuit from Naselle along Willapa Bay to Seaview and back. For an even longer ride, continue south at Seaview, following US 101 up the Columbia to Chinook and Megler before turning north and returning to Naselle on Hwy 401.

A word to the wise for mountain bikers: Enjoy your ride on the beach, because next time you come back to do it, your machine will be a pile of rust.

Horseback Riding

Clomp off (do they clomp on sand?) into the sunset on a rental equine unit from Kotek Skip (Ninth Street S and Beach Boulevard; (360) 642-3676). Those who bring their own can put them up for a fee at the Rodeo Grounds in Long Beach.

Kite Flying

This is the tangled string capital of the Northwest. Visit some of the many good local shops in Long Beach, such as Long Beach Kites (at the stop-light; (360) 642-2202); or Stormin' Norman's (one block south; (800) 4-STORMIN). Just looking? Kite lovers can visit the Long Beach World Kite Museum and Hall of Fame (Third and N Pacific Hwy, (360) 642-4020) or buy their own at August's **International Kite Festival,** which brings thousands of soaring creations to the skies. The entire peninsula swells with visitors for this event, so plan ahead; (360) 642-2400.

outside in

Attractions

After many years of dormancy, **Long Beach** is bustling. New buildings are going up at warp speed and new businesses abound. Increased tourism is inevitable, so if you visit during the summer, prepare for the onslaught. A popular hangout is the half-mile-long elevated **boardwalk** (with night lighting) stretching between S 10th and Bolstad Streets, accessible to wheelchairs, baby strollers, and, of course, pedestrians. **Milton York Candy Company** (on the main drag; (360) 642-2352) purveys chocolates and ice cream; while nearby **Plain Jane's**, (360) 642-4933, offers tasty chocolate chip cookies and other sweets. For some Tex-Mex fast food, also on the main drag, head for **Dos Amigas Cafe** (Second and Pacific Hwy; (360) 642-8365). Farther out, **Clark's Nursery** grows fields of rhododendrons; (360) 642-2241.

Some of the peninsula's prettiest stretches (and a couple of its finest restaurants and lodgings) are tucked into the small beachfront bedroom community of **Seaview.** Almost every westward road leads to the beach, where you can park your car, stroll the quaint neighborhoods, and traverse the rolling dunes. The **Charles Mulvey Gallery** (46th Place and L Street, (360) 642-2189) displays the quintessential peninsula watercolors of ocean, beach, and bay. **Campiche Studios** (3100 S Pacific Way; (360) 642-2264) features watercolors, sculptures, and photography.

Founded as a religious settlement, **Ocean Park** now is a tranquil retirement community with a quiet beach—except in June, when the **Garlic Festival** takes over the town. Needless to say, there's lots of stinkin' good food at this event; (800) 451-2542. The **Wiegardt Watercolors Gallery** (2607 Bay Avenue; (360) 665-5976) displays Eric Wiegardt seascapes in a restored Victorian house. Nearby (at 25712 Sandridge Road; (360) 665-4382) the **Shoalwater Cove Gallery** exhibits nature scenes done in soft pastels.

Nahcotta has become almost synonymous with oysters. At the **Nahcotta Oyster Farm** (270th and Sandridge Road on the old rail line), you can pick up some pesticide-free 'sters (or gather your own for half-price); **Jolly Roger Seafoods** (across from The Ark; (360) 665-4111) is also a good bet. The **Nahcotta Natural Store** (270th and Sandridge Road;

(360) 665-4449) is a pleasant stop for beverages and grub. Two places help explain the oyster story: the **Willapa Field Station** (267 Sandridge Road; (360) 665-4166) has outdoor interpretive signs, maps, and info; **Willapa Bay Interpretive Center** (on the Nahcotta pier, open in summer only) features a viewing deck and indoor exhibits.

The picturesque burg of **South Bend** is perched on the evergreen bluffs along Willapa Bay, one of America's most pristine estuaries. Ruling over the town is the historic **County Courthouse** with its splendid stained-glass dome. (It was denounced by some fiscal sourpusses as a "gilded palace of extravagance" when it opened in 1910.) On Hwy 101 just north of town, the **H & H Cafe**, (360) 875-5442, is still the place to stop for pie.

Set on the long peninsula reaching into northern Willapa Bay, the crabbing community of **Tokeland**, named after 19th-century Chief Toke, is the loneliest part of the southwest coast, where the omnipresent tackiness of contemporary resort life is least apparent. The tiny Shoalwater Bay Indian Tribe hopes to open a casino, so don't bet on the status quo. In the meantime, pick up a container of crabmeat and some cocktail sauce from **Nelson Crab** (open daily 9am to 5pm) to enjoy while sitting on a driftwood log at the beach across the street.

Nestled on the shores of Baker Bay, part of the broad Columbia River estuary, **Chinook** was formerly a profitable salmon fish-trapping center. The too-efficient fish traps were outlawed earlier this century; today, most of the thousands of wooden pilings visible in the bay at low tide are all that remains of these harvesting contraptions.

Nearby, on Scarborough Hill, **Fort Columbia State Park** is a collection of restored turn-of-the-century wooden buildings that once housed soldiers guarding the mouth of the Columbia River from the threat of foreign invasion. The former commander's house is now a military museum (nearby is the youth hostel); ominous concrete bunkers once held huge cannons. The park also claims some of the area's largest rhododendron bushes. Open daily, mid-May to September, but hours vary; (360) 777-8221.

The **Ilwaco Heritage Museum** (115 SE Lake Street, in the Convention Center; (360) 642-3446) is a fine example of a small-town museum. It not only offers a look at southwest Washington history (including Native American artifacts and a scale model of the peninsula in the 1920s) but also contains an excellent research library, art gallery, and a separate building of train memorabilia. Near Fort Canby State Park, the U.S. Coast Guard's Cape Disappointment motor lifeboat station is home to the nation's only heavy-surf marine training center. It's not open to the public, but serves as an interesting sidelight for visitors to nearby Cape Disappointment Lighthouse.

Oysterville dates to 1854, and was the county seat until (legend has it) a group from South Bend stole the county records in 1893. South Bend remains the county seat to this day, but Oysterville has its own charm. It's listed on the National Register of Historic Places and features a distinctive row of shoreside homes, surrounded by stately cedars and spruce trees. (Follow Sandridge Road north to the Oysterville sign.) Oysterville is, of course, known for its bivalves, and **Oysterville Sea Farms,** (360) 665-6585, at the old cannery in Oysterville, sells 'em by the dozen (open weekends, year-round).

Restaurants

The Ark ☆☆   Accolades from up and down the West Coast have built The Ark up to legendary status; unfortunately, such renown is hard to uphold, and the restaurant has gained some snob appeal but lost some epicurean excitement. Most of the time, however, the restaurant with the picture-perfect setting is still quite good. The legendary Ark oyster feed, an unlimited amount (the record is 100) of Willapa Bay bivalves lightly breaded and pan-fried, continues to be the best in, at least, our universe. *On the old Nahcotta dock, next to the oyster fleet; (360) 665-4133; 273rd and Sandridge Rd, Nahcotta; $$$.*

Bubba's Pizza   It's not much to look at, inside or out, but the aroma of fresh-baked pizza dough, garlic, provolone, and pepperoni will entice you through the door. Once inside, the chef's artistry, wit, and showmanship (every pie is hand-tossed) will keep you entertained. *On the Ilwaco waterfront at SE Howerton; (360) 642-8750; 177 SE Howerton Way, Ilwaco; $.*

42nd Street Cafe ☆☆   Cheri and Blaine Walker, late of Shoalwater restaurant fame (she ran the kitchen; he was the manager), have taken over this popular dinner house. Cheri is transforming the kitchen, slowly but surely. But never fear: the comfy-cozy decor, the cheerful waitresses, and the hearty portions of home cooking are still here. *42nd Pl and Pacific Hwy 103; (360) 642-2323; Seaview; $$.*

Gardner's ☆☆   South Bend, the sleepy county seat of Pacific County, bills itself as "The Oyster Capital of the World." That's a classic bit of boosterism, but the Willapa Bay oysters *are* world-class. After the courthouse, the next best roadside attraction is Gardner's, where succulent pan-fried oysters—and almost everything else—are prepared with wonderful attention to detail. *On Hwy 101 in South Bend; (360) 875-5154; 702 W Robert Bush Dr, South Bend; $$.*

The Heron and Beaver Pub ☆   There's a feeling of serendipity here. You might slip in for a beer as you wait for your table at the Shoalwater, across the foyer, then discover that most of the pub's patrons aren't going anyplace else. They're here because the handsome, pint-size Heron and Beaver is a destination in its own right. Light meals are available, all prepared with the same meticulousness as the food next door. *In the Shelburne Inn, Pacific Hwy 103 and N 45th; (360) 642-4142; 4415 Pacific Hwy, Seaview; $$.*

The Lightship Restaurant and Columbia Bar ☆☆   The Lightship is a rare find: a view restaurant with good food. It's housed on the top floor of a boxy Nendel's Inn, and looks like just another poor-quality, high-priced, ocean-front eatery. Disregard all that, because the ocean view, fair prices, and, especially, the food make it all worthwhile. *Between 10th St and the beach; (360) 642-3252; 410 SW 10th, at Nendel's Inn, Long Beach; $$.*

My Mom's Pie Kitchen   The name says it all. This is a small establishment that serves a host of homemade pies. Before savoring a slice, satisfy yourself with a steamy bowl of chowder or a silky Dungeness crab quiche. *Pacific Hwy 103 and 44th St; (360) 642-2342; 4316 Pacific Hwy, Seaview; $.*

Pastimes   What began as a hip espresso house with lots of books and board games is now a restaurant, too. *5th St and Pacific Hwy 103; (360) 642-8303; 504 Pacific Hwy S, Long Beach; $.*

The Sanctuary ☆   You dine in a deified setting, an old Methodist church complete with pump organ, stained-glass windows, statues of angelic cherubs—even pews to sit in, for God's sake. Amid the finery, owner/chef Joanne Leech serves an eclectic array of food, from steak and seafood to the area's best fresh-baked bread. *Hwy 101 and Hazel St; (360) 777-8380; Hwy 101 and Hazel St, Chinook; $$.*

The Shoalwater (The Shelburne Inn) ☆☆☆☆   The Shoalwater is the finest eating establishment on the Northwest coast. Under the direction of the owners and head chef Francis Schafer, this exquisite eatery has helped to establish Northwest cuisine as a nationally recognized method of choosing and preparing food. The seasonal menu is a treat to peruse, and the wine list is superlative. Schafer continually produces imaginative, artful offerings, always using the Northwest's finest ingredients. *Pacific Hwy 103 and N 45th; (360) 642-4142; 4415 Pacific Hwy, Seaview; $$$.*

Cheaper Eats

Jessie's Ilwaco Fish   Take their fresh fish to the city park and have a fisherman's barbecue. *(360) 642-3773; West End and Port Docks, Ilwaco.*

Lodgings

Boreas Bed & Breakfast ☆☆   Boreas is a picturesque lodging in a post-card-perfect setting. A remodeled 1920s beach house, its rooms are tastefully decorated with art and antiques and appointed with handsome furnishings. The beach is a short walk through the dunes. *One block west of the main drag; (360) 642-8069; 607 N Blvd, Long Beach; $$.*

Chick-a-dee Inn at Ilwaco ☆   Located atop a quiet dead-end street overlooking the town, this bed and breakfast is housed in the old Ilwaco Presbyterian Church. Privacy seekers will find the walls unfortunately thin. A couple of rooms can accommodate two twin beds, a good choice for families. In the spacious public room, guests take their ample breakfast and read the morning papers. *Off 4th at Williams; (360) 642-8686; 120 Williams St NE, Ilwaco; $$.*

Klipsan Beach Cottages ☆   This cozy operation, a row of nine small, well-maintained older cottages, faces the ocean in a parklike setting of pine trees and clipped lawns. Since these are individually owned condominiums, interior decoration schemes vary widely, but all of the units feature fireplaces (or wood stoves), full kitchens, and ocean-facing decks just a couple of hundred feet from the beach. *Pacific Hwy 103, 2 miles south of Ocean Park; (360) 665-4888; 22617 Pacific Hwy, Ocean Park; $$–$$$.*

Moby Dick Hotel   Although it looks fairly institutional, this friendly place is one of those that grows on you. It's quite beachy (without really having a beach), with a couple of spacious public rooms, several small and modest bedrooms, and a sauna house. Pets welcome. Dinners are offered if the chef is in residence (call ahead). *South of Bay Ave on Sandridge Rd; (360) 665-4543; 25814 Sandridge Rd, Nahcotta; $$.*

The Shelburne Inn ☆☆   You can't see the ocean from here, but you most definitely can feel its allure throughout the historic Shelburne, a creaky but dignified century-old structure. Trouble is, there's a busy highway out front, with a well-lit supermarket across the way—request a westside room to assure peace and quiet. Breakfasts are superb. The separately owned **Shoalwater** (see above) is the dinner restaurant. *Pacific Hwy 103 and N 45th; (360) 642-2442; 4501 Pacific Hwy, Seaview; $$$.*

Sou'wester Lodge ☆   This place is definitely not for everyone, but those who appreciate good conversation, a sense of humor, and rambling lodgings on the beach will find this humble, old-fashioned resort just what the doctor ordered. You can stay in the main structure (the former summer home of a U.S. Senator), fully equipped cabins, or a classic trailer. The hosts are as much a draw as the lodgings. *1½ blocks southwest of*

Seaview's traffic light on Beach Access Rd (38th Pl); (360) 642-2542; 38th Pl and Jay Pl, Seaview; $.

Tokeland Hotel ☆   This chaste, century-old structure teetered for several years on the edge of genteel collapse until a series of rescues. A Seattle couple bought "the oldest resort hotel in Washington" and made major improvements in both the food and the plumbing. Some of the rooms offer views of Willapa Bay. Breakfast is included (kids will love the pigs in a blanket). *Kindred Ave and Hotel Rd; (360) 267-7006; 100 Hotel Rd, Tokeland; $$.*

Cheaper Sleeps

Arcadia Court   A modest, crisply appointed motel with small but cozy rooms, perky flower boxes, and kitchenettes in some rooms, located dead-bang in the middle of the Long Beach action. *(360) 642-2613; 401 N Blvd, Long Beach.*

Fort Columbia Hostel   A former men's dormitory during the Spanish-American War; a great beach is just a short walk away, and Long Beach Peninsula is 6 miles west. Couples should reserve the nice private room. Open summers only. *(360) 777-8755; Fort Columbia State Park, Chinook.*

The Lighthouse Motel   Each room feels like your own cabin. Dogs allowed. Trail to the beach; fireplaces and kitchenettes. *(360) 642-3622; Pacific Hwy, Long Beach waterfront, Long Beach.*

Our Place at the Beach   A modest motel squeezed between the Long Beach strip and the dunes. Get a top-floor room, facing west. Dogs allowed. *(360) 642-3793; 1309 S Blvd, Long Beach.*

Pacific View Motel   Tidy units with the self-contained feel of cottages, close to all the attractions of Long Beach. Pets allowed in some units. *(360) 642-2415; 203 Bolstad, Long Beach.*

More Information

Long Beach Peninsula Visitors Bureau: *(800) 451-2542.*
Long Beach Peninsula Chamber of Commerce: *(800) 642-2400.*
Port of Ilwaco: *(360) 642-3143.*
South Bend Chamber of Commerce: *(360) 875-5231.*
Willapa National Wildlife Refuge: *(360) 484-3482.*

Olympic
National Forest
and the East Slope
Olympics

From Lake Cushman west to O'Neil Pass in Olympic National Park, north along the eastern Olympic crest to Gray Wolf Ridge, and east to Hood Canal, including the Lake Cushman/Staircase area; Lake Cushman State Park; the Buckhorn, Brothers, Mount Skokomish, and Wonder Mountain Wildernesses; and the Gray Wolf, Dungeness, Dosewallips, Duckabush, Quilcene, Hamma Hamma, and North Fork Skokomish river drainages.

Many of the nation's most scenic wild lands have federal land managers lurking in the corners. It's a bit less subtle than on the Olympic Peninsula, where the U.S. Forest Service has the Olympic Mountains in nothing short of a headlock.

Like it or not, most of the lower-elevation slopes of Washington's most scenic mountain range are controlled by timber-hungry Olympic National Forest, which virtually surrounds the wilderness lands of Olympic National Park. Just as it has been elsewhere around the United States, that federal designation has been both good and bad for wild lands inside the 632,000-acre Olympic National Forest. Okay, mostly bad. But it really depends where you look.

Look at the formerly great lowland rain forest on the peninsula's west side, and you see a picture of devastation: too much old growth cut too fast in too short a time with too little regard for the impact on fisheries and wildlife. Get airborne and see for yourself: virtually all of the Forest Service land is clearcut, right up to the Olympic National Park border. Surrounded as they are by thousands of acres of shrubby second growth, the national park's preserved highlands loom like an island of life in a rather dead lowland sea. For that reason—and also because better, untrammeled national park lands are available nearby—Olympic National Forest lands on the west side of the peninsula have been largely ignored by recreators.

Not so on Olympic Forest's east-peninsula lands, where the picture is more mixed, and recreation opportunities are many. To be sure, massive clear cutting also has been undertaken here, often with the same sort of reckless disregard as on the west side. In the hearts and minds of longtime visitors, logging swaths here cut even deeper, because they blazed right through areas already heavily used for recreation—mostly hiking, backpacking, and fishing. A system of long river-drainage trails that stretched from Hood Canal west to the Olympic crest was replaced by a patchwork quilt of shorter trails, abruptly bisected by clearcuts and their accompanying logging roads. That's why many East Slope Olympic trails now have an "upper" and a "lower" portion, the upper usually running through old growth to the alpine country, the lower winding through second growth, a potholed road forever dividing the two.

This equation has more than one upside, though. Logging has slowed to a crawl here, and the roads left by decades of clearcutting have shortened the walking distance to some of the Olympic Mountains' most spectacular alpine country. And on this side of the forest, not all of that splendor lies within national park boundaries. Olympic National Forest's east-peninsula lands contain four high-country wilderness areas. (Don't fool yourself into believing the government set them aside out of guilt for the carnage below. Most of the areas are too high and too rugged to be logged.) From north to south, the 44,000-acre Buckhorn Wilderness, the 16,000-acre Brothers Wilderness, the 13,000-acre Mount Skokomish Wilderness, and the 2,300-acre Wonder Mountain Wilderness add a bit of long-term preservation insurance for fans of the eastern Olympics.

In spite of their checkered land-management past, the east slope Olympics remain one of the more diverse outdoor playgrounds in Western Washington. Some second-growth forests are now unusually large. And the small forest patches spared from logging are magnificent, with massive Douglas fir, hemlock, and western red cedar trees thundering skyward, while clustered groups of bright pink wild rhododendrons explode in the broken sunlight below. Rivers flowing east from the mountains to Hood Canal are uncommonly beautiful and undeveloped. Wild streams of liquid glass such as the Duckabush, Dosewallips, Hamma Hamma, Gray Wolf, Big Quilcene, and Dungeness are spectacular in their own right, but the mountains-meeting-the-sea setting makes them all the more memorable.

Generations of Washingtonians have been drawn to this rich, wild mix. Given their close proximity to Seattle, it's surprising that the east slope Olympics don't draw even more hikers, campers, and anglers. One possible reason: logistical confusion. People can't quite figure out how to navigate these parts. Unlike the west side, where access to the high country is concentrated in a few well known places, the east side is rife with openings. Credit—or blame, as the case may be—goes to the maze of logging roads. More than 2,500 miles of gravel roads wind through Olympic National Forest, most of them poorly marked and maintained. Staring at a Forest Service map detailing the squirming-wormpile road structure can give you a headache. There's no obvious focal point here: just a series of river drainages stacked end to end from Sequim to Shelton, all flowing toward salt water, and concealing miles of backcountry wonders.

This is a big, diverse area. Don't expect to see it all, or even a fraction of it, in a single visit. Our best advice is to get a Forest Service map and navigate by river drainage. Pick a river, visit for a weekend, hike the trails, camp the campgrounds, drive the roads. Come back and do another drainage. By the time you've worked through all of them, you'll be amazed—and the river you started with probably will have changed dramatically, forcing you to begin anew.

That's the inspiring—and disconcerting—thing about the east slope Olympics. Like it or not, change—often radical—is a fact of life in the Olympic National Forest. No area in Washington exemplifies the double-edged sword of multiuse better—or worse—than this one.

Getting There

Most eastern slope Olympic National Forest trailheads and campgrounds are reached via US 101 on the west shore of Hood Canal (see the Hood Canal chapter). From that highway, access roads lead west into the forest in the Quilcene, Duckabush, Hamma Hamma, and Skokomish river drainages. A major access route to the interior east slope Olympics is Lake Cushman Road, which leads west to the Lake Cushman area from Hoodsport.

Adjoining Areas

NORTH: **Sequim and the Dungeness Valley**

SOUTHWEST: **Grays Harbor: Westport and Ocean Shores**

EAST: **Hood Canal**

WEST: **Olympic National Park: Overview**

inside out

Olympic National Forest Rules and Regulations

Because all Olympic National Forest lands share at least one border with Olympic National Park, many visitors assume rules are the same throughout. Not true. Some key differences:

Dogs, a definite no-no in the national park backcountry, are allowed on trails in the national forest. Free backcountry **permits** are required for camping anywhere inside the national park backcountry. They're not required in the national forest. **Hunting,** particularly for black-tailed deer and Roosevelt elk, is allowed in most of the national forest (something to be mindful of when hiking in the fall). It's illegal in the park.

Backcountry **party size** in the national park is limited to 12 people and eight stock animals; there's no restriction in the national forest, *except* in its designated wilderness areas, where the 12 persons/eight stock rule (or just 12 living beings, which lumps people and stock together) applies. **Campfires** are allowed in national forest backcountry, except in designated wilderness. They're prohibited above 3,500 feet in most areas of the national park. State **fishing licenses** are required in the national forest, and state regulations apply. With the exception of permits for razor-clam digging and catch-record cards for salmon and steelhead, state licenses are not required in the national park. **Firearms** are allowed in the national forest, forbidden in national parks. **Roadside camping** is allowed in the national forest, forbidden in national parks.

An organizational note: Because the bulk of recreation opportunities in Olympic National Forest lie within the Hood Canal and Quilcene Ranger Districts on the east slopes of the Olympics, we've focused the outdoors listings in this chapter on that geographic area. Details about the recreation offerings in the western ranger districts—Sol Duc and Quinault—can be found in the chapters on Lake Crescent and the Upper Soleduck; Forks and La Push; and Lake Quinault and the Quinault Valley.

Hiking/Backpacking

Simply put, this is one of the best and most diverse places to put foot to trail in Washington. The lower slopes of the leeward Olympics are mostly logged, but the upper hills are fantastic, and—mostly protected by wilderness or national park designation—likely to stay that way.

Hikers should note that national forests, wilderness areas, and national parks all have different backcountry restrictions (see Olympic

National Forest Rules and Regulations, above). That's particularly important in this area, where it's possible to begin hiking in the national forest, stumble into a wilderness area, then pass through to the national park—all on the very same trail. If you have any doubt about the rules, consult one of the ranger district offices listed below.

That said, the hiking menu here is like the wine list at a fine restaurant: almost overwhelming, but a joy to sample, sip by sip. Generally, this isn't the best place to come for a short day hike (although plenty are available for the persistent). Most trails here begin in the deep lowland woods and follow a stream drainage west, where they enter wildflower- and view-rich alpine areas in the high Olympics. If you're day hiking, consider that great views or notable destinations often aren't found for a dozen or more miles up the trail—assuming drop-dead gorgeous mountain streams and valleys don't count. Those same features, however, make this a superb backpacking area, whether you're out for an overnighter or a two-week, cross-Olympics jaunt.

A note on seasons: Many of the best trails here begin fairly high in the mountains and end even higher. Most are likely to be snowed in from November through the spring. High alpine areas in the leeward Olympics generally aren't passable to casual hikers and backpackers until June or later, although from year to year this can vary by as much as a month. Ask a ranger.

An important note on access: Most trailheads in the Olympic National Forest are reached by traveling a series of often baffling Forest Service roads. They often wash out, and the government is fond of changing road numbers, just to confuse us. For road closure information and detailed driving directions to trailheads, we *strongly* urge you to call a local ranger district office before setting out.

Trail specialists at these offices also can help you pick a specific hike. A comprehensive—though by no means complete—list of favorites follows. They're listed by river drainage, north to south.

Gray Wolf drainage

Quilcene Ranger District; (360) 765-2200.

The **Gray Wolf River Trail** (moderate; various lengths) is a magnificent walk up one of the least-spoiled river drainages on the Olympic Peninsula. The trail's lower half is a great beginner/intermediate backpack terrain. From a trailhead near Dungeness Forks Campground (see Camping, below), it follows the silvery river about 10 miles upstream to a major trail junction, Three Forks. Good backcountry campsites are located along the river all along the way; go until you run out of gas, then make camp.

From the trail junction at Three Forks, high-country trails lead north to **Deer Park** (difficult; 4.3 miles one way; see the Port Angeles and Hurricane Ridge chapter); southwest up beautiful Cameron Creek Trail to **Cameron Pass** (difficult; 11 miles one way); and south along the bubbling upper Gray Wolf to **Gray Wolf Pass** (difficult; 9.5 miles one way). Strong backpackers can combine the Lower Gray Wolf, Cameron Creek, Dosewallips, and Upper Gray Wolf Trails for a six- to eight-day, 50-mile Olympic backcountry loop. But sticking to the Gray Wolf itself is tough to beat. A round-trip hike to Gray Wolf Pass is about 39 miles. (Name trivia note: Yes, there used to be gray wolves here. This was one of their last refuges from bounty hunters. They're now extinct.)

Dungeness drainage
Quilcene Ranger District; (360) 765-2200.

On its route north, the Gray Wolf dumps into the **Dungeness River,** which has its own pleasant trail system. From a trailhead on Forest Service Road 2860, the Upper Dungeness Trail follows the upper river to **Camp Handy** (moderate; 6.4 miles round trip) and on to **Boulder Shelter** (difficult; 6.8 miles round trip), near the junction with the Marmot Pass/Big Quilcene Trail. This rain-shadow area is a very good backpack destination, particularly when weather is questionable elsewhere on the peninsula. Note that cougars have been very active in this area in recent years.

A mile up the Dungeness Trail is a junction with a path to one of Olympic National Park's most notable backpacking destinations, **Royal Basin** (moderate; 14 miles round trip). The trail empties into a stunning alpine valley beneath 7,788-foot Mount Deception. Campsites are exceptional in the beautiful, wildflower-enriched basin. If you're lucky, you might see a mountain goat on the upper ridges. If you're looking for a great weekend backpack trip to familiarize yourself with the area, this is it.

In the lower Dungeness drainage, a good day hike—and an increasingly popular mountain bike route—is the **Gold Creek Trail** (moderate; 12.8 miles round trip), which follows the Dungeness drainage about 2,000 feet up from a lower trailhead on Forest Service Road 2860 to a trailhead farther up the same road. It can be ridden or walked one way for a fairly easy, 6.4-mile day hike that's especially nice in spring, when wild rhododendrons are in bloom.

Near that trail's upper trailhead is the **Tubal Cain Mine Trail** (moderate; various lengths) which follows Copper Creek beneath Iron and Buckhorn Mountains to the stunning alpine terrain of 6,100-foot **Marmot Pass** (difficult; 17.6 miles). It's a long, tough haul to the pass, 3,300 feet above the trailhead—but worth the climb if you're in shape. (The trail continues south from there into Olympic National Park, over Constance Pass, and down to the Dosewallips Trail.) The Tubal Cain Trail also can be hiked as a nice day hike to abandoned mine sites turned into beautiful alpine meadows, about 4 miles up the trail.

Access note: Most trailheads in the Dungeness drainage are reached by following Palo Alto Road west from US 101 near Sequim Bay State Park to Forest Service Road 28, then connecting Forest Service roads. Call for specific directions.

Quilcene drainage

Quilcene Ranger District; (360) 765-2200.

Much of this area is logged over, but a couple of notable trails stand out. The **Mount Townsend Trail** (difficult; 11 miles round trip) is a popular thigh-burner that gets you to truly stunning views atop a 6,280-foot peak. You can see all the way to Seattle and Mount Rainier, and the wild rhododendron display here in the late spring might be the best in the state. If the 3,400-foot elevation gain sounds like a bit much, make it a two-day trip. Decent campsites are available at **Camp Windy** (3.5 miles) and at nearby **Silver Lakes** (2.5 miles south on a connecting trail). The trailhead is on Forest Service Road 2760, reached via Penny Creek and Big Quilcene roads out of Quilcene.

Another very popular day hike—probably the best short one in the Quilcene area—is the climb to the old fire lookout atop **Mount Zion** (moderate; 3.6 miles round trip). The trail is fairly steep, but short enough to get most people to the top, where views of Hood Canal and Puget Sound are nothing short of awesome. This is another good place to hike among blooming wild rhododendrons in the late spring. The trailhead is on Forest Service Road 2810. Take Lords Lake Loop Road and Forest Service Road 28 north of Quilcene.

Also in this area, the **Upper Big Quilcene Trail** is yet another steep route to **Marmot Pass** (difficult; 10.5 miles round trip); and the **Lower Big Quilcene Trail** has become a popular mountain-bike route (see Mountain Biking, below).

Dosewallips drainage

Hood Canal Ranger District; (360) 877-5254.

This is the heart of the leeward Olympics, and some of the best hiking trails are found here. Most trailheads are reached by following Dosewallips Road west from Brinnon.

The **West Fork Dosewallips Trail,** which begins as the **Dosewallips River Trail** near Dosewallips and Elkhorn Campgrounds (see Camping, below), is a favorite here. It follows the beautiful, clear river to a grand backpacking destination—**Honeymoon Meadows** (moderate; 17.6 miles round trip), then climbs to 4,400-foot **Anderson Pass** (difficult; 21 miles round trip). Wiser hikers camp in the meadow and day hike to Anderson Pass. Cross-Olympic hikers continue west from here, dropping down the East Fork Quinault Trail to Enchanted Valley (see the Lake Quinault and the Quinault River Valley chapter). For a very nice, fairly easy day hike, follow the Dosewallips River Trail 1.4 miles to the major trail junction at Dose Forks, then a short distance beyond on the West Fork trail to a spectacular high footbridge over the West Fork Dosewallips.

Backpackers who continue straight at Dose Forks, and follow the main channel Dosewallips west, have several options. About 2.5 miles from the main trailhead, the Constance Pass trail turns north, climbing steeply over the pass and continuing to **Boulder Shelter** (difficult; 11.5 miles one way). This is a popular connecting route between the Dosewallips and Dungeness drainages. Or proceed west from Dose Forks up the mainstem Dosewallips, a beautiful, isolated area. Popular destinations include the grand views and wildflower meadows at **Dose Meadows** (moderate; 26 miles round trip) and the alpine terrain of **Hayden Pass** (moderate/difficult; 31 miles round trip). Another trail drops 8.5 miles west of Hayden Pass to a junction with the Elwha River Trail (see the Port Angeles and Hurricane Ridge chapter).

A short, very steep trail that begins on Dosewallips Road near the national park border leads to **Lake Constance** (very difficult; 4 miles round trip), one of this area's most heavily (over)used backcountry campgrounds. Don't let the short distance fool you; the trail is an absolute beast, gaining 3,400 feet in its 2-mile ascent. The lake is nice, but overuse here has led to restrictions of 20 overnighters per day. Permits (free, so far) can be reserved through Staircase Ranger Station; (360) 877-5569. You pick them up at Dosewallips Ranger Station near the trailhead (it has no phone). Day hikers don't need a permit. Just thighs of iron.

Duckabush drainage
Hood Canal Ranger District; (360) 877-5254.

Two good day-hiking trails are found in the lower Duckabush drainage. **Interrorem Interpretive Trail** (easy; 1/3 mile loop), which begins near the Interrorem Guard Station about 4 miles west of US 101, is a cool loop trail through lush second-growth forest (with plenty of massive stumps to remind you of the first). Connecting to this trail is the equally popular **Ranger Hole Trail** (easy; 1.6 miles round trip), which leads from the Guard Station to a stunningly beautiful fishing hole on the Duckabush (once extremely productive for fishing, now mildly so, on a good day). Nice picnic grounds near the historic 1907 Guard Station—a former wilderness outpost—make this a good place to spend an afternoon with the kids.

Up the road a bit, the **Duckabush River Trail** (moderate/difficult; various lengths possible) is a lovely river walk, snow-free much of the year. The trail climbs 23 miles to the majestic alpine country around Marmot Lake and LaCrosse Basin, which provide access to the O'Neil Pass Trail down into Enchanted Valley in the Quinault drainage. But day hikers and overnighters enjoy the easier, lower sections of the Duckabush, which ventures into fine stands of old-growth timber. Good campsites are found along the route. The first 2.5 miles are easy, then huffing commences.

Hamma Hamma drainage
Hood Canal Ranger District; (360) 877-5254.

Some of the region's most popular trails are found here. One of them, **Lower Lena Lake** (easy; 7 miles round trip), is so easy (1,200-foot elevation gain) and so scenic that it's been virtually trampled in the past decade. Revegetation work is going on here; use established campsites only. Fishing can be good in the lake, and the setting is idyllic. The campground here is a major staging area for climbers headed to the 6,866-foot summit of The Brothers. A connecting trail leads from the north end of the lake up East Fork Lena Creek to a bivouac base camp. Another connecting trail leads from Lower Lena Lake up—2,800 feet up—to **Upper Lena Lake** (difficult; 14 miles round trip). It's worth the effort: views and wildflowers are stunning here, and camping space more plentiful.

Also in the area is a rough, rarely maintained trail to **Mildred Lakes** in the Mount Skokomish Wilderness (difficult; 9 miles round trip). Not highly recommended, but potentially a great source of solitude.

North Fork Skokomish drainage
Hood Canal Ranger District; (360) 877-5254; or Staircase Ranger Station; (360) 877-5569.

Easy access via mostly paved roads to good camping facilities around Lake Cushman make this area an east-slope Olympics favorite. One of the big draws is the **North Fork Skokomish Trail,** which leads up the river from Staircase Ranger Station to superb alpine backpack campsites at **Home Sweet Home** (moderate; 27 miles round trip). Here—and in countless other areas along this trail—alpine wildflowers and views of the interior Olympics are sublime. Side trips can be made to Mount Steel or Mount Stone, and through hikers can follow the path all the way to a junction with the Duckabush Trail, O'Neil Pass, and ultimately Enchanted Valley in the Quinault drainage. Trout fishing in the Skoke is very good.

A popular side trip from that trail leads to **Flapjack Lakes** (moderate; 16.2 miles round trip from Staircase), where nice campsites await with awesome views of the knife-edged Sawtooth Range of the Olympics—a challenging rock-climbing venue. Side trips to Black and

White Lakes or Smith Lakes are possible, and might be desirable: Flapjack Lakes is so popular that it's now limited to 30 overnighters at a time. Permits can be reserved at the Staircase Ranger Station; (360) 877-5569. If it's a sellout, one backcountry option remains. **Wagonwheel Lake** is only about 3 miles from Staircase—but it's also 3,200 vertical feet, making it one of the steeper Olympic trails you'll find. Brace yourself.

Staircase campers looking for a great day hike shouldn't miss the **Staircase Rapids Trail** (easy; 2-mile loop), which begins near the ranger station and follows the cool, clear North Fork Skokomish up one side, then returns down the other. A great walk on a hot day.

A challenging day hike in the same vicinity is the trail to the top of **Mount Ellinor** (difficult; 6.2 miles round trip). For well-equipped hikers with experience in the snow, this is a fun early-spring trip. Then, you can walk 2.5 snow-free miles from the lower trailhead (there are two for this hike, the lower one is on Big Creek Road and melts out earlier) to Chute Flats, then climb the snow chute straight up to the summit, where truly memorable views of Hood Canal and the inner Olympics await. In the summer, it's safer to stay on the trail around the east side of the peak. And the view is just as grand. You can trim nearly half the round-trip distance off this hike by starting at the upper trailhead, off Spur Road 014. But it's not as much fun.

See the Lake Quinault and the Quinault River Valley chapter for details on National Forest trails around **Lake Quinault** and the nearby **Colonel Bob Wilderness.**

Camping

Like most Forest Service campgrounds, Olympic National Forest sites in the leeward Olympics are far from fancy: pit toilets, running water (maybe), and not much else. But you've gotta love the packaging. Most of these campsites are streamside, in old-growth or mature second-growth forest. They're quiet, remote—and usually worth the effort to locate. A popular state park and two Olympic National Park campgrounds round out the picture.

Lake Cushman campers flock to **Lake Cushman State Park,** on the east shore of the Tacoma City Light reservoir. The park straddles the lake's Big Creek Inlet (which used to be a stream canyon before the river was dammed). Tent sites are on the north shore, RV sites and the picnic area on the south. In all, the park has 80 campsites (30 with hookups; maximum RV length, 60 feet). A smooth, fine-gravel beach and a boat ramp make this a popular summer hangout for sunbathers, water skiers, canoeists, and trout anglers. About 4 miles of marked hiking trails wind through the park, although nicer ones are just up the road at Staircase. Lake Cushman is open daily in summer months; weekends and holidays only from December 1 to March 31. Winter camping is allowed in the day-use area only. Campsites can be reserved up to 11 months in advance by calling (800) 452-5687. *On Lake Cushman Road 7.5 miles west of Hoodsport; (360) 877-5491 or (800) 233-0321.*

Nearby, at the head of the lake, is **Staircase Campground,** an Olympic National Park site. Staircase, nicely situated near the North Fork Skokomish Trailhead, has 59 sites (no hookups; maximum RV length 21 feet). It's very popular with hikers and backpackers. The campground is open all year. *17 miles west of Hoodsport via Lake Cushman Road and Forest Service Road 24 (Jorsted Creek Road); (360) 452-0330 or (360) 877-5569.*

Two smaller alternatives are nearby. **Big Creek Campground,** just up the road from the state park, has 23 sites (no hookups; maximum RV length, 30 feet) in a wooded area. Big Creek is open from May to November. Campsites cannot be reserved. *Near the intersection of Lake Cushman Road and Forest Service Road 24, 9 miles west of Hoodsport; (360) 877-5254.*

Lilliwaup Creek, a state Department of Natural Resources site, has 13 campsites for tents or small trailers (no hookups). It's open all year, and campsites cannot be reserved.*On Forest Service Road 24, 6.5 miles west of Big Creek Campground (above); (360) 902-1234.*

A more remote site on the South Fork Skokomish is **Brown Creek,** which has 19 sites (no hookups; maximum RV length, 21 feet), a horse camp, and access to hiking trails. It's open all year. Campsites cannot be reserved. The road is rough, and you'll need a Forest Service road map to find this place. *On Forest Service Road 2353, 6 miles north of Shelton; (360) 877-5254.*

One river drainage north, **Hamma Hamma** has 15 sites (no hook-ups; maximum RV length 21 feet). Nothing fancy, but it's a nice spot, set on one of the region's most gorgeous rivers. Nearby **Lena Creek,** another Forest Service riverfront campground, has 14 sites (no hookups; maximum RV length, 21 feet). It's near the Lena Lakes Trailhead. Both campgrounds are open summer months only, and campsites cannot be reserved. *On Forest Service Road 25 (Hamma Hamma River Road) 6.5 and 8 miles, respectively, west of US 101; (360) 877-5254.*

In the Duckabush drainage, the only option is **Collins,** a Forest Service camp with six sites (no hookups; maximum RV length, 21 feet). It's open summer months only. Sites cannot be reserved. *On Forest Service Road 2510 (Duckabush River Road), 5 miles west of US 101; (360) 877-5254.*

The Dosewallips drainage has two nice campgrounds. **Elkhorn,** a Forest Service camp, offers 18 riverfront sites (no hookups; maximum RV length, 21 feet). It's open summer months only (the road up the river closes just beyond here in the winter, because Olympic National Park doesn't maintain the part inside its borders). Campsites can be reserved by calling the campground's private concessionaire; (360) 796-4886. *11 miles west of Brinnon via US 101, County Road 10, and Forest Service Road 2610; (360) 765-2200.*

Dosewallips, an Olympic National Park campground, is a pretty spot, and a bit more centrally located, at least if you're a hiker (the Dosewallips Trailhead is right across the parking lot). You'll find 30 tent sites (no hookups) near the river, and they're often full on summer nights. Dosewallips is open summer months only. Campsites cannot be reserved. *At the end of Forest Service Road 2610, 16 miles west of Brinnon; (360) 452-0330.*

Near the confluence of the Dungeness and Gray Wolf Rivers, **Dungeness Forks,** a Forest Service campground, has nine tent sites (no hookups), near the popular Gray Wolf Trailhead. It's open summer months only. Campsites cannot be reserved. *On Forest Service Road 2880, 11 miles south of Sequim; call (360) 765-2200 for directions.*

Just to the south, **East Crossing**'s nine tent sites (no hookups) are set along the Dungeness River. The campground is open summer months only; sites cannot be reserved. *On Forest Service Road 2860, 13 miles south of Sequim; call (360) 765-2200 for directions.*

For information on Olympic National Forest campgrounds near **Soleduck,** see the Lake Crescent and the Upper Soleduck chapter. For details on Olympic National Forest campgrounds on **Lake Quinault,** see the Lake Quinault and the Quinault River Valley chapter.

Fishing

All of the **streams flowing into Hood Canal** through Olympic National Forest offer outstanding rainbow trout fishing during the summer stream-fishing season (June 1 to October 31, unless otherwise posted). Limits typically are two trout a day, minimum size 12 inches. Flies and light spinning tackle do well, but check on local gear restrictions. Access to each river is good, particularly at the many streamside Forest Service campgrounds listed in Camping, above.

Most **rivers** in this region also have local sea-run cutthroat and very fishable, often productive winter and summer steelhead runs. Seasons and restrictions change frequently. Check with the state Department of Fish and Wildlife, or pick up a state fishing pamphlet at a tackle or sporting goods store.

Backpacking anglers usually find fair-to-good trout-fishing conditions at **alpine lakes** listed under Hiking/Backpacking, above. Note that you don't need a state fishing license for streams and lakes inside Olympic National Park, but licenses are required for all waterways in Olympic National Forest. Most of these lakes are frozen until June.

Lake Cushman, a massive, 10-mile-long reservoir, is rife with fish, including cutthroat, rainbow trout, landlocked salmon, and some bass. But they're fairly stubborn about leaving the water. Cushman is very deep and normally very, very clear. Lightweight leaders are usually necessary, and most of the fish caught here are hooked by boat anglers trolling pop gear along the lake banks.

For salmon fishing and shellfish gathering tips on **Hood Canal,** see the Hood Canal chapter.

Mountain Biking

At last count, 30 Olympic National Forest **trails** were open to mountain bikes, with about 85 total miles of terrain. Check with the ranger district offices listed in More Information at the end of this chapter about local restrictions. Two particular Forest Service trails in this area—**Gold Creek,** with trailheads in two places along Forest Service Road 2860, and **Lower Big Quilcene,** off Forest Service Road 2700-080—have emerged as mountain-biking favorites. The latter is only 6 miles one way, but riding local Forest Service roads that connect the upper and lower trailheads creates a very scenic 18.5-mile loop. Beware, however, of dirt bikes.

Actually, trail riding is but a fraction of the lure here. The Olympic National Forest is literally laced with gravel logging roads, most of which are rarely traveled by cars. **Roadways** in the **upper Dungeness** area, near East Crossing and Dungeness Forks Campgrounds, are excellent mountain-biking tracks, as are the many **side roads around Lake Cushman.**

Canoeing/Kayaking

Lake Cushman is a great canoe getaway, particularly if you can snare a campsite at Lake Cushman State Park or Staircase (see Camping, above).

Attractions

The Hood Canal strip of US 101, which parallels the east slope Olympics, offers a great mix of oyster farms, some charming country stores, a winery, and a classical music venue that's world-class. See the Hood Canal chapter for details.

Restaurants and Lodgings

For recommendations on restaurants and lodgings, see the Adjoining Areas to this chapter.

More Information

Olympic National Forest Headquarters: *1835 Black Lake Blvd. SW, Olympia, WA 98512-5623; (360) 956-2400.*

Hood Canal Ranger District: *(360) 877-5254.*

Quilcene Ranger District: *(360) 765-2200.*

Quinault Ranger District: *(360) 288-2525.*

Soleduck Ranger District: *(360) 374-6522.*

Hood
Canal

The Hood Canal shoreline area from Port Ludlow south to Union and east to Belfair, including Mount Walker, Potlatch, Dosewallips, Belfair, and Twanoh State Parks; and the Skokomish, Dosewallips, Hamma Hamma, Quilcene, and Duckabush Rivers.

If mountain ranges had brakes, giant smokin' skid marks would still be visible at the mouth of the Dosewallips River.

That's how dramatic the collision between mountain and sea seems along Hood Canal, 60 miles of saltwater serenity stretching from Admiralty Inlet south toward Shelton. Even in a state known for its thousands of miles of stunning shoreline, Hood Canal (it's really not a canal at all, but the nation's longest fjord) is a place of uncommon beauty. The waterway's gentle shores are sheltered (especially along the north end) from the open-ocean elements by the Olympics, which tower above the west shore like protective big brothers. Some of the Olympics' most impressive alpine peaks—The Brothers, Mount Constance, Mount Washington, and others—loom here, providing a stop-the-car backdrop for one of the state's most intriguing marine playgrounds.

Hood Canal's eastern shores, in Kitsap and North Mason Counties, have been heavily home-ownered. But the west side— marked by the mouths of still-free rivers such as the Hamma Hamma, Dosewallips, and Duckabush—remains relatively green and blue. Granted, most of the uplands between the Olympics and the shore have been logged, courtesy of Olympic National Forest (another "land of many uses": chief among them wood production). But except for a string of private summer homes and residences along the beach, the waterway is comparatively unspoiled.

Recreation is focused on a string of Washington State Parks along US 101, which runs the length of the west shore, usually within view of the salt water. They're some of the most relaxing campground getaways in the state. Also some of the most diverse—just about every Hood Canal campground offers a chance to fish, dig clams, gather oysters, hike, swim, cycle, kayak, or just plain relax—all from the same spot. The canal also is a wildlife-rich area, with many shorebirds, raptors, and marine mammals popping into view.

Whether you're drawn more strongly to the water or to the mountains (see the Olympic National Forest and the East Slope Olympics chapter), Hood Canal is a dependable fresh-air destination. And it's a good year-round draw. Winter months, when shellfish gathering is best, are magnificently quiet, and the shoreside campgrounds rarely receive snow. Summer months are equally alluring, especially for boaters and swimmers. Unlike deep, murky Puget Sound, Hood Canal is a fairly shallow waterway—it warms substantially in late summer. The farther south you drive, the warmer the water gets. This is the best place in the state for a saltwater swim, and one of the best places to learn saltwater kayaking.

Perhaps best of all, the location is ideal. The canal is just close enough to Seattle for weekend-getaway convenience, just far enough away to escape the shadow of the Columbia Tower. Look at it this way: The cell phone will still work. But you'll lose the desire to use it.

Getting There

The west side of Hood Canal is accessed by US 101, which stretches along the shoreline for 53 miles between the Hwy 104 junction north of Quilcene and the Hwy 106 junction on the Skokomish Indian Reservation. (Hwy 106 continues 18 miles east along the canal's "Great Bend," ending in Belfair.)

To get there from the north, take the Seattle-Bainbridge, Seattle-Bremerton, or Edmonds-Kingston ferry to Kitsap County, cross the Hood Canal Floating Bridge, and continue 16 miles on Hwy 104 to the US 101 junction. (For ferry schedules and information, call (206) 464-6400 or (800) 84-FERRY.) To get there from the south, follow US 101 about 30 miles north from Interstate 5 at Olympia, or follow Hwy 3 from Bremerton to Belfair and proceed 18 miles west on Hwy 106.

Adjoining Areas

NORTH: **Port Townsend; Sequim and the Dungeness Valley**

SOUTHWEST: **Grays Harbor: Westport and Ocean Shores**

WEST: **Olympic National Forest and the East Slope Olympics; Olympic National Park: Overview**

EAST: **Kitsap Peninsula**

inside out

Beaches

Near the east end of the Hood Canal's southern "hook," **Belfair State Park** has 1,300 feet of saltwater shoreline, much of it at the site of a long-since abandoned commercial oyster bed. Commerce has fled, but many oysters still remain, making this a favorite spot for oyster pickers. In recent years, however, pollutants have closed the beach here. Conditions have improved of late, and Belfair had its first oyster season in years two years ago. But check with the park or the state Department of Fish and Wildlife for information about closures, whether from local contaminants or red tide.

Even if you can't pick oysters, Belfair's beach is a pleasant spot. The wild, marshy beach uplands are a favorite tromping place for kids, and the terrain draws a wealth of bird life. Just inland from the beach, Belfair has another unique feature: a tidal "swimming pool" that fills with warm salt water when the tide comes in. This is the best—and cleanest—place for a dip in the park. In midsummer, the water actually gets quite warm. The park is 3 miles southwest of Belfair. Its campground is a local's favorite (see Camping, below).

A short distance down Hwy 106, **Twanoh State Park** is best known for its sunny beach area and its unusually clean, warm saltwater swimming on Hood Canal. The park has 3,200 feet of shoreline on the canal, with a large bathhouse, children's wading pool, a boat launch and boat dock, and good picnic facilities. Across the highway is a nice campground. (See Camping, below).

Three miles south of Hoodsport (just north of the Hwy 106/Hwy 101 junction) is another picturesque beach area, **Potlatch State Park.** If you have time for only one rest stop on a tour around Hood Canal, make it this one. At Potlatch you'll find an impressive 10,000 feet of saltwater beach, much of which turns into a sprawling mudflat at low tide. That makes this a favorite park for oyster picking and clam digging, when tides and seasons are right. When the tide's in, the gravelly beach is equally popular with boaters (who can tie up to moorage buoys) and kayakers, who can explore the saltwater estuary at the mouth of the Skokomish River. The area is particularly rich with seals, birds, and other wildlife. On the beach, the grassy picnic facilities are first rate, and a small campground is located across Hwy 101 (see Camping, below).

Triton Cove State Park, a small, former resort site 6 miles south of Brinnon, has a waterfront picnic area and boat launch.

Just south of Brinnon, **Dosewallips State Park,** on the southern banks of its namesake river, is a large, very popular day-use and camping destination. From the campground, a trail leads beneath US 101 to the mouth of the Dosewallips River, where plenty of shorebirds and small animals are seen in the marsh grass. Kayaks are common sights in this minidelta. The beach itself isn't a good one for lounging; it's fairly marshy and ripe-smelling. But it always has been a healthy clam and oyster producer. Until recently, that is, when high levels of fecal contamination have turned up in local shellfish. Harbor seals, drawn to the river mouth to feed, have proliferated, and biologists believe their waterborne feces contaminated the clams and oysters. Meanwhile, clamming beaches have been closed here, but might reopen when anti-seal measures—such as fencing—are put in place. Dosewallips also has a large, well-developed campground (see Camping, below).

A short distance up the road, **Seal Rock Campground,** an Olympic National Forest site, is one of our favorites in this region. This is the only Forest Service Campground in the state that offers saltwater shore access. And it's a beauty of a shore. The rocky tidelands here offer excellent oyster gathering, clam digging, and crabbing. Don't be alarmed by the sea monsters: gigantic Trident submarines, each as long as the Space Needle is high, often cruise just offshore, bound for their deep-water testing ground in Dabob Bay. A picnic area has great views across the canal to Mount Rainier. And the campground (see Camping, below) is first-rate.

Another nice—and lightly used—beach site is **Bywater State Park,** which has a primitive campground, a boat launch, and a day-use area at the north side of the Hood Canal Floating Bridge's west end. It's a pleasant picnic spot, with views north to Mount Baker.

Finally, several beach stretches along Hood Canal are controlled by Washington State Parks, but have no developed facilities. Most have boat access only. But one, **Lilliwaup Tidelands** just north of Lilliwaup, is accessible from US 101. It's a popular clam-digging site.

Camping

Belfair State Park is a Hood Canal favorite. The southern-canal park has 184 campsites (47 with full hookups; maximum RV length, 75 feet). The sites are divided into two areas: a broad, open, flat area just off the beach, with planted lawn and imported shrubs and trees; and a more natural (though darker) wooded area just to the north. Usually full for much of the summer (reservations are a good idea), Belfair is open all year. Campsites can be reserved up to 11 months in advance by calling Reservations Northwest; (800) 452-5687. *3 miles southwest of Belfair; fol-*

low signs from Hwy 3; (360) 275-0668 or (800) 233-0321.

Twanoh State Park, best known for its day-use beach area on the north side of Hwy 106, has a nice, secluded camping area on the south side. Among the big second-growth trees, you'll find 62 campsites (9 with hookups; maximum RV length, 35 feet) and a 100-person group camp. The sites are divided, with smaller tent sites in one loop, RVs in the other. The scenery is nice, with cool shade along Twanoh Creek. Several miles of trails follow the creek through the greenery on the hillside above (bring your bug dope). Also note the old stone buildings here; most were built by CCC crews in the 1930s. Twanoh is open all year (some parts of the park are shut down in winter). Some facilities are wheelchair-accessible. Campsites cannot be reserved. *On Hwy 106, 5 miles east of Union; (360) 275-2222 or (800) 233-0321.*

Potlatch State Park's extensive beach area is even more popular, making its smaller campground across US 101 a popular destination. Potlatch has 35 campsites (18 with hookups; maximum RV length, 60 feet). It's open all year. Campsites cannot be reserved. *On US 101, 3 miles south of Hoodsport; (360) 877-5361 or (800) 233-0321.*

Hoodsport is the turnoff for Lake Cushman, where **Lake Cushman State Park** and **Staircase Campground** are popular overnight spots. See the Olympic National Forest and the East Slope Olympics chapter for details.

Dosewallips State Park, less than a mile south of Brinnon, is likely the most popular campground on the canal. The park's 130 campsites (40 with hookups; maximum RV length, 60 feet) are situated in flat, grassy loops on the west side of US 101. There's not a huge amount of privacy between sites, but the cushy grass feels mighty nice under the backs of tent campers. A trail leads down to the beach, and 4 to 5 miles of trails wind through the shady upland area east of the park. The park often fills up in the summertime; reservations are a good idea. Dosewallips is open all year. Campsites can be reserved up to 11 months in advance by calling Reservations Northwest; (800) 452-5687. *On US 101, 1 mile south of Brinnon; (360) 796-4415 or (800) 233-0321.*

A short mountain-bike ride up the road is **Seal Rock Campground,** one of our favorite Forest Service camps. The park has 35 sites (no hookups; maximum RV length, 21 feet, although we've seen longer ones squeezed into the pullout waterfront sites), nicely spread through a wooded area just off Hood Canal. Sites are very private, and most have beautiful, sand-filled, perfectly level pads for pitching tents. A major bonus for tenters! The spaces down along the beachfront fill first. The rocky beach area (see Beaches, above) is a particular asset, as is the short boardwalk interpretive trail along the beach bluff. Seal Rock is open from mid-April to November. The park is fully wheelchair-accessible. Sites can be reserved by calling (360) 796-4886. *On US 101, 2 miles north of Brinnon; (360) 765-2200.*

Near Quilcene, **Falls View Campground,** another Olympic National Forest site, has 35 sites (5 with hookups; maximum RV length, 21 feet) in a nice wooded area, with the rushing Big Quilcene River below to lull you to sleep. A trail leads a short distance to the picturesque falls. The park is open from May to mid-September. Sites can be reserved by calling (360) 796-4886. *On US 101, 3.5 miles south of Quilcene; (360) 765-2200.*

Not far away is **Rainbow Campground,** which has nine primitive sites (no hookups; tents only), day-hiking trails, and some picnic facilities. The park is open all year. Individual campsites cannot be reserved, but the entire campground can be reserved for up to 50 people. Call (360) 796-4886. *On US 101, 5 miles south of Quilcene; (360) 765-2200.*

Bywater State Park, at the west end of the Hood Canal Floating Bridge, has 20 primitive campsites, but they're very exposed to wind, as well as Hwy 104 and boat-launch traffic. A nice day-use area, but last-resort-only for camping, unless you're in an RV.

For information on **Scenic Beach** and **Kitsap Memorial** State Parks, both on the Kitsap Peninsula side of Hood Canal, see the Kitsap Peninsula chapter.

Hiking

Although some of them can be downright frustrating to locate, many of Washington's finest mountain hikes are found in the valleys of rivers that drain east into Hood Canal. The North Fork Skokomish, Dosewallips, Hamma Hamma, Quilcene, and Duckabush drainages contain dozens of long trails, most of which begin in Olympic National Forest and continue into—and sometimes all the way through—Olympic National Park. For trip advice in the Hood Canal area, stop by the Hoodsport or Quilcene Ranger District offices. Also see the **Olympic National Forest and the East Slope Olympics** chapter, which contains extensive hiking information.

The Hood Canal lowlands have their own hiking charms, however. Most of the state parks listed above have at least several miles of wooded hiking trails, few of which receive heavy use. **Twanoh** and **Dosewallips** have particularly well developed trail systems (see Camping, above).

Want to sample the local forest environment without investing too much time (or logging too many Forest Service Road miles)? Try **Hoodsport Trail State Park** (easy/moderate; various distances), 3 miles west of Hoodsport on Lake Cushman Road. The state-protected forest has several miles of trails, open summers only. This is a good short-day-hike opportunity for campers at Potlatch State Park.

Hiking is perhaps more scenic along the canal's north end, however. From US 101 about 5.5 miles south of Quilcene, watch for signs for **Mount Walker Lookout** (difficult; 4 miles round trip) on the east side of the highway. In the summer, when the gated road is open, you can drive 5 miles to the top of this 2,750-foot hill, which offers sweeping views of Hood Canal, the eastern Olympics, and all the way east to Seattle and south to Mount Rainier. But a trail that runs up one side of the mountain is a fun, although lung-busting, hike. The road is a great thigh-burner of a **mountain bike** ride, especially when it's gated to traffic. As you wheeze, just keep thinking of the ride down.

Nearby **Rainbow Campground** (5 miles south of Quilcene on US 101) has a good leg-stretcher hiking trail that drops a half-mile to a waterfall in Rainbow Canyon on the Big Quilcene River. **Falls View Campground** (3.5 miles south of Quilcene on US 101) also offers short day-hiking trails. And a unique, wheelchair-accessible boardwalk nature trail runs along the beach in **Seal Rock Campground** (2 miles north of Brinnon on US 101).

Canoeing/Kayaking

Hood Canal is a surprisingly underutilized sea kayak playground. Day-use areas at the state parks listed above all have convenient launch sites. Keep in mind that most of these areas are desirable only during higher tides, particularly in the south end of the canal, where tidal fluctuation is extreme. Show up at low tide, and you're launching into an ocean of mud.

For much of the summer, canoeists will find the near-shore waters of Hood Canal calm enough for safe paddling. But all small-craft users should keep in mind that winds can whip up swiftly—and quite dramatically—in the canal. Don't venture too far from shore in an open craft, particularly if the weather is iffy. On those days, a good destination is **Dabob Bay,** near Seal Rock Campground south of Quilcene. It's usually protected from bad weather. But beware the submarines. This deep-water cove is one of the Navy's primary test areas for Trident ballistic subs. Also, keep in mind that nearly all beach areas inside the bay are private property. A good launch site is **Point Whitney Shellfish Lab,** which is marked on US 101.

Some other popular spots:

Mats Mats Bay, a small, protected waterway near Port Ludlow, is a favorite day trip and a good area for beginners. Follow Oak Bay and Verner Roads north from Port Ludlow to the public launch ramp on the bay.

Farther south, the **Hood Head** area, just north of the west end of the

Hood Canal Floating Bridge, includes a protected lagoon that's fun to explore during high tides. It's easy enough for beginners, as long as you stay in the calm waters south of Hood Head. Access is from **Bywater Bay State Park** (the road sign at the end of the bridge says "Shine Tidelands").

Quilcene Bay is a pleasant protected stretch of water. Launch at the ramp on Linger Longer Road. Paddlers who launch at **Dosewallips** or **Pleasant Harbor** State Parks can explore the shoreline between the two, as well as the protected cove inside Pleasant Harbor. Stronger paddlers can cross the canal (about 1.5 miles) for lunch at Scenic Beach State Park near Seabeck (see the Kitsap Peninsula chapter).

At the far south end of the canal, the **Skokomish River delta** is a popular exploring spot, with good launch sites at Potlatch State Park and the boat launch in Union.

Rental kayaks are available at Poulsbo's Olympic Outdoor Center (18971 Front Street; (360) 697-6095).

Fishing/Clamming/Oyster Picking

The clear, relatively clean waters of Hood Canal are rightly famous as an **oyster** producer with few equals. Oyster season on Hood Canal generally runs from September through May, but you'll need to check local seasons and restrictions. **Clams** can be dug on Hood Canal public tidelands any time of the year, but diggers should check the state Red Tide Hotline; (800) 562-5632. Good beaches include Potlatch State Park, Cushman Beach, Lilliwaup Tidelands, Pleasant Harbor State Park, Dosewallips State Park, and Seal Rock Campground.

The canal has waned significantly as a **salmon-fishing** spot. The recreational season here has become almost nonexistent, because of large-scale shutdowns ordered to protect troubled wild coho stocks. Some winter blackmouth are caught on early morning tide changes, but not as many as in Puget Sound. Sea-run cutthroat also are found here, but in declining numbers.

One exception is the popular beach fishery at the **Hoodsport Hatchery,** where anglers cast for incoming **chum** and **pink salmon** in the fall. (Pinks are in good supply during August and September of odd-numbered years only. Chum runs arrive every October.) These fish are very finicky, but a determined caster often can coax one to hit on a bright pink or chartreuse lure, spinner, or salmon fly, or just a plain black hook with a Day-Glo bobber and fluorescent yarn. Rules require single barbless hooks only. (Tip: Use lightweight, trout-size tackle in this ultra-clear water.) You're usually allowed to keep two of these fish, but many anglers voluntarily make this a catch-and-release event. The area around the hatchery is best fished with chest waders. And the crowds here can get out of control on weekends. You'll think you're in Alaska.

Another famous Hood Canal sea creature, the **shrimp,** is a prized prey in these waters. Shrimp in the canal's deeper spots—most notably the Dabob Bay area—are unusually large, plump, and tasty, and they've become highly sought-after delicacies. The shrimp season is short and sweet. It's usually in May, for about a week only, or until a state-determined shrimp quota has been met. Consult a local tackle shop such as Seabeck Marina, (360) 830-5179, for gear (a shrimp pot and float), a license (required), and bait (believe it or not, smelly fish-flavored canned cat food is the weapon of choice). Fishing tackle and supplies also are available at Cove Park Grocery near Brinnon, (360) 796-4723, and at other marinas along the canal. (See Boating, below.)

Boating/Sailing

Hood Canal's broad, generally smooth waters are a grand place for boaters, although a lack of well-developed support facilities seems to limit most marine traffic to locals only. **Pleasant Harbor State Park,** midway up the canal off US 101, is a favorite boater's destination. It offers good, protected moorage, with state park day-use facilities in the upland section. **Pleasant Harbor Marina,** (360) 796-4611, also has moorage, supplies, and bait and tackle. Across the canal, **Seabeck Marina,** (360) 830-5179, has rentals (bring your own motor) and fishing gear. **Hood Canal Marina** near Union, (360) 898-2252, also has a launch ramp and supplies. **Hoodsport Marina,** (360) 877-9657, has moorage and rest rooms. On the north end, **Quilcene Boathaven,** (360) 765-3131, has fuel, guest moorage, and supplies.

Other launch ramps are found at Potlatch State Park, Twanoh State Park, Belfair State Park, Triton Cove State Park, Allyn Dock, Union, Quilcene Bay, Bywater Bay State Park, Mats Mats Bay, Hoodsport, and Tahuya.

Wildlife

Believe it or not, **seals** often are seen off the beach at Seal Rock. Also **bald eagles.** Both species also are usually in good supply at other local beachfront sites, particularly the beach around Potlatch State Park.

A major state fish hatchery at Hoodsport affords a rather rare, up-close encounter with homecoming Hood Canal **salmon.** Runs of chinook, chum, and pink often can be seen splashing through a causeway into the hatchery during fall months. Keep your eyes open as you drive by: large numbers of pickups parked along the road usually indicate a run is underway, and fishermen will be lined up in the canal outside the hatchery. The hatchery is right on US 101 in Hoodsport.

outside **in**

Attractions

The **Union Country Store** (E 5130 Hwy 106; (360) 898-2461) offers wonderful carryout entrees (though servings may be heated up on the spot, to be devoured while casing this friendly store). A great variety of wines, and an interesting selection of groceries and produce. Shucked oysters may be purchased at **Hama Hama Oyster Company,** just before the Hamma Hamma River, (360) 877-5811; **Triton Cove Oyster Farms** near Brinnon, (360) 796-4360; and **Coast Oyster Company,** at the end of Linger Longer Road in Quilcene, (360) 765-3474. Call ahead to make sure they're open. **Hoodsport Winery,** about a mile south of its namesake town, will match its wine to your oysters; (360) 877-9894. The tasting room looks right out over the canal, and the tastable selections include a cabernet sauvignon, several white varietals, and some half-dozen fruit wines.

In rhody season the **Whitney Gardens** in Brinnon are blindingly beautiful, but a walk through the 6.8-acre gardens is delightful anytime, with azaleas, magnolias, evergreens, and maples—brilliant in fall. There's a small fee. The gardens are open every day, except in December and January when it's by appointment only; (360) 796-4411.

Near the Mount Walker (see Hiking, above) turnoff from US 101, the **Walker Mountain Trading Post** crams into a onetime pioneer home a variety of antiques, crafts, and locally made jewelry. A good place to grab a bite and buy some fresh seafood is **Hood Canal Seafood Marketplace and Brager's Barnacle Seafood & Chowder Bar,** 294963 Hwy 101; (360) 765-4880. Enjoy soup, a sandwich, and coffee on the glassed-in porch.

Quilcene has the world's largest oyster hatchery and, in its bay, what's said to be the purest salt water in the West. The venerable **Whistling Oyster Tavern** is where the sociable locals hang out. North of town, the **Olympic Music Festival** holds forth starting at 2pm on Saturdays and Sundays, June through Labor Day, in a turn-of-the-century barn turned concert hall. Listeners sit inside on hay bales or church pews, or outside on the grass. Picnics may be assembled from the well-stocked deli on the premises. The music is sublime, performed by the Philadelphia String

Quartet with guest artists from around the world (11 miles west of the Hood Canal Bridge on Hwy 104, then a quarter mile south from the Quilcene exit; (360) 728-6411).

Restaurants

Half-Way House Restaurant ☆   Brinnon is a town you can miss if you blink, but keep your eyes open for the Half-Way House, especially on Tuesday around dinnertime. That's the night that chef Joseph Day puts on a gourmet five-course champagne dinner. If you can't make it on Tuesday (the only night reservations are required), the food is still good, especially the homemade soups and pies. *On the west side of Hwy 101 in Brinnon next to post office; (360) 796-4715; 41 Brinnon Lane, Brinnon; $ ($$ on Tues).*

Timber House   The Timber House is surrounded by cedar and hemlock, and descriptive logging scenes are painted on the hand-carved tables and counterledges. Roast beef dinners, Quilcene oysters from right down the road, and other goodies from the waters around the Sound. *1/2-mile south of Quilcene on Hwy 101; (360) 765-3339; Hwy 101 S, Quilcene; $$.*

Victoria's at Robin Hood ☆☆   The stone-and-log structure on the east bank of Hood Canal has been a stopover spot since the early 1930s. Locals remember it as a lively dance hall and tavern, but in the last decade it has evolved into one of the better eateries on the Canal. *On Hwy 106, 1 mile west of Alderbrook Inn; (360) 898-4400; E 6791 Hwy 106, Union; $$.*

Lodgings

Inn at Ludlow Bay ☆☆   The Inn at Ludlow Bay guards the head of Hood Canal and is a place to go and be peaceful. The rooms themselves are mini-retreats. Erratic reports about service at the inn leave us slightly tentative, but the inn's restaurant is quietly becoming one of the better places to dine on the peninsula. *On west side, 5 miles north of Hood Canal Bridge; (360) 437-0411; One Heron Rd, Port Ludlow; $$$.*

Port Ludlow Golf & Meeting Retreat ☆☆   This popular resort facility caters especially to groups, with a marina, tennis courts, championship golf course, hiking and cycling trails, and year-round swimming pool on 1,500 acres. The individually decorated suites are very livable (stay away from the standard rooms). The Harbormaster Restaurant has a pleasant bar and a delightful deck. *On west side, 6 miles north of Hood Canal Bridge; (360) 437-2222; 200 Olympic Pl, Port Ludlow; $$$.*

Cheaper Sleeps

Mike's Beach Resort   An unassuming resort that offers an almost bewildering range of activities on Hood Canal. Lodgings are almost as varied: cabins sleeping one to four, a dormitory, a youth hostel, RV spaces, and campsites. *(360) 877-5324 or (800) 231-5324; N 38470 Hwy 101, Lilliwaup.*

More Information

Olympic National Forest, Hood Canal Ranger Station: *(360) 877-5254.*

Olympic National Forest, Quilcene Ranger Station: *(360) 765-3368.*

Shelton/Mason County Chamber of Commerce: *(360) 426-2021.*

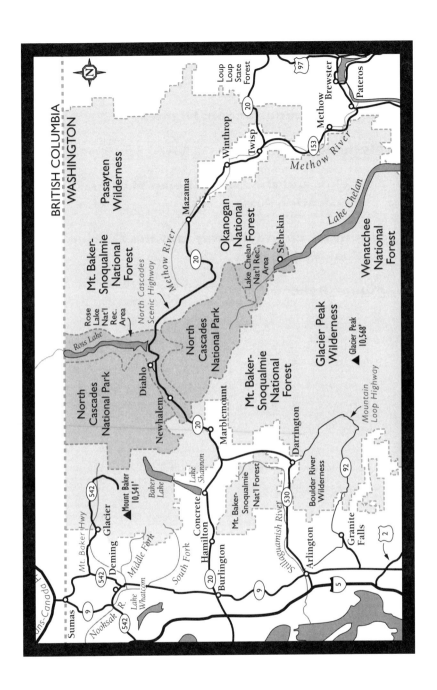

North Cascades

North
Cascades

North Cascades National Park: Overview

Nearly 700,000 acres of rugged, mostly unpopulated wilderness immediately south of the U.S.–Canadian border.

Follow the ice. That's a good general rule of thumb if you're looking for the wildest mountain lands in Washington. And it's particularly appropriate in the North Cascades National Park region, which contains the greatest collection of nature-cut crystal in the Lower 48 states. About 600 active glaciers are found in the United States outside Alaska, and more than half—318—are inside North Cascades National Park. The park, which includes the connected Ross Lake and Lake Chelan National Recreation Areas, is 684,500 acres of the wildest, roughest, and most inspiring mountain valleys in the country.

Like its wild state cousin to the west, Olympic National Park, North Cascades was explored late in the local history of white settlers. The North Cascade range wasn't crossed by early trekkers until 1814, when an exploring party crossed Cascade Pass, following a route used for centuries by Native Americans. Development, such as it was, didn't hit the area until the late 19th century, when gold, lead, zinc, and other minerals drew miners high into the mountain valleys, where they left traces still evident today. When the claims petered out, so did the human presence in the North Cascades—at least until the 1920s, when visionary City of Seattle engineer James Delmage Ross oversaw construction of the first of three Upper Skagit River dams, which continue to light the city today.

The hydropower project—an engineering marvel then and now—put a permanent group of residents in the upper Skagit, and tourists followed. The raw, craggy peaks, stunning alpine valleys, and sprawling glaciers in the area caught the eye of the 1920s and '30s adventuresome set, and much peak-bagging followed. In spite of frequent climbing treks, the North Cascades' interior peaks are so numerous and inaccessible that many were never scaled until 20 to 40 years later—an inordinate number of them by legendary Washington climber Fred Beckey, whose *Cascade Alpine Guide* series remains the region's climbing bible.

As is often the case in the mountains, where climbers led, hikers followed. Lots of them. Thanks in no small part to these backcountry pioneers, including prolific Washington guidebook author Harvey Manning, the North Cascades won national park status in 1968. Succeeding generations have trekked into the fantastic alpine terrain ever since, harvesting the fruit of these conservationists' indefatigable efforts.

Do the same yourself, and be prepared to be overwhelmed. The North Cascades is, with little argument, the wildest single place left in the Northwest, if not the United States. Ninety-two percent of its lands are designated wilderness, meaning only feet and the occasional hoof ever mar its surface. But impressive as it is, the park is but a portion of the larger wilderness picture here. It is surrounded by other protected lands: the Mount Baker and Noisy-Diobsud wilderness areas to the west, the Glacier Peak Wilderness to the south, and the Pasayten and Lake Chelan–Sawtooth Wilderness areas to the east. It's an impressive package, one that could consume a lifetime of exploration.

Around Puget Sound, many of us have pledged large amounts of our free time to that very pursuit. In the spring, we hike and camp in the Ross Lake Valley, admiring the all-around mountain view, gulping down the clean air. In the summer, we lumber, curse, and grin our way high into the backcountry to stunning, wildflower-splashed vistas atop Desolation Peak, Cascade Pass, or Devil's Dome, rub our sore feet, and count our blessings. In the fall, we sneak out of the office at noon and drive the North Cascades Scenic Highway, past golden larches and blue skies, to a waiting bed or campsite in the Methow Valley. If we're feeling lucky, we call in well the following Monday, hop the boat up to Stehekin, walk into the backcountry, and take a world-class nap beneath the butterflies.

And all around, all year long, the glaciers are grinding away, beckoning, gleaming in some of the most memorable mountain vistas we've found, proving a universal mountain truth: for all its flaws and crevasses, ice is in good taste. A taste easily acquired.

Getting There

Only three main access routes lead into the wild backcountry of North Cascades National Park. The most heavily used is Hwy 20, a wagon-path-turned-two-lane-highway that cuts through the mountains between Mount Vernon in the Skagit Valley and Winthrop in the Methow Valley. Primary national park hiking trails, campgrounds and scenic vistas are reached via this highway, which closes between Ross Lake and Early Winters between November and April due to heavy snows. See the North Cascades Scenic Highway chapter for full details.

A popular alternate access is by tour boat or private boat to Stehekin, a mountain outpost at the north tip of Lake Chelan. Stehekin, reached by driving US 2 and US 97 to Chelan, then catching a boat up the lake, isn't actually in North Cascades National Park. But the Stehekin Valley Road, which cuts west from Stehekin into the mountains, deposits hikers, cyclists, and campers at a string of remote trailheads and campgrounds inside the park's southern sector. See the Stehekin and Lake Chelan chapter for details.

The only other road into the park is the uneven, rocky Cascade River Road, which leaves Hwy 20 at Marblemount and penetrates 22 miles into the park's southern quadrant. From here, many hikers climb to Cascade Pass and drop down into the Stehekin Valley, linking with the Stehekin Valley Road, a park shuttle bus, and ultimately, Stehekin Landing on Lake Chelan. The walk across Cascade Pass is about 9 miles.

Another foot route into the park, from the Hannegan area east of Mount Baker, is the trail over Whatcom Pass through the high country west of Ross Lake.

Adjoining Areas

Portions of North Cascades National Park are described in each chapter of the North Cascades section.

Hiking/Backpacking

Without question, the best way to witness the wonders of North Cascades National Park is by hoofing it. The vast majority of rugged territory inside the park is reached only by trail, and some of it is reached only by scrambling off the trail for many miles. Park experts at the North Cascades Visitors Center in Sedro Woolley, (360) 856-5700, can advise you on suitable hikes. Two **trail guides** also will serve you well here. The definitive work is *100 Hikes in Washington's North Cascades National Park Region*, by Ira Spring and Harvey Manning (The Mountaineers). *Pacific Northwest Hiking*, by Ron C. Judd and Dan A. Nelson (Foghorn Press), also contains descriptions of most popular North Cascades hikes, as well as dozens more in the surrounding Glacier Peak and Pasayten Wilderness areas. For a quick list of our favorite North Cascades hikes from Hwy 20 and the Stehekin area, consult the North Cascades Scenic Highway and the Stehekin and Lake Chelan chapters in this guide.

During many times of the year, your hiking choices will be dictated by **weather.** Although some lower-elevation trails (notably those in river valleys) are snow-free by June, many of this area's most popular hiking destinations are off-limits until July or later. The North Cascades receive unusually heavy amounts of snow, and Hwy 20 doesn't open until April or early May. Some alpine areas in the heart of the park don't melt out until late summer, if at all.

North Cascades hikers should be prepared for bad weather, any time of the year. And backpackers bound for high-mountain passes above 6,500 feet should pack an ice ax and know how to use it for snowfield crossings, for most of the summer. If you're unsure whether your chosen trail will require snow crossings, consult a park official at one of the visitors centers listed below. *Never* attempt to cross a steep snowfield without proper training and equipment. This mistake claims several lives in the Cascade high country every summer.

A word about rules. Like Olympic National Park, many trails in the North Cascades National Park area will pass through as many as three federal land-use jurisdictions: national park, wilderness area, and/or national recreation area. **Backcountry permits,** free and available at all park visitors centers and most trailheads, are required for all overnight stays inside the national park. Limited numbers are available for some of the more popular backcountry destinations, including the Pelton Basin and Sahale areas of Cascade Pass; Thornton and Monogram Lakes, Boston Basin; Copper Ridge; and the Sulphide Glacier climbing route on the south side of Mount Baker. Overnight permits are not required in the adjacent Glacier Peak and Pasayten Wilderness areas, but **group size** and **stock-use limits** and other special restrictions apply there. Permits are not required for **day hiking** in any portion of the national park, national recreation area, or wilderness areas.

Other considerations: **Group size** is limited to 12 living beings (people and stock) throughout much of the area; 6 beings in others. **Leashed dogs** are allowed only in campgrounds (note: on leashes here as well) and on trails in the Ross Lake and Lake Chelan National Recreation Areas. One exception is the Pacific Crest Trail, which cuts through the southern sector of the park. **Mountain bikes** are forbidden on all wilderness and national park trails, but allowed in the national recreation area (but not on all trails). **Hunting** and **firearms** are forbidden in the park, but allowed according to state seasons in the national recreation areas. Confused? Employ the fail-safe method: Ask someone in a position to have the answers.

Scenic Drives

Probably 90 percent of visitors to North Cascades National Park see most of it by car. Only one paved road ventures into the park. But it just happens to be one of the most magnificent in the state. The **North Cascades Scenic Highway**, a.k.a. Hwy 20, leaves Interstate 5 north of Mount Vernon and follows the Skagit River upstream through a steep, rocky gorge, culminating in the City of Seattle's extensive upper Skagit hydropower development. Guided tours of the area by railway and tour boat are conducted daily in summer by city crews. They're well worth the time, and a great introduction to the North Cascades ecosystem. (See the North Cascades Scenic Highway chapter for details). From there, Hwy 20 climbs into the heart of the North Cascades, past 24-mile-long Ross Lake, the reservoir behind Ross Dam, and through mile after mile of inspiring mountain scenery. Notable pullouts are found at Rainy Pass and Washington Pass, where short trails lead to spectacular scenic vistas, with views you'd normally expect to see only at the end of a long, arduous hike. The highway then drops dramatically into the high, dry terrain of Mazama and the Methow River Valley at Winthrop.

That entire route can be driven easily in one day from Seattle, although doing so will leave little time to explore the high country on one or more of the many excellent day-hiking trails. Many Puget Sound area visitors make this a weekend trip, either camping in one of the park's campgrounds or picking from the many overnight spots in Winthrop. Hwy 20 is closed between Ross Lake and Early Winters from November to April or May. But in the summer, it makes a great northern leg on a two- or three-day **Cascade Loop**. To make the full circle, drive north on I-5 to Hwy 20, travel east through the Methow Valley to its confluence with the Columbia at Pateros, then follow US 97 south to Wenatchee, and return west via either Hwy 2 (Stevens Pass) or US 97 (Swauk and Blewett Passes) and Interstate 90. The loop is particularly popular in the fall, when slopes burst with colors both on Hwy 20 and, especially, US 2.

Camping

The park has a number of good campsites along the Hwy 20 access route, and a wealth of nice, though primitive, walk- or shuttle-in backcountry camps in the Stehekin area. See the chapters on North Cascades Scenic Highway and Stehekin and Lake Chelan for details.

Wildlife

The North Cascades are a rich wildlife environment, and the full range of typical Cascade wild animals are found here: **black bears, coyote, cougars, bobcats, deer, elk, mountain goats,** and dozens of other, smaller species, most of which will crawl into your tent if you're not careful. The difference here is that they're more dispersed, and rarely visible from established viewing sites. Wildlife viewing up here is more by happenstance—usually on trails—than by careful planning.

The park's two most highly publicized creatures—northern gray wolves and the fabled grizzly bear—are rarely, if ever, seen. The U.S. Fish and Wildlife Service and the state Department of Fish and Wildlife have tracked one small family of **wolves** in the Hozomeen area, at the north end of Ross Lake near the Canadian border. Few wolf sightings have been reported by hikers in North Cascades backcountry. But biologists know wolves pass through the Cascades, whether or not they take up permanent residence there: reliable wolf sightings farther south in the Cascades have verified this. Park officials believe—and hope—that Canadian wolves will repopulate this former hunting territory. If you see one in the high country, give it a wide berth—and consider yourself very, very lucky.

Grizzly bears are yet more elusive. Even people charged with setting out for weeks at a time to find one have consistently come home empty-handed. Bear scat and fur found in some high, remote backcountry areas suggest the big carnivores do tour through the park—or at least have—probably on their way to or from permanent homes in British Columbia. But no hiker has come back with a grizzly photograph, and no qualified observer has yet seen one in the North Cascades. That could change before the turn of the century. The U.S. Fish and Wildlife Service continues to mull plans to reintroduce the majestic beasts to the North Cascades, a former habitat. The plan has prompted a mixed reaction from backcountry users. But many North Cascades aficionados are excited at the prospect. They point out that grizzlies in the North Cascades would have much more isolated terrain in which to roam, play, and reproduce than do other Lower 48 populations in national parks such as Glacier in Montana.

Stay tuned—and keep practicing good bear-country safety techniques, such as making plenty of noise out on the trail, cooking a considerable distance from your tent, and hanging all food and cooking supplies on a bear wire. Some North Cascades veterans would love to see a grizzly someday. But preferably not inside their tent vestibule.

A final wildlife note: Many people are surprised to learn that the park's critter list includes a squirmy one—the **rattlesnake**. They're not common, but rattlers are occasionally seen along trails and roads in the Stehekin Valley. Keep eyes and ears open.

Other Activities

Trout fishing is a favorite summertime activity in many of the park's lakes, most notably Ross Lake, Diablo Lake, and Gorge Lake in the Ross Lake National Recreation Area. Good trout fishing also is found on the Stehekin River and at Domke Lake in the Stehekin area. **River rafting** is a popular spring and summer activity on the upper Skagit River, below Newhalem. **Mountain biking** is a great way to see the Stehekin River Valley, thanks to the 22-mile Stehekin River Road. Mountain bikes are forbidden on nearly all trails in this area, however. See the North Cascades Scenic Highway chapter and the Stehekin and Lake Chelan chapter for details.

Restaurants/Lodgings

Lodging and food are minimal inside the park. See suggestions in the following North Cascades Scenic Highway and Stehekin and the Lake Chelan NRA chapters.

More Information

North Cascades National Park Headquarters/Visitors Center, Sedro Woolley: *(360) 856-5700.*

North Cascades Visitors Center, Newhalem: *(360) 386-4495.*

Wilderness District Office/Ranger Station, Marblemount (May through September): *(360) 873-4500.*

Glacier Public Service Center (summer only): *(800) 627-0062 or (360) 599-2714.*

Golden West Visitors Center, Stehekin: *(360) 856-5703.*

Stehekin Ranger Station: *(360) 856-5700, ext. 340.*

North Cascades Scenic Highway

From Sedro Woolley east to Washington Pass, north to Hozomeen at the Canadian border, and south to Cascade Pass in North Cascades National Park, including the Skagit River Valley, Baker and Shannon Lakes, Diablo and Ross Lakes, Rockport State Park, Colonial Creek Campground, and Rainy and Washington Passes.

The howl of the wolf and the grunt of the grizzly don't sound at all out of place in Washington's North Cascades. Both creatures, previously believed to be extinct, are now thought to be reinhabiting this raw wilderness, one of the wildest expanses of glaciated peaks in the Lower 48 states. Wolves have been seen and heard in the heart of this region, near Hozomeen Campground along the Canadian border. The griz have been more circumspect, leaving only small evidence of their incursions into Washington, probably on foraging commutes from the Cascades of British Columbia.

Seeing or hearing either one in the North Cascades would send a chill up your spine—either out of fear, respect, or both. But it could hardly be considered surprising. If there's one mountain region left in the United States that looks, smells, and feels like wild carnivore habitat, this is it. The North Cascades—divided into a national park, two national recreation areas, two Forest Service Districts, and a large, remote wilderness—are big, bad, beautiful—and mostly untouched. Major exceptions come to mind, of course, such as the occasional abandoned mine shaft. And, most prominently, the City of Seattle's massive—almost mind-boggling—Skagit River hydropower project, which dammed the upper Skagit River, creating a valley-filling backwater, Ross Lake, that stretches north all the way into Canada.

The most amazing thing about this man-made foothold in the North Cascades wilderness is not so much what it's done to the environment. It's how the environment's raw power accommodates it all with little more than a shrug. One of the most impressive construction projects in the history of the Northwest almost gets lost up here. *That's* how awesome the North Cascades appear, particularly to visitors who venture out into the backcountry.

Hwy 20, the only major road in the area, provides a drive-through tour of all the best and worst of this majesty. From Mount Vernon, the highway leads up through the broad, fertile valley to a well-developed recreation area, Baker and Shannon Lakes (also the result of hydro handiwork, this time by Puget Power), then twists and turns along the upper Skagit's narrow gorge to Rockport, Marblemount, Newhalem, and Diablo, the latter two rare examples of true "company towns" constructed for and by Seattle City Light crews building and maintaining Ross and Diablo Dams.

Viewing the massive hydro project from above brings mixed emotions. It's sad to see this river—one of the mightiest in the Northwest before its damming in the early 1920s—blocked by concrete. It's sad to see salmon stacked up below the Gorge Powerhouse in Newhalem, waiting in vain for the water to rise enough to allow their passage to the upper river. Old genes die long, slow, painful deaths.

But it's also a thrill to realize even such a heavily altered area can remain so uniquely wild. The truth is that the power project here (aside from providing a century of cheap power, some of which produced this book and a billion other conveniences) opened an otherwise walled-off treasure trove to Washington recreators. If not for a handful of early City Light engineers with big plans, most of us likely would never witness the unforgettable view from the top of Desolation Peak, encounter a family of black bears beneath Devil's Dome, or watch in wonder as a glacier slowly carves away the face of Johannesburg Mountain. Those who take the time to study the area's early history will be impressed by the degree to which this area's sheer beauty turned its original human conquerors—the hydro crews—into its most ardent defenders, its most vigorous promoters.

Now as then, the North Cascades get under your skin. And there they stay. No area in the Northwest—and probably in the country—is as wild as this. As Hwy 20 crosses the Cascade Crest and proceeds east, all other signs of human presence disappear. Animals outnumber drivers. The nat-

ural order here is as natural, and orderly, as it gets. Whether your visit is
a short day trip to watch bald eagles feed on the Upper Skagit or a month-
long cross-country trek around, beside, and over countless 8,000-foot
glaciated peaks, it likely will create a yearning for another.

The cure is simple: pick a trail, forge ahead, and keep your ears open.
That grunt or howl you hear might be a wandering carnivore—or just
another backcountry pilgrim with too big a load. Either way, it's a cry of
freedom.

Getting There

*The North Cascades Scenic Highway (Hwy 20) turns east from I-5 at exit 230
near Mount Vernon, 63 miles north of Seattle. To reach the Baker Lake and
Shannon Lake area, continue to Baker Lake Road (Forest Service Road 11),
about 14 miles east of Sedro Woolley, which leads north to the lake. Other
recreation sites in this chapter are farther east along Hwy 20, which continues over Rainy and Washington Passes to Mazama and ultimately the Methow
Valley. Note: Hwy 20 is closed between Marblemount and Mazama from
November through April.*

Adjoining Areas

NORTH: **Mount Baker Highway**
SOUTH: **Mountain Loop Highway and the Glacier Peak Wilderness**
EAST: **Methow Valley**
WEST: **Skagit Valley**

inside out

Hiking/Backpacking

Hiking trails are so numerous—and so remarkable—in this area, we can
only hit the highlights here. For full trail information, we strongly suggest
a stop at the National Forest and National Park visitors center in Sedro
Woolley, (360) 856-5700, or the North Cascades National Park Visitors
Center at Newhalem, (206) 386-4495. Both are along Hwy 20. Remember
that overnight permits, free and available at ranger stations and trailheads,
are required for North Cascades National Park trails. No permits are
needed for surrounding National Forest or Ross Lake National Recreation
Area trails.

What follows is a list of perennial favorites, beginning in the Baker
Lake and south slope Mount Baker area in the North Cascade foothills
north of Concrete and heading east, concluding at trailheads at or near

Washington Pass, at the Cascade Crest. This emphasis is on day hikes, although the most popular backpack routes are included.

Baker Lake and south slope Mount Baker

An easy hike along a chain of lakes in the shadow of the mountain culminates at **Elbow Lake** (easy; 7 miles round trip), where fishing can be good for trout. The trailhead for this trail system, which includes a dozen miles of other trails to lakes in the Middle Fork Nooksack drainage, can be reached from the north or south, via Forest Service Road 38 or Forest Service Road 12. Another good day hike for Baker Lake campers is the **Baker River Trail** (easy; 6 miles round trip), which winds through a rain forest environment along the river to **Sulphide Camp** in North Cascades National Park. Follow signs to Trail 606 from Forest Service Road 1168 at the north end of Baker Lake.

High above in the same area, two trail systems climb to fantastic alpine territory on the south slopes of Baker. The **Park Butte Trail** (difficult; 7 miles round trip) is a walk into alpine heaven, climbing 2,250 feet through beautiful mountain parklands filled with wildflowers and backed by wonderful mountain views. The trail culminates at Park Butte Lookout, 5,450 feet. But surrounding areas, such as the adjacent Mazama Park and the nearby rugged Sulphur Moraine (accessible from a connecting path, the Scott Paul Trail), are worth a day's exploring on their own. Also from Park Butte Trail, a connecting path leads up the **"Railroad Grade"** (actually a glacial moraine) to the tip of the Easton Glacier, at about 7,000 feet. This is a primary Mount Baker summit route. Campsites in **Morovitz Meadows,** about midway up the trail, make a good base camp for mountainside exploration. The trailhead is on Forest Service Road 13, reached by turning north from Hwy 20 on Baker Lake Road, about 14 miles east of Sedro Woolley.

Just to the west, another spectacular alpine route is the **Cathedral Pass and Mazama Park Trail** (moderate/difficult; 10 miles round trip), which is an alternate route into the same high-country glacial meadow area reached via the Park Butte Trail. Good campsites are found in beautiful Mazama Park. Buggy in summer, this hike is at its best in early fall. The trailhead is on Forest Service Road 12, also reached from the Baker Lake Road.

Near Baker Lake itself, try the newly expanded **East Bank Baker Lake Trail** (easy; up to 12 miles round trip), which runs along the shore of this scenic reservoir to Maple Grove Camp (see Camping, below), offering nice Mount Baker views. This is a good cross-country ski route in the winter. The trailhead is near Upper Baker Dam, on Forest Service Road 1107.

Three other good routes are within a short drive of Baker Lake campgrounds. On the lake's west shore, along Baker Lake Road, look for the **Shadow of the Sentinels Nature Trail** (easy; .5 mile round trip), a nice, family-friendly loop through one of this heavily manhandled valley's last stands of old-growth Douglas fir. (Note: In 1996, strong winds brought down some of the old-growth trees on the Shadow of the Sentinels trail, blocking the path in places. Call (360) 856-5700 for repair updates.) A good day hike from Rockport State Park is the **Sauk Mountain Trail** (moderate; 4.2 miles round trip), which climbs gradually to a 5,537-foot viewpoint (try it in late spring, when wildflowers are in bloom). Another good family hike is the trail to **Watson Lakes** (easy; 5 miles round trip), a nice summer walk to a string of alpine lakes below Anderson Butte in the Noisy-Diobsud Wilderness. The trailhead is on Forest Service Road 1107-22, east of Baker Lake.

Marblemount area

Cascade Road, which leaves Hwy 20 at Marblemount and winds 22 rough (no RVs) miles into the southern district of North Cascades National Park, gets heavy traffic in the summer, and most people are headed for the same place. The **Cascade Pass Trail** (difficult; 7.4 miles round trip) is widely considered one of the top day hikes in the North Cascades. Hard to argue with that assessment. From the steep trail's 5,400-foot summit, you'll make eye contact with magnificent, 8,065-foot **Johannesburg Mountain,** whose front face contains a very active hanging glacier, that often spits chunks into the valley below. The only drawback here is the crowds. How many other alpine day hikes end at a viewpoint with its own composting toilet? Sidetrips from the summit provide refuge for solitude seekers. They include the spectacular ridge walk up **Sahale Arm** to the **Sahale Glacier,** a trek to **Doubtful Lake,** the ridge walk south to **Mixup Peak,** and a trail northeast to lovely **Horseshoe Basin.** Through hikers can venture east 9 miles (from the Cascade Pass Trailhead) down the upper Stehekin River valley to **Cottonwood Campground,** at the end of the road leading to **Stehekin** on Lake Chelan (see the Stehekin and Lake Chelan chapter). Note: No camping is allowed at Cascade Pass.

Newhalem area

Just west of Newhalem on rocky Thornton Creek Road is the **Thornton Lakes Trail** (moderate/difficult; 10.6 miles round trip), a popular walk to some nice alpine lakes (snowed-in until late summer). Closer to Newhalem itself, take the kids to the **Trail of the Cedars Interpretive Loop** (easy; 1/3 mile round trip) or the **Newhalem Campground Loop** (easy; .5 mile round trip). Or better yet, stop on the edge of town at the Gorge Powerhouse, cross the footbridge, and embark on a fascinating historical/natural journey to **Ladder Creek Falls** (easy; .5 mile round trip), a fascinating rock garden built in the early 1920s by J. D. Ross, Seattle City Light's first superintendent. The falls themselves are a graceful showstopper.

Diablo area

Day trippers who arrive early for the Diablo ferry can stretch their legs on the **Stetattle Creek Trail** (easy; 7 miles round trip), a nice forest walk that begins near the Stetattle Creek bridge in Diablo. Near the tugboat pickup dock itself, the **Diablo Lake Trail** (easy; 7.6 miles round trip) climbs at a leisurely pace above the aqua-green lake and meanders east to Ross Dam. Consider making this a one-way trip by taking the tugboat up the lake, then walking back. See Attractions, below, for boat schedule information. For a climb that will test anyone's mettle, set out from "downtown" Diablo on the **Sourdough Mountain Trail** (difficult; 7 miles round trip), which climbs nearly 4,000 feet to the site of an antenna tower with sweeping views of the Upper Skagit Valley. The trailhead is behind the Diablo swimming pool.

Nearby, along Hwy 20 between Diablo and Colonial Creek Campground, look for the **Pyramid Lake** (difficult; 4.2 miles round trip) pullout parking area on the north side of the road, with the trail on the south side. The trail leads very steeply up to the picturesque lake, set below aptly named Pyramid Peak, 7,182 feet. No camping is allowed at the lake. Watch for climbers on Pyramid Peak and nearby Colonial Peak.

Up the road at Colonial Creek Campground, the **Thunder Creek Trail** (moderate; 12 miles round trip) is a main hiker's thoroughfare in this area, following the creek south all the way to the **Cascade River** drainage. Day hikers and overnight backpackers use the lower portion only, cruising along Diablo Lake's Thunder Arm and passing through the cool, green forest to McAlester Camp, 6 miles in. Long-distance trekkers continue on to connecting trails to **Easy Pass,** spectacular (and highly popular) **Fourth of July Pass** (difficult; 10.5 miles round trip), or **Park Creek Pass** (difficult; 39 miles round trip), which serves as another trail entrance to the Stehekin area. Consult a trail map to consider the many loop-trip backpacking possibilities off this trail, which begins near the Colonial Creek Campground amphitheater.

Ross Lake

The giant reservoir cradled beneath stunning mountain peaks behind Ross Dam is one of Washington's most impressive wild areas. It's also one of the least accessible. To reach most of the wondrous lakeside campgrounds and trail systems on either side of this amazing Skagit River reservoir, you must take a boat (rentals and water-taxi drop-off are available through Ross Lake Resort; (206) 386-4437; see Boating, below) or do it the old-fashioned way: walk. The shortest route is the **Ross Dam Trail** (moderate; 5 miles round trip), which drops from a trailhead near mile-post 134 to a small landing near Ross Dam. From here, you can cross the dam and continue 1.5 miles to Ross Lake Resort, where rental boats are available. Some hardy hikers carry kayaks in via this route, but heavy gear is best brought in by packing it onto the Diablo Lake tug (see Attractions, below), which stops at the foot of Ross Dam, then arranging for a truck pickup and portage (also contact Ross Lake Resort) from lower Ross Dam to the lake on the other side.

If you're boating up the lake, consider one of North Cascade National Park's classic backpack loops: the **Big Beaver and Little Beaver Loop** (difficult; 28.2 miles round trip; allow 4 to 5 days). The best way to get here is to arrange a water-taxi drop-off at Little Beaver Camp trailhead, about 10 miles up the lake. You can also hike the Ross Dam Trail over the dam and about 6 miles up the lake's shore to Big Beaver Trailhead and hike the loop in the other direction, arranging for a water-taxi pickup at Little Beaver. Either way, the route is challenging (trail maintenance is rare) but unforgettable, with awesome mountain views, 1,000-year-old western red cedars, and plentiful wildlife (black bears are common). You can also follow either the Big Beaver or Little Beaver Trails west to Whatcom Pass, for a one-way traverse with an exit near Mount Baker (see Whatcom/Hannegan Pass, in Hiking in the Mount Baker Highway chapter).

Some of the North Cascades' most memorable hiking awaits on the east shore of the lake. The **East Bank Ross Lake Trail** (moderate; 31 miles one way; allow 4 to 5 days) is a Northwest classic, winding along the reservoir through a series of beautiful lakefront camps. You can design a backpack trip of any length on this trail by arranging for a boat pickup at one of the campsites, most of which are equipped with docks. But to do it right, consider walking the entire length, hitting midway showstopper highlights such as **Desolation Peak** on your way to the destination, Hozomeen Campground, where you can arrange a boat pickup or a car pickup by a very, very nice friend who drove all the way through southern British Columbia just to get you. To reach the East Bank Trail, hike the Panther Creek trail (the trailhead is near Panther Creek Bridge, near milepost 138 on Hwy 20) about 3 miles to its junction with the East Bank Trail. Consult a map and go wild with this one. (See note on lake level fluctuations under Boating below.)

If that sounds a bit too time consuming, you can sample the best of the region by hiking the **Desolation Peak Trail** (difficult; 9.4 miles round trip). It's possible to hike to the Desolation Trailhead by walking 18 miles in from Hwy 20 via the Panther Creek and East Bank Ross Lake Trails. But most people make this a weekend trip by arranging a water-taxi ride to Desolation Landing or lakefront Lightning Creek Campground, then making the steep (4,400 vertical feet in less than 5 miles) hike to the top from a base camp at Lightning Creek or Desolation Camp (3.75 miles up the trail). Note that starting at Lightning Creek Campground adds about 4 miles to the round-trip hike, but provides a more convenient camping base for a weekend trip. Whichever route you choose, the summit is truly spectacular, with Ross Lake at your feet, wildflowers all around, and jagged Hozomeen Mountain (8,066 feet), Jack Mountain (9,066 feet), and its Nohokomeen Glacier in your face. At the meadow top is a fire look-out, occupied in 1956 by a then-unknown seasonal worker named Jack Kerouac. His stay here is described in his later beat-generation classic, *Desolation Angels*.

Other classic North Cascades backpack loops lead from the Ross Lake area into the Pasayten Wilderness to the northeast. The **Devil's Dome Loop** (very difficult; 41 miles round trip; allow 8 days) is one of the most spectacular. Study your maps and eat your Wheaties for this one. For more Pasayten Wilderness backpack adventures, see the Methow Valley chapter.

Upper Highway 20/day hikes

On the south side of the highway in the eastern North Cascades high country is one of the more spectacular day hikes in the state. **Easy Pass** (difficult; 7.2 miles round trip) really isn't, whether you go in via the long route (20 miles from Colonial Creek Campground via the Thunder Creek Trail) or the short (3.6 miles from Hwy 20 on the east side). But it's worth it. If you have steely thighs, don't mind company, and want to do *the* North Cascades day hike, this is probably the one. Views at the 6,500-foot pass are stupendous, particularly in the fall, when larch trees paint the rocky slopes gold. Wildlife is plentiful (the last known grizzly bear in Washington state was shot not far from here in 1968), water is scarce. Be prepared for snow in the upper reaches well into summer. The trailhead is about 22 miles east of Colonial Creek.

A similarly popular hike with dual access is **Fourth of July Pass,** which can be reached via the Thunder Creek Trail (see above) or via the Panther Creek Trail, from a trailhead 8 miles east on Hwy 20 (near milepost 138). The latter route is longer (11.5 miles round trip; difficult), but more direct. But many people do both by hiking the entire route as a 10.5-mile, one-way through hike.

Another good day hike, this one easier, is **Lake Ann and Maple Pass** (easy/moderate; 6.2 miles round trip), which gives you the choice of lounging at a pleasant lake (Lake Ann, stocked with cutthroat trout) or continuing 2 miles up the trail to superb views at Maple Pass, elevation 6,800 feet. The trailhead is in the Rainy Pass south parking lot. From the same spot, this highway's most heavily traveled path, the **Rainy Lake Nature Trail** (easy; 1.8 miles round trip) is a wheelchair-accessible path to a beautiful lakeside picnic spot, with views across the water of the Lyall Glacier and a nearby waterfall. Also from Rainy Pass, a popular day hike leads up the Pacific Crest Trail to **Cutthroat Pass** (moderate; 8 miles round trip).

Finally, another short-but-sweet walk is the **Washington Pass Overlook** (easy; .5 mile round trip), a paved path offering a close-up look at Liberty Bell Peak, Silver Star Peak, the Wine Spires, and Early Winter Spires. Perhaps nowhere else in the state is the dramatic difference between eastside and westside climates so evident from a single viewpoint. Watch for signs along Hwy 20.

Camping

In the Baker Lake area any of the six National Forest campgrounds are worth visiting:

Horseshoe Cove has 8 tent sites and 34 RV sites (no hookups; maximum RV length, 35 feet). It's open from May to October, and has this area's best swimming beach. Sites can be reserved by calling (800) 280-CAMP. *Hwy 20 to Birdsview, north on Baker Lake Road to Forest Service Road 1118; (360) 856-5700.*

Panorama Point has 16 sites (no hookups; maximum RV length, 21 feet). It's open from mid-May to mid-September. Sites can be reserved by calling (800) 280-CAMP. *Hwy 20 to Birdsview, north on Baker Lake Road to Forest Service Road 1144; (360) 856-5700.*

Park Creek has 12 sites (no hookups; maximum RV length, 15 feet). It's open from mid-May to mid-September. Sites cannot be reserved. *Hwy 20 to Birdsview, north on Baker Lake Road to Forest Service Road 1144; (360) 856-5700.*

Shannon Creek at the far north end of the lake on Baker Lake Road is a primitive site with 2 tent sites and 20 RV sites (no hookups), and **Maple Grove** is a paddle- or walk-in site on the east side of the lake, with 6 campsites along the East Bank Baker Lake Trail (see Hiking/Backpacking, above). It's free. **Boulder Creek,** 1 mile west of the lake on Baker Lake Road, has 10 tent sites and no drinking water or fees; *(360) 856-5700.*

Farther east along Hwy 20, **Rockport State Park** has 61 sites (50 with hookups; maximum RV length, 60 feet) amid a beautiful old-growth Douglas fir forest. Good hiking is available on the premises, with a wheelchair-accessible Skagit River view trail and a trail at nearby Sauk Mountain (see Hiking/Backpacking, above). It's a short walk from here to the banks of the Skagit, where bald eagles can be viewed in winter months. With its equally nice picnic facilities and group camp, this is one of the most pleasant campgrounds in the area. Hikers note: Showers! The park is open from April to late October. Campsites cannot be reserved. *North of Hwy 20 near Rockport, 9 mi east of Concrete; (360) 853-8461 or (800) 233-0321.*

In Rockport proper, if there is such a thing, is **Howard Miller Steelhead Park,** a city campground with 100 sites (60 with hookups; no maximum RV length). The park, near the confluence of the Skagit and Sauk Rivers, is open all year and popular with steelheaders and eagle-watchers in the winter. *Near the Hwy 20 and Rockport-Darrington Road junction; (360) 853-8808.*

Continuing east, Cascade Road leaves Hwy 20 at Marblemount and leads to three remote campgrounds. **Cascade Island,** a Department of Natural Resources camp, has 15 sites (no hookups), no fees, and is open all year; *(360) 902-1000.* The next two campgrounds are National Forest camps. **Marble Creek** has 23 sites (no hookups; maximum RV length, 31 feet), with no piped water and no fees. It's open from mid-May to mid-September; *(360) 856-5700.* **Mineral Park** has 8 primitive sites (no hookups; maximum RV length, 15 feet), with no piped water, and it's open from mid-May to mid-September; *(360) 856-5700.* The latter is used mainly as a staging area for hikes into the Glacier Peak Wilderness.

Back on Hwy 20, the Newhalem area has two North Cascades National Park campgrounds. **Goodell Creek** has 22 campsites (no hookups; maximum RV length, 22 feet). It's open all year, and is a popular stopover for Skagit River rafters. This park also offers a very rare road view of the North Cascades' jagged Picket Range, a string of 8,000-foot peaks south of Whatcom Pass. *Follow signs from Hwy 20 at Newhalem; (360) 873-4500.*

Across town, **Newhalem Creek Campground** is a major summertime (mid-June to Labor Day) stopover, with 129 standard sites (no hookups), a short nature trail, and nice forested environs. It's within walking distance of Newhalem, just across the suspension bridge. *Follow signs from Hwy 20; (360) 873-4500.*

Near Diablo Lake is the national park's most popular overnight spot, **Colonial Creek Campground**, right on the lake banks and just off Hwy 20. The park has 164 sites (no hookups; maximum RV length, 22 feet). Many good hiking trails begin right in the campground (see Hiking/Backpacking, above), and the park offers great small-boat/canoe access to eerily turquoise Diablo Lake. You could swim here, too—for about 4 seconds, which is how long it will take you to feel frostbite take hold in this bracing, glacial water. Colonial Creek is open from mid-April to mid-October; campsites cannot be reserved. *On Hwy 20 east of Diablo; (360) 873-4500.*

Gorge Creek, a tiny, peaceful riverfront campground near the town of Diablo itself, is a good alternative.

Wildlife

The lower Skagit River Valley is **bald eagle** central during winter months. Viewing the regal raptors has become such high sport for Puget Sound area residents, in fact, that the Forest Service recently proposed new restrictions to limit the number of bird-lovers' rafts on the river. Those proposals were less than warmly embraced by anglers, whose drift boats use the same stretches of river to pursue Skagit steelhead. They squawked; the feds balked, delaying the restrictions until another study is completed. While that process sorts itself out, people and eagles will continue to flock to the Skagit.

Eagles arrive here in late November and peak in January, clearing out and heading for saltwater hunting grounds by early spring. (The Upper Skagit Bald Eagle Festival is in January; (360) 853-7009.) Roadside viewing can be good at times from Hwy 20 pullouts between Rockport and Marblemount. You'll need binoculars or a spotting scope; no wild eagle will let you get closer than about 50 yards without flying off. (Photographers note: Unless you're very, very lucky, you'll need at least a 600-mm lens for good closeups.) The designated pullouts are at **Washington Eddy** and a rest area a short distance to the east. A good place to watch the birds without standing along the road is the **Skagit View Trail,** a wheelchair-accessible loop inside Rockport State Park (see Camping, above.) The park is on the border of the Skagit Bald Eagle Sanctuary. **Howard Miller Steelhead Park** at Rockport is another popular viewing site.

For some reason, birds seem less wary of waterborne craft, which means a raft seat is the best place from which to view the eagles. Many outfitters book mellow, eagle-oriented raft trips on the river from November through January. Leading companies are Downstream River Runners, (206) 483-0335; Northern Wilderness River Riders, (206) 448-RAFT; or Orion Expeditions, (206) 547-6715. Expect to pay about $50 per person. For a full list of outfitters, or for information about running the river yourself via raft, canoe, or kayak, contact the Forest Service's Mount Baker Ranger District in Sedro Woolley; (360) 856-5700.

If you've already been to the Skagit bald eagle view-a-thon, or the thought of crowds makes you itch, consider driving one river drainage north to view birds in the less-known, less-popular **North Fork Nook-sack** drainage (see the Mount Baker Highway chapter). Or take your binoculars north to Lake Shannon near Concrete, home to one of the state's largest populations of resident **ospreys.**

While you're in the upper Skagit, don't overlook the very prey that bring the eagles here. Spawning **salmon** can be viewed from several stops along this route, including the **Puget Power Visitors Center** in Concrete, where sockeye salmon are trapped for hauling around the two Baker River dams to Baker Lake, where they used to wander on their own. Farther east, the **Marblemount Salmon Hatchery** is open to the public all year. Stop here in the fall to see spawning coho. Also check the waters at the **Gorge Powerhouse** in Newhalem for late-fall spawners, often schooled up here at the very end of the navigable Skagit, wondering why they can't go any farther.

Photography

For very scenic shots with minimal effort, hoof it down the short trails to **Rainy Lake** or the viewpoint at **Washington Pass** (see Hiking/Back-packing, above). Both are best photographed in early morning or evening light, as midday brightness washes out both scenes. Also, **Diablo** and **Ross Lakes** can be photographed from high above, from a series of pull-outs along Hwy 20. Another photographer's favorite is Easy Pass (see Hiking/Backpacking, above), where golden larch trees in autumn make a spectacular complement to the awesome mountain scenery. The ultimate wide-angle perch in this region, however, is the meadow atop 6,000-foot **Desolation Peak,** where surrounding mountain views are simply stunning. Our favorite time to pack the tripod to this region is October, when larches are golden, other fall colors are present, and the first dusting of snow coats peaks higher than 7,500 feet.

Fishing

Fishing for trout and kokanee (landlocked salmon) is good in **Baker** and **Shannon Lakes,** each a reservoir behind a Puget Power dam on the Baker River. Note that the minimum-size limit for kokanee is 18 inches. Boat rentals are available from Baker Lake Resort; (360) 853-8325. Watch for submerged stumps. **Ross** and **Diablo Lakes** also hold trout, and rental boats are available at each lake. Diablo also has a popular boat launch inside Colonial Creek Campground.

For best results at Ross Lake, rent a boat at Ross Lake Resort and troll a flatfish behind a flasher or pop gear. Note that Ross Lake is a "selective fishery" that's open only from July 1 through October 31, with a 13-inch minimum-size restriction and a three fish daily limit. The lake has some huge Dolly Varden, but they must be released. Fishing is best around creek inlets, such as the deep, eerie Lightning Creek Gorge.

Other good spots for rainbow and cutthroat trout are **Gorge Lake,** which is stocked with rainbows; and **Watson Lakes, Thornton Lakes, Rainy Lake, Cutthroat Lake,** and **Lake Ann,** all alpine lakes that can be reached by trail by late summer (see Hiking, above).

The **upper Skagit** holds a decent run of winter steelhead, with best results in January and February, and fewer numbers of summer-run steelhead. Fishing isn't as productive as lower-river sites below Concrete, however (see the Skagit Valley chapter). You'll find launch ramps in both Rockport and Marblemount.

Boating/Canoeing/Kayaking

The cold, clear reservoir waters of **Baker Lake, Shannon Lake, Ross Lake, Diablo Lake,** and **Gorge Lake** are all popular with canoeists and kayakers. The best access is at Baker and Shannon Lakes, both of which are ringed by campgrounds and launching points, and Diablo Lake, where a public boat launch is found at Colonial Creek Campground. See Hiking, above, and Lodgings, below, for information on paddle or boat trips on Ross Lake.

Waterborne adventures on **Ross Lake** deserve a special mention. Canoe or boat trips on the 24-mile waterway are a unique thrill. With careful planning, you can create a long backcountry itinerary combining paddling or boating with magnificent lakefront campsites (Ross Lake is ringed by an almost embarrassing assortment of campgrounds, all but one unreachable by road, therefore rarely crowded) and spectacular backcountry day hikes. A paddle up the narrow, winding Lightning Creek Gorge on the east side of the lake is fascinating—almost surreal.

Keep in mind that Ross Lake is a reservoir, with large fluctuations in water level. Trips planned for spring, when the lake is drawn down and shores are expansive mud flats, are much less pleasant than in the late summer or fall, when the reservoir is full. Call Ross Lake Resort, (206) 386-4437, or one of the information centers listed at the end of this chapter, for trip-planning guidance.

Kayakers often take to the waters of the **upper Skagit,** a Class II/Class III river most often floated downstream from Goodell Creek Campground (see Camping, above).

Rafting

The upper **Skagit River** contains Class II/Class III waters run by a number of professional river outfitters. Most trips begin near Goodell Creek

Campground (see Camping, above) and continue 8 to 10 miles downstream. See Wildlife, above, for information on eagle-viewing raft trips and outfitters.

Attractions

Since the only road access to Ross Lake is south from Hope, BC, the best way to get to the southern end of the lake—save by a 3.5-mile hike—is on the **Seattle City Light tugboat** from Diablo. Here Seattle City Light built an outpost for crews constructing and servicing the dams on the river. The tugboat leaves twice daily (8:30am and 3pm), runs from mid-June through the end of October, and the ride costs $2.50; (360) 386-4393.

Worth visiting are the dams themselves, built by a visionary engineer named James Delmage Ross. **Skagit Tours** offers 4-hour journeys through the Skagit Project, including an informative slide presentation, a ride up an antique incline railway to Diablo Dam, then a boat ride along the gorge of the Skagit to Ross Dam, a construction of daring engineering in its day. Afterward, a lavish chicken dinner is served back in Diablo. Ninety-minute minitours also are available. Six miles down the road in New-halem are inspirational walks to the grave of Ross and to **Ladder Creek Falls,** with plantings gathered from around the world (see Hiking/Back-packing, this chapter). The falls are lighted at night. Tours (summer only; reserve well in advance) are arranged through Seattle City Light, 1015 Third Avenue, Seattle, WA 98104; (360) 684-3030.

Restaurants

Buffalo Run Restaurant ☆   What used to be Mountain Song Restaurant is now Buffalo Run, but rumor has it it's still a nourishing stop along the North Cascades Hwy. A casual menu of sandwiches and soups is welcome here at milepost 106. *In middle of Marblemount on Hwy 20; (360) 873-2461; 5860 Hwy 20, Marblemount; $.*

Cheaper Sleeps

North Cascades Inn   Kids are free and the pie is perfect (sometimes we wish it were the other way around) at this roadside inn. Stop in anytime for the homemade pie and coffee, or stay in one of their 14 motel rooms. *(360) 853-8870; 4284 Hwy 20, Concrete.*

Ross Lake Resort   This resort is entirely afloat on the deep waters of Ross Lake just behind Ross Dam. Access is by walking in via the Ross Dam Trail (see Hiking/Backpacking, above) or by riding the Diablo Lake tug to the base of Ross Dam, then arranging for a truck pickup and water taxi to the resort. The cabins are plain, many with wood stoves for heat. No phones; bring your own food. Motorboats, kayaks, and canoes for rent. *(206) 386-4437; Behind the dam on Ross Lake, Rockport.*

The Skagit River Resort   Located near the entrance to North Cascades National Park, the resort (formerly known as Clark's Skagit River Cabins) borders the Skagit, offering plenty of opportunities to keep hikers and fishers happy. The standard cabins are cozy, clean and authentic. *(360) 873-2250; 5675 Hwy 20, Rockport.*

More Information

North Cascades National Park Headquarters/Visitors Center, Sedro Woolley: *(360) 856-5700.*

Ross Lake National Recreation Area, Skagit District (Marblemount): *(360) 873-4500.*

Seattle City Light Diablo Tours: *(360) 386-4393.*

Methow Valley

From Washington Pass east to Loup Loup Ski Area, north to the Canadian border, and south to Pateros, including Winthrop, Mazama, the Methow Valley Community Trail System, Sun Mountain Lodge, the Pasayten and Lake Chelan–Sawtooth Wildernesses, Pearrygin Lake State Park, the Chewuch and Twisp river valleys, and portions of the Okanogan National Forest.

The Methow Valley fits like an old flannel shirt. Thousands of us revel in its familiar warmth every year. Whether we're pulling the valley's sleeves on for a day of blissfully lonesome fly-fishing, silent cross-country skiing, or high-altitude mountain biking, the Methow always leaves us with a massage-like afterglow.

The valley, which unofficially begins in Mazama and follows the liquid-crystal Methow River downstream to shake hands with the Columbia at Pateros, hasn't changed all that much in the past several decades. Our appreciation for it certainly has. Once a mishmash of mining camps, trappers' cabins, hunting lodges and apple orchards, the valley is fast becoming the favorite mountain getaway for wet-side cross-country skiers, mountain bikers, hikers, and yellow-leaf lovers. High, jagged North Cascades peaks loom over rocky river valleys filled with pine, aspen, and other dry-side flora, painting magnificent mountain canvasses all year long: The valley explodes in greens in the spring, when melting snows turn the peaceful Methow into an imposing force of nature, luring whitewater rafters and kayakers who ride it from top to bottom. In the summer, valley skies are dry and clear, and local mountains draw faithful legions of mountain bikers and hikers, who set out north into the Pasayten Wilderness, one of the best places in Washington to enjoy an extended backpack trip. The Methow is exceedingly beautiful—and pleasantly quiet—in the fall, when skies and apples turn crisp and the valley floor is colored a brilliant yellow and red. It is no less stunning in the winter, when the weather turns beastly cold but ample coats of fresh, dry snow coat a 175-kilometer Nordic ski trail system that ranks as one of the most magnificent in the country.

Local residents have made some smart decisions in the Methow, joining forces to create a recreation-based industry that draws a year-round stream of visitors to the valley's just-right number of inns and lodges. Collectively, the towns of Winthrop, Mazama, and Twisp have achieved a thriving ecology-based economy. Like other prospering mountain towns in the U.S. west, the Methow is taking full advantage of the nation's recreation-based vacation boom. Unlike most of them, it has managed to do so without the accompanying plague of overbuilt vacation homes, ugly commercial development, and corporate resort overkill.

Do yourself a favor and plan a cycling, hiking, fishing, or skiing trip to the valley in the near future. Do the rest of us a favor and don't spread the word around too much: every time we get one of these flannel shirts nice and broken in, somebody else is constantly wearing it.

Getting There

The best access to the Methow Valley depends on the season. Between April and November, Hwy 20, the North Cascades Scenic Highway, is the preferred route, crossing Washington Pass and entering the upper Methow Valley at Mazama. From Winthrop, Hwy 153 travels south along the Methow Valley floor to a junction with US 97 at the Columbia River at Pateros. In the winter, Hwy 20 is closed between Mazama and Marblemount, and the best Methow Valley access route is east via US 2 to US 97 at Wenatchee, then north to Pateros and Hwy 153. Allow 3 to 4 hours for the trip via either route. Call (360) 856-5700 for US 20 snow updates.

Adjoining Areas

SOUTH: **Chelan and the Middle Columbia**

EAST: **Okanogan Highlands and Sherman Pass**

WEST: **North Cascades National Park: Overview; North Cascades Scenic Highway**

Cross-Country Skiing

Anyone who says Washington has no truly world-class skiing has never been to the Methow Valley in the dead of winter. The valley, tucked into the dry side of the North Cascades, garners little attention on the national ski scene because it has no high-profile alpine ski resort (although more than one developer has tried, and failed, to produce one at Early Winters). But the valley's cross-country skiing terrain and facilities just might be the best Nordic skiing combination in the country.

The winter's cold skies and abundant dry snow create perfect cross-country touring conditions, while the Methow Valley Sport Trails Association, a conglomeration of skiers and local businesses, maintains a 175-kilometer trail system that literally winds through the entire valley, offering ski terrain ranging from easy loops near cozy Sun Mountain Lodge to experts-only mountain ascents and deep-powder telemark plunges. The trail system largely falls into three separate, groomed chunks: Sun Mountain's trail network on the slopes of Gobbler's Knob, just west of Winthrop; the Mazama system near Mazama, between the Methow River and Early Winters Creek; and the Rendezvous Trail System in the highlands between Rendezvous and Grizzly Mountains, northwest of Winthrop. In between is a long, connecting trail system that runs the length of the Methow River from Mazama to a trailhead near Winthrop.

Just how you go about choosing your starting point depends largely on your choice of accommodations. Most visitors to Sun Mountain Lodge can work full time for several days and never ski the same trail twice on the 50 miles of Sun Mountain loops. Likewise for those staying around Mazama/Early Winters, where major trailheads are found at Mazama Country Inn and near the (closed in winter) Early Winters Ranger Station. Suffice it to say that wherever you choose to roost in the Methow Valley during winter, a great cross-country ski trail is nearby, with your name on it. In one part of the valley, lodging is even more closely tied to the ski trail. In fact, it sits on it. Hut-to-hut skiing is a favorite activity on the Rendezvous trail system. Rendezvous Outfitters, (800) 422-3048, can make the arrangements to ski between three spartan huts, each of which bunks up to eight people and comes equipped with wood stove and propane cookstove.

Use of the valleywide trail system requires a ski pass, widely available for $12.50 a day on weekends, as of this writing. Valley skiing usually begins in December and lasts into March. Keep in mind that the Sun

Mountain trail system, most of which is about 1,000 feet higher than the Methow Valley floor, usually opens first. A variety of ski-related festivals and races take place throughout the winter, including biathlons, a ski rodeo, and numerous distance races. Ski rentals are widely available, but Winthrop Mountain Sports (257 Riverside Avenue, Winthrop; (509) 996-2886) rates as one of the finer full-service Nordic shops in the state. It's open every day except Thanksgiving, when employees stay home to wax the bases and file the edges of their turkeys. Lessons also are widely available, but the **Sun Mountain Lodge Ski School,** (800) 572-0493, is a noted beginner's favorite.

For ski conditions, call the **Methow Valley Sport Trails Association,** (800) 682-5787. **Central reservations** for the entire valley can be made at (800) 422-3048. Sun Mountain Lodge ski packages are available by calling (800) 572-0493 (see Lodgings, below).

Two large cross-country trail systems are found at Loup Loup Ski Bowl between Twisp and Okanogan on Hwy 20. **Loup Loup Sno-Park,** on the north side of Hwy 20, has 21 kilometers of mostly easy-to-intermediate trails. Trail fees are charged only when the ski area is running on Wednesdays, Sundays, and holidays. **South Summit Sno-Park,** across Hwy 20, has 30 kilometers of trails for all abilities. State Sno-Park parking permits, available at outdoor retailers and ranger stations, are required.

Downhill Skiing

Alpine skiing in the Methow is mostly limited to backcountry telemark trips—unless you're willing to fly to the powder. North Cascades Heli-Skiing is your express ride to vast powder fields rarely touched by skis. Heli-skiing is pricey, but owner Randy Sackett's rates are actually quite reasonable compared to similar services to the north in British Columbia's Bugaboos, Selkirks, and Monashees. Mazama-area lodging packages are available. Call (509) 996-3272 for reservations and information.

A couple of state Sno-Park areas also offer limited downhill not far from the Methow Valley proper. **Loup Loup Ski Bowl,** between Twisp and Okanogan on Hwy 20, has two poma lifts and a rope tow to service about 1,200 feet of vertical as well as 30 kilometers of groomed cross-country trails (and many more at the nearby Sno-Park, see below). The lifts run on Wednesdays, Sundays, and holidays; (509) 997-5334. **Sitzmark,** 21 miles northeast of Tonasket, is smaller yet, with two lifts covering about 650 vertical feet. The area also has about 6 kilometers of cross-country trails; (509) 486-2700.

Mountain Biking

The very same community trail system that thrills cross-country skiers in the winter turns into a mountain-biking fast track once the snow clears. The Methow is increasingly becoming a favorite mountain-bike destination, offering rides for literally all abilities. The hilly, challenging, single-track terrain in the **Rendezvous Trail System** draws many expert riders, while novices and intermediates love the long, relatively flat course of the **Methow Valley Community Trail** between Mazama and Winthrop. Riders who begin at Mazama can ride the entire 17-mile course to Winthrop, following the river on its downhill journey through the scenic valley. Guests at Sun Mountain Lodge have their own 30-mile trail system that serves all skill levels.

Infinite loop possibilities present themselves. Consult **Methow Valley Sport Trails Association,** (800) 682-5787, for trail conditions and suggestions. There's plenty of riding outside the trail system, too. **Pipestone Canyon** southeast of Winthrop is a popular backcountry road-riding destination, with a wide variety of terrain in the state-managed Methow Wildlife Area. From Winthrop follow Center Street and Park Avenue south to Bear Creek Road. Turn left and proceed to the end of the pavement, about 2 miles beyond the golf course. The variable-distance **Buck Lake/Buck Mountain Loop** is another old-time favorite. From US 20 at Winthrop, take the West Chewuch River Road about 10 miles to a parking area at the junction with Eightmile Creek Road. Ride north on Eightmile Creek Road to Road 100, where signs indicate Buck Lake. The route is fairly steep, but the lake and a nearby campground are a nice reward. Riders can turn around at the lake for a 6-mile round trip or continue on Road 100 for another 6 miles, connecting once again with Eightmile Creek Road for an easy, paved voyage back to the car. The latter loop is about 16 miles. Another popular road ride is the 12-mile round trip from Winthrop to **Pearrygin Lake State Park** (see Camping, below). A fair number of trails in the surrounding Okanogan National Forest also are open to mountain bikes. Consult the Methow Valley Ranger District in Winthrop, (509) 996-2266, or Twisp, (509) 997-2131, for a list of open trails.

Prime time for mountain biking in the valley is the first weekend in October, when valley businesses host the annual **Methow Valley Mountain Bike Festival.** A full range of rides—both for fun and for hot competition—introduce riders to the valley trail system, and a series of competitive races take place on Sun Mountain Trails. Call the Methow Valley Sport Trails Association, (509) 996-3287, for details. Rental bikes and valley maps are available at Methow Mountain Sports, (509) 996-2886, and The Virginian Resort, (509) 996-2535.

Hiking/Backpacking

The dry alpine country on the east slopes of the North Cascades is a favorite of many Washington hikers, particularly backpackers making extended journeys to the headwaters of the Methow, Pasayten, and Chewuch Rivers in the half-million-acre **Pasayten Wilderness,** one of Washington's loneliest wildlands. More than 400 miles of trails wind through this sprawling, meadow-dominated highland area. Two favorite backpack routes on the west side of this massive wilderness are the **West Fork Pasayten** (moderate; 31 miles round trip) and **Robinson Pass** (difficult; 55 miles round trip), both of which begin just north of US 20 on Hart's Pass Road and wind into the heart of the wilderness, which is particularly beautiful in the fall. Another pair of trails provide quick access to the wilderness from Forest Service Road 51 north of Winthrop. **Andrews Creek** (difficult; 31 miles round trip) and **Peepsight** (moderate; 28 miles round trip) are both outstanding backpack routes that follow pretty streams to scenic alpine meadows loaded with wildflowers, wildlife, and good campsites.

But you don't have to devote a week's worth of walking to see the mountain splendor in the upper Methow drainage. The east side of US 20 west of Mazama offers a series of great day hikes. The very popular hike to **Cutthroat Pass** (difficult; 11.5 miles round trip) begins at Rainy Pass on US 20 and follows the Pacific Crest Trail to mind-blowing views at the pass, which PCT through hikers say is one of the more spectacular spots on the entire route. The elevation gain is about 2,000 feet, and you can venture off on a side trip to Cutthroat Lake. A much easier walk and free of barriers, **Lone Fir Trail** (easy; 2 miles round trip) begins in Lone Fir Campground 11 miles west of Mazama and winds along—and over, via four very stylish wood bridges—Early Winters Creek. It's a great family walk. **Blue Lake** (moderate; 4.4 miles round trip) is a nice day hike to a very pretty lake just west of Washington Pass. Another very easy walk in the area is the paved trail to the **Washington Pass Overlook,** which provides grand views of Early Winters Spires, the Wine Spires, Liberty Bell Peak, and Silver Star Peak. Another local hike is the **Monument Creek Trail** (moderate/difficult; up to 51 miles round trip), a good backpack trip that begins at Lost River Trailhead off Hart's Pass Road and climbs up the Monument Creek drainage to a ridgetop with sublime views. Day hikers will find even the lowest several miles an enchanting walk, and stronger hikers can get to great views and back in a single day.

Around Winthrop itself, the **Methow Valley Community Trail,** even though it's often dominated by the sounds of whirring spokes and schussing skis (see the Mountain Biking and Cross-Country Skiing sections, above), makes for great day hiking between Mazama and Winthrop. Pick up a map at Methow Mountain Sports or any inn or lodge in the valley. A number of good day and overnight hikes are also found west of Twisp in the Twisp River drainage, which provides the primary access to the east side of the **Lake Chelan–Sawtooth Wilderness.** Popular day hikes in the area include the Eagle Creek Trail (moderate; 14.5 miles round trip), which follows a placid, quiet creek valley to good views at Eagle Pass; and **War Creek South** (moderate; 12 miles round trip), which follows the stream through a forest to an alpine area rich with mule deer and other wildlife. Contact the Methow Valley Ranger District at Twisp, (509) 997-2131, for more guidance on hikes in this remote, wild area.

Camping

Winthrop area

Pearrygin Lake State Park is the premier campground in the region. The 580-acre lakefront park has 85 sites (30 with full hookups, 27 with water only), a 48-person group camp, good picnic sites, a swimming beach and bathhouse, and a boat launch. It's very popular with anglers and boaters, and usually remains full through the summer. Pearrygin is open from April through mid-November. Campsites can be reserved up to 11 months in advance by calling Reservations Northwest; (800) 452-5687. *Four miles northeast of Winthrop, follow signs from Bluff Street; (509) 996-2370 or (800) 233-0321.*

North of town in the Chewuch River Valley is a string of Forest Service campgrounds. They're open summers only and offer limited facilities, but most are very scenic sites along streams or lakes with decent trout fishing. The campgrounds are reached by following Forest Service Roads 51, 5130, and 5130100 north of Winthrop. In the Eightmile Creek drainage, **Buck Lake,** 12 miles north of Winthrop on Road 100, has 9 standard sites (no hookups; maximum RV length, 16 feet). **Flat,** 11 miles north of Winthrop on Road 5130, has 9 sites (no hookups; maximum RV length, 16 feet). **Nice,** 13 miles northwest of Winthrop on Road 5130, has 4 tent sites, as does **Ruffed Grouse,** 4 miles farther up the same road. Nearby **Honeymoon** has 6 tent sites. In the Chewuch River drainage along Forest Service Road 51 are **Falls Creek** (7 sites and a short hiking trail to the waterfall) and **Chewuch** (4 tent sites). Call the Methow Valley Ranger District in Winthrop, (509) 996-2266.

Mazama/Early Winters area

Three Forest Service campgrounds offer good camping just off US 20 in the area. **Lone Fir,** near milepost 168 (27 miles northwest of Winthrop) has 27 standard sites. **Klipchuck,** near milepost 175 (19 miles northwest of Winthrop), has 46 standard sites. **Early Winters,** near milepost 177, has 13 standard sites. Call the Methow Valley Ranger District in Winthrop, (509) 996-2266, or Early Winters Information Center (summers only), (509) 996-2534, for information.

Similar campsites are found in the Twisp River drainage. **War Creek Campground,** 14 miles west of Twisp on Forest Service Road 44, has 11 standard sites; **Mystery,** 18 miles west of Twisp, has 4 sites; **Poplar Flat,** 20 miles west of Twisp, has 15 sites. **Smith Creek** and **Roads End,** farther up the same road, are free primitive sites. East of Twisp, just off US 20, are **Loup Loup** (20 standard sites) and **JR** (6 standard sites). For more information, call the Methow Valley Ranger District at Twisp, (509) 997-2131.

In the lower valley, a favorite stopover spot is Alta Lake State Park near Pateros. See the Chelan and the Middle Columbia chapter.

Rafting/Kayaking

The **Methow River** has a split personality. The upper stretch, from Carlton to just north of Methow, is fast in the spring, but fairly tame. The lower section downstream from Methow to the Columbia River is fast and raucous, earning an honest Class IV rating for many rapids in Black Canyon. Contact the Methow Valley Ranger District in Winthrop, (509) 996-2266, for a list of qualified river outfitters.

Fishing

The Methow drainage is prime-time fly-flipping territory, with many clear, cold streams and lakes cranking out good numbers of rainbow and cutthroat trout, plus a few steelhead. Favorite local spots are **Buck, Twin, Patterson,** and **Pearrygin Lakes;** the **Twisp River** and the **Chewuch River,** a selective fishery (artificial flies and lures/single barbless hooks only) stream accessible from many campgrounds north of Winthrop (see Camping, above). Pearrygin Lake is the most popular, both because of the state park on its banks and the extra-plump trout it seems to produce every year.

In the lower part of the valley, the **Methow River** itself is a noted steelhead stream, with a decent run of summer steelies that somehow manage the incredibly long journey through the Columbia River's hydropower gauntlet, out to sea and all the way back again. Methow River fish usually show up in September and October, but luring a Methow steelhead is no easy task. The water here is often so low and clear that the fish can see you coming a mile away. Very light leaders and a dose of good luck are required. Camouflage is optional. Many anglers fare better by fishing with bobbers and jigs on the lower river at its confluence with the

Columbia near Pateros. Remember: All wild steelhead (if there are any left) must be released, and selective fishery regulations are in effect along most of the Methow.

Horseback Riding

The upper Methow River drainage and Pasayten Wilderness look like they're right out of some old Western movie. You can put yourself in one by signing up for a guided jaunt with Early Winters Outfitters, (800) 737-8750, which arranges trips ranging from 1-hour rides to week-long pack trips into the heart of the Pasayten Wilderness.

Attractions

Methow Valley Central Reservations is a booking service for the whole valley—Mazama to Pateros—as well as a good source of information on things to see and do and on current ski conditions. Write PO Box 505, Winthrop, WA 98862, or call (800)422-3048 or (509) 996-2148.

Stroll through the Western-motif town of **Winthrop** and stop in at the **Shafer Museum,** housed in pioneer Guy Waring's 1897 log cabin on the hill behind the main street. Exhibits tell of the area's early history and include old cars, a stagecoach, and horse-drawn vehicles. It is said that Waring's Harvard classmate Owen Wister came to visit in the 1880s and found some of the material for *The Virginian* here. An excellent **Winthrop Rhythm and Blues Fest,** (509) 996-2111, in the summer brings in such talents as John Mayall and the Bluesbreakers and Mick Taylor. And after you've had a big day outside, quaff a beer at the **Winthrop Brew Pub,** (509) 996-3174, in an old schoolhouse in downtown Westernville, a favorite local hangout. With a sociable espresso counter, products from Tim's chips to Orvis fishing rods, a clever goat logo on everything from water bottles to T-shirts, and a picnic area (complete with grillmeister in the summer), **Mazama Country Store,** the only store in Mazama, has become a favorite hangout for valley locals and travelers alike; (509) 996-2855.

Restaurants

Cafe Bienville ☆☆   You can find select Creole, Cajun, or classic French eats from the menu, which has more entrees than the restaurant has tables. There's lots of flavor here, and great wines too. *Can't miss it; (509)* 923-2228; *Hwy 20, Methow; $.*

Duck Brand Cantina, Bakery, and Hotel ☆   Built to replicate a frontier-style hotel, Duck Brand is a Winthrop standby for good, filling meals at decent prices: bulging burritos to fettuccine to sprout-laden sandwiches on whole-grain breads. *On the main street; (509) 996-2192; 248 Riverside Ave, Winthrop; $.*

Lodgings

Early Winters Cabins   Six classy country cabins on Early Winters Creek with handsome river-rock fireplaces. It's all just the beginning of something more grand: the Early Winters Cabins, the Freestone Inn (which opened in July 1996), and the two-to-three bedroom Lakeside cabins are all part of a growing complex called Arrowleaf Resort. *15 miles west of Winthrop just off Hwy 20 in Mazama; (509) 996-2355; 17798 Hwy 20, Mazama; $$.*

Mazama Country Inn ☆☆   With a view of the North Cascades from nearly every window, this spacious 14-room lodge makes a splendid year-round destination (especially for horseback riders and cross-country skiers). Winter packages include three family-style meals. Four cabins with kitchen and bath are available for families or groups of up to 14. *14 miles west of Winthrop just off Hwy 20; (509) 996-2681 or (800) 843-7951; 42 Lost River Rd, Mazama; $$.*

Sun Mountain Lodge ☆☆   This massive timber-and-stone resort has a dramatic location, set on a hill high above the pristine Methow Valley and backed by the North Cascades. Lodging options include 13 cabins just down the hill at Patterson Lake. Amenities include a restaurant, cross-country ski instruction, two hot tubs, and, in summer, a heated pool, tennis courts, guided nature hikes, trail rides, and pack trips. *9 miles southwest of Winthrop on Patterson Lake Rd; (509) 996-2211; Patterson Lake Rd, Winthrop; $$$.*

WolfRidge Resort ☆   Twelve condo-style log units are designed to allow flexibility: rent an entire unit (complete with kitchen), a suite, or just a single room—whatever suits your needs. The 50-acre setting includes a pool, hot tub, playground, and barbecue area (and a warming hut in winter for skiers). *5 miles northwest of Winthrop on Wolf Creek Rd; (509) 996-2828; 412B Wolf Creek Rd, Winthrop; $$.*

More Information

Methow Central Reservations: *(800) 422-3048.*
Methow Valley Ranger District, Twisp: *(509) 997-2131.*
Methow Valley Ranger District, Winthrop: *(509) 996-2266.*

Methow Valley Sport Trails Association: *(800) 682-5787.*
Twisp Chamber of Commerce: *(509) 997-2926.*
Winthrop Chamber of Commerce: *(509) 996-2125.*
Methow Mountain Sports: *(509) 996-2886.*
North Cascades Heli-Skiing: *(509) 996-3272.*
Sun Mountain Lodge: *(800) 572-0493.*

Stehekin
and the Lake Chelan National
Recreation Area

From Stehekin east to the Glacier Peak Wilderness and north to Rainbow Lake, including portions of North Cascades National Park and the Lake Chelan–Sawtooth Wilderness.

Stehekin is the only place in this guide—and one of the few in this outdoor-blessed state—that you can't get your car anywhere close to. Enough said.

Well, almost. Stehekin, year-round population 70, is a special place in an unforgettable setting. Accessible only by foot, passenger ferry up Lake Chelan, or floatplane, the sprawling backcountry in the Stehekin River Valley east of town is virtually unchanged from the time of the first white settlement (if you can call miners "settlers") here in the 1850s.

The Stehekin Valley, filled with fresh, cold streams, peaceful meadows, awesome gorges, and rocky peaks so high your neck will be hurting, has changed little, in fact, since long before that. The valley has provided a convenient access route from east Cascades to west for millennia. When early peoples moved from one climate to the other to hunt, trade, or perhaps just vacation, they came through here, using the same general route—Stehekin River to Cascade Pass, then down the west side to the Skagit drainage and Puget Sound—as many backpackers do today.

Backpacking trails in the upper valley mostly lie in the Lake Chelan National Recreation Area (NRA), with many reaching into North Cascades National Park and Glacier Peak Wilderness. Some legendary routes are found here, many crossing fantastic alpine passes to Highway 20, though the average Stehekin admirer never dons anything heavier than a fanny pack. The town itself is a great retreat, a charming mountain village that would be spectacular anyplace. But its physical dislocation from the rest of the world enhances its adventure/intrigue factor at least tenfold. Setting out from Stehekin with your weekend gear, you get the feeling you're really *out there*.

Once in your life, before you die or have both knees scoped, you owe it to yourself to pack a duffel with a firm set of boots, a stout book, a sleeping bag, a pack of moleskin, some beef jerky and your favorite doorag and set out for a week in the wilds around Stehekin. Compared to most other alpine destinations, this area is tricky to get to, requires some advance planning, and therefore is easy to bypass. That's the *whole idea*. So, make a commitment, make a reservation, make a memory. For at least 150 years, Stehekin has specialized in those.

Getting There

Access to the village at the head of Lake Chelan and the foot of the North Cascades is by boat, floatplane, or foot only. By boat is the preferred route. From Chelan, you can take the old-fashioned tour boat, The Lady of the Lake II, *or the zippier* Lady Express. *The slower tour boat departs Chelan at 8:30am daily mid-April to mid-October, arriving at Stehekin by 12:30pm, setting sail again at 2pm and pulling into Chelan by 6pm. Round-trip fare is $22; no reservations needed. It stops at Lucerne—and at any of the Forest Service campgrounds/trailheads on the lake—by request in summer. The* Lady Express *shortens the daily trip to just over 2 hours, with a 1-hour stop in Stehekin before heading back. Round trips cost $41; reservations are suggested. The* Express *takes the full load in the winter, running five days a week. In the summer, it's possible to combine passage on the two boats to lengthen your time in Stehekin or for a change of transportation scenery. Call the Lake Chelan Boat Company, (509) 682-2224, for prices and information. If time is short, you can fly up to Stehekin by floatplane, tour the valley, and be back the same day via Chelan Airways, (509) 682-5555.*

From Hwy 20, several routes for those on foot lead south into the Stehekin River Valley—and to the Stehekin Valley Road, where you can hijack the bus back to the lake. But the shortest route is the one people have used for thousands of years, Cascade Pass, east of Marblemount (see the North Cascades Scenic Highway chapter). It's a 9-mile crossing—and a stunning one at that—from Cottonwood Campground at the end of Stehekin Road to the Cascade Pass trailhead, 22 miles east of Newhalem.

Once you're in Stehekin, the only way around is by shuttle bus. The National Park Service runs a 14-seat van twice a day from Stehekin Landing.

How far it takes you depends on how late in the year you visit. In a typical year, the bus goes as far as High Bridge from May to mid-June; to Bridge Creek until early July; and all the way to Cottonwood from July through September. One-way fare is $5 per zone (there are two zones on the road, above and below High Bridge Campground). Reservations are required, and can be made up to two days in advance at visitors centers, or farther in advance by calling the Golden West Visitors Center; (360) 856-5703, ext. 14. You'll need to reconfirm the reservations two to four days before you leave, or they'll be canceled. A private contractor, Stehekin Adventures, runs a 36-seat bus four times a day from Stehekin Landing to High Bridge from June to mid-September. Seats are $4, reservations not needed, bikes and packs accommodated. Ask about the special doughnut run—it costs only a buck to get you as far as Stehekin Pastry Company.

Seasonal note: Prime time in Stehekin generally is late June through September. To miss the crowds, consider a visit in late May/early June or—better yet—September, just before the shuttles shut down.

Adjoining Areas

NORTH: **North Cascades National Park: Overview; North Cascades Scenic Highway**

SOUTH: **Wenatchee National Forest: Overview**

EAST: **Methow Valley**

WEST: **Mountain Loop Highway and the Glacier Peak Wilderness**

inside out

Hiking/Backpacking

Most people come here to hike. And most people who don't come here to hike wind up hiking, in spite of themselves. That's how alluring the sunny, wildflower-painted high country around Stehekin is. Listed below are some of the Stehekin Valley's most popular hikes. For full trail information, particularly for longer backpack routes, contact the North Cascades Visitors Center in Sedro Woolley, (360) 856-5700 (all year), or stop at the national park's Golden West Visitors Center at Stehekin Landing (summers only).

Right at Stehekin Landing, find the **Chelan Lakeshore Trail** (moderate; up to 18 miles), a pretty shoreside walk with a split personality. You can make it a brief, 4-mile (one way) walk to a nice campsite, or tighten down your pack and walk the whole thing, 18 miles to Prince Creek Campground, where you can hitch a ride home on *The Lady of the Lake* (make prior arrangements). Or arrange a drop-off at Prince Creek and hike it north to Stehekin. Either way, a fine walk, hilly in a sore-knee (but not cartilage-shredding) kind of way. Good campsites are found all along the way.

If you have an hour to kill, walk, ride, or shuttle up the valley road to the Rainbow Creek Bridge and find the trailhead to **Buckner Orchard** (easy; 1 mile), one of the older (1889) valley homesteads, complete with a still-producing apple orchard. Nearby is a short walk to **Rainbow Falls,** which leaps a remarkable 312 feet into the Stehekin River.

The popular **Rainbow Loop** (moderate; 6.5 miles) begins (or ends) at an upper trailhead a half-mile beyond Harlequin Bridge and ends (or begins) at a lower trailhead about 3 miles up the road from Stehekin Landing. Good views and wildflower meadows are found only a short distance up this trail. About 2.5 miles from the upper trailhead is a junction with the **Rainbow Lake Trail,** which leads to High Camp and McAlester Pass (8 miles) and connects to the Pacific Crest Trail. You can use this trail to make a one-way through hike from Stehekin to Rainy Pass on Highway 20. If you have time, wander up this trail just a half-mile beyond its junction with the Rainbow Loop to a scenic overlook; views are well worth the walk.

For serious oat burners who brag about vertical gain, the **Goode Ridge Lookout** hike (painfully difficult; 10 miles round trip) just might be the ticket—to fame or breakdown, depending on your pain threshold. The path gains a rather remarkable 5,000 vertical feet in just under 5 miles, and much of it comes in the final 2 miles. It ends at a 6,600-foot lookout site. We've heard the views are grand. The trailhead is near the Bridge Creek Bridge.

Another brutal, but extremely rewarding, high-altitude haul is **McGregor Mountain** (difficult; 7.6 miles). From the trailhead near High Bridge Ranger Station, it zigs, zags, zigs, zags—144 times (really) and 6,400 vertical feet (ditto) *straight up* to Heaton Camp, 6.6 miles, where you can set up the tent and perhaps recover for the mile-long scramble (for experienced hikers only, even then only late summer) to the summit, an 8,000-foot former lookout site that will blow what's left of your oxygen-deprived mind.

On a lighter scale, walk the trail from High Bridge Campground to **Agnes Gorge** (easy; 5 miles). The trail follows the west bank of Agnes Creek, with great views into the steep creek gorge and of 8,115-foot Agnes Mountain. A good picnic spot waits at the end.

Backpackers should consider several marvelous loop trips in this area. The **Rainbow Lake Trail** (moderate; 20 miles round trip), makes a fine weekend backpack trip to McAlester Pass. The **Park Creek Pass**

Trail (moderate; 16 miles round trip) is an occasionally steep (the trail gains 3,900 feet), but spectacular, route through a valley surrounded by 9,000-foot peaks, including 9,160-foot Goode Mountain, one of the highest peaks in the Cascades. Good campsites are found at Five Mile Camp, and from Park Creek Pass, you can continue west 19.4 miles to Colonial Creek Campground on Highway 20 (see the North Cascades Scenic Highway chapter).

Other favorites for backpackers are the **Company/Devore Creek Loop** (difficult; 28 miles round trip), a long, delightfully lonesome backcountry walk that's best in fall; **North Fork Bridge Creek** (moderate; 19 miles round trip), a very scenic backpack getaway to a fantastic glacial cirque. It's suitable for the more aerobically challenged, with good views throughout and great early season access; and the **Chelan Summit Loops** (difficult; 19 to 48 miles), a design-it-yourself trip up Chelan Summit Trail and down any number of creek drainages to a water pickup (or walk out via the Lakeshore Trail) on Lake Chelan.

Speaking of water pickups, good hiking trails also emanate from Lucerne, farther south on the Lake, and Holden Village, 11 miles up a gravel road. Near Lucerne, pack the fly rod and follow the Railroad Creek Road a short distance to the **Domke Lake Trail.** It leads an easy 1.5 miles to Domke Lake—which has a private fishing resort—then continues another 3 miles—gaining 3,000 feet—up to good views on Domke Mountain. For a pleasant overnighter, follow signs from the Domke Lake Trail to the **Emerald Park Trail** (moderate; 16 miles round trip). This is a beautiful valley walk into the eastern Glacier Peak Wilderness, with lighter crowds than Stehekin-area trails. You can make it a one-way trip to a car pickup in the Entiat River drainage.

From Holden, the **Railroad Creek Trail,** a major eastern access to the Glacier Peak Wilderness, climbs to spectacular **Lyman Lakes** (moderate; 19.4 miles round trip), at the foot of the Lyman Glacier. From there, very experienced hikers can climb along the glacier and pass through 7,100-foot Spider Gap, then drop to Spider Meadows and an eventual exit on US 2. Bunk-style lodging can be arranged at Holden Village, operated as a Lutheran Conference Center; (509) 687-3644.

Camping

A string of 11 fine (primitive, but anything else would seem out of character here) North Cascades National Park campsites await all along the Stehekin Valley Road and the northern lakeshore. You'll need to stop at the Golden West Visitors Center and pick up a free permit on your way there.

Choose from **Purple Point,** a short walk from the landing; **Weaver**

Point, a boat-in site; or **Harlequin, Rainbow Bridge, High Bridge, Tumwater, Dolly Varden, Shady, Bridge Creek, Flat Creek, Cottonwood,** or a half-dozen other walk-in sites. Consult a ranger, and try to get a campsite nearest any hikes or sites you're most interested in. Remember that upper-valley campsites don't melt out until early July.

Campers seeking RV shelter before taking on the boat ride to Stehekin should consider **Lakeshore Park,** (509) 682-5031, in Chelan (reservations suggested); or **Lake Chelan State Park** on S Lakeshore Road. Sites can be reserved by calling (800) 452-5687. For other Chelan-area camps, see the Chelan and the Middle Columbia chapter.

Mountain Biking

Stehekin Valley Road is the one, the only, route to ride up here. But you could do a lot worse. Mountain bikes actually are the preferred mode of transportation up here, unless you ride the shuttle bus. Many people find a ride up the valley road from Stehekin Landing a perfect way to sample Stehekin's beautiful valley floor without gearing up for a full backpack adventure. You can bring your own bike on the tour boat from Chelan, but it'll cost you $13 round trip. It's easier to rent at Stehekin; both Stehekin Lodge and Discovery Bicycles have ample supplies of mountain bikes and helmets right near Stehekin Landing. Rates are about $15 a day.

For a fun day trip, consider Stehekin Day Tours' cycle trip. For $12, they haul you and your (provided) bike up the road to Harlequin Campground, and leave you to ride back down. Call (509) 682-4584.

Fishing

Pack the fly gear. The **Stehekin River** and its many feeder streams are a decent cutthroat and rainbow trout fishery, with some absolutely gorgeous waters. It's catch-and-release from March through June, but you can catch and keep from July through October (minimum size is 15 inches). The Stehekin is closed to fishing above Agnes Creek; most anglers take the bus there and work their way down. The river also has a chinook salmon run in late August and September. For gear, licenses, advice, and the occasional lie, call North Cascades Stehekin Lodge, (509) 682-4494; or inquire at McGregor Mountain Outdoors at Stehekin Landing.

Fair trout fishing for rainbows and cutthroat also can be found at **Domke Lake** (see Hiking/Backpacking, above).

Cross-Country Skiing

Stehekin is a lonely place in the winter, but you can stay at North Cascades Stehekin Lodge and explore some remarkable cross-country touring terrain, even if you never venture from the snowed-over Stehekin Valley Road. Dress warm, and bring your own food and supplies. The rest of the town is mostly gone 'till summer.

outside in

Attractions

What's outside is what's important in the Stehekin Valley. But the village area itself is fun to explore. The **Golden West Visitors Center** has a good local historical display and art gallery, and puts on an interesting nature or history program every evening in the summer. Inquire within.

Cheaper Eats

Supplies of chips, salsa, and other basic summer food groups can run pretty thin at the local store. If you plan to be here for a while, stock up in Chelan.

Stehekin Pastry Company   It fills the void the Honey Bear Bakery left when it migrated to Seattle. A favorite spot for ice cream, sweet desserts, rich conversation—and general replenishing of fat cells after hiking to the top of Goode Ridge. *Two miles up the road from the Landing, Stehekin.*

Stehekin Restaurant   The eatery attached to North Cascades Stehekin Lodge. Reasonable breakfasts; days open vary seasonally and according to when the boat comes in. *(509) 682-4494; near the Stehekin Landing.*

Stehekin Valley Ranch   Dinner by reservation only, if you're not staying there. *(509) 682-4677; see Cheaper Sleeps, below.*

Lodgings

Silver Bay Inn ☆☆   Located where the Stehekin River flows into Lake Chelan, this wonderful retreat has a spectacular setting: 700 feet of water-front with a broad green lawn rolling down to the lake. Two separate lake-side cabins can sleep four and six, and bicycles, canoes, croquet, and hammocks are available. A hot tub has a 360-degree view. *Take The Lady of the Lake to Stehekin; (509) 682-2212 or (800) 555-7781 in Washington only; Stehekin; $$.*

Cheaper Sleeps

Stehekin Valley Ranch   The Courtney family picks you up at Stehekin in an old bus and takes you to the farthest end of the valley for seclusion and hearty family-style meals at their ranch. Open in the summer months, their rustic tent-cabins offer a place to bunk and just the basics, plus hearty, simple food at a decent price. **Cascade Corrals,** also run by the family, arranges horseback rides and mountain pack trips. *Take* The Lady of the Lake *to Stehekin; (509) 682-4677; Stehekin.*

More Information

Chelan Ranger District, Wenatchee National Forest: *(509) 682-2576.*

Glacier Public Service Center (summer only): *(800) 627-0062 or (360) 599-2714.*

Golden West Visitors Center, Stehekin: *(360) 856-5703.*

North Cascades National Park Headquarters/Visitors Center, Sedro Woolley: *(360) 856-5700.*

North Cascades Visitors Center, Newhalem: *(360) 386-4495.*

Stehekin Ranger Station: *(360) 856-5700, ext. 340.*

Wilderness District Office/Ranger Station, Marblemount (May through September): *(360) 873-4500.*

Lake Chelan Boat Company: *(509) 682-2224.*

North Cascades Stehekin Lodge: *(509) 682-4494.*

Mountain Loop Highway
and the Glacier Peak Wilderness

Highways 92 and 530, from Granite Falls north to Arlington, and east to the Glacier Peak Wilderness.

The Mountain Loop is our recreational backyard. The fact that the Loop, on the east edge of Snohomish County, is not exactly the kind of place for croquet and pink flamingos says a lot about where we live—on the edge of true wilderness.

The Mountain Loop, actually more of a square, is a grand collection of tall mountains, magnificently clear, strapping rivers, and patches of wondrous old-growth forest on the western foothills of the Cascades. It is an area defined by, and indeed still shaped by, wild rivers flowing out of the high, wet Glacier Peak Wilderness just to the east.

The bold, bubbling Stillaguamish reigns supreme here. The Mountain Loop's north edge is defined by its North Fork, which cuts a broad, fertile valley from the foothills town of Darrington to the lowland town of Arlington along Interstate 5. The Loop's south edge is marked by the South Fork Stilly, a swift, clear, boulder-strewn stream that always seems to be flowing straight off one nature calendar and onto another. In between is the raucous Sauk, blasting its way north as if perpetually late for a downstream meeting with the Skagit.

Entire generations of Washingtonians have spent lifetimes exploring what lies in between these flowing crystals. The Mountain Loop is one of the greater Seattle area's favorite hiking getaways, for obvious reasons. More than three dozen quality, old-growth to alpine hikes are found along its borders—most within an hour's drive of the major Puget Sound population areas. Longer trails provide the quickest access to the lands around 10,568-foot Glacier Peak—one of the most pristine alpine areas in the Cascades. Hiker pressure along the Mountain Loop is very heavy in the summertime. Often disconcertingly so.

As the population continues to mushroom, particularly in Snohomish County suburban areas, the pressure on Mountain Loop trails will continue. Not good news for anyone who's hiked the Mount Pilchuck Lookout trail on a recent summer weekend. Mount Pilchuck, in that sense, illustrates one constant about human interaction with the Mountain Loop area: it's where suburbia meets the wilderness, literally and figuratively. This is where civilized Washington, whether it plans to or not, goes to learn about life in the woods. All too often, the lesson comes the hard way. Every year, it seems, half a dozen people get lost on Mount Pilchuck, which to a veteran hiker seems a simple ascent on a well-marked trail. Not so if it's your first or second time in the high country, fog sets in, and panic follows. Year after year, decade after decade, people head to the fabulous backyard playground of the Mountain Loop. Year after year, goof after gaffe, some don't come back.

It's a point worth bearing in mind. The mountains inside the mountain loop are *mountains,* no more or no less beautiful—or fearsome—than their cousins 50 miles from the nearest road. Approach them with respect, and they'll provide a lifetime of memories. Approach them with disregard, and you'll be film at 11.

End of sermon. For most of us—the practical, the cautious, the fun-loving, and especially, the overworked—the Mountain Loop is a godsend, a quick escape from reality. Or to it, depending on one's degree of mountain Zen. Hiking, rafting, kayaking, fishing, and camping here are surprisingly fine, especially for a place within short reach of Seattle. Just driving the loop on a sunny summer day makes you feel like you've done something wholesome.

Go forth and recreate. It's too close at hand to ignore. Even if time is short, take a half day, drive the loop, get out of the car, and do what we do. Walk to the water and launch into a good riverbank daydream, letting the effervescent bubbles at the tail of a whitewater washboard scrub, boil, and wash away the knots in your nerves.

Remember, it's your backyard. And yardwork is good for the soul.

Getting There

The Mountain Loop Highway is actually more of a square, consisting of I-5 (or Hwy 9) on the west, Hwy 530 on the north, Forest Service Road 20 (nar-

row, unpaved; summer only) on the east, and Hwy 92 on the south. Recreation sites are centered on the upper portion of Hwy 530 near Darrington, along Forest Service Road 20, which follows the Sauk River, and all of Hwy 92 from its east end at Barlow Pass west to Verlot.

Most Puget Sound area visitors arrive from the south, taking I-5 north to exit 194 in Everett and following US 2 and Hwy 9 north to Granite Falls, where the "loop" begins by following the South Fork Stillaguamish upstream. To approach from the north, drive north on I-5 to Arlington, follow Hwy 530 east to Darrington, and turn south on Forest Service Road 20. Remember: The loop is closed at Darrington and Barlow Pass (or lower) in the winter.

Adjoining Areas

NORTH: **North Cascades Scenic Highway**

SOUTH: **Snoqualmie Pass Corridor (Mountains-to-Sound Greenway)**

EAST: **Stehekin and the Lake Chelan National Recreation Area**

WEST: **Skagit Valley**

inside out

Hiking

The Mountain Loop slices through some of the best close-in Cascades day hiking in the Puget Sound region. Expect crowds in the summer, and remember to go prepared. Just because these trailheads are less than an hour from home doesn't mean you can't get lost—or worse—if you're ill prepared.

Listed below is a sampling of the more popular hikes here. Dozens more trails are maintained in this mountainous region, which includes the Darrington Ranger District of Mount Baker–Snoqualmie National Forest, the Boulder River and Henry M. Jackson Wilderness areas, and western portions of the Glacier Peak Wilderness. For full trail information, contact the Verlot Public Service Center, 33515 Mountain Loop Hwy, (360) 691-7791 (summer only); or the Darrington Ranger District, 1405 Emmons Street, Darrington, (206) 436-1155.

Near the start of the Mountain Loop's southern leg are three of its most popular day hikes. **Mount Pilchuck Lookout** (moderate/difficult; 6 miles round trip) offers a great mountaintop view of the entire Puget Sound area from the 5,300-foot lookout site. This trail is one of the most underestimated in the state. Every summer brings a report of lost hikers on Mount Pilchuck. Usually, they're people who've strayed off the trail on one of many "shortcuts" and lost their way in bad weather or fog. Go prepared. The trailhead is on Mount Pilchuck Road, which turns south about a mile beyond the Verlot Public Service Center. Also on Mount Pilchuck Road is the trail to **Heather Lake** (moderate; 3.8 miles round trip), a very pretty alpine lake set in old-growth forest below Mount Pilchuck. This heavily used trail usually is accessible all year. Just to the east, **Lake Twenty-two** (moderate; 4 miles round trip) is an equally popular family hike, this one climbing through more old-growth trees and a half-dozen waterfalls on the way to a sterling lake on Pilchuck's northeast ridge. The trailhead is well marked on the Mountain Loop, about 1.5 miles east of Verlot Public Service Center.

Farther up the road, the trail to **Big Four Ice Caves** (easy; 2 miles round trip) is another year-round draw. These actually aren't ice caves at all, but wind- and stream-melted tunnels beneath a remnant snowfield on the north face of 6,153-foot Big Four Mountain. Access to their tempting, ice blue arches is probably too easy. Many people ignore warning signs and logic, and venture into the caves. Bad idea. They can, and do, collapse suddenly. The short trail to the ice caves is a popular cross-country ski and snowshoe route in the winter, and hikers often trudge over the snow to get here in the spring. But visitors should *never* venture out of the forest and into the slide plain around the ice caves while snow is present on Big Four. Avalanches off the mountain are very frequent, and very deadly.

On the north side of the highway, two arduous, but rewarding, day hikes head north from the Mountain Loop. **Mount Forgotten Trail** (moderate; 7.8 miles round trip) passes pleasant waterfalls (Perry Creek Falls, 2 miles in, is a good short-trip turnaround spot) before opening to vast meadows—and a steeper grade—below 6,005-foot Mount Forgotten. Experienced scramblers can swallow hard, climb all the way to the summit, and take a memorable mental picture of the great view. **Mount Dickerman** (strenuous; 8.6 miles round trip) is a good overnight trip to open meadows and a grand, 5,723-foot summit with views of Del Campo, Glacier, Sloan, and Monte Cristo Peaks. This is a favorite hike in the fall, when the meadows are filled with ripe huckleberries and crimson berry bushes. Bring the Backpacker Oven and a boxed crust, and you're in business.

South of the highway at the end of Forest Service Road 4065 (Sunrise Mine Road) is the **Sunrise Mine Trail** (difficult; 5.2 miles round trip), which climbs to 4,700-foot Headless Pass, among the triple spires of Del Campo, Morning Star, and Vesper Peaks. Not for the faint of heart or those untrained in the art of snowfield crossing.

At Barlow Pass, the pavement ends and the fun begins for many hikers and mountain bikers. The **Monte Cristo Road** (easy; 8.6 mi round trip), now closed to traffic, is an easy walk into Monte Cristo, the mostly ghost-town remnants of an early-century bustling mining village. A walk-in campground is open near the townsite, and a slew of great Cascade backcountry hikes depart from the same area. Among them: **Gothic Basin** via the Weden Creek Trail (difficult; 10 miles round trip from Barlow Pass); **Poodle Dog Pass to Twin Lakes** (difficult; 16.8 miles round trip from Barlow Pass); and **Glacier Basin** (difficult; 12.2 miles round trip from Barlow Pass). All three are tough climbs up rocky trails, but serve up stunning alpine views as a reward. Consider camping around Monte Cristo and hiking them as day hikes.

Popular hikes on the northern (unpaved) leg of the Mountain Loop include **Squire Creek Pass** (moderate; 7.4 miles round trip) at the end of Squire Creek Road, south of Darrington; **Old Sauk River** (easy; 6 miles round trip), a nice river walk near the Clear Creek Campground; and **Mount Pugh and Stujack Pass** (difficult; 7 miles round trip), a late-summer scramble that begins 1 mile up Mount Pugh Road.

East of Darrington, the wild Suiattle River drainage contains several great day hikes and longer backpack routes providing westside access to Glacier Peak. The **Huckleberry Mountain Trail** (difficult; 14 miles round trip) is a tough climb through old-growth forest to a 5,900-foot lookout site. Warning: The views don't begin until right near the top. Most people make this an overnighter. The trailhead is near Buck Creek Campground (see Camping, below). Nearby **Green Mountain** (moderate; 8 miles round trip) is an area favorite, thanks to its extensive wildflower meadows and lakeside campsites in the valley below the summit. At the 6,200-foot top is a still-functioning lookout site with the best mountain views in this area. A winner.

Farther down Suiattle River Road, a backpacker's favorite is the **Downey Creek and Bachelor Meadows Trail** (moderate; 13.2 miles round trip). This trail has it all: old-growth forest on the Suiattle, and a stunning alpine meadow below 8,264-foot Spire Peak in the Glacier Peak Wilderness. The trailhead is near Downey Creek Campground. Another popular day hike in the same area climbs up **Sulphur Creek** (moderate; 3.6 miles round trip) to a hot springs, of sorts (too small and too cool to soak in, but fun to look at). At the end of Suiattle Road, the **Suiattle River Trail** (moderate; various lengths possible) leads up the river and onto the northwestern flanks of Glacier Peak itself. Some of the most popular destinations in the Glacier Peak Wilderness—**Image Lake, Suiattle Pass**, and a very scenic stretch of the **Pacific Crest Trail**—are reached via this trail system. Ambitious backpackers can cross through the entire wilderness north of Glacier Peak, east to **Holden** and ultimately to **Lake Chelan**.

One drainage to the south, backpackers flock to the **White Chuck**

River Trail (moderate/difficult; various lengths possible) which leads to the popular (and scummy, by our taste) **Kennedy Hot Springs** and beyond to the Pacific Crest Trail on Kennedy Ridge. Alpine campsites, explorable moraines of the Kennedy and Scimitar Glaciers, and up-close views of 10,541-foot **Glacier Peak** are simply stupendous. A very memorable, 18-to-20 mile round trip, if the weather cooperates. A very horrible one if it doesn't.

Camping

A dozen, count 'em, 12, Forest Service campgrounds are offered for your tent-pitching pleasure (this isn't really good RV territory, although those little Barbie Toyota Campers will fit into some of these). In addition, the Darrington Ranger District handles eight small, **reservation-only** campsites along the Mountain Loop. Call (360) 436-1155 for information on all the campgrounds listed here.

Turlo has 19 sites (no hookups; maximum RV length, 31 feet) near the South Fork Stillaguamish. Campsites can be reserved by calling (800) 280-CAMP. Turlo is open mid-May to late September. *On Mountain Loop Hwy near Verlot Public Service Center, 10.8 miles east of Granite Falls.*

Nearby **Verlot** has 26 sites (no hookups; maximum RV length, 31 feet), some with river views. The Lake Twenty-two and Mount Pilchuck trails are nearby. Verlot is open from mid-May to late September. Campsites can be reserved by calling (800) 280-CAMP. *On Mountain Loop Hwy near Verlot Public Service Center, 11 miles east of Granite Falls.*

The largest and most popular campground in the area, **Gold Basin**, is several miles east. The campground has 93 sites (no hookups; maximum RV length, 31 feet) along the South Fork Stillaguamish. It's open from mid-May to late September. Campsites can be reserved by calling (800) 280-CAMP. *On Mountain Loop Hwy, 13.5 miles east of Granite Falls.*

Boardman Creek has 10 large sites and access to the popular Boardman Lake Trail. It's open mid-May to early September. This is a reservations-only group camp. *On Mountain Loop Hwy, 16.6 miles east of Granite Falls.*

Red Bridge, a very pretty but primitive South Fork Stillaguamish site, has 16 campsites (no hookups; maximum RV length, 31 feet). Hiking trails are nearby. No piped water. The park is open late May to early September. Campsites cannot be reserved. *On Mountain Loop Hwy, 18 miles east of Granite Falls.*

Higher on the South Fork, **Perry Creek** has 8 campsites and is open from May to October. Sites cannot be reserved. *On Mountain Loop Hwy, 25 miles east of Granite Falls.*

On the north-south (unpaved) highway portion is **Bedal,** which has 16 sites (no hookups; maximum RV length, 21 feet) near the confluence of the north and south forks of the scenic Sauk River. The campground is free, has no piped water, and is open from June to early September. Campsites cannot be reserved. *Southeast of Darrington 19 miles (about 6 1/2 miles north of Barlow Pass) on the Mountain Loop Hwy.*

Closer to Darrington, **White Chuck** (five sites), at the confluence of the Sauk and White Chuck Rivers, and **Clear Creek** (nine sites), 3 miles south of Darrington, are small seasonal campgrounds with no fees or piped water.

On the Suiattle River Road (Forest Service Road 26) east of Darrington, choose from **Buck Creek** (25 sites), **Downey Creek** (10 sites), or **Sulphur Creek** (20 sites), all free, seasonal (June through October) campgrounds with no piped water, but with good river and hiking access.

Fishing

The rivers defining the Mountain Loop itself—the North and South Fork Stillaguamish, Sauk, and Suiattle—are wild, unspoiled waterways, with plenty of good rod-bending opportunities.

The **Stillaguamish**—or "Stilly," as it's locally known—is a famous steelhead waterway. The North Fork is a particularly notable fly-fishery, for both summer and winter fish. The river also holds cutthroat trout. The **Sauk** also is a locally famous steelhead stream, known for its occasional large fish. Catch rates aren't what they used to be, though. The **Suiattle** produces a fair number of steelhead itself. Be sure to check steelhead regulations before you fish. Sections of all these rivers now are closed during part of the year and open only to catch-and-release fishing during other periods.

The Mountain Loop offers a wealth of alpine lake fishing for rainbow and brook trout. Easy-to-reach lakes such as **Lake Twenty-two** and **Heather Lake** offer decent fishing amid fantastic alpine scenery. Other good bets are **Boardman Lake, Island Lake, Lake Evan, Goat Lake**, the many small lakes accessible by short trails off the **Suiattle River Road** (Forest Service Road 26), and the string of lakes in the **upper Suiattle** and **White Chuck** river drainages inside the **Glacier Peak Wilderness**. More than two dozen are there for the choosing, and many are periodically stocked with packed-in fingerlings. See Hiking, above, for access ideas.

Rafting/Kayaking

The **Sauk** and **Suiattle** are two of the favorite whitewater haunts of Seattle-area rafting companies. Both receive heavy spring use. The Suiattle is a better choice for novices, although the mostly Class II/Class III stream shouldn't be considered tame, by any means. The Sauk is the wild child in this area, with a score of Class III/Class IV rapids from Bedal to White Chuck, and a serious set of Class IV/Class V rapids between White Chuck and Clear Creek Campground, a popular get-out-and-check-for-missing-body-parts spot. Generally, it gets tamer the farther north you go. Many kayakers will be found racing the rafts through these chutes. This is not for beginners, however. Rookies should stick to the rafts. A large number of good commercial rafting companies run these rivers. For references, contact the Darrington Ranger District, (206) 436-1155.

Most kayakers and canoeists in search of calmer waters float the **North Fork** and **South Fork Stillaguamish** downstream from Granite Falls and Darrington, respectively, to Arlington. The **lower Sauk River** along Hwy 530 between Darrington and Rockport is a scenic, semi-advanced paddle route, with good takeout access.

Mountain Biking

The **Monte Cristo Road** at Barlow Pass (see Hiking, above) is one of the best family-friendly mountain bike routes in the near Cascades. It receives heavy use in the summer; consider a weekday. Mountain bikes are forbidden from most trails in this area, but a wealth of **Forest Service Roads** await the more serious biker looking for a healthy dose of vertical. Check with the Darrington Ranger District, (206) 436-1155, for road conditions, including washouts and logging truck traffic.

Skiing/Snowshoeing

Snow levels can be iffy along the Mountain Loop. But when the freezing level drops, some good cross-country ski/snowshoe trails stand out in the white. The **Big Four Trail** (see Hiking, above) is a popular 2-mile round trip on the south side of the Mountain Loop. The first half-mile, in particular, is flat and suitable for beginners. Remember: In the winter it's never safe to ski or snowshoe into the open area near the Big Four Ice Caves. It's an avalanche zone.

Other good cross-country ski routes are the **Monte Cristo Road** at Barlow Pass, **French Creek Road,** or the portion of the **Mountain Loop** (Forest Service Road 20) that's closed in winter.

Restaurants/Lodgings

For recommended restaurants and lodgings, see the Adjoining Areas to this chapter.

More Information

Darrington Ranger District, Darrington: *(206) 436-1155.*
Verlot Public Service Center (summer only): *(360) 691-7791.*

Mount Baker Highway

From north Bellingham east to Artist Point near Mount Shuksan, including Highway 542, Glacier, Mount Baker Ski Area, Heather Meadows, Glacier Ranger District of Mount Baker–Snoqualmie National Forest, and portions of North Cascades National Park.

This is the back-door entry to Washington's alps. Arguably the most rugged, untamed mountain slopes in the Northwest, if not the country, the North Cascades are the truest test of many a recreator's mettle. Everything about them is raw, from their awesome, jagged peaks to their massive glaciers, charging rivers, and inhospitable access routes.

Lucky for us, the Mount Baker Highway is a fairly civilized crack in the North Cascades' stony armor. From the outskirts of Bellingham, the wandering two-lane road does its best imitation of the Nooksack River it follows into the craggy mountains—winding, curving, climbing, and falling through a beautiful river valley surrounded by snowy peaks. All along its route are places to pull off the road and into Washington's wild natural past.

No matter what time of the year you drive it, the Mount Baker Highway locks onto your alpine guidance system and begins priming your adrenaline pump, ultimately dragging you to a spectacular destination—the alpine ridgeline between 10,778-foot Mount Baker and 8,268-foot Mount Shuksan, two of the state's most magnificent alpine peaks. In the summer and fall, hiking, camping, and climbing from this area are outstanding. Backcountry areas are rich with hundreds of acres of wildflowers, chill-raising alpine views, and secluded backcountry campsites. This is rugged, wild country—the kind you normally have to hike for days to reach. The summer season is short but sweet. Most of Mount Baker's alpine area doesn't melt out until August.

In the winter, access gets tough, but the tough keep going—directly to Mount Baker Ski Area, which has a well-earned national reputation for steep slopes and deep snow. The mountain's average annual snowfall— more than 700 inches, or 60 feet—is tops among North American ski resorts. That gives Mount Baker the longest ski season in the state. And one of the best.

At Baker, however, the very term "ski season" is a misnomer. This is one place where the number of snowboarders typically equals—if not surpasses—skiers. In the past 15 years, Baker's wild, rugged terrain has made it an international snowboarding mecca, turning the tiny valley town of Glacier into a snow-rider's enclave. Craig Kelly, snowboarding's first international superstar, is a local here. Nowhere else in the state is a large recreation area so vividly and accurately personified by a single user group: in this case, Baker's clan of highly skilled, mildly motivated (at least in traditional senses) snowboard hounds, many of whom forsake all else to get their regular mountain fix.

Watching a world-class snowboard rider float in graceful, sweeping arcs down Shuksan Arm is a unique thrill, even for nonriders. Without so much as a sound, their descents say all there is to be said about the special place Mount Baker holds in the hearts of Washington recreators: poetic grace in the midst of natural chaos.

On Mount Baker, whether you're on a snowboard or skis, Vibram soles or a river raft, a boat or a rope, the game can be risky, but the payoff is always rich. Baker is often moody, occasionally ugly, and always challenging. It is alternately relentless and magnificent. But in the end, it usually is simply inspired. It's easy to see why we feel its pull: that's the way a lot of us like to think of ourselves.

Getting There

The Mount Baker Highway is 100 miles north of Seattle on Interstate 5. From I-5 north of Bellingham, take exit 255 (Hwy 542) and drive east. Another option is to take I-5 exit 230 at Burlington, travel to Sedro Woolley, and follow Hwy 9 north to its junction with Hwy 542 near Deming. All activities in this chapter are reached via Hwy 542, which ends at Artist Point, a scenic vista 58 miles east of Bellingham. Note: In the winter, Hwy 542 ends at Mount Baker Ski Area, just below Austin Pass. In an average year, the final 2 miles of road to Artist Point don't melt out until late July or August.

Adjoining Areas

SOUTH: **North Cascades Scenic Highway**

EAST: **North Cascades National Park: Overview**

WEST: **Bellingham and Lummi Island**

inside out

Hiking

The Mount Baker and Mount Shuksan area at the end of Hwy 542 is one of the most awe-inspiring hiking areas in the state. From this region's high, rugged ridges, you'll find mile-long blankets of wildflowers, goose-bump-popping views of glacier-shrouded alpine peaks, and heavenly backcountry campsites.

The only catch: none of these come easy. The very topography that makes the heart soar will make the thighs scream. Most long hikes in this area are steep day hikes, some of them being old miner's trails. (Which, incidentally, is the correct answer to the Jeopardy question: "Why are there no old miners anymore?") In that sense, many of the Baker area's woods-to-views climbs are classic Northwest ascents. Even a day hike here can send you home feeling like you've conquered something. The burn in the legs is a good one.

But you don't have to kill yourself to sample the North Cascades alpine country. The Mount Baker Highway ends at a parking lot/viewpoint between Mounts Baker and Shuksan that ranks right up there on our list of Most Amazing Places You Can Drive to in the State. The Heather Meadows, Austin Pass, and Artist Point area is true high-alpine country, interlaced with short day-hiking trails that loop to and from the parking lot. If you're not into sweating, this is your spot.

Two important visitor's tips: On the average, this area of the North Cascades receives as much snowfall as any auto-accessible (or even chair-lift accessible; see Skiing/Snowboarding, below) site in the United States. The Artist Point parking lot doesn't melt out until early August. Call the Glacier Public Service Center at the number below to check road conditions. Also, once the snow melts, the bugs proliferate. Mid-August in the Baker high country can be a miserable experience in years when black flies are particularly bad. They bite. They're fast. They're relentless. You've been warned. The swarms die down in early autumn—a prime time to visit and stroll through alpine fields of ripe wild blueberries.

A list of our favorite Baker-area hikes follows. For more information on these and others, call the Glacier Public Service Center; (360) 599-2714.

Starting at the top, several good day hikes emanate from the parking lot at Artist Point. At the south end of the parking lot, the **Chain Lakes Loop** trail (moderate; 6.5 miles round trip) makes a circle around Table Mountain, with starting points either at Artist Point or the Heather Meadows parking lot, just south of Mount Baker Ski Area. You'll pass by a string of sparkling alpine lakes—Mazama, Iceberg, Hayes, and Arbuthnot, then climb steeply over Herman Saddle before dropping to another lake and an exit through beautiful Heather Meadows. For a full loop, walk back up the road about 2 miles to Artist Point. Even the road is a pleasant walk, with stunning views. Allow about 4 hours to take it all in. And do *not* forget your camera.

Also from the Artist Point lot, the **Table Mountain Trail** (difficult; 3.5 miles round trip) will take you to the top of its namesake peak, where some truly memorable views of Mount Shuksan await. This is a steep one. You'll zigzag up what seem like several hundred switchbacks, most of them chipped into rugged volcanic rock. And no matter when you go, there's likely to be snow at the top. (Chances are you'll find snowboarders up here, riding down the far side of the mountain.) If you're up for the climb, this one is well worth it.

Nearby, the route up **Ptarmigan Ridge** (difficult; 9 miles round trip) doesn't really follow a trail at all. This is a ridge walk, up the north flanks of Mount Baker. The lower portion is snow-covered for much of the year, and its upper reaches are under snow all year long. That makes it a favorite path of summertime backcountry skiers or snowboarders, or climbers looking for snowfields on which to practice self-arrests. But for experienced hikers who know how to use an ice ax, this is a beautiful late-summer snow walk: follow the cairns or trail markers. The route leads to Camp Kiser, a bivouac camp for climbers taking this secondary route to the summit of Mount Baker. Mountain goats are often seen in the area.

On the highway just below Artist Point but above Heather Meadows, a wide spot in the road marks the parking area for the trail to **Lake Ann** (moderate; 8 miles round trip). The trail drops down for 2 miles to Swift Creek, then climbs up a boulder-strewn (and marmot-inhabited) meadow before dropping into a basin holding jewel-like Lake Ann. Behind the lake, the view is drop-dead amazing. You're looking right at the Lower Curtis Glacier and the full glory of 8,268-foot Mount Shuksan. Campsites are found around the lake. A well-used climber's trail continues on, up the south flank of Shuksan. It's a great day trip; the trail takes you right above Curtis Glacier.

A wealth of long day hikes or weekend backpack routes can be found lower on the Baker Hwy, in the upper Nooksack drainage. Two favorites are **Skyline Divide** (moderate/difficult; 6 miles round trip), which is an express route to a lovely ridgeline painted with purple lupine; and **Heliotrope Ridge** (difficult; 6.5 miles round trip), the main climbing route on the mountain, but a good day hike for strong hikers who want a close look at the Coleman Glacier. The trailheads are on Forest Service Roads 37 and 39, respectively—both just east of Glacier.

Other great view hikes in this region are **Church Mountain** (difficult; 8.4 miles round trip), off Forest Service Road 3040; **Welcome Pass** (difficult; 3.6 miles round trip), a 2,200 vertical-foot climb to a great mountain viewpoint above Forest Service Road 3060; **Excelsior Pass** (difficult; 6 miles round trip), an alpine lookout site off Forest Service Road 31; **Yellow Aster Butte** (difficult; 6 miles round trip), **Winchester Mountain** (easy; 4 miles round trip), and **Tomyhoi Lake** (difficult; 10 miles round trip), all off Forest Service Road 3065; **Goat Mountain** (moderate; 6 miles round trip), a hike with stunning views, off Forest Service Road 32; and **Whatcom/Hannegan Pass** (easy/moderate; 10 miles round trip), a popular backpacker's entry into Ross Lake and the remote backcountry of North Cascades National Park. For the latter hike, which begins on Forest Service Road 32, overnighters will need a backcountry permit. They're available at the Glacier Public Service Center.

Camping

Three small-but-pleasant Mount Baker–Snoqualmie National Forest campgrounds are found along Hwy 542. **Douglas Fir** has 15 tent and 15 RV sites (no hookups; maximum RV length, 31 feet) in a wooded loop near the Nooksack River. The park is open from May to October. Sites can be reserved by calling (800) 280-CAMP. *2 miles east of Glacier; (360) 599-2714.* On Hwy 542, **Silver Fir**'s 21 sites (no hookups; maximum RV length, 31 feet) are on the North Fork Nooksack. The campground is open from May to October. Campsites can be reserved by calling (800) 288-CAMP. *On Hwy 542 14 miles east of Glacier; (360) 599-2714.* **Excelsior Group Camp** has 13 tent sites, and must be reserved through the Forest Service. *On Hwy 542 6.5 miles east of Glacier; (360) 599-2714.*

One of the nicest camping (and lodging; see Lodgings, below) venues in the area is **Silver Lake Park,** a Whatcom County facility on a quiet mountain lake with acres of green space. The park has 25 tent sites and 53 RV sites. Fishing and canoeing in the calm lake are family favorites. Rental craft are available. Campsites can be reserved by calling (360) 599-2776. *On Silver Lake Road, 3.5 miles northwest of Maple Falls; (360) 599-2776.*

Picnics

Heather Meadows, the general name for the gardenlike alpine area at Austin Pass, has been a favorite Washington lunch spot for decades. Austin Pass, in fact, was the site of a grand lodge in the 1920s, but it burnt and never was replaced. In the winter, this is the end of the road for Mount Baker Hwy, and only cross-country skiers and snowshoers make tracks here. But in the late summer and fall, the road continues to Artist Point. Picnickers, however, often gather in the newly revamped **Heather Meadows** or **Austin Pass** parking areas for lunches.

Lower on the mountain, the **Shuksan Picnic Area** at the beginning of Forest Service Road 32 is an enjoyable spot.

Skiing/Snowboarding

Mount Baker taught the Northwest—and by extension, a lot of the world—how to ride a snowboard. Its unusually steep slopes, deep snow, and laid-back air have made **Mount Baker Ski Area** (actually on the foothills of Mount Shuksan) a cult favorite among deep-powder skiers for decades. But in the early 1980s, a new breed of snow play was born here, mostly at the inquisitive whim of young Bellingham-area adventurers and college students seeking to mix their skateboard and surfing affinity with the mountain's deep, steep powder snowfields.

Most people in the snow business will swear snowboarding as we know it today was invented by Jake Burton Carpenter at Stratton Mountain, Vermont. The truth is that snowboarding was bursting out at Stratton and Mount Baker simultaneously. But it blossomed most quickly at Baker, which was the first established ski area in the country to embrace the sport.

The snowboard relationship has only flourished over the past decade. Most of the first professional and world champion–caliber snowboarders (including Amy Howat, daughter of ski-area manager Duncan Howat) sprang from the deep-powder pockets of Mount Baker in the mid-'80s, and it continues to be a globally recognized snowboard mecca. Craig Kelly, widely regarded as the sport's first superstar, is a longtime Glacier resident.

Dozens of these top riders and snowboard pros gather at the mountain every year to compete in the **Legendary Baker Banked Slalom**, a rather amazing slalom-gate race down a steep, high-walled creek bed. (It's on Super Bowl Sunday, and the Slalom makes for a great spectator event for skiers who line the course.)

None of which means Baker is any less of a draw to legions of faithful ski fans. Recent additions at the mountain, such as the fixed-grip quad chairlift to the shoulder of Shuksan Arm, have increased its draw among Seattle-area skiers. Baker is not the most rookie-friendly area (the chair system remains tricky to negotiate, at least until you learn its intricacies). But intermediate-to-advanced skiers love the mountain's ungroomed glades and deep-powder chutes. And beginner terrain has improved in the past several years.

So have the mountain's creature comforts. The new **White Salmon Day Lodge**—a winner of architectural awards for its Cascade styling that incorporates local timber, stone, and other trappings—is destined to become a Northwest classic. Its front-window view of Mount Shuksan will thrill even the nonskiers among us.

Baker's main lure, however, remains the same: snow. Lots of it. The mountain's average annual snowfall—between 650 and 750 inches—is the highest average of any ski area in the United States. By far. That gives Baker the state's longest ski season: It usually opens by Thanksgiving and runs strong until early May (although the schedule shifts to weekends-only late in the year).

The ski area's biggest drawbacks: access and lack of slopeside lodging. Most of the winter, the drive to Baker is a long haul (3 to 4 hours, depending on weather) from Seattle. And the nearest lodging is down the mountain in Glacier. But the pros outweigh the cons here. The skiing is fantastic, and the setting might be unequaled in the country. Anyone who's stood atop Shuksan Arm on one of those clear, crisp, 20-degree January mornings will be a changed person.

Mt. Baker Ski Area is at the end of Mount Baker Hwy 542; (360) 671-0211 (**snow phone**); (360) 734-6771 (**business office**). Call for hours and rates. Full ski and snowboard rentals, sales, repairs, and lessons are available on the mountain. Mount Baker also has a small maintained cross-country ski area.

Climbing

Both **Mount Baker** and **Mount Shuksan** are popular spring and summertime alpine climbs. Both are semitechnical ascents but negotiable by most climbers with basic glacier-climbing experience, and both are used extensively as training routes by climbing schools preparing alpinists for larger peaks. Baker, in particular, is a popular climb, drawing 100 to 200 climbers a day on spring weekends. Two primary routes are used: the Coleman Glacier, on the mountain's northwest slopes, and the Easton Glacier, on the south side. For details on permits, logistics, and conditions, contact the Glacier Public Service Center, (360) 599-2714; or Base Camp Inc. in Bellingham, (360) 733-5461. And if you're looking for instruction, this is a good place to find it. The American Alpine Institute in Bellingham, (360) 671-1505, is one of the best climbing schools in the country, offering novice-to-expert instruction, as well as guided climbs on Baker and Shuksan.

Mountain Biking

Road riding is not impossible on **Mount Baker Highway.** But it is not advisable. The highway, particularly the upper stretches, is narrow and winding, and shoulder space is nil. Lower portions of the highway, between Bellingham and Glacier (31 miles), are more manageable, but less than optimal.

Mountain bikers, however, have a choice of a few backcountry trails and many, many miles of Forest Service roads. Call the Glacier Public Service Center, (360) 599-2714, to find out which roads are open, either by regulation or by snowmelt.

Wildlife

For a river basin less than 30 miles from a fairly large population center, the **North Fork Nooksack** is surprisingly wild. The best evidence is found on its banks in the winter months, when hundreds of **bald eagles** arrive to feed on spawning chum salmon.

The North Fork is often overlooked by Puget Sound–area eagle watchers, who flock instead to the Skagit River, one drainage basin to the south. But the Nooksack, thanks to its lighter crowds, actually may be a better place to view eagles in their habitat. The big birds begin to arrive here in November and stay through January, feasting on hatchery runs of winter **chum salmon.** Public access to the riverbanks is far from ideal. But good viewing points are found at the Nooksack Salmon Hatchery (a mile south of Kendall along Hwy 543) and at the Welcome Bridge on Mosquito Lake Road (turn east from Hwy 542 about 2.5 miles east of the Hwy 9 junction). Recent winter counts on the river have shown as many as 500 eagles on the 4 miles of river between the hatchery and the bridge. For more information, call the state Department of Fish and Wildlife; (206) 775-1311.

In past years, wintering **elk** often were seen in valley fields along the North Fork Nooksack. This herd has been badly depleted by overhunting in recent years, however, so sightings have become more rare.

Fishing

Trout fishing is usually excellent in Silver Lake, which has ample dock and shore access from Silver Lake Park (see Camping, above). The lake gets a hefty spring plant, and less fishing pressure than many other west-side ponds. Silver Lake also is said to hold some **cutthroat trout.** The season opens the last Saturday in April, and it's best early on.

Most of the Nooksack River is also a fair trout fishery. Check the state regulations pamphlet for seasons and special restrictions. Other potential trout haunts are the region's alpine lakes, including Tomyhoi and the Galena Lakes chain (see Hiking, above).

If they're feeling lucky, **steelheaders** can give the Nooksack system a try. The river's north and middle forks are accessible from Hwy 542, and hold some winter-run fish. Catch numbers in recent years have been very low, however, particularly on this upper-river portion. Most of the Nooksack's steelhead now come out of the lower river, near Lynden and Everson. The river also can be a fair **chinook, coho**, and **chum salmon** fishery. For conditions and information, call the Coast to Coast store in Ferndale; (360) 332-4077.

Photography

One of the most often snapped photos in the state is the view of **Mount Shuksan** from a small reflecting pond just below Mount Baker Ski Area. It's a winner—even if you *can* shoot it from the front seat of your car. Walk a ways, and the views get even better. Morning shots of Mount Shuksan from the **Lake Ann** area, and afternoon wildflower meadows at **Skyline Divide, Chain Lakes**, and other local day-hiking trails offer fabulous shutterbug possibilities (see Hiking, above). This is a particularly beautiful area in the fall, when alpine berry bushes turn brilliant crimson.

Rafting

All that melted snow charging down the **North Fork Nooksack** makes for hot whitewater-rafting action in the summer. The most commonly floated stretch on this mostly Class II river is between Douglas Fir Campground and Maple Falls. For a list of rafting vendors, contact the Mount Baker–Snoqualmie National Forest's Mount Baker Ranger District; (360) 856-5700.

Attractions

Cloud Mountain Farm (6906 Goodwin Road; (360) 966-5859) is a noted fruit orchard and nursery. Just up the road on Hwy 542 is **Mount**

Baker Vineyards, a quaint winery that offers tastings 11am to 5pm Wednesday through Sunday. This attractive, cedar-sided, skylit facility specializes in some of the lesser-known varietals, such as Müller-Thurgau and Madeleine Angevine. Their plum wine, made from local fruit, is delightful; 11 miles east of Bellingham on Mount Baker Highway; (360) 592-2300. A short distance down Hwy 9, in the tiny burg of Van Zandt, is **Everybody's Store,** which offers a shocking array of exotic foods and organic produce, herbs, baked goods, and the like; (360) 592-2297. Farther up the highway on Kendall-Sumas Road is **Cloudy Mountain Pottery,** an aptly named co-op gallery in an old gas station/grocery store. It's usually open weekends only; (360) 988-8645. The **Lake Whatcom Railway**—located not on Lake Whatcom, but at Wickersham on Hwy 9—makes scenic runs in July and August using an old Northern Pacific engine; (360) 595-2218.

Restaurants

Carol's Coffee Cup   Carol's is a local institution: a pleasant little hamburger joint/bakery/cafe, long a favorite with loggers, skiers, and hikers. The hamburgers are fine, but the big cinnamon rolls and homemade pies are best. *1½ miles east of Deming at Mt. Baker Hwy; (360) 592-5641; 5415 Mt. Baker Hwy; $.*

Deming Restaurant and Lounge ☆   In operation since 1922, this is one of the few real steak houses left hereabouts. It's not a fancy place, but everyone (a mix of loggers, suburbanites, and Bellingham city slickers) comes for the steak. *Off Mt. Baker Hwy at Deming Rd and 1st St; (360) 592-5282; 5016 Deming Rd, Deming; $$.*

Milano's Market and Deli ☆   Popular with locals and carbo-loading hikers, skiers, and snowboarders alike, this tiny restaurant is really three: a deli (with meats and sandwiches), a casual Italian restaurant (with hearty pastas and a well-priced wine selection), and a nice place for dessert and coffee. *Mt. Baker Hwy in Glacier; (360) 599-2863; 9990 Mt. Baker Hwy, Glacier; $$.*

Lodgings

The Logs ☆   A rustic retreat at the confluence of the Nooksack River and Canyon Creek. Cabins are comfortable, not luxurious, and sleep up to 10. Each has a large stone fireplace, kitchen, and grill. There's a pool and a volleyball court for summer. A great place to bring the kids and the family dog. *30 miles east of Bellingham on Mt. Baker Hwy; (360) 599-2711; 9002 Mt. Baker Hwy, Deming; $$.*

Cheaper Sleeps

Circle F   Five-and-a-half miles east of Bellingham, this castlelike farm-house has three rooms for rent under $50—including breakfast—on 330 acres with cows, horses, pigs, chickens, cats, dogs, and more. Great location for hikers and skiers. *(360) 733-2509; 2399 Mt. Baker Hwy, Bellingham.*

Glacier Creek Motel & Cabins   Hikers and skiers will love the proximity to slopes and backcountry of this motel—nestled among tall firs next to a rushing stream—and appreciate soaking tired bones in the hot tub. Restaurants and a store are within walking distance, as is the Glacier Public Service Center. *(360) 599-2991; 10036 Mt. Baker Hwy, Glacier.*

Mount Baker Chalet Inc.   This service rents privately owned cabins, chalets, and condos just outside of Glacier, with good access to all local attractions. Lodgings range from small, rustic A-frames to deluxe four-bedroom chalets. Rates vary, but you can get a good deal on weekly rates in summer, which is the off season in Glacier. *(360) 599-2405; 9857 Mt. Baker Hwy, Glacier.*

Silver Lake Park Cabins   Six rustic but comfortable mountain cabins on the shores of Silver Lake, a Whatcom County Park. No bathrooms, no hot water, no bedding; but there are equipped kitchens and outbuildings with baths. In addition, the 400-acre park offers hiking, camping, and fishing (see above). *(360) 599-2776; 9006 Silver Lake Rd, Sumas.*

More Information

Glacier Public Service Center: *(360) 599-2714.*
Mount Baker Ski Report: *(360) 671-0211.*
Sedro Woolley National Forest and National Park Information Center: *(360) 856-5700.*
Whatcom County Sheriff: *(360) 676-6911.*
Base Camp Inc. (gear, supplies, rentals), Bellingham: *(360) 733-5461.*
Carter's Carving Edge (rentals and repairs), Bellingham: *(360) 671-9738.*
Fairhaven Bike & Mountain Sports, Bellingham: *(360) 733-4433.*
Mount Baker Snowboard Shop (rentals, repairs, gear, and mountain information), Glacier: *(360) 599-2008.*
Pedersen's Ski & Sports, Bellingham: *(360) 734-7955.*

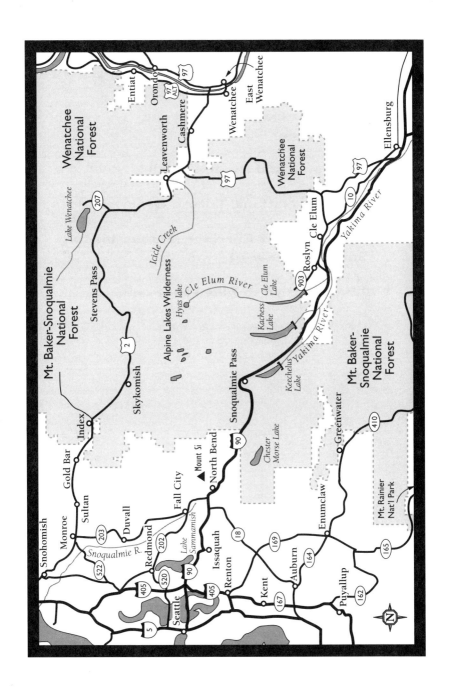

Central Cascades

Alpine Lakes Wilderness: Overview

A 393,000-acre, mostly alpine wilderness backcountry area in the Central Cascades between Snoqualmie and Stevens Passes.

It's the ultimate Washington paradox: The kind of mountain solitude you hope to find in the Alpine Lakes Wilderness is the very reason many nature lovers move to Washington. But on some sunny summer afternoons, you might think every last one of them is up here.

Occupying most of the high Central Cascades between Interstate 90 and US 2, the Alpine Lakes Wilderness contains some of the most splendid alpine territory in the Lower 48. It's also the most heavily trod wilderness in the country, thanks—or no thanks—to its proximity to more than 4 million Puget Sound residents, most of them card-carrying REI members.

Veterans of this beautiful alpine territory know its popularity has been more curse than blessing. The Alpine Lakes, which received federal wilderness designation in 1976, includes 393,000 acres, more than 600 lakes, 500 miles of trails, and countless rugged alpine peaks, many of them glaciated. Yet dozens of its most popular hike-in destinations are overused to the point of serious permanent damage. The sheer weight of hundreds of thousands of hikers and their accompanying gear, tents, candle lanterns, and the like has pounded fragile lakeshores into permanent mud fields. Human waste has fouled once-pristine waterways. Trail maintenance can't keep pace with trail use.

As a result, the Forest Service has announced sweeping new back-country permit regulations, stock and pet restrictions, and other safe-guards for more fragile areas. Most of these new restrictions are being phased in during the summer of 1997 and in subsequent years, as (or if) budgets allow (see Alpine Lakes Wilderness Rules and Regulations, below, for details). Trail-use fees of some form also are likely to be experimented with on many Alpine Lakes Wilderness trails in the near future. Tougher access rules probably won't reverse damage already done. But they should limit future degradation, saving this awesome wilderness for those lucky enough to gain access to it in succeeding generations.

Let's be honest, the notion of phoning a vendor (heaven forbid TicketMaster!) in advance for permits, entering your name in a lottery, or paying a trail-use fee for a weekend hike sounds frightfully alien to many backcountry fans. But take a trip into the Alpine Lakes interior, and it's easy to see why so many endure so much bureaucracy to get here. The glacier-carved terrain—an endless chain of clear lakes surrounded by bursting meadows framed by magnificent granite peaks—truly is spectac-ular. Some of Washington's most precious natural features are found here—the Enchantment Basin, considered one of the nation's most beau-tiful backcountry destinations; the Necklace Valley; Chain Lakes; Tuck and Robin Lakes—the list goes on and on. Cascade peaks here are the stuff of Washington mountaineering legend: the Tooth, Chair Peak, Summit Chief, Mount Snoqualmie, Kendall Peak, Mount Alta, Three Queens, Chikamin Peak, Big Snow Mountain, Bears Breast, Cathedral Rock; and the most impressive granite structures of all—Mount Stuart, the Stuart Range, and the Enchantment Crags.

Topography in the wilderness ranges from lush, green rain forest on the west slopes to dry, ponderosa-pine-and-big-skies country on the east. Most Alpine Lakes territory is snowbound for all but a brief, August-to-October recreational window (porthole might be more appropriate). That means seeing the best of this region requires careful planning, not only to avoid foul weather and deep snowfields, but to time your visit between road washouts and permit hangups.

Somehow, that makes spending time here all the more special, that much more desirable. In future years, we hope, some of the hiker pressure will be taken off the wilderness area by developing more trails on all sides of it. The Mountains-to-Sound Greenway effort—which seeks to develop much of the I-90 corridor (and the Middle Fork Snoqualmie Valley) for hiking, camping, and mountain biking—is the best hope toward that end.

In the meantime, exercise special caution on the trails, around the lakes, and on the mountaintops of the Alpine Lakes Wilderness. Consider visiting your favorite area as a day trip, not a backpack venture. Tread even more lightly than normal. The Alpine Lakes Wilderness is worth every ounce of extra effort.

Getting There

Most of the interior Alpine Lakes Wilderness is reached by a combination of Forest Service logging roads and hiking paths, most originating on US 2 on the north side of the wilderness or Interstate 90 on the south side. From the south, the most widely used access roads are I-90, Middle Fork Snoqualmie Road, Taylor River Road, Forest Service Road 9030, Lake Kachess Road, Salmon La Sac Road, and North Fork Teanaway Road. From the north, the primary access points are along US 2, Miller River Road, Foss River Road, and Icicle Valley Road near Leavenworth. The eastern portion of the wilderness is best reached via US 97, Blewett Pass Hwy.

Adjoining Areas

NORTH: **Stevens Pass Corridor and Lake Wenatchee**

SOUTH: **Snoqualmie Pass Corridor (Mountains-to-Sound Greenway)**

EAST: **Wenatchee National Forest: Overview; Chelan and the Middle Columbia**

WEST: **Greater Seattle**

Alpine Lakes Wilderness
Rules and Regulations

In 1994, after many years of study, the Mount Baker–Snoqualmie and Wenatchee National Forests, which co-manage the Alpine Lakes Wilderness, published a list of new user rules for overused areas in the wilderness. However, it turned out that the Forest Service couldn't afford to enforce its own rules. Forest officials now say the new rules will be phased in "as budgets allow."

In spite of all that, there are some things we do know about life in the Alpine Lakes Wilderness in the near future. It's critical to check with a local ranger district about permit requirements and use restrictions for any Alpine Lakes venture, even if it's a simple day hike. A phone call could save you a major headache—not to mention a wasted trip if your destination turns out to have been booked up a year in advance by other hikers who *were* savvy to the rules. See More Information at the end of this chapter for a list of numbers, and note the following:

Day hikers must fill out trail permits, which at least for now are free, unlimited, and available at all trailheads and ranger stations. The permits are required between May 1 and October 31.

Backpackers also must have a backcountry permit between May 1 and October 31. At this writing, these permits are free and available at trailheads for most Alpine Lakes trails. Some major exceptions:

Limited overnight permits are available for the popular **Enchantments Basin** southwest of Leavenworth. In the summer of 1996, the traditional Enchantments Permit Area nearly doubled in size, and now includes Eightmile and Caroline Lakes, the Upper Ingalls drainage, and the Mount Stuart area. When this book went to press, those permits were being dispensed by Reservations Northwest, the camping reservation system employed by Washington and Oregon state parks. The reservation system, which replaced an old mail-in permit system, is reached by calling (800) 452-5687. As mentioned above, call the ranger district to make sure this venture was more than a one-year experiment. The phone-reservations plan sets aside 25 percent of each day's permits, which are dispensed on a first-come, first-served basis for same-day hikers who show up at the Leavenworth Ranger District; (509) 782-1413.

Other wilderness areas are expected to begin limiting overnight backpackers beginning in the summer of 1997 under a similar advance-reservation permit system. They include the **West Fork Foss River** drainage in the Skykomish Ranger District and a large area **north of Snoqualmie Pass** including **Snow Lake** and **Rampart Ridge**. The latter permit area is the largest and will be by far the most significant because it's less than 1 hour from Seattle and its trails are the most heavily used in the wilderness area. At this writing, it is unclear how permits for these two new areas will be made available for advance reservations. It is clear that overnight use in both areas is likely to be restricted, for the first time, quite soon. Call the Leavenworth, North Bend, or Skykomish Ranger Districts at the numbers listed under More Information for current permit information.

Mountain bikes, or any other "mechanized" mode of transport, aren't allowed (and likely never will be) in the Alpine Lakes, or any other federal wilderness area.

Other **no-nos** that apply to all wilderness areas: cutting switchbacks; caching food or equipment; cutting any trees or portions thereof; washing dishes or bodies in streams and lakes; dumping litter in backcountry toilets; or burying human waste less than 200 feet from a water source.

The maximum number of living souls allowed in one **party** (human or stock) is 12. In the Enchantments Permit Area, it's 8 humans (stock is not allowed).

Campfires are prohibited above 4,000 feet west of the Cascade Crest and above 5,000 feet east of the Crest. (If you can't locate the Crest, you shouldn't be operating a fire anyway.) Campfires are prohibited at most lakes and popular backcountry camps. Also, consider that just because you are allowed to have a fire in some areas doesn't mean you should. Stoves are recommended throughout the wilderness.

Camping is allowed only in designated areas at most backcountry sites. Check with your local ranger district for a list of affected areas. Whenever possible, camp on snow, rock, or bare ground. Camping is not allowed within 200 feet of Cradle Lake, Lake Edna, Cup Lake, Larch Lake, or Escondido Tarns.

You can't lead a **horse** to water unless you make him drink: pack and saddle animals are not allowed within 200 feet of lakes, except to get a drink. Go figure. Bring your own horse feed, and make sure it's seed-free (we don't want to know how the rangers check this after the fact). Consult ranger districts for other stock restrictions.

Dogs are allowed in the wilderness, but must be leashed on all trails off I-90 and US 2 west of Stevens Pass. No dogs are allowed in the Enchantments Permit Area.

Hiking/Backpacking

This is the big-ticket item. Some of Washington's most spectacular high-country destinations lie within the Alpine Lakes Wilderness. You can hike all the way across the wilderness on any of several routes, one of which is the 69-mile north-south stretch of the Pacific Crest Trail between Snoqualmie Pass and Stevens Pass. But even a short enumeration of the best hikes in the region is too long to list here. (For a healthy start, consult the Snoqualmie Pass Corridor, I-90 East: Roslyn to Ellensburg, Stevens Pass Corridor and Lake Wenatchee, and the Leavenworth and the Icicle Valley chapters.)

Camping

No organized campgrounds lie within the Alpine Lakes Wilderness. Backcountry campsites are sublime, but most are subject to "low-impact" restrictions (see Alpine Lakes Wilderness Rules and Regulations, above). A large number of excellent Forest Service campgrounds ring the wilderness border, however. (See the Camping sections of the Snoqualmie Pass Corridor (Mountains-to-Sound Greenway), I-90 East: Roslyn to Ellensburg, Stevens Pass Corridor and Lake Wenatchee, and Leavenworth and the Icicle Valley chapters for details.)

Fishing

The Alpine Lakes are a high-lake angler's paradise. Many of this region's 700 lakes and tarns contain rainbow or brook trout, most of them brought here in tanks packed in on the backs of volunteers. Keep in mind, however, that most high lakes don't fully melt out until July or later, and even then fishing can be slow until waters warm in the very late summer.

Anglers 15 and older need a Washington fishing license to fish all Alpine Lakes Wilderness rivers, lakes, and streams. (See the Camping sections of the Snoqualmie Pass Corridor (Mountains-to-Sound Greenway), I-90 East: Roslyn to Ellensburg, Stevens Pass Corridor and Lake Wenatchee, and Leavenworth and the Icicle Valley chapters for more information, or call a local ranger district.)

Climbing

Many of Washington's best-known climbing routes and pitches lie on granite peaks within the Alpine Lakes Wilderness. (Consult the Snoqualmie Pass Corridor (Mountains-to-Sound Greenway), I-90 East: Roslyn to Ellensburg, and Leavenworth and the Icicle Valley chapters for details.)

Wildlife

You won't find designated animal-watching sites in the Alpine Lakes Wilderness. You won't need them. The wilderness itself is a wildlife refuge in its own right, containing healthy populations of **black-tailed deer, black bears, cougars, mountain goats, raccoons,** and even the occasional migratory **northern gray wolf.** Some people will swear **grizzlies** dip this far south from their journeys though the North Cascades. Doubtful. We'll believe it when we see one. In general, the biggest predators in the Alpine Lakes Wilderness are black bears and cougars, and troublesome human encounters with either species are exceedingly rare. Still, it's a good idea to exercise good backcountry food-storage and -preparation techniques, such as hanging all food and cook gear from a bear wire, and refraining from sleeping with slabs of fresh bacon.

Horseback Riding

Much of the Alpine Lakes Wilderness is open to stock use. Guided tours are available in some portions. (Consult the I-90 East: Roslyn to Ellensburg chapter for trip information.)

Restaurants/Lodgings

For recommended restaurants and lodgings, see the Adjoining Areas to this chapter.

More Information

Mount Baker–Snoqualmie National Forest Headquarters: *21905 64th Avenue SW, Mountlake Terrace, WA 98043; (206) 744-3401.*

Wenatchee National Forest Headquarters: *PO Box 811, Wenatchee, WA 98801; (509) 662-4335.*

Cle Elum Ranger District: *(509) 674-4411.*

Lake Wenatchee Ranger District: *(509) 763-3103.*

Leavenworth Ranger District: *(509) 782-1413.*

North Bend Ranger District: *(206) 888-1421.*

Skykomish Ranger District: *(360) 677-2414.*

Snoqualmie Pass Visitors Center: *(206) 434-6111.*

Stevens Pass Corridor and Lake Wenatchee

From Gold Bar east to Hwy 207 near Lake Wenatchee, north to Dishpan Gap on the Pacific Crest Trail, and south to Deception Lakes in the Alpine Lakes Wilderness.

They don't call it a National Scenic Byway for nothing. Perhaps no other Northwest highway is as deserving of that moniker as Stevens Pass Highway (US 2), a road that mimics the rivers it follows from the Puget Sound lowlands to headwaters high in the Central Cascades. Like the nearby lumbering Snoqualmie River, US 2 begins as a boring four-laner through cow country in the lower Snoqualmie Valley, gets narrower and more interesting between Monroe and Sultan, then downright skinny and squirrelly between Gold Bar and Skykomish.

The roadside views as you enter this upper Skykomish River gorge say more about this region than any words ever mustered. Coming around a bend on an autumn day, motorists are blindsided by the sudden presence of Mount Index, the most impressively jagged slab of rock in the Cascades. Snow clings to a handful of narrow ledges on this near-vertical beast, one of many similar behemoths forming the walls of the upper Skykomish drainage.

In a mountain setting like this, the beauty and mystique of every inch of land is magnified. The Skykomish is a federally designated Wild and Scenic River, and rightly so. Hiking trails leading north into the Henry M. Jackson and Glacier Peaks Wildernesses and south into the Alpine Lakes Wilderness are packed with mountain lakes and alpine meadows as majestic as any in North America. Skiers harden thigh muscles—and strain smile muscles—on trails and ski lifts near the Stevens Pass summit. Anglers wade into the Skykomish and Wenatchee systems, which drain the west and east slopes of this region, respectively, and come home with sizable fish and unwieldy tales.

The Stevens Pass Corridor is wild by accident. Unlike some other state mountain areas set aside early for conservation regions, this one is so rugged that it largely preserved itself. Miners, railroads, developers, and contractors have given their all on both sides of this corridor, but here the rivers and mountains continue to reign supreme. Mine shafts have crumbled. Roads routinely wash out. More than one railroad has picked up its ties and gone home.

A single thin ribbon of concrete—the Stevens Pass Highway—is the lone enduring human presence in this geographic center of the Central Cascades. For recreationalists, that's the ideal compromise. Thanks to the highway, reaching the heart of the mountains is easy. Thanks to the mountains, a lot of us still have trouble getting back out.

Getting There

All destinations in the Stevens Pass Corridor are reached via US 2, Stevens Pass Hwy, which runs east from Interstate 5 at Everett to Wenatchee on the central Columbia River. Stevens Pass summit is some 80 miles northeast of Seattle; allow about 2 hours. Lake Wenatchee is an additional 20 miles to the east. Snow often socks in Stevens Pass near the summit, where one 10-mile stretch can be particularly hazardous for drivers. The pass rarely is closed by snow, but chains sometimes are required. Call (888) SNO-INFO for road updates.

Adjoining Areas

NORTH: **Mountain Loop Highway and the Glacier Peak Wilderness; Stehekin and the Lake Chelan NRA**

SOUTH: **Alpine Lakes Wilderness: Overview; Snoqualmie Pass Corridor (Mountains-to-Sound Greenway)**

EAST: **Leavenworth and the Icicle Valley; Chelan and the Middle Columbia**

WEST: **Greater Seattle**

inside out

Hiking/Backpacking

Trails in this region run the gamut, from close-in, overcrowded day hikes (Wallace Falls) to lonely treks through some of the more remote wilderness areas in the state. From US 2, hikers can head north into the Glacier Peak or Henry M. Jackson Wilderness areas, or south into the heavily traveled, but still spectacular, Alpine Lakes Wilderness.

For full trail information, including ever-evolving permit requirements and reports on high-mountain roads (which often wash out in this area), contact the Skykomish Ranger District (westside trails; (360) 677-2414) or Lake Wenatchee Ranger District (eastside trails; (509) 763-3103). But just to get your mind drooling, here's a short list of popular hikes on both sides of US 2.

Gold Bar area, north side

Everyone should haul themselves up to **Wallace Falls** (moderately difficult; 7 miles round trip) at least once. Visible from US 2 in the winter, the falls have been luring Stevens Pass travelers for decades. From a trailhead in Wallace Falls State Park just north of Gold Bar, the path climbs fairly steeply, coming to a fork. The left route follows an old railroad grade to the top. It's a mile longer, but a bit easier on the lungs. The right fork is the direct route, direct meaning painful if you're not in shape. The paths meet at a bridge over the North Fork Wallace, then take you another mile or so to a lower-falls viewpoint. Stop here, or continue another 1.5 miles to an upper-falls viewpoint. Either way, the payoff is rich. Wallace Falls, a 250-foot drop on the South Fork Wallace, is arguably the most magnificent in the Cascades. The mist is a great elixir.

Skykomish area, north side

The **Iron Goat Trail** (easy; 8 miles round trip), a newly reclaimed Great Northern Railroad right-of-way, is a great family hike, or a good leg-stretcher for Stevens Pass travelers. From US 2, 6 miles east of Skykomish, take the old Cascade Hwy (Forest Service Road 67) 2.3 miles north to Road 6710, turn left, and find the trailhead at road's end, 1.4 miles farther on. Awaiting your strolling pleasure are about 8 miles of reclaimed railroad trail, complete with interpretive signs to link the present ruins (collapsed snowsheds and long-abandoned tunnels) with the railroad past. This particular stretch was abandoned by the Great Northern in 1929, when the second Cascade Tunnel, a 7.8-mile passage beneath Stevens Pass, rendered it obsolete. Today, it's a fascinating walk, and one of the best places in this area to enjoy blooming wildflowers in the spring and early summer. Much credit goes to Volunteers for Outdoor Washington and other trail groups, who have built this trail system almost exclusively with volunteer labor.

North Fork Skykomish River drainage

Follow Road 63, the North Fork Skykomish River Road, east from Skykomish:

A pleasant backpack route is the **West Cady Ridge Trail** (moderate; various loop distances possible) in the North Fork Skykomish drainage. From a trailhead 21 miles up Road 63, the path climbs through thick forest before breaking out on a scenic, 5-mile-long stretch of ridge-top meadows. Highlights include Benchmark Mountain and access to a spectacular stretch of the Pacific Crest Trail that passes Skykomish Peak and skirts Lake Sally Ann on the way to Dishpan Gap in the Henry M. Jackson Wilderness. Pick up a copy of Green Trails' Monte Cristo and Benchmark Mountain maps (numbers 143 and 144) and plan your own route. Don't tell anyone, but you can find summer solitude here.

For a more direct, river-valley access to the same area, the **Dishpan Gap Trail** (moderate; 14.6 miles round trip) begins at the end of Road 63 and follows the North Fork Skykomish directly to Dishpan Gap. A trying day hike in the same area is the **Blanca Lake Trail** (difficult; 7 miles round trip), which climbs about 2,700 feet in the first 3 miles before dropping to the lake, which offers beautiful views of Columbia, Monte Cristo, and Reyes Peaks in the Henry M. Jackson Wilderness.

Beckler River drainage

Take Beckler River Road 65 north from Skykomish, then Rapid River Road 6530 east:

Fortune Ponds (moderate; 17 miles round trip) is a very popular backcountry destination in the heart of the Henry M. Jackson Wilderness. The trail climbs gently from the Rapid River along Meadow Creek to the ponds, a series of lakes in the shadow of Fortune Mountain. Lots of good—and overused—campsites. You can make a long shuttle hike out of this one by joining the Pacific Crest Trail near the ponds and hiking south about 12 miles to Road 6700, which exits on US 2 near Stevens Pass. Or continue south on the PCT for a total of about 20 miles, exiting at Stevens Pass.

Little Wenatchee River drainage

Follow Road 6500 west from the Lake Wenatchee area:

Little Wenatchee Ford is the staging area for a number of excellent Glacier Peak Wilderness hikes. One of the more popular is the **Cady**

Creek/Little Wenatchee Loop (difficult; 18.8 miles round trip). Take the Cady Creek Trail to Cady Pass, turn north for a 5.7-mile walk along the Pacific Crest Trail to Dishpan Gap, proceed 1 mile to Meander Meadows, then turn south and return on the 7-mile Little Wenatchee Trail. It's a spectacular loop, through the heart of a rather amazing alpine wilderness. Also from Little Wenatchee, the **Poe Mountain Trail** (excruciatingly difficult; 5 miles round trip) climbs 3,000 feet in 2.5 miles to a 6,015-foot viewpoint. Eat your Wheaties—twice.

White River drainage

Anybody who survived the hike up Poe Mountain—and enjoyed it—shouldn't miss the trail up an even higher peak four mountains to the east, **Mount David** (difficult; 14 miles round trip). From a trailhead at the end of Road 6400 (northwest of the Lake Wenatchee area), hike the Panther Creek Trail to the Mount David Trail—and muster up some courage. The trail gains more than 5,000 feet on its way to what's left of an old lookout tower (basically, an outhouse with a billion-dollar, 7,400-foot view). This is a tough climb in places, with the trail sometimes lost in scree or snow. Don't go before late summer, and don't ever go unprepared. Also from this trailhead, the **White River** and **Indian Creek** Trails depart east and north into the heart of the Glacier Peak Wilderness.

Lake Wenatchee area, north side

About 9 miles east of Stevens Pass on US 2, watch for the **Rock Mountain Trail** (painfully difficult; 10 miles round trip) near milepost 73. This is the direct—very direct—route to the top of Nason Ridge, which runs from Stevens Pass east to Lake Wenatchee. It climbs 3,500 feet in the first 4 miles, black flies are deadly, and there's little water. Still game? The ridge-top view (from 6,200 feet) is grand, and you can drop several hundred feet and about a mile down to Rock Lake. Conscience forces us to advise you that there's an easier way to get here. The **Snowy Creek Trail,** reached via Smith Brook Road 6700 (it turns off US 2 about 4 ½ miles east of Stevens Pass), is a much gentler, 4.5-mile route. But you wouldn't have nearly the same blisters to show for it.

　　Merritt Lake (moderate; 6 miles round trip), on the other hand, is a rather pleasant day trip for Lake Wenatchee visitors. The trailhead is on Spur Road 657, marked "Merritt Lake," just off US 2, about 12 miles east of Stevens Pass. You'll gain about 1,700 feet in the first 2 miles climbing to a junction with the Nason Ridge Trail. Stay right and climb another 500 feet or so over the final mile to Merritt Lake, which holds some trout.

　　Closer to Lake Wenatchee itself, the **Dirty Face Trail** (difficult; 9 miles round trip), which departs near the Lake Wenatchee Ranger Station on Hwy 207, is a fine place to work off all those s'mores from last night.

This is another major gasser, gaining 4,000 feet on its 7.6 billion-switch-backs route to a 6,000-foot summit lookout. Carry lots of water on this one; little is available.

More sensible day hikers will enjoy the **South Shore Trail** (easy, 2.4 miles round trip) and the short walk to **Hidden Lake** (easy; 1 mile round trip), both of which begin near Glacier View Campground (see Camping, below). Campers or day visitors to **Lake Wenatchee State Park** will find a pair of short, easy hiking trails up both banks of the Wenatchee River as it flows from the lake.

Miller River drainage

Follow Miller River Road 6410 south from US 2 near Money Creek:

The trail to **Lake Dorothy** (easy; 3 miles round trip) is a big hit, thanks to the fact that you can practically drive to it on logging roads. This trail is almost too easy, drawing large crowds to the alpine lake. Keep going for a good example of how logging roads very nearly cut the Alpine Lakes Wilderness in two. Those who continue around the east side of Lake Dorothy can proceed another 6.5 miles up the trail, passing Bear and Deer Lakes on the way to Snoqualmie Lake, in the Taylor River drainage. If you were so inclined, you could walk another couple of miles west down the Taylor River and—voilà!—be back on road, the abandoned Road 5630, which ultimately leads to Forest Service Road 56. Before you know it, you're all the way down the Middle Fork Snoqualmie and into North Bend for a hot-fudge sundae.

Important road note: The Miller River Road was washed out during severe flooding in the spring of 1996. At this writing, its opening has not been rescheduled. Check with the Skykomish Ranger District before departing.

West Fork Foss River drainage

Follow Foss River Road 68 south from US 2, about a half mile east of the Skykomish Ranger Station:

Tonga Ridge (easy; 9.2 miles round trip) is a great way to sample the Alpine Lakes high country, because it starts out high. The first mile or so is in second-growth forest, then the trail breaks out into meadows. You'll find good campsites at Sawyer Pass (3.5 miles), amid one of the largest blueberry patches you'll ever find (a major early autumn bonus). A side trail leads to pretty Fisher Lake. Limited overnight permits are likely to be imposed on this area in the near future. Inquire at the Skykomish Ranger District, which also can give you directions to the trailhead on Spur Road 310, reached via Foss River and Tonga Ridge Roads.

Higher in the same drainage, the **West Fork Foss Lakes** (moderate; 13.5 miles round trip) are one of the most popular destinations in all the

Alpine Lakes Wilderness. Expect major limits on overnight use of this area, beginning as early as the spring of 1997. (For more on Alpine Lakes permits, see the Alpine Lakes Wilderness: Overview chapter.) It's easy to see what draws the crowds. This chain of beautiful alpine lakes, surrounded by stunning peaks and fed by waterfalls, begins with Trout Lake at 1.5 miles and ends more or less at Delta Lake, 7.5 miles in. Day hikers will find that crowds thin measurably after Trout Lake. The trailhead is on Road 6836, a Foss River Road offshoot.

The string of jewel-like lakes in the nearby **Necklace Valley** (moderate/difficult; 15 miles round trip) is another loved-nearly-to-death destination. From a trailhead 4.1 miles up Foss River Road, this trail climbs to Jake, Locket, Jewel, Emerald, Opal, and a half-dozen other too-small-to-name lakes, nearly all set in dramatic alpine cirques in the very heart of the Alpine Lakes Wilderness. The walk is easy for the first 5 miles, following an old miner's railroad grade up the East Fork Foss River. Then the path crosses the river and zooms (okay, *plods*, if you're an average hiker laden with backpack) straight up, gaining about 2,500 feet in just over 2 miles to the first of the lakes. This area, too, is likely to see limits on permits in coming years. Ask at the Skykomish Ranger Station, where you should also be sure to ask about road conditions.

Stevens Pass Vicinity, south side

Deception Creek Trail (moderate; various lengths possible) is a great midsummer, hot-day hike, mainly because it'll keep you out of the sun. The trail, following Deception Creek through deep forest, makes for a steady-but-moderate pace. You can hike it a mile to break in the new boots—or new kid—or keep going about 3 miles to some nice campsites. Shuttle-hiking backpackers (assuming it's late July or beyond, and the snow is melted) can continue south all the way through the Alpine Lakes Wilderness to Deception Lakes, the Pacific Crest Trail, Deception Pass (10.5 miles), and, ultimately, an exit in the Upper Cle Elum River drainage above Salmon La Sac (see the I-90 East: Roslyn to Ellensburg chapter). It makes for a one-way north-south Alpine Lakes Wilderness crossing of about 17 miles. (Note: The upper portions of Deception Creek must be crossed several times on foot logs, which may or may not have survived the winter storms and spring floods before you visit. Check with a ranger.)

Surprise Creek Trail (moderate; 8 miles round trip to Surprise Lake), which begins near Scenic, about 10 miles east of Skykomish, is another grand hot-day excursion. This very pretty creekside trail climbs about 2,300 vertical feet through cool, waterfall-lined forest to the lake. Call it a day there, or continue beyond to the Pacific Crest Trail, 6,000-

foot Pieper Pass, and Deception Lakes (about 10 miles).

Chain Lakes (difficult; 24 miles round trip), reached by hiking the Pacific Crest Trail south from Stevens Pass Summit (park near the ski area), are among the more dramatic backpacking destinations in this area. The trail, occasionally very steep and always snowbound until late summer, climbs to Chain and Doelle Lakes, which lie in a cirque below 6,807-foot Bull's Tooth peak. This area also can be reached by hiking the Icicle Creek Trail west from Icicle Road, crossing Frosty Pass. Through hikers can do a one-way Stevens Pass to Icicle trip of about 31 miles. It's a beauty.

Camping

Lake Wenatchee State Park is the camp-o-rama in this region. One of the few state parks in a truly alpine-lake setting, it's a perennial favorite of hikers, boaters, anglers, and regular old chaise-lounge power snoozers. Spread across both sides of the Wenatchee River's outlet from the lake, this park is big and diverse, with 197 standard campsites (no hookups), an 80-camper group camp, extensive picnic facilities, a boat launch and moorage, swimming area, and horse stables. Good hiking, mountain biking, cross-country skiing, kayaking, and fishing await nearby (see appropriate sections in this chapter). Lake Wenatchee is open all year. Camping loops are closed in the winter, but camping is allowed in the day-use area for those with Sno-Park winter ski permits. Sites can be reserved up to 11 months in advance by telephone; call (800) 452-5687. *On the east side of Lake Wenatchee (take Hwy 207 north 3.8 miles from US 2 east of Stevens Pass); (800) 233-0321.*

Other public camping facilities in the Stevens Pass corridor consist primarily of Forest Service campgrounds, with varying levels of service.

Skykomish Ranger District (west side of Stevens Pass)

Money Creek, west of Skykomish on US 2, has 12 tent and 13 tent/RV sites (no hookups). Open summers only, it's in a pretty setting beside the Skykomish River. Some sites can be reserved in advance by calling (800) 280-CAMP. *On US 2, 4 miles west of Skykomish; (360) 677-2414.*

Beckler River, just north of US 2, has 7 tent sites and 20 tent/RV sites (no hookups; maximum RV length, 21 feet) scattered along the tantalizing—and often unruly—Beckler River. The campground is open summers only. Some sites can be reserved in advance by calling (800) 280-CAMP. *On Forest Service Road 65, 2 miles north of Skykomish; (360) 677-2414.*

Two more remote campgrounds in the North Fork Skykomish area are reached via Forest Service Road 65 from the south or the Index-Galena Road from the west. **Troublesome Creek** has 19 tent spots and 12 tent/RV spaces (no hookups; maximum RV length, 21 feet). **San Juan** has 7 tent sites and 4 tent/RV sites (no hookups; maximum RV length, 21 feet). Neither campground has piped water, but they're both free. Troublesome Creek and San Juan are open summers only. Campsites cannot be reserved. *On Index-Galena Road (summer only) 12 and 14 miles, respectively, east of Index; (360) 677-2414.*

Lake Wenatchee Ranger District (east side of Stevens Pass):

Three remote, primitive campgrounds on the south side of Glacier Peak, near the headwaters of the Wenatchee River, serve as staging areas for fishing and backpacking expeditions. The first is **Soda Springs,** which has 5 tent sites and no running water, but it's free. It's open summers only, and sites cannot be reserved. *Follow Forest Service Road 6500 approximately 7 1/2 miles west from Lake Wenatchee's North Shore Drive (Hwy 207); (509) 763-3103.*

The second, **Lake Creek,** has 8 tent sites (no hookups), pit toilets, no water, and no fee. Lake Creek is open summers only, and sites cannot be reserved. *Follow Forest Service Road 6500 approximately 10 1/2 miles west from Lake Wenatchee's North Shore Drive (Hwy 207); (509) 763-3103.*

Nearby, at the end of the road, is **Little Wenatchee Ford,** which has 3 tent sites, a pit toilet, and lots of solitude. This is a staging area for many Glacier Peak Wilderness hikes, such as the Cady Creek/Little Wenatchee Loop (see Hiking/Backpacking, above). It's open summers only, and sites cannot be reserved. *Follow Forest Service Road 6500 approximately 12 1/2 miles west from Lake Wenatchee's North Shore Drive (Hwy 207); (509) 763-3103.*

One river drainage north, another major Glacier Peak drainage, the White River, is the site of two more quiet campgrounds. The first, **Napeequa Crossing,** has 3 tent sites and 2 tent/RV spots (no hookups). This free campground is another popular staging area for expeditions into the Glacier Peak Wilderness. The Twin Lakes Trail is nearby. Napeequa Crossing is open summers only. Campsites cannot be reserved. *From Hwy 207 north of Lake Wenatchee, drive 7 miles northwest on Forest Service Road 6400 (White River Road); (509) 763-3103.*

The second, **White River Falls,** has 5 tent sites, pit toilets, no running water, and no fee. It's located near the falls of the same name (very impressive), and is open summers only. Campsites cannot be reserved. *From Hwy 207 north of Lake Wenatchee, drive approximately 11 miles northwest on Forest Service Road 6400 (White River Road); (509) 763-3103.*

Two other Forest Service camps are near Lake Wenatchee itself: **Glacier View,** on the lake's southwest shore, has 23 tent sites, 15 of which are walk-in sites near the lake, making this a popular boater/angler camp.

The campground also has a boat launch and piped water. It's open summers only, and campsites cannot be reserved. *Follow Forest Service Road 6607 5.5 miles west from Hwy 207 south of Lake Wenatchee; (509) 763-3103.*

Nason Creek, on the Wenatchee River just south of the lake, has 26 tent and 45 tent/RV sites (no hookups; maximum RV length, 31 feet). A popular alternative to Lake Wenatchee State Park, Nason Creek is open summers only. Campsites cannot be reserved. *Just off Hwy 207 near Lake Wenatchee; (509) 763-3103.*

Downhill Skiing

Stevens Pass Ski Area, a longtime favorite of Seattle-area day-skiing commuters, is the main attraction here, offering some of Washington's best all-around skiing when snow conditions cooperate. Stevens, with 2,000 feet of vertical spread broadly across both sides of the Stevens Pass Summit, has a great mix of alpine terrain. That, coupled with an improving chairlift system and quite consistent snowfall, makes the mountain a must-visit for the serious Puget Sound–area skier.

Stevens offers something for every skier. Options on the front side range from broad, smooth beginner and intermediate runs to a set of downright nasty bump runs under the lifts and, for the experts, the knee-shaking steeps of Seventh Heaven. The back side, a portion of Mill Creek Valley opened to lift skiing several years ago, is equipped with two fixed quad chairs—and many acres of groomed and ungroomed fun. The back side is medium-steep, a touch wild, and usually not as heavily skied as the front, making it the location of choice among fans of unbroken snow. When it's open (often not until a month's worth of skiing on the front side has passed), the back side is the place to be.

Stevens took another step toward regional ski-resort respectability in 1997 with the installation of its first high-speed detachable quad lift, the Skyline Express, which replaced the popular front-side Barrier chair. It should be a boon both to intermediate skiers, who love Barrier's long, flowing runout, and experts, who now can zip to the base of the Seventh Heaven chair without the use of an annoying midmountain rope tow.

The base area at Stevens offers full services, including a quality ski school, a rental and gear shop, several restaurants, a nice brown-bag lunch area, and an efficient ski-check (use it; stolen skis are as much a problem here as anywhere else).

Skiing typically begins here around Thanksgiving (in recent years, the mountain has given perennial early opener Mount Baker a run for its money, although veterans know the skiing usually doesn't get really good until January) and lasts through the first week of April. The base area is

3,800 feet, not exactly high as ski resorts go, but a full 800 feet higher than competing Snoqualmie Pass areas. Stevens tops out at about 5,800 feet.

Snowboarders are warmly welcomed at Stevens, and have proliferated on the slopes. They like the same things about the mountain as skiers: lots of mixed terrain, room to spread out—and relatively reasonable lift rates. Midweek skiing at Stevens has always been one of the better bargains in the state.

The biggest drawback to skiing Stevens is the drive. For much of the winter, it's an easy 90-minute to two-hour commute from the Seattle area. But when the weather turns sour, US 2 can be a hellish drive, particularly for the 10 miles or so on either side of the summit. Carry chains, or you'll regret it.

Stevens is open 9am to 10pm daily during ski season. Adult weekend lift tickets were $32 at this writing. The closest lodging is in Skykomish on the west side, and at Lake Wenatchee and Leavenworth on the east. Mountain information: (360) 973-2441. Snow report: (206) 634-1645.

Cross-Country Skiing

Nordic skiers have three options at Stevens Pass. The first is the increasingly popular **Stevens Pass Nordic Center,** 5 miles east of the main ski area along US 2. The Nordic Center has 27 kilometers of groomed trails running up Mill Creek Valley. It's a nice trail system, the primary drawback being the high-tension power lines that run through the valley, making you wonder what all that snap, crackle, and pop is doing to your brains as you slide underneath.

Even so, this is an enjoyable day outing. Some longtime Stevens Pass Nordic fans lament the construction of this facility in the early '90s (the Mill Creek Valley formerly was an unpatrolled backcountry ski area, with parking access provided by a state Sno-Park). But trail fees have remained reasonable ($7.50 per day at this writing). That seems like a fair tradeoff, considering how much trail grooming is done here now. The Nordic Center is open Fridays through Sundays, plus holidays, from 9am to 4pm. For information, call (360) 973-2441.

Another option is the extensive trail system at **Lake Wenatchee State Park,** where a Sno-Park provides trail access all winter long for skiers whose autos have a Sno-Park parking sticker ($20 annually). This is one of the better Sno-Park areas in the state, with 30 kilometers of trails spread out across lands owned by Washington State Parks, the Forest Service and a couple of private timber companies. The tracks lead to six main loops, ranging from 1 to 4 kilometers in length. The most scenic is the easy 1K lake loop, which skirts the shore of (frozen) Lake Wenatchee.

This isn't the quietest Sno-Park, however. It's a huge staging area for snowmobilers bound for backcountry trips on local logging roads. But there's something here for everybody in the Nordic-skiing family. Call the Leavenworth Ranger District, (509) 782-1413, for snow conditions and information.

The third great backcountry ski option is truly in the backcountry. **Scottish Lakes Back Country Cabins,** reached only by skiing or by riding a snow-cat 8 miles north of US 2, offers a unique ski experience. Skiers are shuttled into a cluster of seven rustic cabins and a newly expanded day-use building in the heart of the high, dry forest. A very extensive (24 kilometers, total) and well-maintained trail system awaits for skiers of all abilities. Backcountry telemarkers also find a nice range of fresh powder in the local mountains. It's a reservation-only affair, so call early: High Country Adventures, PO Box 2023, Snohomish, WA 98291-2023; (800) 909-9916.

Fishing

The middle flanks of the rushing **Skykomish River** settle into a string of deep pools just east of Gold Bar, forming the fabled **Reiter Ponds,** one of the state's most active steelhead-fishing venues. The Sky's winter run is one of the largest in the state. It usually peaks in December and January, but can remain productive until early March, when fishing switches to catch-and-release through April. The Sky also has a very productive summer-run fishery. Reiter Ponds can—and often does—get ridiculously crowded. But there are many other good shore-fishing spots on the river from Sultan downstream to the Hwy 203 bridge at Monroe. This river also has a healthy autumn return of coho, chum, and (during odd-numbered years) pink salmon. Check the state's fishing regulations pamphlet for information on seasons, limits, and conservation closures. If you're a newcomer who's really serious about learning the Sky, consider one of the guided float trips run by most Puget Sound–area river guides. Inquire at any local tackle shop.

The east side of the Stevens Pass Corridor offers an interesting mix of kokanee, trout, and occasionally sockeye salmon fishing. In a good year, **Lake Wenatchee** holds all three. The sockeye run is a spotty one—no surprise, considering the obstacles these fish must endure to return here (see notes on migratory salmon and steelhead in the Leavenworth and the Icicle Valley chapter). When it's open, most anglers employ the same method used successfully for salmon in Lake Chelan and Lake Washington—a bare hook trolled behind a flasher or spinner. The lake's kokanee population is quite healthy, a fact reflected by large bag limits in recent years. Best success comes in a boat, trolling with pop gear or active, flashy spinners.

Both the **Little Wenatchee** and **White Rivers,** the lake's two tributaries, offer decent trout fishing. The White, true to its name, often carries glacial silt from the Glacier Peak Wilderness downstream, so fishing can be tough. No bait is allowed above the Napeequa River confluence. The Little Wenatchee, conversely, can make trout fishing seem like child's play—particularly if you arrive just after the state plants catchable rainbows there. The river opens in late June, and can be productive all summer. (See Camping, above, for a list of good access points to the upper river.)

Trout fishing also can be very good on nearby **Fish Lake,** which holds rainbows and some big brown trout, as well as perch and bass. Decent bank access for fly anglers can be found at various points around the lake, and boats can be rented at The Cove Resort; (509) 763-3130.

If the crowds at these spots are a turnoff, consider that most of the high-country lakes in the **Alpine Lakes Wilderness** offer some semblance of a sport fishery. Check with the Lake Wenatchee or Skykomish Ranger District offices for information on which lakes are open, accessible—and thawed. State licenses are required for all freshwater fishing in this region.

Mountain Biking

In the Skykomish drainage, hundreds of miles of abandoned or nearly abandoned logging roads provide good fodder for fat-tire fans. A popular ride just off US 2 is **Money Creek Road 6420,** reached by turning south at Money Creek Campground (10 miles east of Index; see Camping, above) and following the Old Cascade Hwy and Miller Creek Road a short distance to the road start at a gate (open in summer if the road isn't washed out). You can climb about 12 miles on this road, with grand views along the route, all the way to **Lake Elizabeth.**

Other good day or multiday trips can be made on the **Beckler River Road,** which, combined with the **North Fork Skykomish Road** heading north from Index, creates a loop of about 30 miles off US 2. Riders can make it a multiday trip by camping at Beckler River, Troublesome Creek, or San Juan Campgrounds (see Camping, above).

In the summer, the **Mill Creek Valley,** wintertime site of Stevens Pass Nordic Center (see Cross-Country Skiing, above), is a worthy mountain-biking destination, with more than 15 miles of roads and trails.

Other good mountain-bike routes can be found all around

Lake Wenatchee, where winter ski and snowmobile trails become summer bike and off-road-vehicle routes. If you don't mind some gas-powered company, abandoned and rarely used logging roads on Nason Ridge, Pole Ridge, Minnow Ridge, and up Chikamin Creek all are easily accessible from the Lake Wenatchee area. Get a recent Forest Service map and consult the rangers at the Lake Wenatchee Ranger District for road information.

Rafting/Kayaking/Canoeing

The **Skykomish River** between Gold Bar and Skykomish is one of the state's more notable and frequently ridden whitewater stretches, with many Class III rapids and one particularly hairy obstacle—Boulder Drop, a notorious Class IV-to-V rapid. Whitewater kayakers and rafters run it regularly, but it's no place for wannabes. The river is numbing cold all year long, and its treacherous waters seem to claim a handful of ill-advised amateur river-runners every year. Helmets and life jackets are required by law.

Also rated expert is the Sky's North Fork, often run by experienced whitewater paddlers between Galena on the North Fork Skykomish Road and the river confluence just below Skykomish. If running any portion of the Sky is on your to-do list, go with a pro. Consult the Skykomish Ranger District for a list of qualified guides and outfitters.

On the east side, even more disconcerting are the frothing whitewater drops in Tumwater Canyon, where the **Wenatchee River** plunges from Lake Wenatchee to Leavenworth. Look, admire—and stay out. Rapids in this stretch are Class IV to VI—and there are a lot of them. Relatively placid float trips can be taken on the lower Wenatchee, below Leavenworth. (See the Leavenworth and the Icicle Valley chapter.)

Canoeists will find **Lake Wenatchee** to their liking, although excessive motorboat traffic can be a hassle. **Glacier View Campground** (see Camping, above) near the head of the lake is a great canoe camp. The walk-in sites allow easy access to the lakeshore for launching.

Cheaper Eats

Zeke's   In this region, all roads lead to Zekesville. The enduring roadside burger, fries and homemade shake joint, east of Gold Bar on US 2, is the unofficial National Scenic Byway eatery. (To be honest, we forgot who Zeke is—or was—and we don't care.) Everybody is hereby allowed one

Zeke's chocolate-peanut butter shake per decade. *(360) 793-2287; 43918 State Rte 2, Gold Bar.*

Lodgings

For recommended lodgings, see the Adjoining Areas to this chapter.

More Information

Department of Transportation pass report: *(888) SNO-INFO.*
Lake Wenatchee Ranger District: *(509) 763-3103.*
Northwest Avalanche Hotline: *(206) 526-6677.*
Skykomish Ranger District: *(360) 677-2414.*
Stevens Pass Ski Area: *(360) 973-2441; snow report, (206) 634-1645.*

Leavenworth
and the Icicle
Valley

From Leavenworth south to Mount Stuart, north through the Chiwawa River drainage, west to the Chelan–King County border, and east to Cashmere.

Everyone together now: Do the polar-fleece polka! If there were such a jig, it would feature lots of wheezing accordions played by hefty, pasty-faced mountain boys swilling dark German beer after a long day's free-climb up a rock called "Cruel Thumb." Which means it could be written, produced, and performed only in Leavenworth, the tiny Bavarian (hunch your lips up horse-style and say "Bah-VAHR-ian") village clinging to the edge of one of the Northwest's grander wilderness areas.

Indeed, hang around Leavenworth long enough, and that cornball license-plate-frame slogan "Washington, America's Alps" might begin to seem downright appropriate. If the Bavarian-kitsch town doesn't have you reaching for the lederhosen, the local hiking trails probably will. As with a real Bavarian village, the beauty of Leavenworth is mostly outside it.

Generally, it's in the Icicle Valley, stretching south, then east from town. Specifically, it's in Icicle Creek Canyon, which reaches into the eastern heart of the Alpine Lakes Wilderness. Bordered on the north by Icicle Ridge and on the south by the Stuart Range, the Icicle drains a truly Alps-like highland heaven. The south side is dominated by 9,415-foot Mount Stuart, a freak of nature whose angry face is marked by 2,000-vertical-foot granite scowls.

But the lands around the fantastic peak are more famous than the old mountain itself. Lying in a basin below Enchantment Peak, one mountain east of Stuart, is fabled Enchantments Basin, a string of high-country lakes surrounded by soaring, knife-edged granite spires. This is one of the most awe-inspiring backpack destinations in the country. The Enchantments' soaring popularity, in fact, made it the first alpine area in Washington with enforced limits on overnight visitors. The area has created many a lifetime memory, both among backpackers weary from the long, steep haul in to the 7,000-foot basin, and rock climbers who challenge the basin's magnificent granite spires, collectively known as the Cashmere Crags. In a state filled with many valuable outdoor jewels, this is one of the true irreplaceable treasures.

In the summertime, few backcountry areas in the country rival the sheer beauty of the Icicle Canyon and its guardian Stuart Range. In the winter, most of that backcountry is locked away, but Leavenworth and its surroundings take on what in many ways is an even greater charm. For Puget Sound residents, Leavenworth's always-frosty winter face is a welcome one—a chance to escape the wet, windy winter warmth for a brief taste of good old-fashioned, dry-air mountain shivers; a place to go ski hard all day beneath the silent pines, then build a fire in the wood stove and curl up with a good book (or even this one) at night. Thanks to its relative wealth of lodging options, Leavenworth is perhaps the best place to do just that within 2 hours of Seattle.

This mondo-lodging scenario is crucial for us outdoors enthusiasts. If it wasn't for the Bavarian Blitz, your mothers, fathers, aunts, and uncles would never bother to come to Leavenworth, and many of the hotels, B&Bs, and eateries that make the town such an easy-to-book weekend adventureland would dry up and blow to Peshastin.

Several years ago, nature very nearly accomplished that on its own. In the summer of 1994, many of the local wildlands around Leavenworth were charred by the Rat Creek and Hatchery Creek wildfires, which burned nearly all summer, destroying thousands of acres of timber and blackening earth right to the gates of Little Bavaria. But a rebirth is taking place in the valley, with acres of wildflowers and young trees sprouting forth and prancing in spring breezes created by helicopters hauling out the last of downed "salvage" timber.

Nature, in other words, continues to do its thing here. And the Leavenworth Bavarian Chamber of Commerce continues to do its thing too. For lovers of the pure and natural, the high and quiet, these accordion-huffing lowlands can be a shock to the system. Like unnaturally dark beer, Leavenworth prompts an initial shudder. But after a while...well, it sort of grows on you.

Which is not to suggest that the polar-fleecers and the polka dancers are, or ever will be, in *perfect* step with each other. But they have made something of an art of avoiding one another's toes.

Getting There

Leavenworth is about 100 miles east of Everett on US 2. Recreation sites in Icicle Canyon are reached via Icicle Road (Forest Service Road 7600), which turns south from US 2 on the west side of Leavenworth.

Adjoining Areas

NORTH: **Chelan and the Middle Columbia; Wenatchee National Forest: Overview**

SOUTH: **I-90 East: Roslyn to Ellensburg**

EAST: **Wenatchee and Mission Ridge**

WEST: **Stevens Pass Corridor and Lake Wenatchee**

Hiking/Backpacking

As mentioned above, Leavenworth has become the launching point for some of the Northwest's most memorable backcountry jaunts. Thankfully, they don't all require the extensive advance preparation—or thigh muscles—needed for long trips into the Enchantments.

Some of them, in fact, start right next to your favorite downtown doodad shop. A new Leavenworth **city-center trail system,** used as a cross-country skiing byway in the winter, leads along the Wenatchee River and over wheelchair-accessible ramps to Blackbird Island. Connecting paths lead up into the Icicle drainage and the Leavenworth Golf Course. A good starting point for the **Waterfront Interpretive Trail** is Front Street Park.

Just about every other trail outside town—the good ones, anyway—requires a permit, either the day-use kind (free and unlimited at trailheads) or the overnight kind (call ahead and pray). Beginning in the summer of 1996, additional Alpine Lakes Wilderness destinations accessible from Leavenworth joined the Enchantments on the advance-reservations-required list. These included the Stuart and Colchuck Lakes area, as well as an expanded zone around the Enchantments. If you're planning an overnight hike anywhere in the region, check permit requirements with the Leavenworth Ranger District. (For more on Alpine Lakes permits, see the Alpine Lakes Wilderness: Overview chapter.)

Once you're thoroughly permitted, all that remains to trip you up is nature, and this area has seen more than its fair share of natural temper tantrums in the 1990s. Nearly all the trails in the Icicle drainage—everything from flat, easy creekside paths to trying alpine routes over mountain passes—were, for better or worse, altered by the awesome Rat Creek and Hatchery Creek wildfires in the summer of 1994. Much of the Icicle Canyon burned in those fires, taking thousands of acres of forests with it. A lot of the downed timber has been removed by helicopter "salvage logging," and most Icicle Canyon trails have reopened, with new looks. Expect ramifications from the fires, however, to be felt for years, in the form of washed-out roadways, increased trail erosion, and other difficulties. The fire had its upside, too. Spring visitors to the Icicle will encounter proliferations of wildflowers and wildlife perhaps never before seen here.

For full details on the range of hikes available around Leavenworth, call or stop by the Leavenworth Ranger District; (509) 782-1413. For further pondering, trail guides worthy of consultation are *Pacific Northwest Hiking,* by this author and Dan A. Nelson (Foghorn Press), and The Mountaineers' *100 Hikes in Washington's Alpine Lakes Wilderness.* Two excellent topographic maps of the region are Green Trails Nos. 177 and 178, Chiwaukum Mountains and Leavenworth.

Here's a list of some favorites.

North side Icicle Road

A longtime favorite of early-summer wildflower fiends, the **Icicle Ridge Trail** (moderate/difficult; 26 miles one way) is a Leavenworth-area classic that ties all other north-side trails together. From a trailhead about 1 ½ miles down Icicle Road, this trail gets serious fast, zipping and zagging to the ridge top, which it follows northwest nearly all the way to Stevens Pass. Views from along the route are grand, and backpack loops of various distances through the Chiwaukum Mountains can be made by combining the Icicle Ridge Trail with northern connecting trails such as **Hatchery Creek** (moderate; 13 miles round trip from Tumwater Canyon), **Chiwaukum Creek** (moderate/difficult; 24 miles round trip from Tumwater Canyon to Ladies Pass), or **Frosty Creek** (moderate; various distances), which connects in the north valley at Frosty Pass. Day hikers also might find themselves at high viewpoints on the Icicle Ridge Trail by climbing the **Chatter Creek/Lake Edna Trail** (moderate; 10 miles round trip) or **Fourth of July Creek Trails** (difficult; 10.6 miles round trip) both of which begin on the north side of Icicle Road. For much of its length, the ridge trail is a great place to survey the path of the Hatchery Creek fire, which burned on both sides of the ridge, nearly all the way to Lake Augusta.

South side Icicle Road

The **Snow Lake Trail** (moderate; 13 miles round trip) is best known as the primary access to the Enchantment Lakes Basin. But it's a superb overnight backpacking or long day-hike destination in its own right, often serving as a second option when Enchantment permits are all booked up. The trailhead is about 4 miles down Icicle Road, on the left. Strong hikers won't be disappointed by an in-and-out trip to the two Snow Lakes, which are much like the Enchantments higher up.

The **Enchantment Lakes Trail** (difficult; 29 miles round trip) actually begins as the Snow Lake Trail, switching names—and degree of difficulty—after upper Snow Lake. The difference between backpackers and day hikers on this trail is that backpackers die more quickly and get it over with. Switchbacks climb up, up, up through the trees into the Enchantments, which will be beautiful if you can stay awake long enough to see them. Remember: This is a limited overnight permit area. Call well in advance of your trip (six months is minimum) to find out about permits. No fires, no dogs, no trombones.

Win or lose, you win: that choice awaits visitors to the **Stuart/Colchuck Lakes** area (difficult; 8 to 9 miles round trip). The trail—which begins at the end of Forest Service Road 7601 (an Icicle Road offshoot)—climbs steeply up Mountaineer Creek, coming to a fork at about 2 1/2 miles. Stuart Lake, with awesome views of the north face of Mount Stuart, is 2 miles to the right; Colchuck is 1.6 miles to the left. From Colchuck, a way trail skirts the lake and climbs nearly 4 miles along a high-ridge route over Aasgard Pass, then down into Isolation Lake, easternmost of the Enchantments. This "back door" access to the Enchantments can be a stunning trip, but the pass is snowbound much of the year and shouldn't be crossed by neophytes. Note that Stuart and Colchuck Lakes, like the Enchantments, are limited-permit backcountry areas. Call well in advance for permits. No fires, no dogs, etc.

A trailhead slightly lower down Road 7601 is the start of a popular valley day hike to **Eightmile Lakes** (moderate; 6.6 miles round trip). The short round-trip distance is the key, and the destination, Little Eightmile and Eightmile Lakes, is well worth the walk. But keep in mind that only the last portion of the trail is inside the Wilderness. Much of the lower portion has been logged and, more recently, burned.

A very pretty, and easily accessible valley hike is **Icicle Gorge Trail** (easy; 3 miles round trip), which makes a loop through lovely old-growth forest along Icicle Creek. From a trailhead near the Chatter Creek Guard Station, the trail follows the river to Rock Island Campground, then returns on the other side.

Backpackers, meanwhile, cluster along three upper-valley trails. The

Trout Creek Trail (difficult; 12.6 miles one way) allows a unique, one-way shuttle hike through the area. The path runs south 3 miles, then turns back east and climbs to amazing views at 7,200-foot Windy Pass before dropping to Eightmile Lakes (see above) and a shuttle-hike exit on Road 7601.

The nearby **Jack Creek Trail** (moderate; 24 miles round trip) is a beautiful walk south to a meeting with the mountain gods at Stuart Pass, where you can continue on into the Ingalls Creek drainage (see the I-90 East: Roslyn to Ellensburg chapter) in the US 97 corridor near Blewett Pass. Hikers up for a long, luscious valley walk can do the entire 27-mile route and walk nearly all the way around—but never into—the Stuart Range. The trail is a relaxing, moderately paced, valley-bottom walk, with good campsites all along the route. Short-trip backpackers will be more than happy with overnight jaunts on its lower portions.

A similar valley-bottom hike is the **French Creek Trail** (moderate; 22.8 miles round trip), which follows a peaceful creek drainage south to Paddy Go Easy Pass, a 3-mile downhill walk away from the headwaters of the Cle Elum River in the Salmon La Sac area (see the I-90 East: Roslyn to Ellensburg chapter). French Creek's lower portions are commonly employed as one leg on an upper Icicle drainage loop trip when combined with the **French Ridge, Snowall Creek,** or **Meadow Creek** Trails to the south. The trailhead is 1.5 miles up the Icicle Creek Trail, which begins near Blackpine Horse Camp (see Camping, below) at the upper end of Icicle Road.

Camping

The Forest Service will leave the light on for ya. Well, maybe a citronella candle or something. A string of seven Forest Service camps are the primary camping venues in this area. All have piped water and vault toilets, and all charge a fee. In order, along Icicle Road, they are:

Eightmile—oddly enough, just about 8 miles down Icicle Road—offers 46 sites (no hookups; maximum RV length, 21 feet) and a group site. It's a nice little campground, not far from the trailheads to Stuart/Colchuck and Eightmile Lakes. Eightmile is open summers only. Campsites cannot be reserved. *On Icicle Road 8 miles southwest of Leavenworth; (509) 782-1413.* **Bridge Creek,** a mile farther, is tiny, with 6 tent sites and 1 group site (must be reserved). It's open summers only, and campsites cannot be reserved. *On Icicle Road 9 miles southwest of Leavenworth; (509) 782-1413.*

Johnny Creek, split into upper and lower loops, has a total of 8 walk-in tent sites and 65 tent/trailer sites (no hookups; maximum RV length,

21 feet). Great river access. Johnny Creek is open summers only. Campsites cannot be reserved. *On Icicle Road 12 miles southwest of Leavenworth; (509) 782-1413.* **Ida Creek** has 5 tent spots and another 5 tent/trailer sites (no hookups; maximum RV length, 21 feet). It's open summers only, and campsites cannot be reserved. *On Icicle Road 14 miles west of Leavenworth; (509) 782-1413.*

Chatter Creek is as centrally located as any campground in this area. It has 12 sites (no hookups; maximum RV length, 21 feet) and 1 reservation-only group site. The Chatter Creek, Icicle Gorge, Jack Creek, and Trout Creek trailheads all are nearby, making this a favorite bivouac spot for backpackers. Chatter Creek is open summers only. Campsites cannot be reserved. *On Icicle Road 16 miles west of Leavenworth; (509) 782-1413.* **Rock Island,** in the upper Icicle Canyon, offers 12 tent sites and 10 tent/RV spots (no hookups; maximum RV length, 21 feet). It's open summers only, and campsites cannot be reserved. *On Icicle Road 17 miles west of Leavenworth; (509) 782-1413.*

At the head of the valley (and the end of the road) is **Blackpine Horse Camp,** which has 6 tent sites and 2 tent/RV sites (no hookups; maximum RV length, 21 feet). The camp, located at a major trailhead for excursions into the heart of the Alpine Lakes Wilderness, is horse-packer central. It's the valley's only campground with horse facilities. Non-horse people: your mission, should you choose to accept it, is to put your ground cloth down between those road apples without getting any on you. Blackpine is open summers only; campsites cannot be reserved. *At the end of Icicle Road, 18 miles west of Leavenworth; (509) 782-1413.*

Tumwater, another local option, is an expansive campground back on the main route (US 2). Tumwater has 84 tent/RV sites (no hookups; maximum RV length, 22 feet). The camp also has a group site with a kitchen shelter. This is an almost-always shady, peaceful site along the Wenatchee River in Tumwater Canyon, with nearby access to the Hatchery Creek and Chiwaukum Creek trailheads (see Hiking/Backpacking, above). Tumwater is open summers only. Campsites cannot be reserved. *On US 2, 10 miles west of Leavenworth; (509) 782-1413.*

Cross-Country Skiing

A wealth of overnight lodgings and quick access from Seattle make the Leavenworth area one of the leading winter weekend getaways for fans of the quiet sport of Nordic skiing. The big catch is snow. Leavenworth gets plenty of it, but ice, a four-letter word to the skinny-ski set, can be a problem here. And the season is rather unpredictable. It generally gets under way by Christmas and extends into March. But in some years, the season might be over by January. Call to check snow conditions before you make the drive.

That said, the abundance of good, impeccably maintained trails makes Leavenworth and the Icicle Canyon a great ski getaway, particularly for families and groups. Facilities are scattered around town, which is good, because so is lodging. If you're staying in Leavenworth in the winter, chances are some nice groomed tracks are not far away. All the ski trails are well maintained by the Leavenworth Winter Sports Club, which sells trail passes (at this writing, $7 per day, with children 12 and under free) at the following ski venues:

The **Icicle River Trail,** south of town, has 10 kilometers of groomed tracks and skating lanes in two loops at the mouth of Icicle Canyon. This is a family favorite. It's beautiful, especially on a crisp, sunny day, and the terrain is gentle. The 5K Meadow Loop is lovely and a good place to spot winter wildlife (true beginners, beware Dune Hill—take the bypass!). To get there, take Icicle Road south from US 2 and watch for the thicket of Range Rovers and Explorers.

The **Leavenworth Golf Course,** closest to town, has the most extensive trail system, with 10 kilometers of trail in three chunks. Choose from the 3K, aptly named Lazy River Loop; the 5K Tumwater Loop (a bit more curvy and challenging); and the 2K Waterfront Park trail, the winter version of the Waterfront Interpretive Trail (see Hiking/Backpacking, above). The latter crosses a bridge to Blackbird Island and connects to downtown at the end of Ninth Street. The golf course is located a short distance down Icicle Road.

Aggressive intermediates, free-wheeling free-heelers, and suicidal beginners congregate up the road at **Leavenworth Ski Hill,** which has 5 kilometers of trail split into a 2K and a 3K loop. Both are challenging, hilly, and—if you know what you're doing—lots of fun. A bonus when the weather cooperates is an oh-gosh view of icy-topped Mount Stuart. Ski Hill's 2K loop is lighted for skiing until midnight—or beyond, if diehards are present. Ski Hill is 1.5 miles north of downtown Leavenworth on Ski Hill Road.

Ski passes are sold from 8am to 4pm daily at each venue. For snow conditions, general information, and placing orders for homemade peanut brittle by ticket-booth personnel, call the Leavenworth Winter Sports Club; (509) 548-5115.

For a more natural ski setting, hop in the rig and head out of town to one of several local Sno-Park areas. (You'll need a Sno-Park pass, available at ranger stations and ski shops.) Popular areas are **Swauk Pass,** 25 miles south of Leavenworth on US 97 (watch for snowmobiles); **Lake Wenatchee State Park,** which has 35 kilometers of groomed tracks in two very extensive cross-country ski-trail complexes; and other turnouts along **Chiwawa Road** north of Leavenworth. Shuttle buses run from downtown Leavenworth to Lake Wenatchee State Park. Call the Leavenworth Ranger District, (509) 782-1413, for Sno-Park ski conditions. Some Leavenworth overnighters drive back west to the Stevens Pass Nordic Center to do their skiing. (See the Stevens Pass Corridor and Lake Wenatchee chapter.)

Ski rentals are available at several Leavenworth shops.

Climbing

Mount Stuart, a 9,415-foot wall of solid granite, is climbed via more than 10 separate ice-and-rock summit routes. Some of them go straight up the mountain's 2,000-foot vertical faces, which rank right up there with the Northwest's most challenging alpine routes. The peak and its stony companions—**Sherpa Peak** (8,605 feet), **Argonaut Peak** (8,453 feet), and **Ingalls Peak** (7,662 feet)—shouldn't even be considered by less-than-experienced climbers.

Smaller granite spires in the Enchantments and elsewhere in the Icicle drainage are famous among rock aficionados. The legendary **Cashmere Crags** in Enchantment Valley are among the most challenging pitches in the country, drawing ratings from 5.0 to a couple of off-the-scale 5.11 routes (such as one Dragontail Peak route). Many climbers come here for a lifetime and never summit all of these routes. Their names are enough to scare most people away. Notable rocks in this forest of granite spires include Prusik Peak, Razorback Spire, Cruel Thumb, Crocodile Fang, and Bloody Tower.

Other popular local rock-climbing venues are Icicle Buttress, Memorial Buttress, Eightmile Buttress, Egg Rock, Trick or Treat, Rat Creek Boulder, Condor Buttress, The Sword, Bridge Creek and Little Bridge Creek walls, and the Fourth of July Group. If you're even thinking about setting out on Icicle Canyon rock, consult the bible—Fred Beckey's *Cascade Alpine Guide* series (The Mountaineers). And you'll need a permit, available at the Leavenworth Ranger District.

About 8 miles east on US 2, rock climbers increasingly gather at **Peshastin Pinnacles,** the only Washington State Park designed specifically for that activity. Actually, the climbers were here long ago, when these were just big rocks sticking up in the middle of orchard territory. Frustrated farmers sold the property to the state in 1991, and the state had the good sense to leave the area basically au naturel, adding only a few signs, outhouses, and parking areas. A dozen or so climbing routes make this a favorite practice site for climbers of all abilities (the highest-rated pitch here is about 5.8), especially in the off season when other rocks are under snow. Note, however, that Peshastin Pinnacles is closed in December and January. No camping. Follow signs from US 2, 8 miles east of Leavenworth.

Beginners seeking a list of qualified guides should contact Leavenworth Ranger District; (509) 782-1413.

Mountain Biking

Most local trails are closed to fat tires, but a good selection of Forest Service roads is available. A few time-honored favorites:

Wenatchee River Road (Forest Service Road 7903), which begins on US 2 just west of Tumwater Campground, is a pretty ride, with several good river-access points. You can only go about 5 miles before the road turns private, but it makes for an enjoyable round trip of just under 10 miles.

A series of Forest Service roads in **Derby Canyon** near Peshastin (just east of Leavenworth) have become popular fat-tire hangouts. Loops of various lengths are possible on these rolling, dry public roads. In addition, most of the side roads beginning on US 97 near **Swauk Pass** are prime mountain-bike territory, as long as you don't mind sharing the road with motorcyclists. And many more good routes run through the Lake Wenatchee area (see the Stevens Pass Corridor and Lake Wenatchee chapter). Finally, right in Leavenworth, a couple of decent riding loops can be found at **Leavenworth Ski Hill** (see Cross-Country Skiing, above).

For more information, inquire at the Leavenworth Ranger District. Cycle rentals are available at several outdoor stores (listed in More Information at the end of this chapter). For bicycle pickup and drop-off service, contact Gator's Gravity Tours, (509) 548-5102, or Leavenworth Outfitters, (800) 347-7934.

Rafting/Canoeing/Kayaking

The big melt-off makes for lots of whoops and cheers on the **Wenatchee River** each spring. March through April, a number of commercial rafters take thrill-seekers down the Wenatchee, which is narrow, fast, and scary higher upriver, and wide, fast, and exciting down lower. Float trips continue through the summer on the lower river. For a list of outfitters, contact the Leavenworth Ranger District; (509) 782-1413. The lower river (downstream from Leavenworth) is a popular canoe and kayak route during summer months. For raft pickup and drop-off service, contact Gator's Gravity Tours, (509) 548-5102, or Leavenworth Outfitters, (800) 347-7934.

Wildlife

For those middle-of-the-week, resting-your-bones days, ride or bike down to the fish hatchery on Icicle Creek (12790 Fish Hatchery Road, off Icicle Road; (509) 548-7641) to watch the **chinook salmon** run (June and July) and spawn (August and September). The spawning season prompts (what else?) another Leavenworth festival, the Wenatchee River Salmon Festival in late September.

Icicle Canyon itself—one of the deepest in Washington, with more than 8,000 feet separating the floor from the highest peak—is a wildlife treasure trove. It's a state-designated wildlife area, with common sightings of **mule deer, golden eagles, harlequin ducks, ospreys,** and **great blue herons.** A 2-mile interpretive trail near the fish hatchery is a good starting point. But any of the many trails listed (see Hiking/Backpacking, above) will get you into the animals' home turf.

Fishing

Without question, the most highly sought scaly creatures in this region swim in the **Icicle.** They're spring chinook salmon—hatchery fish that return each year at the end of a flat-out astonishing journey from the Pacific *way* up the Columbia, up the Wenatchee, then 2 miles up the Icicle from its mouth to the hatchery. Spring chinook are the cream of the salmon crop, and some of these fish are the crème de la crème. Some big ones (25 pounds or more) make it up the Icicle, but the run usually is so brief (a few weeks in May) that proper amounts of luck and skill must meet before you take one home. When the Icicle kings are running, lay those egg clusters out there and hang on tight. The Icicle also produces a handful of steelhead every year—not many, considering the number of smolts sent downstream, probably to meet their maker in a hydroelectric turbine.

Steelhead and sockeye salmon in the **Wenatchee River** seem to suffer the same fate, but a few summer runs return every year to swim up Tumwater Canyon. The upper river (above the Icicle) is a selective fishery, with barbless hooks and artificial flies or lures required. Wild steelhead must be released. This stretch is popular with fly fishers, but steelheaders who are looking for something to keep generally fish the lower river, downstream from Leavenworth. A short section of the Wenatchee near Leavenworth (downstream from the Icicle) also is open for spring chinook fishing most years.

Mountain-stream trout fishing can be decent around Leavenworth. Most streams are overfished, but the quality of the experience makes up for results that at best are spotty. The **upper Wenatchee River** (above

Lake Wenatchee) is a fair bet, and **Chumstick Creek** and **Eagle Creek,** both crisp streams that flow into the Wenatchee near Leavenworth, produce a few fish in the summer.

Horseback Riding

Hourly, daily, and multiday horse-riding adventures can be arranged with Eagle Creek Ranch, (800) 221-7433, or Icicle Outfitters, (800) 497-3912. Hay rides and sleigh rides are offered all year round at Mountain Springs Lodge, (800) 858-2276, or Red Tail Canyon Farm, (800) 678-4512.

Dogsledding

You—yeah, you—can do it, December through March. Contact Enchanted Mountain Tours, (509) 763-2975.

Attractions

A railroad-yard-and-sawmill town that lost its industry, Leavenworth, with its stunning alpine setting in the Cascade Range, decided years ago to recast itself as a Bavarian-style town with tourism as its primary industry. The architecture in the city center features some excellent craftsmanship in the Bavarian mode. Popular festivals are the **Autumn Leaf Festival** the last weekend in September and the first weekend in October, the **Christmas Lighting Festival** the first two Saturdays in December, the **Bavarian Ice Fest** (snowshoe races, dogsled pulls, and the like) in mid-January, and **Maifest** the second weekend in May. And not to be outdone, every mid-August brings—our ears are running for cover at the mere thought—the **Leavenworth International Accordion Celebration.**

We recommend browsers head to the **Gingerbread Factory** (828 Commercial Street) for authentic decorated gingerbread cookies and a delightful village of gingerbread houses; **Images and Sounds** (Ninth and Commercial) for distinctly non-Bavarian posters, prints, and notecards; **A Book for All Seasons** (639 Front Street) for an excellent collection of books and a special-order service; the **Wood Shop** (719 Front Street) for colorful wooden children's puzzles and Christmas tree ornaments; **Die Musik Box** (837 Front Street), which has such an array of music boxes that you might turn the store's name into a shouted command before you leave; **Alpen Haus** (downstairs at 807 Front Street) for a fascinating collection of dollhouse furniture and miniatures; and **Country Things** (221 Eighth Street) for folk art, antiques, furniture, tinware, and linens.

Restaurants

Edel Haus Inn ☆   Edel Haus got its start as a Leavenworth bed and breakfast; however, today it's a quiet, pleasant restaurant with an international menu. The menu changes about once a month. *On 9th between Commercial and the river; (509) 548-4412; 320 9th St, Leavenworth; $$.*

Cheaper Eats

Homefires Bakery   Homefires is famous for its German-style wood-fired oven (the nine-grain bread is the thing to get, but don't pass up the dark German rye bread). *(509) 548-7362; 13013 Bayne Rd, Leavenworth.*

Katzen Jammers   This steak and seafood house is a popular gathering spot. *(509) 548-5826; 221 Commercial St, Leavenworth.*

Leavenworth Brewery   The brewery has six or seven beers made on the premises on tap (the types of beers rotate with the season), and offers daily tours of the small brewery itself. *(509) 548-4545; 636 Front St, Leavenworth.*

Oberland Bakery and Cafe   Oberland relies largely on whole-grain breads (try some with chicken salad), but also does a great raspberry Danish. *(509) 548-7216; 703 Front St, Leavenworth.*

Lodgings

All Seasons River Inn ☆☆   Each of the 6 guest rooms in this outstanding inn takes advantage of the Wenatchee River view with a private deck or patio and an indoor seating area in front of sliding glass doors. Mountain bikes are available. *1 mile off Hwy 2 on Icicle Rd; (509) 548-1425 or (800) 254-0555; 8751 Icicle Rd, Leavenworth; $$$.*

Enzian Motor Inn   This is the best hotel/motel place in town (and the price includes your breakfast). Stair rails and ceiling beams are hand-carved by a true Bavarian woodworker. The suites offer in-room spas and fireplaces; even the standard rooms are tasteful and a cut above most "motor inns." *On the north side of Hwy 2 near the center of town; (509) 548-5269 or (800) 223-8511; 590 Hwy 2, Leavenworth; $$.*

Haus Lorelei Inn ☆   The 2-acre site, surrounded by towering pines and flanking the Wenatchee River, is only two blocks from Leavenworth's main street. The inn offers 8 bedrooms furnished in comfortable

European tradition. *2 blocks off Commercial on Division; (509) 548-5726; 347 Division St, Leavenworth; $$.*

Haus Rohrbach Pension ☆   Tucked at the base of Tumwater Mountain, the lodge has a nearly Bavarian view over the valley farmland back toward town and the snow-clad mountains. Most rooms open onto a flower-decked balcony facing the majestic vista. Bring the kids—there's a swimming pool and a sled hill. *About ½ mile off Ski Hill Dr; (509) 548-7024; 12882 Ranger Rd, Leavenworth; $$.*

Mountain Home Lodge ☆   Although you can drive to this remote lodge in the summer, in the winter a heated snow-cat picks you up from the parking lot at the bottom of Mountain Home Road. Miles of cross-country ski trails leave from the back door; you can also snowshoe and sled. The 10 rooms are very plain, and there is now a rentable cabin as well. No kids. *2 ½ miles up Mountain Home Rd off E Leavenworth Rd (at Wenatchee River Bridge) and Hwy 2; (509) 548-7077 or (800) 414-2378; 8201-9 Mountain Home Rd, Leavenworth; $$$.*

Mrs. Anderson's Lodging House ☆   Although it originally opened in 1903 as a boardinghouse for sawmill workers, this 9-room inn right in the center of Leavenworth has charm to spare and very friendly operators. It's a real bargain. *Just off the center of town at Commercial St; (509) 548-6173 or (800) 253-8990; 917 Commercial St, Leavenworth; $.*

Natapoc Lodging ☆☆   For the city dweller who dreams of a weekend home on the Wenatchee River, Natapoc is the next best thing. Each log cabin claims one to five piney acres and at least 200 feet of riverfront, and all are fully stocked with amenities. Lots of outdoorsy things to do, from fly-fishing to cross-country skiing. *4 miles east of Lake Wenatchee on Hwy 209; (509) 763-3313 or (888) 628-2762; 12338 Bretz Rd, Leavenworth; $$$.*

River Chalet ☆   An ideal vacation spot for groups of couples, this contemporary guest house on the east side of Leavenworth is right on the Wenatchee River, with large windows looking out toward the mountains. Four bedrooms sleep 10 comfortably (but slumber parties of 22 sleeping-baggers have occurred); wood stoves keep you warm. *4 miles west of Leavenworth off Hwy 2; (509) 663-7676; 1131 Monroe St, Wenatchee; $$$.*

Run of the River ☆☆   On the banks of the Icicle River, this log-construction bed and breakfast (Leavenworth's finest) boasts such solitude and comfort that you may want to spend the entire day on the deck of one of its 6 guest rooms. Hearty breakfasts emphasize seasonal discoveries from a local organic farmer and the inn's own herb garden. *1 mile east of Hwy 2; (509) 548-7171 or (800) 288-6491; 9308 E Leavenworth Rd, Leavenworth; $$.*

Sleeping Lady This former CCC camp from the 1930s has been transformed into what may become the Northwest's foremost conference facility. Designed to be extremely efficient, with an awareness of nature, the facilities include a performing arts theater and a library. Individual guests on a space-available basis. *2 ¹/₂ miles south of Leavenworth on Icicle Rd; (509) 548-6344; 7375 Icicle Rd, Leavenworth; $$.*

Cheaper Sleeps

Cougar Inn Most people come to this inn on Lake Wenatchee for the all-you-can-eat prime rib on Friday nights or the champagne brunch on Sundays. What many of them don't know is that if you purchase a dinner for two on Sunday, Monday or Thursday, you can stay in the lodge for half price—and even full price ain't bad. *(509) 763-3354; 23379 Hwy 207, Leavenworth.*

Edelweiss Hotel This Front Street hotel, the first building in town to go Bavarian, is now owned by Eva Rhodes. Her son, John Rhodes, oversees the 14 rooms (5 with private bath) and keeps the prices more than reasonable. *(509) 548-7015 or (509) 548-5010; 843 Front St, Leavenworth.*

Ingall's Creek Lodge Built in 1960, Ingall's Creek sports 4 little rooms (with private baths) and makes a good base camp for skiing any of the 210 miles of trails in the winter or for heading into the Enchantments via the Ingall's Creek Trail in summer. *(509) 548-6281; 3003 US Hwy 97, Leavenworth.*

More Information

Lake Wenatchee Ranger District: *(509) 763-3103.*
Leavenworth Chamber of Commerce: *(509) 548-5807.*
Leavenworth Ranger District: *(509) 782-1413.*
Leavenworth Winter Sports Club: *(509) 548-5115.*
Der Sportsman (gear and rentals): *837 Front Street; (509) 548-5623.*
Leavenworth Outfitters Outdoor Center (gear and rentals): *(800) 347-7934.*
Leavenworth Ski and Sports Center (gear and rentals): *US 2 and Icicle Road; (509) 548-7864.*
Vertical Adventure Sports (gear and rentals): *US 2 at Icicle Road; (509) 548-9104.*

Wenatchee National Forest: Overview

More than 2 million acres of eastern Cascade lands from the North Cascades to the Goat Rocks Wilderness.

Here's a national forest with big potential. Make that huge. As in, 2.2 million acres worth of high, mostly dry alpine territory that ranks right up there on the outdoor-inspiration scale. Wenatchee National Forest, Washington's largest single forest jurisdiction, controls (or has a hand in managing) almost half of the state's prime forest lands.

Sadly, much of Wenatchee's potential is unrealized. Although some wilderness areas under its full or partial care—such as the Alpine Lakes, Glacier Peak, and Lake Chelan–Sawtooth Wildernesses—draw large numbers of visitors, Wenatchee's non-wilderness lands are foreign territory to many Western Washington campers, hikers, and backpackers. Why? Dirt bikes and other off-road vehicles, for starters. This national forest has 2,500 miles of trails, but all too many of them have been turned into high-speed raceways for smoke-belching race bikes. These trails—which dominate most of the forest's prime Central Cascades hiking territory—are euphemistically called "dual-use" paths by the Forest Service. But no hikers in their right minds want to risk their bones amid the madness of dirt bikery.

The result: in spite of the fact that Washington hikers outnumber off-road violators exponentially, hundreds of thousands of acres of national forest lands have essentially been reserved for the few. This made no sense during the 1960s, when Wenatchee's forest brain trust was converting many forest trails to "dual use." It makes even less sense now that the state's hiking population has mushroomed in the past two decades. Write your congressman. Write your ranger (for an address, see More Information at the end of this chapter). Write your mother. Write *someone*—and hope for change.

None of which is meant to suggest that the entire Wenatchee National Forest is unworthy of your recreation time. Hardly. Not even the U.S. Forest Service could fully screw up an area this large and unpatrollable. Many of the forest's hiking trails are closed to motorized vehicles. And a slew of other mountain-high recreation gems can be found throughout the forest, particularly in its isolated, often-primitive, but frequently beautiful campgrounds. More than 150 of them dot the pine-treed landscape of this national forest, which fans out north, south, and west from its headquarters in Wenatchee.

The most popular, not surprisingly, are in the forest's Central Cascades heartland. An example is the **Cle Elum Ranger District,** the closest jurisdiction to Seattle. The Cle Elum and Teanaway River valleys, in particular, are premium getaways, with many gorgeous campgrounds near hiking trails climbing into the southeastern Alpine Lakes Wilderness. Both areas are an easy, 2-hour drive from Seattle on I-90. Consult the Snoqualmie Pass Corridor (Mountains-to-Sound Greenway), I-90 East: Roslyn to Ellensburg, Alpine Lakes Wilderness: Overview, and Leavenworth and the Icicle Valley chapters for recreation details.

Equally popular are the lush alpine lands overseen by the **Leavenworth** and **Lake Wenatchee Ranger Districts,** which administer eastside Stevens Pass areas such as Lake Wenatchee, the Wenatchee River, and Icicle Creek drainages, and northeastern fringes of the Alpine Lakes Wilderness. Campgrounds and trails in this region are among the most heavily used in the state—for good reason. It's beautiful here, and overuse is the primary concern of forest rangers. Primary access is via Stevens Pass Highway (US 2) and Blewett Pass Highway (US 97). (Consult the Leavenworth and the Icicle Valley, and Stevens Pass Corridor and Lake Wenatchee chapters for full details.)

To the south, under the watch of the **Naches Ranger District,** are similarly lush, popular campgrounds and trails around Bumping and Rimrock Lakes and on the east side of the Norse Peak, William O. Douglas, and Goat Rocks Wilderness areas. Access, at least in summertime, is easy via Chinook Pass (SR 410) and White Pass (US 12) highways. (Consult the White Pass Corridor and Mount Rainier National Park chapters for recreation details.)

To the north, the **Entiat** and **Chelan Ranger Districts** manage the dry Cascade valleys between Leavenworth and Lake Chelan, as well as eastern approaches (by trail) to the Glacier Peak Wilderness. These rugged lands are primarily the home of small-stream anglers, mountain campers, long-distance backpackers, off-road vehicle enthusiasts, and, in the fall, hunters. Major access is via US 97A and the Entiat River Road, Hwys 207 and 209 and the Chiwawa River Road north from Plain, and via the Lake Chelan water-taxi service. (For details, consult the Chelan and the Middle Columbia, and Stehekin and the Lake Chelan NRA chapters.)

The Chelan Ranger District also administers the wild lands of the **Lake Chelan–Sawtooth Wilderness** north of Lake Chelan. Access is via the Lake Chelan water taxi or Twisp River Road. (Consult the Methow Valley, and Stehekin and the Lake Chelan NRA chapters for details.)

Also, don't overlook the forest lands around **Wenatchee** itself, home to some fine camping, hiking, and skiing. (See the Wenatchee and Mission Ridge chapter for details.)

Getting There

The only major roadway that samples this vast area is US 97, which roughly parallels the forest's eastern border from Yakima to Okanogan. As mentioned above, interior portions of the forest are reached via the White Pass, Chinook Pass, Snoqualmie Pass, and Stevens Pass Highways, as well as Entiat Valley Road, Twisp River Road, and the water-taxi service on Lake Chelan.

Adjoining Areas

Most sections in the North Cascades, Central Cascades, and South Cascades sections of this guide share one or more borders with lands in the Wenatchee National Forest.

inside out

The Wenatchee National Forest is home to many of Washington's most remote, wild recreation lands, which are particularly popular with fans of high, pine-dominated mountain slopes and small, rocky, sparkling creek valleys. **Camping** (151 campgrounds), **fishing** (1,800 miles of streams and rivers), **hiking** (2,500 miles of trails), **skiing** (seven ski areas), **whitewater rafting** (primarily on the Wenatchee River), **climbing** (on Alpine Lakes Wilderness peaks), **canoeing** (nearly 250 lakes and reservoirs), **kayaking** (nine rivers under Wild and Scenic River review), **mountain biking** and other activities too numerous to count all are popular in Wenatchee National Forest.

For full details on all those and more, consult these chapters: Methow Valley; Alpine Lakes Wilderness: Overview; Stevens Pass Corridor and Lake Wenatchee; Wenatchee and Mission Ridge; Leavenworth and the Icicle Valley; Snoqualmie Pass Corridor (Mountains-to-Sound Greenway); I-90 East: Roslyn to Ellensburg; and White Pass Corridor.

Restaurants/Lodgings

Primary services are in Wenatchee, Chelan, Leavenworth, Yakima, Cle Elum, and Ellensburg. (Consult the Outside In sections in these chapters for restaurant and lodging details.)

More Information

Wenatchee National Forest Headquarters: *215 Melody Lane, Wenatchee, WA 98801; (509) 662-4335.*

Chelan Ranger District: *(509) 682-2576.*

Cle Elum Ranger District: *(509) 674-4411.*

Entiat Ranger District: *(509) 784-1511.*

Lake Wenatchee Ranger District: *(509) 763-3103.*

Leavenworth Ranger District: *(509) 782-1413.*

Snoqualmie Pass Corridor (Mountains-to-Sound Greenway)

From Issaquah east to Lake Easton along Interstate 90, including the Issaquah Alps, Iron Horse Trail State Park, Snoqualmie Summit ski areas, and southern portions of the Alpine Lakes Wilderness.

This is wilderness made easy. Too easy, actually. And hence, not so wild anymore. Detect a pattern?

For as long as Seattleites have called themselves Seattleites, the upper Snoqualmie River drainage—a convenient crack in the otherwise impenetrable wall of the Central Cascades—has been a backyard playground. Early exploring clubs such as the Mountaineers cut their climbing teeth and hiking boots in an area which, over time, evolved from the "Yellowstone Highway" to the "Sunset Highway" to Interstate 90. The I-90 corridor's rich collection of trails, creeks, waterfalls, and forests allows Seattleites to be out away from it all in less than 30 minutes—a temptation many have found impossible to resist. As the city and highway have grown, so have crowds of hikers, skiers, horseback riders, and other "solitude" lovers seeking escape. Few metropolitan areas in the United States have a wild, wooded land so close to their back door, and few have taken advantage of it to the extent of Seattle-area residents.

The lure of these woods has been so great, in fact, that not even the systematic clearcutting of the upper Snoqualmie River's once-grand forest system was enough to dissuade us. By the late 1980s, the Snoqualmie Pass corridor had become an unlikely combination of ugly, vegetation-mined slopes and a nonstop stream of hikers, who figured a clearcut trail close to home beat an old-growth hike 4 hours away. Worse yet, the clearcutting acted as a springboard to send hordes of hikers farther east, into the pristine but fragile lands of the Alpine Lakes Wilderness, which have been badly trampled in some places.

In this case, however, two bads have combined to create what ultimately could be a greater good. In 1991, a group of business and community leaders—headed by attorney Jim Ellis, the father of the Metro plan that cleaned up Lake Washington in the 1950s—formed the Mountains-to-Sound Greenway Trust, whose purpose was to create a broad swath of green on both sides of I-90 from Seattle to Cle Elum. From the beginning, the group's approach has been subtle. They persuade rather than coerce. They shape development rather than oppose it. And people have listened. Greenway's vision has evolved into a plan, and the plan is getting results.

Land swaps have been made with timber companies, trading small amounts of visible forest for larger plots hidden from sight. Key historical and natural sights have been preserved. The Greenway, as the Snoqualmie Pass corridor increasingly is known, is slowly taking shape. How it will end up is anyone's guess. For the time being, though, the group has succeeded in at least maintaining status quo in the battle to preserve recreation lands in Seattle's forested backyard. Eventually, they hope to develop newly protected lands for recreation use, easing the substantial burden on existing forest lands and reestablishing what's lacking here: a wilderness ethic—a caring connection between people and land.

Today, as you drive east from Seattle, you can squint a little and actually sort of see it: green lands on both sides of the highway, beginning with the Issaquah Alps and continuing to North Bend, the front door to the upper Snoqualmie. From there, devastated forest lands are slowly coming back to life, painting the corridor a bit greener every year. Tiny steps in trail construction could lead to giant leaps in future years, when the state's Iron Horse Trail State Park will link the entire Greenway in one long, skinny string (it currently is only one washed-out railroad bridge away). The corridor already is, thanks to decades of exploration and exploitation, a highly developed outdoor getaway. The Greenway plan promises to make it better. But only time will tell if improvement can outpace growth, and whether the Greenway, which is being closely watched by other national groups, will be remembered as a brilliant success or just a nice try.

Unfortunately, no one with the Greenway group or outside it has answered the Big Question posed by the use/abuse pattern: Can freeways and greenways coexist? Doesn't attracting more people to a natural area—

no matter how thinly they're dispersed and how well they behave—ultimately lead to its degradation?

History says yes. Greenway optimists say no. The reality will probably be somewhere in the middle. And when the middle is as scenic, resilient, and fun to explore as Snoqualmie Pass, there are worse places to be.

Getting There

The Mountains-to-Sound Greenway's easy access from Seattle is its biggest draw. From anywhere in the Seattle area, hop on Interstate 90 and drive east. Hundreds of recreation chances await between Issaquah (10 miles east of Seattle) and Easton (80 miles east). Seasonal note: Snoqualmie Pass is frequently snowed upon during the winter, but chains rarely are required and road closures are unusual. (Even so, it's a good idea to carry chains between October and May.) Typically, drivers won't encounter snowy roads until about 4 miles west of the summit, where the highway begins a 1,000-foot climb to Snoqualmie Summit, elevation 3,022. For road conditions, call (888) SNO-INFO or tune car radios to 530 AM at Eastgate or 1610 AM at North Bend.

Adjoining Areas

NORTH: **Alpine Lakes Wilderness: Overview**

SOUTH: **Mount Rainier National Park**

EAST: **I-90 East: Roslyn to Ellensburg**

WEST: **Greater Seattle**

inside out

Hiking

The Snoqualmie corridor's proximity to greater Seattle makes it a natural first choice when sunny Saturday morning skies crash through the blinds and implant the word "hike" on the brain. That is both this area's greatest blessing and its greatest curse. In the early part of the century, trails leading up peaks along the corridor were familiar only to hardy, wool-covered explorers from get-out-and-get-wet adventure groups such as the Mountaineers. (Mountaineers' hiking parties, in fact, carved out many of the best trails still in use here today.) But these days, the Mountaineers' old haunts are familiar to everybody, from young rock climbers and mountain bikers to your weak-kneed Aunt Ethel. You're liable to run into both age groups—and about 400 others—on many I-90 corridor trails on a given weekend.

Without question, **overcrowding** is a problem in these parts. It's not unusual to see 400 cars in the Mount Si parking lot on a sunny Sunday, an equal number at Snow Lake, and perhaps even more at the High Point Trailhead for Tiger Mountain, near Issaquah. The amazing—and for many local hikers, frustrating—thing is that more obscure trails in between also will be packed from end to end with hikers. There is, it seems, no way to escape the crush of humanity along I-90 in the summer.

Take that as a given. For most people, particularly those who manage to sneak off during midweek, the short drive makes up for crowded conditions. And it is still possible to find little-used trails in this area. Besides, there's one major upside to the intense trail use here: intense pressure to keep the trails up to snuff and build new ones in the future. Many I-90 trails have been "adopted" by Seattle-area corporations, whose workers, coordinated by groups such as Washington Trails Association, devote weekends to fixing bridges, cutting brush, hauling gravel, and shoring up switchbacks. Consider joining one. Good for the soul, if not the back.

A word about **permits:** Some trails on the north side of I-90 enter the Alpine Lakes Wilderness. Permits are required, for both day hikes and overnighters. They're free, unlimited (so far), and available at trailheads. No sweat, but fill them out. In the near future, limits on overnight campers are expected in some highly popular areas, such as Snow Lake north of Alpental. Check with a local ranger district office about these and other restrictions. (For more on permits, see the Alpine Lakes Wilderness: Overview chapter.)

Permits are not required for nonwilderness trails in this area, most of which are governed by the Mount Baker–Snoqualmie National Forest. **Dogs** are allowed on most trails, but be courteous and keep the beast on a leash. Remember, not everyone is a dog lover, and prudent doggie-watching helps quiet voices crying out for more extensive dog bans.

Finally, a word about **seasons:** Declaring when a trail will be snow-free and walkable is a risky business. Snow levels vary enough from year to year to make those dates shift by a month or more. But some things you can (pretty much) count on when it comes to seasonal snow levels. Valley trails that begin below 1,000 feet in elevation—such as Tiger Mountain near Issaquah, and Little Si, Twin Falls, and Rattlesnake Ledge near North Bend—are snow-free virtually all year. Each makes a nice, if sloppy, winter walk. Lower sections of the Iron Horse Trail also usually are free of snow all year.

Midlevel trails beginning between 1,000 and 2,000 feet *usually* open by May. Note that trails with southern exposure melt off much more quickly than those along north-facing slopes. Higher-elevation trails, such as those beginning at between 2,000 and 3,000 feet in the Snoqualmie

Pass area, often don't melt out until July. The only way to know for sure is to ask at the appropriate ranger district (listed in More Information, below.)

So you're ready to walk. Where? Good question. Choices are rich here, and we won't attempt to list them all. For a full inventory, we recommend *Hiking the Mountains-to-Sound Greenway,* by Harvey Manning (The Mountaineers). The book, chock-full of color and local history, has full details on hikes from Snoqualmie Summit west. Or consult *Pacific Northwest Hiking* (Foghorn Press), by this author and Dan A. Nelson, which contains a long list of hikes in the Greenway area. But here's a healthy sampling of the best.

Issaquah to North Bend

In the world of hiking, closest is busiest. That's certainly the case at **Tiger Mountain State Forest** (easy/moderate; various distances), whose green slopes are laced by the most heavily trod trail system in the region. From the main trailhead at High Point (I-90 exit 20, 2 miles east of Issaquah), trails fan out in many directions, making loops of 1 to 12 miles through mostly deciduous forest, with occasional grand views of the valley, Lake Washington, and, from the 3,000-foot top, Mount Rainier. You'll find more than 60 miles of trails here, all best discovered through the art of trial and error. A popular introductory route is the Tradition Lake Loop, a 2.5-mile walk from the High Point Trailhead. Additional Tiger Mountain trailheads are located near Issaquah High School and along Hwy 18. (From the High Point Trailhead, you can cross under the freeway and catch the old rail-trail to Preston and beyond to Snoqualmie Falls and North Bend.) For maps and details, call the Department of Natural Resources, (360) 825-1631.

Up the road a piece, actually 15 miles of pieces, is North Bend, home of the **Mount Si Trail** (difficult, 8 miles round trip). Everyone, it seems, at one time or another puts foot to trail on Mount Si, the single most overused trail in the state, with as many as 50,000 people a year huffing and puffing their way to the top. On sunny summer days, the Mount Si trailhead looks like the parking lot at Larry's Market: overcrowded with misbehaving yuppies. The trail up Mount Si, named for local settler Josiah "Uncle Si" Merritt, is nothing to write home about. It's almost entirely in dark second-growth forest until the summit. But it does go up 3,200 feet in 4 miles—a good workout pace for training hikers, climbers, and backpackers. That, coupled with its easy access and grand summit view, makes it irresistible to most of us. To give into your own urge, take the main drag out of North Bend and turn north on Mount Si Road. Look for the Amazing Colossal Trailhead Parking Lot on the left in about 2 1/2 miles.

One easier, though nearly as crowded, alternative is **Little Si** (moderate; 5 miles round trip), the 1,500-foot thumb of a peak sticking up on Mount Si's south shoulder. Park in the signed lot just across the Middle Fork Snoqualmie on Mount Si Road and walk a short distance down the residential street (you guessed it, residents aren't thrilled with all you hikers) to the signed trailhead. The path climbs steeply for the first half-mile, then winds through the cool, dark glacier-carved valley between Si and Little Si before climbing steeply again for the final half-mile. Nice views of the upper valley from the top. Little Si's inside walls also are a longtime practice hotbed for rock climbers. You'll see them—or at least hear them—directly overhead.

On the opposite side of the valley, a trail system is ever expanding on Rattlesnake Mountain, that long hulk of green south of North Bend that looks like it lost a knife fight with logging companies. (It did.) The mountain's top ridgeline, thankfully, was recently purchased and reserved for public use. A good way to see its tremendous potential is by walking (climbing, actually) the **Rattlesnake Ledge Trail** (difficult; 2.6 miles round trip). From a trailhead near Rattlesnake Lake (take exit 32, drive 3 miles south), this recently improved route climbs steeply through mostly second-growth trees to an exposed rocky knob with awesome views of the upper valley, and into the marvelously protected forests of the City of Seattle's Cedar River Watershed. Try to imagine what it looked like when a great glacier, crushing south from Canada, climbed all the way up the valley and filled the gap between the Ledge and Mount Washington, the next peak east. The moraine is still visible below. Careful around the top. It's a looooong (400 to 500 feet) way down. Not a good place for kids or dogs. But a very good workout for the rest of you.

Below and a short distance east along a side road is a way trail serving as the westernmost access to **Iron Horse Trail State Park** (see Mountain Biking, below). A major Iron Horse trailhead is planned for this area in the near future by State Parks and the City of Seattle.

North Bend to Snoqualmie Summit, north side I-90

A string of good valley-to-peak hikes is lined up along the north shoulders of I-90. In order: **Bandera Mountain** (moderate; 7 miles round trip) begins at the end of Forest Service Road 9031 (take exit 45) and climbs 2,800 feet to nice views of Rainier from the fire-scarred, 5,200-foot summit. This trail melts out sooner than many of similar height in the area. Also from exit 45, you can follow Forest Service Road 9030 to its end to find the trailhead for one of the Greenway's more popular destinations, **Talapus** and **Olallie Lakes** (easy; 4 miles round trip). Lots of campsites here. Lots of overused, always full campsites.

Two miles east, take exit 47 (Denny Creek/Asahel Curtis), cross the freeway to the north, and turn left to the signed Pratt Lake Trail parking lot. This is a dual-purpose trailhead, with access to **Pratt Lake** (moderate; 11 miles round trip) to the west and **Granite Mountain** (difficult; 8.6 miles round trip) above and to the east. Pratt Lake, also reachable via the Talapus and Olallie Lakes Trail, is a very nice walk along this route, climbing about 1,600 feet to the lake, whose many campsites are shockingly trampled. Make this a day hike. Granite Mountain is a bear of a climb, a leading source of chronic *Thighus Fryus*. You'll huff, puff, and claw 3,800 feet in 4.3 miles to an old fire lookout at the 5,600-foot summit. The upper slopes often are snowbound (and very prone to avalanche) until midsummer. Is the view worth it? Absolutely.

Also from exit 47, take a right at the T on the north side of the freeway and drive beyond Denny Creek Campground, past some private homes, a total of about 3 miles, to the road's-end trailhead for **Denny Creek Trail** (moderate; 9 miles round trip to Melakwa Lake). This is one of the more pleasant walks in the region, offering a choice of a short stroll along Denny Creek to lovely Keekwulee (1.5 miles) or Snowshoe (2 miles) Falls, or a longer day hike to Hemlock Pass (4,800 feet) or another half-mile down to Melakwa Lake. The trail continues 3 miles west around Tuscohatchie Lakes and connects to the Pratt Lake Trail (see above). Another wildly popular local hike, particularly for parents with youngsters, is the short (half-mile) walk to spectacular 75-foot **Franklin Falls**, on Road 58 off Denny Creek Road. Note: Heavy flood damage struck Denny Creek trails in the winter of 1995–96. Check road and trail conditions with the North Bend Ranger District before setting out.

At Snoqualmie Pass proper, take exit 52 (West Summit), turn north under the freeway and follow the Alpental Road 2 miles to its end at Alpental Resort parking lot, aka the summertime (July onward) trailhead for **Snow Lake** (moderate; 7 miles round trip). A grand alpine walk, this. And absolutely mobbed on your average weekend. On the relatively gentle (1,300 vertical-foot gain) ascent, you'll find great views of craggy Cascade peaks such as Chair Peak and The Tooth, then wonderful shoreline lounging along the mile-long lake. The lake is inside the Alpine Lakes Wilderness, so special camping restrictions (follow signs and use established sites only) are in effect. Limited overnight permits are on their way to this overused spot. But there's no getting away from the fact that it's a great day hike.

Also from exit 52, follow signs a short distance on the north side of I-90 to the **Pacific Crest Trail** parking lot, where several hiking options await. Of course, you're welcome to hitch up your shorts and walk north to Canada or south to Mexico. But most of us prefer shorter day jaunts, such as the popular hikes to lovely **Commonwealth Basin** (moderate; 5.5 miles round trip), view-rich **Red Pass** (moderate; 10 miles round trip), or the cliff-clinging **Kendall Katwalk** (difficult; 10.5 miles round trip). The "Katwalk" section of the latter hike is a narrow ledge blasted from solid rock, with stone walls above and lots of open air below. Definitely *not* for the faint of heart or people with really wide packs. The trail is dangerous until all snow is gone, usually by July.

North Bend to Snoqualmie Summit, south side I-90

Parents and baby-sitters of visiting Nebraskans, pay attention. If the recalcitrant interlopers of whom you're in charge want a dose of Northwest-style fresh air (possibly including eye-to-radula encounters with banana slugs as long as your hand), you needn't venture all the way to, say, Stehekin to do it. The long, skinny public place known as Twin Falls/Olallie State Park just east of North Bend should do the trick. From the park's western entrance (take exit 34, Edgewick Road, turn right, and follow signs), the **Twin Falls Trail** (easy/moderate; 2.6 miles round trip) is a nice, family-friendly walk. You'll pass through an actual moss-draped rain forest (90 inches of rain a year) along the South Fork Snoqualmie River, pass some rare old-growth trees, then climb moderately (about 500 feet) up the river gorge to an overlook of the lower of two (actually, there are three) Twin Falls. The waterfall, once known as Upper Snoqualmie Falls, isn't as grand as it used to be. A small power plant now robs much of its thunder, diverting water underground through an invisible turbine. But it's still a splendid sight. Continuing, you'll reach an impressive bridge spanning the 125-foot gorge just above the lower falls. Look pretty pricey for a State Parks trail? It was. The power company undoubtedly paid to helicopter this baby in as part of its public-impact funding in exchange for a hydro permit. Proceed beyond the bridge, up one more switchback, for a view of the upper falls. Most people turn around here, but you can go on to connect to the Iron Horse Trail, which leads east to Olallie State Park.

Olallie State Park, the upper portion of the South Fork Snoqualmie gorge public/hydropower area, offers several hiking options. To get there, take exit 38, turn right and follow the old highway three-quarters of a mile to a road veering left, near a brown house. A parking lot here provides access to the river on the short, flat, very peaceful **Olallie Nature Trail** (easy; 1 mile round trip). It's a nice walk for kids, or for adults who want to escape the big-city noise for an hour or so. At trail's end is another parking lot, this one near the Olallie hydro project. Just beyond, Weeks Falls, another formerly awesome cascade, can be viewed in its now muted state. A sign on the turbine house says the project, which siphons a goodly portion of the South Fork underground, provides enough power to light about 800 homes. You decide if it was worth it.

Olallie State Park also offers the most convenient west-end access to **Iron Horse Trail State Park,** the old Milwaukee Road right of way now being converted to a cross-state walking, cycling, and equestrian path. The trail actually begins near Rattlesnake Lake, where a new trailhead should open in 1997. Until then, where you get on the Iron Horse in Olallie State Park depends on which way you're going. If you're headed west, walking the 4 miles or so toward Rattlesnake Lake, take a right below the exit 38 off-ramp and an immediate hard right up the hill to a trailhead parking lot. From here, it's about a mile west to a dramatic trestle over a waterfall on Washington Creek. Pleasant spot. But those headed east toward Snoqualmie Summit won't get very far. About a half-mile east of the trailhead, you'll cross a trestle over Change Creek, round the corner, and arrive at Hall Creek trestle, the middle third of which is gone—washed out by dead logs, the result of a blatant timber strip-mining of this drainage (the land is denuded as far as the eye can see up and around the small valley). You shouldn't have to be told, but . . . keep off the trestle! It's 150 feet straight down, and there's no idiot fence at the drop-off. Everybody should walk up here and take a look, though. It's a grand example of the cut-first, worry-later thinking that's in evidence all the way over Snoqualmie Pass. If and when they repair the trestle, the Iron Horse will be walkable or rideable all the way from Rattlesnake Lake to Easton and beyond.

If eastern Iron Horse destinations (such as the McClellan Butte and Annette Lake trailheads, or the west entrance of Snoqualmie Tunnel) are your destination, park near the main Olallie parking lot near the river (see above) and follow the way trail up the east bank of Hall Creek. It climbs to the Iron Horse grade on the east side of the washout, and saves you the trouble of going up, down, then back up again.

Next stop east is exit 42 (West Tinkham Road), where a right turn off the exit takes you past a Transportation Department office and to the **McClellan Butte** (difficult; 9 miles round trip) Trailhead. This one can suck the life out of you. It starts steep and stays steep, gaining 3,700 feet on the way to the spectacular 5,100-foot summit perch. North-facing slopes make the upper portions dangerous well into summer. Don't try it before July, and say no thanks to the final couple hundred feet unless you're adept at rock scrambling. That said, the view from the ridge top just below the summit is stupendous in both directions: north all the way up the Cascade Range; south into the lovely green carpet of the Cedar River Watershed and into the glaring north face of Rainier.

Five miles east, take exit 47 (Denny Creek/Asahel Curtis), turn right to the T, then left about a half-mile to the trailhead for highly popular **Annette Lake** (moderate; 7 miles round trip). The trail climbs about three-quarters of a mile beneath a thick canopy (a "recovering" clearcut) to a junction with the Iron Horse Trail, then switchbacks steadily upward through older forest to a pretty alpine lake. Some nice (overused) camp-sites are found on the north shore, probably occupied by Boy or Girl Scouts wearing Glad Trash Bags in a feeble attempt to keep dry. This trail receives heavy use. (Note: The lower portion is a good I-90 exit route for one-way hikers from the Snoqualmie Tunnel. See below.)

People can argue until their Scarpa boots rot off about the Evergreen State's best hiking trails. But there's little quarrel over its most unusual. The **Snoqualmie Tunnel** (easy but creepy; 5.6 miles round trip from Keechelus Trailhead) is proudly billed by its overseers, Washington State Parks, as "the longest hiking tunnel in the United States." Well, okay. That's either saying a whole lot or very little, considering how much underground hiking takes place in the United States. But this historical oddity, in its time an engineering marvel, has attracted thousands of Puget Sound–area walkers since 1994, when its heavy wooden doors swung open for the first time in decades. The tunnel is 2.3 miles long, and cuts a straight path from Hyak, beneath millions of tons of rock (and the Snoqualmie Pass ski areas), to a western portal hidden in the trees just south of I-90, where the highway curves and begins to climb steeply to Snoqualmie Summit. The tunnel was built in 1912—blasted and chipped by crews cutting through the mountain from both ends. Legend has it they met in the middle only several feet apart. The walls are lined with concrete, and trail crews have replaced the old flooded floor with smooth gravel.

Walking the tunnel is a unique experience, to say the least. It's chilly inside, the temperature hovering in the 50s even on 90° days. And a con-stant wind funnels from west to east. It's also nearly pitch dark. There are no lights in the tunnel, only a small pinpoint of daylight visible at the far end. A strong flashlight, extra batteries, and warm clothes are required, no matter when you visit. Those easily inclined to cases of the willies should consider taking a friend. The tunnel is spooky, perhaps because of the lin-gering ghosts of railroad workers past. Or perhaps because the tunnel itself looks, smells, and feels alive. The wind blasting from its eastern por-tal makes a constant roar. When it reaches the warm eastside air, it bil-lows out as steam, like the breath of a snoozing mountain dragon. This giant west-to-east suckage has been a problem in the tunnel since its early days. The wooden doors were kept closed between trains in the winter-time to block the wind, which, combined with seepage from the roof, cre-ated 8-foot icicles. The doors are still kept closed in the winter by State

Parks, which shuts the tunnel from November to May.

The best tunnel access is from the Keechelus Lake/Iron Horse Trailhead near Hyak. (Take exit 54 and follow signs.) From the parking lot, walk a half-mile west to the tunnel entrance, hidden in the weeds just below the parking lot for Hyak Ski Area. You can walk the 2.3-mile tunnel down and back in about 90 minutes. But for a fun day trip with more mileage, bring two cars. Leave one at the trailhead for Annette Lake (see above), take the other to the Keechelus Trailhead. It creates a one-way, moderately downhill walk (or mountain bike ride) of just over 5 miles from car to car.

Downhill Skiing

Snoqualmie Pass taught the Northwest to ski. And it continues to do so. Skiing at the summit began in the 1930s, when a weekly ski train from Seattle brought hordes of weekend warriors to the snowy slopes to make big, heavy turns on even bigger, heavier wooden skis. These days, the equipment has improved (a lot) and the lifts are better (a little), but the setting—and the attraction—is the same: reliable skiing, only 45 Interstate minutes east of Seattle. Together, the four summit ski areas—Snoqualmie Summit, Alpental, Ski Acres, and Hyak (known collectively as "The Pass")—form one of the largest ski operations this close to a major metropolis in the country. Little surprise that perhaps more youngsters learn to ski and snowboard here than at any other single place in America.

When it comes to snow, the Pass, only about a racing ski higher than 3,000 feet, is no Alta, Utah. It's no Mount Baker, for that matter. The borderline altitude makes snow conditions iffy; in the peak season, rain is just as likely as (generations of soggy ski-school students will say more likely than) snow. But the base is reliable, usually providing a Thanksgiving-to-spring-break ski season. That's good enough for ski schools, dozens of which operate at the four areas (mainly Snoqualmie Summit and Ski Acres).

Snoqualmie's other big draw? Night skiing. All things being equal, skiing at night is pretty much the same wherever you do it: cold, dark, icy. Squint a bit on a run at Hyak, and you could very well be in Aspen—so, many skiers who spit in the general direction of Snoqualmie Pass in the daylight lower their standards and head up I-90 at night. Prices are good, access unbeatable: barring major I-90 traffic problems, Seattle workers can go from the 76th floor of Columbia Seafirst Center to a summit chairlift in 1 hour. Try doing that in New York, Chicago, Los Angeles, or even Denver. The snow usually is wet, the vertical drop (1,100 feet at Ski

Acres) puny by Western U.S. standards. But as much as Seattle skiers trash the Pass, we'll probably continue to sneak up there, because, well, we love to ski, and it's too close to resist.

The Pass is a full-service operation, with ample ski schools, rentals, cafeterias, and the like. All of which are in need of repairs—which should arrive soon. Just as this book went to press, the Pass was purchased outright by George Gillett Jr., former chairman of Vail/Beaver Creek, Colorado. The new owners promise new lifts, day lodges, and even a hotel. Slopeside lodging, in the meantime, is limited to the Snoqualmie Summit Inn; (206) 434-1600. A single lift ticket ($28 on weekends and holidays, less for kids and on weekdays) gets you access to lifts at all four areas. Snoqualmie, Ski Acres, and Hyak are connected by ski trails, and can be viewed as one large area. Terrain at all three is similarly nondescript: wide open, untreed, and not very steep. The longest—and arguably best—runs are those on the upper portion of Ski Acres.

Not so at Alpental. This small, tucked-away area, a 2-mile shuttle bus ride away on the north side of I-90, is the demon seed of this ski family. Alpental strains thigh muscles throughout its respectable 2,200 feet of vertical. Its slopes, particularly upper knee-knockers such as Internationale, are as steep as any in the Northwest. For experts, Alpental's unpatrolled backcountry areas can provide incredible, Rocky Mountain–quality experiences when snow conditions are good. Really.

For ski schedules, lift rates and the like, call The Pass Hotline; (206) 236-1600.

Cross-Country Skiing

Cross-country skiing in the I-90 corridor comes in two flavors: commercial and public. The commercial offering is the **Ski Acres Cross Country Center,** one of the best full-service Nordic skiing operations in the Northwest. Choose from 55 kilometers of nicely groomed trails, some in the lower areas near Ski Acres, but most on the plateau atop Snoqualmie Summit's three downhill ski areas. The upper areas, reached by riding a chairlift near the Cross-Country Center, are a joy to intermediate and advanced skiers. On a sunny day, the Mount Catherine Loop is a grand cross-country tour, with stunning views. Lift tickets are $9 for the upper mountain, $5 for the lower track.

Ski Acres offers another rare cross-country bonus: night skiing. The lower track area is lighted on Wednesday nights and weekends. Call (206) 236-1600 for details.

Public opportunities, found at a string of Washington State Parks–maintained "Sno-Parks," are rich all along the I-90 corridor. Sno-

Parks (roadside pullouts or trailheads kept plowed for winter parking) are a great recreational bargain for Washington skiers. An annual Sno-Park pass ($20 at this writing) grants seasonal access to more than 50 of them, as well as dozens more in Oregon. Buy the sticker at any ski shop and stick it on your windshield. Then pick a Sno-Park and kick-glide away. The permit fees pay for parking-area plowing, plus machine grooming on many of the tracks.

Popular Sno-Parks include **Cabin Creek North** (easy/difficult; 10K) and **Cabin Creek South** (easy; 2K), both off exit 63; **Lake Keechelus** (easy; 11.2K on west shore of Lake Keechelus) off exit 54; **Gold Creek** (moderate; various lengths) off exit 54; **Crystal Springs** (easy; 11.2K connecting to Lake Keechelus Sno-Park); and **Lake Easton** (easy; 5K) off exit 70. The grooming crew for these trails operates out of Lake Easton State Park. Call (509) 656-2230 for a recorded message.

Snow Play

Snowshoers generally make their own trails from one of the Sno-Park areas listed above. Snow-tubers bound for Snoqualmie Pass are in luck. Old-fashioned, pull-off-the-road-and-slide opportunities are few, and usually dangerous. But Ski Acres' **Snowflake Tubing Area** is a tuber's delight. Rope tows. Rental tubes. Hot chocolate. Heaters! The discarded innards of truck tires don't get much more fun than that. Snowflake, located just east of the main Ski Acres parking area, generally operates weekends and holidays during ski season. A new day lodge recently opened there. Details: (206) 236-1600.

Mountain Biking

Most I-90 corridor hiking trails are off-limits to mountain bikes. But Forest Service and fire roads emanating from I-90 offer a wealth of gravel mountain-bike opportunities. Ask about open roads at the North Bend Ranger District, (206) 622-8378, or Snoqualmie Pass Visitors Center, (206) 434-6111 (summers only).

Two other grand mountain-bike opportunities are available. **Iron Horse Trail** is an ideal beginner's path, with a broad, smooth surface that never gets steep. A good starting point is the Lake Keechelus Trailhead (see Hiking, above). From here, the trail can be ridden east all the way to Easton, or west through the Snoqualmie Tunnel to a pickup car at one of several trailheads: Lake Annette (5.5 miles), McClellan Butte (16 miles), or Olallie State Park (about 20 miles). Riders who bypass the washed-out

Hall Creek Trestle near exit 38 can continue another 5 miles to Rattle-snake Lake, just south of North Bend off exit 32.

A second option is the summer mountain-bike operation at **Ski Acres,** which opens its upper-mountain cross-country ski trails (see Skiing and Snow Play, above) to cyclists during summer months. A chair-lift ride up the hill puts you into an intermediate mountain biker's heaven. Call (206) 236-1600 for details.

Camping

Choices are limited here. On the west side of the pass, three small Forest Service campgrounds are the only options. **Denny Creek** (20 tent sites) off exit 47 has repeatedly been closed by washouts in recent years. **Tinkham** (46 sites, no hookups; maximum RV length, 21 feet), off exit 42, also has been flood-damaged. Check with rangers. Near the summit, **Commonwealth** (6 tent sites) is a small campground off Forest Service Road 58 (take exit 52). When they're open, sites at Denny Creek and Tinkham can be reserved by calling (800) 280-CAMP.

Things get a bit better on the east side. **Crystal Springs** has 30 sites (no hookups; maximum RV length, 21 feet) near Lake Keechelus. The campground is open summers only. Campsites cannot be reserved. *Take I-90 exit 62, 10 miles east of Snoqualmie Summit; (509) 674-4411.* **Kachess,** on a large reservoir northeast of Easton, is the largest local campground, with 182 sites (no hookups; maximum RV length, 32 feet). This Wenatchee National Forest camp has a summer store, a boat launch, and boat rentals. It's a good base camp for exploring many Alpine Lakes Wilderness trails (the Rachel Lake trailhead is nearby; see Alpine Lakes Wilderness: Overview chapter). Kachess is open summers only. Campsites can be reserved by calling (800) 280-CAMP. *From I-90 east-bound, take exit 62 (Crystal Springs), cross over the freeway, and follow signs; (509) 674-4411.*

The lone local state park, **Lake Easton,** is a very nice one, with 137 sites (45 with hookups; maximum RV length, 60 feet). And it's located just off I-90 (convenient, but noisy). Spaces are spread through wooded loops on bluffs above Lake Easton, a reservoir on the upper Yakima River. The park has a boat launch, and Lake Easton is a decent late-summer trout fish-ery. The park is open all year, but camping loops are open summers only. Campsites can be reserved up to 11 months in advance by calling Reser-vations Northwest; (800) 452-5687. *From I-90 eastbound, take exit 70 and follow signs a short distance to the park; (800) 233-0321 or (509) 656-2230.*

Wildlife

No established wildlife-viewing areas grace the Mountains-to-Sound Greenway, but it's a rich wildlife zone. Hikers and backcountry trekkers (lucky ones) might encounter one of the dozen or so **mountain goats** happily at home on the north side of Mount Si. **Black bears** are sporadically seen on local trails, as are **deer** and, increasingly, **cougars.** It's common to see **coyotes** in the upper Snoqualmie Valley, and people who know what they're seeing have spotted **wolves** even this far south in the Cascades.

Many of these local critters are spillover from the Cedar River Watershed, a vast protected area hidden one ridge to the south. The watershed's **Rocky Mountain elk** herd is particularly infamous, both among hunters, who drool over the 600-animal herd's massive bulls (hunting is forbidden inside the watershed), and among upper Snoqualmie Valley residents, who frequently chase the nosy beasts out of their carrots and peas. Seeing a local elk is a hit-and-miss proposition. But hang out in the area between Rattlesnake Lake and Mount Washington in the winter long enough, and the odds get pretty good.

Picnics/Swimming

First, the essentials: stop at George's Bakery (main street, North Bend) and stock up on fresh bread and buttermilk crullers. Properly equipped, proceed up I-90 to one of several good picnickeries.

The grassy shores of **Rattlesnake Lake,** just south of North Bend, are a pleasant place to partake of sandwiches, frosty beverages, and giant monkey-shaped clouds floating overhead. Where you sit depends on when you get here. The lake is fickle, filling itself right to the roadway in the winter and early spring, then shrinking away in the summer until it's just a big puddle by autumn. You have only yourselves to blame—at least if you live in Seattle. Rattlesnake Lake was an unexpected by-product of the Seattle watershed operation on the nearby Cedar River. The city's Masonry Reservoir, a holding pond for Seattle drinking water, sits 1.3 miles to the south and—more importantly—about 600 feet above Rattlesnake Lake. When the reservoir is full, so is the lake, which is connected by glacial gravel. Result: spring and early summer visits are best, when the lake is full-up. This is a very pleasant, peaceful spot. Good picnic spots are found near the main parking area (watch for goose leavings) and around the corner to the right, where there's a shaded area. *Take I-90 exit 32, continue 4 miles south on SE Cedar Falls Road.*

Up the road a piece is **Olallie State Park** (see Hiking, above), where nice, grassy picnic spots are found near the old house along the South

Fork Snoqualmie River. *Take I-90 exit 38, turn right, and watch for the access road in about ³/4 mile on the left.*

The **Denny Creek Campground** (see Camping, above) is a good picnic spot. And near the Snoqualmie Pass summit, a peaceful but seldom used rest area on **Gold Creek Pond** is a fine summertime picnic spot. *Take exit 54, follow the frontage road north under the freeway, then east to signs for Gold Creek Rest Area.*

To the east, **Lake Easton State Park** (see Camping, above) has a delightful waterfront picnic area, complete with a children's play area and rest rooms with running water.

Canoeing/Kayaking

Whitewater kayakers and canoeists are a common sight on both the **South Fork** and **Middle Fork Snoqualmie.** The activity is heavily dependent on water levels, which vary rapidly and generally are too low during summer and fall months. Both streams provide multiple access points. Most kayakers hit the Middle Fork by following Middle Fork Road to one of a half-dozen decent put-in spots (take exit 34, turn north, and follow signs). The South Fork, when it's high enough, can easily be run between Twin Falls State Park (see Hiking, above) and downtown North Bend. Another put-in can be found about midway on this route—just off 432nd Avenue, reached by turning south from exit 32. This one requires a tricky portage down from a bridge over the river, however.

Canoeists and beginning kayakers will love the placid waters of **Rattlesnake Lake,** which are almost always smooth. A Seattle Water Department park around two sides of the lake allows excellent flat bank access. **Lakes Keechelus, Kachess,** and **Easton** also are popular canoe destinations, especially for campers.

Fishing

The Snoqualmie River is a major destination for Seattle-area steelheaders. Its lower portions that is. Nearly all the fishable waters below Snoqualmie Falls are mined regularly in winter months by steelhead enthusiasts. Two spots draw the biggest crowds—and, not surprisingly, the highest catch totals. One is the confluence of the Snoqualmie and Tokul Creek, where a strong run of winter steelhead returns each year to the Tokul Creek Hatchery. This is a productive fishery, but way down there on the aesthetics scale. Most of the fish hooked here are caught within yards of the inlet stream to the hatchery, and the banks of **Tokul Creek** below the hatchery come as close as anyplace in the state to approximating shoulder-to-shoulder Alaskan "combat fishing" conditions. But if you want your steelhead badly enough, you'll probably find yourself here at least once. The run typically peaks in late December or early January. Tokul Creek has one other major advantage over other local streams—it's relatively flood-proof. Even when the mainstem Snoqualmie and other local rivers are blown out by winter flooding, the shallow waters of Tokul Creek are usually fishable. Take Hwy 203 east from Fall City or west from Snoqualmie to Fish Hatchery Road, near the Tokul Creek Fish Hatchery.

Another productive and popular Snoqualmie River fishery—probably more because of its easy access than any other single factor—is the area on either side of the **Fall City bridge.** You'll find good bank access here, and anglers properly equipped (with hip waders) will usually find good drifts just below the confluence with the Raging River. Skunkees should proceed directly up the street to the Short Fries drive-in for a pleasing infusion of hot grease.

Trout anglers can fish the Snoqualmie after it opens in June (check regulations pamphlet for special restrictions and limits in some areas). Most of the river above the falls, including most of the fishable South Fork and Middle Fork, is a selective fishery, with single, barbless hooks only, and no bait is allowed.

Those same restrictions apply at **Rattlesnake Lake** (see Picnics/Swimming, above), a very popular fly-fishing venue. Flytiers, particularly those who like to fish from float tubes, love Rattlesnake for its ample parking, unparalleled bank access, and convenient, lightly sloping shores. (For cheap entertainment on windy summer nights, those of us who live close to Rattlesnake Lake will drive down to watch the evening breeze kick up and push all those float-tubers, like overgrown rubber duckies, all the way to the far end of the lake, where they have to get out and walk back.) Fishing can be pretty good. The lake gets a plant of 12,000 pan-size rainbows every spring. And unlike many Puget Sound–area lakes, this one usually isn't fished out on Opening Day in late April. The bite tends to pick up later in the summer when waters warm. Remember: No bait or gas motors.

At higher elevations, the **Keechelus** and **Kachess Lakes** hold some kokanee, rainbows, and even burbot, although fishing in both is generally slow because of their massive acreage and slow-warming waters. Keechelus has the added challenge of being nearly impossible to launch a boat into in late summer, when the water level drops far below the lone boat launch near Hyak at Snoqualmie summit. **Lake Easton** is another fair-to-good summer bet for state-planted rainbow trout. Bank access here isn't great—a small boat makes fishing easier.

outside in

Attractions

Twin Peaks is over with, but the valley where it was taped still has the same rural, Sound-meets-mountains charm. Snoqualmie and North Bend, the upper valley's two primary destinations, are growing suburban areas with their feet in an agricultural past and their eyes on a telecommuter future. **North Bend** is a splendid example. Not 500 yards from Tollgate Farm, site of the valley's first major homestead, sits a bigger-than-life Nintendo plant, cranking out who-knows-what-kind of high-tech gadgetry. *Twin Peaks* fans will have to look fairly hard to find remnants of the David Lynch TV series. The downtown souvenir shop still has a stack of "Who Killed Laura Palmer?" T-shirts. (If you don't go buy one, they might be there forever.) And you can still get Twin Peaks Pie at the **Mar-T Cafe** (137 W North Bend Way; (206) 888-1221), although it's not highly recommended, and **George's Bakery,** several doors down, serves more notable baked goods. On the west side of town, the **Snoqualmie Winery,** under the ownership of Stimson Lane, is a splendid stop on the way through the Cascades, with tours, tastings, and a marvelous view; 1000 Winery Road; (206) 888-4000. To satisfy that hankering for a new pair of shoes or some unnecessary plastic objects, swing into **Factory Stores of America** (exit 31 off I-90; (206) 888-4505).

Two miles down Hwy 203 is **Snoqualmie,** whose backyard boasts the state's number-one tourist attraction (sorry, Planet Hollywood): **Snoqualmie Falls,** 268 feet of head-over-spray water power, an awesome sight for first-timers. And a pretty fabulous site for 200-timers, as well. Puget Power, which runs a power plant hidden underground below the falls, manages small, unimpressive Snoqualmie Falls Park, which has an observation deck. Trails lead downward to the base of the falls. They're steep. **The Salish Lodge** (see Lodgings, below) is adjacent. Railroad artifacts and old engines are on display at Snoqualmie Depot, where on weekends from April through October you can board the **Puget Sound Railway** for a scenic round-trip train tour through the upper Snoqualmie Valley. (Call (206) 746-4025 for fares and schedules.) Across Snoqualmie's main drag, **Isadora's** (8062 Railroad Avenue SE; (206) 888-1345) is a funky little country collectibles shop with a cozy cafe. Nearby **Northwest Cellars** (8050 Railroad Avenue SE; (206) 888-6176) presents tastings of the Northwest's best wines and microbrews, and packages splendid gift baskets of the Northwest's finest specialty foodstuffs, while **Big Foot Donut Shop and Bakery** (8224 Railroad Avenue SE, (206) 831-2244) is a good sweets stop.

Restaurants

For recommended restaurants, see the Adjoining Areas to this chapter.

Lodgings

The Salish Lodge ☆☆☆   The falls may be the initial draw, but the rooms themselves are enough reason to come. Designed in a tempered country motif, each has light wooden furnishings, window seats or a balcony, flagstone fireplace with wood and kindling, and a jacuzzi. The dining room features a Northwest-inspired menu, as well as an excessive brunch and an almost legendary wine list. *Exit 27 off I-90, follow signs to Snoqualmie Falls; (206) 888-2556; 37807 SE Fall City-Snoqualmie Rd, Snoqualmie; $$$.*

Cheaper Sleeps

Wardholm West Bed and Breakfast   This red chalet offers rooms with a country-house clutter about them, but they're comfortable, pleasant, *and* there is a hiker's special (you need to call in advance). The owners know all about fishing nearby Lake Keechelus or Denny Creek, hiking the Pacific Crest Trail, and getting cheap lift tickets. *(206) 434-6540; 861 Yellowstone Trail Rd, Snoqualmie Pass.*

More Information

Cle Elum Ranger District, Wenatchee National Forest: *(509) 674-4411.*

Department of Transportation pass report: *(888) SNO-INFO.*

Mountains-to-Sound Greenway Trust: *(206) 382-5565.*

North Bend Ranger District, Mount Baker–Snoqualmie National Forest: *(206) 888-1421.*

Snoqualmie Pass Hotline (skiing): *(206) 236-1600.*

Snoqualmie Pass Visitors Center: *(425) 434-6111.*

I-90 East: Roslyn to Ellensburg

From Easton east to Cle Elum, north to the Stuart Range, and south to the Yakima River Gorge, including portions of Alpine Lakes Wilderness.

If you listen hard, you can almost hear the thud. Right here smack-dab in the center of the state, the wet, cold Cascades collide headlong with the dry, crisp plateau country, sending magnificence flying every which way. Giant pieces of that splendor remain lodged in the high, spectacular mountain-meets-plateau lands between Roslyn and Ellensburg.

This is ponderosa country, both in the tree sense (pine) and in the squishy old TV series sense (we keep expecting Hoss and Little Joe to ride out of the woods somewhere in the Teanaway River Valley). This land also happens to offer perhaps the most user-friendly backcountry interface to the Alpine Lakes Wilderness, which otherwise is forever locked away from the longing gaze of the nonbackpacking public.

Here at ground zero in the state's early-century mining explosion, you can drive right to the edge of that vaunted wilderness—even inject yourself through its skin by hiking one of many fairly easy trails. And once you're in, you're in for good. The sprawling, splendid lands north of I-90 between Easton and Ellensburg are some of the "last best places" in Washington. And we steal that phrase from writer William Kittredge on purpose: this land comes as close as any we've found in the Evergreen state to duplicating

Northwest Montana. It's Big Sky without big (Hollywood) stars. And whether you're a hiker, fly caster, camper, or just an unrepentant cloud-gazer, that's a good thing.

These lands boast some of the highest critter-per-capita ratios of any in the Northwest. The steep, narrow valley of the upper Cle Elum and the broad, peaceful plains of the Teanaway drainage are teeming with deer, elk, cougar, bear, raccoon, beaver, and other mammals too numerous to count. The area, in fact, has far more year-round hooved residents than shoed ones. So many, in fact, that extra caution should be taken driving here. Deer and elk are the main roadside attraction. Trust us: if you ran one over, both you and it would feel very, very bad.

This is a brittle, desolate land in the wintertime, when everything and everyone freezes solid and most mountain roads close to all but snowmo-biles, four-legged creatures, and a few Jim Bridger throwbacks. (You know you're really in the mountains when roadside speed limits are posted for cars *and* snowmobiles.) But this land is vigor personified in the spring and early summer, when the snow melt-off creates a high-mountain waterfall crescendo that echoes all the way down to overflowing lower-valley lakes and reservoirs.

Our favorite time to visit, though, is fall, when the bugs are dead, and the "tourons" from Ohio and the kids from everywhere are back where they belong: at work and at school, respectively. Fall colors are beautiful in these mountains. Fall skies are crisp. Fall travel is slow but unencum-bered. Falling in love with this place is easy. For the nature lover, it's too close to home to ignore and too close to the heart to forget.

Getting There

Roslyn is an easy 80-mile drive east of Seattle on Interstate 90. Cle Elum and Ellensburg are on the same route, 85 and 110 miles, respectively, on I-90.

Adjoining Areas

NORTH: **Alpine Lakes Wilderness: Overview; Leavenworth and the Icicle Valley**

SOUTH: **White Pass Corridor**

EAST: **Columbia Basin**

WEST: **Snoqualmie Pass Corridor (Mountains-to-Sound Greenway)**

inside out

Hiking/Backpacking

The I-90 corridor of Snoqualmie Pass will transport you into some of the most glorious hiking terrain in the Central Cascades. The mountainous land north of Roslyn is drained by the Cle Elum and South Fork Teanaway Rivers, both favorites among fans of this region's pine-dominated forest valleys. And the Middle and North Fork Teanaway River valleys stretching north from Cle Elum provide backdoor access to the spectacular Stuart Range in the Alpine Lakes Wilderness.

Hundreds of trails fan out to explore this area. For full details on area trails and roads, as well as permit requirements for trails in the Alpine Lakes Wilderness, contact the Cle Elum Ranger District (see More Information for this chapter, below; for more on permits, see the Alpine Lakes Wilderness: Overview chapter). Below is a sampling of some of the area's best hikes.

Cle Elum River drainage

The Cle Elum Lake/Salmon La Sac area north of Roslyn is a hiking/camping paradise. One popular overnight route is the **Deception Pass Loop** (difficult; 15 miles round trip), at the end of Forest Service Road 4330 in the upper Cle Elum River valley, 28 miles north of Roslyn. The alpine scenery is stunning. Hiked clockwise, the loop follows Cathedral Rock Trail to Cathedral Pass (5,600 feet), turns north on the Pacific Crest Trail to Deception Pass, then exits south on the Deception Pass Trail, past Lakes Hyas and Little Hyas, back to the Cle Elum River valley. A side trip on the way out is the short, trampled path to Tuck and Robin Lakes, below Mount David. Strong day hikers can do an in-and-out trip on this trail to Cathedral Rock, but it's 18 miles round trip, with a lot of vertical (about 2,200 feet, one way) to complete in a single day.

More sensible day hikers might consider walking the latter portion of the Deception Pass Loop in the reverse direction for a family-friendly, beautiful excursion into the Alpine Lakes Wilderness. From the trailhead at the end of Road 4330, it's an almost level walk to **Hyas Lake** (easy; 4 miles round trip), which has some nice lakeshore campsites, and a pleasant (though crowded) hike on the same trail to **Deception Pass** (moderate; 10 miles round trip). This route usually is snow-free by July, and campsites at Hyas Lake make a good first backpacking trip for the kids. Ask at the Cle Elum Ranger District about permits.

For another taste of the same alpine splendor, try the popular day hike to **Paddy Go Easy Pass** (difficult; 6 miles round trip), which begins on Road 4330 2 miles north of Scatter Creek Campground. It's a gasser: the trail gains 2,700 feet in 3 miles. But the view from the top is stupendous. This trail is the entry route for a long cross-Cascades trek to the Icicle Creek drainage via the French Creek and Meadow Creek Trails (see the Leavenworth and the Icicle Valley chapter).

Campers at Salmon La Sac Campground (see Camping, below) can (and should) take advantage of the beautiful long day hike or pleasant overnight trip into **Waptus Lake** (moderate; 16 miles round trip). The trail follows the Waptus River to the lake, one of the grandest in the wilderness. A trail junction there provides access to greater glories on the Pacific Crest Trail, Waptus Pass, and Dutch Miller Gap. From lakeside campsites, views of local peaks such as Summit Chief will melt your synthetic Thor-Lo socks. The truly adventurous can make a side trip from Waptus Lake's north shore up a steep, nasty path to **Spade Lake** (3.5 miles, one way), a usually frozen tarn below Mount David. Remember, you'll need an overnight permit to camp in this area, and they might be limited in the near future. Inquire at the Cle Elum Ranger District.

Owners of monster thighs, however, should settle for nothing less than the trail to **Jolly Mountain** (difficult; 12.5 miles round trip), which begins near Cayuse Horse Camp in the Salmon La Sac area and goes straight up, up, up to a grand viewpoint. The trail gains more than 4,000 feet in its 6-mile climb, and hikers should pick up a good trail map (Green Trails' Kachess Lake and Snoqualmie Pass maps are a good choice) to avoid getting lost on the confusing, interlaced trail system. As an added challenge, you'll need to cross Salmon La Sac Creek, which can be an unruly gush monster during the spring melt-off. Those who keep their heads above water, their eyes on the path, and their lunches in their stomachs will be rewarded with a postcard view of the Stuart Range to the north, and just about every other peak within gazing distance of this high perch. Plant the flag and scarf a PowerBar. You will have earned it.

Also from Salmon La Sac, a nice day trip is the 5-mile trail to **Cooper Lake**, where you'll find a pleasant walk-in campground (Owhi, see Camping, below) and another major trailhead for hikers bound for **Pete Lake** (moderate; 15 miles round trip).

Teanaway River drainage

Day hikers seeking a quick fix of some of the most scrumptious scenery the Alpine Lakes Wilderness has to offer should proceed immediately to the **Ingalls Lake/Esmerelda Basin/Longs Pass** (easy/moderate; 4 to 8 miles round trip) trailhead high in the Teanaway Valley at the end of Forest Service Road 9737 (Teanaway River Road). This single trailhead is the front door to a trio of great alpine destinations. From the parking lot, what begins as an old mining road turns into a pleasant trail. Less than a mile in, a side trail climbs to the Esmerelda Basin/Fortune Creek Pass area, home of a spectacular summer wildflower display. The main trail continues 2 miles to a second fork, where one trail leads 1.5 miles up and over Ingalls Pass to **Ingalls Lake,** where views of ruggedly handsome Mount Stuart are sublime. The other path leads a half-mile to the right to **Longs Pass,** elevation 6,250 feet, with its own seemingly stone's-throw views of Stuart. Each is a winner in its own right. And all are used rather heavily most of the summer.

The **Beverly-Turnpike Trail** (difficult; 13 miles round trip) is probably more heavily used by Mount Stuart climbers than by hikers. But it makes for a great long day trip in the upper Teanaway drainage, passing through many spectacular wildflower meadows. This path also is the primary western access route to the Ingalls Creek Trail (see below), which leads to Stuart Pass. Backpackers making shuttle hikes from the Blewett Pass area to the North Fork Teanaway often take advantage of this route. To reach the trailhead from Hwy 970 east of Cle Elum, drive north on Teanaway River Road, which becomes Road 9737 at 29 Pines Campground. Proceed about 16 miles to Spur 112 and turn right.

Longer-distance backpackers should strongly consider the **Ingalls Creek–to–Stuart Pass Traverse** (moderate; 29 miles round trip), one of the longest valley hikes in the Alpine Lakes Wilderness. From a trailhead on Ingalls Creek Road (off US 97 near Blewett Pass), this trail follows an easy grade through a long, luscious alpine valley, all within the shadow of the mighty Stuart Range looming to the north. Good first-night campsites are found at Falls Creek (6 miles; good turnaround for day hikers). The trail continues through gorgeous meadows (most with good campsites) in the Falls, Cascade, Hardscrabble, Fourth, and Turnpike creek drainages, each of which is flanked by its own steep side trail. The main route continues west, skirting the edge of 9,415-foot Mount Stuart and climbing steeply to Stuart Pass, 6,400 feet. This is a good turnaround point for a 4-to-5-day backpacking trip, but experienced hikers can find an off-trail route down to the Lake Ingalls area for a shuttle-hike exit in the North Fork Teanaway drainage via the Esmerelda Basin Trail (see above). This is a limited-permit wilderness area. Consult the Cle Elum Ranger District.

Camping

The primary campsites in the area are small, limited-facility (but quite beautiful) campgrounds maintained by Wenatchee National Forest. A half-dozen of them are strung along Hwy 903 (Salmon La Sac Road) along the Cle Elum River north of Roslyn. Also, wide areas along the north shoulder of that road often turn into unofficial campgrounds during the busy summer months, when hundreds of visitors rough it in riverside pullouts between Salmon La Sac and Scatter Creek Campground.

The first campground, **Wish-Poosh,** has 17 tent sites and 22 RV sites (no hookups; maximum RV length, 21 feet). This attractive campground is on Cle Elum Lake, a reservoir, which is often full right up to the campground in the early summer. The north side of Wish-Poosh has the busiest boat launch on Cle Elum Lake. An added treat in the camping loop: 4 "double-wide" spots, able to accommodate two RVs. Perfect for families camping out together. Wish-Poosh is open summers only. Campsites cannot be reserved. *On Hwy 903 (Salmon La Sac Road) 6.5 miles north of downtown Roslyn; (509) 674-4411.*

Next in the valley is **Cle Elum River,** which has 2 tent sites and 33 RV sites (no hookups; maximum RV length, 21 feet). The campground is at the head of Cle Elum Lake and is open summers only. Campsites can be reserved by calling (800) 280-CAMP. *On Hwy 903 (Salmon La Sac Road) 12 miles north of downtown Roslyn; (509) 674-4411.* About a mile upstream is **Red Mountain,** which offers 13 sites (no hookups; no piped water) and some small group sites. It's primitive, but free. Red Mountain is open summers only. Campsites cannot be reserved. *On Hwy 903 (Salmon La Sac Road) 13 miles north of Roslyn; (509) 674-4411.*

One of the most popular is **Salmon La Sac,** a pretty spot on the west bank of the Cle Elum River. The campground has 127 spots (no hookups; maximum RV length, 21 feet). The camp is wheelchair-accessible, and has a horse camp and group camp (but no horse group camp). It's a prime location for hikers (see Hiking/Backpacking, above) and anglers (see Fishing, below). Salmon La Sac is open summers only. Twenty-six Salmon La Sac campsites can be reserved by calling (800) 280-CAMP. *On Hwy 903 (Salmon La Sac Road) 15.5 miles north of downtown Roslyn; (509) 674-4411.*

Beyond Salmon La Sac, the road turns to (steep, rough) gravel, and the campsites become more, well, rustic. Two established campsites are found here, **Scatter Creek,** at the south end of Tucquala Lake, and **Fish Lake,** at the north end of the marshy valley. Both are more open, grassy areas than actual campgrounds, and tenters seem to fan out just about everywhere. The first site, Scatter Creek, is particularly heavily used. In the early summer, a stream running over the road just beyond the Scatter Creek camp prevents most campers from venturing farther north. For more solitude, cross the stream (the crossing has a paved bottom, and usually can be driven by cars and trucks with moderate to high clearance—but be conservative in your guessing!), and camp in an area farther up the valley, near Fish Lake. Camping in this area is free, but facilities are few (no tables, very few outhouses, water from the river only). The area is open summers only. Campsites cannot be reserved. *Near the end of Salmon La Sac Road (Forest Service Road 9330), 29 miles north of downtown Roslyn. The access road can be treacherous; trailers and RVs are not recommended; (509) 674-4411.*

Equally far afield is **Owhi,** a 22-site walk-in campground on the Cooper River. This is a beautiful spot, primitive but free, open summers only. It's a short walk from the parking lot to the campsites, scattered in the woods above lovely Cooper Lake. The backdrop, the snow-clad Three Queens peak, is magnificent. Cooper Lake also is home to a popular trailhead for backpackers bound for Pete or Spectacle Lakes (see Hiking/Backpacking, above). Owhi campsites cannot be reserved. *21 miles northwest of downtown Roslyn via Salmon La Sac Road and Forest Service Road 46; (509) 674-4411.*

To the east, **Beverly,** in the North Fork Teanaway River valley, has 13 tent sites and 3 RV spots (no hookups; maximum RV length, 16 feet). Decent stream fishing can be found nearby, and this is a prime launching spot for Alpine Lakes hikers. Beverly is open summers only. Sites cannot be reserved. *On Forest Service Road 9737, 25 miles north of Cle Elum; (509) 674-4411.*

Mineral Springs, along US 97, has 5 tent sites and 7 RV spots (no hookups; maximum RV length, 21 feet). The campground, which has running water, is at the confluence of Medicine and Swauk Creeks. It's a popular winter-sports stopover. Mineral Springs is open summers only. Campsites cannot be reserved. *On US 97, 21 miles northeast of Cle Elum; (509) 674-4411.*

Swauk, the major campground along US 97, offers 23 sites for tents or RVs (no hookups). It's close to many popular hiking trails. The campground is open summers only. Campsites cannot be reserved. *On US 97, 27 miles northeast of Cle Elum; (509) 674-4411.* Nearby small but very scenic **Red Top** is a primitive spot with 3 campsites. Red Top is a notable wildlife-watching area (see Wildlife, below). *At the end of Road 9702, near Red Top Lookout, 28 miles northeast of Cle Elum (509) 674-4411.* Farther north is **Tronsen,** which has 25 sites and piped water. It's open summers only, and sites cannot be reserved. *On US 97, 23 miles south of Leavenworth; (509) 782-1413.*

If you're stuck in Ellensburg visiting the kid in college, your best bet is the **Ellensburg KOA**; (509) 925-9319.

Fishing

The **Yakima River,** which flows through the heart of this region, is one of the state's best trout-fishing streams, drawing increasing numbers of fly casters each year. The Yakima may be as close as Washington State can come to a classic dry-country, high-mountain, Montana-style trout stream. Fishing for wild rainbows is good, the setting sublime. The catch: you can't keep a trout caught between Easton and Roza Dams—it's catch and release only. This is a selective fishery, with bait forbidden and single barbless hooks (either on flies or small spinners or spoons) the only acceptable hardware. Access is good from I-90 downstream from Easton. For information on the Yakima River Gorge south of Ellensburg, see the Yakima Valley chapter. For fly-fishing guide service, call the Evening Hatch; (509) 962-5959.

The waters of the **upper Cle Elum River** along Salmon La Sac Road look like they should be a fly-caster's heaven, but fishing, by most accounts, is fairly slow. The river and its large valley reservoir, Cle Elum Lake, do yield some rainbows, however.

Cooper Lake, which has a boat launch at Owhi Campground (no gas motors), is usually a fair summer bet for brook and rainbow trout and a few kokanee. Several backcountry Alpine Lakes Wilderness Lakes, such as **Hyas, Waptus,** and **Spectacle,** also can provide fair trout fishing.

Biking

Mountain bikers can ride long, uninterrupted stretches of the **John Wayne Trail** in Iron Horse State Park in either direction from a major trailhead at Easton.

Road cyclists should strongly consider a **Cle Elum–to–Salmon La Sac tour,** which makes a great day trip. Park at the Cle Elum Ranger District (or nearby Safeway) on the west side of town, and follow Hwy 903 several miles north through Roslyn, then on up the Cle Elum River Valley. Numerous rest/lunch stops are found all along the route, notably at Wish Poosh and Cle Elum River Campgrounds. The scenery is gorgeous, and Salmon La Sac Campground, at about 15 miles, is a great turn-around spot. Shoulders are narrow on this highway, but sightlines are very good, and traffic generally not too frantic (the speed limit is 35mph for long stretches and never higher than 50). This trip should become more interesting in a few years. Cle Elum, Roslyn, and Kittitas County, with help from the Mountains-to-Sound Greenway Trust, have purchased the old Burlington Northern Railroad right of way between Cle Elum and Ronald. The plan is to convert it to a multiple-use trail.

Salmon La Sac campers have a grand mountain-bike option: Road 9330 turns to gravel at the campground, climbing sharply to the **upper Cle Elum River Valley.** The first steep stretch is the worst—it's mostly rolling hills after that. Traffic is light (and dust-raising), and the mountain and river-gorge views are fantastic. This is a great mountain-bike ride in the late season, such as in September and October, when few cars are encountered and the air is cool enough to prevent cranial overheating. There are lots of great rest stops along this 18-mile (one way) route, and other Forest Service roads will take you even higher into the valley's east-side mountains.

Canoeing/Kayaking

Camping canoeists would be hard-pressed to find a better getaway than Owhi Campground at **Cooper Lake** (see Camping, above). The portage distance from campsite to lake is very short, and paddlers with heavy boats can drop them right at the lakeshore using the campground's boat launch. From the lake center, views of the Three Queens and other Alpine Lakes Wilderness peaks are splendid.

The shallow, quiet waters of **Tucquala Lake** near the headwaters of the Cle Elum River also are good, though fairly confined, canoeing waters. In the early summer melt season, waterfalls roar right overhead down the sheer westside walls of the Cle Elum River valley. Views of Cathedral Rock and other peaks are magnificent, lake waters are shallow and clear.

Wildlife

Savvy hawk fans already know about the spot, and casual bird lovers should discover it: Red Top Mountain on Teanaway Ridge (off US 97) is one of the state's top **hawk-watching** posts. Also seen in this locale are **ospreys, eagles, turkey vultures, Rocky Mountain elk,** and **mule deer.** The experts suggest visiting in September and October for birds, and right after the spring melt if you're after mammals. A small campground is found near the Red Top Lookout. From US 97 near Blewett Pass, follow Forest Service Roads 9738 and 9702; (509) 674-4411.

In the winter, the state Department of Fish and Wildlife feeds a large **elk** herd in Joe Watt Canyon, near Thorp. Feeding is at 8am daily. Take the Thorp exit from I-90 and follow Old Thorp Cemetery Road to Joe Watt Canyon Road.

Horseback Riding

This is some of the most spectacular country in the Northwest for extended mountain horse-packing trips. Two outfitters, 3 Queens Outfitter/Guide Service, (509) 674-5647, and High Country Outfitters of Issaquah, (425) 392-0111, run day or multiple-day trips into the high country above Roslyn and Cle Elum. High Country Outfitters operates a summer alpine base camp in the North Fork Teanaway drainage, while 3 Queens specializes in the upper Cle Elum/Salmon La Sac area. In addition, Hidden Valley Ranch, (509) 857-2087, offers 90-minute guided rides on its 780-acre ranch.

Rafting

The **Yakima River** between Cle Elum and the large diversion dam near Thorp is a popular, not-too-wild float of about 14 miles. Contact the Cle Elum Ranger District for guide information.

Photography

The upper **Cle Elum** and **Teanaway River valleys** are shutterbug's paradises. Since both valleys are sheer-walled, the best summertime light is early morning when sunlight from the east lights western peaks. The Teanaway River valley, in particular, puts on a spectacular autumn color display.

Cross-Country Skiing/Snowshoeing

For skiers who don't mind commingling with snowmobilers, the Swauk/Blewett Pass area (US 97) offers good winter opportunities. The main attraction, **Swauk Creek Sno-Park,** is a large trailhead to dozens of miles of backcountry ski, snowshoe, and snowmobile roads for all ability levels. Some of these trails are machine-groomed when equipment and staff are available. The Sno-Park is 25 miles east of Cle Elum on US 97. Skiers need a state Sno-Park vehicle pass, available at ranger stations and outdoor stores.

A number of other, smaller parking areas along US 97 also offer ski opportunities. Check with the Cle Elum Ranger District, (509) 674-4411, to see which have been plowed out and are accessible.

A good long-day or overnight ski tour can be made by following Forest Service Road 46 from the Salmon La Sac Road 6 miles into **Owhi Campground** at Cooper Lake (see Camping, above). Strong skiers can continue another 5 miles from Cooper Lake to **Pete Lake.** Avalanche danger exists along this route. Call the Northwest Avalanche Hotline, (206) 526-6677, before setting out.

Climbing

The Alpine Lakes Wilderness in the northern part of this region is home to several noteworthy alpine ascents, including the **Three Queens** (6,678 feet), **Chikamin Peak** (7,000 feet), and **Lemah Mountain** (7,840 feet). In the upper Cle Elum drainage, experienced climbers get all the mountain they can handle from **Bears Breast Mountain** (7,197 feet), **Mount Daniel** (7,899 feet), **Mount Hinman** (7,500 feet), and **Cathedral Rock** (6,725 feet). Most ascent routes on these peaks are rated between 3.0 and 5.7. For a list of qualified guides, contact the Cle Elum Ranger District; (509) 674-4411.

Adventure Calendar

Ellensburg's **Whisky Dick Triathlon,** in late July, is a major annual event. It combines a 1-mile swim, a 26-mile bike ride, and a 9-mile run. The course, up and down Whisky Dick Ridge, is not for the faint of heart. Ellensburg Chamber of Commerce; (509) 925-3137.

Attractions

Until the TV series *Northern Exposure* introduced **Roslyn** to the nation (and called it Cicely), it was just a sleepy reminder of its rough-and-tough days as a thriving coal-mining town. Modest turn-of-the-century homes have become weekend places for city folk, and the former mortuary is now a video store and movie theater, but the main intersection still offers a cross-section of the town's character: the historic Northwestern Improvement Company building (which once housed the company store) occupies one corner, while the old brick bank across the way still operates behind the original brass bars and oak counters. It will be interesting to watch what happens to this town now that the series is over.

The old stone tavern, inexplicably called **The Brick,** has a water-fed brass spittoon running the length of the bar; (509) 649-2643. Down the road, behind the town's junkyard, you'll find **Carek's Market,** one of the state's better purveyors of fine meats and sausages. Notable are the Polish sausage, the pepperoni, and the jerky; 4 South A Street; (509) 649-2930.

Easy access brings travelers from the freeway to **Cle Elum,** a former coal-mining town now undergoing a modest rediscovery. **Cle Elum Bakery** is a longtime local institution, doing as much business these days with travelers as with locals. From one of the last brick-hearth ovens in the Northwest come delicious torchetti, cinnamon rolls, and great old-fashioned cake doughnuts. Closed Sundays. First and Peoh; (509) 674-2233. **Cle Elum Historical Telephone Museum,** open Memorial Day to

Labor Day only, incorporates the area's original phone system, which was operating well into the 1960s; First and Wright; (509) 674-5702.

If you get away from the tourist ghetto by the freeway, as you should, the college-and-cowboy town of **Ellensburg** projects a pleasant ease. Its famous Labor Day rodeo draws many for its slice-of-life view of rural America.

Ellensburg has more than its share of interesting buildings. The downtown area was rebuilt after a devastating fire in 1889. Among the handsome structures still standing are the **Davidson Building,** on the corner of Pearl and Fourth, and the **Masonic Temple,** with its intriguing asymmetrical facade. On the fringes of town, at Third and Wenas, is a prime example of the **Great American Train Station,** built late in the last century for the Northern Pacific. Art deco is represented by the **Liberty Theater,** at Fifth and Pine, and by the **Valley Cafe.**

For modern architecture, turn to the campus of **Central Washington University,** which displays **Fred Bassetti's** library and dormitory compound and **Kirk/Wallace/McKinley's** fine-arts complex. The campus makes for a wonderful stroll, especially through the serene **Japanese Garden,** designed by Masa Mizuno. The curious should call ahead and arrange a Saturday or Sunday workshop with the **Chimpanzee and Human Communication Institute** (at 14th and D at the north end of campus). Here you can observe a human and chimps communicating through American Sign Language. Call in advance for workshop times and prices; (800) 752-4380.

Sarah Spurgeon Gallery, on 14th Street in the fine-arts complex at Central, presents regional and national exhibits in all media, Monday through Friday (closed in September); (509) 963-2665. The **Clymer Museum and Gallery,** at 416 N Pearl Street, honors Ellensburg's own chronicler of the Western frontier, John Clymer, whose work appeared on several covers of the *Saturday Evening Post;* (509) 962-6416. **Community Art Gallery** (408 N Pearl; (509) 925-2670) has nice quarters in an old building, displays good contemporary art, and sells local crafts; open 11am to 5pm Monday through Saturday.

Central Washington's only professional repertory theater presents over 35 performances by the energetic **Laughing Horse Company** during July and August (Wednesday through Saturday at 8pm); for reservations, call (509) 963-3400. Plays are staged in the architecturally stunning **Tower Theater** on the Central campus.

Close to the Central Washington campus along Ninth Street are tree-lined blocks of attractive turn-of-the-century homes. For something a bit out of the ordinary, check out the **Ellensburg Bull** statue by Richard

Beyer, located in the historic downtown business district; the **cowboy sculpture** by Dan Klennard that guards the corner of Fifth and Pearl; or stop by 101 N Pearl for a gander at **Dick & Jane's Spot,** a blend of unusual yard art, including reflector gyros, statues, and other unique offerings. Or perhaps treat the kids to an ice cream straight from the dairy at **Winegar Family Dairy** (419 W 15th; (509) 925-1821), Monday to Saturday 11am–6:30pm. Or down an espresso while sitting in the saddle at the **Cowboy Espresso Bar** in **Jaguar's;** 423 N Pearl; (509) 962-5995.

The hills surrounding Ellensburg are speckled with blue agates found nowhere else in the world but in the Kittitas Valley. If you don't stumble upon any, you can purchase some at any of the local gem shops, particularly the **Ellensburg Agate Shop;** 201 S Main; (509) 925-4998.

Olmstead Place, 4 miles east of town on Squaw Creek Trail Road (off I-90), is a cottonwood log cabin from an 1875 cattle ranch now coming back to life; tours Saturday and Sunday noon to 4pm, and by appointment; (509) 925-1943. Not too far from Ellensburg is the **Thorp Mill,** an 1883 gristmill still in mint condition after 110 years. Open for tours by appointment; (509) 964-9500 or write PO Box 7, Thorp, WA 98946.

The big event in Ellensburg is the **Ellensburg Rodeo,** held Thursday through Monday of every Labor Day weekend at the fairgrounds; (509) 962-7639.

Restaurants

Giovanni's on Pearl ☆   Ellensburg lamb, a good sampling of fish, and lotsa pasta. Candlelight, flowers on the tables, and green chintz tablecloths add a slight English country air to a fresh and relaxing atmosphere. Desserts are outstanding. *1 block east of Main in the historic district; (509) 962-2260; 402 N Pearl, Ellensburg; $$.*

Mama Vallone's Steak House & Inn ☆   Talk to the regulars at this Cle Elum steak house, and they'll tell you about the warm welcomes, great steaks, and good homemade pasta at Mama Vallone's. *On the main drag at the west end of town; (509) 674-5174; 302 W 1st St, Cle Elum; $$.*

Roslyn Cafe ☆   The Roslyn Cafe remains the kind of funky eatery that every picturesque, slightly chic town like Roslyn should have. It's best at lunch, when you can get really good burgers, a fine corn chowder, or a super Philadelphia steak sandwich. Breakfast is also worth the side trip. *2nd and Pennsylvania; (509) 649-2763; 28 Pennsylvania Ave, Roslyn; $.*

The Valley Cafe ☆☆   This 1930s-built bistro, with mahogany booths and back bar, would be an oasis anywhere—but is especially so in cow country. People traveling on business to Ellensburg arrange to arrive around lunchtime just to eat at this airy art deco spot (take-out, too). *Near the corner of 3rd and Main; (509) 925-3050; 105 W 3rd, Ellensburg; $$.*

Lodgings

Circle H Holiday Ranch ☆☆   A small herd of horses, and sweeping views of the Kittitas Valley and the Cascade foothills, are the big draws to the Circle H. The bunkhouses have been converted into 2-room suites; each sleeps four and contains a kitchenette and bath. Meals, included in the price of your stay, are served family-style. Hiking, biking, horseback riding, fly-fishing, and lazy-day river rafting. *Exit 101 off I-90; (509) 964-2000; 810 Watt Canyon Rd, Thorp; $$$.*

Hidden Valley Guest Ranch ☆   On a pastoral 700 acres a short hour from Seattle is the state's oldest dude ranch. The cabins are quite rustic, but miles of wildflower-lined trails, horseback riding, nearby trout fishing, a pool, a hot tub, and splendid cross-country skiing terrain make up for the basic accommodations. All meals are served as country-style buffets (open to the public by reservation). *Off SR 970 at milepost 8, Hidden Valley Rd; (509) 857-2322; 3942 Hidden Valley Rd, Cle Elum; $$.*

The Moore House ☆   Now on the National Register of Historic Places, this bed and breakfast was originally built in 1913 to house employees of the Chicago, Milwaukee, St. Paul & Pacific Railroad. The bunkhouse with 10 guest rooms and a honeymoon suite is light, airy, and pleasantly furnished with reproduction antiques. *Adjacent to Iron Horse State Park Trail at 526 Marie St; (509) 674-5939 or (800)22-TWAIN; 526 Marie St, South Cle Elum; $$.*

More Information

Cle Elum Ranger District: *(509) 674-4411.*
Ellensburg Chamber of Commerce: *(509) 925-3137.*

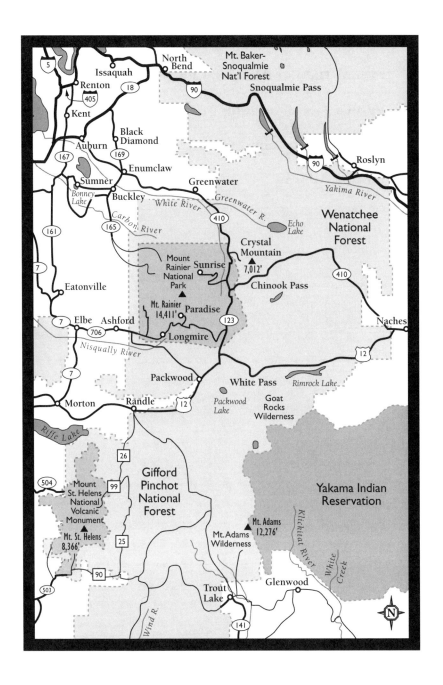

South Cascades

South
Cascades

Mount Rainier National Park

From Elbe west to Cayuse Pass, north to the Carbon River Valley, east to Crystal Mountain Resort, and south to the US 12–Highway 123 Junction.

Those magical Tahoma moments strike swiftly and, it seems, always at the least opportune time. In heavy freeway traffic, for example.

Anyone who's lived here very long has been there: Driving down Interstate 5, focused on the bumper ahead, trapped in the permafunk gloom of a Washington winter. Suddenly, storm clouds part to the south, a shaft of light slices through and—*whoa*—there she is, Mount Rainier. The Northwest's most powerful, enduring landmark thrusts its head through the clouds and reminds us all why we live here. It's enough to make you cry, and some of us occasionally do. For those of us whose homes lie scattered helter-skelter below its heavily glaciated slopes, the mountain is a source of inspiration, fear and respect. This personal, often emotional connection to a hulking, 14,411-foot rock defies explanation. But it is undeniable. Just *look* at the thing, and you'll know. This is a mountain that truly moves people.

Mount Rainier—or Tahoma, as it is known to Native Americans—is all things to most people. Some of us are dabblers, visiting only on sunny summer days and fighting the crowds in visitor-center parking lots to give the Pennsylvania relatives a quick glimpse of Sunrise or a taste of Paradise. Some of us are fair-weather regulars, meeting with Rainier each year to sample its crystal streams, camp beneath its old-growth hemlocks and firs, hike its 300 miles of trails, and sleep in its endless meadows. Some of us, preferring to face the mountain one-on-one, avoid the summer crush altogether and visit only in winter, when the peak's full face stays hidden and only one road goes in and out of the park. Some of us have become downright hard core, swinging through the national park's developed facilities just long enough to park the car, and heading by foot, ski, or snowshoe into the true heart of the mountain's wilderness. And for some of us, none of that is enough: we can no longer bear the sight of the mountain from afar without knowing we've set foot on top of it.

Rainier clearly is one of the most diverse outdoor haunts in the United States. The mountain's high-altitude visitors centers at Paradise and Sunrise are spectacular enough, but the backcountry can be mind-numbingly beautiful when weather cooperates. It also can be deadly when the weather does not. Mount Rainier, it is often (correctly) said, creates its own weather, and in doing so, rarely seems to take our vacation plans into account. People die from exposure every year—occasionally in August—in Rainier's deceptively beautiful alpine country. And not all of them are climbers. Backpackers and backcountry skiers, in particular, should heed the advice of Rainier veterans and never—at any time of the year—venture far into the wilds without overnight gear and the good sense to use it.

That said, something about days spent outside on the slopes of Mount Rainier sets the park apart from all other sections of the state. The hills seem steeper here, the ice a bit slicker, the sun a lot brighter, and the air thinner. Lifetimes have been spent exploring this magnificent rock, extremely rich lifetimes. It's our firm belief, based on years of trying, that no day spent poking around Rainier is a wasted one. Whether you're a climber or a loafer, more often than not you will go home with a self-satisfied glow.

Entire books have been written about Rainier's many special fresh-air nooks and deep-snow crannies. We offer instead a mere outline—a road map to get you rolling. Trust yourself, respect the mountain, and for heaven's sake, carry extra long johns. Which brings to mind a rule about the rarity of those "Tahoma moments," and about enjoying Rainier's hard and soft sides—a rule that might well fit the Washington outdoor experience as a whole: The only thing worse than underestimating Mount Rainier is taking it for granted.

Getting There

In the summer, Mount Rainier is approached by two main access routes: Hwys 7 and 706 from the Puyallup/South Tacoma area (to the Nisqually entrance,

Longmire, and Paradise); and Hwy 410 from Enumclaw (take Hwy 18 to Enumclaw from Interstate 5) to Crystal Mountain Resort, the White River entrance, and Sunrise. Allow about 2 ½ hours from the Seattle area via either route when snow isn't a concern. In the winter, Hwy 410 (Chinook Pass Hwy) closes near the National Park border, at the Crystal Mountain Boulevard turnoff. That leaves Hwy 706 as the only winter park entrance—the Park Service keeps 706 open to Longmire all winter. The road beyond, to Paradise, is open daily as soon as plows have cleared it—usually by 10am, but sometimes as late as noon. The road is closed during periods of particularly heavy snow or avalanche danger. Always carry chains when entering the park in the winter. Cheating not only is ill-advised, it's basically impossible: park rangers check for chains or four-wheel drive. If you don't have either, you're going back home.

The park has three other entrances. The Stevens Canyon entrance is on Hwy 123 (Cayuse Pass Hwy) on the southeast side of the park. This entrance can be reached via US 12 from the south or Hwys 410 and 123 from the east, via Enumclaw or Yakima. Hwys 410 and 123 are closed in the winter. On the northwest side of the park, both Mowich Lake Road and Carbon River Road are unpaved entrances to the scenic (and less heavily visited) north side. Both are accessed via Hwy 165, which runs south into the park from Buckley and Wilkeson. These roads are open summer only, and often are in rough condition. Particularly bad flooding in the spring of 1996 washed out both roads; Mowich Lake Road reopened in midsummer, but at this writing, Carbon River Road still has not been repaired. For updates on road conditions, call (360) 569-2211, the park's recorded information line.

Daily-use fees (presently $10 per carload) are collected at the Nisqually, Stevens Canyon, White River, and Carbon River entrances—unless you arrive very early or late, in which case you can sneak by without paying. Frequent park visitors usually fork over $20 for an annual pass or $25 for a pass granting admission to all U.S. national parks for one year.

Gray Line Tours of Seattle, (800) 426-7532, runs summer tours of the park.

Adjoining Areas

NORTH: **Snoqualmie Pass Corridor (Mountains-to-Sound Greenway)**

SOUTH: **White Pass Corridor**

EAST: **Wenatchee National Forest: Overview**

inside out

Scenic Drives/Visitors Centers

The vast majority of Mount Rainier's 2.2 million annual visitors pack a lunch, grab a map, and make a day trip to the mountain. And most of them wind up at one of two places, Paradise or Sunrise.

Longmire/Paradise

Hwy 706, the road to Paradise on the southwest side of Rainier, passes through the Nisqually entrance and climbs gradually to Longmire, a small village where you'll find the National Park Inn, (360) 569-2275; a small wildlife museum with plant and animal displays; several day-hiking trails (see Hiking/Backpacking, below), and a hiking information center; and a rental outlet for cross-country skiing. The restaurant at the National Park Inn is very familiar to backcountry skiers, who often bide their time here waiting for snowplows to finish their work on the Paradise Hwy.

From Longmire, the road climbs steeply, crosses the massive rubble path of the Nisqually Glacier and river drainage, then climbs to Paradise, elevation 5,400 feet. (Notable spots to pull off the road on the way up are beautiful Narada Falls—a good picnic spot—and the Canyon Rim Viewpoint, which overlooks the upper Nisqually River.) You'll know you've arrived at Paradise when you happen upon the other 217,000 cars parked in the massive lot. Okay, maybe not that many, but on summer weekends, Paradise is so heavily visited that you'll likely have to patrol, shopping-mall-the-week-before-Christmas style, for a parking spot.

The attractions here are obvious: an up-close view of the mountain (too close, really, for photographers, because you're standing on the mountain rather than looking at it), many hiking trails through beautiful alpine meadows (see Hiking/Backpacking, below), picnic sites with killer views, and the Henry M. Jackson Visitors Center, housed in a saucer-shaped building that looks as if it just arrived from the planet Zendar. The Jackson Visitors Center exhibits are interesting, but most people never see them, so impressed are they by the view of the mountain. Nearby, the folksy Paradise Inn offers accommodations from May to October; call (360) 569-2275 for reservations.

Paradise is a treat for many southern-clime visitors, because snow is present nearly year-round. The largest single-season snowfall in history—1,122 inches, or 93 feet—was recorded here in the winter of 1971–72, and the average is about 700 inches a year. It's not unusual to find accumulated snow on the ground from October through April; 20 feet of snow on the ground by midwinter is not unusual. Only in late summer and early autumn do the slopes above Paradise completely clear of snow, and even then permanent snowfields and glaciers remain to entice visitors. Generally, hiking trails around Paradise are free of snow by early July, but this varies widely with weather conditions.

Paradise also is the departure point for most climbing expeditions headed up the mountain (see Climbing, below), creating a fascinating parking-lot mishmash of hardened mountaineers and tourists in RVs with Nebraska plates. People-watching here is almost as good as mountain-viewing. In the winter, the Paradise parking lot takes on an entirely different, and by this we mean nasty, character. Weather can turn brutal in an instant, with winds gusting routinely to 30mph, and snowstorms a constant threat. Woe is the winter Paradise visitor who ventures more than 100 feet from the car without a pack full of basic survival gear. Still, Paradise is surprisingly busy in the winter, when cross-country and telemark skiers flock here for some of the best backcountry skiing in the Northwest. Inner-tubers and snowboarders also flock to Paradise in the winter (see skiing and snow sections, below).

Sunrise

The park's second most-frequented—and arguably its most beautiful—auto-accessible spot is the Sunrise area at 6,400 feet on the northeast side of the mountain. Sunrise, which opens only after snow melts off the access road (usually in late June or early July), has a historic day lodge, a ranger station, and a substantial picnic area. But most visitors come for the stunning views of the mountain—the best from any vista in the park. A multitude of both short and long hiking trails fan out from the parking lot (see Hiking, below), most winding through alpine meadows. Naturalists lead guided walks daily; stop by Sunrise Ranger Station for a schedule, or set out on your own. If you venture more than a couple of miles from the car, there's a better than even chance that you'll encounter deer, mountain goats, Rocky Mountain elk, or marmots.

Remember to bring your binoculars or spotting scope. From the parking lot, you can see the entire Emmons Glacier climbing route, where ant-size climbers inch their way up and down steps kicked into the snow. If you can't spot the route yourself, stop by Sunrise Ranger Station, which monitors climbing expeditions with a spotting scope. The station can turn into a beehive of activity if a mountain rescue operation is under way.

Additional summer ranger stations are located at Ohanapecosh, White River, Carbon River, Nisqually and Longmire. All dispense park information, hiking permits, and other information. See More Information in this chapter for phone numbers.

Hiking/Backpacking

The slopes around Mount Rainier, though heavily visited, contain some of the most splendid hiking terrain in the Northwest, if not the country. More so than other parks that share its stature, Rainier is best experienced on foot, either on one of its many short, paved interpretive trails, or on its magnificent 93-mile Wonderland Trail, which circles the entire mountain.

All hikers should note, however, that weather on Rainier is even more unpredictable than in most other Cascade hiking destinations. It can snow on the mountain any time—and we do mean *any* time. Hikers should never set out on a Rainier trail of any significant length without carrying extra clothing and the other "10 essentials" of backcountry travel (see the Washington Outdoors Primer chapter). Many trails in the park are at high altitudes, where skin can sunburn quickly and dehydration and minor altitude sickness are significant concerns. Route-finding can become difficult when snow and fog set in. If that's not enough, flash floods are not uncommon in the park's heavily glaciated valleys. You've been warned.

Also, heed the rules, which are consistent with those in most other fragile wilderness areas: no dogs, no bikes, no fires. Groups are limited to 12 people. Day-hiking permits aren't required, but you must have a free backcountry permit to stay overnight, and they're limited for some popular backpacking areas. Overnight permits also are required for winter snow camping, which is allowed in virtually all of the park (at least as much of it as you can get to). Permits are available at all ranger stations, but your best bet is to shoot for one of the park's Hiker Information Centers, found at Longmire, White River, and Carbon River.

All that said, enjoy yourself. We've rarely completed a hike on Rainier that wasn't memorable in some way—good or bad. This is raw, unfiltered Washington at its alpine best. Entire books have been written about Mount Rainier hiking and climbing trails, so we won't attempt to list the entire 300 miles here. That's what your spare time and hiking boots are for. Below are some favorites to get you started, grouped into the most popular park destination areas.

Longmire area

One of the most popular day hikes in the park is the **Comet Falls/Van Trump Park Trail** (moderate; 5.5 miles round trip), which begins at a trailhead on the Paradise Hwy about 4 miles beyond Longmire, just before the Christine Falls Bridge. The trail, which doesn't melt out until mid-summer, climbs steeply about 1 1/2 miles to great views of the 320-foot falls. The path continues up to Van Trump Park, a lovely alpine meadow-land. Watch for mountain goats. Lower on the road, about 3 miles inside the park, is the **Kautz Creek Trail** (moderate/difficult; 11.4 miles round trip), which showcases the magnificent devastation wrought by a 1947 flood from a burst ice dam at the foot of the Kautz Glacier. The trail climbs steadily to **Indian Henry's Hunting Grounds,** one of Rainier's most beautiful alpine parklands, and a great place to see wildflowers in the summer.

From Longmire itself, options include the moderately scenic **Rampart Ridge Loop** (easy/moderate; 4.5 miles round trip), with connections to the Wonderland, Van Trump Park, and Comet Falls trails (see above); and the kid-friendly **Trail of the Shadows Nature Trail** (easy; ³/₄ mile round trip), an interesting walk to the former site of the Longmire Springs Hotel, as well as the ruins of an 1888 homestead cabin once occupied by the Longmire family. The trailhead is across the highway from the National Park Inn. Also near Longmire, a trail on the far side of the suspension bridge over the Nisqually River leads to **Eagle Peak** (difficult; 7.2 miles round trip), where views of Rainier and the Nisqually drainage are sublime. It's a steep hike, though, gaining some 3,000 feet in the 3.6 miles to the 5,700-foot saddle just below the summit.

North of Longmire near Cougar Rock Campground is the **Carter Falls Trail** (easy; 2 miles round trip), which leads along the Paradise River to the remains of an old hydropower plant, then through a nice forest to Carter Falls.

West Side Road

Great hiking terrain in the Puyallup River drainage on the west side of Rainier is a bit lonelier than most other mountain locales, largely because the West Side Road, which turns north from Hwy 706 (Paradise Hwy) about a mile beyond the Nisqually entrance, is washed out and permanently closed at Fish Creek, about 3 ¹/₂ miles. The closure adds as much as 8 miles of road walking (one way) to the most popular trails in this area, turning short day hikes into long ones, or even overnighters. Some hikers ride mountain bikes up West Side Road beyond the washout to the trailhead of their choice.

A good destination here is **Klapatche Park** (difficult; 21 miles round trip), a spectacular backpacking route. Campsites on this route at Aurora Lake, Saint Andrews Lake, and Saint Andrews Park are so great they're overused, even with the washout's addition of 16 miles of road walking. A long but spectacular day hike in the same area is **Emerald Ridge Trail** (difficult; 16 miles round trip), which begins 4.5 miles up from the washout and climbs steeply to a connection with the Wonderland Trail. Go left to Saint Andrews Park or right to the Tahoma Glacier and Glacier Island. Both are magnificent. A bit shorter, but only slightly less scenic, is the **Gobbler's Knob/Lake George Trail** (moderate; 12 miles round trip), which begins 3 miles up from the washout and follows a very easy path to Lake George, a pleasant lunch spot. Fully fortified, you can proceed another mile up the hill to a fire lookout site atop Gobbler's Knob, where the view of the Tahoma Glacier on the western face of Rainier is likely the best in the park.

Paradise

A number of short nature trails begin at the Paradise Visitors Center. All pass through alpine meadows and offer great views of Rainier and other Cascade peaks. They include the **Alta Vista Loop** (easy; 1.5 miles round trip), which climbs through some nice meadows to a viewpoint; and nearby Nisqually Vista Trail (easy; 1.2 miles round trip), a similar walk. Both can be hiked in about an hour. For a slightly longer walk, take the **Deadhorse Creek** and **Moraine Trails** about 1.25 miles to a great viewpoint high above the Nisqually Glacier. To get more altitude and better views, hop on the Skyline Trail and climb about 600 vertical feet in a mile to the **Glacier Vista Loop.**

For a more serious day hike, **Skyline Loop** (moderately difficult; 5.8 miles round trip) is a great option. The trail climbs north beyond the Alta Vista Trail and short Glacier Vista Loop before coming to a fork at about 2 miles. The lower route leads across a permanent snowfield—if it's early in the day or cold, making the snow hard and slippery, take the upper route, which climbs around the snow and adds about 3/4 mile to the trip. The steep climb to Camp Muir (see below) begins nearby. The trail tops out at about 7,000 feet, granting superb views at Panorama Point before connecting with the Golden Gate Trail (the quickest way back) or the Mazama Ridge Trail, which can be followed to the Lakes Trail, then back to the parking lot. The latter option adds about 2 1/2 miles to the loop distance.

Another great day hike is the **Mazama Ridge/Lakes Loop** (moderately difficult; 5 miles round trip), which begins above Paradise and follows the Mazama Ridge to the Reflection Lakes area, then climbs back to the Paradise parking lot. This is a busy, beautiful trail, offering the best mix of terrain and views in the Paradise area. Another popular day trip, particularly among backcountry skiers who flock here in spring and early summer, is **Paradise Glacier** (moderately difficult; 6 miles round trip), which begins on the Skyline Trail before branching off up Mazama Ridge and climbing to the toe of the Paradise Glacier, 6,400 feet. The path continues up the glacial moraine, which can be difficult to negotiate. Venturing out on the glacier—where the Paradise Ice Caves remain buried—is very hazardous, particularly in the late summer when hidden crevasses might lie just below the surface. The view is awesome, however, making this a great place to pack in a lunch and escape some of the Paradise-area masses.

The ultimate Paradise day hike, of course, is the straight-up climb to **Camp Muir** (difficult; 9 miles round trip), the 10,000-foot base camp for summit expeditions. The route begins on the Skyline Trail, then turns straight north up the mountain from either Pebble Creek or Panorama Point. From there on, it's a snow slog most of the year. This isn't for the meek. The route gains 4,600 feet—much of it in snow—from the Paradise parking lot. Don't do it if you're not properly trained and equipped for snow travel.

Two great day hikes begin just below Paradise, in the Reflection Lakes parking area on Stevens Canyon Road. The trail to **Bench** and **Snow Lakes** (easy; 2.6 miles round trip) is extremely crowded, largely because it's immensely beautiful and very accessible. The lakes, jewel-like ponds below Tatoosh Ridge, about 700 feet below Paradise, don't thaw out until late July, and the trail stays quite muddy most of the summer. Wildflowers are beautiful here through August. Some campsites are found here, but the trails are too busy to allow any semblance of an enjoyable overnight stay. Pick another trail for that.

To escape some of the crowds, you can get up on Tatoosh Ridge by following the **Pinnacle Peak Trail** (moderate; 2.6 miles round trip) from the same parking area. The trail climbs steadily to 6,000-foot Pinnacle Saddle, between Pinnacle Peak (6,562 feet) and Plummer Peak (6,370 feet). Because it's detached a bit from the peak, this might be the best place in the Paradise area to photograph Mount Rainier.

Many hikers also choose the Paradise area as their departure point for hikes on the **Wonderland Trail** (very difficult; 93 miles round trip), the spectacular route that skirts the entire mountain. This is one of the nation's most magnificent backpacking adventures, requiring significant planning (food caches and campsites must be arranged with rangers before departure) and substantial stamina. The route passes through every conceivable Cascade Mountain landscape on its long journey, from placid meadows to deep forest to open snow and ice to frustrating, rocky moraines, and harrowing stream fords. In many respects, circumnavigating Rainier on the Wonderland Trail is more difficult than climbing the mountain: the trail gains and loses about 20,000 feet of elevation on the loop, and gains and losses of 4,000 feet in a day's hike are not uncommon. Contact park rangers for information about cache points and designated campsites. And carry plenty of moleskin.

Sunrise

Many short, easy trails lead from the Sunrise parking lot to Emmons Glacier views. They include the half-mile **Emmons Vista Trail** and the placid **Sunrise Rim Trail,** which makes a nice, 1 1/2-mile (one way) stroll into the walk-in campground near Shadow Lake. Wildflowers, deer, and elk are thick here in the summer. The most popular day hike from Sunrise very likely is the **Fremont Lookout Trail** (moderate; 5.6 miles round trip), which leads to great views of the entire central Cascade Range. Mountain goats often are seen in this area. By branching in different directions from the same trail, you can pack your lunch to **Grand Park** and **Berkeley Park** (moderate; 13 miles round trip), or up the steep, occasionally dangerous route to **Burroughs Mountain** (difficult; 7 miles round trip), where views are magnificent (but don't try to cross the permanent snowfield without an ice ax).

Lower on the mountain, near the White River entrance station, are two memorable mountain routes. Both are great overnight backpacking routes—which naturally makes them among the most crowded trails in the park. The **Glacier Basin Trail** (moderate; 7 miles round trip) begins at White River Campground, following the White River past some old mining-operation remnants to a side path that leads to the foot of the massive Emmons Glacier, the largest ice sheet by surface area in the Lower 48. The trail ends at Glacier Basin Camp, a staging area for summit climbs via the Emmons/Winthrop Glacier route. Nearby, from a small parking lot near the Fryingpan Creek Bridge, is the **Summerland/Panhandle Gap Trail** (moderate; 8.6 miles round trip), which climbs 4 miles through the Fryingpan Creek drainage before breaking into open slopes and, ultimately, the alpine wonderland of Summerland, rich with wildflowers and jaw-dropping views of Rainier, Little Tahoma, Goat Island Mountain, and the Fryingpan Glacier. Watch for mountain goats. If you've strategically placed another car or consider yourself an ace hitchhiker, you can make a longer trip by proceeding from Summerland to the Wonderland Trail and heading south to Indian Bar and an exit on the Stevens Canyon Road. It's a one-way hike of about 16 miles, and a great way to get away from the crowds. (Another good option is to hike it with another party starting from the opposite end and swap car keys in the middle.)

Carbon Glacier

The northern slopes of Rainier are extremely rugged and extremely beautiful. They're also extremely popular, although the steep, rocky nature of many trails here tends to weed out all but the most determined backcountry travelers. (Note that at this writing, the Carbon River Road was washed out about 5 miles below Ipsut Creek Campground. If it hasn't been repaired, add 10 miles to the round-trip distance for any of these hikes.)

An uncharacteristically easy, and lovely, day hike is the **Green Lake Trail** (easy; 3.6 miles round trip), which begins at Ranger Creek, 3 miles beyond the Carbon River entrance station. This is a grand family hike, passing through a wonderful old-growth forest, and beyond gushing Ranger Creek Falls to placid Green Lake, where (thankfully) no overnight camping is allowed.

From the main trailhead near Ipsut Creek Campground, hikers can venture up one leg of the Wonderland Trail to the impressive Carbon Glacier and beyond to magnificent alpine backcountry. Options include **Windy Gap** (difficult; 13 miles round trip), a strenuous but beautiful backpack trip; and the **Carbon Glacier/Mystic Lake Trail** (moderate/difficult; up to 15.2 miles round trip). The latter can be either a moderately easy (except for the rickety suspension bridge) 7-miles-round-trip hike to the toe of the lowest-elevation glacier in the Lower 48, or a curse-inducing haul to Mystic Lake, where you can stare directly into Rainier's magnificently sheer north face, the Willis Wall. You can also follow the Wonderland Trail south from here to the meadowlands of **Seattle Park** and **Spray Park.**

Mowich Lake

Rough, gravelly Mowich Lake Road ends at a walk-in camping area that also serves as trailhead for the **Spray Park Trail** (moderately difficult; 6 miles round trip). This extremely popular day-hiking trail drops slightly to the Wonderland Trail, then climbs steeply through the forest to Spray Falls before opening to the wildflower meadows and parklands of Spray Park. It's beautiful in midsummer, providing easy off-trail access to snow-play and skiing areas on the remnant Flett Glacier. Backpackers can continue north on the Wonderland Trail to Seattle Park and Ipsut Campground, then take the connecting Ipsut Creek Trail back to Mowich Lake, for a loop of 15.5 miles. Another popular day hike leads to **Tolmie Peak Lookout** (moderate; 6.4 miles round trip), which offers great views of the northwest side of Rainier. Many hikers walk only as far as Eunice Lake, a pretty spot about 3 miles up the trail. The short access trail to the lookout is very steep. No camping is allowed at the lake, although a few permits are issued for designated sites nearby.

Stevens Canyon/Ohanapecosh

Day hiking trails in the southeast corner of the park don't offer views of the mountain, but they're scenic, nonetheless. The **Grove of the Patriarchs** (easy; 1.3-mile loop) is a resilient stand of ancient Douglas fir, hemlock, and western red cedar trees that have been nursing on the rich, clean waters of the Ohanapecosh River for centuries. The trail crosses the river on a suspension bridge and loops through trees as big as 35 feet in circumference. Some are believed to be 1,000 years old. The trailhead is on Stevens Canyon Road, just north of the Ohanapecosh Visitors Center. This is a popular cross-country skiing destination in the winter (see Cross-Country Skiing, below).

For a longer taste of the same, get on the nearby **Eastside Trail** (moderate; 9 miles one way), which follows the river between Ohanapecosh Campground and a second trailhead about 6 miles north on Stevens Canyon Road. Another easy, primo day hike, the **Silver Falls Loop** (easy; 3 miles round trip), begins near the Ohanapecosh Visitors Center and leads to a former hot springs resort site and 75-foot Silver Falls. The trail also is accessible from Loop B of the Ohanapecosh Campground and the **Laughingwater Creek Trail** off Hwy 123.

Climbing

We look up there every day (well, at least in the summer) and see the Mountain. And some of us just can't resist climbing it. Mount Rainier is attempted by thousands of climbers every year, with skill levels ranging from world-class alpinist to first-time weekend warrior. Many people make it, many don't. Nearly all who do make it come home at least partially whipped, saying the summit trek was the most difficult physical thing they've ever done—and ever plan to do. While the primary climbing route on the south face of Rainier isn't technically difficult, the elevation, 14,411 feet, is enough to make a summit climb very challenging. Altitude affects many climbers, and fickle weather can very quickly turn a sunny snow slog into a wintry hell.

Generally, the summer climbing season is relatively safe. Good-weather days can see dozens of climbers reach the summit. But would-be summiteers should not underestimate the mountain's considerable peril. Many climbers—including many experienced alpinists—have died on Rainier. And many, many more have turned back, exhausted.

Thanks largely to the considerable expertise of Rainier Mountaineering, Inc., one of the nation's top climbing-guide services, you don't need climbing experience to get up Rainier. You do need to be in good shape and to have the good sense to follow the directions of a veteran guide. The typical **guided climb** on Rainier includes a partial day of training, followed by a long trek from Paradise to Camp Muir, at 10,000 feet. Climbers rise early and head for the summit via Disappointment Cleaver and the Ingraham Glacier. For guide information, call RMI at Paradise, (360) 569-2227, in the summer, or Tacoma, (206) 627-6242, in the winter.

You can also climb the mountain without a guide, although anyone who does so without considerable experience is a fool. A $15 climbing fee is charged. Call the park at (360) 569-2211. Rainier can be, and is, climbed all year round, but peak climbing season is from May to July.

Camping

Campers are limited to 14 days at all Mount Rainier campgrounds. And after the trouble you go through to score a space, you'll want to stay the full two weeks. Nabbing a midsummer campsite at Rainier can be a lot like winning the lottery. Everybody's looking for one, and only a fraction wind up happy when the sun goes down. Rainier's campgrounds are open summers only, except for Sunshine Point, which is open all year. They provide water and flush toilets, but no showers or RV hookups. No reservations are offered.

Paradise-area visitors can choose from **Sunshine Point** (18 sites along the Nisqually River) or **Cougar Rock** (200 sites, about 2 ½ miles beyond Longmire). Sunrise visitors head for **White River,** which has 117 sites near the White River entrance. If you're entering at Stevens Canyon, **Ohanapecosh** is the best bet, with 232 sites along this pretty river. An alternative is **La Wis Wis,** a Forest Service campground near Packwood (see the White Pass Corridor chapter).

On the north side of the park, **Ipsut Creek** (if and when the washed-out Carbon River Road reopens) offers 31 campsites, plus a group camp. A large walk-in campground is at **Mowich Lake.** Campers need back-country permits, available on-site on weekends or from the Carbon River Ranger Station other times. Mowich Lake has no piped water.

Downhill Skiing

Widely regarded as the state's premier alpine ski resort, **Crystal Mountain** is not inside the national park—but you can see Rainier from its summit. Crystal, 39 miles southeast of Enumclaw via Hwy 410, has the state's biggest vertical drop, most lifts, and by far the most diverse terrain. This is a big ski area, offering an in-bounds terrain with enough variety to keep any skier happy and an unpatrolled backcountry area that ranks with the best in the West.

The resort also offers a small number of condominium-style slope-side lodgings—a rarity for Washington skiers. That's a particular blessing, given how difficult Crystal can be to drive to. Thousands of people make it on winter weekends, but the commute to Crystal can be trying. Most of the drive is two-lane road, the upper portions of which get nasty when the snow is dumping.

The mountain also seems to have been plagued in recent years by inconsistent management; skiers gripe that lifts are shut down without warning, and the resort has done little in improving facilities to keep up with its Northwest competitors. Lift lines are a significant problem on weekends—a good problem to have if you're a resort owner, but a bad one if you're a skier who has driven 2 ½ hours to get here. Crystal fans hope that will change in the near future. The resort's owners have been negotiating to sell to a larger ski-resort operator, which could mean an infusion of badly needed capital-construction money.

In the meantime, in spite of its small problems, Crystal on a good snow day is tough to beat. The ridgetop view of Mount Rainier from the top of the Rainier Express lift is truly spectacular, and the mountain's open bowls provide a great mix of fast, steep ski terrain. Experts usually ride the Rainier Express and turn right, headed for areas such as Green Valley or the North or South Backcountry.

Most of that, however, depends on good snow, which can be wildly inconsistent here. A bare base area has been a consistent problem at Crystal, although upper-mountain lifts typically have a very reliable base from early December through mid-April. It can dump hard and fast here. A major storm in the winter of 1994 dumped 65 inches of snow on the resort in a single 24-hour period. Astonishing, but unfortunately fairly rare. Crystal's most consistently heavy snowfall comes late in the winter, during February and March. That makes it a great spring skiing area.

The resort also has a small summer operation, ferrying hikers, mountain bikers, and Summit House diners to the top of the Rainier Express lift for a fee.

Crystal stats: Elevation: 4,400 to 7,000 feet. Lifts: One high-speed quad, nine fixed chairs, one surface lift. Prices: Adult weekend tickets are $33 at this writing, less expensive on weekdays. Hours: 9am to 4:30pm weekdays, 8:30am to 4pm weekends. Night skiing to 10pm Fridays, Saturdays, Sundays, and holidays. Lodging reservations: (206) 663-2558. Mountain information: (360) 663-2265. Snow phone: (206) 634-3771.

Cross-Country Skiing

Mount Rainier is the backcountry skiing capital of the Northwest. For **cross-country skiers** and **snowshoers,** an abundance of great terrain is found both inside and outside the park. Paradise usually has skiable snow by late October, and almost always by Thanksgiving.

Whenever you go, make sure you're equipped with tire chains. The road to Paradise is plowed and kept open all winter, but it can be treacherous above Longmire, and rangers will turn you away if you attempt it without four-wheel drive or chains (see Getting There, above).

Inside the park, **Paradise**—the only National Park area open all winter—is the skiing focus. Many good cross-country and telemark routes begin here. Beginners will enjoy the flat, easy pace of the Stevens Canyon Road, which is closed to auto traffic (and buried in about 30 feet of snow) at the Paradise parking lot. The road drops about 500 feet in a 3-mile descent through Paradise Valley to Reflection Lakes. There's no grooming here, but it's usually easy to follow the tracks made by previous skiers. Stronger skiers can continue on a trail to Narada Falls parking lot, where a cozy, heated changing room is open all winter. If you have friends nice enough to come pick you up, you can thaw out and ignore the steep ski back up the hill. Also good for beginners is the 1.2-mile Nisqually Vista Loop from Jackson Visitors Center.

When there's enough snow down low, ski-touring trails also can be found at **Longmire,** 2,700 feet lower on the mountain. Another popular ski route is the east end of the Stevens Canyon Road, which can be skied from the Stevens Canyon entrance to the Grove of the Patriarchs Trail (see Hiking/Backpacking, above). Similarly, many of the Longmire- and Paradise-area trails listed under Hiking can also be skied in the winter. Check with rangers about avalanche danger. Ski rentals are available at Longmire Ski Touring Center; (360) 569-2411.

More advanced cross-country and telemark skiers go straight up the mountain from Paradise to any of a number of wide-open winter snowfields. The **Paradise Glacier** above Mazama Ridge is a particularly popular destination, weather permitting. Make no mistake: Backcountry skiing is an inherently risky activity made even more dangerous by the weather at Paradise. Avalanche danger is considerable, and winter storms often are so strong that skiers are completely blinded very quickly. It's easy to get lost, even if you think you know where you're going. Don't ski alone. Newcomers should hook up with at least one other skier who's expert at route-finding. Always carry a pack with survival gear sufficient to wait out a long storm. Many telemarkers in this area carry avalanche transceivers.

Outside the park, the **Mount Tahoma Scenic Trails Association** maintains an extensive 145-kilometer (103-mile) trail network, mostly on logging roads and trails on both sides of Hwy 706, below Rainier's south slopes. The trails are free, and reservations are available for overnight stays in the association's yurts and backcountry cabins. About 32 kilometers of trails are groomed. Skiers parking in trail lots must have state Sno-Park stickers, available at outdoor retailers, ranger stations, and ski shops. Stop by the MTSTA office in Ashford, or call (360) 569-2451, for a trail map and information.

Snowshoeing/Snow Play

Paradise isn't just a snooty skinny-ski heaven. Kids love it, too, particularly those of the **inner-tube persuasion.** The park makes a fuss every year about kids scalping off trees and colliding with themselves and other objects as they hurtle down the lower slopes at Paradise. But they ultimately wind up establishing a semiorganized area for inner-tubing every winter. Before you go, call the park to make sure the tubes are flying. Tubing often doesn't get good at Paradise until mid- to late December, when the snow gets deep enough to cover the small trees and fragile alpine plants above Paradise.

Paradise is a **snowshoer's** dream, with walkable snow available at least nine months out of the year. Newcomers to the sport are welcome here. Park rangers lead guided snowshoe walks from Paradise on weekends and during holiday seasons. The walks are free, with the park usually requesting a small donation to cover snowshoe rentals. No experience is necessary. It's a lot of fun. Call the park information line, (360) 569-2211, for details. If you want to go it on your own, rental snowshoes are available at Longmire Ski Touring Center; (360) 569-2411.

Biking

Rainier's highways are open to cyclists, and some park roads—notably the Stevens Canyon Road between Paradise and Ohanapecosh—make beautiful summertime rides. But none of Rainier's 300 miles of trails are available to the fat-tire fans—largely because virtually all of the park is designated wilderness. The only place mountain bikes are commonly seen in Rainier is **West Side Road** above the washout 3.5 miles up from the Paradise Hwy. There, hikers often bring bikes to reduce their time walking up the abandoned roadway to several popular trailheads in the Puyallup River drainage (see Hiking/Backpacking, above).

Fishing

An angler's paradise Rainier is not. Some trout are caught in **Green Lake,** in the Carbon River drainage, and in nearby **Mowich Lake** (see Hiking/Backpacking, above). But like all other lakes in the park, these don't receive planted fish. **Dewey Lake**—a popular backpacking destination south of Chinook Pass, along the Pacific Crest Trail—holds some brook trout.

Wildlife

Mount Rainier National Park is one of the richest wildlife areas in the state. **Mountain goats** are frequent visitors to alpine campsites along the park's

300 miles of trails. The easiest to negotiate probably is the Mount Fremont Lookout Trail from Sunrise Visitors Center. Backpacking destinations such as Summerland/Panhandle Gap and Van Trump Park also are consistently reliable goat haunts. See Hiking/Backpacking, above, for details.

The Sunrise area in general is rife with wildlife. We almost always see friendly **black-tailed deer** here, and very often encounter **Rocky Mountain elk.** Spring and fall are the best times to spot elk.

Photography

Any fool with a camera should come home with at least one great photograph from a summertime visit to Mount Rainier. Pick a direction, pick a time of day, pick an exposure. Everywhere you look, Rainier is photogenic. Some nature photographers we know have spent the better part of their lifetimes exploring the nooks and crannies of Rainier. They keep coming back for more, swearing the mountain is one of the most diverse nature-shooting havens on the planet.

Generally, it's a given that the very best pictures produced at Mount Rainier have two characteristics. They're usually taken some distance off the road, often on one of the park's 300 miles of trails. And they're usually *not* picture of the mountain, which is too close to be squeezed into a fitting landscape from most areas of the park. What to shoot, then? Wildlife. Wildflowers. Ice formations. Waterfalls. Clouds. Marmots. Rivers. Big trees. Ferns. Park rangers' Smokey Bear hats or mint green patrol cruisers. You name it. Rainier is a Kodachrome gold mine.

If you insist on shooting the mountain—and who among us has ever been able to resist?—don't go to Paradise to do it. The Sunrise Visitors Center on the northeast side of the mountain provides far better vistas. Or try the Pinnacle Peak Trail (see Hiking/Backpacking, above). As usual, very early or very late light is best. Rainier sometimes lights up in brilliant crimson alpenglow just after sunset. Choose your spot and bring a tripod.

Attractions

Stop in at the **Lindon Bookstore** (1522 Cole Street, **Enumclaw;** (360) 825-1388) for an espresso and browse through the large, well-considered selection of books.

The advent of the Morton Dinner Train (and an enterprising restaurateur) has turned the onetime sawmill town of **Elbe** into more of a museum (some say graveyard) for antique cabooses. The **Morton Dinner Train**—$55 per person, (360) 569-2588—is a 4-hour, 40-miles-round-trip train ride from Elbe to Morton. The dinner (shrimp cocktail, prime rib, and the works) is surprisingly good, and the conductor is well versed in the area's lore. You don't get dinner on the hour-long **Mount Rainier Scenic Railroad** excursion—summers only, (360) 569-2588—but the scenery (to Mineral and back) is just as attractive. A new convention resort is in the works on 300 acres just outside of Elbe.

Northwest Trek is a "zoo" where animals roam free while people tour the 600-acre grounds in small, open-air trams. The buffalo herd steals the show. You can also combine your visit with breakfast at the food service concession, the Fir Bough. Open daily February through October, weekends only the rest of the year. Group rates are available. On Hwy 161, 17 miles south of Puyallup; (360) 832-6116.

Restaurants

Naches Tavern   Now *this* is the way to do a country tavern. The fireplace is as long as a wall and roars all winter long to warm the Crystal Mountain après-ski crowd. The group assembled in this Greenwater gathering spot is a peaceable mix of skiers, hunters, loggers, and locals, and the food is homemade and modestly priced (deep-fried mushrooms and four-scoop milkshakes!). *North side of Hwy 410; (360) 663-2267; 58411 SR 410E, Greenwater; $.*

Lodgings

Alexander's Country Inn ☆☆   This quaint country inn has gained such a following that it now rivals the mountain itself as the best reason to visit Ashford. A large wheelchair-accessible suite has been added on the second floor—very private, with its own deck. The dining room is your best bet in these parts for a perfectly pan-fried trout—caught out back in the holding pond. *4 miles east of Ashford on Hwy 706; (360) 569-2300 or (800) 654-7615; 37515 Rte 706 E, Ashford; $$.*

Nisqually Lodge ☆   Reasonably priced and clean, this lodge just a few miles before the west entrance to Mount Rainier offers a welcome respite. This 24-room, two-story lodge is well visited—returnees like the stone fireplace in the lobby, the air conditioning in the summer, and the hot tub outside (though we hear reports about the thin walls). *Hwy 7 to Rte 706, 5 miles from park entrance; (360) 569-8804; 31609 Rte 706, Ashford; $$.*

Paradise Inn ☆   The hotel at Paradise, just above the visitors center, is a massive, old-fashioned 1917 lodge, full of exposed beams, log furniture, and American Indian rugs. The Paradise Inn has 125 rooms, but the greatest advantage to staying here is the proximity to the summit (the expensive meals in the restaurant tend toward routine beef and frozen seafood dishes). Open late May to October only. *Hwy 706 to Paradise in Mt Rainier National Park; (360) 569-2275; Mount Rainier Guest Services, PO Box 108, Ashford, WA 98304; $$.*

Wellspring   For more than a decade, Wellspring has quietly greeted outdoor enthusiasts with two spas nestled in a sylvan glade surrounded by evergreens. A soothing hour or two at Wellspring has become almost de rigueur for folks coming off Mount Rainier. Owner Sunny Thompson recently built three log cabins on her wooded south slope. Now you don't need to drive home in the cold and you can wake up to a basketful of breakfast. *On Kernahan Rd 2 ¹/₂ miles east of Ashford toward the park; (360) 569-2514; Kernahan Rd, Ashford; $$.*

Whistlin' Jack Lodge ☆☆   Ideal for all manner of outdoor activity, this mountain hideaway has all the comforts of home and then some. There are six cabins, two bungalows, and eight motel units here, but best are the cabins. Access via Chinook Pass near Mount Rainier is restricted almost seven months a year, but lodge patrons (many families) are used to driving the winding road from Yakima instead. *40 miles west of Yakima on SR 410; (509) 658-2433 or (800) 827-2299; 20800 SR 410, Naches; $$.*

Cheaper Sleeps

Hobo Inn   We like this place, if only because it's fun to stay in a caboose. So what if it's right on the road to Rainier and rooms are $70 to $85 during high season—squeeze in four and you've got a genuine train experience. *(360) 569-2500; 54106 Mountain Hwy E, Elbe.*

More Information

Department of Transportation pass report: *(888) SNO-INFO.*
Mount Rainier National Park Headquarters: *Tahoma Woods, Star Rte, Ashford, WA 98304; (360) 569-2211.*
Ranger stations: *(360) 569-2211 and the following extensions:*
    Carbon River: *ext. 2358.*
    Longmire: *ext. 3305.*
    Nisqually: *ext. 2390.*
    Ohanapecosh: *ext. 2352.*
    Paradise: *ext. 2314.*
    Sunrise: *ext. 2327.*
    White River: *ext. 2356.*

White Pass Corridor

From Packwood east to Naches, north through the William O. Douglas Wilderness, and south through the Goat Rocks Wilderness, including Rimrock Lake, the Tieton River, and White Pass Ski Area.

Be prepared to undergo conversion. White Pass visitors who aren't geology buffs when they leave Packwood likely will be before they arrive in Naches. The White Pass corridor provides the state's most intriguing slice into the violent volcanic past of the South Cascades. Evidence is everywhere you look, from fascinating layers of volcanic rock in highway roadcuts to 6,000-foot cinder cones that look like they might have erupted only recently—and could once again at any time.

Most who explore the White Pass area on foot, however, are struck less by the area's volcanism than by the stunningly beautiful alpine terrain it has left in its wake. White Pass is the drive-through window for Washington wilderness. As you travel east between Packwood and White Pass summit, you're literally surrounded by it. To the north is Mount Rainier National Park and the 167,000-acre William O. Douglas Wilderness, named for the late Supreme Court justice who hiked extensively here, chronicling his journeys in *Of Men and Mountains*. The volcano-pocked wilderness is dotted with small lakes, sprawling meadows, and fantastic alpine ridges. To the south is the spectacular 105,000-acre Goat Rocks Wilderness, whose centerpiece, the Goat Rocks, is a series of impressive 8,000-foot crags that mark the site of an ancient extinct volcano.

Both wilderness areas are reached by hiking a short distance north or south of US 12. This rugged country lures hikers up steep mountain paths to stunning vistas and down cool, quiet paths along the Clear Fork Cowlitz and Tieton Rivers. But you don't have to invest a lot of sweat to be awed by the sights of White Pass. Hwy 12 through White Pass is one of the more beautiful mountain highways in the state, particularly in the autumn, when aspens, alders, and larches on the east side of the pass burst into a brilliant yellow. It is perhaps even more fantastic in the winter, when deep snows lure skiers to one of the state's most scenic alpine ski areas.

White Pass is open all year, except for occasional snow closures near the 4,500-foot summit. A central stretch of about 20 miles often is coated with packed snow and ice. Carrying chains is a must in the winter. No matter when you visit, the roadside views are grand. A short distance from the highway are vistas of the Goat Rocks and the massive Rimrock Lake, a prominent wildlife-viewing area, and a string of serene campsites along the liquid-crystal Tieton, a favorite of anglers and whitewater rafters.

The total package is impressive enough for the mixed-in volcanic remnants to be a bit troubling. Normally we take it for granted that the wonders left in the wake of volcanoes are potentially temporary (see Mount St. Helens for proof). But we'd hate to see White Pass go before we do.

Getting There

The White Pass Hwy (US 12) turns east from Interstate 5 south of Chehalis, continues about 85 miles to White Pass and another 35 miles to Naches, east of Yakima. Allow 3 hours' travel time from Seattle to White Pass summit.

Adjoining Areas

NORTH: **Mount Rainier National Park**
SOUTH: **Mount Adams; Mount St. Helens**
EAST: **Yakima Valley**

Hiking/Backpacking

The White Pass Highway is the primary access route to dozens of good short day hikes and extended backpack trips into the William O. Douglas Wilderness to the north and the spectacular Goat Rocks Wilderness to the south. For a full trail inventory, maps, and current permit information, contact the Packwood Ranger District, (360) 494-0600, or Naches Ranger District, (509) 653-2205. Following is a list of favorites, arranged from west to east beginning at Packwood.

Just north of Packwood is **Tatoosh Ridge** (difficult; 9 miles round trip), a prominent high point popular for its awesome views of Mount Rainier. The trail begins on Forest Service Road 5272 and climbs steeply to a spectacular view at the old Tatoosh Lookout. Hikers with two cars can walk the entire ridge as a through hike, exiting at a southern trailhead along Road 5292. There are more good day hikes a short distance to the north, near the Stevens Canyon entrance to Mount Rainier National Park.

For a sampling of the greater wonders that await south of the highway, drive about 4 ½ miles east of Packwood, turn south on Roads 4610 and 4612, and try the **Bluff Lake Trail** (difficult; 13.2 miles round trip). The going is very steep at first, but relents somewhat after the first couple of miles. Your reward is a beautiful lake and beautiful views of the Goat Rocks Range from the ridgeline of Coal Creek Mountain. Nearby, the **Three Creeks Trail** (moderate; 10.8 miles round trip), which begins on Road 1266, is a fairly uneventful trail, but views of the Packwood Lake area are good from the top.

Moving east, two delightful day-hiking trails weave through the cool forests of the upper Cowlitz River drainage. The first, **Clear Fork** (easy; up to 19.2 miles round trip), begins on Forest Service Road 46, about 5 miles east of Packwood, and follows the Clear Fork of the Cowlitz on a very flat trail (it gains only about 1,200 feet in 8 miles). It's an easy walk, suitable for children most of the year. Trout fishing is fair in the river, and small Lily Lake is a nice bonus attraction. The **Clear Lost Trail** (moderate; up to 13.2 miles round trip), on US 12 about 17 miles east of Packwood, drops steeply for about 2 miles to the Clear Fork. Here, it ends—unless you're willing to get wet. Hikers who ford the river can proceed up the other side of the valley to fine views from Coyote Ridge.

White Pass is a crossing for the **Pacific Crest Trail,** which can be hiked south from here through the entire Goat Rocks Wilderness—a stretch that many through-hikers say is among the most spectacular sections of the 2,600-mile Mexico-to-Canada trail. If you're heading south, you'll climb up Hogback Ridge and find great campsites at Shoe Lake (about 6 ½ miles). The route continues south past Lutz Lake and Elk Pass, and ultimately to Cispus Pass in the Mount Adams Wilderness (about 13 miles in). Northbound hikers head into the heart of the William O. Douglas Wilderness on a grade that's uncharacteristically flat for the PCT. Many good campsites are found on this 29-mile stretch between White Pass and Chinook Pass. Highlights include Deer Lake, Sand Lake, Cowlitz Pass, Snow Lake, and Dewey Lakes, which is a popular backpack destination for Mount Rainier National Park visitors. Backpackers usually can hike the stretch from one pass to the other in about three days.

A mile farther east on US 12, near Leech Lake, is the trailhead for the **Dumbbell Lakes Loop** (moderate; 15.7 miles round trip), a popular overnight trip that starts on a leg of the PCT and continues to a plethora of lakes in this volcanic area. The best campsites are at Buesch Lake (3.8 miles) and Dumbbell Lake (4.3 miles). It's a beautiful area, but mosquitoes are intolerable here in midsummer. Try it in the fall, after the first freeze. Five miles farther east, also on the north side of the highway, is **Spiral Butte** (difficult; 12 miles round trip), a steep climb to the top of an interesting old cinder cone. The 5,900-foot summit offers grand views of the Goat Rocks Range and beyond. Just east of Rimrock Lake, between Hause Creek and Riverbend Campgrounds (see Camping, below), Forest Service Road 1500 heads north to Road 199, where you'll find the Cash Prairie Trailhead and the **Ironstone Mountain Trail** (moderately difficult; up to 13 miles one way). This is a very quiet, scenic trail that stays high on an east-west ridgeline, with a multitude of possibilities. Day hikers can proceed just a couple of miles to great William O. Douglas Wilderness vistas; backpackers can drop into the Rattlesnake Creek drainage or find great views and camping meadows on the flanks of Burnt Mountain (6,536 feet) and Shellrock Peak (6,835 feet). A highlight, and the best camping destination, is Fox Meadow below Ironstone Mountain, at about 6 1/2 miles. You can return the way you came or continue north to an exit in the Bumping Lake area, for a one-way trip of about 10 1/2 miles.

Some of the most beautiful hikes in the White Pass Corridor lie farther south, in the upper Tieton River drainage of the Goat Rocks Wilderness. A joint trailhead for three of them is reached by driving 29 miles east of Packwood to Forest Service Road 12 near Clear Lake, turning south, and proceeding to Road 1207. From the end of this road, the **Tieton Meadows Trail** (moderate; 9.4 miles round trip) is a great midsummer hike for wildflower fans, with meadows full of blossoms a short distance down the trail. Then it gets serious, climbing sharply up 7,000-foot Pinegrass Ridge, which offers great views, but no water or campsites. From the same trailhead, the **North Fork Tieton Trail** (moderate; 9.8 miles round trip) winds through a nice forest for a couple of miles before breaking into open, boulder-strewn meadows, where the grade gets steep but the wide-open alpine scenery is spectacular. The trail climbs all the way to Tieton Pass, where it joins the Pacific Crest Trail. A third enticing option here is **Hidden Springs Trail** (moderate; 7 miles round trip), which branches off the North Fork Tieton Trail at about 1 1/2 miles and climbs steeply to beautiful alpine campsites in a meadow around a coldwater spring. Great side trips are available on the nearby PCT.

From the nearby Conrad Meadows Trailhead (at the end of Road 100, a Road 12 offshoot), hikers can take **Bear Creek** (moderate; 15 miles round trip) and **South Fork Tieton** (moderate; 9 miles round trip) trails. The first climbs to breathtaking views at a former lookout site atop 7,336-foot Bear Creek Mountain; the second is a top-notch backpacking route through some beautiful (and relatively flat) meadows, then moderately uphill to lovely Surprise Lake.

The other highly popular Goat Rocks Wilderness area is reached by driving south from US 12, 2 miles east of Packwood on Forest Service Roads 21 and 2150 to Chambers Lake. Here, a connecting path leads about 5 miles to **Snowgrass Flat** and a nearby junction with the Pacific Crest Trail on its most spectacular local stretch, past the Goat Rocks themselves and a beautiful alpine vista at Cispus Pass. You can combine the trail with the PCT and the Goat Ridge Trail for a memorable backpacking loop trip. Mountain goats are frequently seen in the Goat Rocks.

Camping

West-side White Pass (Packwood Ranger District; (360) 494-0600): The largest campground in the region, **La Wis Wis,** is on the Ohanapecosh River, just north of US 12 about 7 miles east of Packwood. This Forest Service camp, which sits at 1,400 feet, has 118 sites (no hookups; maximum RV length, 18 feet), as well as picnic grounds and a scenic river overlook. It gets a lot of overflow traffic from Mount Rainier National Park (only about 7 miles away), so sites can be tough to come by in the peak summer season. La Wis Wis is open from late May through September. Campsites cannot be reserved. *On Forest Service Road 1272, about 7 miles east of Packwood.*

Another option is the private **Packwood RV Park,** with showers, hookups, and full services. *On US 12 at Packwood; (360) 494-5145.* Two smaller Forest Service camps, **Summit Creek** and **Soda Springs,** are free campgrounds along Summit Creek, open summers only, with no piped water. *About 20 minutes east of Packwood via US 12 and Forest Service Roads 45 and 4510.*

At White Pass summit, the local cross-country ski venue (see Skiing, below) turns into a campground in the summer, when it's the site of **White Pass Lake Campground.** The primitive (no piped water) camp has 16 sites (no hookups; maximum RV length, 15 feet) on the east side of pretty Leech Lake. The Pacific Crest Trail (see Hiking/Backpacking, above) is a short walk away, as is a boat launch. An adjacent horse camp has 6 campsites, hitching rails, and other equestrian facilities.

East-side White Pass (Naches Ranger District; (509) 653-2205): On the north side of the highway just east of White Pass is **Dog Lake,** another small (10 sites) free campground with no piped water. Farther east on the south side of the highway is **Clear Lake,** which has 67 sites spread throughout two separate campgrounds (north and south) on Clear Lake, part of the Rimrock Lake reservoir. Fishing and wildlife viewing are the primary activities here (see appropriate sections in this chapter, below).

Three other Forest Service campgrounds encircle scenic Rimrock Lake reservoir. **Indian Creek** (39 sites; maximum RV length, 32 feet), **Peninsula** (19 sites), and **South Fork** (15 sites) all are on or near Rimrock Lake, which is massive when it's full in the early summer, but becomes a large mudflat by late fall. All these campgrounds are open summers only, and campsites can't be reserved.

Farther down the Tieton drainage are four more small campgrounds: **Hause Creek** (42 sites), **River Bend** (6 tent sites), **Wild Rose** (8 sites), and **Willows** (16 sites). These are wild, fairly primitive campgrounds, but exceptionally beautiful in the fall, when aspen, alder, and larch trees burst into brilliant gold. They're popular with anglers and, in the fall, river rafters (see Rafting, below). Farther east is **Windy Point** (15 sites), the campground closest to Naches and the Oak Creek Wildlife Area (see Wildlife, below). These campgrounds also are open summers only, and campsites can't be reserved.

Skiing

Long one of Washington's better-kept skiing secrets, **White Pass Ski Area** is best known for being where Phil and Steve Mahre, regarded by many as the greatest U.S. alpine racers ever to strap on boards, honed their considerable skills. The Mahres still ski here, but they've been joined by plenty of skiing-purist compadres in recent years, now that White Pass has added a high-speed, detachable quad lift to the top of the mountain.

Nestled along the northern boundary of the Goat Rocks Wilderness, White Pass is treated to healthy doses of snow that's typically drier than the normal Northwest fare. Even on weekends, the mountain's slightly remote location leaves it far less crowded than nearby areas such as Crystal Mountain. Show up here on a crisp, clear, winter midweek day, and you'll feel like you have the place all to yourself.

The terrain is mostly intermediate, making this a great destination for families, beginners, and cruisers who love smooth, uncrowded runs. But it's far from boring. While no super-steeps exist to prime the adrenaline pumps of experts, they'll find plenty of short, steep, powder-filled chutes to keep them entertained.

The ski area's primary disadvantage—an extra hour of driving time from Seattle, compared to Crystal Mountain—is largely overcome by slopeside lodging, a rare feature for a Washington resort. The 55 Village Inn condos right across Hwy 12 from the base area are privately owned, but many are available nightly through the mountain's rental office; (509) 672-3131. If you're not up for longish commutes for day skiing, this is a good way to go. White Pass is a great, very quiet weekend getaway. But be warned: Weekends book up fast. There are alternate lodgings in Packwood (see Lodgings, below) and Yakima, 51 miles east.

White Pass gets solid amounts of snow from early December through early April. An annual highlight is the **White Pass Winter Carnival** the first weekend in March, which includes a Children's Hospital charity event during which you can actually race Phil Mahre. Hey, you never know: he might fall.

White Pass facts: Elevation: 4,500 to 6,000 feet. Lifts: Five. Lift tickets: $32 adult daily on weekends at this writing; substantially lower midweek. Hours: Daily 8:30am to 4pm; night skiing until 10pm. Mountain info: (509) 453-8731. Snow phone: (509) 672-3100.

The most convenient **cross-country skiing** in the corridor is at White Pass Ski Area, which maintains 15 kilometers of mostly intermediate groomed trails, open Thursdays through Sundays from 8:45am to sunset, and daily during the Christmas holiday season. Rentals, lessons, and other services are available.

For more remote skiing and snowshoeing, two state Sno-Parks are found on the east side of White Pass Highway. They are **Goose Egg,** 22 miles west of Naches on Road 1201; and **North Fork Tieton,** 32 miles northwest of Naches on Road 1207. A string of similar Sno-Parks is found on Highway 410 east of Naches. Another popular option is the ski up **Stevens Canyon Road** from the Stevens Canyon entrance to Mount Rainier National Park, north of Packwood.

Wildlife

The Oak Creek Wildlife Area, just east of Naches on US 12, is one of the state's most popular wildlife-viewing areas. This is the winter feeding site for the giant Yakima elk herd, the thriving descendants of a couple dozen **Rocky Mountain elk** released here decades ago to start a population for hunting. The elk—which have few natural predators in this area—prospered, and many began moving down the valley in search of feeding grounds just as homes and orchards were creeping up it. The Oak Creek feeding program, coupled with miles of 12-foot elk fences, solved that problem. The elk now venture only as far down the valley as the feeding station, where they're fed every morning through the winter by sportsmen's club volunteers. It's an impressive sight, to say the least. Several hundred elk typically line up for their hay here every day, and visitors can stand as little as 20 or 30 yards away behind a wood fence. It's a great place to photograph or just watch elk. Feeding typically begins as soon as snows creep down to 3,000 feet, and lasts through the winter. The feeding area is just beyond the Hwy 410/US 12 junction east of Naches. A separate feeding area for bighorn sheep, which are fewer in number but still often seen, is just off US 12 on Old Clemens Road, at the base of Clemens Mountain near the US 12/Hwy 410 junction.

Farther west, **mountain goats** often are spotted from the old lookout site atop Timberwolf Mountain, reached by driving Road 1500 north from US 12 to Forest Service Road 190. **Mule deer** and **elk** also are commonly seen at the mountain and along the road on the way up. Rimrock and Clear lakes also are rich wildlife areas. Watch for nesting **bald eagles** and **osprey** around Peninsula Campground. Clear Lake Campground (see Camping, above) is usually a good place to spot wildlife. An interpretive trail along the lake has wildlife-viewing information, and the North Fork Tieton, which flows out of the lake, is a great place to watch spawning **kokanee** (land-locked sockeye salmon; they'll be bright red).

Rafting

The **Tieton River** is alive with whoops and screams of river rafters every September, when irrigation water released from Rimrock Lake creates a wild ride down the canyon toward Naches. About two dozen Seattle-area outfitters run trips down the Tieton in September, when it's really the only game in town for Washington whitewater fans. Contact the Naches Ranger District, (509) 653-2205, for a list of qualified guides.

Fishing

The **Tieton River** receives annual state plants of rainbow trout, and bank access is excellent from the Forest Service campgrounds along US 12 (see Camping, above). The lower river also has a productive winter whitefish season. Nearby **Oak Creek** produces some trout. Farther up the pass, **Rimrock Lake Reservoir** has a very beautiful kokanee (landlocked sockeye) fishery. The limit is 16, and many people get there during the hot fishing season in midsummer. The lake becomes unfishable late in the summer, when irrigation water is released from Tieton Dam and the reservoir shrinks to a puddle. Just upstream, **Clear Lake** also is planted with rainbow trout.

Near White Pass summit, **Dog Lake** and **Leech Lake** (see Camping, above) are decent trout lakes (once the ice melts). Note that Leech is fly-fishing only. Backpackers with portable rods will find plenty of good fishing in the **William O. Douglas Wilderness** north of White Pass. The Pacific Crest Trail north from White Pass, or the Dumbbell Lake Loop, both described under Hiking/Backpacking, above, are good routes for backpacking anglers.

outside in

Attractions

White Pass is one of the most fascinating geologic areas of the state. Evidence of heavy volcanic activity is everywhere, and several unique features can be driven to. Examples are **The Palisades,** a large columnar basalt wall visible from a roadside viewpoint about 2 miles east of the Hwy 123 junction; **Clear Creek Falls Scenic Viewpoint** just east of White Pass; and **Goose Egg Mountain, Chimney Peaks,** and **Kloochman Rock,** all off Tieton Road (Forest Service Road 1200) at the south end of Rimrock Lake. The scale of these creations is a testament to the unimaginable power of the volcanic forces that shaped the Cascades.

Cheaper Eats

Ma and Pa Ruckers   Locals favor Ma and Pa Ruckers, an old drive-in (with inside seating, too) serving home-made ice cream, good pizza, and burgers. Especially good, they say, is the Ma Burger. *(360) 494-2651; 13015 US Hwy 12, Packwood.*

Lodgings

Packwood Hotel   Just 10 miles west of White Pass Ski Area, Packwood makes a good base camp for wintertime skiers and summer hikers into the Goat Rocks Wilderness. A couple of motels in town may have more modern appliances, but this spartan lodge (open since 1912) remains a favorite. A small narrow staircase climbs to the simple shared-bath rooms. *On Main St; (360) 494-5431; 104 Main St, Packwood; $.*

More Information:

Department of Transportation pass report: *(888) SNO-INFO.*
Naches Ranger District: *(509) 653-2205.*
Packwood Ranger District: *(360) 494-0600.*
White Pass Ski Area: *(509) 453-8731.*

Mount
St. Helens

From Randle on US 12 south to Swift Reservoir, east to the monument boundary, and west to Silver Lake.

Words cannot do it justice. Nor can photos, slide shows, fancy interpretive exhibits, or even a big-screen IMAX movie. The colossal volcanic explosion of Mount St. Helens on May 18, 1980, was one of the most cataclysmic natural events in recorded history, and succeeding years have done little to minimize the awe visitors feel upon exploring the Mount St. Helens National Volcanic Monument.

The only way to begin to imagine the spectacular force of the eruption is to poke through the rubble of what's left. And in that sense, Washington nature lovers are fortunate. Rather than lock the curious public out of this remarkable, blasted-apart mountain, managing federal agencies have, in effect, invited all of us to act as our own scientists. The Mt. St. Helens National Volcanic Monu-ment—a specialized federal designation that includes elements of both natural parks and federal research sites—is with few excep-tions wide open for public use.

Nearly two decades after the eruption, St. Helens has gone relatively dormant, and the volcano—one of the youngest and still most active in the country—calls out for exploration. Just about the only place you can't go on foot around Mount St. Helens is a restricted zone inside the crater itself. And nobody in their right mind would want to go there, anyway. The volcano may be dor-mant, but the ominous black lava dome inside its mouth still looks like a living, breathing creature—one prone to violent tantrums with little or no warning.

In a way, that's a large part of the allure of hiking, biking, or fishing around the volcano, or just warily watching it. It's a little like the scary—but oddly welcome—feeling you get when hiking in grizzly country: there's a constant element of danger here, a unique sense that the world through which you walk is one over which you have absolutely no control. For many recreationists, that's the very definition of a "wild" encounter. At Mount St. Helens, where the evidence of nature's power is present everywhere you look for 50 miles around, the feeling is impossible to ignore.

It lives in the eyes of hikers standing on the shores of Spirit Lake, amid an otherworldly landscape—a city-size circle of land that was rearranged from top to bottom in one volcanic blink of an eye. It lives in the minds of visitors who walk into one of the mountain's interpretive centers and attempt to assimilate the numbers: 6.6 billion tons of mud, ice, and rock moving at 150mph and settling 650 feet deep; 500 degree winds blasting at 650mph; ash and rock bursting 12 miles into the sky before circling the earth; 230 square miles laid waste. It lives in the souls of those of us who remember the mountain as it once was—a pristine, symmetrical cone standing as a shrine in one of the most beautiful, forested recreation playgrounds of the Pacific Northwest. Then Mount St. Helens was a thing of beauty, a place to escape to and relax. Now it is the ultimate monument to humility, a place to stand in awe and reflect.

There will be no attempt here to describe the event, the result, or the rebirth now taking place in its wake. The only way to know is to go. The St. Helens National Volcanic Monument does an excellent job—especially considering the unprecedented logistical obstacles—of providing human access to an incredible natural work-in-progress. It's a pilgrimage everyone who loves and reveres the natural world ought to make.

Getting There

The primary access to Mount St. Helens National Volcanic Monument is from the northwest, via Hwy 504, the Spirit Lake Memorial Highway, which turns east from Interstate 5 at Castle Rock (exit 49) and travels 53 miles into the heart of the volcanic blast zone. Hwy 504 is the only paved route into the blast area; allow at least 3 hours from Seattle. The northeast side of the mountain, including popular hiking trails and viewpoints near Norway Pass and Windy Ridge, is reached by following Forest Service Roads 25 and 99 about 45 miles south from Randle on US 12. Allow about 4 hours from Seattle, and note that winter flood damage to roads is common in this area.

Adjoining Areas
NORTH: **White Pass Corridor; Mount Rainier National Park**
SOUTHEAST: **Mount Adams**

Scenic Drives

The vast majority of those visiting Mount St. Helens do so in a daylong auto tour from the Seattle or Portland areas. The most popular route is **Hwy 504,** which leads east into St. Helens National Volcanic Monument from Castle Rock. Hwy 504, the only paved highway into the monument, connects with four interesting visitors centers. The other popular access route, Forest Service Road 99, reached by driving 45 miles on forest roads from Randle, is more difficult, but leads to Windy Point, which has the best drive-to views of the volcano. The volcanic monument will begin charging **access fees** in 1997 to offset maintenance costs. A 3-day pass will cost $8 and cover all sites; it will be available at all visitors centers, as well as at area stores. (Hikers heading into the backcountry need not pay.)

A good first stop is the **Mount St. Helens Visitors Center,** (360) 274-2100, 5 miles east of Castle Rock on Hwy 504 (follow signs from I-5, exit 49). The center, open daily, has impressive interpretive displays, maps, literature, and—most important—rangers and specialists who can help you get the most out of your visit. On very clear (rare) days, the volcano itself can be seen in the distance from an area behind the center.

Hwy 504 is an impressive piece of construction. As you wind your way high above the Toutle River Valley, several pull-off viewpoints offer impressive overlooks of the massive mudflow that scoured the valley, which now is being revegetated in a forest of green shrubs and trees. Bring binoculars: you might spot some members of St. Helens' burgeoning elk herd below.

The first views of the volcano are at **Hoffstadt Bluffs Visitors Center,** (800) 752-8439, near milepost 27, which has a memorial to mountain characters such as Harry Truman, the stubborn Spirit Lake man who refused to leave before the eruption that took his life. Also at the center is a gift shop filled with cheesy volcano memorabilia, a snack/espresso bar (naturally), and a large restaurant—the only sit-down dining in the monument. A bit farther up the road, the **Forest Learning Center** is another worthwhile stop, with plenty of hands-on exhibits particularly popular with children.

The **Coldwater Ridge Visitors Center** (43 miles east of Castle Rock; (360) 274-2131) offers the first good naked-eye views of St. Helens, as well as Coldwater Lake, a large, eruption-formed lake directly below. Inside, the interpretive displays feature a lot of whiz-bang gadgetry (including a theater with an eruption film you shouldn't miss) that's highly informative, and impressive on its face. Ultimately, however, all the glass, steel, and electronics (not to mention the obligatory gift shop) seem wildly out of character with the stark, moonscapelike terrain that surrounds the modern building. A series of trails begins here—most of them dropping steeply into the blast zone (see Hiking/Backpacking, below). Coldwater Ridge is open daily, although snows can close Hwy 504 in winter. Note: Bring your jacket. Coldwater Ridge is 5,000 feet above sea level—higher than just about any of Washington's major mountain passes.

The newest section of Hwy 504 proceeds beyond Coldwater Ridge and drops to Coldwater Lake (where there's a small boat launch and interpretive trail; see Fishing and Hiking/Backpacking, below). The road then climbs through the blast zone to the new **Johnston Ridge Observatory,** scheduled to open in 1997. Views from here are straight into the gaping, fractured north face of the volcano, and should be the best in the monument available from a paved highway.

From the north, Forest Service Roads 25 and 99 lead 45 miles south from US 12 at Randle to the aptly named **Windy Ridge Viewpoint,** which looks directly into the crater from the south shore of volcano-revamped Spirit Lake. This also serves as one of the monument's major trailheads (see also Hiking/Backpacking, below). Note: The road to Windy Ridge washed out during heavy flooding in the winter of 1995–96, and is prone to doing so again. Call monument headquarters in Amboy, (360) 247-3900, before you go. On your way, stop by the **Woods Creek Information Center** on Road 25 south of Randle.

Visitors entering the monument from the south, via Hwy 503, can get visitors information at the summers-only **Pine Creek Information Center,** near Swift Creek Reservoir at the junction of Forest Service Roads 90 and 25 (about 45 miles east of Woodland).

Hiking/Backpacking

Setting off on foot in the St. Helens blast zone is an unforgettable experience. The sheer magnitude of destruction in evidence all around (including in your hair and under your fingernails, if you're hiking when winds stir the volcanic ash) is overwhelming, the rebirth of plant and animal populations inspiring. It's an experience you won't find anywhere else on the continent, and in few places on the planet.

A hike around the volcano can be *particularly* unforgettable if you don't go prepared. This is still very much an active volcano. While geologists say large-scale eruptions aren't likely to happen without seismographic warnings, smaller steam and ash eruptions are not uncommon. It's vital to carry **survival gear,** which should consist minimally of "10 essentials" supplies (see the Washington Outdoors Primer). Footing is shaky, at best, on some trails. Use your head. Also keep in mind that the gritty ash can destroy your camera, clog your water filter, and perhaps render your cookstove inoperable. Carry repair kits for the filter and stove. Backup iodine tablets for treating water are a good idea.

Hiking trails inside the volcanic monument are in a constant state of flux, due to the instability of both the area itself and of the federal budget. **Trail maintenance** is a problem here, because of a lack of funding and an abundance of open slopes and unstable soils highly prone to erosion. The same is true of roads, particularly the Forest Service access roads in the north monument area, south of Randle. Flood damage closed many of them in 1996. Call monument headquarters in Amboy, (360) 247-3900, before you set out.

Generally, however, more and more trails are being added, and Northwest hikers only recently have begun to catch on to the thrill of climbing near, on, or all the way around an active volcano. As of this writing, more than 200 miles of trails are open inside the Volcanic Monument.

Some rules: Mountain bikes are allowed on some trails. Keep in mind that the restricted area is a living laboratory. Pack out everything you pack in, and practice very low-impact travel techniques. Backcountry camping is allowed, but with restrictions (consult monument headquarters). Fires are prohibited. Group size is limited to 12. Permits aren't required unless you're bound for blast-zone areas above 4,800 feet between May 15 and October 30 (see Climbing, below), although limited overnight permits might be issued soon for the Mount Margaret backcountry north of the volcano. Dogs are prohibited on many trails, and must be leashed on all others.

For maps, trail reports, and a full list of routes, contact monument headquarters or stop at any of the visitors centers described above. Following are some popular routes, divided by area.

Coldwater Ridge

The volcano's most heavily visited area is the launching point for three short, worthwhile interpretive trails and a longer hike through the blast zone. The **Winds of Change Trail** begins just outside the visitors center and loops along the ridgeline, with interpretive signs describing landscape changes under way here. A short distance down the road is the

Birth of a Lake Trail, another short, easy path on a boardwalk above Coldwater Lake, which was formed by a massive mud slide that dammed the creek drainage. Both trails are barrier-free. A short distance farther down the road, the **Hummocks Trail** (easy; 2.5-mile loop) begins just beyond the Coldwater Lake pullout. The trail winds through the hummocks—hilly remnants of the massive landslide that swept this area the day of the eruption. An overlook of the area is found a short distance down the trail. Keep your eyes peeled for elk. Similar trails are likely to be built at the new Johnston Ridge Observatory, scheduled to open in 1997.

Back on the ridge near the visitors center, the **Coldwater Lake Trail** (moderate; 12 miles round trip) drops steeply to Coldwater Lake, then follows its north shore. (This trail was closed by 1996 flood damage, and its repair date was uncertain at press time.) The first portion of the trail is an access route used by trout anglers (see Fishing, below). It's an interesting walk through what once was a pretty, forested valley and now looks like a massive, bare crater with a water-filled bottom.

Norway Pass area

Access south from Randle on Forest Service Roads 25, 99, and 26:

The **Goat Mountain Trail** (moderate; up to 12 miles round trip) begins on Forest Service Road 2612 near Ryan Lake and climbs steeply to a ridge with excellent views into the volcano crater. It's a good place to compare what's left of St. Helens with the dormant (for the time being), snow-covered dome of Rainier, visible to the north. The first views of the crater are less than a mile up the trail, but you can continue along the ridge top, weaving into and out of the blast zone, to Deadman's Lake and ultimately Vanson Peak.

The **Boundary Trail (West)** (moderate; up to 10 miles round trip) is the remnant western portion of the Boundary Trail that bisected the Gifford Pinchot National Forest before the volcano wiped out much of the western end. This section draws less attention from backpackers than the longer eastern route. From Road 26 near Norway Pass, the trail climbs to Bear Pass and 5,858-foot Mount Margaret, where views into the volcano are unforgettable. The counterpart **Boundary Trail (East)** (difficult; 30 miles one way) begins at the same place, but heads east along the ridge tops all the way to Council Lake Campground near the Mount Adams Wilderness. It's a popular one-way backpack route, with several good campsites along the way. Volcano views are good, but not as easily accessible as on the West Boundary Trail. A short, easy hike in the same area is the **Ryan Lake Interpretive Loop** (easy; .6 mile round trip).

Windy Ridge area

Access through Randle on Forest Service Roads 25 and 99:

A great primer on the survival and recovery of life in the blast zone is the **Meta Lake Trail** (easy; ½ mile round trip), where much of the plant and animal life was spared from the May 1980 eruption by a 10-foot blanket of snow. If you're looking for good crater and Spirit Lake views without investing many hours and gallons of sweat, the **Independence Pass Trail** (moderate; up to 7 miles round trip) is a good option. From its Road 99 trailhead, the path climbs a short distance to a fine viewpoint, then proceeds to a junction with the Boundary Trail. For a close look at the volcano-remodeled Spirit Lake, proceed about a mile up Road 99 to the **Harmony Trail,** (moderate; 2 miles round trip) which drops about 600 feet through blast-devastated forest to the lakeshore. This currently is the only way to hike all the way to Spirit Lake, and it's a stunning experience, particularly for those who remember Spirit Lake in its former pristine state. The eruption raised the lake level 200 feet, creating a giant wave of water that destroyed everything standing on the far shore. Harmony Falls, a once-magnificent cascade, is now half its former height, thanks to the millions of cubic yards of earth, logs, and muck that reshaped the lake.

At the end of the road near Windy Ridge, the **Truman Trail** (moderate; up to 13 miles round trip), named for the Spirit Lake Lodge owner who died in the eruption, drops through the blast zone on the south shore of Spirit Lake, then climbs to a junction with the Boundary Trail above the west side of the lake. It's also a common entry point to the Loowit Trail (see below), which connects several miles down the path via the Windy Trail. The Truman Trail is one of the best, most direct footpaths into the very heart of the blast zone. Be aware that there's no shade or water, making this a very hot, dry walk in midsummer. It's a particularly fine autumn hike, however.

A similar experience can be had on the nearby **Plains of Abraham Trail** (moderate; up to 8 miles round trip), which turns south into the blast zone from the Truman Trail just before that path turns north, up to Spirit Lake. The Abraham Trail continues south to a junction with Loowit Trail. A 9-mile loop can be made by combining the upper Truman, Loowit, and Windy Trails (if you haven't already done so, consult a map!).

Many hikers also favor the Windy Ridge Viewpoint as a drop-off/starting point for their journey all the way around St. Helens on the **Loowit Trail** (very difficult; 28 miles round trip), which roughly circles the volcano. Loowit, the native name for this volcano, is the granddaddy of all St. Helens backpack routes, exposing hikers to a bewildering array of environments, old and new. We advise starting at Windy Ridge and traveling clockwise, although other popular starting points are reached via the **Ptarmigan Trail** near the Climber's Bivouac on the south slope (see Climbing, below) and the **June Lake Trail,** off Forest Service Road 83. This is a rough, often treacherous route. Middle sections through the blast zone are marked only by cairns. Don't attempt the hike unless you're well equipped and proficient at route-finding. If you are, by all means do it. This is one of the most fascinating backpack routes on the planet today. Give yourself a week, though.

South side

Access from Cougar via Forest Service Roads 83, 8303, 81, and 8122:

This lesser-ravaged side of the volcano is still interesting, as evidenced by the awesome **Lava Canyon Interpretive Trail** (easy; ½ mile round trip), which leads you on a tour of the Muddy River Canyon, an ancient lava flow remodeled by floodwaters from the 1980 eruption. The trailhead is on Road 83, north of Cougar, and guided interpretive hikes sometimes are offered in the summer. The trail continues down this steep gorge in spectacular fashion, ending at a second trailhead on Road 8322 below. The 3-mile walk between them is very difficult and very spectacular, clinging to steep canyon walls and at one point crossing the chasm on a wobbly suspension bridge.

For a look at a St. Helens forest spared from the blast, try the **Jackpine Shelter Interpretive Trail** (easy, .8 mile round trip), which winds through a lovely stand of old-growth firs. The trail begins on Road 83 and includes some views of the volcano and its eruption floodpath in the Pine Creek drainage. A nice day hike nearby is the **June Lake Trail** (moderate; 2.8 miles round trip), which climbs moderately from Road 83 to a small, picturesque lake, also connecting to the Loowit Trail. Another interesting interpretive trail, the **Trail of Two Forests Loop** (easy; ¼ mile round trip), begins on Road 8303, a half-mile from the Road 83 junction.

A half-mile farther up Road 8303 is one of the most popular trails in the monument, if not in all southwest Washington: **Ape Cave** (moderate; 1 mile one way). You can take two routes into the cave, the longest intact lava tube (12,800 feet) in the continental United States. Explorers can walk through a lower (.75-mile) or upper (1.25-mile) section of the caves, then return on a mile-long trail. The lower section is by far the easiest (best for kids), with a relatively smooth floor surface. The upper cave requires scrambling over large rocks and one particularly steep rock face. Oh, yes: don't expect any apes. The cave is named after an outdoor club, the Mount St. Helens Apes, who first explored it in the 1950s. Kids love the cave, but beware the uneven cave-floor surface and the temperature: it's quite cold (about 42 degrees, year-round) inside. Strong flashlights and good hiking shoes are a must. Lantern rentals and guided walks are available daily at the parking area in the summer.

A very nice southside weekend backpacking destination is **Butte Camp** (moderate; up to 6.8 miles round trip). The trail, which begins on Road 81 at Red Rock Pass, crosses an ancient lava flow and mudflows from the recent eruption before climbing through an old-growth forest to Butte Camp, a pretty backcountry site that serves as a climber's bivouac for an alternate route to the summit. The campsite is a good launching point for a 1.25-mile side trip through scenic alpine meadows to a junction with the Loowit Trail, which offers views of the jagged southside crater rim. For more easily attainable views in this area, the **Sheep Canyon Trail** (easy; up to 4 miles round-trip) has a fine viewpoint of the upper Toutle Valley about a quarter-mile from the trailhead on Road 8123. The trail, which passes through a nice noble fir forest and offers views of a 75-foot waterfall, connects with the Loowit Trail at 2.2 miles, 4,600 feet. (For a scenic loop of about 5 miles, follow Loowit Trail north to the Toutle Trail, which can be followed south back to Sheep Canyon Trail.)

Climbing

If you think St. Helens is impressive from 5 miles away, try looking straight down into its throat. About 15,000 climbers get that opportunity every year by following the **Monitor Ridge route** up the southwest side of St. Helens. The climb to the top isn't technical at all in the summer, when it's mostly free of snow. It's a mildly technical snow-trudge in the winter and spring, accessible to anyone with an ice ax and basic snow-travel skills. The most popular climbing time—by far—is spring, when stable snowfields cover the upper portion of the route. Why? Footing. Ironically, for even moderately experienced trekkers, footing is better—certainly easier—on the snow than on the aggravating, loose pumice that dominates the upper route in summer. Climbing in the pumice is like hiking up a sand dune. You feel like you're sliding 2 feet back with every one step up.

The vast majority of climbers follow the established route from **Climber's Bivouac,** reached by following Forest Service Roads 8100 and 8100-830 a total of 14 miles northeast from Cougar. It's common practice to drive to Cougar one day, snare a climbing permit (see below), and set up camp at the Bivouac (bring your own water!), elevation 3,765 feet, then set out for the summit early the next morning.

The route—just over 2 miles up Ptarmigan Trail and about 3 miles on open slopes—isn't technically challenging. But it is relentless, gaining about 4,500 feet in 5 miles to the crater rim. There, peering over the rocky lip, you literally are gazing into the depths of the earth. The crater's steaming lava dome looks very much alive, and large rockslides and steam eruptions are common. It's awesome to consider that, from the point where you're standing, the former Mount St. Helens rose an additional 1,300 feet before the blast. Be very careful near the 8,350-foot rim, where rock and snow often are unstable. It's 2,000 feet straight down off the other side, and no one—we do mean no one—will be coming to pick up your remains.

In the spring or early summer, climbers trained with an ice ax and comfortable with self-arrest skills will find the return trip an absolute hoot. It's basically a 3-mile, uninterrupted glissade, one of the longest and best in the Northwest. This is a serious way to get hurt if you don't know what you're doing, however. Bringing along slick plastic or some other sliding device to facilitate your speed, as some foolhardy guidebooks suggest, is only for those with a death wish.

Permit roulette: The monument issues **permits** for 100 climbers a day during the peak spring and summer climbing season. Sixty of these permits can be reserved in advance. Call the monument's climbing hotline, (360) 750-3961, for details. Reserved permits (one advance permit covers up to 12 climbers) can be picked up at Jack's Restaurant and Store on Hwy 503 west of Cougar, (360) 231-4276. To get one of the remaining 40 spots, show up at Jack's the day before you intend to climb and sign the list for a daily 6pm drawing. You must be present to claim your prize. A single lottery permit covers up to 4 climbers: if you have a party of 12, 3 reasonably warm bodies must play the odds at Jack's. Permits are good for 24 hours and cost $15. All parties must sign in at Jack's before climbing and sign out on the way home. Otherwise the search-and-rescue army will come looking for you—and they won't be too happy if they find you back home in Bothell.

Cross-Country Skiing

Many of the backcountry trails described in Hiking/Backpacking, above, are gaining favor with backcountry skiers. Call monument headquarters for ski-trail information, which changes significantly with snow levels throughout the winter.

The most commonly skied cross-country areas are on the south side of the mountain, north of Cougar. The focal point is the **Cougar Sno-Park,** 8 miles east of Cougar on Forest Service Road 83. The lot has spaces for 30 cars; state Sno-Park passes are required. Trails here are not groomed, but good skiing can be found on snowed-under Forest Service roads. Several other unofficial backcountry skiing pullouts are found farther up Road 83, including the **Lahar Viewpoint Trailhead** in Ape Canyon. Rental skis are available at Jack's Restaurant and Store on Hwy 503 west of Cougar; (360) 231-4276.

Fishing

Some of us used to kid the fish biologist in Mount St. Helens National Monument about having the easiest job in the world: Watching over fish in a blast zone where everything within 10 miles is dead? The joke was on us. The fact is that many fish species survived the 1980 blast because they were protected beneath alpine lakes still covered with spring ice. Not only that, but the volcano—by completely wiping clean the local landscape and starting over—gave biologists a unique opportunity to study marine-life development in waterways relatively uninfluenced by other living organisms. A good example is 700-acre **Coldwater Lake,** which formed in Coldwater Creek valley after the volcano mudflow built a natural dam at its mouth. State Fish and Wildlife biologists planted rainbow trout here in 1989, and the population has flourished, with many now measuring 24 inches or more. Fishing is allowed all year in the lake, but selective fishery regulations are in effect (single, barbless hooks; no bait; one-fish limit; minimum size 16 inches). The lake can be fished in a couple of places from the west shore along the Coldwater Lake Trail (see Hiking/Backpacking, above), but most anglers launch float tubes or small boats at a parking area at the south end of the lake on Hwy 504. Amazingly, Coldwater also contains cutthroat that just might be the hardiest creatures in the state. Scientists believe they rode out the blast in one of several local lakes protected by ice, later migrating through blast-zone streams into Coldwater Lake. You can fish here for cutthroat, too—but after all that, how could you possibly kill one?

Another popular monument fishing spot, this one much tougher to reach, is **Castle Lake,** which holds a healthy stock of rainbows. It's also under selective-fishery rules. Call monument headquarters for details on access to this lake, which is reached by driving a string of old Weyerhaeuser logging roads off Hwy 504. The other notable trout fishery here is in the **Upper Green River Lakes,** which lie north of the volcano in the upper Green River drainage. Brook trout and some big rainbows are caught in this string of five small lakes, which also are reached by navigating a string of Weyerhaeuser roads.

Steelhead action can be found here, too. A decent summer hatchery steelhead run is beginning to reestablish itself in the **South Fork Toutle River,** which can be reached from Weyerhaeuser Road 4100. Wild fish (those with intact adipose fins) must be released. (The North Fork, more heavily scoured by volcanic mudflows, also holds some steelhead, but usually is too cloudy to fish easily.) A Toutle tributary, the **Green River,** also has a small summer steelhead run.

Silver Lake, a shallow, broad wetland near Castle Rock, is open all year for largemouth bass fishing, and some hefty ones are landed here. The lake also holds crappie, perch, and a few rainbow trout. Bank access is fairly good at any of several resorts here, or at the state boat launch.

Photography

It goes without saying that St. Helens is on the must-do list for every Washington shutterbug—novice, pro, or in-between. For a big mountain with a gaping crater, St. Helens can be surprisingly difficult to photograph well. Good panoramic vistas are available at the **Coldwater Ridge, Johnston Ridge,** and **Windy Ridge** viewpoints. But some of the best scenic shots of the blast zone actually are taken from a bit farther back, on high ridge-top trails north of the volcano (see Hiking/Backpacking, above). The advantage is height and perspective: photos from here can show not only the volcano, but the broad blast zone in relation to the forest that survived on the edges. As with most scenic shots, very early or late light will bring best results here. The volcano crater is almost always photographed looking south, so midday light is troublesome.

If you're serious about capturing the entire volcano experience on film, take a walk on one of several trails that lead into the blast zone. In some areas, felled trees laid out like matchsticks and the nearly black-and-white moonscape environments create fascinating landscape scenes. Increasingly, though, local photographers have turned their attention to the rebirth of life here. The blast zone gets a little greener every year. Forest Service Road 99, which ends at the Windy Ridge overlook, is a good place to photograph **Spirit Lake,** now packed with dead trees.

Important note: The fine, gritty volcanic ash in the blast zone can wreak absolute havoc with camera gear, particularly zoom lenses with moving parts. Keep your camera and all lenses *sealed away tight*—not only inside a camera bag, but sealed in zipper pouches—anytime you're near the ash. And try to minimize the number of times you open your camera to change film or lenses.

Camping

Options are limited here. The best destination by far for campers is **Seaquest State Park** on Hwy 504, near the National Volcanic Monument Visitors Center. The park, which includes a nice grove of old-growth trees, has 100 campsites (16 with hookups) and a large day-use area with picnic grounds and playfields. Silver Lake, one of the state's better bass fisheries, is across Hwy 504. That, coupled with the convenient location for volcano visitors, makes this a very busy park. Seaquest is open all year. If you're counting on a campsite here in the summer, reserve up to 11 months in advance by calling Reservations Northwest; (800) 452-5687. *On Hwy 504 (follow signs from Interstate 5 exit 49) 6.5 miles east of Castle Rock; (360) 274-8633 or (800) 233-0321.*

On the north side of the Monument is **Iron Creek,** a Forest Service campground with 99 campsites (no hookups) and piped water. It's not fancy, but the location is good for north-side volcano hikers. It's open summers only. Some campsites can be reserved by calling (800) 283-2267. *10 miles south of Randle via Forest Service Roads 23 and 25; (360) 497-1100.*

The other camping options around the mountain are on the far south side—out of easy reach if you're visiting the volcano via Hwy 504. Several campgrounds are available in the Gifford Pinchot National Forest north of Carson. A handful of others operated by Portland's Pacific Power and Light—**Swift, Crescent Bay, Cougar, Saddle Dam**, and **Beaver Bay**— are located near the Swift Creek and Yale Reservoirs along Hwy 503; call (503) 464-5035.

Wildlife

Many mammals began moving back into the St. Helens blast zone almost as soon as the ash cooled. But none took advantage of the outdoor remodeling job to the extent of the Toutle River **Rocky Mountain elk** herd. Mudflows scoured out the entire floor of this broad river valley in 1980, but thousands of acres of grass and shrubs—primo grazing fodder— sprouted the following spring. Elk, needless to say, were ecstatic, and the herd now is proliferating on the valley floor. Bring your binoculars, and you might see them from any of a number of pullouts along Hwy 504. Elk also often are seen on the bare (of trees, anyway) slopes around Coldwater Lake.

Mountain Biking

Frankly, the ubiquitous ash and stark terrain don't appeal to many mountain bikers. But some surprisingly good riding can be found on monument trails (not all are open to bikes; check at headquarters first) and local logging roads. Some bikers' favorites are the **Plains of Abraham Trail** from Windy Ridge Viewpoint (see Hiking/Backpacking, above) and the **Ape Canyon Trail** on the southeast side of the mountain off Forest Service Road 83. Another very popular route south of the volcano is the

Upper Lewis River Trail, a 14-mile single-track ride up or down the river through a beautiful old-growth coniferous forest. Access is off Forest Service Road 90.

Also, several private outfitters have been running guided tours on Weyerhaeuser roads north of the volcano, above Coldwater Ridge, in recent years. Contact monument headquarters, (360) 247-5473, for referrals.

Kayaking/Canoeing

Silver Lake, near Seaquest State Park (see Camping, above), is an interesting place for paddlers, with lots of old snags, and fields of grass and pond lilies. It's a big lake, but it's less than 10 feet deep almost all the way across. Small boats and canoes also can be launched in **Coldwater Lake** (see Fishing, above). Be advised that it's often windy here. If your craft is blown down the lake, there's no convenient way for you to get out and walk back.

outside in

Attractions

Close to the freeway, before you begin the ascent to the ridge, you can stop in to see the Academy Award–nominated film *The Eruption of Mount St. Helens* projected onto the **Cinedome**'s three-story-high, 55-foot-wide screen. The rumble alone, which rattles your theater seat, is worth the price of admission. Just off I-5 at the Castle Rock exit; (360) 274-8000.

Restaurants

For recommended restaurants, see the Adjoining Areas to this chapter.

Lodgings

Mount St. Helens Motel, (360) 274-7721, and **Timberland Inn & Suites,** (360) 274-6002, are both conveniently located in Castle Rock near I-5. For recommended lodgings, see the Adjoining Areas to this chapter.

More Information

Mount St. Helens National Volcanic Monument Headquarters: *4218 NE Yale Bridge Road, Amboy, WA 98601; (360) 247-5473.*
Coldwater Ridge Visitors Center, Hwy 504: *(360) 274-2131.*
Mount St. Helens Climber's Hotline: *(360) 750-3961.*

Mount St. Helens Information Line: *(360) 750-3900.*
Mount St. Helens Visitors Center, Silver Lake: *(360) 274-2100.*
Randle Ranger District, US 12: *(360) 497-1100.*
Wind River Ranger District, Carson: *(509) 427-3200.*

Mount Adams

From Trout Lake north through the Mount Adams Wilderness, west to Takhlakh Lake, and east to the Yakama Indian Reservation.

They should issue head nets at this wilderness boundary. The rough, volcano-forged lands around Mount Adams lead the state in mosquitoes-per-capita. The whiny little critters (and by that we mean bugs, not forest rangers) buzz incessantly in the early summer, forming in clouds at the door to your Explorer before you even slow to a stop. It's enough to make you scream, pull a U-turn, and drive back to the Vancouver Holiday Inn. Assuming you found your way here, that is. Mount Adams is as hard to get to as it is bug-ridden. No matter which way you drive here, it's a long trip, requiring the better part of a day.

Discouraged yet? Well, we tried.

Those factors do discourage a good number of would-be Mount Adams explorers. But they don't even faze hard-core wilderness fans. And that, more than anything, shapes the confused degree of activity at Mount Adams, in many respects the most alluring of the state's string of Cascade volcanoes. Generally, the mountain's reputation for being the loneliest, wildest, and least-seen of the bunch is true: it's visited by far fewer tourists, largely because it's difficult to get to. On the other hand, it's a misnomer to think of Adams as a remote, lonely wilderness. Some areas of the mountain, such as the popular Around the Mountain Trail and South Spur summit climbing route, have become so crowded that limited-use permits are being mulled by Forest Service managers.

All things considered, though, the Mount Adams area offers a much more remote experience than its neighboring peaks. Rainier, St. Helens, and Hood, which form a volcanic triangle around Adams, are all overrun by tourists and hikers in the summer. Adams is Mayberry RFD by comparison. Hikers, campers, climbers, and skiers who do happen upon the peak tend to get hooked. The bait is appealing. At 12,276 feet, Adams is the second-highest peak in the state. But it wins the sheer bulk award hands down. This is a huge mountain, with shoulders broad enough to wear some of the Northwest's most magnificent hanging glaciers.

The peak and much of the surrounding volcanic plain is protected territory. The Mount Adams Wilderness, nearly 43,000 acres, surrounds the mountain to the north, west, and south. The Yakama Indian Nation controls all access to the east, where some truly wild lands still exist.

The natural beauty that brought wilderness protection in 1964 had been attracting nature lovers for nearly 100 years. Mount Adams was first scaled in 1854, and quickly became a destination for weekend mountaineers drawn to one of several early-century outpost hotels. The word got out—the big, beautiful peak just up the road from the Columbia Gorge had an easy summit route. Adams has drawn large numbers of mountaineers ever since.

More than two dozen ascent routes have been climbed and reclimbed. They range from the extremely difficult to the fairly easy snow trudge up the south side. Climbing, however, no longer is the sole focus of activity here. The mountain's north, west, and south slopes make magnificent backpacking territory for strong hikers. Much of the terrain here is even more spectacular than mountainside routes on Mount Rainier. Word of the wonders of Adams is spreading fast, and backcountry use has increased rapidly in the past decade.

In the western shadows of the mountain lies one of the state's most fascinating geologic areas. The South Cascades are a volcanic wonderland, with broad lava plains, extinct craters, collapsed mountain peaks, and long lava tubes dotting the landscape. This is among the most rugged, least-visited land west of the Cascade Crest. Intrepid visitors willing to put in their time on winding Forest Service roads will happen upon some true gems: forest lookouts with stunning mountain views, little-used trails, and lakefront campgrounds with nature-calendar views out the tent flap.

The *zipped* tent flap, that is. Like a lot of other Adams fans, we might have been trying to scare you away to save the place for ourselves. But we weren't kidding about the bloodsuckers. If you're visiting in early to midsummer, pack an extra plasma unit in your fanny pack. You're going to need it.

Getting There

No matter how you hold the map, there's no really easy way to drive to Mount Adams. Primary access ("primary" meaning most pavement) is from the south. Take Hwy 14 east from Vancouver to White Salmon, then travel north on Hwy 141 to Trout Lake. From there, Forest Service Road 23 leads to the west side of the mountain, while Forest Service Roads 80 and 82 lead north to most south-side Mount Adams trailheads. The Yakama Indian Nation's Bird Creek area (Tract D, open July 1 to September 30 only) on the mountain's southeast side is reached from the east through Glenwood or from the south via Roads 82 and 8290. A fee is charged to enter Tract D. Finally, you can get here from the north by driving Forest Service Road 23 south from Randle on US 12. It's the short-est route, in terms of mileage, and the best way to reach campgrounds in the Takhlakh Lake area. But if your destination is Trout Lake, Road 23 is a long, slow haul. Note that many Forest Service roads in this area are closed in win-ter and often washed out by spring. Call the Mount Adams Ranger District at Trout Lake, (509) 395-3400, for road conditions before setting out.

Adjoining Areas

NORTH: **White Pass Corridor**

SOUTH: **Bridge of the Gods: Stevenson and Beacon Rock; White Salmon and Bingen**

EAST: **Goldendale and Maryhill**

WEST: **Mount St. Helens**

inside out

Hiking

The north, west, and south slopes of Mount Adams have a lot of what we all sweat to get to: fantastic hanging glaciers, sprawling alpine meadows, and broad views of the rest of the Cascade Range. Mount Adams Wilderness hiking trails in many ways have the feel of alpine routes on Mount Baker—except you'll generally find fewer people down here in the oft-overlooked South Cascades. Dozens of quality hiking trails skirt the lower and middle slopes of Adams, particularly on the south and west sides. They range from short climbs to great mountain viewpoints to long, spectacular backpack routes above 7,000 feet. (Some, such as the Around the Mountain Trail, are so popular that limited-use permits are being con-templated by rangers.) Don't forget the bug dope. This land, heavily scarred by both volcanic and glacial forces, is pitted with little lakes and swamps, which become full-fledged mosquito factories in the summer. For a full trail roster, trail reports, and road information, contact the Mount Adams Ranger District at Trout Lake; (509) 395-3400.

The star of the Adams trail system is its most popular backpack route—the somewhat misnamed **Around the Mountain Trail (Trail 9)** (difficult; 16.6 miles round trip). The trail doesn't go around the mountain at all (although you can go halfway around by combining this trail with the Pacific Crest Trail, which runs up the west side), but it does skirt a large portion of Adams's south slopes. And a spectacular portion, at that. This is an excellent two- to three-day backpack route. From a trailhead on Forest Service Road 8810, the route follows the Pacific Crest Trail 5 miles, then climbs steadily to good campsites at Horseshoe Meadows, 8 miles. It then continues around the mountain, passing through some beautiful alpine meadows, with grand views all along the route. As you travel east, the trail passes junctions with trails connecting to Morrison Creek and Cold Springs campgrounds—allowing one-way through hikes if you've arranged to leave a car. The trail ends at the Yakama Indian Reservation Tract D border—the turnaround point unless you've obtained tribal permission and paid an access fee to hike on and exit in the beautiful Bird Creek Meadows on the southeast side of the mountain. The Bird Creek Trailhead is reached via Forest Service Road 8290.

A similarly beautiful—and challenging—route on the north side of the mountain is the **Highline Trail** (moderate/difficult; 16 miles round trip), which begins on the Killen Creek Trail along Forest Service Road 2329 near Takhlakh Lake and climbs very steeply to a route that partially follows the Pacific Crest Trail. This is a tough trail, looping up and down steeply across rocky moraines and ravines and climbing as high as 7,500 feet. But the terrain is spectacular, as are the views from this glacier-carved mountainside.

Day hikers also will find plenty to keep them busy on the northwest side of the mountain. **Divide Camp** (moderate; 5.6 miles round trip), on Forest Service Road 2329 southeast of Takhlakh Lake, is a surprisingly easy hike, considering the payoff: up-close views of the Adams Glacier at about 6,000 feet. Campers at Takhlakh Lake itself don't have to walk very far for their own great views of the mountain. **Takhlakh Loop Trail** (easy; 1.1 miles round trip) begins in Takhlakh Lake Campground (see Camping, below) and skirts the lakeshore. For a similarly good view of Adams from just outside the wilderness area, try the **Steamboat Viewpoint Trail** (moderate; 1.4 miles round trip), west of Trout Lake on Forest Service Road 8854-021, which climbs to a former lookout site on Steamboat Mountain. Goats are often spotted in the area.

If you're looking for day hikes on the mountain's south side,

Stagman Ridge (moderate; 8.6 miles round trip), on Forest Service Road 8031-120, is a moderate climb to a nice lunch/view spot at a junction with the Pacific Crest Trail, elevation 5,800 feet. (If you can ignore the big clearcut on the trail's lower stretches, it's almost a real wilderness experience.) The **Shorthorn Trail** (easy/moderate; 5.6 miles round trip), which begins in Morrison Creek Campground (see Camping, below), is a not-too-tough walk to a 6,200-foot view of Mount Adams's south face. The **Snipes Mountain Trail** (moderate; 11.4 miles round trip) on Forest Service Road 8225-150 climbs up extensive lava beds, offering good views of the mountain. Bring plenty of water.

Many more trails are within a moderate driving distance in the buggy-but-beautiful **Indian Heaven Wilderness** southwest of Trout Lake.

Climbing

The very best high-altitude hike in this region actually qualifies as a climb. It's the Mount Adams summit route. The climb up 12,276-foot Adams, the second-highest point in Washington (and arguably its loveliest peak, now that St. Helens has taken itself out of the running), requires plenty of stamina, but only basic alpine-climbing skills. It's one of the most climber-friendly summits we've found in the Northwest—basically a long, steep snow trudge, much like the route to the summit of the South Sister in Central Oregon. That doesn't mean it's easy, or—when the weather turns nasty—even safe. The easy routes on Adams are south-face climbs such as the South Spur from Cold Creek Campground. No matter which way you go, you're exposing yourself to about 6,000 vertical feet of above-treeline steep snow climbing. Don't attempt it unless you know what you're doing. For experienced climbers—or rookies climbing with veterans—the south slopes of Adams often turn into an early-season training ground. Adams is famous for its early-summer climb-up, ski-down trips. Registration at Randle or Trout Lake is required (both in and out). At this writing, the Gifford Pinchot National Forest is considering requiring climbing permits, and limits on the number issued for the overused South Spur route seem inevitable. Contact Mount Adams Ranger District at Trout Lake, (509) 395-3400.

Camping

Some very nice, relatively untrampled backcountry campgrounds are found in this area—uncrowded largely because they're not easy to drive to from any major highway. All these campgrounds are open summers only, charge a fee, and offer no utility hookups or campsite reservations.

Mount Adams northwest side (Randle Ranger District, (360) 497-1100):

The nicest spot in the area is **Takhlakh Lake Campground,** where 54 campsites ring a lovely lake, with good fishing (see below) and drop-dead gorgeous views of Mount Adams. It's 34 miles southeast of Randle via Forest Service Roads 23 and 2329. Nearby **Olallie Lake Campground** is similar but much smaller, with only 6 sites. A good option in the same area is **Chain of Lakes Campground,** a walk-in camp area with 3 established sites. Just to the south, **Council Lake Campground**'s 11 sites also are on a small, scenic lake, with primitive boat-launch facilities. It's 35 miles southeast of Randle via Roads 23 and 2334.

Farther north, in the Killen and Spring Creek drainages, are **Horseshoe Lake** (10 sites), **Keenes Horse Camp** (15 sites and a corral), and **Killen Creek** (8 sites). All are reached via Roads 23 and 2329 south from Randle.

South side Mount Adams (Mount Adams Ranger District, (509) 395-3400):

Cold Springs Campground is a high (4,200 feet) site with 9 campsites and not much else, unless you count lots of huckleberry bushes and good access to south-side hiking trails and climbing routes (see the Hiking and Climbing sections, above.) Follow Roads 80 and 8040 north from Road 23. Nearby is **Morrison Creek Campground,** a very small campground/horse camp at 4,600 feet.

The Yakama Indian Nation also operates three small campgrounds in the Bird Creek drainage on the south side of the mountain: **Bird Lake** (20 sites), **Mirror Lake** (12 sites), and **Bench Lake** (44 sites) are east of Trout Lake via Roads 82 and 8290. Call the Yakama Nation's Forestry Development Program, (509) 865-5121, ext. 657, for information.

Berry Picking

The alpine meadows on and around Mount Adams are Washington's most prolific **huckleberry** producers. The sweet, juicy berries thrive on the region's marshy, volcano-pocked landscape—the same factors that combine to create bumper crops of mosquitoes. Peak picking time is mid-August to mid-September, although this varies from year to year depending on the weather. Your best bet is to call the Mount Adams Ranger District at Trout Lake, (509) 395-3400, to find out what's ripe, when, and where. (You'll need to get a free picking permit there, anyway). Prizes go to anyone who can pick enough berries for an 8-inch pie—then successfully bake it on a Whisperlite camp stove. Also please note: Black bears like huckleberries, too, and they were here first!

Fishing

Takhlakh, Council, Horseshoe, and **Olallie Lakes,** all easily accessible from Forest Service campgrounds in the Randle Ranger District (see Camping, above), offer decent spring and summer trout fishing. Stocked with cutthroat, brown, and brook trout, they're fun to fish from canoes or other small craft launched from the campgrounds. If you don't catch anything, you won't care, so spectacular is the view of Mount Adams on a clear day.

Cross-Country Skiing/Snowshoeing

Two maintained Sno-Parks are northeast of Trout Lake on Forest Service Road 82. **Smith Butte** is a small (10-car) parking area providing access to a number of ungroomed backcountry trails. **Pineside** is more developed, with intermediate 8 kilometer and 2.2 kilometer loops on either side of Road 82. For the deluxe treatment, however, the place to go is **Flying L Ranch** near Glenwood. The ranch maintains about 3 kilometers of groomed trails, but a much more extensive trail network (about 14K) is on nearby state Department of Natural Resources land. (See Lodgings, below.)

outside in

Attractions

Volcanic activity long ago left this region flooded with lava and honeycombed with caves and lava tubes. Two of the most fascinating remnants are found near Trout Lake. The **Ice Cave,** a 650-foot-long lava tube filled with icy stalactites and stalagmites, is best viewed from the Ice Cave Picnic Area, on Forest Service Road 24 west of Trout Lake. Amateur spelunkers can drop down a staircase into the cave near an interpretive exhibit here. The cave floor is icy and can be treacherous. Bring sturdy boots, a helmet, warm clothes, and extra flashlights.

To the southwest of Trout Lake, in the Wind River drainage north of Carson, is **Big Lava Bed,** a 12,500-acre lava field filled with cracks, crevasses, rock piles, and unusual lava formations. This lava floodplain, part of a 45-volcano string in the South Cascades known as the Indian Heaven Rift, is 10 miles long and covers nearly 20 square miles. It's hardly a developed tourist attraction. In fact, few official trails lead into it, and many people drive by it without realizing what it is. Intrepid lava fans can view much of the lava bed from Forest Service Road 60 (Carson Guler Road), which winds through the South Cascades between Trout Lake and the Wind River Hwy north of Carson. Better yet, set out for the fire lookout atop Red Mountain, reached by driving Road 60 and turning north on Road 6048, near Crest Horse Camp. At 4,977 feet, it looks straight down on the Lava Bed; spot the actual crater, near the north end, near Goose Lake. The lookout, staffed during the summer, also provides memorable views of Mount Rainier and Mount Hood. For more information, contact the Mt. Adams Ranger District at Trout Lake, (509) 395-3400.

Restaurants

For recommended restaurants, see the Adjoining Areas to this chapter.

Lodgings

Flying L Ranch ☆   We love the Flying L; this 160-acre ranch is like a big kids' camp in some of the most spectacular country around. Bike the backroads, hike the trails, observe the birds in the Convoy Wildlife Refuge, or ski Mount Adams. Darvel and Darryl Lloyd can point you in the right direction for anything. Dinners for large groups can be prepared with advance notice. *1/2 mile off Glenwood-Goldendale Hwy; (509) 364-3488; 25 Flying L Lane, Glenwood; $$.*

More Information

Mount Adams Ranger District, Trout Lake: *(509) 395-3400.*
Randle Ranger District, US 12: *(360) 497-1100.*
Yakama Indian Nation, Forestry Development Program: *(509) 865-5121, ext. 657.*

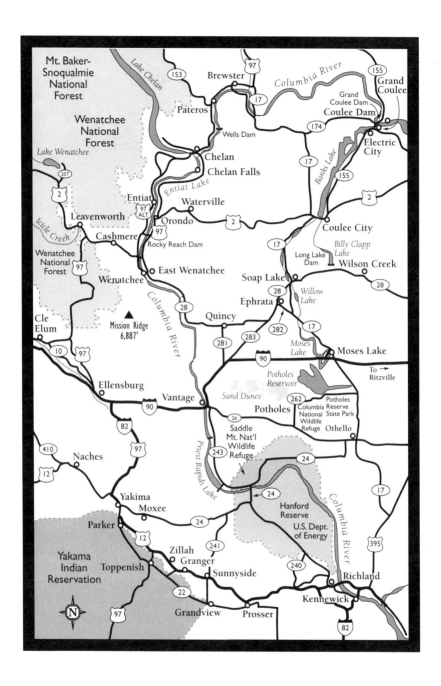

Central
Washington

Central
Washington

Wenatchee and Mission Ridge

From Cashmere east to Wenatchee Confluence and southwest to Mission Ridge.

Make no mistake: for a city that lies at the junction of the spectacular Wenatchee and the mighty Columbia Rivers, the greater Wenatchee area isn't great at all. It's miles of strip malls, truck stops, apple warehouses, and a maddeningly slow, one-way thoroughfare through downtown. Wenatchee's cluttered sprawl (a unique land-use achievement!) can make you downright loopy, particularly if you're fresh off one of the many 70-mph highways leading into town.

Yet we're forced to admit that some local amenities—one old, a couple new—are making the Apple Capital a tasty year-round destination, particularly for cyclists, campers, and skiers. The key to Wenatchee's new recreation luster is its smartly designed Apple Capital Loop trail, which winds along and over the Columbia River. The trail has encouraged both use and sprucing up of existing Columbia River waterfront parks in the north section of Wenatchee. Spend a day on the path, and Wenatchee's ugly side fades from view, literally and figuratively.

Depending on your taste in skiing, Wenatchee also can be a worthy winter destination. When the deep, dry stuff collects on Mission Ridge (which is not nearly as often as anyone would like), the local ski mountain turns into a high, dry, downhill racecourse guaranteed to test your base wax.

Granted, getting there means doing the downtown Wenatchee

crawl, which is only slightly more pleasant than driving through Lynn-wood at rush hour. But if you squint really hard, it looks like paradise...or you just rear-ended a big ol' pickup truck. In Wenatchee, save yourself some time and look north and south of town.

Getting There

Wenatchee is 138 miles (about 2 1/2 hours) east of Seattle via US 2, the Stevens Pass Hwy. It can also be approached via I-90 east and then north on US 97 over Blewett Pass. Recreation sites in the Mission Ridge area are 13 miles south of town. Follow Mission Street south from downtown Wenatchee.

Adjoining Areas

NORTH: **Chelan and the Middle Columbia**

SOUTH: **Yakima Valley**

WEST: **Leavenworth and the Icicle Valley**

EAST: **Columbia Basin; Grand Coulee: Coulee Dam to Soap Lake**

inside out

Camping

Campers in the Wenatchee area have their choice of only two sites, but they're nice ones. **Wenatchee Confluence State Park,** just north of town on US 97A, is a six-year-old park that sits at the confluence of the Wenatchee and Columbia Rivers. This sunny, flat space, surrounded on two sides by cool waters, is a superb spot for family campers, particularly those with kids on bikes. The Apple Capital Loop trail (see Cycling, below) runs right through the campground, providing year-round riding fun, not to mention easy pedal or foot access to downtown Wenatchee. The park's 59 campsites (51 with full hookups; maximum RV length, 65 feet) are spread throughout a nicely manicured, grassy field (exposed to sun until the planted shade trees gain a few stories in height) that's a delight for tent campers. Also on site are a volleyball court and play area, boat launch on the Columbia River, swimming area, and nice waterfront picnic sites. Wenatchee Confluence is open all year. Campsites can be reserved up to 11 months in advance by calling Reservations Northwest; (800) 452-5687. *Immediately north of the US 2/US 97A junction near Wenatchee, follow signs north on US 97A; (509) 663-6373 or (800) 233-0321.*

West of town along US 2 is **Wenatchee River County Park,** which has 41 tent sites and 64 RV sites with hookups in shaded rows near the

Wenatchee River. The park is open April through October. Campsites cannot be reserved. *On US 2 near Monitor, about 5 miles west of Wenatchee; (509) 662-2525.*

Another nearby campground, **Squilchuck State Park,** near Mission Ridge Ski Area, is a reservation-only group camp for up to 168 people. It reverts to a ski hill operated by Wenatchee Valley College on winter weekends (see Skiing, below). *Follow Mission Street south from Wenatchee, then follow signs along Squilchuck Road; (800) 233-0321.*

Cycling

At first blush, Wenatchee seems an unlikely destination for two-wheelers. Its topography—rolling hills and hot, sunny summertime skies—is fairly pedestrian (sorry), and most roads in the area are either busy interstates or dusty backroads. The **Apple Capital Loop,** however, turns that image on its head. The loop, which runs through Wenatchee Confluence State Park (the best parking area and starting point; see Camping, above), crosses the Wenatchee River on a newly constructed bridge and rolls through some lovely green city and utility-company waterfront parks near Wenatchee before crossing the Columbia on a railroad-bridge-turned-footbridge. On the east side, it follows the Columbia's shoreline north for 4 or 5 miles, then recrosses the river on a concrete highway bridge and returns to Wenatchee Confluence. The total loop of about 14 miles makes a great day trip for campers at Wenatchee Confluence, or for any travelers who find themselves in Wenatchee for a day. It's all asphalt, with smooth riding, few hills, and plenty of walkers and in-line skaters for company. Even on hot days, a cooling breeze off the river makes this path a treat. Plans call for a northern extension of the trail to Rocky Reach Dam.

Hiking

For downtown Wenatchee visitors, the **Apple Capital Loop** (see Cycling, above) offers a pleasant walk along the Columbia and Wenatchee Rivers. From downtown, a walk north on the trail, through the city's waterfront parks and over the Wenatchee River footbridge to Wenatchee Confluence State Park, makes a perfect half-day round trip of about 7 miles.

Outside town, many unmarked fire trails lead into the dry forest area around **Squilchuck State Park** (see Camping, above), and fire roads and hiking trails also emanate from **Mission Ridge Ski Area** (see Skiing, below), some connecting with trails and roads in the Swauk Pass area to the west, along US 97.

Rafting/Kayaking/Canoeing

The lower **Wenatchee River** is perhaps Washington's whitewater favorite. It's easy to see why. From Leavenworth downstream through Cashmere to, ultimately, the Columbia River confluence, the Wenatchee is a broad, rushing stream throughout the spring and early summer, when it carries millions of gallons of Central Cascades snowmelt from Tumwater Canyon and Icicle Gorge. Peak months are April through June, and most commercial rafters focus on the 18 miles of rapids between Leavenworth and Monitor. The river's appeal: big; fast water, lots of speed; pleasant, sunny surroundings (high bluffs topped by apple orchards) and good put-in and take-out spots below Leavenworth and at Cashmere. A large number of commercial rafting companies run trips on the lower Wenatchee. Contact the Leavenworth Ranger District, (509) 782-1413, for references.

Kayakers and experienced whitewater canoeists are drawn to the same waterway for the same reasons. Good put-ins are found just east of Leavenworth, at Peshastin, in downtown Cashmere, and at the Monitor Wildlife Area. You'll see plenty of kayakers in the area throughout the summer. Even after water levels drop too low to make large rafts practical, this remains runnable water for kayak paddlers. Note: There's a necessary portage over an irrigation dam at Dryden, just below Peshastin Creek, and several Class III to IV rapids to negotiate.

Skiing

Mission Ridge, 13 miles southwest of Wenatchee, is a favorite of many Washington dry-snow skiers. The mountain indeed gets dusted with a much drier-than-usual base, and a small-but-efficient resort creates a nice, homey feel here. Mission, under new management for the past several years, has taken some major customer-service strides, such as regrading and widening the once-narrow ski trails and upgrading the day lodge and other base facilities. The resort's goal: Convince all those Seattle-area skiers Mission is worth driving another 90 minutes beyond Stevens Pass, a longtime state favorite.

To that end, they've organized some very economical weekend packages with Wenatchee-area motels. Hit Wenatchee on that one midwinter weekend when the sky is blue and powder is deep, and you'll have a true Rocky Mountain–style ski getaway—at a fraction of the price. Chronically light snowfall continues to plague Mission Ridge, however. And mountain managers in recent years have only exacerbated the problem by refusing to divulge Mission's snow depth to statewide media and national snow-reporting systems. That makes them unique—in the way you don't really want to be unique—among ski areas in the West, if not the nation. And it has created distrust among hard-core Western Washington skiers, who suspect that any mountain afraid to divulge its snow depth has something to hide. The resort's response: depth doesn't matter, it's how well it's groomed and prepared. The top half-inch is the only important part, they say. True enough, but not if that half-inch is the only half-inch.

Physically, Mission is somewhat unique among Washington ski resorts. The upper mountain is distinguished by a panel of steep canyon walls—the Bomber Cliffs—sometimes jumped from by hard-core ski vaulters (not recommended). Upper-mountain chutes and glades collect deep snow, and make excellent expert skiing after snow dumps. Below, most runs are long, fairly narrow trails through mixed forest. Most of this mountain is a treat for intermediate cruisers and lovers of light, groomed surfaces. Favorite fast cruiser run: Bomber Bowl. Favorite white-knuckle, jump-turn run: Wa Wa or Ka Wham Chutes.

Mission has no slopeside lodging, but plenty is available in Wenatchee, which runs a shuttle bus to the mountain. Call the ski area, or the Wenatchee Visitors Bureau, for package-deal information (see More Information, below).

Mission Ridge facts: Elevation: 4,600 to 6,740 feet. Skiable acreage: 2,080. Lifts: Six (two rope tows, four double chairs). Hours: Daily, 9am to 4pm. Mountain information: (509) 663-7631. Snow phone: (800) 374-1693. To get there: Mission Ridge is 13 miles southwest of Wenatchee on Squilchuck Road. Follow Mission Street south from downtown and watch for signs.

Just down the road a few big GS turns is **Squilchuck Ski Bowl,** a small (one rope tow) operation run by Wenatchee Valley College. It's a fun beginner slope, and a grand place to rent out for the weekend (the 200-person ski lodge can be reserved through State Parks; see Camping, above). A series of unimproved cross-country trails also begins at Squilchuck.

Fire trails and snowed-in Forest Service roads in the hills above Mission Ridge Ski Area are favorites of **backcountry telemarkers.**

Wildlife

The South Confluence area, a marshy natural set-aside at the Wenatchee-Columbia confluence, is a productive creature-spotting venue. Park at Wenatchee Confluence State Park, follow the trail south over the Wenatchee River Footbridge, and turn left on the waterfront interpretive trail. Watch for **blue herons, pheasants, hawks, eagles, ducks,** and small mammals such as **beavers** and **raccoons.** This 100-acre, rich wildlife spot has an equally rich history: it's an **ancient campsite** of

Columbia River tribes, who were here more than 10,000 years ago. The first white settlers in the Wenatchee area also took up residence here.

Adventure Calendar

The **Ridge-to-River Pentathlon,** held on the third Sunday every April, is one of the state's better multisport marathons. It begins at the top of Mission Ridge and ends on the Wenatchee waterfront after furious downhill skiing, cross-country skiing, cycling, running, and canoeing legs.

Attractions

Wenatchee is the heart of apple country, with an **Apple Blossom Festival** the first part of May. **Ohme Gardens,** 3 miles north on US 97A, is a 600-foot-high promontory transformed into an Edenic retreat, with a natural alpine ecosystem fastidiously patterned after high mountain country. Splendid views of the valley and the Columbia River; (509) 662-5785. **Rocky Reach Dam,** 6 miles north on US 97, offers a beautiful picnic and playground area (locals marry on the well-kept grounds), plus a fish-viewing room. Inside the dam are two large galleries devoted to the history of the region.

The little orchard town of **Cashmere** gives cross-mountain travelers not in a Bavarian mood an alternative to stopping in Leavenworth. The main street has put up Western storefronts; the town's bordered by the Wenatchee river and a railroad. **Chelan County Historical Society and Pioneer Village,** 600 Cottage Avenue; (509) 782-3230, has an extensive collection of Native American artifacts and archaeological material; the adjoining pioneer village puts 19 old buildings, carefully restored and equipped, into a nostalgic grouping. **Aplets and Cotlets,** confections made with local fruit and walnuts from an old Armenian recipe, have been produced in Cashmere for decades. You can tour the plant at **Liberty Orchards** and (of course) consume a few samples (117 Mission Street; (509) 782-2191).

Restaurants

Garlini's Ristorante Italiano ☆   There's nothing fancy about the outside of this restaurant tucked away on one of the main streets in East Wenatchee. But inside, the dark, heavy wood, dim lighting, and festive music bring Italy to the senses. The Garlini family cooks up all the old

Italian favorites. *1 block north of the Wenatchee Valley Mall; (509) 884-1707; 810 Valley Mall Parkway, East Wenatchee; $.*

Golden East   A remodeled bank is now a vault of red vinyl booths, paper lanterns, and Chinese food. Both Cantonese and more potent Sichuan favorites are available at this East Wenatchee restaurant. Ask for a window table with a view of the Wenatchee River and Mission Ridge beyond. *Across the Columbia River and up Grant Rd; (509) 884-1510; 230 Grant Rd, East Wenatchee; $.*

Greathouse Springs Cafe   The noontime hot spot for Wenatchee 9-to-5ers. Belly up to the sandwich bar and place your order, or have a seat at one of the cedar picnic benches. Panini sandwiches are the specialty. There's a Greathouse Springs in East Wenatchee, too, (509) 886-3128. *Follow Wenatchee Ave till it branches at N Miller; (509) 664-5162; 1505 N Miller St, Wenatchee; $.*

John Horan's Steak & Seafood House ☆☆   The feel of the early 1900s remains in this house near the confluence of the Wenatchee and Columbia Rivers. The menu features fresh fish and meat dishes, including marvelous Columbia River sturgeon in season. The Carriage House Pub next door has lighter fare and is a friendly stop for a glass of wine, a Northwest microbrew, or a game of cribbage. *Just south of the K-Mart plaza along the Wenatchee River; (509) 663-0018; 2 Horan Rd, Wenatchee; $$$.*

Mickey O'Reilly's Sports Bar & Grill ☆   Modeled after Seattle's Jake O'Shaughnessey's, this East Wenatchee sports bar doubles as a family restaurant and gathering place. It's a take-me-out-to-the-ball-game kind of place. The bar is separate from the main dining area, but TV screens with the hottest sporting events are visible from any perch. *Across from the Wenatchee Valley Mall in East Wenatchee; (509) 884-6299; 560 Valley Mall Pkwy, East Wenatchee; $.*

The Pewter Pot   Here in Cashmere you can get Early American food such as apple country chicken topped with apple cider sauce, Plymouth turkey dinner, and New England boiled dinner. Desserts are tasty and dishes use local ingredients. If you want dinner, arrive early; the place closes promptly at 8pm even on Saturdays. *Downtown Cashmere in the business district; (509) 782-2036; 124 ½ Cottage Ave, Cashmere; $$.*

Steven's at Mission Square ☆☆   One of Wenatchee's premier restaurants, serving Northwest cuisine, with a few international excursions, in a handsome setting. Pasta and seafood dishes are served with pride and a flourish. Bread is freshly baked and warm, and desserts are first-rate. *1 block off Wenatchee at 2nd and Mission; (509) 663-6573; 212 N Mission St, Wenatchee; $$.*

Visconti's Italian Restaurant ☆   All the standards are on the menu, from spaghetti to caesars to thick slabs of lasagne. Fresh garlic and herbs permeate each generously sized dish at this Wenatchee eatery. *At the west end of town on Wenatchee; (509) 662-5013; 1737 N Wenatchee Ave, Wenatchee; $.*

The Wenatchee Roaster and Ale House ☆   High atop the West Coast Wenatchee Center Hotel, the Roaster serves up a variety of meals in a venue that shouts "corporate chain." The spit roaster and fruitwood smoker display whole chickens and turkeys rotating slowly, and you'll find prime rib (guaranteed to be the best in Wenatchee or your money back) and "all-clam clam chowder." Twenty-four beers on tap. *1 block north of the Wenatchee Convention Center; (509) 662-1234; 201 N Wenatchee Ave, Wenatchee; $.*

The Windmill ☆☆   A constantly changing number on a blackboard keeps track of the steaks sold at this celebrated Wenatchee steak house. Not the number of steaks sold since the Windmill opened 72 years ago, but since January 1982, when new owners took over—and we haven't heard of even one that wasn't terrific. *1 ¹/₂ blocks west of Miller, on the main thoroughfare; (509) 663-3478; 1501 N Wenatchee Ave, Wenatchee; $$.*

Lodgings

Cashmere Country Inn ☆☆   A first-class inn in the middle of Aplet-and-Cotlet country. The 5 guest rooms are a bit small, but attention to detail is large. Breakfasts are an accomplished cook's delight, and you can also get a lovely candlelit five-course dinner with advance notice. *Off Hwy 2, turn right and follow Division to Pioneer, continue past the cemetery; (509) 782-4212 or (800) 291-9144; 5801 Pioneer Dr, Cashmere; $$.*

The Chieftain Motel   This Wenatchee motel stands out for its dependable quality year after year (since 1928). It may need a new paint job, but it's popular with the locals who come for the famous prime rib evenings. The rooms themselves are large. And you can bring your pet with advance notice. Ugly views. *On Wenatchee off 9th; (509) 663-8141 or (800) 572-4456; 1005 N Wenatchee Ave, Wenatchee; $$.*

The Warm Springs Inn ☆   The Wenatchee River is a perfect backdrop, and the pillared entrance and dark green and rustic brick exterior lend a certain majesty to these 4 guest rooms with private bath. A path behind the two-story inn (which served as a hospital in the 1920s) leads through a wooded area to the river's edge. *Head toward Cashmere and turn left off Hwy 2 onto Lower Sunnyslope Rd; (509) 662-8365 or (800) 543-3645; 1611 Love Lane, Wenatchee; $$.*

West Coast Wenatchee Center Hotel ☆   This is the nicest hotel on the strip, with its view of the city and the Columbia River. It's Eastern Washington—elegant, but not overdone. The nine-story hotel has three nonsmoking levels. Rates may rise if most rooms are already booked the day you call, so make advance reservations and be sure to ask about package rates. *Center of town on Wenatchee Ave; (509) 662-1234; 201 N Wenatchee Ave, Wenatchee; $$.*

Cheaper Sleeps

Hillcrest Motel   Hillcrest has 16 rooms up on Sunny Slope Hill above Wenatchee. The owners have been slowly refurbishing and every year the place looks better. There's an outdoor pool (summers only). *(509) 663-5157; 2921 School St, Wenatchee.*

More Information

Wenatchee Visitors and Convention Bureau: *(800) 572-7753.*
Mission Ridge Ski Area: *(509) 663-7631.*
Ski Link Bus: *(509) 662-1155.*
Arlberg Sports (outdoor gear; in-line skates rentals): *(509) 663-7401.*
Second Wind (cycle rentals): *(509) 884-0821.*

Chelan
and the Middle
Columbia

From Rocky Reach Dam north to Pateros, west to the Glacier Peak Wilderness, and east to US 97.

By all rights, this area should be one mondo mudhole. Consider the ingredients: Thousands of square miles of empty, dry land. Billions of gallons of clear, standing water. Nowhere else in the Northwest will you find so much wet surrounded by so much dry. Get the two together, and you should have a first-class slophole on your hands. But wet and dry stay nicely separated, thank you, in the middle Columbia area, which is distinguished mainly—okay, only—by two of the more impressive waterways in the state.

One is the middle Columbia River itself, a once-magnificent stream now relegated to lake status by an endless series of hydropower dams. Even in its dammed state, the Columbia, once the greatest free-flowing Western river, is an impressive waterway. Surrounded by massive, crumbling cliffs, it provides the water to irrigate millions of Central Washington apple trees, making this once-barren stretch of drylands an agricultural gold mine.

An equally impressive waterway, Lake Chelan, creates gold of its own—recreation dollars—thanks to the natural handiwork of ancient Central Washington glaciers, which carved a lake trough that ranks among the deepest in North America. Lake Chelan, 55 miles long and never more than 2 miles wide, redefines "deep and-clear." The lake bottom is 1,500 feet down in places, a mark that's surpassed in the United States only by Lake Tahoe and Crater Lake.

That in itself doesn't make Lake Chelan a great outdoor getaway. But its location does. The heavenly waterway just happens to be surrounded on three sides by celestial mountain peaks. To the south rise the magnificent, glacier-draped mountains of the Glacier Peak Wilderness. To the west are the rugged peaks of North Cascades National Park. And due north is the impressive Sawtooth Range and other peaks in the Lake Chelan–Sawtooth Wilderness.

All these mountains are visible on a leisurely trip up the lake, either on the popular *Lady of the Lake* or *Lady Express* tour boats or by private watercraft. The setting is so spectacular, in fact, that many Lake Chelan visitors never leave the lake at all, choosing to while away the days on a houseboat or at a lakeside campsite. Lake Chelan is a watersport wonderland that draws thousands of boaters, sailors, windsurfers, water-skiers, Jet-ski riders, big-fish anglers, and swimmers. The surrounding delights—hiking or backpacking from Stehekin or the mountain village of Holden; cycling down impressive canyons and coulees; riding neverending thermals on a hang glider from tall, open buttes; cross-country skiing on unobstructed, sunny slopes—make the Chelan area one of the state's most richly stocked recreation treasure chests.

And there's no need to rough it in order to drink this all in. The Chelan area's wealth of sunshine and just plain wealth of wealth (imported by retirees and vacation-home builders) have sparked an amenities boomlet here, with condos, hotels, B&Bs, and resorts sprouting in Chelan and Manson. At first glance, in fact, Lake Chelan's southern shores look more like a condo-infested Malibu than a Cascade Mountain getaway. Don't be fooled. Lake Chelan is a massive, cold-water dogleg, and only its southernmost little pinkie is touched by development. Get on the boat to Stehekin, and you leave time—and time-shares—far behind.

Together, the middle Columbia and Lake Chelan represent the best and worst of the Washington experience: An unstoppable river stopped by dams. A prehistoric lake skimmed by Jet-skis. Condos with views of actual wilderness areas. Summertime-dream-worthy campsites—booked up before Valentine's Day. It's Washington in a bottle. Somebody please put the cork in—and by all means, refrain from shaking.

Getting There

The Middle Columbia area is reached by driving US 2 or Interstate 90 east from the Puget Sound area and following US 97 (on the east bank of the Columbia) or US 97A (on the west bank) north to Pateros. Allow 3 to 4 hours for the 170-mile drive from Seattle. In the summer, an alternate route is driving US 20, the North Cascades Hwy, through Winthrop and Twisp, then Hwy 153 south down the Methow Valley to US 97 at Pateros.

Adjoining Areas

NORTH: **Methow Valley**

SOUTH: **Wenatchee and Mission Ridge**

EAST: **Grand Coulee: Coulee Dam to Soap Lake**

WEST: **Leavenworth and the Icicle Valley**

inside out

Camping

Columbia River

A string of modern campgrounds is found on the shores of the Columbia between Wenatchee and Pateros. On the east bank is **Lincoln Rock State Park,** which is typical of the many riverside campgrounds in this region: sprawling grassy playfields, boat launches, a swimming area, and flat, open trailer and tent sites separated by young shade trees. All of these parks are popular with boaters, who flock here in summer months to water-ski and soak up the sun.

Lincoln Rock, within sight of Rocky Reach Dam, has its own unique physical oddity: a rock face across the Columbia which, if you squint pretty hard, looks a lot like a profile of Abraham Lincoln. (We must confess it really *does* look like Lincoln. On the other hand, the fact that someone actually took the time to discover this is more than a little disconcerting.) Lincoln Rock has 94 campsites (67 with hookups), extensive playgrounds and ballfields, two boat launches and moorage floats, and large, well-developed picnic facilities. Just across the river (actually, they call the impoundment behind Rocky Reach Entiat Lake) is the Rocky Reach Dam visitors center, which you can only get to by driving back south to Wenatchee, crossing the river and driving up US 97A. Lincoln Rock State Park is open all year. Campsites can be reserved up to 11 months in advance by calling Reservations Northwest; (800) 452-5687. *On US 97, 1 mile north of Wenatchee; (509) 663-9603 or (800) 233-0321.*

Farther north on US 97, **Daroga State Park** is another welcome oasis in this dry, brown canyon. This relatively new state park is one of the best in the region, with an interesting layout, particularly for tent campers. The park's walk-in tent camp sits on a narrow finger of land jutting into the Columbia, with the river on the outside and a broad lagoon on the inside. The park, which has nearly a mile and a half of riverfront, also has a nice waterfront group campsite on the south border and a neatly kept trailer loop at the far north end. In all, Daroga offers 17 walk-in camp-sites, 25 RV sites with hookups, a 75-person group camp (booked by reservation only), and extensive picnic facilities on the shores of the Columbia. Also on the premises are a swimming area and bathhouse, boat launch and moorage, short cycle paths, and a playground. When the weather cooperates, winds that kick up here are sufficient for windsurfing. Daroga is open April through October. Campsites cannot be reserved. *On US 97, 21 miles north of Wenatchee; (509) 664-6380 or (800) 233-0321.*

Entiat City Park offers 100 tent sites and 31 RV sites with hookups, a nearby boat launch, picnic facilities, and other amenities. It's open April through September. Campsites can be reserved. *On US 97A at Entiat; (509) 784-1500.*

Lake Chelan

Two well-developed state parks on this massive lake's south shores are camper and boater favorites, while a string of walk-in or boat-in camp-grounds farther up the lake are popular with people who don't mind packing in their gear.

Lake Chelan State Park is a boater's heaven. This beautiful camp-ground on the shores of the deep, crystal-clear lake was built with boating in mind, and rates as one of the most popular waterfront campsites in the state. The park has 144 sites (17 with hookups; maximum RV length, 35 feet). The hookup spots are clustered side by side in a grassy upland area of the park. Far nicer are the spectacular walk-in sites along an access road in the park's southern section. Each has a flat tent pad, a table, and a fireplace, all within a lazy rock's-throw of the lakeshore, which is well equipped with modern boat-moorage floats. Absolutely killer views, right from your vestibule.

Also on site are a swimming area, playfields, picnic shelters, a bathhouse, and boat launch. In the winter, the park is a popular snow-play area, with local cross-country skiers using it as a warming base for ski trips on local roads and trails.

Lake Chelan State Park is open all year, but weekends only from late October to late March. You're not likely to get in during the summer without a reservation. Campsites can be reserved up to 11 months in advance by calling Reservations Northwest; (800) 452-5687. *On South Lakeshore Road (follow signs from US 97A) 7.5 miles west of Chelan; (509) 687-3710 or (800) 233-0321.*

Just up the road is **Twenty-five Mile Creek State Park,** an interesting old resort site that became a state park in 1975. Boating also dominates the scene here; the park has a boat launch, ample moorage, a fuel dock, and other amenities. The campground offers 75 campsites (23 with hookups) and an 88-person group camp, all in wooded sites near the lake and along Twenty-five Mile Creek. Kids can test their fishing gear on a fishing pier or in the stream, which holds rainbow trout. Twenty-five Mile Creek is open from May through September. Campsites can be reserved up to 11 months in advance by calling Reservations Northwest; (800) 452-5687. *On South Lakeshore Drive about 10 miles north of Lake Chelan State Park; (509) 687-3710 or (800) 233-0321.*

Lake Chelan's shorelines also offer some of Washington's better walk-in or boat-in-only camping experiences. A string of U.S. Forest Service camps, all administered by Wenatchee National Forest's Lake Chelan Ranger District, rings the lake.

On the southwest shore: **Big Creek, Graham Harbor, Domke Lake, Lucerne, Refrigerator Harbor,** and **Weaver Point.** On the northeast shore: **Deer Point, Prince Creek, Mitchell Creek, Safety Harbor, Flick Creek, Boiling Lake, Cub Lake, Moore Point,** and **Purple Point.** The north-shore campgrounds all are stops on the Chelan Lakeshore Trail, which begins at Prince Creek Campground and runs 18 miles northwest to Stehekin. All the campsites can be reached by private watercraft. Or arrangements can be made for *Lady of the Lake* drop-offs at most of the campgrounds (see Attractions, below, or consult the Stehekin and the Lake Chelan NRA chapter). The most popular drop-off camps are Prince Creek, where Chelan Lakeshore Trail walkers depart; and Lucerne, the drop point for hikers bound for Holden Village along Railroad Creek in the Glacier Peak Wilderness. Call the Lake Chelan Ranger District, (509) 682-2576, for information.

In addition, a series of remote campgrounds northwest of Stehekin on Stehekin Valley Road are accessible only by the shuttle bus from Stehekin. See the Stehekin and the Lake Chelan NRA chapter for details.

Pateros area

A little-known but very nice campground, **Alta Lake State Park,** is tucked away in the foothills of the lower Methow River Valley. The 180-acre park is nestled into a dry pine forest between impressive rock cliffs and peaceful Alta Lake, a popular trout fishing, swimming, and picnicking site. The campground's three loops offer a choice of 190 sites (15 with full hookups) nicely scattered through the thin pine forest. The lakeside picnic area is a great stopover spot for tired travelers, and a short, steep hiking trail leads from the park to a viewpoint of the Middle Columbia Valley. A private resort with a store and boat rentals is nearby. Alta Lake State Park is open all year. Campsites cannot be reserved. *Follow signs from Hwy 153, 4 miles southwest of Pateros; (509) 923-2473 or (800) 233-0321.*

Entiat River Valley

Lovers of dry Central Washington plateau country are drawn to the long, narrow Entiat Valley, which connects the Columbia River Valley to the alluring alpine country in the Glacier Peak Wilderness. A string of picturesque Forest Service campgrounds in the upper valley have few, if any, services. Their attraction is location. They're remote camps, filled in summer months with small-stream anglers, horse or dirt bike riders, or hikers and backpackers headed into the wilderness; in the fall they're filled with hunters.

Unfortunately, much of the heart of the Entiat Valley—as well as thousands of acres in all directions—was devastated by the Tyee Creek Wildfire of 1994, which burned uncontrolled from midsummer to the first snows of October, stretching north nearly all the way to Lake Chelan. Be sure to check with the Entiat Ranger District, (509) 784-1511, on the status of roads, campgrounds, or trails anywhere in this area. The impact of the damage on the valley is likely to last for decades. This area is particularly beautiful in the fall, when aspens, cottonwoods, and maples put on a rainbow display of color. Be aware, however, that local hunting seasons might coincide with peak colors.

The campgrounds, all accessed via Entiat River Road, are **Pine Flat** (5 sites, 15 miles west of Entiat on Mad River Road); **Fox Creek** (16 sites, 28 miles west of Entiat); **Lake Creek** (18 sites, 29 miles west of Entiat); **Silver Falls** (30 sites, 32 miles west of Entiat); and **North Fork** (8 sites, 35 miles west of Entiat). All these campgrounds are open mid-May through mid-November, and all except Pine Flat have drinking water and charge a fee. Most are suitable for tents and small RVs. Campsites cannot be reserved.

For an even more rustic setting, dozens of **unofficial campsites** are found along the river on Entiat River Road, which climbs high into the river's headlands between the Entiat and Chelan Mountains. Many classic Glacier Peak Wilderness backpacking trips begin from this area. (See Hiking/Backpacking, below.)

Boating

Whether the activity of choice is water-skiing, boat camping, hiking, fishing, or just waterborne lollygagging, **Lake Chelan** clearly is one of the state's premier recreational boat getaways. The deep, long lake offers exceptionally clear water and almost always sunny skies. Boater/camper families often queue up for sites at **Lake Chelan** or **Twenty-five Mile Creek** State Parks, both of which offer camping spots with nearby boat moorage. For more solitude, head for one of the many boat-in campgrounds along Lake Chelan, most of which have boat docks (see Camping, above.)

There are public boat launches at **Lake Chelan State Park, Twenty-five Mile Creek State Park, Riverfront Park,** and **Don Morse Park** in Chelan, and at **Old Mill** and **Manson Bay** Parks near Manson. Launches also are available at Wapato Lake and Ross Lake, just northwest of Chelan.

Boats, Jet-skis, and water-skiing gear can be rented at Chelan Boat Rentals, (509) 682-4444, and at Ship 'n' Shore Boat Rentals, (509) 682-5125.

Hiking/Backpacking

The Middle Columbia area doesn't have many interesting hikes inside its borders, but it's the gateway to some of the most spectacular hiking destinations in Washington. Most of these trails are in four primary areas:

Stehekin area

Dozens of scenic mountain trails fan out from the village of **Stehekin,** ranging from short day hikes to long, multiday backpacking adventures into North Cascades National Park. See the Stehekin and the Lake Chelan NRA chapter for a list of good options.

Entiat River drainage

Many mixed-use trails (mixed meaning hikers, horses, mountain bikes, and dirt bikes) emanate from Entiat River Road. But a couple stand out as spectacular.

The **Ice Lakes/Entiat Meadows Trail** (moderate/difficult; 29.5 miles round trip) leads into a fantastic alpine area in the heart of the Glacier Peak Wilderness. From a trailhead near Cottonwood Campground (as far as you can drive up the Entiat), this popular trail follows the river 4.3 miles northwest to the wilderness boundary (bye-bye, mountain and dirt bikes), passes junctions with the Larch Lakes and Snowbrushy Creek Trails, then joins the Icicle Creek Trail about 8 miles in. Options: Turn left and hike just under 4 miles to spectacular Ice Lakes, which lie in a cirque below 9,100-foot Mount Maude. Or continue straight on the Entiat River Trail another 5 miles, into the alpine wonderland of Entiat Meadows. Views of Mount Maude, 9,077-foot Seven Fingered Jack, 9,249-foot Mount Fernow, and the Entiat Glacier are unforgettable. Our advice: Plan enough time to visit both areas. That adds about 8 miles to the round-trip total, which is measured to the end of the Entiat River Trail. Note: Long-distance shuttle hikers can do a truly fantastic through trip by taking the Entiat River Trail to the Snowbrushy Creek Trail, which can be followed over Milham Pass east through Emerald Park (see below) to Domke Lake and a Lake Chelan water-taxi pickup at Lucerne. It's a grand 20-mile (one way) traverse.

Also high in this valley, at the end of Forest Service Road 113, is the **Pyramid Mountain Trail** (difficult; 18.5 miles round trip), a rugged climb with a magnificent payoff: an airplane-seat view of Lake Chelan from an 8,245-foot fire lookout site. Be warned that the road to the trailhead is rough, and the trail itself isn't for slouches. Due to the long climb and big-time vertical, most mortals make this an overnighter, camping on the summit.

Note that this entire valley continues a slow recovery from the massive Tyee Creek Wildfire of 1994. Check trail and road conditions with the Entiat Ranger District, (509) 784-1511, before departing.

East side Glacier Peak Wilderness (Lucerne/Holden Village area)

Lady of the Lake drop-off passengers can combine a stay in the Lucerne or Holden Village area with a trek into the backcountry for a truly unique wilderness weekend. From Lucerne, a trail leads east to **Domke Lake** (easy; 3 miles round trip) and **Domke Mountain** (difficult; 6 miles round trip from Domke Lake). Domke Lake is an easy walk from the main trailhead, a quarter-mile up Railroad Creek Road. You'll find a private resort here, with decent fishing in the lake. Another trail continues about 3,000 vertical feet to the top of Domke Mountain, which has grand Lake Chelan views.

Domke Lake also is a good launching point for backpackers seeking high-altitude solitude at **Emerald Park** (moderate; 16 miles round trip from Domke Lake). This route, the reverse path of the Entiat to Lake Chelan traverse described above under Ice Lakes/Entiat Meadows, is an excellent overnight getaway to some beautiful alpine meadows.

For a more remote backpack getaway, it's tough to beat the **Lyman Lakes** (moderate; 19.4 miles round trip), reached by hiking the Railroad Creek Trail from the old mining village of Holden, which awaits 12 miles up Railroad Creek Road (there's a shuttle bus). The hike up Railroad Creek from Holden, now a Lutheran conference center, is spectacular, passing Crown Point Falls on the way to Lower Lyman Lake, about 7 miles. A side trail leads through beautiful meadows to the upper lakes, near the toe of the Lyman Glacier below Chiwawa Mountain. Many skilled hikers climb a way trail up the glacier to Spider Gap, 7,100 feet, then drop down the **Spider Glacier** to **Phelps Creek Pass** and an exit route in the **Chiwawa River** drainage north of Leavenworth. If you know your way around a glacier and can save yourself and/or a friend with an ice ax, it's a rewarding cross-country jaunt. Few hikers, however, are disappointed with a backpack trip into Lyman Lakes and back. Remember that this is an exceptionally fragile, heavily used area. It's important to practice low-impact camping techniques. To break up a long trip, consider booking lodging at a bunkhouse in Holden Village; (509) 687-3644.

Lake Chelan–Sawtooth Wilderness

The **Chelan Lakeshore Trail** (easy; 18 miles one way) can be walked campground to campground (see Camping, above) for a fantastic, low-difficulty backpack trip all year long except for the deep winter months. Consider a water-taxi drop-off at Prince Creek, then an 18-mile walk north on the trail to Stehekin, where the boat can be reboarded for a return trip to Chelan. Vertical-gain fans have a wealth of other options. Using the Chelan Lakeshore Trail as a shoreline leg, hikers can create a number of challenging loops by climbing any of numerous creek-drainage paths up, up, up to the Chelan Summit Trail in the Chelan–Sawtooth Wilderness. The Summit Trail follows a ridgeline above the lake, never dropping below 5,500 feet on its 28-mile journey from South Navarre Campground high above the lake (reached by a maze of roads from Manson) to War Creek Pass, a 6,800-foot lookout above Stehekin. By combining the Summit and Chelan Lakeshore Trails with routes up and down drainages such as Fish and Prince Creeks, hikers can make loops ranging from 19 to 48 miles.

Free overnight permits (unlimited, at this point) are required for hikes in the Lake Chelan–Sawtooth and Glacier Peak Wildernesses. They're available at the Entiat and Lake Chelan Ranger Districts (see More Information, below). Free overnight permits also are required for trips inside North Cascades National Park, northwest of Stehekin. They're available at the Golden West Visitors Center near Stehekin Landing. No permits are required for hikes within the Lake Chelan National Recreation Area.

Cycling

A hilly but picturesque scenic loop starts right in Chelan, providing a full sampler of the area's rocky buttes, steep coulees, and magnificent lakeshores. Follow **South Lakeshore Road** about 9 miles west of town to **Lake Chelan State Park.** Rest up for the coming onslaught: **Navarre Coulee Road** climbs steeply from the park, eventually dropping into the very scenic coulee and continuing about 8 1/2 miles south to US 97A. From there, it's up again for about 2 miles on US 97A, then down steeply back into Chelan, about 11 1/2 miles from the Navarre Coulee Junction.

For a more relaxing tour from Chelan, consider the 8.5-mile (one way) ride north to **Manson.** Follow Columbia Street to Hwy 150. Manson Bay Park is a nice midpoint lunch stop.

Fishing

Washington's deepest lake holds some of its most highly sought fish. Present and quite often accounted for in **Lake Chelan** are rainbow and lake trout, kokanee and chinook salmon, freshwater lingcod (burbot), and a number of other species. All these are worthy of pursuit, but the chinook fishery is a truly unique one. Chinook have been stocked in the deep, cold lake since the mid-1970s, and now provide a popular all-year fishery. Successful anglers troll herring, often very deep, making downriggers an almost necessary tool. Graybill's Guide Service, (509) 682-4294, is the local expert on lake fishing.

Just up the road in Manson, **Wapato Lake** is a noted trout pond, with a decent reputation among fly fishers. It also holds some largemouth bass. Nearby **Roses Lake** also is a good trout fishery, but it's open winters only. Bring the ice-fishing gear. To the north, up Grade Creek Road, **Antilon Lake** and **Long Jim Reservoir** are popular mixed-species fisheries, and **Dry Lake** is a productive bass-fishing lake.

Trout anglers shouldn't overlook the many clear high-mountain streams in the **Entiat River Valley** and on Wenatchee National Forest land west of Lake Chelan. For details, inquire at the Entiat Ranger Station (see More Information, below).

Wherever you fish in this region, watch where you step. Local anglers say rattlesnakes are commonly encountered in brushy and rocky lakeshores and creek banks.

Picnics

Nearly all of the campgrounds listed above have good picnic facilities, many with reservable group shelters. In the town of Chelan, **Lakeshore City Park** is a nice waterfront picnic venue, as is **Manson Bay Park.** For weary US 97 travelers, **Rocky Reach Dam** has nice picnic grounds, as do **Lincoln Rock** and **Daroga State Parks,** across the Columbia River.

Skiing

The Lake Chelan area is a notable **cross-country** ski destination, provided snow levels drop enough to blanket local hillsides' elevations. Examples of good Nordic tours include the **Stehekin Valley Road,** and roads and trails around **Twenty-five Mile Creek State Park.** Rentals are available at Lake Chelan Sports, (509) 682-2629.

The premier cross-country venue in the area, though, is **Bear Mountain Ranch,** which has more than 55 kilometers of trails on hillsides above the lake. Rentals are available on-site. The ranch is on Country Club Road, about 6 miles west of downtown Chelan. Call for schedules; the area generally is open only late in the week and weekends; (509) 682-5444.

The **Lake Chelan Golf Course** also maintains a small cross-country ski operation; (509) 682-3503. **Echo Ridge,** operated, like Echo Valley (see below), by the Lake Chelan Ski Club, has some cross-country trails, but unfortunately also plenty of snowmobilers.

Downhillers aren't totally out of the picture. **Echo Valley,** northwest of the town of Chelan on Hwy 150, offers rope tows and a poma lift on gentle slopes. It's open Christmas through February; (509) 682-2576.

Photography

It's tough to go wrong with a camera in the **Lake Chelan** area, particularly if you have boat access to the lake. Its aqua blue waters spread out before a magnificent alpine backdrop of peaks in the Lake Chelan–Sawtooth and Glacier Peak Wildernesses. At 3,800 feet, **Chelan Butte Lookout,** 9 miles west of town, provides an almost aerial view of the lake, the Columbia River, and the orchard-blanketed countryside. You're also likely to see hang gliders here, launching off the bluff for extended glides over the lake. Follow Chelan Butte Road from West Chelan.

Wildlife

The Swakane Canyon, reached by turning west on Swakane Canyon Road just north of Rocky Reach Dam on US 97A, is a major habitat for **mule deer** and **bighorn sheep.** The Canyon also is home to **golden eagles** and other raptors, as well as many smaller birds. This is one of the most reliable sites for viewing mule deer and bighorn sheep in the winter. From December to March, both are fed at stations in the canyon, reached by snowshoes or cross-country skis. For feeding and access information, contact the Entiat Ranger District; (509) 784-1511. Entiat River Canyon also is an area rich in wildlife.

Lake Chelan also attracts wildlife. On your boat journey up or down the lake, watch for **mule deer, mountain goats, ospreys, eagles,** and beautiful **harlequin ducks.**

Attractions

Ironically, Chelan's greatest tourist attraction is a trip out of town: a **cruise up Lake Chelan** to Stehekin on an old-fashioned tour boat, *The Lady of* *the Lake II* or the newer *Lady Express.* Both boats include a layover at Stehekin, where you can visit craft shops and eat a barbecue lunch before getting back on board for the return voyage. (See the Stehekin and Lake Chelan NRA chapter for other activities in, around, and outside Stehekin.) *The Lady of the Lake II* tour boat departs Chelan at 8:30am (daily in summer for a 4-hour trip each way, three or four days a week off-season), and returns to Chelan by 6pm; round trips cost $22; kids 6 to 11 years old are half price. No reservations needed. The faster *Lady Express* shortens the daily trip to just over 2 hours each way, with a 1-hour stop in Stehekin before heading back; round-trip tickets are $41, and reservations are suggested. More info: The Lake Chelan Boat Company, (509) 682-2224. Or fly up to Stehekin, tour the valley, and be back the same day via Chelan Airways, (509) 682-5555.

Other local sights: **St. Andrew's Church** in downtown Chelan is a log edifice reputedly designed by Stanford White in 1898, and still in service; at the **Chelan Museum** (Woodin Avenue, 1 to 4pm in summer) you can learn about other restored houses nearby, such as the old **Lucas Homestead. Rocky Reach Dam,** on US 97A about 6 miles north of Wenatchee, has a nice visitors center, with an interesting hydroelectric exhibit, a fish ladder viewing area, and parklike grounds.

Restaurants

Goochi's Restaurant ☆   After years of abuse as a tavern in the historic Lakeview Hotel building, this pretty space with its huge antique cherrywood back bar is now a smart dinner stop. Great for burgers, beer, and pasta. *Across Woodin from Campbell's Lodge; (509) 682-2436; 104 E Woodin, Chelan; $.*

Cheaper Eats

El Vaquero   This place is 7 miles up the east side of the lake in Manson, but it supplies the hungry and the sunburned with authentic Mexican fare. *(509) 687-3179; 75 Wapato Way, Manson.*

Lodgings

Amy's Manor ☆☆   Built in 1928, this enchanting manor is situated at the foot of the Cascades overlooking the Methow River. Rooms are country-quaint, with patchwork quilts and comfortable beds. The 170-acre estate includes a small farm, and the table's bounty, be it breakfast or dinner, never disappoints. *On Hwy 153, 5 miles north of Pateros; (509) 923-2334; 435 Hwy 153, Pateros; $$.*

Campbell's Lodge ☆☆   Chelan's venerable resort continues to be the most popular place for visitors, with prime lakeside properties and 148 rooms, many with kitchenettes. Among the facilities, you'll find three heated pools, an indoor Jacuzzi, a sandy beach, and moorage should you arrive by boat. Campbell House, the most dependable restaurant at the lake, is here. *On the lake at the end of the main street through Chelan; (509) 682-2561; 104 W Woodin, Chelan; $$$.*

Darnell's Resort Motel ☆   Situated right on the shore of the lake, this is a resort especially suited to families, with large, attractive suites for four. Amenities included in the price: putting green, heated swimming pool, sauna, hot tub, exercise room, shuffleboard, volleyball, badminton, tennis, barbecues, bicycles, rowboats, and canoes. *Off Manson Hwy; (509) 682-2015; 901 Spader Bay Rd, Chelan; $$$.*

Kelly's Resort ☆   The original 10 fully equipped cabins are set back in the woods; they're dark and rustic, but they're great for those on a budget ($90 for four) and families seeking a playground. They also have four condo units on the lake. There's a nice deck near the grocery store (a good spot to have a beer) and a knotty-pine common area with table tennis and a fireplace. *14 miles uplake on the south shore; (509) 687-3220; Rt 1, Box 119, Chelan; $$$.*

Cheaper Sleeps

Apple Inn Motel   A clean, well-lighted roadside motel that's one of the least expensive places to stay in the area, probably because it's located 10 blocks from town. There are 3 buildings to choose from, each with its own perks, but we like the oldest with its knotty pine. *(509) 682-4044; 1002 E Woodin Ave, Chelan.*

More Information

Chelan Ranger District: *(509) 682-2576.*
Entiat Ranger District: *(509) 784-1511.*
Lake Chelan Visitors Center: *(800) 424-3526.*
North Cascades National Park, Stehekin District/Lake Chelan National Recreation Area: *(509) 682-2549.*

Grand Coulee: Coulee Dam to Soap Lake

From Coulee Dam south to Soap Lake, west to Jameson Lake, and east to Fort Spokane at the Spokane/Columbia Rivers confluence, including Grand Coulee Dam, the Lake Roosevelt National Recreation Area, Lake Roosevelt, Banks Lake, Dry Falls, and the Sun Lakes area.

The Columbia River is on vivid display here. All incarnations of it.

The old, old Columbia washed through here in a gush unequalled in the prehistoric history of the West. The Big Flow came between 10,000 and 15,000 years ago, when glacial dams holding back a lake that covered much of what is now Montana abruptly gave way, and the lake swept Eastern Washington with a wall of water. Geologists believe this process repeated itself hundreds of times as glaciers advanced and retreated, washing a series of deep coulees—ancient flood scars—into the landscape. These coulees survive today, and the Grand Coulee, true to its name, is the largest. The head of this massive canyon is near present-day Coulee Dam, its foot far to the south, near Soap Lake.

Along the way, the floodwaters wreaked havoc almost beyond imagination, restructuring the landscape and forming a colossal waterfall now known as Dry Falls. At their peak flow, the falls—more than 3 miles wide and 400 feet high—likely created the largest waterfall on the planet. The dry face remains impressive today, even without water. A series of lakes at its base, collectively known as Sun Lakes, remains as a lingering scar of the ever-moving falls' splash pools.

The old Columbia—the river of our era, before it was dammed—took a different path, turning west toward Chelan and leaving the Grand Coulee dry. It stayed that way until the early 1940s, when completion of 550-foot-high Grand Coulee Dam across the head of the coulee created Franklin D. Roosevelt Lake, the 150-mile flooded basin that stretches northeast to Kettle Falls. Water from Roosevelt Lake was (and still is) pumped into the coulee, now sealed off at each end by the North and Dry Falls Dams. The result is a 30-mile-long reservoir—Banks Lake—that serves as a holding pond for irrigation water bound for the Columbia Basin Reclamation Project.

Thus, the new Columbia is a tamed beast, at least for the time being. The damming of the great river and reflooding of the Grand Coulee have helped create an agricultural empire in Eastern Washington. And the soothing waters have proved equally beneficial to outdoor recreators. Today, Roosevelt Lake provides year-round thrills for tens of thousands of boaters, swimmers, sailors, anglers, and houseboat devotees. Banks Lake (see the Wildlife and Fishing sections of this chapter, below) is a noted wildlife refuge, boater's paradise, and fishing venue. Steamboat Rock—another Old, Old Columbia River creation—looms like an island in the center, with one of Washington's most popular state parks at its base (see Camping, below).

Today, this is a place to soak under the big, open sky, drink up the sunlight, and imagine these surroundings before humans set foot here. If not for the behemoth dam, the old land scars would look much the same as they must have 10,000 years ago.

Getting There

The length of the Grand Coulee can be navigated by driving Hwy 17 between Soap Lake and Dry Falls, and Hwy 155 east of Banks Lake between Coulee City and Coulee Dam. For the most direct route (about 200 miles) from Seattle, take Interstate 90 over Snoqualmie Pass and east to George, then follow Hwy 283 northeast to Ephrata and Soap Lake. Allow about 3 1/2 hours. For an alternate route from north Puget Sound, follow US 2 east over Stevens Pass to Wenatchee, US 97 north to Orondo, then US 2 east again over the Waterville Plateau and through the Moses Coulee to Dry Falls. It's slower but more scenic.

Adjoining Areas

NORTH: **Okanogan Highlands and Sherman Pass**

SOUTH: **Columbia Basin**

EAST: **Spokane**

WEST: **Chelan and the Middle Columbia**

inside out

Camping/Swimming/Picnics

The Grand Coulee is one of those rare Evergreen State regions where "the thing to do" is obvious: get on (or in) the water, stupid. Outdoor activities here begin, continue, and end on Roosevelt Lake, Banks Lake, or the chain of lakes below Dry Falls. Following is a rundown of the Grand Coulee's many lakefront parks, all of which offer a combination of camping, fishing, boating, and sunbathing.

Lake Roosevelt

Small campgrounds, managed either by the National Park Service (because they lie within the Lake Roosevelt National Recreation Area) or the Colville or Spokane tribes, literally ring Roosevelt Lake, the massive, 150-mile long reservoir behind Grand Coulee Dam. Stop by the Lake Roosevelt NRA office in Coulee Dam, (509) 633-9441, for a full list. All these campgrounds provide water access, most are open all year, and some have boat launches. Some of the more than two dozen campgrounds are so far up the lake that they land in a separate chapter of this guide (see the Kettle Falls, Colville, and the Pend Oreille chapter). But a few are within a short drive of the Coulee Dam visitors center.

Spring Canyon, just east of Coulee Dam on Hwy 174, is the leading campsite for all those dam visitors. It's a nice one, overlooking the lake just behind the massive dam. The federally managed campground has 87 campsites (no hookups; maximum RV length, 26 feet) spread throughout a series of loops in this dry, sagebrush and light-air country. The park also has a boat launch, making it a favorite home base for anglers and water-skiers. It also has a very popular swimming area, with a lifeguard on duty from July through Labor Day weekend. The campground is open all year. Campsites cannot be reserved. *On Hwy 174 about 3 miles east of Coulee Dam; (509) 633-9441.*

Keller Ferry, at the south side of the Roosevelt Lake ferry crossing on Hwy 21, is off the beaten path unless you're taking the ferry. It has 50 sites (no hookups; maximum RV length, 16 feet). The Colville Confederated Tribes' boat ramp and moorage facility is nearby, and there's a playground for kids. A lifeguard is on duty at the swimming area from July through Labor Day weekend. Keller Ferry is open all year. Campsites cannot be reserved. *On Hwy 21, 14 miles north of Wilbur; (509) 633-9441.*

Farther upstream are **Hawk Creek,** which offers 16 standard sites in a quieter setting; and **Fort Spokane,** which has 67 sites (no hookups; maximum RV length, 25 feet) and interesting historical exhibits describing the late 19th-century Indian wars. Fort Spokane has a noted swimming area (lifeguard included during summer months), a boat launch, and other goodies. Both parks are open summers only, and campsites cannot be reserved. *Follow Hwy 25 north from US 2 to the Spokane/Columbia River confluence, turn south on Miles-Creston Road; (509) 633-9441.*

Banks Lake

And you thought irrigation was only good for growing asparagus. Banks Lake, nature's own holding tank (with a little help from those big pumps at Grand Coulee), offers a whole lot more to recreators—particularly the lie-in-the-sun-till-you-bake type. Banks also is a first-class fishing lake, and most of its shorelines are managed as state wildlife habitat (see Fishing and Wildlife, below).

Most of the focus here is on **Steamboat Rock State Park,** one of Washington's premier sunny-side vacation getaways. It's a mondo park—3,500 acres—with a very well groomed, very well attended campground. Steamboat was one of the first parks in the state to leap onto reservation status, and if you're seeking a campsite between Memorial Day and Labor Day, it's a good idea to get one. The park has 126 campsites (100 with full hookups; maximum RV length, 60 feet) and a dozen or more isolated, boat-in campsites. Most are on flat, grassy land that's well suited for tents (be warned, however, about nasty winds and predatory late-night sprinklers).

Steamboat Rock is a water-sports recreation hub, with boat launches and moorage, a sandy-bottom swimming area, a water-ski float, bathhouses, and extensive waterfront picnic facilities. For water-skiers, the 27-mile-long, 4-mile-wide lake is paradise. If the weather's not baking hot, you can take to the park's trail system, which contains 25 miles of paths on, around, and over Steamboat Rock, the massive, prow-shaped basalt bluff jutting up from Banks Lake. Bring the sunscreen and floppy hat in summer and warm clothes in winter, when ice fishing and cross-country skiing are the only signs of life here. Steamboat Rock is open all year. Campsites can be reserved up to 11 months in advance by calling Reservations Northwest; (800) 452-5687. *On Hwy 155, 9.5 miles south of Electric City; (509) 633-1304 or (800) 233-0321.*

Boaters will find two other public boat launches on the northeast side of **Banks Lake,** just off Hwy 155. One is at Osborne Bay, the other at the mouth of Northrup Creek, both with picnicking and primitive camping facilities nearby. The two sites are jointly managed by State Parks and the Department of Fish and Wildlife. Several other primitive boat-in sites can be found elsewhere on the lake. The entire reservoir is designated as **Banks Wildlife Area,** as it's a significant stopover point for migratory birds.

Park Lake, Blue Lake and Sun Lakes

Sun Lakes State Park, another extremely popular summertime getaway, is an odd mix of private amenities and public facilities amid a gaggle of small lakes at the south end of the Grand Coulee. If you don't mind camping next to a Palm Springs–style golf course, rental cabins, and other businesses, you might enjoy all the commotion. If you do mind, go elsewhere.

The main development is on the south boundary at Park Lake, where you'll find a private resort complex as well as a state park picnic area, camping area, and large group camp. To the north, trails lead to a half-dozen other small lakes, all believed to be former splash pools from the awesome Dry Falls just to the north (see Attractions, below).

In all, the state park offers 193 campsites (18 with full hookups; maximum RV length, 50 feet), a large group camp, and day-use picnic facilities, a boat launch, and more than 16 miles of hiking trails (watch for snakes). The resort adds cabins, a golf course, boat ramps and rentals, a store, laundromat, and other amenities, plus 110 RV sites and a stable for horseback trips to the surrounding lakes. Good fishing is found throughout this multilake park (see Fishing, below). And don't miss the Dry Falls Interpretive Center (see Attractions, below) just up the road or the Lenore Caves (see Hiking, below) just up the trail.

Sun Lakes is open all year. The concession-operated resort is open summers only. State park campsites can be reserved up to 11 months in advance by calling Reservations Northwest; (800) 452-5687. Sun Lakes Resort campsites can be reserved by calling (509) 632-5291. *On Hwy 17, 6 miles south of Coulee City (17 miles north of Soap Lake); (509) 632-5583 or (800) 233-0321.*

In Soap Lake, **Smokiam Campground** is a city facility that makes a decent RV stopover. *On East Beach in Soap Lake; (509) 246-1211.*

Boating

Roosevelt Lake and its neighbor, **Banks,** are among the most popular boating destinations in the state. (See Camping/Swimming/Picnics, above, for a list of launch facilities.) Boaters bound for Roosevelt Lake should note that most of its 16 public boat launches are unusable in the spring, when the lake is drawn down to accommodate the spring meltoff. The waters reach a stable level by early July. A hotline number, (800) 824-4916, gives updated lake levels.

Until three years ago, this big reservoir was untapped by the RV-on-pontoons fleet. Now there are 40 **houseboats** available to explore the 150-mile-long lake, and most book up early for the summer. The service is managed by the Colville Confederated Tribes. The sun's almost guaranteed, and all you need to bring is food, bed linens, towels, fishing gear, and your bathing suit; boats are moored at Kelly Ferry Marina, 14 miles north of Wilbur. Rates vary seasonally, and most of the boats will sleep about a dozen guests; (800) 648-LAKE.

Fishing

The dry shores and deep, clear reservoirs and lakes in the ancient Grand Coulee contain more than a few monstrous, waterborne links with the past. Big fish await anglers in these waters, which hold some of the most prized lunkers in Washington.

Lower **Roosevelt Lake** is known for its productive walleye, rainbow trout, largemouth and smallmouth bass, kokanee, whitefish, and perch fisheries. This is a huge, diverse lake, where a variety of methods will yield different species. The big fish—rainbows, kokanee, and walleye all grow to impressive sizes here—are usually caught trolling spoons or spinners. The state record for kokanee is broken almost annually here. It currently stands at about 5 1/2 pounds. Get after it. Roosevelt also contains some truly massive white sturgeon, which grow to 20 feet in the deep, cold waters. Most fishing action centers around stream inlets or rocky shorelines providing underwater structure. Hot temperatures send many fish scurrying for the lake's depths in mid-summer. Best fishing usually is early and late in the summer season. That's particularly true for bank anglers, who can be successful here, but usually find fishing much more hit-and-miss than do boaters. Keller Ferry Marina, (509) 647-5755, is a good source of supplies and advice.

Banks Lake is another monstrous waterway with a mess of marine life lurking below. Walleye also are the prominent species here, but largemouth and smallmouth bass, crappies, rainbow trout, and whitefish also are solid. Steamboat Rock State Park (see Camping, above) is a great base camp for Banks Lake anglers.

To the west, **Jameson Lake** is a longtime favorite trout-fishing spot, particularly when it first opens in the spring. Then, anybody—and we do mean anybody—should be able to hook into a chunky rainbow or two with a bit of effort, even by bank casting. Flip your glob of Power Bait out there among all the hand-tied flies and hang on tight. (Just don't get your glob hooked up to our glob; this is a favorite guidebook-author fishing spot.) Check the state regulations pamphlet for seasons on Jameson, which closes during midsummer and reopens in the fall. Jameson Lake Resort, (509) 683-1141, dispenses supplies and advice.

Most of the many lakes below Dry Falls in **Sun Lakes State Park** are open from late April through September, and they offer uncommonly good fishing early in the season. The largest, **Park Lake,** is another can't-miss rainbow trout fishery on or around Opening Day. Healthy catches are made here every spring, with most bank and boat anglers limiting on some of Washington's healthiest trout. When the bite is on, just about anything works. Access is good through the state park and along Hwy 17. Rental boats are available at Sun Lakes Resort Lodge; (509) 632-5291. Expect unbelievably huge crowds during the first two weeks of fishing.

Conditions at **Blue Lake,** outside the Sun Lakes Park just to the south, are nearly identical, with excellent bank access, excellent catch rates early in the year, and very large crowds. If the mob scene makes you nuts, try this lake (or any in this area) later in the summer. Crowds thin out—and fishing usually is still productive—before the lakes close in September.

You'll have to work a bit harder in the Sun Lakes cluster's smaller, less accessible lakes, all reached by walking or driving several miles on very rough roads from the state park. But that seems to make the experience more rewarding. **Deep Lake,** at the south end of the Sun Lakes complex, holds planted rainbows, which are fairly bite-happy on Opening Day in late April every year. To the north, **Dry Falls Lake** is a selective fishery. Bait and barbed hooks are prohibited, but the lake has become a favorite of fly casters, who report fair-to-good trout catches. **Perch Lake,** in the center of the Sun Lakes group, also is a hot Opening Day lake, as is nearby **Rainbow Lake.** Both reportedly get fished out pretty early in the season.

To the south, below Blue Lake, is **Alkali Lake,** a warmwater lake that's being groomed as a walleye fishery. Immediately to its south is **Lake Lenore,** home of a fascinating—and amazingly successful—stocking program. Lahontan cutthroat trout planted here have grown huge—some up to 6 pounds or more—and strict selective fishery regulations are in place to prevent overfishing. The lake is fast becoming legendary among fly casters, who flock here in March for the start of a three-month catch-and-release-only fishery. A one-fish bag limit goes into effect for the rest of the summer, but many of Lenore's fly casters have taken to releasing fish all season—a very healthy trend.

Another alternative in this region are three Colville Tribe–controlled lakes north of Grand Coulee Dam: **McGinnis, Buffalo,** and **Rebecca.** Tribal fishing permits are required, but fishing can be quite good in all three, without the big crowds of lakes in the lower Coulee.

Hiking

The impressive Steamboat Rock State Park in the midst of Banks Lake (see Camping/Swimming/Picnics, above) has an interesting trail system, including one short, steep jaunt up a crack in **Steamboat Rock** (difficult; 3 miles round trip) to the broad, flat, 700-foot summit. Nice view! Bring lots of water, however. It's dry, hot, and miserable in the dead of summer.

To the south, **Sun Lakes State Park** has more than 15 miles of trail, although some of it is shared by horses and four-wheel-drive rigs. Roads or paths link all of the half-dozen largest lakes in the Sun Lakes cluster. The region is geologically fascinating (see Dry Falls Interpretive Center in Attractions, below). But it can be very exposed and dry in summer months. Protect yourself from the sun, and watch for snakes. For the most interesting route (moderate; 3 miles one way), follow the path from the end of the campground loop around the east side of Rainbow Lake, past Perch Lake, and on to the shore of Dry Falls Lake, where the massive Dry Falls cliff band is an awesome sight from ground level.

On the east shores of Lake Lenore—just off Hwy 17 about 10 miles south of Dry Falls—a short trail leads to a cliff band concealing **Lenore Caves** (moderate; .5 mile round trip), a series of rock caverns carved by the ancient river. Some of these caves have produced significant archaeological finds, believed left by passing bands of ancient hunters. Pictographs are visible on the rock walls. These caves are worthy of exploration, but be careful.

Wildlife

The entire, 44,000-acre reservoir at **Banks Lake** is a state wildlife area, with access at several primitive camping/boat-launch sites on the east shore (see Camping/Swimming/Picnics, above). The lake attracts a fair number of **waterfowl,** and hunting is allowed here in season. In the winter, keep your eyes peeled for **bald eagles,** which winter here in fairly large numbers.

Cycling

A good day trip suitable for the whole family is the **Down River Trail,** which follows the Columbia downstream from the city park in the town of Coulee Dam. It's about 6 ½ miles one way.

outside in

Attractions

Say hello to the mother of all Redi-mixes. **Grand Coulee Dam** is one of the largest structures on earth—as tall as a 46-story building, with a spillway twice the height of Niagara and a length of nearly a mile. The gargantuan structure contains 12 million cubic yards of concrete. Grand Coulee, completed in 1941, was originally intended more to irrigate the desert than to produce electricity; so much power was generated, however, that the dam became a magnet for the nation's aluminum industry. The north-face extension (completed in 1975) was designed by Marcel Breuer, a great practitioner of the International Style, and the heroic scale of the concrete is quite magnificent, especially when illuminated by the inspirational 35-minute laser light show (summers only). Daily self-guided tours are available, with hours varying according to season; (509) 633-9265.

The dam is so monstrous that you really can't see the entire thing when you're standing atop it. For a broad, overall view of the massive structure, follow Hwy 174 about a mile north to the signed turnoff for **Crown Point Vista,** a state-managed overlook site. It's a good spot from which to view the laser light show.

To the south, eccentric inventor Emil Gehrke amassed an oddly compelling **windmill collection** at North Dam Park on Hwy 155 between Electric City and Grand Coulee. Four hardhats tilted sideways catch the wind, cups and saucers twirl around a central teapot. Check it out, but don't get vertigo.

Dry Falls Interpretive Center, 4 miles south of Coulee City off Hwy 17, is a great place to view the 3-mile-wide face of an almost unbelievably massive ancient waterfall, the largest in the world when the Columbia flowed through this coulee (see the introduction to this chapter, above). The center (Wednesday through Sunday, 10am to 6pm, summer; (509) 632-5214) explains the local geology, which has been compared to the surface features of Mars. From this lookout, you can also see Sun Lakes, puddles left behind by the ancient Columbia (see the Camping/Swimming/Picnics, Hiking, and Fishing sections, above).

At the south end of the coulee, **Soap Lake** is an interesting physical and historical attraction. The lake has an unusually high mineral content, which gives the water a soapy feel. Past generations visited the town of

Soap Lake to soak at the local sanitorium, believing the sudsy water had medicinal effects. You'll still find it piped into some local motels for drinking and/or bathing.

Northeast of Coulee Dam on Roosevelt Lake, **Fort Spokane,** at the confluence of the Spokane and Columbia Rivers, is an interesting historical site, with buildings remaining from the old army outpost here during the late 19th century.

Restaurants

Deb's Cafe   The glory days of Deb Cobenhaver, a world-champion rodeo rider back in the mid-1950s, are kept in a kind of time capsule here in Creston; the place is strewn with trophies, photos, and saddles. The cafe opens at 6am for hearty breakfasts with homemade cinnamon rolls; at lunch there are a few decent sandwiches, served with home-cut fries; steaks at dinner. *Hwy 2; (509) 636-3345; 600 Watson, Creston; $.*

Lodgings

Coulee House Motel   Dam good view and decent amenities. At night you can sit on the tiny lanai outside your room (smoking or non) and watch the animated laser light show (summers only) over one of the largest dams on earth as the water cascades past. *Birch and Roosevelt; (509) 633-1101; 110 Roosevelt Way, Coulee Dam; $$.*

Four Winds   Once a dormitory for dam engineers, the Four Winds is now Coulee Dam's most personable inn *and* within walking distance of the dam itself. There are 11 spotlessly clean rooms with many combinations of baths (shared with one other, down the hall, etc.). At 8:30am there's a virtual smorgasbord. *Lincoln St is across from the Coulee Dam City Hall; (509) 633-3146 or (800) 786-3146; 301 Lincoln St, Coulee Dam; $$.*

Notaras Lodge   On the shores of Soap Lake, you can stay in the Norma Zimmer Room (the bubble lady on the *Lawrence Welk Show*), the Bonnie Guitar Honeymoon Suite (named for a local country-western singer), or the Western Nostalgia Room (featuring a pool table and whirlpool). The healing waters of Soap Lake are available to guests on tap in the bathrooms. *4 miles north of Ephrata on Hwy 28, 1 block west on Main St; (509) 246-0462; 236 E Main St, Soap Lake; $$.*

More Information

Dry Falls Interpretive Center: *(509) 632-5214.*
Fort Spokane Ranger Station: *(509) 725-2715.*

Grand Coulee Visitors Center: *Hwy 155, near Coulee Dam; (509) 633-9265.*

Kettle Falls Ranger Station: *(509) 738-6111.*

Lake Roosevelt National Recreation Area: *(509) 633-9441.*

Lake Roosevelt water-level hotline: *(800) 824-4916.*

Soap Lake Visitor Information Center: *300 Beach Street; (509) 246-1821.*

Columbia
Basin

From Ephrata south to Othello, west to Vantage and east to Ritzville,
including Moses Lake, Potholes Reservoir, and the Gorge amphitheater
area.

Went to see Peter Frampton, got hooked on white pelicans.

That could well be the refrain of music fans who've flocked in recent years to the Columbia River Amphitheater near George, which has emerged as one of the state's leading concert venues. All those people heading to Moses Lake and George have had to scratch and sniff for campsites, and their search has put them on a collision path with a little-known fact about the Columbia Basin: a lot of wildlife passes through this endless flat land. And by that we do not mean Joe Cocker.

The Columbia Basin, Washington's largest stretch of desert before the Columbia Irrigation Project turned it into a fertile agricultural center, doesn't attract many full-time residents. But its singular asset—water—draws plenty of part-timers. The list includes white pelicans and countless other bird species, which flock to the Potholes and the Columbia National Wildlife Refuge every year as they migrate along the Pacific Flyway. That's long been known to the state's avid birders. But the bird species dropping in on the basin are attracting new bird lovers by sheer force of numbers. They're giving the region what it really has long lacked: a long-term tourism draw.

Of course, it doesn't take birds—no matter how many or how fancy—to draw another segment of the outdoors community that's been trekking to the Columbia Basin for years: anglers. The basin's broad waterways and relatively clean environs have combined to create one of the most productive freshwater fisheries in the state.

That's about all there is to offer the outdoor lover in the Columbia Basin. But it's enough for the people of Moses Lake, George, and Ephrata. Bring your tackle box. Bring your spotting glasses. Fish and fowl are taking center stage.

Getting There

Moses Lake, the heart of the Columbia Basin (and arguably the only civilized spot therein), is 176 miles east of Seattle on Interstate 90. It's about a 3-hour drive.

Adjoining Areas

NORTH: **Grand Coulee: Coulee Dam to Soap Lake**

SOUTH: **Tri-Cities**

EAST: **Snake River Country: Clarkston, Pullman, and the Palouse**

WEST: **I-90 East: Roslyn to Ellensburg**

inside out

Camping/Swimming/Picnics

The best thing to do in Moses Lake in the summer is wish it were winter. Well, that's not entirely true, considering that winters are as ferociously cold as summers are hot, and besides—lots of people flock to the Columbia Basin during the hot season specifically *for* its arid, Palm Springs–like climate. But even sun worshippers need a place to cool off once in a while. In the Columbia Basin, a series of waterfront parks are the cool places to be.

Potholes State Park is the hub of waterborne activity in the Columbia Basin. The 640-acre splash of green amid the rather harsh surrounding desert won't be everyone's idea of a grand vacation getaway, but if fishing or canoeing are even medium-high on your list, the place deserves a visit. The water, naturally, is the star here. Most of it is seepage from the grandiose Columbia Basin Irrigation Project, which pumps millions of gallons of water from Banks Lake onto surrounding fields. When earthen O'Sullivan Dam was completed here in 1949, the water backed up and filled a series of low-lying glacial depressions: the Potholes. At about 29,000 acres when full in the spring, Potholes Reservoir is by far the largest body of water here. But literally hundreds of other small ponds and water canals are linked to it by the artificially high water table, creating a navigable paradise for anglers and paddlers.

The park, which sits on the southwest shore of the reservoir, offers 126 campsites (60 with full hookups; maximum RV length, 50 feet), a mondo boat launch and day-use parking area, picnic facilities, and a playground. Potholes State Park is open all year. Campsites can be reserved up to 11 months in advance by calling Reservations Northwest; (800) 452-5687. *From I-90 westbound, take exit 164 to Dodson Road and follow signs about 10 miles to the park; (509) 765-7271 or (800) 233-0321.*

Nearby, a notable private development on the Potholes, **Mar Don Resort,** offers 250 sites (full hookups; no maximum RV length), a store, motel, and extensive boating and fishing services (see Fishing, below). The park is open all year. Campsites can be reserved. *On O'Sullivan Dam Road (Hwy 262) at the west end of O'Sullivan Dam; (509) 346-2651.*

Like the Potholes to the south, the waters of Moses Lake also were augmented by the irrigation project. The diverted Columbia River water expanded the lake to a skinny, 17-mile-long waterway that keeps Moses Lake bearable during the blazing summers.

Moses Lake State Park, just off I-90 in Moses Lake, a day-use area only, is a welcome oasis of rolling green lawns, covered picnic shelters, playgrounds, and other summer fun equipment. The 80-acre park is on the lakeshore, with good access for swimmers, paddlers, and bank anglers. The bathhouse and swimming area (lifeguard on duty during the summer) is one of the best in the region. The park also has a boat ramp and mooring dock. Easy freeway access to this park makes it a popular lunch stopover for road-weary I-90 travelers. In the winter, bring your skates: ice skating on a portion of the frozen lake near the park is a popular activity. Moses Lake State Park is open all year. *Follow signs from I-90 exit 175 in Moses Lake; (800) 233-0321.*

Other nice Moses Lake waterfront picnic spots include **Cascade Park** on Valley Road, **Montlake Park** on Beaumont Road, and **McCosh Park,** at Dogwood and Fourth, which has a popular water slide and outdoor pool complex. Cascade Park also has limited camping facilities.

To the north, in the thriving hub of Ephrata, **Oasis Park Resort** on Hwy 28 is a quiet spot, complete with shaded picnic facilities, a swimming area, fishing ponds, and more than 100 campsites, some with utilities. It's a good possible stopover spot for travelers bound to or from Grand Coulee. The park is open all year. Campsites can be reserved. *On Hwy 28 in Ephrata; (509) 754-5102.*

In the Vantage area, two options await I-90 travelers or Gorge concertgoers. At **Wanapum Recreation Area,** a riverfront site on the west side of the Vantage bridge over the Columbia, you'll find a slew of individual picnic sites, a swimming area and bathhouse, a boat launch, and 50 partially shaded campsites (all with full hookups; maximum RV length, 60 feet). They'd work for a tent in a pinch, but are geared for RV use. The park, the only one in this area along I-90, is crowded during the summer. Ginkgo Petrified Forest State Park (see Attractions, below) is nearby. Wanapum Recreation Area is open all year. Campsites cannot be reserved. *Follow signs from the Vantage exit on I-90; (509) 856-2700 or (800) 233-0321.*

Tent campers likely will be happier by scooting over to the nearby **KOA Vantage,** which offers 125 campsites (100 with hookups) and the usual KOA amenities. The campground is open all year. Campsites can be reserved. *North of Vantage off I-90 exit 136; (509) 856-2230.*

Gorge Amphitheater visitors also might consider another private campground, **Shady Tree RV Park** in George, which offers 50 campsites (44 with hookups). George and Martha Lakes are nearby. The park is open all year. Campsites can be reserved. *At the Hwy 281/283 junction near George; (509) 785-2851.*

Fishing

No other region of the Evergreen State provides the wealth of angling opportunity found in the Columbia Basin. The literal flood of fresh water provided by the Columbia Basin Irrigation Project combines with warm weather and a wealth of species for some of the hottest fishing action in the Northwest. The list of lakes, canals, and reservoirs with good fishing in this region would be monstrous. We've grouped them into overall areas, and urge you to spend some time at each, discovering your own tucked-away fishing water. Take a good map and a state regulations pamphlet. Like the fishing venues themselves, seasons, catch limits, and special restrictions are all over the map here. Anglers who get an itchy casting finger early in the year should note that many Columbia Basin fishing waters are either open all year or have March 1 opening dates, and some of the hottest fishing here is in early spring, before it even gets under way in much of Western Washington.

If you can't catch your favorite fish at **Potholes Reservoir,** you're just plain unlucky. Chances are, the one you want is down there. The Potholes are famous for their production of largemouth and smallmouth bass, walleye, trout, kokanee, crappie, perch, and other species. Finding your way around this massive jigsaw waterway is the tricky part. It comes with experience (either your own or hired, through one of the local guide services). The south end of the Potholes near the dam is the most easily negotiated by boat, and also offers plenty of good bank access. Fishing for bass and walleye can be very good from the bank here. The north end is a maze of small waterways, making it easy to get lost if you're not careful. Still, fishing for warm-water species is excellent in these shallower waterways, which are guaranteed to provide a memorable day on the water, at the very least.

Trout anglers take some hefty ones home from the Potholes, either by trolling deep in the south end, or by fishing from the bank at deep-water drop-offs or the fishing pier at Mar Don Resort (see Camping/Swimming/Picnics, above). Boat-launch facilities are found at Potholes State Park (also see above) and Mar Don, which offers guide services and serves as the best information and gear source for Potholes fishing; (509) 346-2651.

An equally impressive—and equally bewildering—array of "seep lakes" and waterways is found to the south in **Columbia National Wildlife Refuge** (see Wildlife, below). Many of these lakes and ponds are very productive fisheries for trout, whitefish, perch, bass and other species. The largest, Warden, opens March 1 for an extremely popular fishery of planted rainbow trout. Many smaller lakes are stocked with rainbow trout. You can find good fishing just about any time of the year here. Many of the lakes are open all year, including Upper and Lower Goose, which are among the most popular for warm-water species. Call Columbia National Wildlife Refuge, (509) 488-2668, for access information.

Lenice, Merry, and **Nunnally,** three tiny lakes off Highway 26 near Beverly, have a reputation beyond their size among fly casters, who flock to the selective-fishery (single barbless hooks, no bait) lakes for monster-size rainbow and brown trout. The lakes are open April through October, but veterans say the best fishing almost always is early in the season.

On the western side of the basin near George, **George** and **Martha Lakes** provide decent fishing for planted rainbows. Like many lakes in this region, they open March 1.

Wildlife

Pelicans like the taste of Columbia River irrigation water every bit as much as potatoes do. The Columbia Basin's vast array of open waterways is visible from miles up in space, so it's no surprise that migratory birds on the Pacific Flyway include the region on their annual travel itinerary. So do most Washington birders. Springtime visits to the Potholes, Columbia National Wildlife Refuge, and the Channeled Scablands are rites of the season for bird lovers. These rich bird refuges, in fact, have converted many otherwise disinterested visitors into bird lovers, simply on the strength of overwhelming numbers of species. Birds and other wildlife are commonly seen in fields and on waterways throughout the basin, but viewing is best in these areas:

Potholes Reservoir may well be the single richest bird-viewing area in the state. The sprawling waterway is home to large numbers of migratory **Canada geese, mallards,** and other **waterfowl** in the fall and winter. Also watch for **cormorants, herons, egrets,** a variety of **songbirds,** and some **white pelicans. Avocets** are commonly seen on the Winchester Wasteway during the spring. A trail along the Frenchman Hills Wasteway near the southwest corner of the reservoir is another popular bird-viewing spot, although serious birders will enjoy the best success by launching a canoe or other quiet craft from Potholes State Park (see Camping/Swimming/Picnics, above.) Spring is the peak viewing time in the Potholes. From Moses Lake, take Hwy 17 southeast to Hwy 262 (O'Sullivan Dam Road).

To the south, Columbia National Wildlife Refuge is a sprawling, 23,000-acre refuge comprising hundreds of small lakes and waterways with adjacent nesting fields. This is migratory waterfowl central, with hundreds of thousands of **geese** and **ducks** stopping over in the fall migration. Wading birds such as **avocets** and **curlews** also are commonly seen, and **sandhill cranes** are often spotted in March and April. An overlook site is maintained at Royal Lake, in the south end of the refuge, and trailheads are found along Morgan Lake Road. Because the refuge is large and access roads often confusing, it's best to stop first at refuge headquarters (44 S Eighth Street in Othello) for maps and information. The Moses Lake Visitors Center (324 S Pioneer Way; (509) 765-7888) dispenses copies of an Audubon Society brochure and map detailing bird-viewing in the area.

A more remote, but no less fascinating site is Crab Creek Coulee, which contains the famed Lenice, Merry, and Nunnally fishing lakes (see Fishing, above). The Coulee is home to large numbers of **raptors, waterfowl,** and **range birds,** as well as **coyotes** and **badgers.**

The **Channeled Scablands,** a bizarre mix of gullies, rocks, caves, and cliffs on the high, dry east side of the Columbia Basin, were formed by the same series of prehistoric floods that carved out the Grand Coulee and created Dry Falls. They're now home to various waterfowl; hundreds of desert songbird species; range birds such as **partridge** and **quail;** and large numbers of raptors, including **great horned owls, golden eagles, falcons,** and numerous **hawks.** This area—roughly bordered by Wilbur, Davenport, Odessa, and Ritzville—is best experienced by following a 150-mile wildlife-viewing loop from Ritzville. A visitors guide to the loop, which takes about 5 hours and includes six major stops on a mix of public and private property, is available from the Odessa Economic Development Council; (509) 982-2232.

For single-stop viewing of the same type of shrub-steppe environment, visit Wilson Creek Canyon, south of US 2 off Govan Road (just west of Wilbur). A short trail leads to an overlook where various **hawks, owls, eagles,** and **falcons** are often seen, as well as waterfowl such as the beautiful **redhead duck** and the **cinnamon teal.**

Canoeing/Kayaking

Both Moses Lake and Potholes Reservoir are popular with canoeists and kayakers, particularly those interested in viewing wildlife. (See Wildlife and Camping/Swimming/Picnics, above, for major access points.)

Hiking

Hiking "trails" per se are a rarity out here. Why build a trail through a wide-open, flat space? But plenty of hiking can be done by the enterprising walker, particularly one with a set of field glasses and a bird guide. **Potholes Reservoir** (see Camping/Swimming/Picnics, above) is a good place to set out for a stroll, as is the **Columbia National Wildlife Refuge,** where several short trails lead to bird-viewing blinds.

Ginkgo Petrified Forest State Park (see Attractions, below) has a mile-long interpretive trail and a 2.5-mile loop trail through brushy desert that is home to more rattlers and lizards than people. (It's said to be nice in the spring, when some wildflowers are in bloom. But we suspect "nice" is a relative term here.)

outside in

Attractions

Situated on a splendid stretch of the Columbia, **Vantage** has nothing much in the way of food, but the view from the parking lot of the A&W surpasses that of all other known root-beer stands.

The town notwithstanding: Nearby **Ginkgo Petrified Forest State Park** is a must-see for natural-history buffs. The park's interpretive center—open daily in summer, 10am to 6pm (by appointment only otherwise); (509) 856-2700—takes you back to the age of dinosaurs; then you can go prospecting yourself on a mile-long interpretive trail that weaves through a fascinating "forest" of petrified wood. The park is one of only a few places on the planet where fossilized remains of the ginkgo tree—which thrived here about 200 million years ago—have been found. These and other trees in what once was a thick forest were decimated by lava flows, then sealed in mud beneath an ancient lake. A fascinating place, and not a bad picnic spot. Follow signs from I-90 exit 136.

A naturally terraced amphitheater near **George** looking west over the Columbia Gorge offers a spectacular summer-evening setting for musical performances that attract thousands of people to see big-name performers ranging from the stars of Lollapalooza to the Moody Blues, Def Leppard to Crosby, Stills, and Nash, Bonnie Raitt to George Thorogood. You can bring a picnic, but no booze (they'll search your packs and toss it, so don't bother). Arrive early; the one country road leading to the Gorge amphitheater is not fit for crowds of this kind. For tickets, call Ticketmaster in Seattle, (206) 628-0888. George is a 3-hour drive from Seattle; you may find camping nearby (see Camping/Swimming/Picnics, above, or, for a small fee, camp at a partitioned area just above the concert site), but the closest lodgings are in Ellensburg, Vantage, or Ephrata.

Restaurants

Multnomah Falls Lodge   Now a National Historic Landmark, the lodge houses a popular naturalists' and visitors' center. It has a large restaurant that is a good stop for breakfast (weekends only in winter), but dinners are unremarkable (better to just go for dessert). *At the foot of the Multnomah Falls; (503) 695-2376; Hwy 30E at Multnomah Falls, near Bridle Veil; $$.*

Lodgings

For recommended lodgings, see the Adjoining Areas to this chapter.

More Information

Moses Lake Visitor Center: *324 S. Pioneer Way; (509) 765-7888.*

Yakima Valley

From Ellensburg south through Yakima Canyon, west to Naches, and southeast to Toppenish, including Prosser and Sunnyside and the Yakima Wine Country.

Here's the best place, bar none, to live and play in Washington. Assuming you're asparagus.

The Yakima Valley, which for our purposes begins in the Yakima River Canyon south of Ellensburg and stretches southeast to Toppenish, truly is Washington's fertile crescent. Some of the most productive soils in the state make the valley a national leader in cranking out apples, cherries, asparagus, corn, grapes, and other crops. All of this is made possible, of course, only by the cooperation of the Yakima River, which bubbles to life high on Snoqualmie Pass and leaves a swath of green in its wake as it flows southeast to the Columbia. The river, or at least that portion of it not siphoned off for irrigation, also serves as the recreation lifeblood of the Yakima Valley.

The Yakima also provides a world-class trout fishery—and regionally significant wildlife habitat—in the Yakima River Canyon. It's the star attraction along the Yakima River Greenway, this valley's leading recreation venue, as well as in most valley campgrounds.

It's hard to imagine life here without it. *Any* life. The Yakima Valley sans river would be a dust bowl. It rains less than 10 inches a year here (less than you might get in three days during the occasional Western Washington winter storm). Vegetation is sparse and—unless you get really excited about sage and tumbleweeds—nondescript. Take away the Yakima River, and all that's left is a long downtown strip of motels, ringed by more bowling alleys than you'll find anywhere this side of Omaha, Nebraska.

Lucky for you the river is here to stay, at least in some form. And the recreation venues it creates are surprisingly interesting, some even unique. The key to visiting this area—even more so than in most other places—is timing. The valley has become one of our favorite weekend getaways during the spring or late autumn, when local temperatures have cooled and conditions elsewhere (on the coast or in the mountains) are inhospitable. The Yakima River Canyon, in particular, is stunningly beautiful in both of these "shoulder seasons," decked out in bright fall leaves or brilliant spring wildflowers. Trout fishing in the river may be as pure an angling thrill as you can get in Washington, with catch-and-release restrictions designed to keep it that way. Hikers, particularly those who enjoy sweating a bit to share space with wild birds and mammals, can find refreshingly under-visited wildlife habitat in and around the valley, and a world of mountain exploration awaits a short distance to the east, in the Tieton River drainage.

The Yakima Valley, like the asparagus that sprouts from its floor, is a great natural product hampered by bad packaging. It might look funky and unappealing, but get it while it's fresh, and the flavor is hard to beat.

Getting There

Yakima is 142 miles east of Seattle via Interstate 90 and Interstate 82—an easy, all-freeway drive of about 2 1/2 hours. If there's time to spare, don't hesitate to drive Hwy 821, the Yakima Canyon Road, between Ellensburg and Selah, rather than take I-82 over the hill. It's one of the state's more visually lovely drives, and adds only about 30 minutes to the trip. In the summer, highly scenic routes to Yakima skirt Mount Rainier, via either Cayuse or Chinook Passes or US 12 (White Pass). Note: White Pass is the only Rainier-area mountain pass open all winter.

Adjoining Areas

NORTH: **I-90 East: Roslyn to Ellensburg**
SOUTH: **Goldendale and Maryhill**
EAST: **Tri-Cities**
WEST: **White Pass Corridor**

Fishing

It might be dry. It might be dusty. It might be hot and windy. But there's fishin' to be done here. The **Yakima River** north of Roza Dam is an intergalactically famous trout stream. The river's gentle pace, brushy bank cover, ample highway access, and Montana-like terrain make it an absolute favorite of fly casters. The Yakima is home to a healthy population of plump wild rainbow trout, which you must catch and release. This is a selective fishery, meaning only single, barbless hooks can be used, and no bait is allowed. A wide variety of flies is effective, but you can also fish with light spinning lures, provided they're equipped with single barbless hooks. The Yakima will test your casting mettle: most of the river's feisty trout hide from the sun under brushy bankside cover, which provides constant target practice. The river is open all year, and access is quite good from all along the Yakima Canyon Road. The Umtanum Creek parking area is popular because a suspension bridge allows foot access to the west side of the river. Watch for snakes!

Not far from the canyon's south outlet at Selah (take Wenas Road west) is **Wenas Lake,** an irrigation reservoir that holds some lunker-size brown trout, plus a mess of nice rainbows. It's open all year, and boat trollers have the best success.

West of Yakima in the Tieton River Valley, both the **Tieton River** and one clear, swift tributary, **Oak Creek,** offer decent rainbow trout fishing. Both receive annual rainbow plants from the state Department of Fish and Wildlife. Follow Hwy 12 west from Yakima.

Closer to town, **Cowiche Creek** (see Hiking and Wildlife, below) is a very scenic stream with good trail access and a healthy number of smaller rainbows. Outstanding bank access can be found at all seven of the **Freeway Ponds,** just west of I-82 between Union Gap and Zillah. This chain of small lakelets offers productive fishing for nearly every species imaginable. Warm-water fish—bass, walleye, perch, and the like—are very active here, but you can also find brown and rainbow trout.

A unique kids-only fishery is found at **Yakima Sportsman State Park** (see Camping, below), where ponds stocked with rainbows are open to anglers 15 and younger. Follow signs from I-82 exit 34.

Gary's Fly Shoppe (1210 W Lincoln; (509) 457-3474) is your best local-expert contact.

Camping

Yakima Sportsman State Park is the leading campground in the Yakima Valley, where campsites are sparse, to say the least. The park, with good access to the Yakima River, has 64 sites (36 with full hookups; spaces are pull-throughs!), a playground, kids' fishing ponds, and extensive (shady) picnic facilities. Yakima Sportsman is open all year. Campsites can be reserved up to 11 months in advance by calling Reservations Northwest;

(800) 452-5687. *Take I-82 exit 34 and follow signs from Hwy 24; (509) 575-2774 or (800) 233-0321.*

The **Yakima KOA** is the other major campground in the area, with 50 tent sites and 90 RV sites with full hookups and the usual KOA amenities. The riverside campground is open all year, and campsites can be reserved. *On Keyes Road in Yakima (take I-82 exit 24); (509) 248-5882.*

West of the city, in the **Ahtanum Creek** drainage, the state Department of Natural Resources maintains four small, free campgrounds. Unless you're riding a dirt bike or really enjoy the exhaust from other people's, don't bother.

Hiking

The dry, dusty lands around the Yakima Valley don't seem like hiker heaven, but some choice slices of it can be found by the industrious lugged-soler.

The **Yakima Greenway National Recreation Trail** (easy; 7 miles one way) is a pleasant, mostly paved walkway along the Yakima River's west bank between Selah Gap and Nob Hill Boulevard in Union Gap. The trail also is an excellent bikeway and wildlife-spotting venue. Major access points are at the Resthaven Road exit off I-82, Harlan Landing in Selah Gap, and Sarge Hubbard and Sherman Parks in Yakima. The Yakima Greenway folks—who developed and maintain this trail through a nonprofit agency—have done a great service to the valley. Pick up trash, follow the posted rules, and keep it pleasant.

A very interesting diversion, **Cowiche Canyon Conservancy Trail** (easy; 3 miles round trip), follows an abandoned railroad right of way along (and over, 11 times) Cowiche Creek, which cuts through basalt and andesite cliffs. This is another prime wildlife-watching area, with more than 50 bird species spotted in the canyon (also some rattlesnakes). At last check, the trail ended where a bridge is out, just over 1 1/2 miles from the start. But it should extend along the full 3 miles of right of way in years to come, and plans call for a connecting link to the Yakima Greenway Trail. It's a very nice walk, particularly in morning or evening, out of the harsh sunlight. The trailhead is off Weikel Road, three miles northwest of the city limits (take Summit View Avenue).

In the Yakima River Canyon, a number of trails skirt the high cliffs of **Umtanum Ridge,** with views of the river. A good day hike is the short, steep climb up the old road from the Umtanum Creek Recreation Area parking lot, about 12 miles south of Ellensburg (cross the river on the suspension bridge). The trail leads about 1 1/2 miles to the ridge top, which offers sweeping views of the canyon. On the same (west) side of the river, the **Yakima Rim Skyline Trail** (moderate; 15 miles one way) stretches along the ridge top. The best of several tough-to-find accesses to this high, dry (no water) trail is the northern trailhead, found on the old Jacob Durr Wagon Road (from Selah, take North Wenas Avenue and Wenas Creek Road, turn right on Sheep Company Road, and proceed to Durr Road). This mostly flat ridge-top hike with sweet mountain and canyon views is very popular in the spring, when wildflowers are aburst along the path, and other Cascade trails remain snowed in. The surrounding lands are part of the L. T. Murray Wildlife Area.

A wide range of scenic hikes in the **Tieton River Valley** is found off of Hwy 12, about 1 hour east of Yakima. (See the White Pass Corridor chapter.)

Cycling

The most popular cycling out here involves following the grape: riders can enjoy loop tours of the Yakima Valley by visiting its wineries (see Attractions, below). Contact the Yakima Valley Wine Growers Association (PO Box 39, Grandview, WA 98930) for maps and information.

Wildlife

The Yakima Valley is a standout on the Washington Watchable Wildlife tour. Two popular trails, the Greenway Trail and the Cowiche Canyon Trail (see Hiking, above), are great places to see a wide range of birds and small mammals. The Greenway Trail, which runs along the west bank of the Yakima, is an increasingly popular **bald eagle** hangout. Many of the regal birds are attracted here to feed on fish. The Yakima Arboretum, near the south end of the 3,600-acre Greenway, is another rich bird-watching spot. Take I-82 exit 34. Yakima Sportsman State Park's ponds and Yakima River banks also are prime bird-watching territory. (See Camping, above.) The entire length of the Yakima River Canyon, reached by driving Hwy 821 between Ellensburg and Yakima, is rich with wildlife. Broad expanses of canyon uplands west of the river are managed as wildlife habitat in the L. T. Murray Wildlife Area. It's mostly designed as a reserve for **mule deer, elk,** and **California bighorn sheep,** but the high cliffs and valley shrub steppe also draw large numbers of **raptors.** Twenty-one raptor species have been observed here, and 10 are known to nest in the valley. As you drive the canyon, use roadside pullouts as a chance to get out of the car and watch for **bald eagles,** any of 11 **hawk** or **falcon** species, 5 **owl** species, and other rare birds, such as **American kestrels** and **osprey.** If you want to get out on foot, consider the Umtanum Canyon Trail, which begins across the suspension bridge from the Umtanum Recreation Area parking lot. (Watch for snakes.)

For an excellent booklet detailing the bird species of the canyon—and better yet, when they're likely to appear—write the Bureau of Land Management's Wenatchee Resource Area, 915 Walla Walla Avenue, Wenatchee, WA 98801. The free booklet and a pair of binoculars can make for a very inexpensive, but quite memorable, daylong outing. Birders also will enjoy the Boise Cascade Park and Bird Sanctuary, 5 miles west of Selah on Wenas Road. It's a 40-acre preserve where more than 100 bird species have been spotted.

Finally, one of Washington's most popular wildlife-watching venues, the Oak Creek Wildlife Area just east of Naches, is only a 30-minute drive from downtown Yakima. It's the annual winter home to the state's biggest single herd of **Rocky Mountain elk,** which are fed here daily as soon as snows drive the herd down from high areas. Without the hay-feeding program—largely financed by sportsmen's groups—most of these elk would starve. Hundreds of miles of game fences lock them out of valley lowlands where they'd normally congregate in the winter to feed on grass—and crops. The feeding station is definitely worth a trip in the winter. It's as close to wild elk as you're likely to get, and kids absolutely love it. A **bighorn sheep** feeding station is nearby, at the base of Clemens Mountain. Follow Old Naches Road from the US 12/Hwy 410 junction.

Rafting

Very scenic, not-too-raucous float trips can be made down the **Yakima River Canyon** between Ellensburg and the Roza Dam. Call River Raft Rentals in Ellensburg, (509) 964-2145, for rentals. These are relaxing, beautiful trips, with a good chance of spotting deer, elk, bighorn sheep, and other wildlife. Good public access is along Hwy 821.

To the west, the scenic **Tieton River** becomes a raging gusher in September, when water is released from the reservoir above. It's one of Washington's most popular whitewater-rafting venues, particularly since it's about the only whitewater show in town at the end of summer. Contact Naches Ranger District, (509) 653-2205, for referrals to the dozens of commercial raft companies that book trips on the river.

Skiing

Terrific downhill and cross-country ski facilities are less than 1 hour's drive west of Yakima at **White Pass** on US 12. (See the White Pass Corridor chapter for details.)

outside in

Attractions

Welcome to Napa Lite. If your last visit to the Napa Valley recalled rush-hour traffic on the freeway to Disneyland, you may be ready for the less traveled, more organic pleasures of the **Yakima wine country.** Get off the freeway at virtually any point between Union and the Tri-Cities and you'll find a scene of unspoiled pastoral splendor. (See also the Tri-Cities chapter.) Vineyards and orchards follow the meandering Yakima River. Cattle graze the pastures. And the small towns scattered here and there provide constant surprises and unexpected small pleasures. The burgeoning wine industry (you'll find close to two dozen wineries in the valley, and more on the way) has encouraged small businesses to go after the tourist trade. Warm welcomes in the shops and tasting rooms are genuine; they really are glad to see you.

Since vineyards were first planted about two decades ago, the valley's unique weather patterns—warm days, cool nights, with seemingly more daylight than down in Napa—have encouraged winemakers to develop new approaches to their craft. A Northwest style has emerged: bright fruit flavors underscored by crisp acids. The white wines are mostly dry (even the rieslings tend that way) and firmer than their counterparts in California, while the reds are rich and textured, with the structure of fine Bordeaux. Prices are low, and wineries often sell special bottlings unavailable elsewhere.

The Yakima Valley Wine Growers Association (PO Box 39, Grandview, WA 98930) publishes a useful brochure that lists member wineries along with tasting-room hours, easy-to-follow maps, and a bit of history. Big or small, all offer a taste of what's new and a chance to chat about the vintage in the most relaxed circumstances.

Yakima's **Front Street Historical District** includes a 22-car train that houses shops and restaurants, and the renovated Pacific Fruit Exchange Building, which holds a local farmers market. The restored, 1906 **Interurban Trolley** provides summer evening and weekend rides around Yakima. Call (509) 575-1700 for schedules. For fans of horse racing, **Yakima Meadows** has live races November through March. It's a dandy place to watch small-town, Old West racing (1301 S 10th; (509) 248-3920.) The **Yakima Valley Museum** has handsome pioneer pieces, plus a collection from Yakima's most famous native son, Justice William O. Douglas. (Open every day; 2105 Tieton Drive; (509) 248-0747.)

Western artist Fred Oldfield was raised here and returns occasionally at the request of the **Toppenish Mural Society,** (509) 865-6516, to lead a mural-painting posse. As a result, the whole town is an art gallery, with 10 large walls covered in murals and more planned. Clusters of Western shops, antique stores, and galleries make strolling and shopping pleasant, and there are rodeos scheduled throughout the summer months.

The **Yakama Nation Cultural Center,** located on ancestral grounds, houses a Native American museum and reference library, plus a gift shop, a Native American restaurant, a commercial movie/performing arts theater, and the 76-foot-tall Winter Lodge for conventions and banquets. Open every day (closed January and February). (On Fort Road off Hwy 97, Toppenish; (509) 865-2800.) **Fort Simcoe** was built in 1856, and its Gothic Revival officers' quarters still stand in desolate grandeur; 28 miles west of Toppenish on Route 220.

Cherries have always grown well in the Yakima Valley, except when the weather doesn't cooperate. Too much rain cracks cherries, too little leaves them small. **Chukar Cherries** turns imperfect fruit into a year-round delicacy—dried cherries. In the showroom of their production center you'll also see chocolate-covered cherries, cherry poultry sauce, and even cherry waffle mix (306 Wine Country Road, Prosser, (509) 786-2055.)

Restaurants

Birchfield Manor ☆☆   Birchfield Manor offers elegant French country dining right in Yakima. Ambitious and imaginative, they let the food set the mood for a formal evening, and offer a one-of-a-kind experience here in Central Washington. There are five B&B rooms upstairs, and two fireplace suites for a chunk more change. An outdoor pool and hot tub are for guests only. *Take exit 34 off I-82 onto Hwy 24, head east 2 miles, then south on Birchfield; (509) 452-1960; 2018 Birchfield Rd, Yakima; $$$.*

Deli de Pasta ☆   The North Front Street area is a comfortable blend of the old, the funky, and the hip. A half block south of The Brewery Pub, this intimate Italian cafe is quite popular with the locals. Fresh pastas and sauces, made on the premises, can be mixed and matched to suit your mood. *1/2 block off Yakima on N Front St; (509) 453-0571; 7 N Front St, Yakima; $.*

Dykstra House Restaurant   Who can resist a restaurant that features bread made from hand-ground whole wheat grown in the Horse Heaven Hills? Rich desserts and a few choice Washington State wines complement this 1914 Grandview mansion's simple menu, which changes daily. *Exit 73 off I-82, 1 1/2 miles on Wine Country Rd; (509) 882-2082; 114 Birch Ave, Grandview; $$.*

Gasperetti's Restaurant ☆☆☆   This Northern Italian restaurant in Yakima continues to be one of the most innovative in the region. The space is intimate, casual and elegant, and the wine list has an excellent selection of Washington wines, as well as many Italian labels. Service is informed, unobtrusive, and a world away from the busy street outside. *6 blocks south of the N Front St exit off I-82; (509) 248-0628; 1013 N 1st St, Yakima; $$.*

Grant's Pub ☆   Bert Grant, one of the creators of the Northwest's boom in microbreweries, has brought back full-flavored, fresh, locally made ales and stouts. The pub is in the old train station in Yakima, where small experimental batches are brewed (the bulk of the beer is made 2 miles south). British pub menu. A good place to meet friendly residents. *Head west on Yakima, turn right on Front St; (509) 575-2922; 32 N Front St, Yakima; $.*

Santiago's ☆   A Mexican courtyard in downtown Yakima! The chalupas and the tacos Santiago are especially popular. Steak picado (their version of fajitas) was on the menu long before the sizzling sirloin strips became chic at every other Mexican restaurant. *Close to the intersection of 1st and Yakima; (509) 453-1644; 111 E Yakima Ave, Yakima; $.*

Cheaper Eats

El Ranchito   Here in hops- and fruit-growing country, home to many Mexican Americans, is a jolly Zillah tortilla factory-cum-cafeteria that makes a perfect midday stop. You eat in the large dining area or in the cool, flower-shaded patio during the summer. There is a Mexican bakery on the premises, but no cerveza. *Exit 54 off I-82, follow the signs; (509) 829-5880; 1319 E 1st Ave, Zillah; $.*

Taqueria La Fogata   Here in Sunnyside is a small, simple roadside Mexican taqueria doing a lot of things right. The clientele is clearly local, the help clearly Mexican, and the menu expansive. The service is friendly and prices prehistoric. *In Sunnyside; (509) 839-9019; 1204 Yakima Valley Hwy, Sunnyside; $.*

Lodgings

Rio Mirada Motor Inn ☆   This Yakima Best Western motel, just off the I-82 freeway and right next to the shimmering Yakima River, doesn't look like much from the road. Once inside, you'll find 96 attractive, moderately priced rooms, each with a small balcony and a view of the river. A few rooms have kitchenettes. A pleasant 7-mile path runs along the riverbank. *Exit 33 off I-82; (509) 457-4444; 1603 Terrace Heights Dr, Yakima; $$.*

Sunnyside Inn Bed and Breakfast ☆   The 8 bedrooms in this 1919 home are huge (so big they sometimes feel empty), 4 have outside entrances, and all come with phones, cable TV, air conditioning, and enormous private baths with Jacuzzi tubs. For those who like the friendliness of B&Bs but need their fair share of privacy, this place is a godsend. *Exit 63 or 69 off I-82; (509) 839-5557; 804 E Edison Ave, Sunnyside; $.*

Cheaper Sleeps

Wine Country Inn Bed & Breakfast   A welcome addition to the limited overnight options in Prosser, this riverside home has 3 rooms upstairs and 1 down. The river winds lazily by the front door and the adjoining restaurant turns out terrific country breakfasts, lunches, and ample, hearty dinners. *Exit 80 off I-82, near bridge in Prosser; (509) 786-2855; 1106 Wine Country Rd, Prosser.*

More Information

Yakima Visitors and Convention Bureau: *(800) 221-0751.*
Naches Ranger District: *(509) 653-2205.*

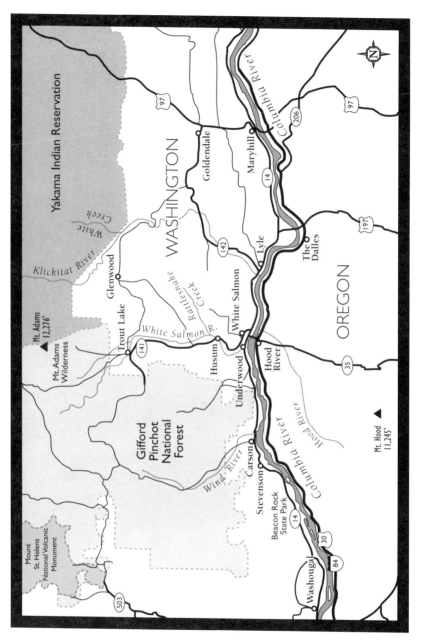

Columbia
River
Gorge

Bridge of the Gods: Stevenson and Beacon Rock

From North Bonneville east to Dog Mountain, and north through the Wind River Gorge, including Beacon Rock State Park, Home Valley, and the Skamania Lodge area.

If Lewis and Clark could see all these boardheads, they'd probably make careful notes, sketch out a drawing or two—then run like hell.

Not that they were unaccustomed to new sights. On their long, slow journey through these then-inhospitable parts in 1805, the pair of explorers encountered unfamiliar wilderness, weather, and Native cultures.

But the speeds of the board sailors would have thrown the canoe-and-barge-trained explorers for a loop or two. When winds, as they often still do, howled at 40mph through the Columbia River Gorge, Lewis and Clark parked the boats and waited. When gale-force winds howl through the Gorge these days, surf's up for the region's thousands of wind surfers, who launch from the beaches on both the Washington and Oregon sides to chase after the hottest board-sailing action in the country, if not the world. The Gorge, particularly this stretch of it, is board-sailing central, U.S.A. The sport has turned the little town of Hood River, just across the Columbia, into a thriving sports hub with year-round action, and much of that activity spills across Columbia River bridges to the Washington side.

Windsurfing is the hottest participatory and spectator sport in this region, but it's far from the only one. To the north, a rich, volcano-forged mountain wonderland in the Gifford Pinchot National Forest provides top-rate camping and hiking action, in the Wind River drainage south of Mount St. Helens. In the summer, you can negotiate the back-roads and drive practically right to St. Helens itself.

But plenty of wonder is found right outside the motel room (or tent) door. The Columbia Gorge is one of the most awesome physical wonders in North America, and this stretch is the most scenic on the Washington side. The Gorge, a river-carved swath through the Cascades so deep and wide that it literally creates its own weather, is a showcase for the awesome natural features of the Northwest. Its walls, sliced cleanly by the most powerful river in the country, are visible cross-sections of the Cascades, revealing volcanic features such as massive Beacon Rock and graced by countless plunging waterfalls and stunning vistas.

A sight even more fantastic exists, however, in the imagination of visitors to the Stevenson area. The small bridge crossing the Columbia today to Cascades Locks, Oregon, is a "Bridge of the Gods" in name only. The real bridge, according to Native American legend, was a natural one: a massive stone arch that bridged the river after a landslide clogged the waterway, forcing the river to tunnel beneath it. The bridge, as the legend goes, eventually gave way, forming the raucous Cascades of the Columbia rapids that Lewis and Clark encountered on their way west (since flooded by Bonneville Dam). Geologists believe the tale has merit, noting that eruptions of Mount Hood and Mount Adams, which loom close by to the south and north, could have caused such massive land shifts. (See the interpretive display in a roadside pullout, just east of the Bridge of the Gods.)

From the top of Beacon Rock, elevation 1,048 feet, it doesn't take much imagination to look east up the Gorge and imagine the natural bridge. The rock is one of the most striking features in the Gorge. That somehow seems comforting. All those hydro plants down below will, like the legendary Bridge of the Gods, give way one day—with as little resistance as the windsurfers flying between them.

Getting There

Stevenson is 40 miles east of Vancouver on Hwy 14, which follows the Washington side of the Columbia River Gorge. Allow about 3 hours from the Seattle area.

Adjoining Areas

NORTH: **Mount St. Helens**

EAST: **White Salmon and Bingen**

inside out

Hiking

Along Hwy 14 itself, several options await weary drivers itching for some vertical followed by great scenery. Beacon Rock State Park has its own 14-mile trail system. The highlight is the **Beacon Rock Trail** (moderate/difficult; 2 miles round trip), which follows a meticulously carved path (most of which is guarded by handrails) up 53 switchbacks to the summit of the ancient, 850-foot volcanic plug. (Keep a tight rein on the kids here; the handrails make the steep trail fairly safe, but short people can slide underneath.) A major-league view awaits at the top of this rock, which is considered the largest monolith in North America, second on the planet only to Gibraltar.

On the north side of Hwy 14, **Beacon Rock State Park** proper offers a dozen miles of other pleasant trails. The most popular one begins in the main day-use area and climbs about a mile up Hardy Creek to beautiful **Rodney and Hardy Falls** (easy; about 2 miles round trip) and ultimately the top of **Hamilton Mountain** (difficult; about 4 miles round trip). These paths, which can be combined with a string of fire roads (see Mountain Biking, below) for daylong loop hikes, make Beacon Rock a great place to spend a day, whether you're camping here, passing through, or staying at Skamania Lodge.

Just to the east on Hwy 14, a little-known interpretive trail that overlooks the Bonneville Dam makes a good leg-stretcher. The **Fort Cascades Trail** (easy; 1.5 miles round trip) loops along the river bluff through the site of the former fort and town of Cascades. The turnoff is near the North Bonneville Powerhouse, just past milepost 38.

Farther along Hwy 14, about 9 miles east of Carson, is the **Dog Mountain Trail** (difficult; 6.5 miles round trip), which climbs swiftly from the Gorge floor to a trail fork (one part of this trail is a former route of the Pacific Crest Trail) about a half mile up. Take either path, but the left one is a steeper, more direct route to the summit, where the view of the Gorge and Mount Hood from a former lookout site is absolutely splendid. This is a beautiful hike in the spring, when wildflowers are blooming on the upper reaches. But bring plenty of water. Total elevation gain is about 2,800 feet. The trailhead is near milepost 53.

Also note that the **Pacific Crest Trail** crosses the Columbia at Bridge of the Gods, then heads northwest through the Gifford Pinchot National Forest. The section of the trail within short day-hiking distance of the Gorge isn't very scenic or interesting. But you can park at the trailhead near the bridge and follow the trail north for several hours or several weeks: it's only about 500 miles to the Canadian border.

Some very scenic hiking awaits in the volcano-shaped lands of the southern Gifford Pinchot National Forest, north of Carson in the Wind River drainage. For a full list, as well as for local road and trail conditions, contact the Wind River Ranger District; (509) 427-3200. Following are a few favorites.

In the upper valley, the **Lava Butte Trail** (easy; 1.2 miles round trip) begins at Paradise Creek Campground on Wind River Road and climbs to a clearcut butte with a good regional view of the surrounding volcanic landscape. It's far from spectacular, but makes a nice day hike for campers in the area. Just off Forest Service Road 64, which turns west of the Wind River Road about 16 miles north of Carson, the **Paradise Trail** (moderate; 5 miles round trip) climbs to the top of Paradise Ridge, then follows it north to a second trailhead. Good views all along. One of the most popular hikes in this area is **Upper Falls Creek** (moderate; 8 miles round trip), which climbs to a 100-foot waterfall plunging from a magical deep, clear pool. The trailhead is on Forest Service Road 3062, which turns east off Wind River Road about 15 miles north of Carson.

On the east side of the Wind River drainage are a handful of other worthwhile Gifford Pinchot National Forest hikes. The **Observation Trail** (moderate; 16.5 miles round trip) climbs through forest before breaking out to grand views on the slopes of Observation Peak and Sisters Rocks. The view from the top of Observation Peak (reached by a short way trail, about 6 miles from the trailhead) is stupendous, with Rainier, St. Helens, and Hood all on display. Decent campsites are found along the route, although the climb to Observation and back (about 11.5 miles) can be made in a day by strong hikers. The trailhead is on Forest Service Road 5401, reached by following Wind River Road 8 miles north to Mineral Springs Road and following it west. Nearby, off Forest Service Road 34, the **West Crater Trail** (easy/moderate; 1.5 miles round trip) climbs along the rim of an ancient volcano crater, a fascinating spot. Follow Wind River and Hemlock Roads to Forest Service Road 54, then turn left on Road 34.

Slightly to the south is **Zig Zag Loop** (moderate/difficult; 1 mile round trip), a short but steep trail through a nice forest to an alpine lake that contains Eastern brook trout. The trailhead is on Forest Service Road 42. An easy hike that's palatable and engaging enough for children is the **Lower Falls Creek Trail** (easy; 3.4 miles round trip), which climbs gently through a cool, mossy forest to a bridge vista of a 100-foot waterfall. Follow Wind River Road north to Road 3062, turn east for 1.5 miles, then turn right on Road 57.

Fans of big, wide-open views won't be disappointed by the **Bunker**

Hill Trail (moderate; 4 miles round trip), which follows the Pacific Crest Trail for about a mile before climbing steeply (about 1,300 feet) to this former fire lookout site, where fantastic views await in all directions. Follow Wind River Road to Hemlock Road, turn west for just over a mile to Road 43, then turn right and drive a half-mile to Road 43-417. Watch for Pacific Crest Trail markers to the trailhead.

Camping

Beacon Rock State Park is the primary campground in this region, with two separate camping areas and a 200-person group camp. In all, the park offers 33 campsites (no hookups; maximum RV length, 50 feet). The best ones are in the main, upland camping area, but a handful of more primitive (also more scenic, also more windy) sites are found across the narrow Hwy 14 bridge in the park's marine area, where a boat launch is located. (Note: The marine area suffered flood damage in the spring of 1996. Call the park for updates.) Beacon Rock is open all year. Campsites cannot be reserved. *35 miles east of Vancouver on Hwy 14; (509) 427-8265 or (800) 233-0321.*

A handful of more primitive, but occasionally quite pleasant Gifford Pinchot National Forest campgrounds are found in the Wind River Drainage, reached by following Wind River Road north from Carson. **Panther Creek** (33 sites) and **Beaver** (24 sites), both near the Wind River Ranger Station, are the closest. Farther north, near the south border of Indian Heaven Wilderness, are **Paradise Creek** (42 sites) and **Falls Creek Horse Camp** (12 small sites). All are open summers only, and campsites cannot be reserved. Call the Wind River Ranger District, (509) 427-3200, for road information. Winter washouts are common in this area.

Windsurfing

The Washington side of the Gorge isn't as widely known for windsurfing as the Oregon side. But savvy riders know several beaches that are as good as the Gorge gets when winds cooperate. Here's a list of Washington windsurfing beaches and vista points for those seeking to get wet or just to watch.

Rock Creek Pond in Stevenson is on a shallow, protected inland lake better suited to beginners than most Gorge locations. It's on Rock Creek Drive between Stevenson and Skamania Lodge. Another local hot spot, **Bob's Beach** at Stevenson Landing, draws large crowds of intermediate-to-expert surfers, who are advised to watch out for the big paddlewheeler that docks here. Farther east, **Home Valley Park** is a favorite beginner-to-intermediate spot, and **Drano Lake** is a noted area for beginners. Follow signs to the Drano Lake boat launch from Hwy 14. In this area, expert sailors usually are found farther east at **Swell City** (see the White Salmon and Bingen chapter).

To discover the world's foremost collection of windsurfing gear, supplies, lessons, and lore cross the Columbia at Bridge of the Gods or White Salmon and trek to Hood River, home to a dozen sailing shops. Beginners: You'll be wasting valuable time if you don't take a lesson. They're available from a dozen board shops in Hood River and usually cost about $125 for full gear and two days of instructions. A leading provider is Rhonda Smith's Windsurf Center in Hood River; (800) 241-2430.

For updated wind conditions, call (800) 562-BLOW from a touch-tone phone anywhere in North America. The reports are mostly centered on Hood River–area beaches, but they're a good general wind indicator. For specific beach weather reports, including many on the Washington side, call Windsight at (900) 860-0600. It costs $1.50 per minute.

Traveling tourists who just want to know where to go to watch should tune radios to 104.5 FM, a Hood River station that offers wind updates and "noteworthy boardhead news" all day long. For planning a Gorge board-sailing vacation, pick up a copy of *The Gorge Guide,* available at most Seattle-area outdoor stores, or contact the Columbia Gorge Windsurfing Association; (541) 386-9225.

Canoeing/Kayaking

Paddlers, particularly sea kayakers, are drawn to the rocky shores, towering cliffs, and interesting inlets of the Columbia River. Frequent high winds, coupled with heavy boat and barge traffic and dangers from dams and river locks, make the Columbia itself an experts-only area. Good launch points include **Beacon Rock State Park, Skamania Landing, North Bonneville boat launch, Rock Creek Park, Stevenson Landing, Stevenson boat launch,** and **Home Valley Park**. The one good beginner area here is **Drano Lake,** also an interesting canoe venue, where waters are calm most of the time. Follow signs to the boat launch from Hwy 14. The **Upper Wind River** is a noted whitewater kayak stretch.

Fishing

The **lower Columbia River** below Bonneville Dam is a world-famous fishery, noted both for its once abundant salmon (now troubled; seasons are truncated) and its healthy steelhead populations. Fishing for steelhead still can be productive here, both from boats and banks. Keep in mind that all wild steelhead must be released.

If you're after the big one—the really, really big one—consider a guided lower-river sturgeon trip. These babies are literally monsters, with some growing to 20 feet. They're uglier than sin, with giant sucker mouths and long, reptilian bodies. You can only keep sturgeon between 42 and 66 inches, but, for the catch-and-release experience of a lifetime, many Columbia guides steer clients to fish that are longer than the boat. The peak season is June and July. Experienced anglers hook a good number of sturgeon from the shore, fishing a shad or smelt bait off the bottom.

An increasingly popular Columbia fishery is the robust lower-river shad run, which peaks in June. The hot spot is the water below Bonneville Dam. Bank casters on both sides of the river do well with just about any kind of cast-and-retrieve tackle. Shad, basically overgrown herring, aren't much for eating. But they're fun to catch, and as of this writing, there's no limit on them.

For years, the **Wind River** was known for a productive chinook salmon run. But as with other Columbia chinook runs, hydropower, over-fishing, and a half-dozen other factors have combined to snuff most of it. The river does still have a semiproductive, hatchery-produced summer steelhead run, with the best fishing in July and August. All wild steelhead must be released here. Reliable river reports sometimes can be had by inquiring at Carson Hot Springs, (509) 427-8292.

Wildlife

For fish fans and kids young and old, the **Bonneville Dam Fishway and Visitors Center** is a must-stop, particularly if you're in the area during a summer **salmon migration**. Fish runs in the mighty Columbia are mere fractions of their former numbers, but because all steelhead and salmon stocks returning to dozens of rivers in eastern Washington, Oregon, and southern Idaho must pass through this hydropower funnel, the fish windows at Bonneville usually are alive with movement. Spring chinook pass through in April and May, but other chinook, coho, sockeye, and steelhead pass through the ladder for most of the summer. The center is open daily until 5pm, 8pm during summer months. Follow signs from Hwy 14 between Beacon Rock and Stevenson; (509) 427-4281.

Another fish-viewing area is the **Carson National Fish Hatchery** near the Wind River Ranger Station on Wind River Road north of Carson. The hatchery, which raises salmon and trout smolts, welcomes visitors.

Mountain Biking

Options are somewhat limited in this water-and-rock dominated landscape. But fat-tire hounds can work up a good sweat on the 13 miles of fire roads in the upland area of **Beacon Rock State Park** (see the Camping and Hiking sections, above). From the main park entrance, follow signs to the group camp area and watch for the gated road on the right. The road leads about 5 miles north, and a 10-mile loop around Hamilton Mountain is possible. Some Forest Service roads in the Wind River drainage also are suitable for mountain-bike touring. Contact the Wind River Ranger District, (509) 427-3200, for information.

Climbing

The front face of 848-foot **Beacon Rock** is a major rock-climbing destination, attracting experts who take on some 60 routes, many among the most technically challenging in the Northwest, with ratings up to 5.10. Climbing was halted recently because of concerns about nesting peregrine falcons on the rock, but it has since resumed. An access trail leads down from the parking area on the south side of Hwy 14.

Cross-Country Skiing

The **Wind River Sno-Park**, at Oldman Pass, 25 miles north of Carson on Wind River Road, is a launching pad to 22.5 kilometers of cross-country trails, which are groomed from December 15 to April 1. The Sno-Park—actually four separate winter parking areas spread along the highway—is a great place for beginner and intermediate skiers; all of the trails are rated easy. The more adventurous skier can head off on an additional 25 kilometers of marked but unmaintained ski trails on local Forest Service roads. Cars must have a state Sno-Park parking permit, available at ski and outdoor stores and Ranger District offices. For snow updates, call the Wind River Ranger District at Carson; (509) 427-3200.

Adventure Calendar

The annual **Gorge Games**, centered in Hood River and including mountain biking, snowboarding, rock climbing, windsurfing, kayaking, running, paragliding, and kite-skiing, are the third week in July; (541) 386-1327.

Attractions

In **Stevenson**, stop by the newly opened **Columbia Gorge Interpretive Center** for a history of the Gorge, including a nine-projector slide show that re-creates the Gorge's cataclysmic formation; Native American fishing platforms; and a 37-foot-high replica of a 19th-century fishwheel. Just west of Stevenson off Hwy 14; (509) 427-8211. Summertime cruises are offered on the **sternwheeler** *Columbia Gorge,* which departs from Stevenson's Marine Park at 10am, 12:30 and 3pm daily. Call (509) 374-8427.

The eccentric **Carson Hot Springs**, established in 1897 and reminiscent of a time when the sickly "took the waters" to improve their health, is today a bit worn. We still, however, recommend the hot mineral bath ($8), after which you're swathed in towels and blankets for a short rest. The women's side is much more crowded than the men's, so if you visit in a mixed group, the men will finish sooner. To avoid this problem, reserve a massage in advance ($32 per hour) and a bath time will also be reserved for you. Don't expect as healthy a treatment from the restaurant. PO Box 370, Carson, WA 98610; (509) 427-8292.

Nature lovers should make the trip north to the **Wind River Nursery,** a working U.S. Forest Service tree farm in existence since 1909. An interpretive trail leads through the large tree-growing facility. It's about 10 miles north of Carson, near the Wind River Ranger Station; (509) 427-5645.

Restaurants

For recommended restaurants, see the Adjoining Areas to this chapter.

Lodgings

Skamania Lodge ☆☆   The lodge was not meant to be a luxury resort; it's a 195-room park resort and conference center, whose main element of grandeur is its massive stone-and-wood lobby. Guests have use of an 18-hole golf course, tennis courts, a lap pool, saunas, and an outdoor hot tub. The U.S. Forest Service's information center in the lobby provides maps and information on Gorge activities. *Just west of Stevenson; (509) 427-7700 or (800) 221-7117; 1131 Skamania Lodge Way, Stevenson; $$$.*

More Information

Columbia Gorge Windsurfing Association: *(541) 386-9225.*
Columbia River Gorge National Scenic Area: *(509) 493-3323.*
Skamania County Chamber of Commerce: *(800) 989-9178.*
Wind River Ranger District: *(509) 427-3200.*

White Salmon
and Bingen

From Drano Lake north to Husum and east to Lyle, including the lower White Salmon and Little White Salmon river valleys.

White Salmon itself isn't an outdoor lover's paradise. But you can certainly see the outdoors from here. Any direction you look, as a matter of fact. Located as it is near the geographic center of the Northwest, White Salmon has a South Cascades wonderland (the Mount Adams Wilderness) to the northwest, Hood River and Mount Hood across the Columbia River to the south, and the Columbia Gorge extending east and west from either end of town.

That makes the outdoor lineup predictable but rich. In the summertime, White Salmon is a good launching point for Gorge windsurfing or fishing expeditions; hiking on Mount Adams Wilderness trails to the north, near Trout Lake; and rafting or just general cavorting on the scenic White Salmon River. In the winter, roads to the north are closed, and White Salmon becomes a quiet, peaceful getaway, with rich wildlife-viewing opportunities in the Gorge and at its many fish hatcheries. All things considered, White Salmon is a good, central location for many days worth of Gorge exploration.

Getting There

White Salmon is 65 miles east of Vancouver on Hwy 14. For travelers driving the Oregon side of the Columbia River Gorge, White Salmon is directly across the Columbia River bridge from Hood River, Oregon.

Adjoining Areas

NORTH: **Mount Adams**

EAST: **Goldendale and Maryhill**
WEST: **Bridge of the Gods: Stevenson and Beacon Rock**

inside out

Windsurfing

The White Salmon area is home to some of the best windsurfing on either side of the entire Columbia River Gorge. When the wind is strong, the bulk of the area's board-sailing faithful might start the day in Hood River, Oregon, but many board sailors quickly become part of the northbound traffic on the Hood River–White Salmon bridge.

One of Washington's board-sailing hot spots, **Swell City,** is found close by, near Hwy 14 milepost 61, 4 miles west of the Hood River Bridge. The spot seems made for windsurfing: a small, protected bay gets you on your feet, and several yards farther south, the big winds turn on the gas. The river here is known for its consistently ripping west gales, making Swell City a top spot for advanced Gorge sailors. Parking is limited and is maxed out quickly on good wind days.

A half-mile east is another mostly experts area, **Spring Creek Hatchery.** Access to the river through the fish hatchery isn't great, and parking is very limited. Launching also can be tricky on the riprap bank. Winds are slightly tamer, amenities certainly more comforting, at the **Klickitat Point** windsurfing beach near **Bingen Marina.** The parking area is spacious, and the site offers plenty of rigging room. Veterans advise: Watch out for deadheads (logs that float just beneath the surface)!

Farther east, 2.5 miles beyond Lyle, is another longtime access point, **Doug's Beach State Park,** named after Doug Campbell of Hood River Windsurfing. Parking is along the south shoulder of Hwy 14, where you'll need to cross the busy Burlington Northern tracks. A small, sandy beach makes a good launching point, and big waves and big winds (30mph gales aren't unusual) make this an experts-only beach. Beware of barge traffic close to the shore.

For more information on windsurfing lessons and supplies and on Hood River, Oregon, see the Bridge of the Gods: Stevenson and Beacon Rock chapter.

Hiking

Hiking terrain is scarce on the floor of the steep-sided Gorge, but many quality hikes are found in the Mount Adams and Indian Heaven

Wilderness areas around Trout Lake. And two Gifford Pinchot trails in the region are a short distance north of White Salmon off Hwy 141.

A fairly easy trail that climbs to nice views at a former lookout site is the **Monte Cristo Trail** (easy; 8 miles round trip), which begins south of Trout Lake and climbs very gradually to the twin summits of Monte Cristo and Monte Carlo. To reach the trailhead from Hwy 141, turn south on Road 80 3 miles west of Trout Lake, then turn west on Road 86-080.

A more difficult hike near Little Goose Horse Camp, the **Little Huckleberry Trail** (moderate/difficult; 5 miles round trip) climbs steeply to a summit with a grand view of the Big Lava Bed and Goose Lake. The trailhead is about 2 miles west of Little Goose Horse Camp on Hwy 141.

A very popular Gorge trail nearby is the **Dog Mountain Trail.** See the Bridge of the Gods: Stevenson and Beacon Rock chapter.

Fishing

Much of the sport-fishing action here centers on **Drano Lake,** at the mouth of the **Little White Salmon River** east of Cook. Seasonal highlights are the spring (April/May) chinook fishery, and the fall (August/September) chinook and steelhead seasons. The spring season has been iffy in recent years because of troubled chinook stocks in the Columbia system, so call the Mt. Adams Ranger District, (509) 395-3400, before you go. A boat launch is located on the north side of the lake.

Conditions are similar on the **White Salmon River** to the west, where strong numbers of steelhead and salmon catches are made around the river's mouth in the spring and fall. Upriver several miles on Hwy 141, decent trout fishing breaks out every spring in **Northwestern Lake,** a reservoir on the White Salmon. Trout also are stocked in **Rowland Lake,** a Columbia River pond bisected by Hwy 14 east of Bingen.

The pooled-up **Columbia River** in this region also is a productive fishery. See the Fishing/Boating section of the Goldendale and Maryhill chapter for details.

Camping

Options are somewhat limited here, unless you want to drive an hour north up Hwy 141 to one of the two dozen small-but-scenic Forest Service campgrounds in the Trout Lake area of the White Salmon River drainage. See the Mount Adams chapter for details.

Closer to the Gorge are two other Forest Service camps, **Moss Creek** (18 sites) and **Oklahoma** (23 sites), which are 8 and 14 miles north of Cook, respectively (drive north on County Road 86). Both are open summers only. Campsites cannot be reserved. *Contact Mount Adams Ranger District in Trout Lake; (509) 395-3400.*

Wildlife

Another good Gorge fish-watching station, the **Little White Salmon National Fish Hatchery,** is at the mouth of the Little White Salmon River between Home Valley and White Salmon. Chinook and coho spawn in the lower river, attracting flocks of **osprey** and **bald eagles,** which feed on the spent carcasses. Eagles are commonly seen here throughout the winter, and salmon are visible in the hatchery ponds. Best viewing times are during the spring chinook run in June and July and the fall chinook run in September and October. The hatchery is managed by the U.S. Fish and Wildlife Service; (509) 538-2755.

Rafting/Kayaking

A popular summertime rafting venue, with some Class III and Class IV rapids, the **White Salmon River** also is a good ride for whitewater kayakers. The upper portion (downstream from Glenwood Road) is extremely hazardous, with many Class V obstacles. Several falls are impassable, and other stretches are navigable only during heavier flows. The middle portion (between BZ Corner and Husum) is an intermediate stretch, with mostly Class III obstacles. The lower portion from Husum to Northwestern Lake is gentler, with a couple Class II rapids. For detailed river information and guide referrals, contact the Mount Adams Ranger District in Trout Lake; (509) 395-3400.

outside in

Attractions

Two local wineries are open to the public. **Monte Elise Vineyards** in Bingen offers tastings on weekends; (509) 493-3001. And **Charles Hooper Winery,** about 10 miles north of White Salmon on Hwy 141, is open weekends and most summer weekdays, 10am to 6pm; (509) 493-2324.

For a quick taste of Gorge history, stop by the **Gorge Heritage Museum,** in an old church at Maple and Humboldt in Bingen; (509) 493-3228.

White Salmon visitors with a day to spend also should consider a drive up the scenic **Klickitat River Gorge** north of Lyle. See the Goldendale and Maryhill chapter for details.

Restaurants

Fidel's ☆   Lively Mexican music sets the mood. Enormous margaritas go with the warm chips and salsa. Portions are generous (often big enough for two), and the chile relleno—encased in a thick layer of egg whites so that it resembles a big pillow—is *muy bueno. 1 mile east of the Hood River toll bridge on Hwy 14; (509) 493-1017; 120 E Stuben St, Bingen; $.*

Lodgings

For recommended lodgings, see the Adjoining Areas to this chapter.

More Information

Columbia Gorge Windsurfing Association: *(541) 386-9225.*
Columbia River Gorge National Scenic Area: *(509) 493-3323.*
Mount Adams Ranger District: *(509) 395-3400.*
Rhonda Smith's Windsurf Center: *Hood River, Oregon; (800) 241-2430.*
Skamania County Chamber of Commerce: *(800) 989-9178.*
Windsight: *(900) 860-0600 ($1.50 per minute).*
For wind conditions anywhere in North America: *(800) 562-BLOW (touch-tone phone only).*

Goldendale
and Maryhill

From Lyle northeast to Goldendale and southeast to John Day Dam, including the Klickitat River Gorge and Horsethief Lake and Maryhill State Parks.

We hate to say a place has a little of everything. But Goldendale really does.

No matter which way you look at it, the little town perched high on a bluff above the Columbia River Gorge is a transition zone. This is where wet turns to dry, flat turns to mountainous, Oregon turns to Washington. The result, for outdoor lovers, is a nice mix of all the activities and ecosystems found up and down the Gorge.

South of Goldendale is the Columbia, where Maryhill and Horsethief Lake State Parks lure campers, anglers, and wind surfers all year round. To the north are the beautiful rocky outcrops and dry pine forests of the Satus Pass area—a past and present home to the Yakama Indian Nation. And the giant, hulking form of Mount Adams, a constant backdrop, is a reminder that a short distance west, the serious mountains begin. The Goldendale area is a prominent gateway to the Mount Adams Wilderness, most frequently explored on its south slopes.

And there's a bonus. If the weather goes haywire on you (not an unusual occurrence in the Gorge), Goldendale offers plenty of tourist curiosities to distract your attention. The intriguing Maryhill Museum, Stonehenge Monument, and other legacies of the late Sam Hill, a quirky industrialist who shaped this area, all are worth a stop, as is the Goldendale Observatory—a bit of everything, and a big telescope to boot.

Getting There

The Goldendale/Maryhill area is a long haul from Seattle, with a choice of two scenic routes. Take Interstate 90 east to I-82, and continue east to Toppenish. Turn south on US 97 and proceed 50 miles, crossing Satus Pass, to Goldendale. Or, from I-5 at Vancouver, follow Hwy 14 about 100 miles east to US 97 at the Sam Hill Bridge over the Columbia. Allow about 4 hours either way.

Adjoining Areas

NORTH: **Yakima Valley**

EAST: **Tri-Cities**

WEST: **White Salmon and Bingen**

inside out

Camping

Maryhill State Park is one of the best-developed and nicest campgrounds in the Columbia River Gorge. Located on a long stretch of riverfront with ample green lawns and mature shade trees, Maryhill is a favorite of road-weary Gorge travelers as well as boaters and wind surfers. Maryhill has a boat ramp, large group picnic facilities, a swimming beach, fishing pier, broad playfields, and 53 campsites (50 have hookups; maximum RV length, 50 feet). The Maryhill Museum and Stonehenge Memorial are nearby (see Attractions, below). Maryhill is open all year. Campsites can be reserved up to 11 months in advance by calling Reservations Northwest; (800) 452-5687. *Immediately east of the Sam Hill (US 97) Bridge; (509) 773-5007 or (800) 233-0321.*

To the west, near The Dalles Dam, is a smaller, less-developed riverfront site, **Horsethief Lake State Park.** The park has 14 campsites (no hookups; maximum RV length, 30 feet) near the Columbia and Horsethief Lake, standing water created by the backup from The Dalles Dam. It's an interesting historical area: Lewis and Clark reported a permanent Indian camp here, and discernible petroglyphs can be seen at the end of a short trail from the park. Another hiking trail leads up Horsethief Butte (see Hiking/Climbing, below). Horsethief Lake itself is a popular spot for windsurfing and fishing (see sections for both, below). The campground is open summers only. Campsites cannot be reserved. *On Hwy 14 1.5 miles east of The Dalles (Hwy 197) Bridge; (509) 767-1159 or (800) 233-0321.*

To the north, **Brooks Memorial State Park** straddles US 97 just south of 3,100-foot Satus Pass. With its group camp, large picnic shelters, and educational facilities, the park is most heavily used by groups. But it has a pleasant area for individual campers in the portion of the park on the west side of the highway. Here, 55 campsites (23 with full hookups; maximum RV length, 50 feet) are scattered through two pine-forested loops. The park's high elevation makes it a popular cross-country skiing/snowmobiling base camp in the winter. Brooks Memorial is open all year. Campsites cannot be reserved. *On US 97 14 miles north of Goldendale; (509) 773-5382 or (800) 233-0321.*

Somewhat primitive, but also usually quite private, camping can be found in the **Klickitat Wildlife Area,** a state Department of Fish and Wildlife preserve west of Goldendale. (See Wildlife, below.)

Windsurfing

A nice mix of beginner and expert waters can be found along the Columbia below Goldendale. From west to east:

A highly popular site is **Doug's Beach State Park** (see the White Salmon and Bingen chapter), home to some of the best expert surfing in the Gorge, thanks to steady west winds. Look for all the cars along Hwy 14, 3 miles east of Lyle.

A good beginner area is **Horsethief Lake State Park,** which has the advantage of a sheltered inland lake large enough for neophyte sailors to roam. From the same location, experts can launch into the Columbia proper. The dual action makes this a good spot for windsurfing families or for campouts for groups whose members are far apart on the skills list. The lake is safe for beginners because there's no boat or barge traffic. But beware of winds that seem perpetually to blow rookie sailors to the far side—with no easy way to return on foot. And be particularly cautious about walking along the very actively used railroad tracks. The park is about 1.5 miles east of The Dalles Bridge.

Avery Park, 6 miles east of The Dalles Bridge, is a primitive Corps of Engineers parking lot/river access. It's an intermediate-skills area with strong west winds and big waves. Steer clear of fishing boats launching here, and of the Indian fishing platform at one end of the park. Also note that most barge traffic is funneled to this side of the river, between the bank and Brown's Island.

Maryhill State Park, immediately east of the Sam Hill Bridge, is a favorite expert's hangout, with plenty of room for rigging, a nice launching beach, and rest rooms. The river here can be a challenge even for the expert wind surfer, with smoking west winds coupled with very strong currents, particularly in the spring.

Two other frequently surfed experts-only areas, **Peach Beach** and

The Wall, are found between Maryhill and the John Day Dam, but access is difficult, launch areas hazardous.

For information on windsurfing lessons, vendors and wind conditions, see the Bridge of the Gods: Stevenson and Beacon Rock and the White Salmon and Bingen chapters.

Kayaking/Rafting

Experienced paddlers can launch at any of the beaches identified in Windsurfing, above, for raucous, whitewater-style action in the big winds and waves of the **Columbia.** The scenic **Klickitat River Gorge,** home to a wealth of Class IV rapids, is frequently run by experienced paddlers. Many commercial rafting companies lead guided expeditions down the Klickitat. Contact the Mount Adams Ranger District at Trout Lake, (509) 395-3400, for references.

Fishing/Boating

The **Klickitat River,** accessible along Hwy 142 between Lyle and Goldendale, consistently ranks as one of the state's favorite summer steelhead streams. Fishing is best early in the season (late June/early July) and late (September). Even when the fishing slows, the setting—in the spectacular Klickitat Gorge—is unbeatable. Note that all wild steelhead must be released. Fishing for fall chinook also can be productive. Most successful steelhead and salmon anglers float the upper part of the river in drift boats. To book a guided trip, call Garrett's Guide Service; (509) 493-3242.

The broad, deep waters of the **Columbia River** in this Gorge midsection used to be famous for spring and fall chinook salmon fishing. Both have been curtailed dramatically in recent years because of concerns over struggling wild salmon stocks. Check the state regulations pamphlet for information about river openers. There's plenty of other fishing to be done here, however. A fair number of sturgeon are horsed ashore at the **Maryhill State Park boat launch** in the early summer, before catch-and-release rules take effect in July. This section of the river also holds walleye, shad, largemouth and smallmouth bass, and steelhead.

Public boat launches are found at **Maryhill, Horsethief Lake State Park, Lyle, Bingen,** and **Drano Lake. Horsethief Lake** is stocked with rainbow trout (best in the spring) and offers a decent bass fishery. Bank access is decent for both, and a launch ramp awaits boaters.

Hiking/Climbing

Several short but interesting trails fan out through **Horsethief Lake State Park.** One climbs a short distance from the day-use area to some interesting ancient petroglyphs on the hillside. Another climbs from Hwy 14 about a mile east of the park entrance to the top of 500-foot Horsethief Butte, which looms east of the lake. It's a 2-mile round trip from the (limited) parking area on the north side of Hwy 14, or a 4-mile round trip walk from the campground. The last part is a rock scramble. Watch for snakes, and please refrain from digging for arrowheads.

Most of the good mountain hiking trails in this region are on the southern slopes of Mount Adams, in the **Mount Adams Wilderness** around Trout Lake. See the Mount Adams chapter for details. The short pitches on the north side of **Horsethief Butte** are popular beginner **rock-climbing** areas.

Wildlife

Black-tailed deer are thick in winter months throughout the Klickitat Wildlife Area, a very scenic mix of grasslands, mountain ridges, and forests of oak and ponderosa pine; (509) 773-4459. This 13,000-acre site west of Goldendale is bisected by the Klickitat River (see Fishing/Boating, above), and also is home to a variety of game birds (including **wild turkeys**) and raptors. To reach the visitors center, follow Hwy 142 north from Lyle or west from Goldendale and turn northwest on Glenwood Road. In the winter, chances of spotting deer on south-facing slopes along this road are excellent. Note that hunting seasons for deer and game birds take place every fall.

Farther north, toward Mount Adams, is Conboy Lake National Wildlife Refuge, home to large populations of migratory **geese, ducks,** and **swans** every spring. This refuge also is the only known state nesting spot for **sandhill cranes,** and **elk** often are spotted in the fall. The headquarters for the 5,600-acre refuge is 6 miles southwest of Glenwood, (509) 364-3410. An interpretive loop trail begins nearby.

Photography

Just about anywhere you go in the Gorge area is rich with photo opportunities, but this particular section shines even brighter. The lower **Klickitat River Gorge,** accessible along Hwy 142, is gorgeous, with plenty of whitewater and canyon scenic spots.

For an overall Columbia Gorge view looking west from the dry side of the state to the wet, the **Stonehenge** memorial (see Attractions, below) offers a grand vista, with the Sam Hill Bridge providing a humbling degree of scale in the foreground.

outside in

Attractions

One of the Evergreen State's oddest curiosities is visible from miles away—a massive stone mansion in the middle of nowhere. **Maryhill Museum,** a stately Palladian structure, perches rather obtrusively upon the barren Columbia River benchlands. Constructed in 1917 by the eccentric Sam Hill, son-in-law of railroad tycoon James J. Hill, Maryhill began as the European-inspired dream home for Hill and his wife, Mary. She was never impressed enough to even come see the place, and the mansion became instead what it is today: a fine art museum. With one of the largest collections of Rodin sculptures in the world, a whole floor of classic French and American paintings and glasswork, unique exhibitions such as chess sets and Romanian folk textiles, and splendid Northwest tribal art, the museum makes for quite an interesting visit. A cafe serves espresso, pastries, and sandwiches; peacocks roam the lovely landscaped grounds. *Hwy 14, 13 miles south of Goldendale; (509) 773-3733.*

Up the road is another of Sam Hill's bizarre creations: a not-quite-life-size replica of **Stonehenge.** Hill built the monument to honor Klickitat County's 13 World War I veterans, operating on the now-rejected theory that the real Stonehenge in England was built as a burial ground or memorial to the dead. Perched high on a bluff above the Columbia River Gorge—drawing crowds of curious tourists and harmonic-convergence celebrants—it remains to this day a fascinating, even haunting, place. Hill is buried in a crypt not far away, down a short side trail.

The region's other claim to fame is the **Goldendale Observatory.** This State Parks–managed site on a hill overlooking town was a popular spot when Halley's comet dropped in. High-powered telescopes, including a 24.5-inch monster that's the largest in the United States open to general-public eyes, give incredible celestial views through unpolluted skies. Open Wednesday-Sunday April through September 2 to 5pm and 8pm to midnight; in winter, open weekend afternoons and Saturday evenings. On US 97, 20 minutes north of Goldendale; (509) 773-3141.

Restaurants

For recommended restaurants, see the Adjoining Areas to this chapter.

Lodgings

Highland Creeks Resort ☆☆   Guests take advantage of the wilderness here—hiking and fishing in summer, cross-country skiing and sleigh riding in winter. The main lodge is situated at the confluence of three creeks, with glass and cedar walls that seem to bring the trees inside. *On Hwy 97 18 miles north of the Columbia River; (509) 773-4026 or (800) 458-0174; 2120 Hwy 97, Goldendale; $$.*

More Information

Columbia Gorge Windsurfing Association: *(541) 386-9225.*
Columbia River Gorge National Scenic Area: *(509) 493-3323.*
Goldendale Chamber of Commerce: *(509) 773-3400.*
Klickitat County Travel Information Center: *(509) 773-4395.*
Mount Adams Ranger District: *(509) 395-3400.*

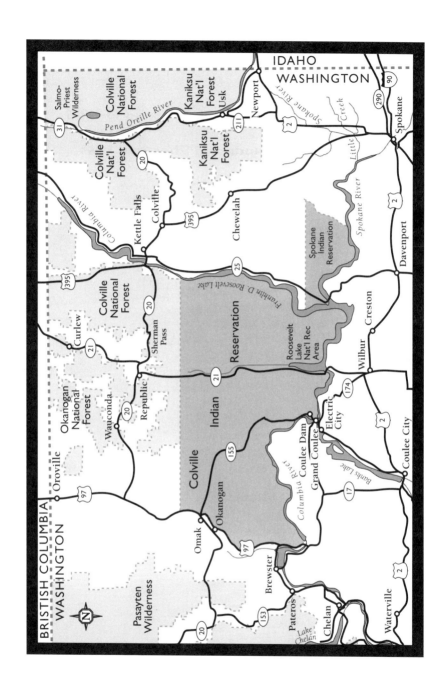

Northeast Washington

Northeast
Washington

Spokane

From downtown Spokane north to Mount Spokane, south to Sprague, east to the Idaho border, and west to Long Lake Reservoir, including the Spokane and Little Spokane Rivers, the Centennial Trail, Riverside State Park, Riverfront Park, and the Turnbull National Wildlife Refuge.

Locals call it "the Capital of the Inland Empire." They point out that it was the site of the first white settlement in the Northwest. They insist it's the biggest city between Seattle and Minneapolis. Big deal. For many of us, the important thing about Spokane is something a lot more practical: it has the only REI between Bellevue and Boise.

Before you summarily dismiss that little fact, consider the implications. They only locate REI (Recreational Equipment Inc.) stores in urban centers containing plenty of A) cash and B) outdoor-recreation enthusiasm. Spokane, it could be argued, from time to time is short on the former. But it certainly suffers no lack of the latter. Long the center of commerce, education, medicine, manufacturing, transportation, and religion for a broad Northwest inland area comprising Eastern Washington, Idaho, Western Montana, Eastern Oregon, and southern British Columbia and Alberta, Spokane also holds the regional focus for outdoor enthusiasts. Many of the Spokane area's 375,000 residents are newbies, and a high percentage of those were attracted by the regional lifestyle. It includes plenty of clean air, medium-size mountains, clear-running rivers, and hospitable pine forests. Not to mention actual seasons. Unlike the state's other major population centers, Spokane has real weather: blazing hot summers, stormy autumns, frequently brutal winters, and magical springs.

Even more so than most other parts of the state, Spokane is a city shaped by its environment. From the time of explorer David Thompson's initial white settlement here in 1810, through the growth boom of Western railroad expansion, the harsh era of the Great Depression, and a current rebirth related to high-tech industry and light manufacturing, the people of Spokane always have been dragged down—and lifted up—by the landscape. It's not a gentle place to live.

That perhaps explains why Spokane residents—and many of their frequent visitors—deal with the natural elements the only way they know how: head on, face first. Whether they're whitewater kayaking on the Spokane River, running till they drop in the Bloomsday Race, backcountry telemark skiing on Mount Spokane, or hauling a state-record cutthroat out of a local lake, Spokane outdoor enthusiasts are serious about their craft. When your environment is constantly in your face, freezing your radiator, challenging your mind, serious is the only way to be. Not that a visit to the Spokane Valley requires wearing your best outdoors game face. Spokane can provide a wonderful, relaxing experience for the visiting recreator. Local fishing, kayaking, recreational running, cross-country skiing, and just plain walking all rate as excellent. The city is rightfully proud of its fine 39-mile Centennial Trail (see Cycling and Hiking, below), which plays a role in each of those activities. It's equally fond of its lakes, streams, wildlife reserves, campgrounds, and even a ski mountain.

Make a visit to this little big city, and you'll see why. Ultimately, you're likely to find yourself in the aisles of REI, rubbing elbows with the locals. You'll be buying maps and lattes, and they'll be buying moleskin and duct tape. Never mind that. Once you step outside, into the river or onto the trail, you're all playing the same game. For once, being the visiting player holds a distinct advantage: when the going gets tough, you can fold up the board and go home.

Getting There

Spokane is 280 miles east of Seattle on Interstate 90. Allow 5 1/2 to 6 hours— less if you're under the influence of caffeine and/or radar-detection devices. Many major airlines, including Horizon, Northwest, Alaska, and Southwest, offer daily flights from Seattle to Spokane International Airport. Other transportation options are Greyhound, (800) 231-2222, and Amtrak's Empire Builder; (800) 872-7245.

Adjoining Areas

NORTH: **Kettle Falls, Colville, and the Pend Oreille**

SOUTH: **Snake River Country: Clarkston, Pullman, and the Palouse**

WEST: **Grand Coulee: Coulee Dam to Soap Lake**

City Parks

Spokane has a very nicely maintained park system, with some of the more pleasant urban parks in the state. **Riverfront Park** is the green heart of the old city. Developed from old railroad yards by Expo '74, the park is now an airy place full of meandering paved paths (see Cycling, below), with entertainments ranging from ice-skating to an IMAX theater.

Manito Park, at Grand Boulevard and 18th, has theme gardens and a duck pond you can splash in. **Finch Arboretum** (west of downtown Spokane), a pleasant picnic site, holds a modest but attractive collection of trees and shrubs among ravines and a stream. For a panoramic vista of Spokane, visit **Cliff Park** at 13th and Grove.

Cycling

By all means, bring the bikes. Perhaps the best urban-to-rural walking-and-cycling path in the state, the 39-mile **Centennial Trail** from Riverside State Park to Coeur d'Alene, Idaho, is the recreational focus of the Spokane area. The trail follows the Spokane River, and its entire length is open to strolling and cycling (in some sections, wheeled and nonwheeled users are channeled onto separate paths), with some portions open to horseback riding. The primary access point is Riverfront Park in downtown Spokane (see City Parks, above.) The trail passes by Gonzaga University, Mission Park, the Walk in the Wild Zoo, and other local attractions. For details and trail events, contact Friends of the Centennial Trail; (509) 624-3430. If you couldn't squeeze the bikes into the van, rentals are available from Quinns in Riverfront Park; (509) 456-6545.

Mountain bikers find plenty of single-track and fire-road riding in **Mount Spokane State Park** (see Camping, below).

Hiking

The **Centennial Trail** (see Cycling, above) is a grand place for a short walk or a very long trek along the Spokane River. The 39-mile trail begins in Riverside State Park northwest of Spokane and runs east to Idaho. By Washington standards, the trail isn't wildly scenic. But it's a walk with plenty of historical flavor. Indian petroglyphs are visible from the trail near Long Lake, and the trail itself follows a route pounded out over the centuries by Native Peoples—and after that, white fur traders. For lovers of wilder territory, the trail portions inside Riverside State Park are the most alluring. Riverside also contains an intricate network of its own hiking trails, with some 36 miles of combined hiking, equestrian, and ORV paths.

A bit more on the wild side is another family-friendly trail, this one winding through the **Little Spokane Natural Area** north of Spokane, adjacent to Riverside State Park (see Wildlife, below). About 6 miles of mostly flat trails lead through this preserve, where deer, beavers, coyotes, blue herons, and other bird species are commonly seen. (No mountain bikes allowed.) The **Turnbull National Wildlife Refuge** and **Dishman Hills Natural Area** also have some hiking trails (see Wildlife, below).

A number of good day hikes are found at **Mount Spokane State Park,** leading from the camping area to the Mount Spokane Vista House, Mount Kit Carson, Smith Gap, and other areas. This is another favorite horseback-riding area. See Camping, below, for directions and other information.

Wildlife

Two areas just a couple of miles outside Spokane's city limits are excellent places to hike and to see birds and wildlife: the **Little Spokane Natural Area,** (509) 456-3964, and the **Spokane Fish Hatchery,** (509) 625-5169. The fish hatchery is at 2927 W Waikiki Road; for the Natural Area, look for the Indian Rock Paintings parking lot on Rutter Parkway.

The **Dishman Hills Natural Area,** a 460-acre preserve in the Spokane Valley, has a network of trails with mixed wildlife habitats. Take I-90 east to the Sprague Avenue exit, go east 1.5 miles to Sargent Road; turn right a half-mile to the parking area. Just 25 miles south of Spokane near Cheney, you'll find the 17,000-acre **Turnbull National Wildlife Refuge,** especially interesting during fall and spring waterfowl migration. A 6-mile, self-guided auto tour leads through the refuge, which—unlike most others in the state—never allows hunting. Take I-90 west, exit at Cheney, go through the town, and turn left on Smith Road; (509) 235-4723.

Camping

Riverside State Park is scattered in separate parcels along 9 miles of the Spokane River. The camping area is in a broad meander curve, in a park section known as the "Bowl and Pitcher area," named for unique rock formations along the river. Offering 101 campsites (no hookups; maximum RV length, 45 feet); it's a popular spot, so consider reserving a site in advance. The campground, however, is only one of a dozen good reasons to venture to Riverside. Inside the park's 7,600 acres are 36 miles of hiking and equestrian trails, a large group camp, multiple picnic areas, fascinating rock formations, Indian petroglyphs, whitewater rapids on the Spokane and Little Spokane Rivers, an off-road vehicle park, a scenic river gorge, and Spokane House Interpretive Center. The latter, which has been open sporadically of late because of budget problems, is on the site of Spokane House, explorer David Thompson's 1810 fur-trading outpost. Riverside State Park is open all year. Campsites can be reserved up to 11 months in advance by calling Reservations Northwest; (800) 452-5687. *From Division Street in downtown Spokane, take Frances Avenue northwest to Hwy 291 and follow signs to the park's multiple entrances. The main park offices and camping area are in the Bowl and Pitcher section; (509) 456-3964 or (800) 233-0321.*

It's known mostly as a day-use area, but **Mount Spokane State Park** has a small campground with 12 sites (no hookups; maximum RV length, 30 feet). The park also has an extensive trail system, and is open in winter for cross-country and downhill skiing. The view from Vista House atop the 5,800-foot mountain is outstanding. Mount Spokane is open all year. Campsites cannot be reserved. *30 miles northwest of Spokane via Division Street (US 2) and Hwy 206; (509) 456-4169 or (800) 233-0321.*

A number of private resorts are located west of town on the shores of **Medical Lake.** Several large private campgrounds, including summer-only KOA Spokane, (509) 924-4722, have reserved sites and other amenities. *Call the Spokane Visitors Center, (800) 248-3230, for a full list.*

Skiing

Only one downhill area, **Mount Spokane**—30 miles north on Highway 206—is within a short drive of Spokane. The day-use area has five lifts and a respectable 2,000 feet of vertical. Weekend lift tickets are $18, and midweek passes are an even better bargain; (509) 238-6281.

A wealth of even better skiing is found within about 2 hours. The list includes **49 Degrees North,** 58 miles north of Spokane near Chewelah, (509) 935-6649 (see the Kettle Falls, Colville, and the Pend Oreille chapter); **Schweitzer Mountain Resort** in Sandpoint, Idaho, (208) 263-9555, with excellent facilities for family skiing; and the region's newest destination ski resort, **Silver Mountain** at Kellogg, Idaho, (208) 783-1111. Any one of these areas can provide a good day's skiing for reasonable prices, but if you have time to sample only one, Schweitzer is the star in this cluster.

For cross-country skiers, **Mount Spokane Sno-Park** is a longtime favorite. A large (180-car) state Sno-Park at the mountain offers 25 kilometers of groomed ski trails for all skill levels, plus two warming huts. A Sno-Park pass, available at local outdoor retailers and ranger stations, is required. Information: (509) 456-4169.

Closer in, two short ski trails are found at the **Indian Canyon Golf Course,** which operates as a state Sno-Park in the winter. Easy .3 kilometer and 4.5 kilometer loops begin near the main parking area at Assembly Street and West Drive. Another good beginner area is the **Downriver Golf Course Sno-Park,** which offers two loops totaling 5 kilometers at 3225 N Columbia Circle. The six-mile **Little Spokane Natural Area** trail (see Wildlife, above) is another popular beginner-to-intermediate area northwest of the city. For other, more remote cross-country venues, see the Kettle Falls, Colville, and the Pend Oreille chapter.

Fishing

Plenty of good trout fishing is available in the greater Spokane area. Noted spring and summer rainbow and brown trout producers are **Medical and West Medical Lakes, Silver Lake,** and **Clear Lake,** all in a cluster southwest of the city. West Medical Lake Resort, (509) 299-3929, is a good contact.

Fishtrap Lake near Sprague is a noted early-season hot spot, and nearby **Sprague Lake** is a good mixed-species fishery. Other good trout lakes are **Fish Lake** near Cheney; **Newman Lake** to the east, via Hwy 290; and **Long Lake,** a Spokane River reservoir west of the city. The **Spokane River** itself, much of which is under selective fishery regulations, is a fair fly-fishing stream.

Kayaking/Canoeing

Kayakers run the **Spokane River** primarily in two sections—an intermediate (Class II) 6-mile stretch below Harvard Park off I-90 east of the city, and an advanced (Class III) stretch on the lower river between Downriver Drive and Riverside State Park. Highlights on the lower stretch are the Class III rapids at Bowl and Pitcher and Devil's Toenail, both viewed from Riverside State Park (see Camping, above). The Spokane is best run in May and June. It's a big, fast river—not for novices.

Reasonably experienced canoeists will enjoy the float along the **Little Spokane River,** in the Little Spokane Natural Area (see Wildlife, above). A good put-in is near the Spokane Trout Hatchery on Waikiki Road. Note that inner-tubing and swimming are prohibited in this area.

Golfing

Golf is very good here. **Indian Canyon,** (509) 747-5353, and **Hangman Valley,** (509) 448-1212, two of the most beautiful public courses in the nation, have recently attracted a number of professional tournaments. **The Creek at Qualchan,** (509) 448-9317, is the newest and most challenging of the city courses. There are nine others.

Horseback Riding

You can rent your own steed or take a guided ride at **Riverside State Park** (see Camping above), where Trailtown Riding Stables, (509) 456-3964, offers 5-mile rides. Indian Canyon Riding Stable (4812 W Canyon Drive, (509) 624-4646) also provides guided rides with scenic views.

Adventure Calendar

Spokane's annual **Bloomsday Run,** the granddaddy of all road races, takes place the third Sunday in May. It has grown into the largest timed race in the country, drawing some 60,000 competitors a year. The 12K (7.6-mile) race kicks off the Bloomsday Lilac Festival. Those who don't register early won't get in; (509) 838-1579.

outside in

Attractions

The friendly city by Spokane Falls is far more attractive to visit than is generally recognized. It is full of old buildings of note, marvelous parks, and splendid vistas, and the compact downtown is most pleasant for strolling. The Gold Rush of the 1880s brought it wealth, and railroads brought it people.

The three blocks on W Riverside Avenue between Jefferson and Lincoln—doubtless the loveliest three blocks around—contain a wealth of handsome structures. The **Spokane Club** on W Riverside is a fine example of the work done by Kirtland Cutter, who rebuilt most of the city after the fire of 1889; the **Spokesman-Review Building,** also on W Riverside, is everybody's idea of what a newspaper building should look like, especially one that is the seat of power for the dominant Cowles family. The **Spokane County Courthouse,** north of the Spokane River on W Broadway, is a Loire Valley clone built in 1895 by Willis A. Ritchie. **City Hall,** on Spokane Falls Boulevard, occupies an old Montgomery Ward building, now elaborately restored in an award-winning use of art deco elegance. Tour **Overbluff Drive** to see the small palaces of the upper crust, and **Cliff Drive** or **Sumner Avenue** on the South Hill to view some splendid older homes. **Browne's Addition,** west of downtown, is full of late-Victorian homes.

Brazilian-born conductor Fabio Machetti has been working with the **Spokane Symphony** since June 1993, and programs—including a pops series—are lively and innovative. An annual free Labor Day concert in Comstock Park draws thousands of picnicking spectators; (509) 326-3136. The **Spokane Civic Theatre** (1020 N Howard; (509) 325-2507) offers a mixed bag of amateur performances each season; the **Interplayers Ensemble Theatre** (174 S Howard; (509) 455-7529) is a professional company with a full season. **Riverfront Park** often hosts concerts of jazz, bluegrass, and popular music during the summer; call (509) 456-4386 for information. The 12,000-seat **Spokane Veterans Arena,** opened in mid-1995, is the home of the Western Hockey League Spokane Chiefs. The venue is also big enough to attract major entertainers and bands to the city; most of the tickets are sold through a local ticket agency, G&B Select-a-Seat; (509) 325-7328 or (800) 325-7328. A Best of Broadway touring performance series is held at the **Opera House** at the south edge of Riverfront Park.

Cheney Cowles Museum displays pioneer and mining relics, and one of the fine old mansions from Spokane's mining era, **Clark Mansion,** is open for viewing; 2316 W First Avenue, (509) 456-3931. Bing-ophiles shouldn't miss the **Crosby Collection,** a display of memorabilia donated by crooner Bing Crosby to his alma mater, Gonzaga University; (509) 328-4220.

Hale's Ales, which now has plants in Spokane and Kirkland, welcomes visitors—when the day's brewing work is done. Call ahead for a reservation for a tour and a taste of Hale's pale ale, bitter, porter, Moss Bay ale, and seasonal specialties, 5634 E Commerce Street; (509) 534-7553. Also open for tours is **Fort Spokane Brewery** (401 W Spokane Falls Boulevard; (509) 838-3809) across from Riverfront Park.

Restaurants

Clinkerdagger's ☆ Clinkerdagger's has broadened its menu to include more Northwest-oriented dishes, but in the end, it's the basic but well-handled (and attractively presented) food that wins us over—especially when fresh seafood is available. Reservations recommended; request the coveted window seats in the spring, when the Spokane River is rushing. *East of Monroe in Flour Mill; (509) 328-5965; 621 W Mallon, Spokane; $$.*

Coyote Cafe The walls of this recently remodeled Mexican place are covered with offbeat art, and the service is prompt and relentlessly cheerful. If you want to be in and out in 20 minutes, that's no problem. Food includes reasonably priced, standard south-of-the-border fare—all of which is enhanced by the large, icy margaritas. *Corner of 3rd and Wall; (509) 747-8800; 702 W 3rd Ave, Spokane; $.*

The Downtown Onion ☆   The Onion set the standard in Spokane for gourmet hamburgers, and they're still local classics. The beer selection and fruit daiquiris are outstanding. Being part of the chaos is part of the fun of this place, so don't take a booth in the sun room. There's also a North Onion at 7522 N Division, (509) 482-6100. *On Riverside at Bernard; (509) 747-3852; 302 W Riverside, Spokane; $.*

Europa Pizzeria and Bakery   Exposed brick walls and bare wood, generous portions of baked pasta entrees, and college students are all in abundance here. The service is cheerful, advice reliable, and the pace relaxed (sometimes too much so for those on a lunch hour). *North side of the railroad trestle downtown, next to the Magic Lantern Theater; (509) 455-4051; 125 S Wall St, Spokane; $.*

Knight's Diner ☆   Eggs the way you want them and crispy hashbrowns have been served up in this renovated circa-1900 railroad car for four decades. In this former Pullman passenger car diners sit on stools and eat at a mahogany counter that runs the length of the car. The very hungry can order the 24 dollar-size pancakes. *At the intersection of N Market and Green St; (509) 484-0015; 2909 N Market, Spokane; $.*

Luna ☆☆   It didn't take long for local diners to embrace this new restaurant with its innovative, eclectic menu, and emphasis on fresh herbs and seasonal fruits and vegetables. A fair-weather patio awaits in summer. Reservations recommended. *South on High Drive to 56th, right 1 block to Perry; (509) 448-2383; 5620 S Perry, Spokane; $$.*

Marrakesh ☆   A meal at this Moroccan restaurant begins with a traditional finger-washing routine and ends with the sprinkling of fragrant rose water over your hands. A set price buys a five-course meal in which you choose only the entree. Plan to go with at least a group of four (or, if it's crowded, you may be seated with other diners). *West of Monroe on Northwest Blvd; (509) 328-9733; 2008 Northwest Blvd, Spokane; $$.*

McGowen's ☆   This cafe's an adjunct to Auntie's Bookstore and Uncle's Games in the historic Liberty Building. On the second floor there's a spacious area for readings, and an art gallery. The cafe offers soups, salads, desserts, and a modest menu of daily hot entrees. *On the corner of Washington and Main; (509) 624-1870; 404 W Main Ave, Spokane; $.*

Milford's Fish House and Oyster Bar ☆☆   Spokane's oldest fish house is simply decorated and offers good food at reasonable prices. Check the fresh list and don't hesitate to ask the waiter for recommendations. Reservations are highly recommended. *Corner of Broadway and Monroe; (509) 326-7251; 719 N Monroe St, Spokane; $$.*

Niko's Greek & Middle Eastern Restaurant ☆   Niko's is deservedly popular locally for traditional Greek food, much of which is homemade. Lamb is well treated here, and the garlicky, smooth hummus is wonderful. Niko's Favorite is ours, too. Thursday is belly-dancing night. Niko II, downtown at 725 W Riverside, (509) 624-7444, is a popular lunch spot. *2 blocks off Sprague; (509) 928-9590; 321 S Dishman-Mica Rd, Spokane; $.*

Patsy Clark's ☆   Locally, we like to show off Patsy's, but not so much for its dinners. An elegant spot it is with marble, wood carvings, and Tiffany stained glass all imported by the original owner, Patrick "Patsy" F. Clark, a miner multimillionaire. You should find some excuse to stop by, even if it's only for a drink (the wine list is one of the best in the area). Sunday brunch is memorable and requires reservations. *15 blocks west of downtown at 2nd and Hemlock; (509) 838-8300; 2208 W 2nd Ave, Spokane; $$$.*

Thai Cafe ☆   A waft of curry greets patrons at the door, and you'll find such seasonings, along with coconut milk and peanuts, in most of the entrees. We've yet to be disappointed with any of the chicken selections. Don't miss the desserts. *Sprague at Washington; (509) 838-4783; 410 W Sprague, Spokane; $.*

Cheaper Eats

Cannon Street Grill   If you get hungry while in Spokane's Browne's Addition neighborhood, stop at Cannon Street Grill for a caesar salad or a Reuben. *(509) 456-8660; 144 S Cannon St, Spokane.*

Lodgings

Cavanaugh's Inn at the Park ☆   This hotel on the bank of the river across from Riverfront Park has 402 rooms, many with southern views of downtown Spokane (and a few, of the hydropower weir). All seven stories of rooms open out to the spacious lobby; it can be noisy, so specify a quiet room. The attractive Windows on the Seasons restaurant overlooks the river. *Division St exit from I-90, north across the bridge and left to N River Dr; (509) 326-8000 or (800) 843-4667; W 303 N River Dr, Spokane; $$.*

Fotheringham House ☆☆   The first mayor of Spokane built this Victorian house, and the details are what make the place (pressed tin ceilings, hundreds of daffodils), and location next to Patsy Clark's mansion doesn't hurt either. Relax in the wicker swing on the wraparound porch, stroll the cobblestone paths through the butterfly gardens, or play tennis on the courts in the park. *Maple St exit from I-90, north to 2nd, turn west, stay in right lane; (509) 838-1891; 2128 W 2nd Ave, Spokane; $$.*

Waverly Place ☆☆   Across the street from lovely Corbin Park (once a racetrack), Waverly Place retains the elegance of the Victorian era. Add a pool and a tall glass of lemonade and call it vacation. There are guest rooms, suites, and marvelous fresh breakfast. *Exit I-90 at Division St, north on Division and Ruby to N Foothills Dr, west to Washington, north to Waverly; (509) 328-1856; 709 W Waverly Pl, Spokane; $$.*

West Coast Ridpath Hotel ☆   The rooms are pleasant and spacious, and those in the tower overlook the city. The downtown location is convenient. This place is popular and sometimes crowded, but the mood here is always convivial. The rooftop restaurant, a predictable Ankeny's, boasts a grand view of Spokane. *In the heart of downtown; (509) 838-2711 or (800) 426-0670; 515 W Sprague, Spokane; $$.*

Cheaper Sleeps

Cavanaugh's Value Inn   This motel's rooms offer the standard motel amenities, and you can stroll through one of Spokane's oldest residential areas to get downtown. Pay a bit more for a larger room with a kitchenette. *(509) 624-4142; 1203 W 5th Ave, Spokane.*

More Information

Spokane Visitors and Convention Bureau: *926 W Sprague; (509) 747-3230 or (800) 248-3230.*

REI (outdoor equipment sales and rentals): *1125 N Monroe; (509) 328-9900.*

Mountain Gear (outdoor equipment sales and rentals): *2002 N Division; (509) 325-9000.*

Kettle Falls, Colville, and the Pend Oreille

From Kettle Falls north to British Columbia, east to Idaho, and south to Newport, including 49 Degrees North ski area, the Salmo-Priest Wilderness, Sullivan Lake, and portions of the Colville and Idaho Panhandle National Forests.

Go where the moose go. Anywhere you go in the West, that's a fairly reliable rule for finding the wildest, least-spoiled mountain areas. It certainly works in Washington, where the moose population largely limits its range to the still-wild hillsides of the Pend Oreille Valley in extreme Northeast Washington.

The moose are not alone in choosing this out-there, away-from-it-all region. The state's most constant population of grizzly bears is believed to roam the rocky peaks of the Selkirk Range. Bighorn sheep are a common sight, and the Lower 48's last herd of woodland caribou live—and struggle to survive—in patches of preserved land such as the Salmo-Priest Wilderness.

This is a last refuge, of sorts. That's true of the wildlife population and of the human one. No other place in the state is less geared for tourists than this one. That's not the result of hostility toward encroachers. It's just that the northeast corner of the state isn't *on the way to anything.* Whether you're measuring distance in miles of asphalt or state of mind, this place is a long way from your local Larry's Market.

Which probably explains why many native Evergreen State outdoor lovers (all seven of them) at some point in their lives make a Pend Oreille pilgrimage. They come to see the animals, taste the luscious alpine meadows of the Shedroof Divide Trail in the Selkirks, fish for trout on lonely mountain streams. They come to breathe the same air their great-great-grandparents might have breathed. Stop looking for the last and only uncivilized part of Washington. This is it: Section 119—the very last page in the *Washington Atlas & Gazetteer*. It's been pushed right up against the back corner, and the minivan caravan is visible on the horizon.

Getting There

The Kettle Falls/Colville area is reached by driving US 2 east to US 97, then Hwy 20, the Sherman Pass Scenic Byway, east from Tonasket. It's a full day's journey from the Seattle area.

Adjoining Areas

SOUTH: **Spokane**

WEST: **Okanogan Highlands and Sherman Pass**

Camping

Most public campgrounds in the area are Colville National Forest sites. Among the more popular in the Sullivan Ranger District (Metaline Falls area) are **Sullivan Lake** and **Noisy Creek,** both on Sullivan Lake northeast of Metaline Falls. Sullivan Lake has 35 sites (no hookups; maximum RV length, 32 feet) on the lake's north shore, near the south boundary of the Salmo-Priest Wilderness. Noisy Creek has 19 sites (no hookups; maximum RV length, 32 feet) on the lake's southeast shore. A bighorn sheep feeding station, which operates in the winter only, is nearby, as are several great hiking trails (see Wildlife and Hiking/Backpacking, below). These two campgrounds are popular with anglers, water-skiers, boaters, and canoeists. Both are open May through September, and campsites can be reserved in advance by calling (800) 280-CAMP. *On Sullivan Lake Road (County Road 9345), 6.5 and 10 miles northeast of Metaline Falls; (509) 446-2681.*

An alternative site not far away on the Pend Oreille River is **Edgewater,** which has 23 campsites (no hookups; maximum RV length, 21 feet) and limited picnic facilities. It's open May through September, and campsites cannot be reserved. *On County Road 3669, 2 miles northeast of Ione; (509) 446-2681.*

In the Colville Ranger District, the area northeast of Colville and north of Highway 20, are five campgrounds, all open summers only and all fairly remote. For directions and information about **Lake Leo** (8 campsites), **Lake Thomas** (15 tent sites), **Big Meadow Lake** (16 campsites), **Gillette** (48 campsites, very nice, so reserve a site in advance by calling (800) 280-CAMP) or **Little Twin Lakes** (20 campsites, quite pleasant), contact the Colville Ranger District; (509) 684-4557. Big Meadow Lake has a wildlife-viewing platform (see Wildlife, below).

In the Kettle Falls Ranger District between Kettle Falls and the Canadian border is another remote campground, **Pierre Lake,** which has 15 sites and good fishing access to the lake. Call the Kettle Falls Ranger District; (509) 738-6111.

Farther south in the Newport Ranger District are **Panhandle** (11 sites), **Brown's Lake** (18 sites), **South Skookum Lake** (25 sites), and **Pioneer Park** (14 sites). All the campgrounds charge a fee, and all are open between Memorial Day and Labor Day. Call the ranger district at (509) 447-3129.

Several state Department of Natural Resources campgrounds offer more options. Most of these campgrounds are open all year, and all are free and offer limited services. For details, call the DNR's Northeast Region office in Colville; (509) 684-7474. **Sheep Creek**—on Sheep Creek Road, just off Highway 25 near the Canadian border—has 11 small campsites along the scenic creek. **Upper Sheep Creek,** just up the road, has 2 primitive sites. Sheep Creek Falls is nearby. **Douglas Falls Grange Park,** on Douglas Falls Road north of Colville, has 8 sites. **Williams Lake,** on Williams Lake Road north of Kettle Falls, has 8 sites. **Rocky Lake,** off Hwy 395 south of Colville, has 7 unimpressive sites, but it's near the Little Pend Oreille Wildlife Area (see Wildlife, below). **Flodelle Creek** off Hwy 20 northeast of Colville has 8 sites—and lots of dirt bikes. Avoid it. **Starvation Lake,** east of Colville off Hwy 20, has 6 small sites and canoe/fishing access. **Skookum Creek,** on the Pend Oreille River near Usk, has 10 sites and access to an Indian painting interpretive site.

In addition, five Coulee Dam National Recreation Area campgrounds on upper Lake Franklin D. Roosevelt are nice facilities with good lake access for boaters, water-skiers, and swimmers. For information about **Kettle Falls** (77 sites), **North Gorge** (10 sites), **Evans** (46 sites), **Marcus Island** (20 sites), or **Kamloops** (14 sites), contact the Coulee Dam National Recreation Area office in Kettle Falls; (509) 738-6266. Kettle Falls, near the junction of Hwys 20 and 395, is by far the most heavily used.

Hiking/Backpacking

The Pend Oreille region offers some of Eastern Washington's finest high-forest day hiking and backpacking, especially in motorcycle-free areas such as the Salmo-Priest Wilderness. A healthy menu of day-hiking trails also is available for campers at any of the dozen state or federal campsites listed in Camping, above. For road and trail reports and full trail information, contact the Sullivan Lake Ranger District; (509) 446-2691. Following is a list of area favorites.

Sullivan Lake/Metaline Falls area

Campers at any of the Sullivan Lake campgrounds will find pleasant walking on the **Sullivan Lake Trail** (easy; 4 miles one way), which extends along the lake to Noisy Creek Campground. Noisy Creek campers are within a short distance of the **Noisy Creek Trail** (moderate; 10.6 miles round trip), which begins at the campground and climbs fairly steeply up the creek drainage to several good viewpoints and ultimately a junction with the Hall Mountain Trail.

If you're here in midsummer, try the **Hall Mountain Trail** (moderate/difficult; 5 miles round trip) which climbs steadily to the summit of the big rock butte, and is one of the most reliable places in the state to view bighorn sheep. State wildlife managers have relocated many of these majestic beasts from Rocky Mountain states to this area, and sometimes place salt licks at the summit peak to supplement the sheeps' diets. Sheep are visible here all year, but the access road (Road 500) is closed from August 15 to June 30 every year to provide solitude for the sheep during fall mating and spring birthing seasons.

East of Metaline Falls, several good vista hikes are found in the Abercrombie-Hooknose Roadless Area. One of the most popular is **Abercrombie Mountain Trail** (difficult; 8 miles round trip), which climbs about 2,000 vertical feet to the 7,300-foot summit of Abercrombie, the tallest Selkirk peak. Views of the entire region are outstanding. The trailhead is on Forest Service Road 350, which turns west from Boundary Road near Flume Creek.

Salmo-Priest Wilderness

The Sullivan Lake/Metaline Falls area also is a good staging ground for treks into the beautiful Salmo-Priest Wilderness, a 40,000-acre wild area that contains some of Eastern Washington's largest remaining old-growth forests. Viewed on a map, the protected area is shaped like a horseshoe, with 6,828-foot Salmo Mountain located at the head. The westernmost prong extends south almost to Sullivan Lake, and the easternmost traces the Idaho border on a route defined by a string of 6,500-foot-plus mountains: Shedroof, Thunder, Helmer, Mankato, and Round Top. The western summit line is defined by Crowell Ridge and Gypsy Ridge, the eastern by Shedroof Divide.

Not surprisingly, trails follow both ridgelines, with a series of short connectors climbing from the heavily clearcut slopes outside the wilderness boundary into the unspoiled highlands. Popular hikes on the north (Hwy 31) side of the wilderness include **Halliday** (moderate; 15.6 miles round trip), a popular wilderness connector trail that climbs from the junction of Hwy 31 and Road 180 to the Halliday Fens, a string of beaver bogs that attracts deer and moose; **Slate Creek** (moderate; 8.4 miles round trip), which begins on Slate Creek Road and goes up, down, up, down, and up a series of ridges that also draw large numbers of wildlife (and autumn hunters); **Red Bluff Trail** (difficult; 10.5 miles round trip), a lowland route that begins near Mill Pond Campground; and **North Fork Sullivan Creek** (difficult; 19.2 miles round trip), a rugged backpackers' route that begins near Lime Lake and climbs steadily up the drainage to the top of Crowell Ridge, where mountain goats sometimes are spotted.

The **Crowell Ridge Trail** (moderate/difficult; 15.6 miles round trip)—a high route that connects with the North Fork Sullivan Trail and other access paths—is a regional highlight. If you start at the upper trailhead off Forest Service Road 245 just below the summit of Sullivan Mountain, this becomes one of those rare backpack routes that starts very high (6,200 feet) and stays there, offering grand views of BC's Kokanees and the Pend Oreille Valley. Lovely meadows surround you all along the route, and good campsites are abundant. Note: Unless you visit very early in the summer, you'll need to carry all your own water. Little is found along the ridgetop, although strong hikers can drop to one of several lakes below the ridge to replenish supplies.

In the more remote, northern portion of the wilderness, **Salmo Loop** (difficult; 18 miles round trip) is a popular two- to three-day backpack route through the South Salmo River Valley to Shedroof Divide Trail, following the divide past Shedroof Mountain and Old Snowy Top, then down a long ridgeline back to the trailhead at the end of Forest Service Road 2220. Good day hikes in the same area include Thunder Creek (moderate; 5.8 miles round trip), which follows the creek through a cool old-growth forest; and Shedroof Cutoff (moderate; 3.4 miles round trip), a steep shortcut to the Shedroof Divide Trail.

In the eastern wilderness, the shining star is the **Shedroof Divide Trail** proper (moderate; 31.4 miles round trip). Like its westside counterpart, Crowell Ridge, the Shedroof trail begins high and follows the ridgeline, this time to a turnaround point near Idaho. Allow four days for a long, memorable walk through this inspiring alpine area. Side trips allow short-but-difficult hikes to the summits of Round Top, Thunder, Helmer, Shedroof, and Old Snowy Mountains (try to find the old lookout access trails, and be careful). The Shedroof Trail is accessible via the Thunder Creek, Salmo Loop, and Shedroof Cutoff Trails, but the main trailhead is near Pass Creek Pass, on Forest Service Road 22. A long day hike in the same area is the **Pass Creek/Grassy Top Trail** (moderate; 15.5 miles round trip), which is a wonderful summer wildflower hike.

Pend Oreille River Valley

Near the southern Colville National Forest boundary on Hwy 20 are three notable trails, each easy and interesting enough for the whole family: **Sherry Loop** (easy; 3.8-mile loop), a very pretty riverside walk near Sherry Lake that's popular with summer anglers and winter cross-country skiers; **Springboard Interpretive Loop** (easy; 2.4 miles round trip), which winds through an interesting old homestead site; and the **Tiger** and **Coyote Rock Loops** (easy; 5-mile round trips), which begin near Frater Lake.

To the south, campers at Skookum Lake Campground shouldn't miss the **South Skookum Loop** (easy; 1.3 miles round trip), which meanders along the lake through a truly beautiful forest and affords the chance to see the occasional wandering moose. At Pioneer Park Campground, try walking the **Pioneer Park Interpretive Trail** (easy; .5 mile round trip), site of a Kalispell tribe camas-root harvesting area.

In the northwest corner of this region, another campground-centered walk, the **Pierre Lake Trail** (easy; 1.6 miles round trip), leads through a nice forested area on the shore of the lake north of Orient off Hwy 395. The trail begins in the campground and follows the west shore. It's a good family walk.

Wildlife

This is where the really wild things are. Some of Washington's—and indeed, America's—rarest creatures roam the woods of extreme northeast Washington. A herd of 30 to 50 **woodland caribou,** an endangered species, divide their time between Washington, British Columbia, and Idaho in the rocky Selkirk Range. Rarely seen, they're struggling to hang on. This is the very last herd of the animals in the Lower 48 states. State Fish and Wildlife biologists have been supplementing the herd with animals from British Columbia, and most of the caribou are tracked and loosely monitored by radio collars. The most recent group of caribou was released in the winter of 1995–1996 at Gypsy Meadows, near the border of the Salmo-Priest Wilderness.

Two other endangered species, the **grizzly bear** and the **northern gray wolf,** also are believed to dip into the area from BC habitats. They're even more scarce, and hikers who encounter either one not only would be extremely fortunate, but important eyewitnesses. Fish and Wildlife managers need all the help they can get to monitor both species. Report any sightings to a ranger district office.

Though not endangered, **moose** are rare in the Lower 48, and the northeast corner of the state is home to as many as 200. Keep your eyes peeled around lakes and boggy areas in this region. Moose sightings aren't common, but they're by no means unusual. If you are fortunate enough to encounter a moose, keep in mind these massive beasts aren't always as genteel as their smaller deer-family cousins. Bull moose and protective cows have been known to charge people, cars, outhouses, radio towers, and anything else they suddenly find offensive. Keep your distance. Two high-cliff dwellers, **mountain goats** and **Rocky Mountain bighorn sheep,** are found in the northeast corner of the Colville National Forest, in and around the Salmo-Priest Wilderness. An excellent place to view mountain goats, moose, and deer is the Flume Creek Mountain Goat Viewing Area, on Boundary Road (Forest Service Road 2975) just north of Metaline Falls. Bighorns are commonly seen in the Hall Mountain area east of Sullivan Lake (see Hiking/Backpacking, above). They're even easier to find in the winter, when many of them feed at Noisy Creek Sheep Feeding Station near Noisy Creek Campground on Sullivan Lake.

Two other popular wildlife-viewing areas are **Big Meadow Lake** (see Hiking/Backpacking, above), where **deer, moose, beaver,** and **osprey** often are seen; and Little Pend Oreille Wildlife Area north of Chewelah, where **deer, bear,** and various **waterfowl** species often are seen. From Hwy 20 about 8 miles east of Colville, turn south on Narcisse Creek Road.

Wherever you go in this region, chances are good you'll eventually encounter **mule** and **white-tailed deer.** This corner of the state is home to the bulk of the state's white-tail population, making this a wildly popular hunting area in the fall.

Fishing

Good trout-fishing waters dot the region. **Deep Lake** near Northport, **Sullivan Lake** near Metaline Falls, and **Pierre Lake** northeast of Orient all are productive trout waters. A string of lakes on either side of Hwy 20 east of Colville—**Rocky, Hatch, Starvation, Little Twin,** and **Black Lakes**—also offers good rainbow and cutthroat trout fishing. In the Little Pend Oreille Wildlife Area, **McDowell Lake** and **Bayley Lake** are fly-fishing–only waters popular with trout anglers. Another popular fly-only venue is **Browns Lake,** north of the **Skookum Lakes** (also good trout fishing) near Usk. For Franklin D. Roosevelt Lake fishing information, see the Grand Coulee: Coulee Dam to Soap Lake chapter.

Skiing/Snow Play

Downhill skiers are in for a treat at **49 Degrees North,** a small but often outstanding day-use ski area on 5,775-foot Mount Chewelah. The area is small, with 1,845 feet of vertical on 16 runs accessed by four double chairlifts. But the snow typically is light, cold, and dry—often as close as snow in Washington state comes to a true "powder" rating. Mountain managers close off some of the best of the ski area for weekend skiing. All-day adult lift tickets are $25; the closest lodging is in Chewelah, 11 miles west. About 9 miles of cross-country ski trails are found nearby. Snow phone: (509) 458-9208. Mountain information: (509) 935-6649.

Two groomed cross-country-skiing areas lure skinny-ski riders near Newport, one long schuss from the Idaho border. **Geophysical Nordic Ski Trails Sno-Park,** on Indian Creek Road east of Newport, has 10 kilometers of groomed trails that wind through a cold, very scenic pine forest. **The Upper Wolf Nordic Trail** system—the winter incarnation of the Wolf Donation Trail north of Newport—offers 4 kilometers of short, often steep, groomed trails. State Sno-Park passes, available at local ranger stations and ski shops, are required. For snow reports, call the Newport Ranger District; (509) 447-7300. The **Sherry Lake** area (see Hiking/Backpacking, above) along Hwy 20 also is a popular, nongroomed cross-country area, as are the **Tiger** and **Coyote Rock Loops** along Hwy 20 at Frater Lake.

Boating/Canoeing/Kayaking

Upper **Franklin D. Roosevelt Lake,** the flooded backwater from Grand Coulee Dam, is a boater and water-skier's dream. See the Camping section above and the Grand Coulee: Coulee Dam to Soap Lake chapter for launch and campground information. **Sullivan Lake** is a clear, beautiful waterway, but jet skiers and fast motorboats can ruin the experience for canoeists. Better bets for quiet paddlers are **McDowell Lake** and **Bayley Lake** in the Little Pend Oreille Wildlife Area (see Fishing and Wildlife, above). The fast waters of the **Kettle River** below Orient Bridge are popular kayak/rafting/inner-tubing rapids when water conditions allow. Call the Kettle Falls Ranger District, (509) 738-6111, for details.

Picnics

A nice roadside stop, **Crystal Falls State Park,** offers views of the cascades on the Little Pend Oreille River; 14 miles east of Colville on Hwy 20.

Adventure Calendar

An annual highlight is July's **Poker Paddle,** a 40-mile canoe journey down the Pend Oreille River; (509) 445-1212.

Attractions

One of the state's least-known but most fascinating subterranean areas, **Gardner Cave,** in **Crawford State Park** north of Metaline Falls, is definitely worth the trip. More than 1,000 feet long, Gardner is one of the longest limestone caves in the Northwest, and State Park tour guides lead visitors through its upper half several times a day when the park is open (from May 1 to September 15). It's named after Ed Gardner, a local bootlegger who, legend has it, found the cave and claimed it as his own, only to lose it in a poker game to Metaline resident William Crawford, who later signed it over to the state. Unfortunately, many of the fantastic stalactite formations in the cave were vandalized before State Parks took over. The tours now follow a path on steel ramps with handrails. Bring a jacket; it's cold all year long. Follow Boundary Road north from Metaline Falls. Nearby **Boundary Dam** offers interesting tours that include treks through its labyrinth of rock tunnels; (509) 446-3073. The access road leads past Flume Creek Mountain Goat Viewing Area (see Wildlife, above).

Kettle Falls Historical Center, just north of Hwy 395 overlooking the Columbia River, tells the story of settlement at the historic falls—once a major salmon-harvesting spot, now a giant lake; (509) 738-6964. Nearby is **St. Paul's Mission,** built in 1848 and open daily; (509) 738-6266.

Restaurants

For recommended restaurants, see the Adjoining Areas to this chapter.

Lodgings

My Parent's Estate ☆ This 120-year-old house has been a mission school, an abbess's home for a Dominican convent, a home for troubled boys, and a private residence; it's now a quiet haven in the woods. The 43-acre estate on the Colville River boasts more amenities than most. Cross-country ski in the winter; float the Colville River in summer, hike, or play in the water at nearby FDR Lake. *7 miles past downtown Colville on Hwy 395; (509)738-6220; 719 Hwy 395, Kettle Falls; $$.*

More Information

Colville Ranger District: *(509) 684-7000.*
Department of Natural Resources, Colville: *(509) 684-7474.*
Kettle Falls Ranger District: *(509) 738-6111.*
Newport Ranger District: *(509) 447-3129.*
Republic Ranger District: *(509) 775-3305.*
Sullivan Lake Ranger District: *(509) 446-2681.*

Okanogan Highlands and Sherman Pass

From Omak north to Lake Osoyoos, east to Highway 395 and south to Highway 20, including Republic, Curlew, and Wauconda, portions of the Okanogan and Colville National Forests, and the Sherman Pass National Scenic Byway.

Anyone who grew up in high country marked by tall, straight ponderosa pines, crisp air, and autumn yellow larch-tree fireworks would call the Okanogan Highlands "God's country." Those of us who grew up anywhere else would be hard-pressed to disagree.

The Okanogan Highlands are rolling ranges of quiet, clean, unpeopled mountains just south of the Canadian border between the Okanogan and Columbia river valleys. This is wide-open country, a place where backpackers can still set out for two weeks— even in midsummer—and meet more bears and deer than people. Spacious, virtually unpopulated (save for a handful of interesting outpost communities), and largely left alone by Washington's recreating masses, this is prime discovery territory for anyone feeling the pinch of population in the "wilderness" closer to home.

You can choose your level of lonely here. The Okanogan Valley clings to the fringe of civilization, drawing occasional campers, anglers, hikers, and skiers from the wildly popular Methow Valley, one river drainage west. It's wild enough to be refreshing, close enough to semi-equipped towns such as Omak and Okanogan to offer comfort. Venture farther north and hang a hard right on Hwy 20, however, and it's easy to throw your mind back to the early 19th century, when the first hardy white explorers began following fur-trapping lines—and insatiable curiosities—down the Pend Oreille, Okanogan, and Columbia Rivers, in search of adventure and a water route to the Pacific.

For them, this was the last great frontier land in what would become the Northwestern United States. For many of us, it still is. Today, it's easy to get swept up in the same awe of discovery by parking the car at Sherman Pass and heading off on a trail into some of the least-traveled wildlands in the state. Hiking and backpacking are a treat in this region, but (and perhaps *because*) they're not the main focus. Fair numbers of Northwest hikers discovered the wonders of this section of the Okanogan National Forest some time ago. But it still never attracts the uncomfortable summer hordes often encountered in the North or South Cascades or the Alpine Lakes or Glacier Peaks Wildernesses.

Most who visit the Okanogan Highlands do so just to drive through and look, following Hwy 20, a National Scenic Byway, to Sherman Pass, at 5,575 feet the highest in the state. Those who stay on for a while usually do so to fish. Trout fishing is legendary in the cold, deep lakes and streams of this region, and more and more anglers are making the discovery—particularly as fly fishing continues to grow in popularity. Skiing, too, is drawing fair numbers of visitors to the Highlands. The rolling mountains and deep forests here have what many westside cross-country-skiing venues lack most: dry snow and profound silence.

Wildlife lovers also find treks to the Okanogan Highlands productive. The woods here are filled with deer, bear, cougar, lynx, and other predators. And lucky visitors might happen upon an even greater rarity, such as a moose, bighorn sheep, or great gray owl.

Choose your reason. Choose your method. But do make the trip. Several days in the Okanogan Highlands are almost enough to restore your faith in the cleansing power of Northwest fresh air.

Getting There

The Okanogan River Valley, which begins at the river's confluence with the Columbia near Brewster and runs north to the Canadian border, is best reached from the Seattle area by driving US 2 east to Wenatchee, then US 97 north. The Okanogan Highlands are crossed by driving Hwy 20, the Sherman Pass National Scenic Byway, east from US 97 at Tonasket. An alternate route for visitors of the Columbia Basin and Grand Coulee Dam is Hwy 21, which runs 53 miles north from Keller Ferry near Coulee Dam to the town of Republic, near Sherman Pass. Allow 4 to 5 hours to make the 225-mile drive from the Seattle area to Omak/Okanogan.

Adjoining Areas

SOUTH: **Grand Coulee: Coulee Dam to Soap Lake**

EAST: **Kettle Falls, Colville, and the Pend Oreille**

WEST: **Methow Valley**

inside out

Camping

On the west side of the broad Okanogan Highlands is the largest and most heavily used campground in the region, **Conconully State Park,** a popular summer fishing spot southwest of Tonasket on Conconully Lake. The park has broad lawns shaded by massive willow trees, making it a favorite summer lounging spot. Waterfront areas for swimming and boating are affected by broad fluctuations in lake levels. The campground has 83 sites (10 with water hookups) divided between a main camping area and a second, more primitive section closer to the lakeshore. Several private resorts ring the lake as well. Conconully is open summers only. Campsites cannot be reserved. *On Conconully Road 22 miles northwest of Omak (follow signs from Okanogan, Omak, or Tonasket); (509) 826-7408 or (800) 233-0321.*

Beyond Conconully Lake, along North Fork Salmon Creek Road (Forest Service Road 38) are four remote Okanogan National Forest campgrounds, **Cottonwood, Oriole, Kerr,** and **Salmon Meadows.** All are small, summer-only sites with water but few other facilities. *For information, call the Tonasket Ranger District; (509) 486-5100.*

Another string of popular Forest Service campgrounds is found in the Okanogan Highlands east of Tonasket, on Bonaparte Lake Road (Forest Service Road 32; turn north from Hwy 20). The Five Lakes area is home to four campgrounds, **Bonaparte Lake** (25 sites), **Beaver Lake** (4 sites), **Beth Lake** (17 sites), and **Lost Lake** (20 sites). The campgrounds all are lakefront areas at about 3,000 feet, with lake access for swimming, fishing, and boating. *For information, call the Tonasket Ranger District; (509) 486-5100.*

Farther east, Hwy 21 turns due north from Hwy 20 just east of Republic and leads up the Kettle River drainage to **Curlew Lake State Park.** The popular park offers great access to the east shore of Curlew Lake (see Fishing, below), a favorite fishing, boating, and swimming spot. Facilities include a boat launch and large day-use area with a swimming beach. The campground has 72 sites (18 with full hookups, 7 with water only) spread throughout a hilly, forested area along the lakeshore. You can fly in, as well: the park has five "fly-in" sites with tiedowns for planes landing at nearby Merritt Field. Several private resorts are located nearby. Curlew Lake is open summers only, although day-use activities such as cross-country skiing and ice fishing are common in the winter. Campsites can be reserved up to 11 months in advance by calling Reservations Northwest; (800) 452-5687. *On Hwy 21 9 miles north of Republic; (509) 775-3592 or (800) 233-0321.*

A handful of other Forest Service campgrounds are found along Hwy 20 itself. **Sweat Creek,** an Okanogan National Forest camp 31 miles east of Tonasket, has 9 sites, piped water, and few other facilities. *Contact the Tonasket Ranger District; (509) 486-2186.* **Kettle Range,** near Sherman Pass, has 9 sites. *Contact the Republic Ranger District; (509) 775-3305.* On the east side of Sherman Pass, **Canyon Creek**—a Colville National Forest camp nine miles west of Kettle Falls—has 12 sites, some short, barrier-free trails, and trout fishing in the creek. And **Trout Lake,** due north on Trout Lake Road, has 4 sites and good fishing access. *Call the Kettle Falls Ranger District; (509) 738-6111.*

The remaining public campgrounds in this region are scattered along either the Kettle River Arm of the backed-up Columbia near Kettle Falls, or on the west shore of the Columbia itself (actually the northern extremes of Franklin D. Roosevelt Lake). **Kettle River** and **Kamloops Island** (north of Kettle Falls on Hwy 395) and **Sherman Creek** and **Haag Cove** (on the west lakeshore south of US 20) are Coulee Dam National Recreation Area sites. *Call the Coulee Dam NRA office in Kettle Falls for information, (509) 738-6266.*

Fishing

The Okanogan Valley and Highlands provide some of the absolute best rainbow, brook, and lake trout fishing in Washington State. The first good example is **Conconully Lake and Reservoir** (see Camping, above), which opens in late April and remains productive through the summer. Both forks of **Salmon Creek** above the lake also are productive for rainbows, but note these are selective fishery waters: single, barbless hooks only; bait prohibited. Check the state regulations pamphlet. Nearby **Blue Lake** also offers good trout fishing. Another Tonasket-area lake worthy of note is **Aeneas Lake,** a fly-fishing–only water that produces some hefty rainbows every summer. It's a must-visit for state fly-casters.

The Five Lakes area at the end of Bonaparte Road (see Camping) is another popular trout-fishing hub. **Bonaparte, Beth, Beaver, Little Beaver,** and **Lost Lakes** all provide good fishing for brook and rainbow trout. Bonaparte, in particular, is legendary among the big-fish crowd. The clear, cold lake holds some truly massive Mackinaw (lake) trout. A handful of trout over 20 pounds have been horsed into boats here, and legend has it one monster weighing upward of 40 pounds was boated many years ago. At least that's what they say at the Bonaparte Lake Resort, where you can call to argue or get fish reports; (509) 486-2828. Bonaparte is open all year, but be warned: We've been here in the winter, and it's *c-c-c-cold*. (If you put your tongue on your fish bonker, it'll stick.)

Another very hot rainbow fishery is **Curlew Lake** north of Republic, which receives annual plants supplemented by fish raised here in net pens. It's open all year.

On the east side of the region, most of the small streams accessible from Hwy 20 provide fair trout fishing (check the regulations pamphlet for seasons). A particularly good access spot is the trail along **Canyon Creek** west of Kettle Falls (see Hiking, below). **Trout Lake** (see Camping, above) has good spring trout fishing, as does the **Kettle River** above the confluence with the Columbia at Kettle Falls (check special regulations and seasons here). For **Franklin D. Roosevelt Lake** fishing details, see the Grand Coulee: Coulee Dam to Soap Lake chapter. The upper portions of the lake are open all year and are particularly known for walleye fishing.

Boating/Canoeing

All the notable fishing lakes mentioned above are navigable by canoe or small craft. **Curlew Lake,** in particular, is a scenic canoe waterway. Rental boats are available from several Curlew Lake private resorts.

Hiking/Backpacking

The Five Lakes/Bonaparte Lake area (see Camping, above) is home to a handful of hiking trails that get you up above the rocky peaks and dry forests that dominate this region, as well as on some easy, family-friendly lakefront and forest paths. Hardcore backpackers won't be disappointed in this region, either. Trails fanning out from Sherman Pass, including the deservedly popular, 60-mile Kettle Crest route, rank among the finest high-country trekking routes in the state. For more detailed information and a full trail list, contact the ranger stations listed below. Following is a list of favorites.

Five Lakes area

Bonaparte Road, Tonasket Ranger District; (509) 486-2186:

The **Strawberry Mountain Trail** (moderate; 3.2 miles round trip), which begins near Lost Lake campground, is a nice walk with a gentle grade, climbing wild-strawberry–dominated slopes to some nice views of Bonaparte and Lost Lakes below and Canadian peaks afar. The crown jewel hike in this region, though, leads to Bonaparte Peak. The **South Side Bonaparte Trail** (moderate/difficult, 11 miles round trip) begins on Road 100 beyond Lost Lake Campground and climbs steadily to the 7,258-foot tiptop of Bonaparte and a stunning, 360-degree view good enough to merit not one, but two summit fire lookouts. An older leg of the trail begins at Bonaparte Campground and is still hikable, but adds another 1,000 vertical feet to the 1,200-foot ascent. Another good view hike in the area, this one much shorter, is the **Pipsissewa Trail** (moderate; 2 miles round trip), which climbs at a very agreeable grade (even for early morning) to a nice, flat overlook high above Bonaparte Lake. The trailhead is on Forest Service Road 100, beyond Lost Lake Campground. Another easy family trail in the Five Lakes area is **Beth Lake** (easy; 3.8 miles round trip), a nearly flat lakeside path along Beaver and Beth Lakes. The trail passes through Beth Lake Campground, but the main trailhead is in Beaver Lake Campground (see Camping, above). Another gem of a trail in the area is the **Big Tree Botanical Loop** (easy; 1.5 miles round trip), which begins on Forest Service Road 33 and weaves through a truly fantastic old-growth forest of larch and various pine trees, some of which are 500 or more years old. Yet another good family walk is the **Virginia Lilly Old-Growth Trail** (easy; 3-mile loop) off Forest Service Road 3240. This interpretive trail winds through a rich wildlife area; watch for deer, woodpeckers, and other creatures, and consider a dusk walk to look for magnificent great gray owls, the largest of North American owls.

Sherman Pass area

Hwy 20, Republic Ranger District; (509) 775-3305:

Some of Eastern Washington's premier high, ponderosa-dominated backpacking routes begin at or near Sherman Pass, the state's highest mountain crossing, at 5,575 feet. The star attraction here is the **Kettle Crest Trail,** which follows the crest of the Kettle Range in two sections north and south of Hwy 20. **The Kettle Crest North Trail** (difficult; 29 miles one way) is best hiked as a one-way through hike (or a dual-party, swap-keys-in-the-middle hike) between Sherman Pass and a northern trailhead on Boulder Creek Road, off US 395 north of Kettle Falls. The route climbs high and stays high, following ridge tops over or around Columbia Mountain, Wapaloosie Mountain, Copper Butte, Profanity Peak, and other prominent peaks. Views all along the route are fantastic, and good campsites are ample. The **Kettle Crest South Trail** (difficult; 29 miles round trip), which begins on the south side of Sherman Pass, is similarly scenic. A highlight is a short side trip to the summit of 7,100-foot Snow Peak.

Sherman Pass has its share of day hikes, too. On the north side, the **Columbia Mountain Trail** (moderate; 4.4 miles round trip) begins on the Kettle Crest North Trail, splitting off to the right about 1.5 miles from the trailhead and climbing to a killer lunch spot, elevation 6,500 feet, views outstanding. Near Kettle Range Campground (see Camping, above), the **Sherman Pass Tie Trail** (easy; 1 mile round trip) is a connector to the Kettle Creek Trail that makes a nice short day-hike on its own.

Eastside Sherman Pass

Kettle Falls Ranger District; (509) 738-6111:

The **Wapaloosie Trail** (moderate; 5 miles round trip) is another conduit to the Kettle Creek Trail that makes a fine day hike on its own. It's a nice walk through pine forest, with a moderate grade and very good views near the top. You almost have to do it, just so you can repeat the name to friends at the office. The trailhead is off Albian Road, which turns north from US 20 about 20 miles west of Kettle Falls. The **Log Flume Trail** (easy; .5 mile round trip) is an educational, though not overly scenic, trail from US 20 about 20 miles west of Kettle Falls. The old log flume, used to float cut pine trees out of the forest, is an interesting site. Nearby, in Canyon Creek Campground (see Camping, above) the **Canyon Creek Trail** (easy; 2 miles round trip) is a beautiful, barrier-free trail along the rushing, clear waters of Canyon Creek. This is a great family day hike, with good river access for anglers (see Fishing, above). Another popular view hike is **Barnaby Butte** (moderate; 3.4 miles round trip), which follows an old road from Forest Service Road 680 to a fine regional viewpoint.

And don't overlook the **Thirteenmile Trail** (moderate; 26 miles round trip), which wanders through a magnificent forest of old-growth ponderosa pine. The grade is moderate to easy, unless you embark on any of a number of side trails to the top of peaks such as Fire Mountain. It's a great route for a three- to five-day backpack jaunt, or just a quick day hike on the lower portions. To reach the trailhead, drive 6.5 miles east of Sherman Pass on Hwy 20, and turn south on Hall Creek Road. Proceed 2.5 miles to Road 300, turn east (left), and continue to the road's end.

Wildlife

Two of Washington's least-seen, but most majestic, beasts roam the hillsides in this region.

The Okanogan Highlands are **bighorn sheep** country, and one of a small handful of areas in the state where you can reliably see them. Little

Vulcan Mountain, off West Kettle River Road west of Curlew, is a prime bighorn habitat. The big sheep often are spotted through binoculars and spotting scopes from the road. If you want to get closer, a steep, unmaintained trail runs up the mountain from Forest Service Road 2114. Your chances improve in spring and fall, when the sheep are more active.

You also have a small chance of meeting up with a **moose.** Occasional sightings are made at the Sherman Creek–Growden Heritage Site, between Kettle Falls and Republic along Hwy 20. **Deer** and **beaver** are more commonly seen here. But you never know when a Bullwinkle might amble by. Short day-hiking trails begin at the interpretive exhibit here.

Skiing

They might not be big, glitzy, or even all that organized, but **downhill** turns can be made at two small day-skiing areas in the Okanogan Valley. **Loup Loup Ski Bowl,** between Twisp and Okanogan on Hwy 20, has two poma lifts and a rope tow to service about 1,200 feet of vertical, as well as 30 kilometers of groomed cross-country trails (and many more at the nearby Sno-Park, see below). The lifts run Wednesdays, Sundays, and holidays; (509) 997-5334. **Sitzmark**—21 miles northeast of Tonasket—is smaller yet, with two lifts covering about 650 vertical feet. The area also has about 6 kilometers of cross-country trails; (509) 486-2700.

Two large **cross-country trail systems** are found at Loup Loup Ski Bowl between Twisp and Okanogan on Hwy 20. **Loup Loup Sno-Park,** on the north side of Hwy 20, has 21 kilometers of mostly easy-to-intermediate trails. Trail fees are charged only when the ski area is running, on Wednesdays, Sundays, and holidays. **South Summit Sno-Park,** across Hwy 20, has 30 kilometers of trails for all abilities. State Sno-Park parking permits, available at outdoor retailers and ranger stations, are required.

Another state Sno-Park, **Highlands,** 16.5 miles northeast of Tonasket, is small (15-car parking lot) and remote, but the snow can be great, and some of the terrain will test even the most serious free-heelers. For snow reports and gear rentals, call Highland Nordic in Tonasket, (509) 485-3483, or Sitzmark Ski Shop, (509) 486-2700. Sno-Park trail access also is available at **Sherman Pass,** where trails aren't groomed or maintained, and at **Deer Creek Summit** 11 miles east of Curlew, where a 37-kilometer trail system (12.2 kilometers groomed) is found. For snow and grooming reports, call the Republic Ranger District; (509) 775-3305.

Scenic Drives

Sherman Pass Hwy 20 is a National Scenic Byway, and it's a well-deserved title. This high road across the Okanogan Highlands is a beautiful drive during spring and summer, but it's downright magnificent in the fall, when larch trees turn golden, traffic is even lighter than usual, and local wildlife is active. Keep your eyes peeled for a once-in-your-lifetime lynx spotting.

A very pretty loop trip off the main highway can be made by driving Hwy 20 east from Tonasket, turning north on **Bonaparte Lake Road** to the Five Lakes area, then continuing on **Tonasket-Havillah Road** past Sitzmark Ski Area and back to Tonasket. Pack a lunch and the hiking boots, and this trip can take all day.

outside in

Attractions

The **Okanogan County Historical Museum** (1410 Second, Okanogan; (509) 422-4272) has exhibits on local pioneer life; free, it's open May to September. On Hwy 155 east of Omak, **St. Mary's Mission** was founded by the Jesuits in the 1890s to minister to local Natives. It's open daily; (509) 826-2097. Another worthwhile historical stop is **Fort Okanogan Interpretive Center** (5 miles east of Brewster on Hwy 17; open Wednesday through Sunday, June through August), where artifacts are on display from the trading post and fort built by John Jacob Astor in 1811 at the confluence of the Columbia and Okanogan Rivers. The fort later became a Canadian Northwest/Hudson's Bay Company outpost, and paved the way for white settlement of the area. Like many historical sites in this part of the state, the fort, along with remains of an ancient Indian village in the same area, was flooded by damming of the Columbia.

An interesting stop in the old mining town of Republic near Sherman Pass is the **Stonerose Interpretive Center** and **Stonerose Fossil Center,** (509) 775-2295, where fossilized plants and animals from a local dig are on display. You can even rent picks and chisels and go out after your own.

Omak's famous—and controversial—Suicide Race is the climax of the **Omak Stampede** the second weekend each August. At the end of each of the four rodeos that take place over the three-day weekend, a torrent of horses and riders pours down a steep embankment, across the Okanogan River, and into the arena. No one's ever been killed during the races since the event started in 1933, but plenty of horses have broken their legs.

Restaurants

Breadline Cafe ☆   Here in the heart of steak and Stampede country, the Breadline offers a country-style menu: steak and scampi, Cajun chicken, and pasta. In the front of an old bottling-works building, the eatery includes a low-tech bistro/nightclub offering live music—from small folk bands to big-name blues artists like Charlie Musselwhite. Big, informal market in the back, too. *Ash and 1st; (509) 826-5836; 102 S Ash St, Omak; $.*

The Riverside Restaurant and Lounge ☆ An oasis in Washington's northeastern corner. The setting is pleasant, there's a view of the river, the produce is fresh, and the food is fairly simple but always good. Where else in this territory can you get a shredded beef enchilada sided by gently steamed asparagus? *On the main drag; (509) 779-4813; 813 River St, Curlew; $$.*

The Wauconda Cafe, General Store and Post Office If you want atmosphere, here it is in this small general store cum gas station cum post office cum restaurant. It's a popular hangout for the local folk, and the view across the rolling meadows is soothing. The food is fresh and simple. *The only place in town; (509) 486-4010; 2360 Hwy 20, Wauconda; $.*

Lodgings

U and I Motel The name suits this family-run place's folksiness. The two-room cabinettes, albeit small, are clean, cozy (with rustic paneling), and a deal, as are one-roomers with a double bed. Best of all, the grassy backyard and flower garden front the tranquil Okanogan. Pets okay. *Off Hwy 97 on old 97; (509) 422-2920; 838 2nd Ave N, Okanogan; $.*

More Information

Colville National Forest, Kettle Falls Ranger District: *(509) 738-6111.*

Colville National Forest, Republic Ranger District: *(509) 775-3305.*

Department of Transportation pass report: *(888) SNO-INFO.*

Okanogan National Forest Headquarters: *1240 Second Avenue S, Okanogan, WA 98840; (509) 826-3275.*

Omak Chamber of Commerce: *(509) 826-1880.*

Republic Chamber of Commerce: *(509) 775-3387.*

Tonasket Ranger District: *(509) 486-5100.*

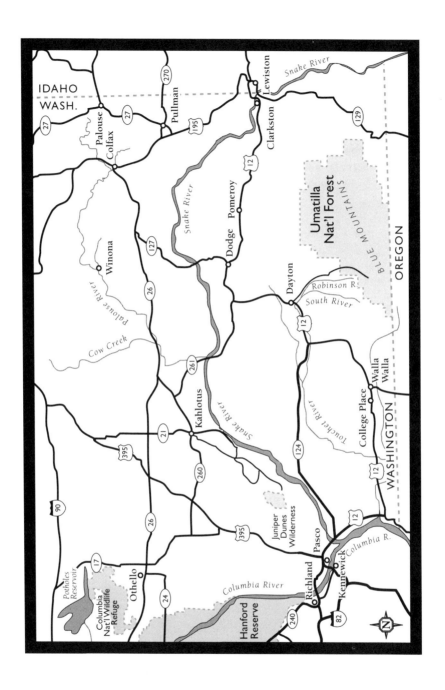

Southeast Washington

Southeast
Washington

Tri-Cities

From Benton City east to Lake Sacajawea, north to the Juniper Dunes Wilderness, and south to Paterson, including the towns of Kennewick, Richland, and Pasco.

You know you're in trouble when you look under the "outdoor recreation" section of the local chamber of commerce brochure and it lists "the tallest treeless mountain in the world" as a regional highlight.

Such is the case in the Tri-Cities of Kennewick, Richland, and Pasco, where the terrain is just barren enough to make a big, bald hump seem special. It's not all that bad, actually. What the Tri-Cities lack in vegetation, they make up for in water. The cities sit at the confluence of three mondo river systems: the Yakima, Snake, and Columbia. All that water power, coupled with a nearby Columbia River dam at Umatilla, Oregon, makes a long, broad lake that separates the three municipalities. Tri-Citians take full advantage of it. The region is a water sport mecca, with waterskiing, Jet-ski riding, fishing, and jet-boat tours leading the way for outdoor recreation. The watery oasis and four large wildlife areas also attract plenty of wildlife, particularly migratory birds.

The grandest Tri-Cities–area wildlife refuge of all, however, isn't even so designated. The Hanford Reach, a long stretch of the Columbia through the Hanford Nuclear Reservation, is the last free-flowing stretch of this oft-dammed super river. Sealed off from development for half a century while the Department of Defense fueled the Cold War arms race with Hanford-produced plutonium, the Hanford Reach is a splendid—and unique—example of the Columbia the way it was when explorer David Thompson set foot here in 1811.

The fate of the reach is up for grabs, with environmentalists arguing for protected status and local agribusinesses urging development. We can only hope the federal government has the good sense to save the last tiny slice of a massive river it has otherwise muted by hydropower development.

Folks in the Tri-Cities should hope so, too. The year after Hanford Reach gets the protected status it deserves, we can almost guarantee that that tall, treeless mountain will seem a lot less seductive.

Getting There

The Tri-Cities are 206 miles east of Seattle via Interstate 90 and I-82. Allow 4 hours.

Adjoining Areas

NORTH: **Columbia Basin**

EAST: **Walla Walla and Dayton**

WEST: **Yakima Valley**

inside out

Boating

The Tri-Cities area is the boat and water sports capital of interior Washington. Thanks to the region's always sunny weather and its great access to the broad Columbia (not to mention the absence of much else to do), Tri-Citians take to the water in huge numbers to water ski, fish, and race. Lake Wallula, the 64-mile-long Columbia impoundment behind McNary Dam near Umatilla, Oregon, makes for a broad, smooth boating track. So does Lake Sacajawea, the Snake River backup created by the Ice Harbor Dam, 9 miles east of Pasco. You'll find three actual yacht clubs in town, and it's not difficult to find boating supplies and services. Major public launches are found at all the waterfront parks listed in Swimming/Picnics, below.

Boatless outdoor lovers searching for the unique heart of this region should consider a jet-boat tour to **Hanford Reach,** the last free-flowing stretch of the Columbia River. This is the upside of the federal government's 50-year experiment with nuclear power on the sprawling Hanford Reservation. Because the river flows through the once heavily protected nuclear reservation, it was locked away from development—and from most human visitation, for that matter—for half a century. Not surprisingly, a wide range of wildlife has taken advantage, making boat or kayak trips through the reach a bird- and animal-watcher's treat. The future of this river stretch is very much up in the air; go soon if you want to see it like it always has been. Contact Jet Boat Adventures in Benton City; (509) 588-5310.

A similarly spectacular boating destination, **Hells Canyon** on the Idaho/Oregon border, is a short trip away. Contact Beamers Hells Canyon Tours and Adventures; (800) 522-6966.

Swimming/Picnics

On the Columbia (aka Lake Wallula), picnicking, swimming, and general lounging sites are available at more than a dozen small parks. The major venue is **Columbia Park,** on Hwy 240 (Columbia Drive) in Kennewick. The sprawling park has boat ramps, hiking/biking trails, picnic grounds, campsites (see Camping, below), and other attractions. **Sacajawea State Park,** near Pasco at the Columbia/Snake River confluence, has interpretive exhibits describing Lewis and Clark's 1805 stopover, plus a boat ramp, extensive moorage docks, and picnic grounds. Follow signs from US 12. Directly across the Columbia in Kennewick is **Two Rivers County Park,** which has a swimming area, boat launch, and picnic facilities. **Howard Amon Park,** along the bank of the Columbia in Richland, is a great spot for picnics, tennis, golf, jogging, or just ambling.

On the lower Snake River (aka Lake Sacajawea), there are picnic and swimming facilities at **Ice Harbor Lock and Dam; Charbonneau Park** and **Fishhook Park,** both off Hwy 124 on the southeast side of the lake; and at **Levey Park** on the lake's northwest shore, off Pasco-Kahlotus Road.

Camping

Many of the waterfront parks listed in Swimming/Picnics above, also offer camping.

Columbia Park has 122 sites (100 with full hookups; 26 drive-through) in an open (often hot), grassy area. It's open from mid-April to mid-October, and campsites may be reserved. *Off Columbia Drive in Kennewick; (509) 783-3711.* **Charbonneau Park** on Lake Sacajawea is a Corps of Engineers–operated campground with 55 sites (full hookups; 18 drive-through) on the lower Snake River near Ice Harbor Dam. The park is open all year, and campsites cannot be reserved. *Off Hwy 124 southeast of Pasco; (509) 547-7781.* **Fishhook Park** has 35 tent sites and 41 RV sites (no hookups; 8 drive-through) on Lake Sacajawea. The park is open summers only, and campsites cannot be reserved. *On Page Road, off Hwy 124 southeast of Pasco; (509) 547-7781.* **Hood Park,** another Corps of

Engineers development, has 69 standard sites on the lower Snake River. Good river access here for swimming and boating. It's open summers only, and campsites cannot be reserved. *Off Hwy 124 near Pasco; (509) 547-7781.*

The state's **McNary Habitat Management Area,** next to the McNary National Wildlife Refuge (see Wildlife, below), has a Fish and Wildlife campground with 24 primitive sites and no piped water. It's open all year, it's free, and it's not your best choice unless you're a very enthusiastic birder. *Southeast of Pasco, follow signs from US 12; (509) 456-4082.*

To the south, **Crow Butte State Park** is a unique site—it sits on an island in the middle of the Columbia River, called Lake Umatilla because of the flooded backwater from John Day Dam. The park is situated on what once was a high bluff. The campground has 50 sites (full hookups), a 60-person group camp, a boat launch and moorage, and a swimming area. Short hiking trails lead to the top of 670-foot Crow Butte, which offers views of Mount Hood. The land on the park's eastern border is a portion of the Umatilla National Wildlife Refuge, a significant migratory waterfowl nesting site. Crow Butte is open all year. Campsites can be reserved up to 11 months in advance by calling Reservations Northwest; (800) 452-5687. *On Hwy 14, cross a bridge to the island; 12.5 miles west of Paterson on Hwy 14; (509) 875-2644 or (800) 233-0321.*

Hiking

Hikes in the Tri-Cities area are limited. They're also a study in extremes. On the soft side, the 6.2-mile trail through **Columbia Park** (see Camping, above) is a paved, smooth walkway through the greenest greenery you'll find in this area: watered park lawns. On the harsher side, fans of open, dry country will find plenty of that—and solitude to match—in the 7,140-acre **Juniper Dunes Wilderness** north of Pasco. The wilderness is so wild, it's tough even to get to. There's one unmarked access road, but no marked trailheads or facilities. Pick up a good map and find the entryway off Peterson Road, reached by driving north from US 12 on the Pasco-Kahlotus Hwy. Your best bet is to contact the BLM office in Spokane, (509) 353-2570, for directions to the single "trail"—an old jeep road that slices through the southern section of the wilderness. Once there, you have to park outside the boundary and bring your own water. You don't need to follow a trail to explore this area. And it *is* worth the trouble, if you're into unique topography, such as the largest sand dunes—up to 130 feet high and a quarter-mile wide—and the largest natural groves of western juniper—some 150 years old—in the state. This pocket of wilderness is all that remains of an ecosystem that once stretched over nearly 400 square miles south to the Snake and Columbia Rivers. The area also is rich with desert wildlife and wildflowers. It's big enough to get lost in, but small enough for you to quickly walk back out. The wilderness is only about 4.5 miles square, so a (fenced) boundary is never more than a couple of hours away.

Most of the other maintained trails in the area wind through the four wildlife refuges surrounding the Tri-Cities. See Wildlife, below.

Wildlife

Four wildlife refuges form a bird- and animal-watching square around the Tri-Cities. Badger Slope, to the west near Benton City, is a Bureau of Land Management area on an antenna-farm bluff overlooking the Yakima River. Its open grasslands and basalt cliffs are a major feeding/nesting site for raptors, including several **hawk** species, **falcons, turkey vultures,** and **golden eagles. Marmots** also are often seen in the fields. Follow McBee Road west from I-82 at Kiona.

Right in the center of the Tri-Cities sprawl is Yakima River Delta Wildlife Park, at the confluence of the Yakima and Columbia Rivers. The site incorporates Richland's Wye Park and Bateman Island, a Columbia River island connected by a short dike. Trails run north, to the Yakima Confluence, and in a loop around Bateman Island. The area is a major waterbird hangout. Watch for **geese, ducks,** and **blue herons.** This is a decent canoeing spot, with some quiet-water shorelines and a boat launch in Wye Park. Off Columbia Drive between Richland and Kennewick.

On the far side of the Columbia south of Pasco is the McNary National Wildlife Refuge, a 3,600-acre reserve near the Snake River confluence. This is a major wetland, with acres of swamps, sloughs, and grasslands that attract a wide variety of **shorebirds. Pelicans** also are frequently seen here in the summertime, and **northern harriers** and **burrowing owls** are occasionally seen. A mile-long interpretive trail at the west end of the refuge is open all year, but other areas are closed periodically during nesting seasons. Follow signs from Hwy 12, south of Pasco.

The Wallula Habitat Management Unit is a significant 2,000-acre wetlands farther south on US 12—a good place to view migratory **geese,** a variety of **ducks,** some **raptor** species, and **pelicans.** There are no maintained trails, but a series of gated access roads skirt three of the area's five ponds. They're open to foot traffic. The area is managed by the Corps of Engineers.

Fishing

Here's a shock: a stretch of the **Columbia River** that you can actually wade out and fish like a river! The waters around Ringold in Hanford

Reach, the last free-flowing stretch of the Columbia, are notable fall steelhead territory, with good success for anglers casting spinning gear from gravel bars. Farther downstream, the deep, slow waters behind McNary Dam also provide good to very good winter steelhead fishing for boat trollers. The river also holds chinook salmon, whitefish, sturgeon, and largemouth and smallmouth bass. Newcomers might be wise to invest in a guide to fish this massive waterway. One local service is King's Fisher Guide Service of Richland; (509) 375-7442.

Fall steelhead action also can be good in the **Lower Snake River.**

outside in

Attractions

The **Tri-Cities wine country** is the hub of the huge Columbia Valley viticultural appellation, which includes both the Yakima Valley and Walla Walla Valley appellations within its borders. Here its three principal rivers (Columbia, Snake, and Yakima) converge. A few miles to the west, at Red Mountain, the Yakima Valley wineries begin; and a few miles to the east is the small cluster of Walla Walla Valley wineries. The Tri-Cities Visitors and Convention Bureau, (509) 735-8486, can provide up-to-date wine-touring maps and tasting-room schedules, and visitors will find some of the state's oldest wineries and vineyards located nearby (90 percent of the state's vineyards are reportedly located within a 50-mile radius of Red Mountain).

Richland was once a secret city, hidden away while the atomic bomb workers did their thing in the 1940s; now "the Atomic City" is the second largest of the Tri-Cities. Interestingly, Hanford now employs more people to dismantle the site than it ever did in its heyday. However, as nuclear reactors close and the controversy over hazardous waste continues, civic leaders are working hard on industrial diversification. **Hanford Science Center** in downtown Richland tells a bit of the saga of atomic energy; the energy displays are quite instructive; 825 Jadwin Avenue; (509) 376-6374. **Allied Arts** (89 Lee Boulevard, (509) 943-9815), located at the edge of the park, displays the work of mostly local artists in the oldest building in Richland.

Restaurants

The Blue Moon   If you don't need atmosphere to enjoy your dinner, you'll appreciate this seven-course prix-fixe meal (call for info about seatings and private parties). The lobster bisque is full-flavored, rich, and spicy, and entree selections often fantastic. Reservations essential. *A block from Washington; (509) 582-6598; 21 W Canal Dr, Kennewick; $$$.*

Casa Chapala   Tri-Cities' most endeared Mexican eatery is in Kennewick and is run by a couple so young that when they opened, they couldn't legally get a liquor license. They're old enough now and have maintained this very festive place where the tortillas are fresh, and you can be sure anything inside of them is too. *Columbia and Washington; (509) 586-4224; 107 E Columbia Dr, Kennewick; $.*

Chez Chaz ☆   A fun collection of salt shakers sits on the counter and every table has its own sodium centerpiece, but that's as whimsical as this restaurant in an office building gets. Most people choose to do Chez Chaz for a well-executed lunch. There is a long list of sandwiches—try the great hot version of the Smoky Tom. *Between Edison and Union on W Clearwater; (509) 735-2138; 5011 W Clearwater Ave, Kennewick; $$.*

The Emerald of Siam ☆☆   One of the most authentic Thai restaurants in Eastern Washington is located in a Richland shopping center. Thai-born Ravadi Quinn and her family run a cultural center for visiting school groups, a display of Thai handicrafts for sale, an Oriental grocery, and Quinn herself teaches occasional cooking classes and has put out her own cookbook, *The Joy of Thai Cooking. William and Jadwin; (509) 946-9328; 1314 Jadwin Ave, Richland; $.*

Giacci's ☆   In Richland's oldest building (1906), wonderful aromas waft from the busy kitchen and Puccini arias float through the air. Good salads and Italian sandwiches comprise the lunch menu at this attractive deli/restaurant. Excellent desserts, and outdoor tables in summer. *Corner of George Washington and Lee; (509) 946-4855; 94 Lee Blvd, Richland; $.*

Lodgings

Quality Inn on Clover Island   It's truly on an island, and thus offers wonderful river views from many of its 150 rooms. The Quality Inn in Kennewick gains our favor for its comparatively inexpensive rates. Otherwise, there's not much to distinguish this well-situated link in the chain (lodgings) from its Red Lion and Holiday Inn cousins. *Columbia Dr and Washington; (509) 586-0541; 435 Clover Island, Kennewick; $.*

Red Lion Hanford House ☆   Location, location, location. For conventions you might do better at the Best Western Tower Inn down the street, but the Hanford House has secured Richland's finest piece of real estate right on the Columbia (aka Lake Wallula) stretched with more miles of park than most guests can manage in an afternoon jog. This is the place to stay in the Tri-Cities. *Take Richland exit off I-82 to George Washington;* *(509) 946-7611; 802 George Washington Way, Richland; $$.*

Red Lion Inn ☆   The large, sprawling Pasco motel in half-timbered style has two outdoor pools, an exercise facility, and an 18-hole municipal golf course that runs right alongside the motel, making it appear to be set in a park—even though it's right on the freeway. One of the few restaurants in Eastern Washington that really knows how to cook seafood *and* beef. *Take 20th St exit off Hwy 395; (509) 547-0701; 2525 N 20th St, Pasco; $$.*

Cheap Sleeps

Nendel's   There's nothing fancy about Nendel's, but you can get a clean room for a fair price with a moderate amount of style. *(509) 943-4611 or (800) 547-0106; 615 Jadwin Ave, Richland.*

More Information

Tri-Cities Visitors and Convention Bureau: *(509) 735-8486 or (800) 666-1929.*

BB&M Inc. (wide range of sporting goods and camping gear): *1382 Jadwin Avenue, Richland; (800) 400-9127.*

Sporthaus Northwest (skis, sporting goods, inline skates): *326 N Columbia Center Boulevard, Kennewick; (509) 735-7555.*

Walla Walla and Dayton

From Walla Walla north to Dayton, east to Chief Joseph Wildlife Area, and south to the Oregon border, including the Blue Mountains, a section of Umatilla National Forest, the Wenaha–Tucannon Wilderness, and Bluewood Ski Area.

The land of the double Walla is the Willie Nelson song of Northwest outdoor venues: high, dry, and lonesome. Walla Walla represents what writer and social historian Richard Rodriguez notes is an ironic modern twist on the nation's westward-ho mentality: Puget Sound–area residents are heading *east* in search of the *real* West—the one of wide-open plains, rugged mountain ranges, awe-inspiring river gorges, and honest, earthbound people. To which proud Walla Walla residents would say, "Welcome, pilgrim."

Of course, like most Eastern Washington regions in this guide, the Walla Walla area certainly isn't for everybody. Whether you're talking about onions (biggest, sweetest), weather (freezing/boiling), or history (rough and occasionally violent), Walla Walla is a land of extremes. You don't perspire here in summer. You power-sweat. You don't shiver in winter. You turn blue. Then again, you're not likely to ever encounter a traffic jam, either on the road, in the campground, or at the local latte stand. Nor are you likely to see more than a dozen other hikers on the nearest local hiking trail, regardless of the season.

Walla Walla is about as far from Seattle as you can get without lapsing into Idaho, which for many visitors is reason enough to make the trek. Once here, however, they discover that this land is more than just far away. The lands surrounding Walla Walla—which sits on a flat volcanic plateau—are downright impressive, with clear streams, deep, rugged canyons, and wide-open skies. Impressive gives way to beautiful a short distance to the east, where the lava-forged Blue Mountains rise from the plains of the Snake River flatlands. Here, high, rocky peaks provide stunning territorial views of a half-dozen river canyons carved by liquid-crystal rivers. Mountain slopes are roamed by Rocky Mountain elk, trophy-size mule and white-tailed deer, impressive bighorn sheep, and unsettlingly brash black bears and cougars. Most of this wild mountainous area lies within the Umatilla National Forest, which straddles the Washington/Oregon border. The heart of the mountains was protected as federal wilderness in 1978. The Wenaha–Tucannon Wilderness (177,000 acres) is a former game preserve that's still home to some of Washington's healthiest elk, deer, and bighorn sheep herds. More elk set foot inside the wilderness every year than people.

Treks here, whether by automobile, foot, ski, snowshoe, or horseback, are some of the most scenic—and least crowded—in the state. This Wilderness provides a classic, wide-open Western experience very reminiscent of the best Wyoming or Montana backcountry. And the busy little city of Walla Walla, which manages a degree of unpretentious sophistication that belies its size and location, is a perfect launching point.

As mentioned above, weather can be a drawback here; Walla Walla bakes in the summer and gets tongue-sticking cold in the winter. Consider trekking this way during the "shoulder seasons," spring or autumn. A trip to the Blue Mountains in the late spring—when the top layer of snow is gone but the most deadly heat is still on its way—brings pleasant weather, mind-boggling bursts of wildflowers, and very few other people. Likewise, an autumn trip—preferably before mid-October, when hunting season begins in earnest, brings fantastic crisp, clear skies and mountain color.

Whenever you go, you're bound to return convinced there's a lot more to the Walla Walla area than meets the faraway eye. If the weather cooperates and the rattlesnakes stay away, you just might head back West with a set of nature-sparked memories which, like many a local onion, are actually bigger than your own head.

Getting There

It might feel like 400, but the odometer says Walla Walla is a mere 260 miles southeast of Seattle via Interstate 90 to Ellensburg, I-82 to Tri-Cities, then US 12. Give yourself a solid 5 hours. From Walla Walla, US 12 continues northeast to Dayton and Pomeroy, the two gateways into hiking, camping, skiing, and fishing venues in the Umatilla National Forest and Wenaha–Tucannon Wilderness.

Adjoining Areas

NORTH: **Snake River Country: Clarkston, Pullman, and the Palouse**

WEST: **Tri-Cities**

Camping

In town, the primary campground is **Walla Walla Campground** at Fort Walla Walla Park, the 1856 Army fort that now houses a museum, playfields, and a nature preserve. The park has 125 sites (76 with hookups; maximum RV length, 35 feet) in an attractively wooded, grassy area with a nearby stream. For an in-city campground, this one's a peach. Or an onion, if you're using the local sweet-food scale. The campground is open all year. Campsites can be reserved. *On Dalles Military Road; (509) 527-3770.*

Up US 12 between Waitsburg and Dayton, **Lewis and Clark Trail State Park** (not to be confused with Lewis and Clark State Park in Winlock) is a small place set in a very pleasant forest of big, straight ponderosa pines with a tinder-dry grassy floor. The park, which fronts on the Tucannon River, is an oasis in this flat, dry area—no doubt one reason the Lewis and Clark Expedition chose it as a stopping point as they returned from their Pacific trek in 1806. The park is split by US 12; day-use areas, playfields, and picnic grounds are on the south side, camping to the north. The two riverside loops contain 34 campsites (no hookups; maximum RV length, 28 feet) and a 100-person group camp. The park also has several hiking trails, including a short interpretive trail from the camping area. Lewis and Clark Trail State Park is open all year, with limited winter camping. Campsites cannot be reserved. *On US 12 4.5 miles west of Dayton; (509) 337-6457 or (800) 233-0321.*

For a remote campout—and we're talking really remote here—consider one of five small **Umatilla National Forest** campgrounds in or near the Wenaha–Tucannon Wilderness. Most of them make excellent jump-off points for wilderness backpacking or fishing treks, and are used most heavily in the fall, when elk and deer hunters flock to the wilderness area. For forest maps and other information, contact the Pomeroy Ranger District; (509) 843-1891.

Tucannon, 20 miles south of Pomeroy on Forest Service Road 47, has 6 sites (no hookups; maximum RV length, 16 feet), a small picnic area, and good access to the Tucannon River, where trout fishing can be excellent (see Fishing, below). It's free, open summers only, and has no piped water. **Camp William T. Wooten State Park,** an Environmental Learning Center with a group camp but no other camping, is nearby.

Alder Thicket, 20 miles south of Pomeroy on Forest Service Road 40, has 6 small sites (maximum RV length, 16 feet). The camp, at 5,100 feet in the Blue Mountains and open summers only, is free and has no piped water. A short distance to the south, **Big Springs,** 23 miles south of Pomeroy on Forest Service Road 42, offers 6 small campsites (no hookups) at a high (5,100 feet) dry location in the Blue Mountains. It's free, open summers only, and has no piped water. A bit farther south and a bit more removed is **Teal Spring,** 26 miles south of Pomeroy on Forest Service Road 40, another high-altitude (5,600 feet) campground in the Blue Mountains. Open summers only, Teal Spring has 8 campsites (no hookups; maximum RV length, 15 feet). It's free and has no piped water. The Clearwater Lookout tower (see Scenic Drives/Photography, below) is nearby.

Godman, 25 miles southeast of Dayton on Forest Service Road 46 (Kendall Skyline Road; see Scenic Drives/Photography, below), is a favorite hiking and horse-packer launching point, with hitching rails and other horse facilities. For campers, there are 8 sites (no hookups; maximum RV length, 15 feet) and few other services. Godman, which lies one creek drainage east of Ski Bluewood, is free, open summers only, and has no piped water.

The easternmost camp, **Wickiup,** is 34 miles southeast of Pomeroy via Forest Service Roads 40 and 44. It has 9 campsites (no hookups; maximum RV length, 16 feet). The campground is free, open summers only, and has no piped water.

Western Washington campers frustrated by big crowds and searching for that one state park really, really out there away from the hordes can stop and plant the flag at **Field's Spring State Park.** This park—located 30 miles south of Clarkston, just north of the Grande Ronde River Canyon, and east of...well, just about everything—lies in a thicket of trees marking the transition from flat plains lands to the high, dry forests of the Blue Mountains. It's a lovely spot, rich with wildflower blooms on mountain slopes in the spring, and with wildlife all year round. Don't miss the hiking trail to the grand view atop Puffer Butte (see Hiking/Backpacking, below). The campground has 24 campsites (no hookups; maximum RV length, 30 feet), as well as playfields and other day-use facilities. It's a very popular winter hangout, with lighted sledding and tubing runs near the park's twin Environmental Learning Centers, and many marked cross-country ski routes on local fire roads (see Skiing/Snow Play, below). Fields Spring is open all year. Campsites cannot be reserved. *30 miles south of Clarkston on Hwy 129; (509) 256-3332 or (800) 233-0321.*

Hiking/Backpacking

For strolling Walla Walla itself, the city has a nice **walking tour,** outlined on a pamphlet available at the Chamber of Commerce, 29 E Sumach Street. If you're just looking to get the kids (or yourselves) out of the car for a stretch, **Lewis and Clark Trail State Park** (see Camping, above) has two nice hiking trails. One is a mile-long nature loop, the other a mile-long bird-watching trail. Interpretive information is available for both.

Another great day hike is found in **Field's Spring State Park** (see Camping, above). It's a long haul from the Walla Walla area, but people camped at the state park should make the time to climb to **Puffer Butte** (moderate; 2 miles round trip). At the top of this 4,500-foot butte, awesome views loom in all directions: the Grande Ronde River Canyon to the south, the Snake River Canyon to the east, and the Blue Mountains to the southwest. It's one of Eastern Washington's best viewpoints.

Some of the dry side's most inspiring countryside can be reached by trail throughout the 177,000-acre **Wenaha–Tucannon Wilderness** and the surrounding Umatilla National Forest in the Blue Mountains east of Walla Walla. This is rugged, spectacular country, with high basaltic peaks separated by steep, deep canyons. It's truly wild, a fact reflected in the rich population of large mammals such as elk, deer, bighorn sheep, and black bear. One of the largest Rocky Mountain elk herds in Washington lives here, drawing crowds of winter hunters, who enjoy "grandfathered" status that allows them to continue hunting in this former game reserve. Most hunting takes place from mid-October to mid-November—a good time to stay clear if you're hiking.

Weather can be extreme here, with summer temperatures often in the high 90s and winters brutally cold and often snowy. Most hikes in this wilderness are far from being easy strolls, but backpack trips can be memorable. Wilderness regulations restrict group size to 12 and prohibit camping within 75 feet of streams. Dogs are allowed, and no permits are required. For road and trailhead updates, maps, and other information, contact the Pomeroy Ranger District; (509) 843-1891.

The Tucannon River Trail (easy; 8.2 miles round trip) is one of the most pleasant hikes in this area, with a gentle grade along the Tucannon River making it a favorite of fly-casters, who come here in pursuit of hefty trout. The Tucannon Trail is a favorite of many Eastern Washington families, who introduce kids to backpacking here. Deer, elk, and bighorn sheep sightings are common, and great campsites are found at Ruchert Camp, about a mile up the trail. The trailhead is reached by driving Tucannon Road south from US 12 to Forest Service Road 4712 and proceeding up the left fork to the end of the road.

Another scenic walk down into the Tucannon River drainage, the **Bear Creek Trail** (moderate; 6 miles round trip) drops south from a ridgetop at Bear Creek Trailhead on Forest Service Road 40 to the Tucannon River Trail. The river is a favorite fly-fishing area, and a good place to wet your whistle before the climb back *up* to the car. In between are clusters of pine and tamarack that conceal the occasional mule deer or grouse.

Not far from Tucannon Campground (see Camping, above) is the **Panjab Trail** (moderate; 11.2 miles round trip), a popular horseback route that begins on Panjab Road (Forest Service Road 4713) and ends at Indian Corral horse camp. Most of the route maintains a moderate pace along Panjab Creek, then climbs steeply at the end to the camp. From the same trailhead, long-distance backpackers can embark on the **Crooked Creek Trail** (moderate; 22 miles one way), one of several trails that cut through a long portion of the wilderness area. The route follows Panjab Creek to Indian Corral, then drops through the Trout Creek, Third Creek, and Crooked Creek Valleys to a southern trailhead at Three Forks, off Forest Service Road 4039 near the Oregon border. This is a scenic wilderness traverse, with peaceful, wildlife-rich valleys and plenty of solitude.

Trailheads in the vicinity of Godman Camp on Forest Service Road 46 offer some of the best day hiking in the area. A good half-day hike with rich regional views, the **Oregon Butte Trail** (moderate; 6 miles round trip) climbs to a magnificent fire lookout that's still staffed during summer months. Views of the Wallowa and Seven Devil ranges are magnificent from the lookout, which is perched at 6,400 feet. The trail begins at Teepee Trailhead at the end of Forest Service Road 4608 (from Godman Guard Station, turn left on Road 4608 and take all right turns for 5 miles to the trailhead). Backpackers needn't turn around at Oregon Butte. For a long, fantastic trip through the wilderness, continue on the same path along the **Smooth Ridge Trail** (difficult; 40 miles round trip), which has good campsites and—a rarity here—plenty of fresh water all along the route. Below, near the Godman Ranger Station, the **West Butte Trail** (moderate; various distances possible) works its way through a number of scenic creek valleys, any one of which makes for a good overnight trip.

In the North Fork Touchet River drainage (the Ski Bluewood resort area), a good day hike can be had on the **Sawtooth Trail** (moderate/difficult; 8 miles round trip). The trail is actually a long, dry traverse to the

Wenaha River drainage, but for the first 4 or 5 miles it follows Sawtooth Ridge south, rewarding hikers with grand views of Squaw Peak, Table Rock, and the upper Wenaha River drainage. The trailhead is near Burnt Flat, about 3.5 miles beyond Ski Bluewood on Forest Service Road 46.

Farther south, the **Slick Ear Trail,** a popular backcountry angler's route (moderate/difficult; 10.5 miles round trip), drops steeply to a junction with the Wenaha River Trail across the Oregon border. The trailhead is near Twin Buttes, south of Ski Bluewood on Forest Service Road 300.

Fishing

The upper **Tucannon River,** which flows through the Umatilla National Forest, is one of Washington's prettiest trout streams, in the classic, dry-country fly-fishing tradition. The river, which bubbles to life in the Blue Mountains of the Wenaha–Tucannon Wilderness and flows north to join the Snake River near Starbuck, is accessible from many points along Tucannon Road, which runs south from US 12 just west of Pomeroy. Much of the challenge of fishing this river is discerning which portions are open when, and with what special regulations. Spend some time with the state fishing pamphlet and a good topographic map when you head out. Some of the river's best, most scenic fishing is in the upper drainage, which holds native and planted rainbow trout. See the list of Wenaha–Tucannon Wilderness campgrounds and hiking trails in Hiking/Backpacking, above, for access information. The lower river, with a decent winter steelhead run, is fished from the Snake River confluence upstream to the Tucannon Hatchery, about midway between Pomeroy and the wilderness boundary.

The **Touchet River** holds German brown trout and steelhead, and access is easy at Lewis and Clark Trail State Park (see Camping, above.)

More fair-to-good rainbow trout action usually can be found on the dozen small lakes and ponds in the **W. T. Wooten Wildlife Area** (see Wildlife, below). All the lakes are small enough to provide good bank access (indeed, boats are prohibited), and one lake, Big Four, is for fly-fishing only. The lakes are stocked with rainbows, and open March 1, but action often doesn't pick up until later, when the ice melts and water warms enough for fish to become active.

In the state's extreme southeast corner, the **Grand Ronde River** gives up a fair number of winter steelhead every year. Good access is available on Hwy 129, which runs south from Asotin.

Finally, if you have a taste for eels, head northeast to **Asotin Creek.** Asotin, legend has it, is a native word for "eel creek," and large numbers of the slithery wonders allegedly were harvested from the creek near its confluence with the Snake River. We're not sure if there's a limit on eels, but the creek mouth also is a known rainbow trout producer.

Picnics

Two nicely maintained city parks, **Pioneer** and **Veterans Memorial,** are good picnic spots, as are the grounds of **Whitman Mission Historical Site** west of town. For parks outside town, see the listings for Camping, above.

Skiing/Snow Play

One of Washington's least-known but most-fun ski areas, **Ski Bluewood** is tucked away in the slopes of the Blue Mountains, 21 miles southeast of Dayton. It's a small area, with only three lifts and 1,100 feet of vertical spread over 26 runs. But Bluewood's greatest drawing card—some of the highest, driest snow in the state—continues to lure skiers from afar, who catch on fast to the delights of Walla Walla and Clarkston skiers' secret powder stash. Weather can be extremely erratic here, as the winter of 1995–96 proved in a memorable way. Bluewood, which normally opens in late November or early December, still hadn't opened by mid-January; the resort sent most of its 150 employees home. Then in late January the snow gods let loose and made up for lost time. Bluewood was hammered by more than 7 feet of snow in seven days, creating some of the best ski conditions since Lewis and Clark staggered through here in 1806. Several weeks later, the season ended just as quickly as it began, when record rains and flooding wiped out Bluewood's only access road, closing the area for the season. The lesson: Call the ski report! If conditions are good at Bluewood (which is often the case), it makes a very relaxing weekend ski getaway for wet-side skiers tired of rain and lift lines, and the mountain is rarely, if ever, crowded.

Bluewood is open from 9am to 4pm Tuesdays through Sundays and all holiday Mondays. Adult all-day lift tickets are $25. From downtown Dayton, drive south on Fourth Avenue, which becomes North Fork Touchet Road at the city limits and Forest Service Road 64 at the forest boundary. Proceed 21 miles to the ski area. Mountain information: (509) 382-4725. Snow phone: (509) 382-2877.

Ski Bluewood also has 5 kilometers of **cross-country**/snowmobile **trails,** as well as access to many miles of backcountry skiing, snowshoeing, and snowmobiling in the Umatilla National Forest.

Many of the campgrounds in or around the **Wenaha–Tucannon Wilderness** (see Camping and Hiking/Backpacking, above) are home to backcountry skiers in the winter. Wilderness trails can provide memorable backcountry ski treks, with magnificent surroundings and plentiful wildlife. But be warned that route-finding is tough in the backcountry if you're not familiar with the terrain. Maps and suggestions are available at the Pomeroy Ranger District; (509) 843-1891.

Field's Spring Sno-Park, the winter incarnation of Field's Spring State Park (see Camping, above) provides 12 kilometers of groomed ski trails in loops ranging from an easy .2K trail to the 3K Grande Ronde Loop. The snow here usually is dry and cold, the scenery outstanding. State Sno-Park passes, available at outdoor stores and ranger district offices, are required to use the groomed trails and to park in the 80-car lot. Snow updates: (509) 256-3332.

Field's Spring State Park (see Camping and Hiking/Backpacking, above) also is a favorite winter family getaway, largely because of the diverse offerings here. The park literally offers one-stop winter fun shopping. There's something for everyone here, whether they're standing by the big fire or trekking far into the local hills on snowshoes. Kids are drawn to several excellent sled/tubing hills, one of which is lighted at night. A nice added touch are picnic shelters heated in the winter for frosty snow revelers. Snow updates: (509) 256-3332.

Mountain Biking

We're not sure if anyone makes a water bottle big enough to sustain an average fat-tire sweatmonger in the hills around Walla Walla and Dayton on your average summer day. It's hot, dry, dusty country. If that's your thing, though, the **Umatilla National Forest** has a hundred miles or so of dry forest roads—and a handful of single-track trails—with your name on them. Popular routes include the **Kendall Skyline Road 46** (see Scenic Drives/Photography, below) and the **Tucannon River Trail** (see Hiking/Backpacking, above). Contact the Pomeroy Ranger District, (509) 843-1891, for information on other open trails and roads.

Horseback Riding

The **Blue Mountains** are known for their dry, wide-open spaces—ideal terrain for short or extended horse-packing trips. The Umatilla National Forest, which manages the area, is well suited for equestrians, providing horse ramps, hitching posts, and other facilities throughout the Forest and the Wenaha–Tucannon Wilderness. Several local firms offer full-service horse-packing trips through this magical area. Call the Pomeroy Ranger District, (509) 843-1891, for outfitter referrals.

Scenic Drives/Photography

For a series of good vistas displaying the volcano- and river-forged wild-lands of the Blue Mountains and Wenaha–Tucannon Wilderness, take a drive on **Kendall Skyline Road 46.** From Dayton, drive south on Fourth Avenue and turn left on Eckler Mountain Road (County Road 9124). Proceed about 28 miles on the road, which turns to Road 46 at the forest boundary, and continue south to Godman guard station and campground, where several good day-hiking trails are found. The Oregon Butte Trail (see Hiking/Backpacking, above) is 5 miles up the road on Forest Service Road 4608.

Another popular day trip in the area is the drive to the 100-foot-high **Clearwater Lookout,** which offers a superb view of the wilderness area. Take Benjamin Gulch Road south from Pomeroy and proceed about 25 miles on Forest Service Road 40.

Wildlife

The William T. Wooten Wildlife Area is a great place to sample the wildlife of the Blue Mountains. **Rocky mountain elk,** big **mule** and **white-tailed deer, bighorn sheep, cougar, turkey,** and **quail** all are abundant in this area. (The Blue Mountains, in fact, are home to one of the state's largest Rocky Mountain elk populations, with more than 20,000 head.) Winter (late December through March) is one of the most productive viewing times; elk, bighorn sheep, and mule deer are commonly seen feeding on the 11,000-acre refuge. Follow Tucannon Road south from US 12 between Pomeroy and Dayton. A number of lakes in the refuge are popular sum-mertime fishing venues (see Fishing, above). The area is managed by the state Department of Fish and Wildlife; (509) 456-4082.

Even farther afield is Chief Joseph Wildlife Area, a beautiful canyon site along the Grande Ronde River—about as far southeast as you can go in Washington State. This remote canyon, a former winter camp of the Nez Perce, is a wintering area for Blue Mountains **mule deer** and **Rocky Mountain elk. Raptors, quail, partridge,** and **bluebirds** often are spot-ted on the cliffs in the spring. From Asotin, follow Snake River Road to Joseph Creek Road—and just keep going until you run out of state.

Nearer to civilization, Whitman Mission National Historic Site, east of Walla Walla, also is a designated wildlife site. A trail to the top of Whitman Memorial Hill often affords glimpses of **red-tailed hawks, pheasants, quail,** or **harriers.** Follow signs from US 12 west of Walla Walla.

Adventure Calendar

A big annual highlight is the **Walla Walla Balloon Stampede,** every May at Howard Park. We're told that, barring an unexpected climatic event, the balloons do not actually stampede. But 40 to 50 of them all gassed up at once create quite a spectacle, nonetheless. The festival's **sheep dog trials** also are a fascinating spectator event.

The city's old-time heritage is celebrated every July during the **Walla Walla Mountain Man Rendezvous** (certainly *not* to be confused with Roslyn's Manly Man Contest) at Fort Walla Walla. Black powder and flying axes everywhere! Call the Walla Walla Chamber of Commerce, (509) 525-0850, for details.

Attractions

The Walla Walla valley is an important historical area: the Lewis and Clark Expedition passed through in 1805 and returned in 1806; fur trappers, following in the canoe path of famed British explorer David Thompson, began traveling up the Columbia River from Fort Astoria in 1811 and set up a fort in 1818. In 1836, missionary Marcus Whitman built a medical mission west of the present town. Later, blamed for an outbreak of measles, Whitman and his wife, Narcissa, and a dozen fellow settlers were slain by a band of Cayuse Indians in the famous "Whitman Massacre" of 1847. The subsequent Cayuse War helped hasten Oregon Territory's statehood in 1848, and settlement in the Walla Walla area was halted until territorial governor Isaac Stevens signed treaties with the Cayuse (and most other Washington tribes) in 1855. The U.S. Army's Fort Walla Walla was built to keep this "peace" in 1856.

The town was founded the same year by fort developer Colonel Edward Steptoe and later named Walla Walla, a derivation of the native word *walatsa,* which means "running water" or "many waters." Main Street was built on the Nez Perce Trail (much to the chagrin of the Nez Perce and other tribes, which had hunted and traveled here for centuries). Washington's first commercial enterprises, banks, and railroads came here in the 1860s, when a flood of settlers came looking for gold in the Northern Rockies.

Since then, Walla Walla has grown into a pleasant vale with a population of 26,000 with fecund wheatlands all around. **Whitman College,** a pretty private college, anchors the city. The campus is a nice place to stroll; (509) 527-5176. The community boasts the oldest continuous symphony west of the Mississippi River, which performs a season of winter concerts.

Whitman Mission National Historic Site, 7 miles west of town, off Hwy 12, sketches out the story of the mission and the massacre; there aren't any historic buildings, but the simple outline of the mission in the ground is strangely affecting. A hike up Whitman Memorial Hill to an overlook (see Wildlife, above) offers the best impression of what the area looked like to the Whitmans and fellow settlers. The mission became an important station on the Oregon Trail, and Narcissa Whitman's arrival was notable in that she and Eliza Spalding, also with the Whitman party, were the first white women to cross the continent overland. Also, this is the place to find out what a real gristmill is. Call (509) 529-2761.

Fort Walla Walla Museum, in Fort Walla Walla Park on the west edge of town, has a collection of 14 historic buildings and pioneer artifacts from the state's Indian wars era. Call (509) 525-7703 for hours; camping and picnicking sites are available at the park adjacent to the museum. Summers only.

A number of old houses are worth a stop. **Kirkman House Museum,** listed on the National Register of Historic Places, is a fine period-home museum; 214 N Colville Street, (509) 529-4373. Mature trees and Colonial architecture lend a New England feeling to **Catherine Street, South Palouse Street,** and **West Birch Street. Pioneer Park** on E Alder Street is a good example of the urban-park style of 80 years ago and was designed by the Olmsted brothers, the landscape architects whose father created New York City's Central Park and Seattle's Lake Washington Boulevard. The park has an excellent open-air aviary with a fine collection of pheasants, pigeons, and native waterfowl.

Lest we forget the onions: **Walla Walla Sweets** are splendid, truly sweet onions, great for sandwiches. (So sweet, in fact, that the author's great-grandfather reportedly ate one every day for lunch, just like an apple.) The onion strain was carried here in 1916 by a European immigrant, and subsequently cultivated for sweetness. The key to good taste, farmers say, is a lack of sulfur in local soils. Those of you who thought you drove all the way for nothing, take note: In Walla Walla, you can get the "number ones," with thin skins. Celebrate all this, plus undoubtedly much more, at the annual **Walla Walla Sweet Onion Harvest Festival** at Fort Walla Walla every July.

The region is also home to some of the state's most brilliant wineries. Most notable is **Woodward Canyon** (Lowden; (509) 525-4129), which produced a cabernet in 1987 that was judged one of the top 10 in the world by *Wine Spectator.* Others are **L'Ecole No. 41,** Lowden, (509) 525-

0940; **Leonetti Cellars,** Walla Walla, (509) 525-0940; **Waterbrook Winery,** Lowden, (509) 522-1918; and **Seven Hills Winery,** (509) 529-3331, with production facilities over the state line in Milton-Freewater, Oregon, (509) 938-7710 (open by appointment only).

It's a lot more than just the Green Giant plant. An impressive **88 Victorian buildings** on the National Register of Historic Places make Dayton worthy of a stop, although don't expect to find all of the buildings restored. Dayton, on the main stage route between Walla Walla and Lewiston, profited from a gold rush in 1861 in Idaho. Merchants and farmers built lavish houses during the boom years. Today the town takes pride in a number of "oldest" records. If you're looking for that out-of-production faucet washer, Dayton boasts the oldest family-run hardware store in the state, **Dingle's.** The town also is home to the state's oldest volunteer fire department, oldest rodeo, and first high school graduating class.

Restaurants

Jacobi's   For dining with a historic ambience, head for the former Northern Pacific Railroad Depot in Walla Walla, home to Jacobi's, a cafe partially located in a former railroad dining car. The college crowd hangs out here, where they talk over espresso and beer (local). For more elegant ambience, ask for a table in the railroad dining car. *Take 2nd St exit off Hwy 12 to the old Northern Pacific Depot; (509) 525-2677; 416 N 2nd St, Walla Walla; $.*

Merchants Ltd. ☆☆   It's a cluttered New York–style deli, with culinary merchandise piled ceiling-high on broad shelves, a deli counter loaded with breads, cheeses, sausages, salads, caviars, and a glass-fronted bakery. The homemade soups are popular, and there is an excellent wine list. *Take 2nd St exit off Hwy 12, turn left on Main; (509) 525-0900; 21 E Main St, Walla Walla; $$.*

Patit Creek Restaurant ☆☆☆   Bruce and Heather Hiebert have turned a small rural cafe into an excellent regional restaurant. Bruce uses only the freshest vegetables and herbs and serves superbly roasted meat in what was a service station in the 1920s and, later, a soda fountain. Heather's homemade pies and desserts are a proper finale. Reservations are crucial on weekends—call ahead. *On Hwy 12 at north end of town; (509) 382-2625; 725 E Dayton Ave, Dayton; $$.*

Lodgings

Green Gables Inn ☆☆   The broad covered porch of this converted Arts and Crafts–style mansion is an ideal setting for relaxing on a warm afternoon, lemonade and book in hand. Names for the 5 guest rooms are from the L.M. Montgomery book *Anne of Green Gables* (a favorite is Idlewild). *Take the Clinton exit off Hwy 12 to Bonsella; (509) 525-5501; 922 Bonsella, Walla Walla; $$.*

The Purple House B&B   Owner Christine Williscroft brought her passion for Chinese antiques and Oriental rugs to her bed and breakfast. She can pack a picnic luncheon for explorers, and there is a patio and a swimming pool. A typical dinner (guests only) would be Hungarian goulash or trout in season when Williscroft goes fishing in the Touchet River. *1 block off Hwy 12 in downtown Dayton; (509) 382-3159; 415 East Clay, Dayton; $$$.*

More Information

Walla Walla Area Chamber of Commerce: *(509) 525-0850.*
Umatilla National Forest: *(509) 843-1891.*

Snake River Country:
Clarkston, Pullman,
and the Palouse

From Clarkston north to the town of Palouse and west to Kahlotus, including the city of Pullman, the Snake River Canyon, and Palouse Falls, Chief Timothy and Lyons Ferry State Parks.

And the wind blows. Man, does it blow. Has for a long, long time, which pretty much explains the great piles of dirt that form the rolling, wheat-growing hills of the Palouse. This loose volcanic dirt—or *loess*, as it's known to geologists—has been carried by thousands of years of southwesterly winds from the Columbia Plateau to here, the Evergreen State's big brown dumping ground.

In a state known for its greens and blues, that's not much of a recommendation. Yet the Palouse—as the collective hilly area is known (ironically, it's a derivation of the French *pelouse*, which means "short, thick grass")—is beautiful in its own right. The broad, rolling hills are unique, sort of a not-so-awful badlands. The superbly rich soil grows thousands of annual barge-loads of wheat and legumes. Without the Palouse, we'd all be short on grass seed and lentils in no time. And nobody wants that.

Still, it's fair to say there's not a lot here for the avid outdoorsperson. It's a good area to roll through once, twice, or thrice, just to see it. But once you're done exploring the area's highlight—waterfront parks in the dam-flooded Snake River Canyon—the Palouse becomes just a long stretch of road on the way to somewhere else.

None of which should be construed to mean we don't *like* the place. It's just that we still haven't quite recovered from an initial visit to the Palouse, an occasion on which we drove for what seemed like four or five days, arrived near Pullman, got out of the car, looked around, and asked: "*This* is it?"

It was. It is. It ever shall be. Until the really big southwesterly kicks up and moves it all over to Central Idaho.

Getting There

Pullman, the spiritual if not geographical heartland of the Palouse, is 288 miles southwest of Seattle via Interstate 90 and Highway 26. It's a long day's drive. For quick trippers, it's only 76 miles south of Spokane, where major airlines can get you from Seattle in less than an hour.

Adjoining Areas

NORTH: **Spokane**
SOUTH: **Walla Walla and Dayton**
WEST: **Tri-Cities**

inside out

Camping/Picnics/Swimming

Not surprisingly, most Palouse campers are out to beat the heat, and the best refuge is along the water. There's a lot more of it here to go around than there used to be, thanks to a series of dams built on the Snake River between the Tri-Cities and Lewiston, Idaho, from the late 1960s through the 1970s. Lower Granite, Little Goose, Lower Monumental, and Ice Harbor dams were built to do something that only a creative federal government would have thought possible (or necessary): turn Lewiston, Idaho, into a port. In the process, the dams also have largely choked off some of the Northwest's most magnificent steelhead and salmon stocks. These fish once migrated hundreds of miles to the Pacific via the Columbia River, then all the way back, surviving even the gauntlet of dams on the lower Columbia to return and spawn in Idaho streams such as the upper Snake, Clearwater, and Salmon Rivers. The Snake River dams have nearly put an end to that. Snake River chinook salmon now are a federally protected species—probably too late to save them.

The fish's loss, however, has been recreation's gain. Not a good trade-off, but a fact of which state parks planners have taken full advantage, developing a string of waterfront parks and recreation areas around the dams.

You'll see lots of boat trailers and swim fins at **Central Ferry State**

Park, which fronts on the Snake River and draws many boaters and water-sport fans. Spaces here often are reserved well in advance. The park is built specifically to take advantage of Lake Bryan, the large waterway created by Little Goose Dam on the Snake River. Two basins were dug to protect moored boats from occasionally nasty winds that whip through the river gorge. The campground has 62 sites (60 with full hookups; maximum RV length, 45 feet), supplemented by several boat launches, a moorage float, a bathhouse, a swimming area, and many nice waterfront picnic sites. Stake those tents down tight, or you might wake up in Washtucna! Central Ferry is open all year. Campsites can be reserved up to 11 months in advance by calling Reservations Northwest; (800) 452-5687. *On Highway 127 about 17 miles south of Dusty; (509) 549-3551 or (800) 233-0321.*

Similar in character is **Lyons Ferry State Park,** which sits on a point at the confluence of the Palouse and Columbia Rivers. As at Central Ferry, the boat that used to cross the wide river here was long ago replaced by a bridge. Unlike Central Ferry, however, the Lyons Ferry is still here, tied up on shore, where it serves as a fishing pier and historical display. The park lies on either side of the north end of the Lyons Ferry Bridge on Hwy 261. On the west side is a plain, poorly landscaped campground with 52 campsites (no hookups). Not exactly a garden spot, but it'd do for an overnight spot, particularly if you're in an RV. In addition to the old ferry, the much nicer day-use area features a long spit of land (a ridge top, before dams flooded the valley) jutting into the lake, providing a wealth of good waterfront picnic spots. Farther south are more picnic grounds, a swimming beach, and a boat launch.

At the north end of the day-use area, a trail leads about a mile up on a bluff to a canyon overlook, where you'll find historical information about **Marmes Rock Shelter,** an ancient Palouse Indian burial cave below here, now flooded by the lake waters. Before the flooding, archaeologists discovered human remains carbon-dated to 10,000 years ago. For a time they were considered the oldest human remains on the continent. Lyons Ferry is open summers only. Campsites cannot be reserved. *On Highway 261, 7 miles north of Starbuck; (509) 646-3252 or (800) 233-0321.*

Chief Timothy State Park near Clarkston is another "waterworld." It sits on an island in Lower Granite Lake, another Snake River dam-formed impoundment. The proximity of the island to the shore creates a nicely protected waterway—an ideal swimming and water-play area made even better by a broad, flat sandy beach. The day-use area has shaded picnic sites, playground equipment, a bathhouse, and ample boat launches and moorage. The campground offers 66 campsites (33 with hookups and large enough to accommodate all RVs) split into three camping loops. A historical display tells of an old Nez Perce village here (Timothy was a Nez Perce chief), followed by the old pioneer town of Silcott, which like many other Snake River historical sites now lies beneath the lake waters. Chief Timothy State Park is open all year. Campsites can be reserved up to 11 months in advance by calling Reservations Northwest; (800) 452-5687. *On Silcott Road 8 miles west of Clarkston; (509) 758-9580 or (800) 233-0321.*

Camping facilities are very limited at **Palouse Falls State Park,** but don't let that deter you from visiting. The 200-foot waterfall is one of Washington's most spectacular natural sights, plunging from a half-circle of wall-like columnar basalt into a deep pool. The falls are at their peak in the spring (usually late March), when the Palouse River is at high flow. The prolific spray at the bottom often forms a rainbow, making this a photographer's dream. The falls are believed to have been formed by the same prehistoric floods that carved other Eastern Washington features such as the Grand Coulee. The park does have 10 primitive campsites, but is used most often as a day-use picnic area. Several hiking trails fan out along the cliffs (see Hiking, below). Palouse Falls is open all year. Campsites cannot be reserved. *16 miles northwest of Starbuck via Hwy 261 and Palouse Falls Road; (509) 549-3551 or (800) 233-0321.*

In the Clarkston area, alternate camping is available at **Wawawai County Park,** on Lower Granite Lake about 25 miles west of Clarkston, and across the river at **Boyer Park and Marina.** Around Pullman, the city's **Pullman RV Park** (South Street; (509) 334-4555) has decent RV spots in the summer. And **Kamiak Butte County Park** (see Hiking, below), 10 miles north on Highway 27, also has camping; (509) 397-3791.

Boating/Canoeing/Kayaking

The **Snake River Canyon,** dammed into a series of large, welcoming lakes (see Camping/Picnics/Swimming, above), provides ample waters for boating and paddling. All of the lakes are broad enough for waterskiing. The best access points are the state parks listed above.

For a wilder, truly memorable river trip, don't overlook a boat trip down spectacular, 6,500-foot-deep **Hells Canyon,** which delineates the Oregon–Idaho border south of Clarkston. The canyon isn't technically a canyon at all; it's a river gorge, and the deepest one on the planet. While most of Hells Canyon is not in Washington, Clarkston and nearby Lewiston are the most common departure points for the dozens of outfitters that explore the canyon via single- or multiday jet-boat, dory, raft, or kayak trips on the Snake River. For a list of qualified outfitters, contact the dual Hells Canyon National Recreation Area and Wallowa–Whitman

National Forest headquarters in Enterprise, Oregon; (503) 426-4978; or contact the Clarkston Chamber of Commerce (see More Information, below).

For canoeists, a popular day trip can be made by launching at Lyons Ferry State Park and paddling upstream several miles to the site of the flooded **Marmes Rock Shelter** (see Camping/Picnics/Swimming, above), where 10,000-year-old cremated human remains were discovered before the valley was flooded by dams.

Photography

Palouse Falls (see Camping/Picnics/Swimming, above) is a natural feature no serious landscape photographer should miss. The highest water volumes are during the spring meltoff, and the best shooting times for the west-facing falls are in the morning.

The Palouse itself can be photographed from many roadside vistas, and is particularly impressive in the spring, when sprouting wheat creates multilevel, multihued green rolling hills. The best—and probably only—overall view is found at **Steptoe Butte,** a day-use state park about 30 miles northwest of Pullman, just off Hwy 195. This big hunk of granite is one of very few to survive the lava flows, floods, and hellacious winds that stripped most of this region clean between 10 million and 20 million years ago. Today, the 3,600-foot butte stands 1,000 feet taller than anything within sight, providing an amazing 360-degree view of the Palouse, the Blue Mountains to the south, and even the Bitterroots of Idaho. The butte, which also is a popular hang-gliding and kite-flying spot, was named for U.S. Army colonel E. J. Steptoe, who was defeated in a nearby 1858 battle with a local tribe.

Geological trivia department: Thanks to the local tribes' choice of places to defeat Steptoe, the colonel's name lives on not only here, but in geology texts everywhere. "Steptoe" now is an accepted geological term for a remnant rock formation surviving amid a new one. Rocks from the butte are hundreds of millions of years old, suggesting it's the sole survivor of an old mountain range (perhaps all that remains of the Selkirk Range) predating the relatively new, 15- to 20-million-year-old volcanic basalt that overlays the rest of the area.

Hiking

Hiking trails are a relative rarity in Palouse Country, where most locals are too busy farming and most tourists are bound for greener climes to the north near Spokane, or to the south, where the Blue Mountains beckon. **Palouse Falls State Park,** however, has a small trail system that's worth cautious exploration. An unmaintained path skirts around the west side of the massive plunge pool, offering the best views of the 198-foot waterfall and the fascinating, castlelike columnar basalt forming the vertical walls of the splash basin. The trail peters out after about half a mile. Use extreme caution here; the trail skirts to the cliffs very closely, and there's no guardrail. A second reason to watch your step: rattlesnakes are common in the area—sometimes even in the parking lot. Definitely *not* a good walk for kids, dogs, or adults under the influence of excessive caffeine! Other trails lead down into the canyon itself. Prudent—make that even minimally rational—hikers will avoid them.

An interesting trail for natural history lovers is the **Marmes Rock Shelter** path (see Lyons Ferry in Camping/Picnics/Swimming, above). A longer (about 2 miles), though unmaintained, trail follows the river to the upper Marmes site itself. The site is easier to reach via the river, however (see Boating/Canoeing/Kayaking, above).

If you're stuck in—er, have the good fortune to be spending some time in—Pullman, the best tree/view hiking option is 10 miles away on the **Pine Ridge Trail** (moderate; 7 miles round trip), which climbs to the top of 3,360-foot Kamiak Butte, a sister formation to nearby and better-known Steptoe Butte (see Photography, above). The trailhead is within Kamiak Butte County Park, about 10 miles north of Pullman on Hwy 27.

It's not technically part of the Palouse, but the 6-mile **Clearwater and Snake River National Recreation Trail** (aka Snake River Bikeway) from Beachview Park in Clarkston to Chief Looking Glass Park near Asotin has many scenic views, including ancient Swallow's Nest Rock, a basalt cliff that—you guessed it—is a primary swallow nesting ground.

Wildlife

Palouse Falls (see Hiking and Camping/Picnics/Swimming, above) also is a noted wildlife area. **Golden eagles, falcons, hawks,** and other **raptors** often are seen in the canyon below the falls.

All the dams on the Snake River are fitted with fish ladders, and the best viewing area is at **Lower Monumental Dam** south of Kahlotus. Spring chinook pass through here—keep your fingers crossed—in April and May. The fall chinook run peaks in September, and steelhead are often seen passing in September and October. The fish-ladder viewing room is open all year, with hours that vary according to the season. Call (509) 547-7781.

Kamiak Butte County Park (see Hiking, above) is a productive **bird-watching** site, as is Swallow's Nest Rock south of Clarkston (see also Hiking, above).

Fishing

The Palouse is a dry spot when it comes to almost everything, but it's *really* a dry spot in the fishing world. The one exception is the **Snake River** downstream from Clarkston. The deep lakes created by the river's four dams provide decent bass, perch, and crappie fishing, and many anglers fish at night for channel catfish. Trolling for steelhead also can be productive, and a few sturgeon are caught in the lakes.

Cycling

This is hot, lonely country for cycling, but a relative dearth of traffic on Palouse roads makes it grand touring territory for devoted cyclists. A popular 24-mile racing route, the **Tour of the Palouse,** begins at Palouse, follows Hwy 27 south to Clear Creek Road, then turns right and proceeds to Hwy 272, which can be followed east back to Palouse.

Another route favored by local cyclists is the **Pullman–Snake River Loop.** The 79-mile tour begins at Wawawai-Pullman Road at Hwy 195, follows Wawawai-Pullman Road to the Snake River Canyon, which is skirted upstream to the Clearwater Bridge and US 12 at Lewiston, Idaho. The route then recrosses the Clearwater, climbs steeply up Lewiston Hill on Old Lewiston Grade, then turns north on Hwy 195 and returns to Pullman. It's a gasser, but the scenery is fine, particularly along the long central Snake River Canyon portion.

Rental cycles are available at Pullman Bikes and Skis, 219 E Main Street; (509) 332-1703.

Attractions

Beautiful downtown **Pullman** is the biggest tourist draw in this area (which might say more about the lack of tourist attractions than it does about beautiful downtown Pullman). The town's population swells in the fall with Washington State University students, while the permanent residents are a mix of wheat farmers and university faculty. The largest of the Palouse towns, Pullman retains some of its cowpoke image but covets an international reputation as a university town. The central business district consists mostly of one main street crowded with shops and some restaurants. There is abundant free parking just off the main street. Browsers might visit the **Nica Gallery** for an excellent representation of Eastern

Washington artists, 246 E Main Street, (509) 334-1213; **Bruised Books** for used books that sometimes include hard-to-find first editions, 105 N Grand, (509) 334-7898; and **The Combine** for deli sandwiches, salads, desserts, espresso, and teas and herbs, 215 E Main, (509) 332-1774.

The **Washington State University** campus is expanding constantly, and is worth a visit. The **Fine Arts Center** is a showcase with a spacious gallery that attracts exhibits of notable artists. **Martin Stadium,** home of the perennial-underdog WSU Cougar football team, holds Pac-10 Conference–size crowds; the baseball team plays on **Bailey Field** near the 12,000-seat **Beasley Performing Arts Coliseum,** which houses both the basketball team and frequent rock concerts; call (800) 325-SEAT for tickets and an events calendar.

Visitors might want to drop by **Ferdinand's,** now located in the Food Quality Building and open weekdays only, which offers ice cream, milk shakes, and Cougar cheese, made from milk and cream from WSU's own dairy herd; (509) 335-2141. Tours of the university, (509) 335-4527, can keep visitors busy for a couple of days. For an impressive insect collection, visit the **Museum of Anthropology** and the **Maurice T. James Entomological Collection** in Johnson Hall. Other campus destinations include the **Marion Ownbey Herbarium** in Herald Hall for a quick course on herbs; the **Beef, Dairy, and Swine Centers;** and the **Jewett Astronomical Observatory;** (509) 335-6868 for tours. Pick up a campus map and a visitor's parking pass from the visitors center adjacent to the fire station (follow the signs on Stadium Way).

Restaurants

Hilltop Restaurant   This motel and restaurant has probably the best steaks in Pullman, family-style chicken dinners Sunday afternoons, Sunday brunch, and a wonderful view of the university and surrounding hills. The food is consistently good, albeit predictable, fare. *At city limits off Hwy 195 between Olson and Davis Way; (509) 334-2555; 928 Olson, Pullman; $$.*

The Seasons ☆☆   No doubt Pullman's finest dining experience. This elegant eatery occupies a renovated old house atop a flower-covered cliff. Dinner is presented in a proper and elegant fashion; chicken and seafood are good choices. Salad dressings are made on the premises and salads are served with scrumptious homemade breads. *On the hill about 1/2 block off Grand; (509) 334-1410; SE 215 Paradise St, Pullman; $$.*

Swilly's ☆☆   Located in what was a 1920s photography studio, Swilly's flanks the Palouse River and sports a small outdoor cafe. Works by area artists decorate the walls. The eatery boasts fresh local ingredients, right down to cream from a nearby dairy and bread from a local bakery. A separate calzone menu is billed as "the freshest and finest in the Palouse." *1 block east of Grand; (509) 334-3395; 200 NE Kamiaken St, Pullman; $$.*

Cheaper Sleeps

CUB Hotel   Washington State University operates 30 simple rooms as a small hotel. Some rooms have tubs and showers; others have only a shower. Open during the regular school session. Parking permit comes with the room. *(509) 335-9444; Compton Union Building (CUB), Washington State University, Pullman.*

More Information

Pullman Chamber of Commerce: *(800) 365-6948.*
Clarkston Chamber of Commerce: *(509) 758-7712.*

Index

Inside Out: Washington
Report Form

Based on my personal experience, I wish to recommend the following trail, route, waterway, area, guide, outfitter, organization, or establishment; or confirm/correct/disagree with the current review.

_____

_____

_____

(Please include address and telephone number of your recommendation, if applicable):

Report:

Please describe the aspects of your experience that made it memorable; for example, the type of trail, outstanding natural features, best season to go, etc. Continue on the other side if necessary.

_____

_____

_____

_____

_____

_____

I am not concerned, directly or indirectly, with the management or ownership of this guide, outfitter, organization, or establishment *(if applicable)*.

Signed _____

Name *(please print)* _____

Address _____

_____

Phone Number _____

Date _____

Send to:

Inside Out: Washington
c/o Sasquatch Books
615 Second Avenue, Suite 260
Seattle, WA 98104

Or email your report to: books@sasquatchbooks.com